EXAM✓CRAM

CompTIA®
Security+
SY0-601
Exam Cram

Marty M. Weiss

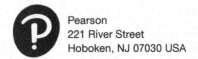

Pearson
221 River Street
Hoboken, NJ 07030 USA

CompTIA® Security+ SY0-601 Exam Cram

ISBN-13: 978-0-13-679867-5

ISBN-10: 0-13-679867-5

Library of Congress Control Number: 2020914528

5 2022

Trademarks

All terms mentioned in this book that are known to be trademarks or service marks have been appropriately capitalized. Pearson IT Certification cannot attest to the accuracy of this information. Use of a term in this book should not be regarded as affecting the validity of any trademark or service mark.

Warning and Disclaimer

Every effort has been made to make this book as complete and as accurate as possible, but no warranty or fitness is implied. The information provided is on an "as is" basis. The author and the publisher shall have neither liability nor responsibility to any person or entity with respect to any loss or damages arising from the information contained in this book.

Special Sales

For information about buying this title in bulk quantities, or for special sales opportunities (which may include electronic versions; custom cover designs; and content particular to your business, training goals, marketing focus, or branding interests), please contact our corporate sales department at corpsales@pearsoned.com or (800) 382-3419.

For government sales inquiries, please contact governmentsales@pearsoned.com.

For questions about sales outside the U.S., please contact intlcs@pearson.com.

Editor-in-Chief
Mark Taub

Director, ITP Product Management
Brett Bartow

Executive Editor
Nancy Davis

Development Editor
Ellie C. Bru

Managing Editor
Sandra Schroeder

Project Editor
Mandie Frank

Copy Editor
Kitty Wilson

Indexer
Ken Johnson

Proofreader
Donna Mulder

Technical Editor
Christopher Crayton

Publishing Coordinator
Cindy Teeters

Designer
Chuti Prasertsith

Compositor
codeMantra

Credits

Figure Number	Attribution/Credit
Figure 2-1	Screenshot of an example of what user's see when they were infected with ransomware © WannaCry
Figure 5-1	Screenshot of an example of an interactive threat map © 2018 AO Kaspersky Lab
Figure 10-4	Screenshot of The AWS Management Console © 2020, Amazon Web Services, Inc.
Figure 12-1	Courtesy of Apple, Inc.
Figure 23-1	Screenshot of Windows local security policy settings for the account lockout policy © Microsoft 2020
Figure 23-2	Screenshot of Windows local security policy settings for the password policy © Microsoft 2020
Figure 24-1	Screenshot of Standard Microsoft Windows file permissions © Microsoft 2020
Figure 25-1	Screenshot of details of a digital certificate © 2020 Apple Inc.
Figure 26-1	Screenshot of using a command-line interface to access a remote computer by using SSH © 2020 Apple, Inc.
Figure 26-2	Screenshot of using the cURL command to return the source code of a web page © 2020 Apple, Inc.
Figure 26-3	Screenshot of using the ping command-line utility © 2020 Apple, Inc.
Figure 28-1	Screenshot of an example of a SIEM system security dashboard © security information and event management
Figure 28-2	Screenshot of Microsoft Windows Event Viewer Security log © Microsoft 2020
Figure 28-3	Screenshot of Activity Monitor for macOS © 2020 Apple, Inc.

Contents at a Glance

Table of Contents

EXAM✓CRAM

The CompTIA® Security+ SY0-601 Cram Sheet

This Cram Sheet contains the distilled key facts about the CompTIA Security+ exam. Review this information as the last step before you enter the testing center, paying special attention to those areas where you think you need the most review.

Domain 1.0: Attacks, Threats, and Vulnerabilities

1. Programming errors can result in system compromise, allowing someone to gain unauthorized privileges. This is known as privilege escalation.

2. Forms of malware include the following:
   - **Viruses:** Infect systems and spread copies of themselves
   - **Worms:** Similar to viruses but do not require a host to replicate
   - **Trojans:** Disguise malicious code within apparently useful applications
   - **Logic bombs:** Trigger on a particular condition
   - **Rootkits:** Can be installed and hidden on a computer mainly for the purpose of compromising the system
   - **Ransomware:** Usually demands money in return for the release of data, which may have also been encrypted using crypto-malware
   - **Spyware:** May monitor browser activity and log keystrokes and may impact computer performance

3. Spyware and adware often result in a computer running slowly and generating pop-ups.

4. An armored virus seeks to make analysis difficult by including a metaphorical layer of armor around the virus.

5. Phishing is a social engineering attack commonly done through email across a large audience.

6. Spear phishing is a social engineering attack commonly done through email that targets an individual or an individual group.

7. Whaling is similar to spear phishing but affects big targets, such as a CEO.

8. In vishing, also known as voice phishing, the attacker often uses a fake caller ID to appear as a trusted organization and attempt to get the individual to enter account details via the phone.

9. The term pharming is based on farming and phishing. Pharming does not require the user to be tricked into clicking on a link. Instead, it redirects victims to a bogus website, even if they correctly entered the intended site.

10. DoS and DDoS attacks involve disruption of normal network services and include attacks based on the ICMP echo reply called Smurf attacks.

11. Spoofing is the process of making data look as if it came from a trusted or legitimate origin.

12. With a an on-path attack, a third system intercepts traffic between two systems by pretending to be the other system.

13. Replay attacks involve reposting captured data.

14. Zero-day vulnerabilities do not have patches yet and aren't detected by antimalware software.

15. Password guessing, brute-force, and dictionary attacks involve repeated guessing of logons and passwords.

16. DNS poisoning allows a perpetrator to redirect traffic by changing the IP record for a specific domain (thus permitting attackers to send legitimate traffic anywhere they choose).

17. ARP poisoning is a Layer 2 attack that deceives a device on a network and poisons the table associations of other devices.

18. XSRF is an attack in which the end user executes unwanted actions on a web application while currently authenticated.

19. XSS vulnerabilities can be used to hijack a user's session.

20. Injection attacks include SQL, LDAP, DLL, and XML. Such attacks insert code or malicious input to try to force unauthorized activity or access.

21. A rogue access point is an unauthorized wireless access point that is set up.

22. A rogue access point can serve as a type of on-path attack that is often referred to as an evil twin.

23. In bluejacking, attackers generate messages that appear to come from the device itself, leading users to follow obvious prompts and establish an open Bluetooth connection to the attacker's device.

24. When a user pairs with an attacker's device, the user's data becomes available for unauthorized access, modification, or deletion. This is an aggressive attack referred to as bluesnarfing.

25. When traffic being sent across a network is unencrypted, packet sniffing enables an attacker to capture the data and decode it from its raw form into readable text.

26. Threat actor attributes include the actor's relationship to the organization, motive, intent, and capability.

27. Threat actor types include script kiddies, insiders, hacktivists, organized crime, competitors, and nation-states.

28. Nation-states and organized crime are likely to have greater capabilities than other threat actors. Competitors are more likely to want to steal intellectual property to gain a competitive advantage.

29. OSINT describes information for collection from publicly available information sources, such as publications, geospatial information, and many online resources.

30. In a black-box test, the assessor has no information or knowledge about the inner workings of the system.

191. Protocol analyzers can be placed inline or in between the devices from which you want to capture traffic.

192. Some of the most common firewall configuration errors include permissions for traffic to run from any source to any destination, unnecessary services running, weak authentication, and log file negligence.

193. A misconfigured web content filter can either prevent legitimate content or allow prohibited content.

194. Written authorization should be required before conducting vulnerability or penetration tests.

195. Incident response plans should include details related to incident categorization, preparation, roles, responsibilities, reporting requirements, escalation procedures, and details on cyber incident response teams and training exercises.

196. The incident response process includes preparation, identification, containment, eradication, recovery, and post-incident events such as lessons learned.

197. Order of volatility describes the order in which evidence should be collected, from the most volatile systems to the least volatile.

198. Data in RAM and swap or paging files is considered the most volatile.

199. Chain of custody ensures that evidence is properly handled.

200. Data acquisition during and after an incident includes capturing system images, traffic logs, video, time offset, hashes, screenshots, and witness interviews.

201. When computers are examined, their date and time settings are recorded and compared with the current time. This can be used to calculate the difference between the two. This difference is then used as an offset and applied to all the time evidence on the computer.

202. MITRE ATT&CK is a framework similar to a kill chain and provides a reference for incident response.

203. The Diamond Model of Intrusion Analysis places the basic components of malicious activity at one of four points: adversary, infrastructure, capability, and victim.

204. Incident responses exercises can be discussion oriented or simulated.

205. BCP and COOP ensure the restoration of organizational functions in the shortest possible time, even if services resume at a reduced level of effectiveness or availability

Domain 5.0: Governance, Risk, and Compliance

206. Generally, controls deter, prevent, detect, or correct. Some controls, such as anti-malware, provide more than one of those functions.

207. A computer login notification is an example of a common preventive control.

208. Compensating controls are used when a business or technological constraint exists and an alternate control is effective in the current security threat landscape.

209. SLA, BPA, MOU, and ISA are types of interoperability agreements that help mitigate risk when dealing with third parties.

210. User types require unique training and awareness. The user types include general users, privileged users, system administrators, executive users, data owners, and system owners. The latter three are in positions that are responsible for creating or managing security policies.

211. Users must be given training in the proper use of their various personal applications, including email and social media networks. This training should address any limitations or expectations regarding their use.

212. RPO designates the amount of data that will be lost or will have to be reentered due to network downtime.

213. RTO designates the amount of time that can pass before a disruption begins to seriously impede normal business operations.

214. MTBF is the average time before a product requires repair.

215. MTTF is the average time before a product fails and cannot be repaired.

216. A privacy threshold assessment determines whether systems contain personal information. A privacy impact assessment is needed for any organization that collects, uses, stores, or processes such information.

217. Risk assessment is largely a function of threat, vulnerability, and impact. It can be considered with this formula:

    Risk = Threat x Vulnerability x Impact

218. Risk identification includes asset identification, risk assessment, threat identification and classification, and identification of vulnerabilities.

219. Regarding risk, qualitative measures are based on subjective values; they are less precise than quantitative measures, which rely on numbers.

220. An identified risk can be accepted, mitigated, transferred, or avoided. Purchasing insurance is a common example of transferring risk.

221. ALE equals the SLE times the ARO.

222. Change management is important because change introduces risk that can impact systems and services.

223. A DRP details considerations for backup and restoration, including secure recovery methods.

224. To be considered PII, information must be specifically associated with an individual person.

225. Data owners determine data's classification level. Data custodians implement the controls for the data.

226. Degaussing is a data disposal method that involves using a tool to reduce or remove the magnetic field of storage media.

227. Benchmarks provide guidance for creating a secure configuration posture.

CHAPTER 15:
Physical Security Controls 239

CHAPTER 16:
Cryptographic Concepts 261

CHAPTER 18:
Host and Application Security Solutions **307**

CHAPTER 19:
Secure Network Design **339**

About the Author

Marty M. Weiss has spent most of his career in information security and risk management, helping large organizations. Marty holds a bachelor of science degree in computer studies from the University of Maryland University College and an MBA from the Isenberg School of Management at the University of Massachusetts Amherst. He holds several certifications, including CISSP, CISA, and Security+. Marty has authored and coauthored more than a half-dozen books on information technology, many that have been described as riveting and Dostoevsky-esque in reviews by his mother. A Florida native, he now lives in New England.

Dedication

This book is dedicated to my parents.

Acknowledgments

Thank you, the reader of this book. It's a pleasure to help others achieve a goal, and I'm thankful for that opportunity. Thank you to the entire team that helped to bring this book together. I'd like to acknowledge, in particular, Carole Jelen, Nancy Davis, Ellie Bru, Chris Crayton, Mandie Frank, and Kitty Wilson. Also, thank you, Diane Barrett. While you weren't directly involved in this edition, many of your words and ideas exist from previous editions. Finally, thank you to my friends and family for their support and understanding through the entire process.

About the Technical Reviewer

Chris Crayton is a technical consultant, trainer, author, and industry-leading technical editor. He has worked as a computer technology and networking instructor, information security director, network administrator, network engineer, and PC specialist. Chris has authored several print and online books on PC repair, CompTIA A+, CompTIA Security+, and Microsoft Windows. He has also served as technical editor and content contributor on numerous technical titles for several of the leading publishing companies. He holds numerous industry certifications, has been recognized with many professional and teaching awards, and has served as a state-level SkillsUSA final competition judge.

We Want to Hear from You!

As the reader of this book, *you* are our most important critic and commentator. We value your opinion and want to know what we're doing right, what we could do better, what areas you'd like to see us publish in, and any other words of wisdom you're willing to send our way.

We welcome your comments. You can email or write to let us know what you did or didn't like about this book—as well as what we can do to make our books better.

Please note that we cannot help you with technical problems related to the topic of this book.

When you write, please be sure to include this book's title and author as well as your name and email address. We will carefully review your comments and share them with the author and editors who worked on the book.

Email: community@informit.com

Reader Services

Register your copy of *CompTIA® Security+ SY0-601 Exam Cram* at www.pearsonitcertification.com for convenient access to downloads, updates, and corrections as they become available. To start the registration process, go to www.pearsonitcertification.com/register and log in or create an account.* Enter the product ISBN 9780136798675 and click **Submit**. When the process is complete, you will find any available bonus content under Registered Products.

*Be sure to check the box to indicate that you would like to hear from us to receive exclusive discounts on future editions of this product.

Introduction

Welcome to *CompTIA® Security+ SY0-601 Exam Cram*, sixth edition. This book helps you get ready to take and pass the CompTIA Security+ SY0-601 exam.

This book is designed to remind you of everything you need to know to pass the SY0-601 certification exam. Each chapter includes a number of practice questions that should give you a reasonably accurate assessment of your knowledge, and, yes, we've provided the answers and their explanations for these questions. Read this book, understand the material, and you'll stand a very good chance of passing the real test.

Exam Cram books help you understand and appreciate the subjects and materials you need to know to pass CompTIA certification exams. *Exam Cram* books are aimed strictly at test preparation and review. They do not teach you everything you need to know about a subject. Instead, the authors streamline and highlight the pertinent information by presenting and dissecting the questions and problems they've discovered that you're likely to encounter on a CompTIA test.

We strongly recommend that you spend some time installing and working with security tools such as Wireshark and Metasploit and experimenting with the many network and security-related resources provided with many operating systems. The Security+ exam focuses on such activities and the knowledge and skills they can provide you. Nothing beats hands-on experience and familiarity when it comes to understanding the questions you're likely to encounter on a certification test. Book learning is essential, but without a doubt, hands-on experience is the best teacher of all!

Let's begin by looking at preparation for the exam.

How to Prepare for the Exam

This text follows the official exam objectives closely to help ensure your success. The CompTIA exam covers 5 domains and 35 objectives. This book is divided into 5 parts and 35 chapters, aligning with those domains and objectives. These official objectives from CompTIA can be found here: https://www.comptia.org/training/resources/exam-objectives.

As you examine the numerous exam topics now covered in Security+, resist the urge to panic! This book you are holding will provide you with the knowledge (and confidence) that you need to succeed. You just need to make sure you read it and follow the guidance it provides throughout your Security+ journey.

Practice Tests

This book is filled with practice exam questions to get you ready! Cram quizzes end each chapter, and each question also includes complete explanations.

In addition, the book includes two additional full practice tests in the Pearson Test Prep software, available to you either online or as an offline Windows application. To access the practice exams, please see the instructions in the card inserted in the sleeve in the back of the book. This card includes a unique access code that enables you to activate your exams in the Pearson Test Prep software.

In case you are interested in more practice exams than are provided with this book, Pearson IT Certification publishes a Premium Edition eBook and Practice Test product. In addition to providing you with three eBook files (EPUB, PDF, and Kindle) this product provides you with two additional exams' worth of questions. The Premium Edition version also offers you a link to the specific section in the book that presents an overview of the topic covered in the question, allowing you to easily refresh your knowledge. The insert card in the back of the book includes a special offer for an 80% discount off of this Premium Edition eBook and Practice Test product, which is an incredible deal.

Taking a Certification Exam

After you prepare for your exam, you need to register with a testing center. At the time of this writing, the cost to take the Security+ exam is US $349 for individuals. Students in the United States are eligible for a significant discount. In addition, check with your employer as many workplaces provide reimbursement programs for certification exams. For more information about these discounts, you can contact a local CompTIA sales representative, who can answer any questions you might have. If you don't pass, you can take the exam again for the same cost as the first attempt until you pass. The test is administered by Pearson VUE testing centers, with locations globally. In addition, the CompTIA Security+ certification is a requirement for many within the U.S. military, and testing centers are available on some military bases.

You will have 90 minutes to complete the exam. The exam consists of a maximum of 90 questions. If you have prepared, you should find that this is plenty of time to properly pace yourself and review the exam before submission.

Arriving at the Exam Location

As with any other examination, arrive at the testing center early (at least 15 minutes). Be prepared! You need to bring two forms of identification (one with a picture). The testing center staff requires proof that you are who you say you are and that someone else is not taking the test for you. Arrive early because if you are late, you will be barred from entry and will not receive a refund for the cost of the exam.

> **ExamAlert**
>
> You'll be spending a lot of time in the exam room. Plan on using the full 90 minutes allotted for your exam and surveys. Policies differ from location to location regarding bathroom breaks, so check with the testing center before beginning the exam.

In the Testing Center

You will not be allowed to take into the examination room study materials or anything else that could raise suspicion that you're cheating. This includes practice test material, books, exam prep guides, and other test aids. The testing center will provide you with scratch paper and a pen or pencil. These days, this often comes in the form of an erasable whiteboard.

Examination results are available immediately after you finish the exam. After submitting the exam, you will be notified if you have passed or failed. I trust that if you are reading this book, you will pass. The test administrator will also provide you with a printout of your results.

About This Book

The ideal reader for an *Exam Cram* book is someone seeking certification. However, it should be noted that an *Exam Cram* book is a very easily readable, rapid presentation of facts. Therefore, an *Exam Cram* book is also extremely useful as a quick reference manual.

The book is designed so that you can either read it cover to cover or jump across chapters, as needed. Because the book chapters align with the exam objectives, some chapters may have slight overlap on topics. Where required,

references to the other chapters are provided for you. If you need to brush up on a topic or if you have to bone up for a second try at the exam, you can use the index, table of contents, or Table I.1 to go straight to the topics and questions that you need to study. Beyond helping you prepare for the test, we think you'll find this book useful as a tightly focused reference on some of the most important aspects of the Security+ certification.

This book includes other helpful elements in addition to the actual logical, step-by-step learning progression of the chapters. *Exam Cram* books use elements such as ExamAlerts, notes, and practice questions to make information easier to read and absorb. This text also includes a Glossary to assist you.

> **Note**
>
> Reading this book from start to finish is not necessary; this book is set up so that you can quickly jump back and forth to find sections you need to study.

Use the *Cram Sheet* to remember last-minute facts immediately before the exam. Use the practice questions to test your knowledge. You can always brush up on specific topics in detail by referring to the table of contents and the index. Even after you achieve certification, you can use this book as a rapid-access reference manual.

Exam Objectives

Table I.1 lists the skills the SY0-601 exam measures and the chapter in which each objective is discussed.

TABLE I.1 **SY0-601 Exam Domains and Objectives**

Exam Domain	Objective	Chapter in Book That Covers It
1.0 Attacks, Threats, and Vulnerabilities	1.1 Compare and contrast different types of social engineering techniques.	Chapter 1
1.0 Attacks, Threats, and Vulnerabilities	1.2 Given a scenario, analyze potential indicators to determine the type of attack.	Chapter 2
1.0 Attacks, Threats, and Vulnerabilities	1.3 Given a scenario, analyze potential indicators associated with application attacks.	Chapter 3
1.0 Attacks, Threats, and Vulnerabilities	1.4 Given a scenario, analyze potential indicators associated with network attacks.	Chapter 4

Exam Domain	Objective	Chapter in Book That Covers It
1.0 Attacks, Threats, and Vulnerabilities	1.5 Explain different threat actors, vectors, and intelligence sources.	Chapter 5
1.0 Attacks, Threats, and Vulnerabilities	1.6 Explain the security concerns associated with various types of vulnerabilities.	Chapter 6
1.0 Attacks, Threats, and Vulnerabilities	1.7 Summarize the techniques used in security assessments.	Chapter 7
1.0 Attacks, Threats, and Vulnerabilities	1.8 Explain the techniques used in penetration testing.	Chapter 8
2.0 Architecture and Design	2.1 Explain the importance of security concepts in an enterprise environment.	Chapter 9
2.0 Architecture and Design	2.2 Summarize virtualization and cloud computing concepts.	Chapter 10
2.0 Architecture and Design	2.3 Summarize secure application development, deployment, and automation concepts.	Chapter 11
2.0 Architecture and Design	2.4 Summarize authentication and authorization design concepts.	Chapter 12
2.0 Architecture and Design	2.5 Given a scenario, implement cybersecurity resilience.	Chapter 13
2.0 Architecture and Design	2.6 Explain the security implications of embedded and specialized systems.	Chapter 14
2.0 Architecture and Design	2.7 Explain the importance of physical security controls.	Chapter 15
2.0 Architecture and Design	2.8 Summarize the basics of cryptographic concepts.	Chapter 16
3.0 Implementation	3.1 Given a scenario, implement secure protocols.	Chapter 17
3.0 Implementation	3.2 Given a scenario, implement host or application security solutions.	Chapter 18
3.0 Implementation	3.3 Given a scenario, implement secure network designs.	Chapter 19
3.0 Implementation	3.4 Given a scenario, install and configure wireless security settings.	Chapter 20
3.0 Implementation	3.5 Given a scenario, implement secure mobile solutions.	Chapter 21
3.0 Implementation	3.6 Given a scenario, apply cybersecurity solutions to the cloud.	Chapter 22
3.0 Implementation	3.7 Given a scenario, implement identity and account management controls.	Chapter 23

Exam Domain	Objective	Chapter in Book That Covers It
3.0 Implementation	3.8 Given a scenario, implement authentication and authorization solutions.	Chapter 24
3.0 Implementation	3.9 Given a scenario, implement public key infrastructure.	Chapter 25
4.0 Operations and Incident Response	4.1 Given a scenario, use the appropriate tool to assess organizational security.	Chapter 26
4.0 Operations and Incident Response	4.2 Summarize the importance of policies, processes, and procedures for incident response.	Chapter 27
4.0 Operations and Incident Response	4.3 Given an incident, utilize appropriate data sources to support an investigation.	Chapter 28
4.0 Operations and Incident Response	4.4 Given an incident, apply mitigation techniques or controls to secure an environment.	Chapter 29
4.0 Operations and Incident Response	4.5 Explain the key aspects of digital forensics.	Chapter 30
5.0 Governance, Risk, and Compliance	5.1 Compare and contrast various types of controls.	Chapter 31
5.0 Governance, Risk, and Compliance	5.2 Explain the importance of applicable regulations, standards, or frameworks that impact organizational security posture.	Chapter 32
5.0 Governance, Risk, and Compliance	5.3 Explain the importance of policies to organizational security.	Chapter 33
5.0 Governance, Risk, and Compliance	5.4 Summarize risk management processes and concepts.	Chapter 34
5.0 Governance, Risk, and Compliance	5.5 Explain privacy and sensitive data concepts in relation to security.	Chapter 35

The Chapter Elements

Each *Exam Cram* book has chapters that follow a predefined structure. This structure makes *Exam Cram* books easy to read and provides a familiar format for all *Exam Cram* books. The following elements typically are used:

▶ Chapter topics

▶ Essential Terms and Components

▶ Cram Quizzes

▶ ExamAlerts

▶ Notes

▶ Available exam preparation software practice questions and answers

> **Note**
>
> Bulleted lists, numbered lists, tables, and graphics are also used where appropriate. A picture can paint a thousand words sometimes, and tables can help to associate different elements with each other visually.

Now let's look at each of the elements in detail:

▶ **Chapter topics:** Each chapter contains details of all subject matter listed in the table of contents for that particular chapter. The objective of an *Exam Cram* book is to cover all the important facts without giving too much detail. When examples are required, they are included.

▶ **Essential Terms and Components:** The start of every chapter contains a list of terms and concepts you should understand. These are all defined in the book's accompanying Glossary.

▶ **Cram Quizzes:** Each chapter concludes with multiple-choice questions to help ensure that you have gained familiarity with the chapter content.

▶ **ExamAlerts:** ExamAlerts address exam-specific, exam-related information. An ExamAlert addresses content that is particularly important, tricky, or likely to appear on the exam. An ExamAlert looks like this:

> **ExamAlert**
>
> Make sure you remember the different ways in which you can access a router remotely. Know which methods are secure and which are not.

▶ **Notes:** Notes typically contain useful information that is not directly related to the topic currently under consideration. To avoid breaking up the flow of the text, they are set off from the regular text.

> **Note**
>
> This is a note. You have already seen several notes.

Other Book Elements

Most of this *Exam Cram* book on Security+ follows the consistent chapter structure already described. However, there are various important elements that are not part of the standard chapter format. These elements apply to the entire book as a whole.

▶ **Practice questions:** Exam-preparation questions conclude each chapter.

▶ **Answers and explanations for practice questions:** These follow each practice question, providing answers and explanations to the questions.

▶ **Glossary:** The Glossary defines important terms used in this book.

▶ **Cram Sheet:** The Cram Sheet is a quick-reference, tear-out cardboard sheet of important facts that is useful for last-minute preparation. The Cram Sheet provides a simple summary of the facts that may be most difficult to remember.

▶ **Companion website:** The companion website for your book allows you to access several digital assets that come with your book, including the following:

▶ Pearson Test Prep software (both online and Windows desktop versions)

▶ Key Terms Flash Cards application

▶ A PDF version of the Cram Sheet

To access the book's companion website, simply follow these steps:

1. Register your book by going to **PearsonITCertification.com/register** and entering the ISBN 9780136798675.

2. Respond to the challenge questions.

3. Go to your account page and select the **Registered Products** tab.

4. Click on the **Access Bonus Content** link under the product listing.

Pearson Test Prep Practice Test Software

As noted previously, this book comes complete with the Pearson Test Prep practice test software. These practice tests are available to you either online or as an offline Windows application. To access the practice exams that were

developed with this book, please see the instructions in the card inserted in the sleeve in the back of the book. This card includes a unique access code that enables you to activate your exams in the Pearson Test Prep software.

Accessing the Pearson Test Prep Software Online

The online version of this software can be used on any device with a browser and connectivity to the Internet, including desktop machines, tablets, and smartphones. To start using your practice exams online, simply follow these steps:

1. Go to **http://www.PearsonTestPrep.com.**

2. Select **Pearson IT Certification** as your product group.

3. Enter the email address and password for your account. If you don't have an account on PearsonITCertification.com, you need to establish one by going to PearsonITCertification.com/join.

4. In the **My Products** tab, click the **Activate New Product** button.

5. Enter the access code printed on the insert card in the back of your book to activate your product. The product will now be listed in your My Products page.

6. Click the **Exams** button to launch the exam settings screen and start your exam.

Accessing the Pearson Test Prep Software Offline

If you wish to study offline, you can download and install the Windows version of the Pearson Test Prep software. There is a download link for this software on the book's companion website, or you can just enter this link in your browser: http://www.pearsonitcertification.com/content/downloads/pcpt/engine.zip.

To access the book's companion website and the software, simply follow these steps:

1. Register your book by going to **PearsonITCertification.com/**register and entering the ISBN 9780136798675.

2. Respond to the challenge questions.

3. Go to your account page and select the **Registered Products** tab.

4. Click on the **Access Bonus Content** link under the product listing.

5. Click the **Install Pearson Test Prep Desktop Version** link under the Practice Exams section of the page to download the software.

6. After the software finishes downloading, unzip all the files onto your computer.

7. Double-click the application file to start the installation and follow the onscreen instructions to complete the registration.

8. When the installation is complete, launch the application and click the **Activate Exam** button on the My Products tab.

9. Click the **Activate a Product** button in the Activate Product Wizard.

10. Enter the unique access code from the card in the sleeve in the back of your book and click the **Activate** button.

11. Click **Next** and then click the **Finish** button to download the exam data to your application.

12. To start using the practice exams, select the product and click the **Open Exam** button to open the exam settings screen.

Note that the offline and online versions will sync together, so saved exams and grade results recorded in one version will be available to you in the other as well.

Customizing Your Exams

In the exam settings screen, you can choose to take exams in one of three modes:

▶ Study Mode

▶ Practice Exam Mode

▶ Flash Card Mode

Study Mode allows you to fully customize your exams and review answers as you are taking the exam. This is typically the mode you use first to assess your knowledge and identify information gaps. Practice Exam Mode locks certain customization options, as it presents a realistic exam experience. Use this mode when you are preparing to test your exam readiness. Flash Card Mode strips

out the answers and presents you with only the question stem. This mode is great for late-stage preparation, when you really want to challenge yourself to provide answers without the benefit of seeing multiple-choice options. This mode will not provide the detailed score reports that the other two modes will, so it should not be used if you are trying to identify knowledge gaps.

In addition to these three modes, you can select the source of your questions. You can choose to take exams that cover all of the chapters, or you can narrow your selection to just a single chapter or the chapters that make up specific parts in the book. All chapters are selected by default. If you want to narrow your focus to individual chapters, simply deselect all the chapters and then select only those on which you wish to focus in the Objectives area.

You can also select the exam banks on which to focus. Each exam bank comes complete with a full exam of questions that cover topics in every chapter. The two Practice Exams printed in the book are available to you, as are two additional exams of unique questions. You can have the test engine serve up exams from all four banks or just from one individual bank by selecting the desired banks in the exam bank area.

There are several other customizations you can make to your exam from the exam settings screen, such as the time you are allowed for taking the exam, the number of questions served up, whether to randomize questions and answers, whether to show the number of correct answers for multiple-answer questions, or whether to serve up only specific types of questions. You can also create custom test banks by selecting only questions that you have marked or questions on which you have added notes.

Updating Your Exams

If you are using the online version of the Pearson Test Prep software, you should always have access to the latest version of the software as well as the exam data. If you are using the Windows desktop version, every time you launch the software, it will check to see if there are any updates to your exam data and automatically download any changes that were made since the last time you used the software. You must be connected to the Internet at the time you launch the software.

Sometimes, due to many factors, the exam data may not fully download when you activate an exam. If you find that figures or exhibits are missing, you may need to manually update your exams. To update a particular exam you have already activated and downloaded, simply select the **Tools** tab and click the

Update Products button. Again, this is only an issue with the desktop Windows application.

If you wish to check for updates to the Pearson Test Prep exam engine software, Windows desktop version, simply select the **Tools** tab and click the **Update Application** button. This will ensure you are running the latest version of the software engine.

Contacting the Author

Hopefully, this book provides you with the tools you need to pass the Security+ exam. Feedback is appreciated. You can follow and contact the author on Twitter @martyweiss.

Thank you for selecting my book; I have worked to apply the same concepts in this book that I have used in the hundreds of training classes I have taught. Spend your study time wisely and you, too, can achieve the Security+ designation. Good luck on the exam, although if you carefully work through this text, you will certainly minimize the amount of luck required!

PART I

Attacks, Threats, and Vulnerabilities

This part covers the following official Security+ SYO-601 exam objectives for Domain 1.0, "Attacks, Threats, and Vulnerabilities":

▶ 1.1 Compare and contrast different types of social engineering techniques.

▶ 1.2 Given a scenario, analyze potential indicators to determine the type of attack.

▶ 1.3 Given a scenario, analyze potential indicators associated with application attacks.

▶ 1.4 Given a scenario, analyze potential indicators associated with network attacks.

▶ 1.5 Explain different threat actors, vectors, and intelligence sources.

▶ 1.6 Explain the security concerns associated with various types of vulnerabilities.

▶ 1.7 Summarize the techniques used in security assessments.

▶ 1.8 Explain the techniques used in penetration testing.

For more information on the official CompTIA Security+ SYO-601 exam topics, see the section "Exam Objectives" in the Introduction.

The requirement to adequately assess the security posture of an enterprise environment and to be able to recommend and implement appropriate security solutions involves many complexities and requirements. Today's networks and computer systems are complex and distributed across varying environments. To be able to assess these environments and make the best decisions about securing them, you must understand the risk associated with them—including attacks, threats, and vulnerabilities across the technology landscape. The chapters in this part of the book explore the many potential threats, the varying attack types, and vulnerabilities to help you understand and identify these potential dangers, as well as important measures and processes that can assist in managing the risk.

CHAPTER 1

Social Engineering Techniques

This chapter covers the following official Security+ exam objective:

▶ 1.1 Compare and contrast different types of social engineering techniques.

Essential Terms and Components

▶ social engineering
▶ phishing
▶ smishing
▶ vishing
▶ spam
▶ spam over Internet messaging (SPIM)
▶ spear phishing
▶ Dumpster diving
▶ shoulder surfing
▶ pharming
▶ tailgating
▶ eliciting information
▶ whaling
▶ prepending
▶ identity fraud
▶ invoice scam
▶ credential harvesting
▶ reconnaissance
▶ hoax
▶ impersonation

> ▶ watering hole attack
> ▶ typo squatting
> ▶ influence campaign
> ▶ principles (reasons for effectiveness)

Social engineering has been around as long as humans. Many people are familiar with face-to-face interactions in which one individual fishes for information in a deceptive way. Social engineering is the process by which an attacker seeks to extract useful information from users, often by just tricking them into helping the attacker. In many circumstances, social engineering is the precursor to more advanced attacks. Social engineering is extremely successful because it relies on human emotions. Common examples include the following:

▶ An attacker calls a valid user and impersonates a guest, temp agent, or new user, asking for assistance in accessing the network or requesting details on the business processes of the organization.

▶ An attacker contacts a legitimate user and poses as a technical aide, attempting to update some type of information. The attacker asks for identifying user details that can then be used to gain access.

▶ An attacker poses as a network administrator, directing the legitimate user to reset the password to a specific value so that an imaginary update can be applied.

▶ An attacker provides the user with a "helpful" program or agent through email, a website, or some other means of distribution. This program might require the user to enter login details or personal information that is useful to the attacker, or it might install other programs that compromise the system's security.

The Social Engineer

In the preceding examples, the attacker is using *impersonation*, a core tactic of social engineers, which simply means someone assumes the character or appearance of someone else. The attacker pretends to be something he or she is not. Impersonation is often used in conjunction with a pretext or an invented scenario. Images of private detectives might come to mind here. In many great movies, such as *Catch Me If You Can* and *Beverly Hills Cop*, the drama or humor

unfolds as a result of impersonation and pretexting. While social engineering is often used to gain information, usually the attacker uses public information sources to first do *reconnaissance* of the target. For example, LinkedIn or an organization's website may be used to identify personnel and their roles and responsibilities within the organization. And while this might seem like just fun and games, in many cases fraud is involved. For example, with *identity fraud*, a person's personal information is used without authorization to deceive or commit a crime. In fact, online impersonation is usually a crime. Even just posing online as someone else without that person's consent is against the law.

> **ExamAlert**
>
> Social engineering often involves impersonation of some sort. Attackers often use impersonation tactics, which are not easily countered via technology. It is important to understand that the best defense against social engineering is ongoing user awareness and education.

Tailgating

Tailgating is a simple yet effective technique in a social engineer's arsenal. It involves piggybacking or following closely behind someone who has authorized physical access in an environment. Tailgating involves appearing to be part of an authorized group or capitalizing on people's desire to be polite. A common example is an attacker following an authorized person and working to get the person to hold open a secure door to grant access. Many high-security facilities employ mantraps (airlock-like mechanisms that allow only one person to pass at a time) to provide entrance control and prevent tailgating.

Dumpster Diving

As humans, we naturally seek the path of least resistance. Instead of shredding documents or walking them to the recycle bin, employees often throw them into the wastebasket. Workers also might put discarded equipment into the garbage if city laws do not require special disposal. Intruders know this and scavenge for discarded equipment and documents in an act called *Dumpster diving*. They can extract sensitive information from the garbage without ever contacting anyone in the organization.

In any organization, the potential risk of an intruder gaining access to this type of information is huge. What happens when employees leave the organization? They clean out their desks. Depending on how long the employees have been there, the material that ends up in the garbage can be a gold mine for an intruder.

Other potential sources of discarded information include the following:

- ▶ Organizational directories
- ▶ Employee manuals
- ▶ Hard drives and other media
- ▶ Printed emails

Proper disposal of data and equipment should be part of the organization's security policy. Companies should have a policy in place that requires shredding of all physical documents and secure erasure of all types of storage media before they may be discarded. Secure erasure is often performed via the use of disk-wiping software, which can delete the data according to different standards.

Shoulder Surfing

Shoulder surfing involves looking over someone's shoulder to obtain information. It may occur while someone is entering a personal identification number (PIN) at an automated teller machine (ATM) or typing in a password at a computer system. More broadly, however, shoulder surfing includes any method of direct observation and could include, for example, locating a camera nearby or even using binoculars from a distance. With many of these types of methods, user awareness and training are key to prevention. In addition, some tools can also assist here. For example, many ATMs now include mirrors so users can see who might be behind them and better-designed keypads to help conceal keypad entry. Special screen overlays are available for laptop computers to prevent someone from seeing the screen at an angle.

The consequences of getting caught shoulder surfing are low. Simply peering over someone's shoulder to learn the combination is less risky than, say, breaking open a safe or attempting to open the safe when unauthorized. In fact, a shoulder surfer might not actually be the one to initiate a subsequent attack. Information security attacks have evolved into an ecosystem. The shoulder surfer's job might be complete after he or she provides or sells the information gleaned to someone else who has more nefarious goals.

Phishing and Related Attacks

In this section, we discuss various attacks—such as phishing, whaling, and vishing—that can also be classified as social engineering but that rely on technical methods to accomplish the goals. Such attacks are attacks on humans and take

advantage of human psychology. People tend to trust others. People tend to want to be helpful to those in need. Because of these tendencies, adequate and ongoing training is required to counteract potential attacks.

These techniques by themselves are first and foremost about *eliciting informa-tion* that can directly or indirectly lead to sensitive data loss or other compro-mise. The information acquired might not have immediate consequences, but the cumulative effect of these techniques combined with other social engineer-ing and technical attacks could have dire consequences for either the individu-als or their organization.

Increasingly, social engineering attacks are being conducted electronically. Social engineering conducted via computer systems has different names depending on the target and the method. Such attempts are often classified as spam by electronic communication security systems and never reach the target. Attackers continue to evolve their channels and techniques. *Spam over Internet messaging (SPIM)*, the delivery of spam through the use of instant messaging (IM) instead of through email, is one example that has increased.

One common method of social engineering via electronic communications is phishing. *Phishing* is an attempt to acquire sensitive information by masquerad-ing as a trustworthy entity via electronic communication (usually email). Phish-ing attacks rely on a mix of technical deceit and social engineering practices. In most cases, the phisher must persuade the victim to intentionally perform a series of actions that provides access to confidential information. As scam artists become more sophisticated, so do their phishing email messages. The messages often include official-looking logos from real organizations and other identify-ing information taken directly from legitimate websites. For best protection, you must deploy proper security technologies and techniques at the client side, the server side, and the enterprise level. Many organizations now prepend to the subject line some sort of notification if the email is external; this practice is known as *prepending*. Ideally, users should not be able to directly access email attachments from within the email application. However, the best defense is user education.

Related social engineering methods with slight differences from basic phishing include the following:

- ▶ **Spear phishing:** This is a targeted version of phishing. Whereas phishing often involves mass emailing, *spear phishing* goes after a specific individual.

- ▶ **Whaling:** *Whaling* is identical to spear phishing, except for the size of the fish. Whaling employs spear phishing tactics but goes after high-profile targets, such as an executive within a company.

▶ **Vishing:** Also known as voice phishing, *vishing* is the use of fake caller ID to appear as a trusted organization and attempts to get an individual to enter account details via the phone.

▶ **Smishing:** Also known as SMS phishing, *smishing* is the use of phishing methods through text messaging.

▶ **Pharming:** This term is a combination of farming and phishing. *Pharming* does not require the user to be tricked into clicking a link. Instead, pharming redirects victims from a legitimate site to a bogus website. To accomplish this, the attacker employs another attack, such as DNS cache poisoning.

ExamAlert

Phishing combines technical deceit with the elements of traditional social engineering. Be sure to know the variants of phishing attacks. For the SY0-601 exam, know the differences between spear phishing, whaling, vishing, smishing, and pharming.

In many instances, sensitive information is acquired for a downstream purpose, such as to simply sell the information to someone else, or to use the information to perpetrate a deeper attack within an organization. *Credential harvesting* is a common goal of phishing campaigns that involves capturing usernames and passwords. A credential harvesting attempt might be in the form of a bogus email designed to get you to log in to your bank. However, the links in the email wouldn't actually go to your bank's website but would go to the attacker's website, which would be designed to look exactly like your bank's site. From there, the attacker's goal would be to get you to input and submit your username and password. After that, the site might just return a server error, but it would have captured your credentials. Typically, all of the credentials gathered through such a campaign would be aggregated and subsequently monetized.

Often an initial phishing attempt could be a means to commit fraud. The advance-fee scam is one example. In this scam, a large sum of money is promised, but the target is asked to make a small payment first in order to complete the transaction. Of course, the victim never sees the large return. *Invoice scams* are another example. In such an attack, the threat actor may use well researched and carefully crafted emails requesting payment. The hope is that the victim will follow standard processes for paying out invoices, without giving much thought to the details of this particular payment.

Watering Hole Attacks

In many ways, a *watering hole attack* is like spear phishing, discussed earlier. However, instead of using email, the attacker attacks a site that the target frequently visits. The goal is often to compromise the larger environment—for example, the company the target works for.

Just as a lion waits hidden near a watering hole that zebras frequent, a watering hole attacker waits at the sites you frequent. In a typical scenario, the attacker first profiles and understands the victim—such as what websites the victim visits and with what type of computer and web browser. Next, the attacker looks for opportunities to compromise any of these sites based on existing vulnerabilities. Understanding more about the victim (for example, type of browser used and activities) helps the attacker compromise the site with the greatest chance of then exploiting the victim. A watering hole attack is commonly used in conjunction with a zero-day exploit—an attack against a vulnerability that is unknown to software and security vendors. By taking advantage of a Cross-site Scripting vulnerability on the visited site, which allows the attacker to execute scripts in the victim's web browser, the attacker can ensure that the trusted site helps deliver an exploit to the victim's machine.

Typo Squatting

Typo squatting, also known as URL hijacking, is a simple method used frequently for benign purposes but it is also easily used for more malicious attacks. Typo squatting most commonly relies on typographic errors users make on the Internet. It can be as simple as accidentally typing *www.gooogle.com* instead of www.google.com. Fortunately, in this example, Google owns both domain names and redirects the user who mistyped the domain name to the correct domain. However, a misspelled URL of a travel website might take a user to a competing website. Certainly, any domain name can be slightly misspelled, but some typos are more common than others.

Imagine that you unknowingly and mistakenly type in the wrong URL for your bank; perhaps you just accidentally transpose a couple letters. Instead of being presented with a generic parked domain for a domain registrar (an immediate tip-off that you are in the wrong place), you are presented with a site that looks just like your bank's. Attackers' variations and motives can vary, but the simplest attack is to simply record your login information. Perhaps after you try to log in, you see a message saying that your bank is undergoing website maintenance and will be back up in 24 hours. What you probably won't realize is that the attacker has access to your credentials and knows which site they can be used on.

Hoaxes and Influence Campaigns

Hoaxes are interesting because although a hoax presents a threat, the threat does not actually exist at face value. Instead, the actions people take in response to the perceived threat create the actual threats. For example, a *hoax* virus email can consume resources as it is forwarded on. In fact, a widely distributed and believed hoax about a computer virus can result in consequences as significant as an actual virus. Such hoaxes, particularly as they manifest themselves in the physical world, can create unnecessary fear and irrational behaviors. Most hoaxes are passed around not just via email but also on social networks and by word of mouth. Hoaxes often find ways to make the rounds again even years later, perhaps altered only slightly. Snopes.com is a well-known resource that has been around since the mid-1990s. If you are ever in doubt or need help in debunking hoaxes, make this site part of your trusted arsenal.

While most hoaxes may appear benign, they have a more sophisticated counterpart: *influence campaigns*. While influence campaigns are nothing new, the web, advertising, and social media have recently given influence campaigns greater visibility and awareness. Broadly, an influence campaign involves coordinated actions that seek to affect the development, actions, and behavior of the targeted population. And while there are campaigns that are perfectly legitimate and ethically run by businesses and organizations, influence campaigns have recently come to include *hybrid warfare*. Conventional warfare is understood to be confrontational and use infantry and weaponry, but cyberwarfare has recently become common among nations.

While influence campaigns, propaganda, and disinformation have been around for many centuries, their use has expanded largely due to the Internet and, specifically, social media. The Internet has provided an opportunity to widely disseminate information, and social media has provided an opportunity for it to spread. Hybrid warfare can and often does include a combination of these methods, but the psychological, economic, and political influence aspects go beyond just distraction to achieving greater goals, such as dividing public opinion by exploiting societal vulnerabilities.

Principles of Influence (Reasons for Effectiveness)

Ready for a psychology cram? As stated earlier, social engineering relies on human psychology. In particular, a social engineer is looking to influence another person to gain something, which is most often not in the target's best

interest. In many cases, social engineering combines influence with manipulation. Given this, let's look at the various *principles* of influence. The following topics are largely based on the work of Robert Cialdini, Regents Professor Emeritus of Psychology and Marketing at Arizona State University. The key challenge for the various principles of influence is that even though people might recognize a specific principle, they may not easily notice when it is being used against them for nefarious purposes. The following points summarize key principles of influence and highlight why they are effective:

▶ **Authority:** Job titles, uniforms, symbols, badges, and even specific expertise are all elements we often equate with authority. With such proclaimed and believed authority, we naturally feel an obligation to comply. For example, flashing red lights would likely prompt you to pull over, and the specific expertise of the IT security administrator or chief information security officer would probably compel you to divulge your password to aid in troubleshooting. In addition to feeling a sense of obligation, we tend to trust authoritative symbols (many of which are easily forged).

▶ **Intimidation:** Authority plays to our sense of duty, and people with authority or power above us are in a position to abuse that power. We might feel that not complying would have a negative impact. Intimidation does not need to necessarily be so severe that one fears physical harm. A social engineer would more likely use intimidation to play on a fear of getting in trouble or getting fired, for example.

▶ **Consensus/social proof:** Because people tend to trust like-minded people such as friends and family members, they often believe what others around them believe. Think of the cliché "safety in numbers." We are more likely to put a tip in a tip jar when it is not empty, for example, and we might hesitate to eat at a restaurant that is empty. A social engineer might mention friends and colleagues to take advantage of this principle; the attacker might say that these trusted people mentioned you, or that they have already complied with whatever you are being asked for. Ambiguous requests or situations are more likely to be acted on with the belief that others are doing the same thing or bought into the same situation.

▶ **Scarcity and urgency:** Scarcity is commonly used as a marketing ploy (sometimes more effectively than in other cases). You have certainly heard a pitch about special pricing available to only the first 50 callers. Or perhaps you have heard tales of companies unable to keep up with demand (either real or illusory). We tend to want or value something more if we believe it is less available. We are likely to be more impulsive if we believe something is the last one. A social engineer might use the principle of scarcity to spur someone to quickly act on a request before giving the

request more thought. Scarcity tends to work when the victim desires something and, in turn, will act with a sense of urgency. Likewise, a social engineer can use urgency to gain support, perhaps saying that dreadful consequences will occur unless action takes place immediately.

▶ **Familiarity/liking:** People tend to comply with requests from those whom they like or have common ground with. Liking often leads to trust. A social engineer might use humor or try to connect more personally through shared interests or common past events and institutions. This can be effective because of our fundamental desire to establish and maintain social relationships with others. Social engineers who can get you to like them often find that you will be helpful because you, too, want to be liked.

▶ **Trust:** Trust plays a large role in all of these principles. We trust those with assigned authority. We trust those with specific expertise regarding their subject. Trust typically follows liking. We trust the consensus. Trust further is established and plays out in the idea of reciprocation. We are taught from an early age the Golden Rule: Do unto others as you would have them do unto you. As a result, a social norm is established to create equity in social situations—to return favors and not feel indebted to any-one. The reciprocation that occurs and the equity that is established help build trust.

ExamAlert

Be sure to understand how social engineers can use these principles for gain and why these strategies are effective.

Cram Quiz

Answer these questions. The answers follow the last question. If you cannot answer these questions correctly, consider reading this chapter again until you can.

1. Many employees fell for a phishing email that appeared to be from a department head and demanded that employees click on a link and complete an online survey by the end of the day. Which one of the following principles of influence did these employees succumb to?

   ○ **A.** Authority

   ○ **B.** Scarcity

   ○ **C.** Whaling

   ○ **D.** Social proof

2. At your place of employment, you are rushing to the door with your arms full of bags. As you approach, the woman before you scans her badge to gain entrance while holding the door for you, but she asks to see your badge first. What has she just prevented?

○ **A.** Phishing

○ **B.** Whaling

○ **C.** Tailgating

○ **D.** Intimidation principle

3. Which of the following is an effective way to get information in crowded places such as airports, conventions, or supermarkets?

○ **A.** Vishing

○ **B.** Shoulder surfing

○ **C.** Typo squatting

○ **D.** Phishing

4. An attacker wishes to infect a website that employees at your company often visit in order to infect them with malware. What type of computer attack strategy is the attacker setting up?

○ **A.** Zero-day

○ **B.** Credential harvesting

○ **C.** Identity fraud

○ **D.** Watering hole attack

5. Which of the following is the best defense against social engineering?

○ **A.** Cross-site Scripting

○ **B.** Intimidation

○ **C.** Awareness and education

○ **D.** Influence campaign

Cram Quiz Answers

Answer 1: A. Employees likely felt obligated to quickly comply based on the perceived authority of the email. Often such an email would attempt to replicate the status of the department head by using the appropriate formatting and signature line. Answer C is incorrect. Whaling is a specific phishing attack against an important specific target. Answers B and D describe other principles of influence but are incorrect. Scarcity relies on a sense of urgency due to limited availability. Social proof involves consensus around the trust of like-minded people.

Answer 2: C. Tailgating involves piggybacking, or following closely behind someone who has authorized physical access. Answers A and B are incorrect as they describe attempts to acquire sensitive information. Answer D is one of the principles of influence and is incorrect.

Answer 3: B. Shoulder surfing involves using direct observation techniques. It gets its name from the tactic of looking over someone's shoulder to obtain information. Answer A is incorrect because vishing involves using a phone to obtain information. Answer C is incorrect because typo squatting relies on typographic errors users make on the Internet. Answer D is incorrect because phishing is an attempt to acquire sensitive information by masquerading as a trustworthy entity via an electronic communication, usually an email.

Answer 4: D. In a watering hole attack, the attacker attacks a site that the target frequently visits. The goal is often to compromise the larger environment—for example, the company the target works for. Answer A is incorrect. A zero-day attack is a cyberattack targeting a software vulnerability that is unknown to the software vendor or to antivirus vendors. Answer B is incorrect. Credential harvesting is a common purpose of phishing campaigns to capture usernames and passwords. Answer C is incorrect. Identity fraud is the use of a person's personal information, without authorization, to deceive or commit a crime.

Answer 5: C. It is important to understand that the best defense against social engineering is ongoing user awareness and education. Cross-site Scripting (XSS) is a client-side code injection attack, so answer A is incorrect. Answer B is incorrect because a social engineer may use the principle of intimidation to play on one's fear of getting in trouble or getting fired. Answer D is incorrect. An influence campaign involves coordinated actions that seek to affect the development, actions, and behavior of the targeted population.

What Next?

If you want more practice on this chapter's exam objective before you move on, remember that you can access all of the Cram Quiz questions on the Pearson Test Prep software online. You can also create a custom exam by objective with the Online Practice Test. Note any objective you struggle with and go to that objective's material in this chapter.

Attack Basics

This chapter covers the following official Security+ exam objective:

▶ 1.2 Given a scenario, analyze potential indicators to determine the type of attack.

Essential Terms and Components

▶ malware

▶ ransomware

▶ Trojan

▶ worm

▶ potentially unwanted program (PUP)

▶ virus

▶ bot

▶ crypto-malware

▶ logic bomb

▶ spyware

▶ keylogger

▶ remote access trojan (RAT)

▶ rootkit

▶ backdoor

▶ rainbow table

▶ rootkit

▶ password attack

▶ skimming

▶ card cloning

▶ adversarial artificial intelligence (AI)

▶ cryptographic attack

Malware

Malicious software, or *malware*, has become a serious problem in today's network environment. Malware is software designed to harm a user's computer or data. The target is not only the information stored on local computers but also other resources and other computers. As a security professional, you must recognize malicious code and know how to respond appropriately. This chapter covers the various types of malicious code you might encounter, including *viruses, worms, Trojans, spyware, rootkits, botnets,* and *logic bombs*. Increasingly malware is taking advantage of weaknesses throughout the system in which the manufacturing and processing of goods occurs. These supply-chain attacks often take advantage of other vendors that organizations rely on. For example, malware may be introduced into equipment such as point-of-sale terminals before they are deployed. Cloud-based services are often part of an organization's supply chain, and malware within a cloud service provider can compromise partner organizations.

The most serious malware typically takes advantage of system vulnerabilities, which makes the malware more dangerous and enables it to spread more effectively. These threats, known as *blended threats*, involve various types of malware.

Endpoint protection technologies defend against malware by identifying and remediating security threats. Such software often provides a first line of defense by identifying that a machine has been targeted or compromised. Other symptoms of infection include unexpected system behavior and system instability. To determine whether a system has been infected, examine the following critical areas:

▶ **Memory:** After malware is executed, it might reside in memory. Tools such as Windows Task Manager and Activity Monitor for Macs provide insight into all running processes in memory and can help identify rogue processes.

▶ **Registries:** The Windows registry, for example, provides various system settings that malware often targets. Specifically, the Windows registry provides various entries that enable software to automatically start upon login. Malware can take advantage of these entries to ensure that malicious executables are run each time the computer starts up.

▶ **Macros:** Office applications such as Microsoft Word provide a powerful ability to automate procedures through the use of macros. However, these macros also give malware an opportunity to automatically generate instructions when such documents launch. Office software offers an option to generate alerts when macros are being run.

Viruses

A *virus* is a program or piece of code that runs on a computer, often without the user's knowledge and certainly without the user's consent. Viruses are designed to attach themselves to other code and replicate. A virus replicates when an infected file executes or launches. It then attaches to other files, adds its code to the application's code, and continues to spread. Even a simple virus is dangerous because it can use all available resources and bring the system to a halt. Many viruses can replicate across networks and even bypass security systems.

Viruses are malicious programs that spread copies of themselves throughout a single machine. They infect other machines only if a user on another machine accesses an infected object and launches the code.

> **ExamAlert**
>
> Viruses are executed by some type of action, such as running a program.

Viruses are classified and subclassified in several ways. The following classifications are based on how a virus lives in a system:

▶ **Resident virus:** This type of virus resides in memory, which means it is loaded each time the system starts and can infect other areas based on specific actions. This method allows a virus to remain active even after any host program terminates. To reside in memory, such viruses usually need to be called up from some type of storage. Fileless viruses, on the other hand, do not.

▶ **Nonresident virus:** Once executed, this type of virus looks for targets locally and also across the network. The virus then infects those areas and exits. Unlike a resident virus, it does not remain active.

▶ **Boot sector virus:** This type of virus is placed into the first sector of the hard drive so that when the computer boots, the virus loads into memory. As a result, the virus loads before the operating system even starts. Boot sector viruses were much more prevalent in the era of floppy disks because inserted disks supplied the means for infection and spread the virus when the computer booted up.

▶ **Macro virus:** This type of virus is inserted into a Microsoft Office document and emailed to unsuspecting users. A macro virus uses the macro language and executes when the document opens.

Viruses exhibit several potential characteristics that further define their classifications:

▶ **Program- and file-infecting virus:** Many common viruses, particularly early ones, are this type. The virus infects executable program files and becomes active in memory. It then seeks out other files to infect. This type of virus is easily identified by its binary pattern, or signature, which works essentially like a fingerprint. Similar types of file-infecting viruses emerged in an effort to evade this signature detection, including polymorphic, stealth, and multipartite viruses (discussed shortly). Fortunately, security vendors are always improving their techniques as well. The evolving technology of security and antimalware vendors can help combat such attacks.

▶ **Polymorphic virus:** A polymorphic virus can change form or signature each time it is executed to avoid detection. The prefix *poly* means "many"; *morphic* means "shape." Thus, polymorphic malware is malicious code that is capable of changing shape. Each time a polymorphic virus infects a new file or system, for example, it changes its code. As a result, detecting the malware becomes difficult without an identifiable pattern or signature to match. Heuristic scanning is one example. Instead of looking for a specific signature, heuristic-based scanning examines the instructions running within a program.

▶ **Armored virus:** As with a polymorphic virus, the aim of an armored virus is to make detection difficult. As the name suggests, armored viruses go one step further by making it difficult to analyze functions, creating a metaphorical layer of armor around the virus. Armored viruses use various methods of operation: Most notably, in addition to seeking to defeat heuristic countermeasures, they try to prevent disassembly and debugging. If a virus succeeds in these latter aims, security researchers have more difficulty analyzing the code and designing better countermeasures.

▶ **Stealth virus:** This memory-resident virus also uses techniques to avoid detection, such as temporarily removing itself from an infected file or masking a file's size. For example, a stealth virus removes itself from an infected file and places a copy of itself in a different location.

▶ **Multipartite virus:** A multipartite virus infects executable files and also attacks the master boot record of the system. If the boot sector is not cleaned along with the infected files, the files can easily be infected again.

When looking at many of these attributes, you might notice that a common goal of viruses is to increase infection and avoid detection. A more recent virus type known as *fileless* malware is a lot like a memory-resident virus but more insidious. While a memory-resident virus requires some components of the virus to be written to disk, a fileless virus does not. Further, these viruses "live off the land" and use legitimate tools that are usually part of the operating system or development packages to do their work, such as Windows PowerShell, Windows Management Instrumentation, and macros.

Worms

Worms are similar in function and behavior to viruses, with one exception: Worms are self-replicating and do not need a host file. A worm is built to take advantage of a security hole in an existing application or operating system, then find other systems running the same software, and then automatically replicate itself to the new host. This process repeats and needs no user intervention. When the worm is successfully running on a system, it checks for Internet connectivity. If it finds connectivity, the worm tries to replicate from one system to another. Keep in mind that the key difference between a virus and a worm is that worms do not need to attach themselves to files and programs and are capable of reproducing on their own. Common methods of replicating include spreading through email, through a network, and over the Internet.

Trojan

Trojans, or Trojan horses, are programs disguised as useful applications. Trojans do not replicate themselves as viruses do, but they can be just as destructive. Code hidden inside an application can attack a system directly or allow the code originator to compromise the system. A Trojan is typically hidden, and its

ability to spread depends on the popularity of the software and users' willingness to download and install the software. Trojans can perform actions without the user's knowledge or consent, including collecting and sending data and causing a computer to malfunction. Trojans are often classified by their payload or function. The most common include backdoor, downloader, infostealer, and keylogger Trojans. Backdoor Trojans open a less obvious entry (or backdoor) into the system for later access.

Downloader Trojans download additional, often malicious, software onto infected systems. Infostealer Trojans attempt to steal information from the infected machine. *Keylogger* Trojans monitor and send keystrokes typed from an infected machine. Trojans can download other Trojans as well; this link is part of how botnets are controlled, as discussed later in this chapter, in the section "Bots."

Trojans are often associated with *backdoors* created intentionally as part of the Trojan. Backdoors are not malicious on their own, however; they are simply application code functions that trusted developers create either intentionally or unintentionally. During application development, software designers often add shortcut entry points to allow rapid code evaluation and testing. If the designers do not remove them before application deployment, such entry points can allow an attacker to gain unauthorized access later. Application designers might purposefully insert other backdoors as well, and those backdoors can present threats to the network later if no other application designer reviews them before deployment.

A backdoor Trojan is also known as a *remote access Trojan (RAT)*. Specifically, RATs installed on a system allow a remote attacker to take control of the targeted system. This approach is similar to remote control programs that allow you to personally access your computer and control it even if you are not sitting at the keyboard. Clearly, the technology itself is not malicious; only the Trojan component is because it is installed without the victim's knowledge.

> **ExamAlert**
>
> Trojans trick users by disguising their true intent to deliver a malicious payload. When executed, a remote access Trojan provides a remotely accessible backdoor that allows an attacker to covertly monitor the system or easily gain entry.

Rootkits

Rootkits were first documented in the early 1990s. Today they are widely used and are increasingly difficult to detect on networks. A *rootkit* is a piece

of software that can be installed and hidden on a computer mainly to compromise the system and gain escalated privileges, such as administrative rights. A rootkit is usually installed on a computer when it first obtains user-level access. The rootkit then enables the attacker to gain root or privileged access to the computer, which can lead to compromise of other machines on the network as well.

A rootkit might consist of programs that view traffic and keystrokes, alter existing files to escape detection, or create a backdoor on the system.

ExamAlert

Rootkits can be included as part of software packages, can be installed through an unpatched vulnerability, or can be downloaded and installed by users.

Attackers are continually creating sophisticated programs that update themselves, making them harder to detect. If a rootkit has been installed, traditional antivirus software cannot always detect it because many rootkits run in the background. You can usually spot a rootkit by looking for memory processes, monitoring outbound communications, and checking for newly installed programs.

Kernel rootkits modify the kernel component of an operating system. These newer rootkits can intercept system calls passed to the kernel and can filter out queries that the rootkit software generates. Rootkits have also been known to use encryption to protect outbound communications and piggyback on commonly used ports to communicate without interrupting other applications. These tricks invalidate the usual detection methods because they make the rootkits invisible to administrators and detection tools.

Vendors offer applications that can detect rootkits, including Rootkit-Revealer. Removing rootkits can be complex, however, because you must remove both the rootkit itself and the malware that the rootkit is using. Rootkits often change the Windows operating system and cause it to function improperly. When a system is infected, the only definitive way to get rid of a rootkit is to completely reformat the computer's hard drive and reinstall the operating system. In addition, most rootkits use global hooks for stealth activity. Using security tools that prevent programs from installing global hooks and stop process injection thus prevents rootkit functionality. In addition, rootkit functionality requires full administrator rights. Therefore, you can avoid rootkit infection by running Windows from an account with lesser privileges.

Logic Bombs

A *logic bomb* is a virus or Trojan horse designed to execute malicious actions when a certain event occurs or after a certain period of time. For a virus to be considered a logic bomb, the user of the software must be unaware of the payload. A programmer might create a logic bomb to delete all code from the server on a future date, most likely after he or she has left the company. In several recent cases, ex-employees have been prosecuted for their roles in this type of destruction. One of the most high-profile cases of a modern-day logic bomb involved Roger Duronio, a disgruntled computer programmer who planted a logic bomb in about 1,000 computer systems of investment bank UBS to delete critical files and prevent backups. UBS estimated the repair costs at $3.1 million, not including downtime, lost data, and lost business. The actions of the logic bomb coincided with Duronio's stock transactions, so the company added securities and mail fraud charges to the computer crime charges. Duronio was found guilty of planting a logic bomb on the systems and of securities fraud. He was sentenced to more than 8 years in jail and fined $3.1 million.

> **ExamAlert**
>
> A logic bomb is also referred to as *slag code*. The malicious code is usually planted by a disgruntled employee.

During software development, it is a good idea to evaluate the code to keep logic bombs from being inserted. Unfortunately, code evaluation cannot keep someone from planting a logic bomb *after* programming is complete.

Bots

A *bot*, short for *robot*, is an automated computer program that needs no user interaction. Bots are systems that outside sources can control. A bot provides a spam or virus originator with a venue to propagate. Many computers compromised in this way are unprotected home computers (although many computers in the corporate world are bots as well). A *botnet* is a large number of computers that forward transmissions to other computers on the Internet. You might also hear a botnet referred to as a *zombie army*.

A system is usually compromised by a virus or other malicious code that gives the attacker access. A bot can be created through a port that has been left open or an unpatched vulnerability. A small program is left on the machine for future activation. The bot master can then unleash the effects of the army by sending a single command to all the compromised machines. A computer can be part of

a botnet even though it appears to be operating normally. This is because bots are hidden and usually go undetected unless someone is specifically looking for certain activity. The computers that form a botnet can be programmed to conduct a distributed denial-of-service (DDoS) attack, distribute spam, or perform other malicious acts. Chapter 4, "Network Attacks," has more information on DDoS and other types of attacks.

Botnets can be particularly tricky and sophisticated because they can make use of social engineering. A collection of botnets known as Zbot stole millions from banks in four nations. The scammers enticed bank customers with a ruse to click a link to download an updated digital certificate. Zbot then installed a program that allowed it to see the next time the user successfully accessed the account. While the victims did their online banking, Zbot automatically completed cash transfers to other accounts.

The main issue with botnets is that they are securely hidden. The botnet masters can perform tasks, gather information, and commit crimes while remaining undetected. Worse, attackers can increase the depth and effect of their crimes by using multiple computers because each computer in a botnet can be programmed to execute the same command.

Crypto-Malware

Crypto-malware is specifically designed to find potentially valuable data on a system and uses cryptography to encrypt the data to prevent access. The decryption key is then required to access the data. Crypto-malware is often associated with ransomware. And just as the name indicates, *ransomware* is a form of malware that attempts to hold a user's information or device for ransom: The attacker provides the decryption key only after the victim has made a ransom payment.

With ransomware, an attacker typically has already compromised a system and demands payment to prevent negative consequences such as deleting files. Payment is typically demanded in cryptocurrency such as bitcoin. (See Chapter 16, "Cryptographic Concepts," for more information.)

Note

This demand for payment is actually an evolved and more demanding form of scareware. Such scare tactics are common with fake antivirus ads that supposedly find malware on a user's machine; making a purchase simply removes the annoying notices.

CryptoLocker is an example of crypto-malware that became prevalent in 2013. CryptoLocker attempts to encrypt a user's data by generating encryption keys and storing the private key on a command-and-control server. Thereafter, the user's data is held for ransom. If the user does not pay, the malware threatens to delete the private key, which is required to unencrypt the files and thus restore access.

In 2017, crypto-malware known as WannaCry affected hundreds of thousands of systems around the world. WannaCry specifically exploited unpatched vulnerabilities on Windows systems. It even targeted hospitals, holding data hostage and demanding that infected users pay for access to their files. Figure 2.1 provides an example of a ransomware demand and is a close approximation of what WannaCry looked like on the machines it impacted. The WannaCry attack resulted in damages of billions of dollars.

> **ExamAlert**
>
> Crypto-malware combined with ransomware is unique, in that the attacker directly demands payment, often through cryptocurrencies. The amount requested often is relatively low to make payment more likely.

FIGURE 2.1   **An example of what users see when they are infected with ransomware**

Potentially Unwanted Programs (PUPs)

A *potentially unwanted program* (*PUP*) is a program that is most likely unwanted, despite the possibility that users consented to download it. PUPs include spyware, adware, and dialers, and these programs are often downloaded in conjunction with programs that users actually want.

Spyware

Undesirable code sometimes arrives with commercial software distributions or downloaded from the Internet. *Spyware* is associated with behaviors such as advertising, collecting personal information, and changing a user's computer configuration without obtaining consent to do so. Basically, spyware is software that communicates information from a user's system to another party without notifying the user.

Much like a Trojan horse (described earlier in this chapter), spyware sends information across the Internet to some unknown entity. However, spyware monitors user activity on the system, potentially including keystrokes typed, and sends this logged information to the originator. The information collected—such as passwords, account numbers, and other private information—is then no longer private.

Some clues indicate that a computer might contain spyware:

▶ The system is slow, especially when browsing the Internet.

▶ The Windows desktop is slow in coming up.

▶ Clicking a link does nothing or takes you to an unexpected website.

▶ The browser home page changes, and you might not be able to reset it.

▶ Web pages are automatically added to your favorites list.

ExamAlert

Spyware monitors user activity on the system, possibly including keystrokes typed. The information is then sent to the originator of the spyware.

Adware

Advertising-supported software, or *adware*, is a form of spyware that gives advertisers an online way to make a sale. Companies offer to place ads in their

web properties. A portion of the revenue from banner sales goes to the company placing the ad. However, this novel concept presents some issues for users. These companies also install tracking software on your system that remains in contact with the company through your Internet connection. The software reports data to the company, such as your general surfing habits and the sites you visit. The company might affirm that it will not collect identifying data from your system. However, the situation is still sensitive because software on your system is sending information about you and your surfing habits to a remote location.

U.S. federal law prohibits secret installation of software that forces consumers to receive pop-ups that disrupt their computer use. Adware is legitimate only when users are informed up front that they will receive ads. In addition, if the adware gathers information about users, it must inform them. Privacy issues arise even with legitimate adware, however. For instance, although legitimate adware discloses the nature of data collected and transmitted, users have little or no control over what data is being collected and dispersed.

Cryptomining Software

Many cryptocurrencies, such as bitcoin, are "mined" using compute resources in a process known as *cryptomining*. Cryptomining software is often on dedicated mining hardware; however, organizations have been concerned about such software being on their systems. Cryptomining software consumes compute resources, making heavy use of the CPU. Criminals have been using malware to deliver malicious cryptomining software in order to use distributed resources of others (often as part of a botnet) to mine for cryptocurrency. Such an attack is known as *cryptojacking*. Cryptojacking compromises a victim's computer and uses its resources to mine for cryptocurrency. Such an attack can also take place in a web browser, when a user visits an infected website or ad that automatically executes a script. In this situation, no files exist on the computer, and as long as the browser remains open, the script runs, consuming CPU resources to mine cryptocurrency for the criminal.

Physical Attacks

In addition to the social engineering techniques covered in Chapter 1, "Social Engineering Techniques," the physical world opens up opportunities for attacks often through the use of or attacks on peripheral devices. As part of a university study years ago, researchers left hundreds of unmarked USB flash drives around the campus and found that about half of them were later plugged in to

computers. If an attacker had loaded malware onto those devices, it would have infected the machines either when users plugged the devices in to their computers or when users opened files from the devices on their computers.

A similar approach goes beyond small storage devices and uses malicious cables and plugs, such as generic USB cables, mobile device charging cables, and wall or power adapters. In addition to potentially infecting a system with malware, these cables and adapters can be fitted with advanced technology such as wireless chips to allow nearby attackers to control or provider further instructions to the now vulnerable device.

Skimming is an attack type that has gained more widespread attention. It involves copying data from a credit or debit card by using a specialized terminal. The card can subsequently be cloned, in a process known as *card cloning*. The terminal where the card is swiped could be an ATM outfitted with a nefarious swipe mechanism over the legitimate one or might be a special-purpose device that is used to quickly store the data when a user presents a card to a third party. In most cases, skimmers read data from the magnetic stripe; chip cards (that is, EMV cards) provide some protection against such cloning attacks. And while proximity access and smart cards employ stronger controls, these too have proven susceptible to physical attacks. In one example, by just having physical access to a proximity reader, it was possible to get the encryption key. With this key, an attacker could read, manipulate, and clone a card.

Adversarial Artificial Intelligence (AI)

Artificial intelligence (AI) involves the application of various techniques to solve a variety of problems and challenges. *Machine learning* (*ML*) is one of the key techniques used in AI. Machine learning, as its name implies, allows a machine to learn. It allows machines to be able to do analysis and perform tasks without specifically being programmed. Machine learning is now everywhere. It is used in many ways across various applications. ML can be applied to applications such as web searching, photo tagging, spam detection, video surveillance, virtual assistants, business decision making, customer support, product recommendations, fraud detection, security automation, and weather forecasting.

Machine learning involves mathematical models that often result in predictions made by a computer. However, these models aren't very useful without data— and good data matters! Data known as *sample* or *training data* serves as input to a machine learning model.

Just as information security has benefited from machine learning, the technology can also be used for nefarious purposes by an adversary. Attackers are not only using machine learning for their gain but are perpetrating attacks against ML algorithms. This can have huge impacts across both information and operational security. Given that these algorithms rely on data, it shouldn't be surprising that tainted data can have negative impacts. Both training data and input received by a system could be tainted. For example, tainted data may be used to trick autonomous vehicles into misinterpreting streets signs; an attacker could simply make minor modifications to physical signs. Data can also be poisoned. Imagine a fraud detection system that is provided with tainted data that will always ignore a specific type of fraudulent transaction. The data might be tainted or poisoned during development. Also, because such systems are constantly learning, data could be tainted while the system is operating. Streaming accounts such as Netflix accounts can be tainted. These services tend to offer unique profiles for each user so they can apply ML to constantly learn about the tastes of each user and make recommendations. With access to someone else's profile, consider how you might be able make future recommendations inaccurate by purposely watching specific content—tainting the input data.

Password Attacks

The most common form of authentication and user access control is the username/password combination, which can be significantly weakened as a security measure if the user selects a weak password. Automated and social engineering assaults on passwords are easiest when a password is short, lacks complexity, is derived from a common word found in the dictionary, or is derived from easily guessable personal information such as birthdays, family names, pet names, and similar details. There are four common methods of attacking passwords:

▶ Dictionary attack

▶ Brute-force attack

▶ Spraying

▶ Rainbow table

Passwords should never be stored unencrypted in plaintext. Access to the password database would then make it quite easy to compromise every account. As a result, cryptographic concepts are heavily used in the storing of passwords. (See Chapter 16 for more information on these important concepts, such as hashing

and salting.) Passwords are typically stored as hashes. A hash is a one-way function, which means you can't turn a hashed value into a password. But if you hash a password, you can compare that output to a previously hashed password.

Attacks against passwords usually fall into two broad categories: online and offline attacks. An online attack might, for example, involve an automated or manual attack against your web-based email account, in which the attacker attempts to log in with your username and password. Or an attacker might gain access to an entire hashed (unreadable) database of passwords from the web-based email provider. The attacker might use techniques offline to crack the hashed passwords before attempting to log in online. Security best practices can help avoid online attacks—for example, locking accounts after several failed attempts—but offline attacks give the attacker the convenience of iterating through different methods and countless attempts. Online attacks occur while connected directly to a system. Users getting locked out of their accounts could be a result of forgetting passwords or could indicate attacks against the accounts. An offline attack occurs when the attacker has access to the material independent of the source system; for example, the encrypted password database might have been downloaded. An offline attack is less risky and affords the attacker the opportunity to circumvent controls without being detected.

Imagine trying every word in the dictionary to gain access to a system. This is a *dictionary attack*. In essence, software tools are available to automate such tasks to perform attacks on passwords. Dictionary attacks can use different and custom dictionaries. Such files can even contain lists of passwords that are not typically found within a traditional dictionary, such as *1234* and *abcde*. Dictionary attacks are most successful on simple passwords because the attack simply tries each word from the supplied list. The word *password*, for example, can easily be compromised through a simple dictionary attack; however, simply changing the letter *o* to the numeral 0, and the letter *a* to the @ sign could thwart a dictionary attack.

Brute-force attacks, however, are quite capable of defeating such passwords. Unlike a simple dictionary attack, a brute-force attack relies on cryptanalysis or hashing algorithms that are capable of performing exhaustive key searches. Brute-force attacks can crack short passwords more quickly than can dictionary attacks. However, a brute-force attack can take a lot of time and computing power with larger, more complex passwords because it attempts to exhaust all possible combinations of letters, numbers, and symbols.

Dictionary and brute-force attacks can also be combined into *hybrid attacks*. A hybrid attack uses the dictionary attack method and then builds on that by adding numbers to the end of the words, substituting certain letters for numbers, and capitalizing the first letter of each word. This hybrid method

can also be a useful tool to help identify weak passwords and controls for audit purposes.

A common countermeasure to mitigate password attacks is account lockouts. Password *spraying* seeks to circumvent account lockouts by spreading the use of a single password attempt across multiple accounts. Password spraying is a slow approach, but what it lacks in speed across a single account it gains in scale across multiple accounts at once. A single failed password across an account may be benign. However, a single failed login across many accounts at the same time should serve as an indication to a security administrator that password spraying may be occurring.

A *rainbow table* can thought of as a very large set of precomputed hash values for every possible combination of characters that is able to reverse a cryptograph hash function. If an attacker has enough resources to store an entire rainbow table in memory, a successful attack on hashed passwords can occur with great efficiency. Further, such an attack can occur offline. Thus, the attacker does not need to hash every potential password, as a rainbow table has already done this, and the attacker only needs to perform a search against the required password hashes. Adding an additional input of random data to the function that creates the hashes is known as a salt and can help make a rainbow table attack ineffective.

> **ExamAlert**
>
> A user being locked out of his or her account may indicate an attack against the user's password—especially if that user has no history of failed repeated logon attempts.

Birthday Attacks

A *birthday attack* is a cryptographic method of attack against a secure hash. Keep in mind that a dictionary attack or a brute-force attack is successful when each guess is hashed, and then the resulting hash matches a hash being cracked. A birthday attack finds collisions within hash functions and so is a more efficient method of brute-forcing one-way hashing.

This type of attack is called a birthday attack because it is based on what is known as the birthday paradox. Simply put, if 23 people are in a room, the probability that two of those people have the same birthday is 50%. Hard to believe? True. That's why it is called a paradox. Without getting into complex math, let's try to simplify the reasoning here (though this is not easy to do!). The birthday paradox is concerned with finding any match (not necessarily a match for you). You would need 253 people in a room to have a 50% chance that someone else shares your birthday. Yet you need only 23 people to create 253 pairs when cross-matched with one another. That gets us to a 50% chance. This same theory applies to finding collisions within hash functions. Just as it would be more difficult to find someone who shares (collides with) your birthday, it is more difficult to find something that would collide with a given hash. However, just as you increase the probability of finding any two birthdays that match within the group, it is easier to find two inputs that have the same hash.

Downgrade Attacks

Cryptographic attacks are made simpler through *downgrade attacks*. The cryptographic protocols used for secure web browsing are a common example. A downgrade attack is often a result of security configurations not being updated. Failure to update often stems from the desire to maintain backward compatibility. When a web browser is communicating over a secure channel with a web server, the two must first agree on the version of the cryptographic protocol to use. The server might require the latest and most secure version of a protocol; however, if the browser does not support this specific method, the connection cannot happen. For this reason, security might give way to preventing operational impact. However, if the server allows negotiation to downgrade to a lesser version, the connection is susceptible to further attacks. An attacker might therefore purposely choose to use a client implementation that supports less secure cryptographic versions.

> **ExamAlert**
>
> A man-in-the-middle attack in which the attacker uses an older browser might indicate a downgrade attack. You should ensure that web servers aren't configured to allow for such backward compatibility with older cipher suites.

Cram Quiz

Answer these questions. The answers follow the last question. If you cannot answer these questions correctly, consider reading this chapter again until you can.

1. A user in finance opens a help desk ticket identifying many problems with her desktop computer, including sluggish performance and unfamiliar pop-ups. The issues started after she opened an invoice from a vendor. The user subsequently agreed to several security warnings. Which of the following is the user's device most likely infected with?

   ○ **A.** Ransomware

   ○ **B.** Spyware

   ○ **C.** Backdoor

   ○ **D.** Adware

2. A user has reported consistent activity delays with his PC only when a specific web browser is open. A quick investigation reveals abnormally high CPU usage. Which of the following types of malware is most likely affecting the user's PC?

   ○ **A.** Cryptomining

   ○ **B.** Worm

   ○ **C.** Macro virus

   ○ **D.** Keylogger

3. Which of the following are unique characteristics of a rainbow table attack but not of a brute-force attack? (Select two.)

   ○ **A.** This attack doesn't require the hashed passwords.

   ○ **B.** This attack involves precomputed hash values.

   ○ **C.** This attack must be conducted online.

   ○ **D.** This attack circumvents account lockout restrictions.

4. Which of the following allow machines to solve problems and do analysis without specifically being programmed? (Select two.)

   ○ **A.** RATs

   ○ **B.** PUPs

   ○ **C.** AI

   ○ **D.** ML

5. Which of the following attacks often occurs when security configurations are not updated?

- ○ **A.** Birthday
- ○ **B.** Downgrade
- ○ **C.** Spraying
- ○ **D.** Skimming

Cram Quiz Answers

Answer 1: C. Because the user opened an attachment that masqueraded as something legitimate and required agreement to various security prompts, it is most likely a backdoor installed on the system. Answer A is incorrect because with ransomware, the attacker would be asking for a ransom payment. While both spyware and adware may cause problems with performance, they would not likely prompt the user with security dialogs. Thus, answers B and D are incorrect.

Answer 2: A. Crypto-malware is most likely. While crypto-malware may have worm-like capabilities, such malware is known for heavy CPU use, and, because this particular issue happens when using the web browser, the problem is likely to be a cryptojacking variant. The other choices may result in anomalous CPU behavior, but that is not as likely as it would be with crypto-malware. Further, a macro virus would involve the use of office software. Thus, answers B, C, and D are incorrect.

Answer 3: B and D. A rainbow table is a large set of precomputed hash values used to reverse cryptographic hash functions, and such an attack may be performed offline. Answer A is incorrect, as the attack needs the hashed password values in order to do a lookup or search. Answer C is incorrect as rainbow table attacks may be performed offline.

Answer 4: C and D. Artificial intelligence (AI) involves applying various techniques to solve a variety of problems and challenges, and machine learning (ML) is one of the key techniques used in AI. Answer A is incorrect because remote access Trojans (RATs) installed on a system allow a remote attacker to take control of the targeted system. Answer B is incorrect. PUPs (potentially unwanted programs) include spyware and adware that are often downloaded with a program the user wants.

Answer 5: B. A downgrade attack may occur when security configurations are not being updated. Often this stems from the desire to maintain backward compatibility. Answer A is incorrect because a birthday attack is a cryptographic method of attack against a secure hash. It is based on what is known as the birthday paradox. Answer C is incorrect. Password spraying is an attack that attempts to access a large number of user accounts with a very small number of commonly used passwords. Answer D is incorrect because skimming involves copying data from a card (ATM or other) by using a specialized terminal. The card can subsequently be cloned, by encoding a blank card with the stolen data.

What Next?

If you want more practice on this chapter's exam objective before you move on, remember that you can access all of the Cram Quiz questions on the Pearson Test Prep software online. You can also create a custom exam by objective with the Online Practice Test. Note any objective you struggle with and go to that objective's material in this chapter.

CHAPTER 3

Application Attacks

This chapter covers the following official Security+ exam objective:

▶ 1.3 Given a scenario, analyze potential indicators associated with application attacks.

Essential Terms and Components

▶ privilege escalation

▶ cross-site scripting (XSS)

▶ injection

▶ directory traversal

▶ buffer overflow

▶ race condition

▶ time-of-check to time-of-use (TOCTOU)

▶ error handling

▶ improper input handling

▶ replay attack

▶ integer overflow

▶ cross-site request forgery (CSRF)

▶ server-side request forgery (SSRF)

▶ application programming interface (API) attack

▶ resource exhaustion

▶ memory leak

▶ Secure Sockets Layer (SSL) stripping

▶ shimming

▶ refactoring

▶ pass-the-hash attack

The attacks discussed so far in this book, such as social engineering, malware, and password attacks, don't always lead to the ultimate objective. Often attackers combine these types of attacks with subsequent application and service attacks. For example, an attacker may tailgate into a sensitive area to gain access and then conduct further attacks.

The evolution of web- or cloud-based application resources available via the HTTP and HTTPS protocols presents an "anytime/anywhere" approach to enterprise network resource availability. As more applications are migrated into a browser, attackers have an increasingly large attack surface area for interception and interaction with user input and for directed attacks against web-based resources.

Race Conditions

A *race condition* involves software and, specifically, the way a program executes sequences of code. A race condition typically occurs when code sequences are competing over the same resource or acting concurrently. *Time-of-check to time-of-use* (*TOCTOU*) is an example of a race condition; it is an asynchronous attack that exploits timing. TOCTOU takes advantage of the time delay between the checking of something and the usage of something. Here's a simple analogy to consider: Say that you want to withdraw $100 from your bank's ATM. First, you check your balance and see that you have $100. Next, you initiate the withdrawal, but you are told that you don't have sufficient funds. Between the "check" and the "use," your spouse used a different ATM to make a withdrawal.

Race conditions can result in unexpected and undesirable results or can even result in malfunction. Race conditions also can cause denial of service. In fact, a race condition can cause null pointer errors. With a null pointer error, an application dereferences a pointer that it expects to be valid but that is really null, resulting in a system crash. Race conditions are also associated with allowing attackers to exploit system processes to gain elevated access to areas that otherwise should be restricted. This is known as *privilege escalation*.

ExamAlert

A race condition exploits a small window of time in which one action impacts another. These out-of-sequence actions can result in system crashes, loss of data, unauthorized access, and privilege escalation.

Improper Software Handling

Software should be designed to ensure proper handling of input into the system, as well as proper *error handling*. Both of the following software errors can have operational impacts on an organization and its users, as well as security impacts:

▶ **Improper input handling:** Solutions that don't properly validate input into the system can affect data flow and expectations; this is called *improper error handling*. An attacker might be able to gain control of a system or inject code for remote execution.

▶ **Improper error handling:** When software is not designed to properly handle errors, the result might be release of message and diagnostic information that is sensitive to the inner workings of the systems. This data can disclose details to an end user and allow an attacker to gain sufficient information to advance an attack.

> **ExamAlert**
>
> Software that is not properly designed to validate input or manage errors is vulnerable to program manipulation and could reveal information that should not be disclosed.

Resource Exhaustion

Computing systems often have finite hardware resources available. Cloud computing systems might offer elasticity in terms of ability to scale, but monetary costs are associated with such scalabilty. If software does not properly manage resources such as memory, CPU, and storage, a system might completely consume or exhaust its resources. The most obvious impact of such a situation is denial of service. Without the required resources, users will not be able to access the system, and processing can be impacted. *Resource exhaustion* can also result from other unexpected events and attacks. For example, with a *memory leak*, all available memory is exhausted from the system, resulting in slow operations or unresponsiveness. At their best, memory leaks reduce the performance of a system. If left unchecked, they can cause an entire application or computer to become unresponsive, thus impacting a system's availability.

Overflows

Buffer overflows cause disruption of service and lost data. An overflow occurs when the data presented to an application or service exceeds the storage space that has been reserved in memory for that application or service. Poor application design might allow the input of 100 characters into a field linked to a variable that is capable of holding only 50 characters. The application would not know how to handle the extra data and would become unstable. The overflow portion of the input data must be discarded or somehow handled by the application; otherwise, it can create undesirable results. Because no check is in place to screen out bad requests, the extra data overwrites some portions of memory that other applications use and then causes failures and crashes. A buffer overflow can result in the following:

▶ Data or memory storage may be overwritten.

▶ An attack may overload the input buffer's capability to cope with the additional data, resulting in denial of service.

▶ The originator might execute arbitrary code, often at a privileged level.

An *integer overflow* is another type of overflow that is specific to whole numbers, known as integers. For example, 12 is an integer, but 12.1 is not. When programs do not carefully account for integer overflows, undesirable behaviors and consequences can result. Imagine a typical vehicle odometer. For example, most vehicle odometers support only six digits, which go to 999,999 miles or kilometers. Many vehicles are lucky to see 200,000 miles, but what happens if a car drives 1 million miles? The odometer suffers from an integer overflow and then shows that 0 miles have been driven. Put another way, a program designed to hold an integer of 8 bits could support a number up to 255, which is 11111111 in binary. The number 256 requires an extra bit and equates to binary 100000000. If this program accepted the decimal number 256, it could interpret 256 as 0 (accepting only the last 8 bits) or as 128 (accepting only the first 8 bits).

Overflows present an opportunity for compromise using privilege escalation. Services require special privileges for their operation. A programming error could allow an attacker to obtain special privileges. In such a situation, two possible types of privilege escalation exist: a programming error enabling a user to gain additional privileges after successful authentication and a user gaining privileges with no authentication.

Good quality assurance and secure programming practices can thwart buffer overflows. Currently, the most effective ways to prevent an attacker from exploiting software are to keep the software patched and updated and to monitor the web for newly discovered vulnerabilities.

Code Injections

A buffer overflow could enable an attacker to execute code outside of a specific application. Code injection, such as *dynamic link library (DLL) injection*, specifically allows an attacker to run code within the context of another process, which makes it difficult for the organization to trace the attack.

Arbitrary code execution can occur when an attacker is able to execute programs and commands on an attacked machine. Exploits are designed to attack bugs in software that provide the methods for running these commands. From a vulnerability standpoint, these types of bugs are significant because they allow the attacker to overtake a process. This capability increases the likelihood that the attacker can then completely take control of the client system. A system vulnerable to such code execution is highly susceptible to malware, which does not require the owner's consent. This problem is compounded with remote code execution. Specifically, such code can run across networks and even the Internet.

Preventing these attacks begins with using secure coding practices. Unfortunately, end users are sometimes at the mercy of their software vendors. Therefore, it is important for end users to keep their systems patched and for organizations to pay attention to the types of software vulnerabilities. Arbitrary remote code execution vulnerabilities need to be prioritized in the remediation process.

Application developers and security professionals need to be aware of the different types of threats from malicious code. Using malicious code *injection*, attackers can perform a variety of attacks on systems. Proper input validation is a primary means of preventing such attacks. Injection attacks can result in modification or theft of data. Examples of common code injection techniques include the following:

▶ **Cross-site scripting (XSS):** By placing a malicious client-side script on a website, an attacker can cause an unknowing browser user to conduct unauthorized access activities, expose confidential data, and log successful attacks back to the attacker without users being aware of their participation. *Cross-site scripting (XSS)* vulnerabilities can be exploited to hijack a user's session or to cause the user accessing malware-tainted Site A to unknowingly attack Site B on behalf of the attacker who planted code on Site A.

▶ **SQL injection:** In this type of attack, malicious code is inserted into strings that are later passed to a database server. The SQL server then parses and executes this code.

▶ **LDAP injection:** With this type of attack, which is similar to SQL injection, malicious input is applied to a directory server, which may result in unauthorized queries, granting of permissions, and even password changes.

▶ **XML injection:** An attacker can manipulate the logic of an application in order to perform unauthorized activity or gain unauthorized access by inserting Extensible Markup Language (XML) into a message.

▶ **DLL injection:** DLL injection involves inserting malicious code into a running process. This code injection technique takes advantage of dynamic link libraries (DLLs), which applications load at runtime. A successful attack occurs when the legitimate process hooks into the malicious DLLs and then runs them.

These attacks take advantage of coding flaws, which are preventable. In fact, many application and web development frameworks provide built-in resources and tools to prevent such errors. The Windows operating system now protects against DLL injection by using a protected process system to prevent attacks by ensuring that only trusted code gets loaded.

Note

Proper input validation cannot prevent DLL injection attacks. Rootkits, covered in Chapter 2, "Attack Basics," use DLL injection to hook themselves into older versions of the Windows operating system.

ExamAlert

If given specific scenarios on the exam, remember that the different injection techniques are based on their targets: SQL injections target databases, LDAP injections target directory servers, and XML and DLL injections target applications.

Driver Manipulation

Kernel-mode device drivers, which most operating systems support, run at a much lower level than the operating system and with the same privileges as the operating system. Driver manipulation is a process that can legitimately be done to help improve performance, ensure compatibility, and improve security.

However, the manipulation of device drivers also has the potential to do the opposite and even completely subvert a system. A driver manipulation attack is often a result of malicious code written specifically for system device drivers in order to modify their behavior.

Two concepts related to driver manipulation are important:

- ▶ **Shimming:** In the case of incompatible device drivers, a developer can either write a shim (a piece of code between two components that is then capable of intercepting calls) to provide compatibility or rework the existing driver through refactoring. *Shimming* can also be used as a sophisticated hack that involves installing a shim. Once calls are intercepted, the shim can handle the operation, make changes, and even redirect the call.

- ▶ **Refactoring:** *Refactoring* helps improve the manageability of code, which also helps reduce complexity and improve code extensibility without changing its outward behavior. Malware can potentially exploit poorly written code that is not refactored and look for vulnerabilities. In addition, a skilled attacker could refactor code and trick the underlying system into using the manipulated driver with malicious intent. It is therefore important to verify trusted code using cryptographic techniques to ensure the integrity of the code components allowed on the systems.

Request Forgeries

You need to be familiar with a couple types of attacks that take advantage of how a web server handles URLs:

- ▶ Cross-site request forgery (CSRF or XSRF)
- ▶ Server-side request forgery (SSRF)

Both of these attacks are made possible by a web server being improperly configured in the way it handles URLs. Otherwise, the two attacks are very different.

A *cross-site request forgery* (*CSRF*) causes end users to execute unwanted actions on a site they are already logged in to. The attacker prepares a specially crafted URL that is initiated on the client side, from the web browser. This could result in the user changing her own password to something the attacker knows or taking some other desired action. Imagine that you are logged in to a social media website. You then browse to another site in a different browser tab. Meanwhile, without your knowledge, that second site sends a request

that includes code to post a status update on your social media account. If you remain logged in and the social media site is not designed to protect against such forged requests, this type of attack is entirely possible.

Keep in mind that with a CSRF attack, the user is tricked into going to a specially crafted URL, either by directly clicking on it or by going to a website under the attacker's control with the embedded URL. This attack relies on the user's identity and a website's trust in that identity. If the user is logged in to a social media account, a subsequent malicious web request can succeed because the social media page trusts the individual who is already logged in. Figure 3.1 shows an example of this type of attack. In the final step, the attacker posts a message to the social media page. If the website involved were a financial institution site, the final request might transfer funds to the attacker.

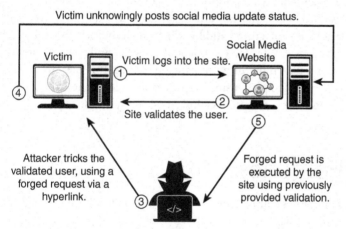

FIGURE 3.1 **An attacker uses CSRF to trick a victim into unknowingly posting a social media status update**

A server-side request forgery (SSRF), unlike a CSRF, is initiated from a web server through a vulnerable web application. With a CSRF attack, the user is tricked into doing something that benefits the attacker. In contrast, an SSRF attack is done for the purpose of compromising information from the web server or enabling other attacks, such as bypassing input validation controls or enabling the attacker to execute further commands. An SSRF attack exploits trust relationships. For example, the vulnerable web application trusts requests coming from the local server on which it's hosted. An SSRF then forces the web server to make a web request, either back to itself or to another server. The following is a simple example of a typical web request in which the

attacker makes a request to retrieve data from another internal web server, which otherwise may not be reachable by users directly (see Figure 3.2):

```
GET http://internal-server-B.example.com/meta-data/ HTTP/1.1
Host: example.com
```

In the following example, the server is making a request using a special file parameter to retrieve a file from itself (in this case, the password file):

```
GET file:///etc/passwd HTTP/1.1
Host: example.com
```

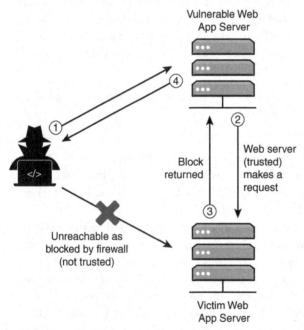

FIGURE 3.2 **Attacker exploits a vulnerable web server to make a request, unknowingly, on the victim's behalf, as the victim web app server trusts the vulnerable web app server**

Proper input validation is vital to preventing SSRF vulnerabilities in web applications. In addition, a list of allowed domains and protocols should be required. This list, known as a *whitelist*, allows only the domains and protocols specified to be fetched locally or from remote resources.

Directory Traversal

Web and application servers vulnerable to directory traversal can potentially expose system directories and files. In the previous section, you saw that an SSRF attack can enable an attacker to access a file on the web server's local filesystem. When possible, applications should avoid passing input from the user to the filesystem interfaces and should at least validate all input. The simplest example of *directory traversal* is a server application being configured in a manner that provides no protection against such attacks.

Directory traversal could allow an attacker to simply view the source code for a website's public directories and files. Or an attacker might be able to look at the path for an image on the site and see, for example, the path https://example.com/images/image.png. An attacker who tries to go to http://example.com/images/ should be denied access. However, a server that allows directory traversal may provide a list of all the images in that directory.

Building on this example, images from a web application are usually loaded from HTML in the following format:

```
<img src="/loadImage?filename=image.png">
```

Image files on the server are located in the var/www/images directory. The source in this case simply returns from this base directory the image it's instructed to load by using a filesystem API that has read access. The attacker now uses the following address in his web browser: https://example.com/loadImage?filename=../../../etc/passwd. If you are familiar with command line operations, you likely know that ../ allows you to go up a level in the directory tree. So this address is asking the server to go up three levels from var/www/images and to the /etc directory and return the passwd file, which contains all the passwords. Therefore, if you were at the command line interface on the server in the /var/www/images folder, the following commands would lead you to the same location:

```
cd /etc/passwd
```

```
cd ../../../etc/passwd
```

By now you might have surmised that web servers have their own root directory that is separate from the operating system that they use to serve content (for example, var/www). Everything in this root directory is accessible to users, and the web server restricts this information, as needed, based on controls such as access control lists. In the second example above, the attacker is able to break outside the web root directory and into other directories in the operating system. As a result, directory traversal may be an undesired vulnerability only within the web root, or the operating system might be vulnerable, potentially

allowing an attacker to attain files and even execute commands from the operating system.

Replay Attack

In a *replay attack*, packets are captured by using sniffers. After the pertinent information is extracted, the packets are placed back on the network. This type of attack can be used to replay bank transactions or other similar types of data transfer, in the hopes of replicating or changing activities such as deposits or transfers. Consider, for example, a password replay attack. In such an attack, the attacker intercepts a password and can later send the password to authenticate as if he were the original user.

Protecting yourself against replay attacks involves some type of time stamp associated with the packets or time-valued, nonrepeating serial numbers. Secure protocols such as IPsec prevent replays of data traffic in addition to providing authentication and data encryption.

A common attack on web applications is a *session replay* attack. A web application assigns a user a session ID (often stored in a cookie) that is good for the session (that is, the visit or use of the application). In this attack, the attacker retrieves the session ID from the user and uses it to appear as that authorized user within the application. Alternatively, an application may not use a cookie to maintain a session but instead might use a unique parameter value that is passed as part of the request. In this situation, an attacker could create a session ID and send it as part of a URL to another valid user (for example, https://example.com/app/login.php?SESSIONID=ATTACKER123). When the user clicks the link and logs in to the application using her own credentials, the attacker can access the account and impersonate the user by using the same URL.

Secure Sockets Layer (SSL) Stripping

Essentially, secure web transactions between a client and a server occur over the Hypertext Transfer Protocol over SSL/TLS (HTTPS) protocol, which incorporates encryption through either SSL or TLS. Most websites today use HTTPS. For example, any transaction on the web between you and your bank would be encrypted and have integrity ensured through HTTPS. With *Secure Sockets Layer (SSL) stripping*, an attacker strips—or removes—the encryption between the client and the website. By acting as a proxy or middleman, the attacker can establish a secure connection between himself and the server.

Figure 3.3 shows an example of this type of attack and how it's possible to trick both the client and the server. Imagine that you are at a coffee shop and connect to the wireless network. To make this attack very simple, say that you unknowingly connect to a wireless hotspot you think is the coffee shop's hotpot, but it actually belongs to an attacker. At this point, the attack is possible because the attacker is able to intercept an unencrypted (HTTP) request you make to your bank. The reason HTTP is used instead of HTTPS is that you haven't established a secure connection to the bank. Most users, either by typing in directly or via a link on another unencrypted website often go to http://www.example.com rather than https://example.com. Normally this is fine, as an HTTP redirect occurs that sends your browser to the HTTPS site. The attacker uses software to intercept the HTTP traffic, and as the traffic is being redirected, the attacker strips away the use of HTTPS. Rather than connecting to your bank, you end up communicating directly with the attacker's computer. At this point, the attacker makes a secure connection to the bank and provides the unencrypted content back to you. At this point, the attacker can capture and read all your information.

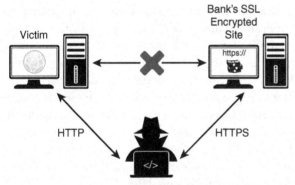

FIGURE 3.3 **Summary of an SSL stripping attack**

A number of countermeasures are available to help mitigate this type of attack. First, most websites have incorporated HTTPS by default. In addition, the introduction of HTTP Strict Transport Security (HSTS) mitigates the risk. Finally, modern browsers have introduced features that make it clear to users when HTTPS has been removed.

Application Programming Interface (API) Attacks

While application programming interfaces (APIs) have been around for decades and web APIs have existed since 1995, concern about *API attacks* in recent years has increased—for good reason. Modern applications across today's mobile web and distributed environments that increasingly rely on smartphone apps aren't monolithically designed the way applications were in the past. Instead, they are modular, composed of individual services, and are expected to provide and get their value from other services. APIs play a critical role in this by exposing application logic and making data available where it's needed. As a result, attackers have naturally looked to APIs for their own use and also found ways to exploit them. Almost since its founding, the Open Web Application Security Project (OWASP) has annually published the *OWASP Top 10* for web application security risks. APIs are so pervasive across web applications that OWASP now annually publishes a similar list for API security. The following is the OWASP's most recent list of the top 10 risks:

▶ **Broken Object Level Authorization:** APIs tend to expose endpoints that handle object identifiers, creating a wide attack surface Level Access Control issue. Object level authorization checks should be considered in every function that accesses a data source using an input from the user.

▶ **Broken User Authentication:** Authentication mechanisms are often implemented incorrectly, allowing attackers to compromise authentication tokens or to exploit implementation flaws to assume other users' identities temporarily or permanently. Compromising a system's ability to identify the client/user compromises API security overall.

▶ **Excessive Data Exposure:** Looking forward to generic implementations, developers tend to expose all object properties without considering their individual sensitivity, relying on clients to perform the data filtering before displaying it to the user.

▶ **Lack of Resources and Rate Limiting:** Quite often, APIs do not impose any restrictions on the size or number of resources that can be requested by the client/user. Not only can this impact the API server performance, leading to Denial of Service (DoS), but also leaves the door open to authentication flaws such as brute force.

▶ **Broken Function Level Authorization:** Complex access control policies with different hierarchies, groups, and roles and an unclear separation between administrative and regular functions tend to lead to authorization flaws. By exploiting these issues, attackers gain access to other users' resources and/or administrative functions.

▶ **Mass Assignment:** Binding client-provided data (e.g., JSON) to data models, without proper properties filtering based on a whitelist, usually leads to Mass Assignment. Either guessing object properties, exploring other API endpoints, reading the documentation, or providing additional object properties in request payloads allows attackers to modify object properties they are not supposed to.

▶ **Security Misconfiguration:** Security misconfiguration is commonly a result of unsecure default configurations, incomplete or ad hoc configurations, open cloud storage, misconfigured HTTP headers, unnecessary HTTP methods, permissive Cross-Origin resource sharing (CORS), and verbose error messages containing sensitive information.

▶ **Injection:** Injection flaws, such as SQL, NoSQL, Command Injection, and so on, occur when untrusted data is sent to an interpreter as part of a command or query. The attacker's malicious data can trick the interpreter into executing unintended commands or accessing data without proper authorization.

▶ **Improper Assets Management:** APIs tend to expose more endpoints than traditional web applications, making proper and updated documentation highly important. Proper hosts and deployed API versions inventory also play an important role to mitigate issues such as deprecated API versions and exposed debug endpoints.

▶ **Insufficient Logging and Monitoring:** Insufficient logging and monitoring, coupled with missing or ineffective integration with incident response, allows attackers to further attack systems, maintain persistence, pivot to more systems to tamper with, extract, or destroy data. Most breach studies demonstrate the time to detect a breach is over 200 days, typically detected by external parties rather than internal processes or monitoring.

Not much on this list is brand new in regard to how attackers would look to attack an application or a system. However, some of these risks may be magnified due to the nature of APIs, which are designed to expose application logic and data—often across a large population group. However, as with any other application or security system, you need to be concerned with things like authentication and authorization, understanding data sensitivity, proper configuration, ensuring availability, adequate documentation, and proper logging and monitoring.

Pass-the-Hash Attack

Most systems do not send passwords in plaintext. Instead, a system is likely to create a digital fingerprint, or cryptographic hash, of a password. Knowing a hash does not allow a system to reconstruct a password; it allows it to verify that an input maps to a particular hash value. In fact, most passwords are stored as cryptographic hashed values.

Chapter 16, "Cryptographic Concepts," explores hashes in detail. The current discussion provides a simplified example of hashing. Imagine that each letter of the alphabet corresponds to a number (A = 1, B = 2, C = 3, and so on). If your password is ABC, then by using your hashing algorithm (that is, adding up the numbers), you arrive at a value of 6. When a password is subsequently entered, it is run through the same algorithm and then compared to the stored value. If you try to enter ABD as the password, the resulting value, 7, does not match the value stored. Of course, actual hashing algorithms are much more complicated than this, but this should help you understand the concepts further.

In a *pass-the-hash attack*, the attacker does not need access to a user's password. Instead, the attacker needs only the hashed value of the password. This type of attack is performed against systems that accept specific implementations of authentication schemes known as NT Lan Manager (NTLM) or LM. In such an attack, the attacker does not need the password as long as she has gained access to the cryptographic hash. The attacker then can pass this hash value to a system for authentication.

Cram Quiz

Answer these questions. The answers follow the last question. If you cannot answer these questions correctly, consider reading this chapter again until you can.

1. An attacker exploited an interactive process in a recently developed and deployed application and was able to gain access to areas of the application from which users are otherwise restricted. Which of the following best describes what occurred?

   - ○ **A.** Driver manipulation
   - ○ **B.** Directory traversal
   - ○ **C.** Buffer overflow
   - ○ **D.** Privilege escalation

2. Which of the following attacks can be related to the length of a variable in an input not being properly checked and contained by an application?

   - ○ **A.** Input validation
   - ○ **B.** Shimming
   - ○ **C.** Buffer overflow
   - ○ **D.** Privilege escalation

3. A security analyst discovered on the dark web a text file containing a list of usernames along with many other attributes belonging to the organization. A review of the web server access logs reveals the following requests:

   ```
   https://example.com/loadImage?filename=../../scripts
   https://example.com/loadImage?filename=.//.//.//etc/shadow
   https://example.com/loadImage?filename=../../../etc/passwd
   ```

   What type of attack occurred?

   - ○ **A.** Cross-site scripting
   - ○ **B.** Refactoring
   - ○ **C.** Race condition
   - ○ **D.** Directory traversal

4. Which of the following can a race condition result in? (Select three.)

   - ○ **A.** Extensively Marked-Up Language
   - ○ **B.** System crash
   - ○ **C.** Unauthorized access
   - ○ **D.** Privilege escalation

5. An attacker removes the encryption between a client and a website server and then establishes a secure connection between himself and the server. What is this technique called?

- O **A.** Replay
- O **B.** Integer overflow
- O **C.** SSL stripping
- O **D.** Cross-site request forgery

Cram Quiz Answers

Answer 1: D. Privilege escalation occurs when an attacker is able to gain elevated access to areas that otherwise should be restricted. Although a buffer overflow may lead to privilege escalation, it's not clear from the question that this is the best description, and so answer C is incorrect. Answer A is incorrect. Driver manipulation is done to improve performance, compatibility, or security of device drivers, and it is sometimes used by attackers with malicious intent. Answer B is incorrect. Directory traversal provides a user or an attacker the ability to list and navigate a web server or an operating system's filesystem.

Answer 2: C. A buffer overflow may result from the length of a variable in an input not properly being checked and contained by an application. Answer B is incorrect. Shimming is a device driver manipulation technique. Answer D is incorrect as privilege escalation occurs when an attacker is able to gain elevated access to areas that otherwise should be restricted. Answer A is incorrect. Input validation is a solution to prevent a buffer overflow by ensuring that input variables are properly formatted.

Answer 3: D. Directory traversal can expose system directories and files. The logs reveal someone making requests to try to access system files from the web server's base directory. Answer A is incorrect because cross-site scripting is a code injection technique that uses client-side scripts. Answer B is incorrect because refactoring is a driver manipulation technique. Answer C is incorrect. A race condition relates to the way a program executes sequences of code.

Answer 4: B, C, and D. A race condition exploits a small window of time in which one action impacts another. These out-of-sequence actions can result in a system crash, loss of data, unauthorized access, and privilege escalation. Answer A is incorrect and invalid because the proper term is Extensible Markup Language (XML), which is a text-based markup language that is both machine and human readable.

Answer 5: C. With Secure Sockets Layer (SSL) stripping, an attacker strips or removes the encryption between the client and the website. Acting as a proxy or middleman, the attacker establishes a secure connection between himself and the server. Answer A is incorrect because in a replay attack, packets are captured by using sniffers. After the pertinent information is extracted, the packets are placed back on the network. Answer B is incorrect. An integer overflow is specific to whole numbers, known as integers. For example, 12 is an integer, but 12.1 is not. When programs do not carefully account for integer overflows, undesirable behaviors and consequences can occur. Answer D is incorrect. A cross-site request forgery (CSRF) causes end users to execute an unwanted action on sites they are already logged in to. The attacker prepares a specially crafted URL that is client-side-initiated from the web browser.

What Next?

If you want more practice on this chapter's exam objective before you move on, remember that you can access all of the Cram Quiz questions on the Pearson Test Prep software online. You can also create a custom exam by objective with the Online Practice Test. Note any objective you struggle with and go to that objective's material in this chapter.

Network Attacks

This chapter covers the following official Security+ exam objective:

▶ 1.4 Given a scenario, analyze potential indicators associated with network attacks.

Essential Terms and Components

▶ evil twin

▶ rogue access point

▶ bluesnarfing

▶ bluejacking

▶ disassociation

▶ jamming

▶ radio frequency identification (RFID)

▶ near-field communication (NFC)

▶ initialization vector (IV) attack

▶ on-path attack

▶ Address Resolution Protocol (ARP) poisoning

▶ Media Access Control (MAC) flooding

▶ MAC spoofing

▶ domain hijacking

▶ DNS poisoning

▶ uniform resource locator (URL) redirection

▶ domain reputation

▶ distributed denial of service (DDoS) attack

▶ malicious script execution

Networks are becoming increasingly distributed and mobile. Not only are there various points of entry, but the idea of a tight perimeter no longer exists as technologies such as wireless, mobile devices, and modern cloud-based web applications have eliminated the idea of the perimeter. It is important to understand the different types of attacks. Keep in mind, however, that most single attacks do not succeed. A combination of attacks is often required. For these reasons, the idea of defense-in-depth is critical to the security of an organization. As you learn about the individual attacks in the sections that follow, think about the situations to which they might apply. Also think about how each of these attacks might be used and when a combination of attacks would be required.

Wireless

Wireless networks present unique security challenges. Wireless networks are subject to the same types of attacks as their wired counterparts, such as MITM, DoS, replay, and crypto attacks. These attacks have become more prevalent as wireless networks have become common. Replay attacks on a wireless network are arguably simpler than replay attacks carried out on wired networks. A wireless sniffer includes a hardware or software device that is capable of capturing the data or packets that traverse the wireless channel. When traffic being sent across the network is unencrypted, packet sniffing enables the attacker to capture the data and decode it from its raw form into readable text.

Wireless networks are further susceptible to being disrupted by other radio sources. Such disruptions can merely be unintentional interference or can be malicious attempts to jam the signal. For example, you might have personally experienced or heard stories about how the operation of a microwave oven can interfere with wireless access to the Internet. This can happen because specific wireless 802.11 devices operate at or near the same wireless band used by the microwave. In addition, specific attacks on wireless networks can be performed by setting up a nearby access point or using dedicated wireless jamming devices.

> **Note**
>
> According to the Federal Communications Commission (FCC), "federal law prohibits the operation, marketing, or sale of any type of jamming equipment, including devices that interfere with cellular and Personal Communication Services (PCS), police radar, Global Positioning Systems (GPS) and wireless networking services (Wi-Fi)."

Counteracting a *jamming* attack is both simple and complicated. It is simple because most jamming attacks require physical proximity. In the case of a cell phone, for example, just moving 30 feet away can make a difference. However, changing location is not always a viable option. Sometimes you must either locate the source of the jamming or boost the signal being jammed. Many enterprise-grade devices provide power levels that can be configured and have the capability to identify and locate rogue devices that are causing interference.

Key to wireless networks are wireless access point devices. Wireless endpoints connect to an access point. The access point typically acts as a bridge to the wired network. A common attack involves the use of a *rogue access point*. In such a situation, an unauthorized wireless access point is set up. In an organization, well-meaning insiders might connect to rogue access points (rogue APs), which create a type of man-in-the-middle attack, referred to as an *evil twin*. Because the client's request for connection is an omnidirectional open broadcast, it is possible for a hijacker to act as an access point to the client and to act as a client to the true network access point. This enables the hijacker to follow all data transactions and thus modify, insert, or delete packets at will. By implementing a rogue access point that has stronger signal strength than more remote permanent installations, an attacker can cause a wireless client to preferentially connect to its own stronger connection by using the wireless device's standard roaming handoff mechanism.

Fortunately, it is simple to detect rogue access points by using software. A common method for detecting rogue access points is to use wireless sniffing applications. As wireless networks have become ubiquitous and often required, organizations have conducted wireless site surveys to analyze and plan wireless networks. These site surveys are often associated with new deployments, but they are also conducted in existing wireless networks. Looking for rogue access points is part of the survey process because these access points can negatively impact not just security but also quality of service for the legitimate wireless network.

When a rogue access point is disconnected, it receives a deauthentication frame and is disassociated from the network. However, this message can be exploited in another common attack that involves a denial of service between wireless users and the wireless access point: a *dissociation* or *deauthentication* attack. By spoofing a user's MAC address, an attacker can send a deauthentication data transmission to the wireless access point.

Some Wi-Fi technologies have been shown to be especially susceptible to *initialization vector (IV) attacks*, which are attacks that use passive statistical analysis. An IV is an input to a cryptographic algorithm, which is essentially a random number. Ideally, an IV should be unique and unpredictable. An IV

attack can occur when the IV is too short, is predictable, or is not unique. If the IV is not long enough, there is a high probability that the IV will repeat after only a small number of packets. Modern wireless encryption algorithms use a longer IV, and newer protocols also use a mechanism to dynamically change keys as the system is used.

> **ExamAlert**
>
> An IV that is repeated with a given key is especially subject to being attacked.

Short-Range Wireless Communications

As the use of wireless networks has increased, so has the use of a variety of wireless technologies. Much of this growth has been spawned by computer peripherals and other small electronics. Consider mobile devices. Most mobile phones today take advantage of Bluetooth and near-field communication (NFC) technology. If you walk into almost any store today, you can find a wide array of Bluetooth-enabled devices, such as speakers and earbuds, that can be used to play music from a phone or any other Bluetooth-enabled device.

Bluetooth

Mobile devices equipped for Bluetooth short-range wireless connectivity, such as laptops, tablets, and cell phones, are subject to receiving photos, messages, or other broadcast spam sent from nearby Bluetooth-enabled transmitting devices in an attack referred to as *bluejacking*. Although this act is typically benign, attackers can use this form of attack to generate messages that appear to come from a legitimate device. Users then follow obvious prompts and establish an open Bluetooth connection with the attacker's device. When paired with the attacker's device, the user's device makes data available for unauthorized access, modification, or deletion, which is a more aggressive attack referred to as *bluesnarfing*.

> **ExamAlert**
>
> Do not confuse bluejacking and bluesnarfing. Bluesnarfing is generally associated with more dangerous attacks that can expose or alter a user's information.

Near-Field Communication

Near-field communication (*NFC*) is a set of standards for contactless communication between devices. Although NFC is considered contactless, in most practical uses, devices establish communication by being close or touching. Currently, varying use cases for NFC exist. Most individuals are familiar with NFC as a smartphone feature. NFC is available on most devices, such as those running the Android operating system and the Apple iPhone.

An NFC chip in a mobile device generates an electromagnetic field. This allows the device to communicate with other devices or with a tag that contains specific information that leverages the electromagnetic field as a power supply to send the information back to the device. For example, an advertisement at a bus stop may be embedded with a tag that is able to communicate with a smart device.

Given NFC's limited range, the types and practicality of attacks are limited by distance. However, NFC still presents potential risks, including the following:

- ▶ **Confidentiality:** Attacks can take advantage of the risks posed by any communications methods, including eavesdropping. Any sensitive data must be encrypted to mitigate such concerns.

- ▶ **Denial of service:** NFC could be subject to jamming and interference disruptions that cause loss of service.

- ▶ **Man-in-the-middle (MITM) attacks:** Theoretically, MITM attacks are possible. But again, given the limitations of proximity, such attacks are uncommon with NFC.

- ▶ **Malicious code:** As with any client device, malware prevention and user awareness are key controls.

Specific concerns about NFC that have surfaced largely stem from lenient configurations. For example, applications of NFC might provide a function to pass information such as contacts and applications, but no confirmation may be required from the receiving end. In other applications, such as with device pairing, in the absence of any type of confirmation, an attacker can easily connect and run further attacks to access the device.

RFID

Radio frequency identification (*RFID*) is a wireless technology that was initially common to supply-chain and inventory tracking. RFID has been around longer than NFC. In fact, NFC is based on the RFID protocols. RFID is commonly

used with toll booths, ski lifts, passports, credit cards, key fobs, and other applications. RFID chips can even be implanted into the human body for medical purposes. RFID uses electromagnetic fields and is one-way. Information is transmitted from a chip, also known as a smart tag, to an RFID reader. There are two types of RFID tags: active and passive tags. An active tag can broadcast a signal over a larger distance because it contains a power source. A passive tag, on the other hand, isn't powered but is activated by a signal sent from the reader.

Cryptography is an important component for RFID security. Without it, an RFID tag is susceptible to attackers writing or modifying data to the tag. Arguably one of the biggest concerns surrounding RFID has been privacy. Even when RFID tags are encrypted, an attacker can read them, for example, to track the movement of a tag or the object to which a tag is applied.

> **Note**
>
> NFC is based on RFID protocols. However, NFC provides peer-to-peer communication, which sets it apart from most RFID devices. An NFC chip functions as both a reader and a tag.

On-Path Attack

The on-path attack, also known as a *man-in-the-middle (MITM) attack* takes place when an attacker intercepts traffic and then tricks the parties at both ends into believing that they are communicating with each other. This type of attack is possible because of the nature of the three-way TCP handshake process, which uses SYN and ACK packets. TCP is a connection-oriented protocol, and a three-way handshake takes place when establishing a connection and when closing a session. When establishing a session, the client sends a SYN request, the server sends an acknowledgment and synchronization (SYN-ACK) to the client, and then the client sends an ACK (also referred to as SYN-ACK-ACK) to complete the connection. During this process, an attacker may initiate a man-in-the-middle attack. The attacker uses a program that appears to the client as the server and appears to the server as the client. An attacker may also choose to alter the data or eavesdrop and pass it along. This type of attack is common with the Telnet protocol and wireless technologies. It is also generally difficult to implement because of physical routing issues, TCP sequence numbers, and speed.

If an on-path attack is attempted on an internal network, physical access to the network is required. Be sure that access to wiring closets and switches is restricted; if possible, such an area should be locked. After you have secured the physical environment, be sure to protect the services and resources that allow a system to be inserted into a session. DNS can be compromised and used to redirect the initial request for service, providing an opportunity to execute a man-in-the-middle attack. You should restrict DNS access to read-only for everyone except the administrator. The best way to prevent these types of attacks is to use encryption, secure protocols, and methods for keeping track of the user's session or device.

> **ExamAlert**
>
> An on-path attack takes place when a computer intercepts traffic and either eavesdrops on the traffic or alters it. Many organizational proxy servers are designed to do this. The clients have digital certificates and trust the proxy.

On-path attacks have declined due to the prevalence of prevention techniques. As a result, a newer type of on-path attack, known as a *man-in-the-browser* (*MITB*) *attack*, has become more common. An MITB attack is a Trojan that infects web browser components such as browser plug-ins and other browser helper objects. MITB attacks are particularly dangerous because everything occurs at the application level on the user's system. These attacks are capable of avoiding web application controls that might otherwise be alerted to a traditional MITM attack at the network layer. MITB attacks can also go beyond mere interception to injecting web code and performing other functions to interact with the user.

Layer 2 Attacks

Layer 2 is the data link layer of the Open Systems Interconnection (OSI) model for computer networks. This is the layer responsible for transferring data between systems on a local network. Computers are often connected to a switch in a wiring closet. Switches operate at Layer 2 of the OSI model. Their packet-forwarding decisions are based on Media Access Control (MAC) addresses. Switches allow LANs to be segmented, thus increasing the amount of bandwidth that goes to each device. Each segment is a separate collision domain, but all segments are in the same broadcast domain.

As you consider network attacks at Layer 2, keep in mind that the OSI model allows each layer to work without having to be considered with the others.

However, lower layers can affect the layers above them. Thus, if the physical layer is hacked, Layer 2 will suffer, and if Layer 2 is hacked, the network layer (Layer 3) is also compromised, and so forth.

MAC Spoofing

Spoofing is a method of providing false identification information to gain unauthorized access. Spoofing a MAC address, called MAC spoofing, involves changing the built-in MAC address of a networked device, which is hard-coded and assigned to each network interface from the factory. In some circumstances, this address can be changed, but most attacks simply mask or spoof the address to something else. Some networks might control access via this address. An attacker able to spoof this address could then gain access. Many wireless networks restrict access to systems with only known MAC addresses. For example, most home wireless access devices provide an option to configure this quite easily. You could, for example, provide a unique address for each device the members of your household use so only they can access the network. You can also provide a user-friendly name to each device as its MAC address doesn't change (unless, of course, it's spoofed). You would see an unknown device on your network if you weren't authorizing by MAC address. If you were blocking by MAC address, the attacker would need to be able to spoof an allowed MAC address.

ARP Poisoning

A unique 48-bit address is hard-coded into every network card. For network communications to occur, this hardware address must be associated with an IP address. Address Resolution Protocol (ARP), which operates at Layer 2 (data link layer) of the OSI model, associates MAC addresses to IP addresses. ARP is a simple lower-layer protocol that consists of requests and replies without validation. However, this simplicity also leads to a lack of security.

When you use a protocol analyzer to look at traffic, you see an ARP request and an ARP reply, which are the two basic parts of ARP communication. Reverse ARP (RARP) requests and RARP replies also are used. A device maintains an ARP table that contains a cache of the IP addresses and MAC addresses the device has already correlated. The host device searches its ARP table to see whether a MAC address corresponds to the destination host IP address. When no matching entry exists, it broadcasts an ARP request to the entire network. All systems see the broadcast, but only the device that has the corresponding information replies. However, devices can accept ARP replies before even

requesting them. This type of entry is known as an *unsolicited* entry because the information was not explicitly requested.

> ### ExamAlert
>
> ARP does not require any type of validation. Thus, as ARP requests are sent, the requesting devices believe that the incoming ARP replies are from the correct devices. Thus a perpetrator may be able to trick a device into thinking any IP address is related to any MAC address.

Address Resolution Protocol (ARP) poisoning is limited to attacks that are locally based, so an intruder needs either physical access to the network or control of a device on the local network. To mitigate ARP poisoning on a small network, you can use static or script-based mappings for IP addresses and ARP tables. For large networks, by using equipment that offers port security, you can permit only one MAC address for each physical port on the switch. In addition, you can deploy monitoring tools or an intrusion detection system (IDS) to alert you when suspicious activity occurs.

MAC Flooding

ARP poisoning can lead to attacks such as DoS attacks, on-path attacks, and MAC flooding. DoS attacks are covered in greater detail later in this chapter. *Media Access Control (MAC) flooding* is an attack that compromises a networking switch. This type of attack is successful because of the way all switches and bridges work. Only a limited amount of space is allocated to store source addresses of packets. When the table becomes full, the device can no longer learn new information and becomes flooded. As a result, the switch may be forced into a hub-like state and broadcast all network traffic to every device in the network.

Port Stealing

A lesser vulnerability of ARP is port stealing. *Port stealing* is an on-path attack that exploits the binding between a port and a MAC address. The idea behind port stealing is that an attacker sends numerous packets with the source IP address of the victim and the destination MAC address of the attacker. This attack applies to broadcast networks built using switches.

Domain Name System (DNS) Attacks

Domain Name System (DNS) translates user-friendly names, such as example. com, to IP addresses, such as 93.184.216.34. Several DNS attacks take advantage of vulnerabilities in DNS and the way in which DNS works. Organizations more than ever before need to protect their domains, especially given that applications and services are provided from these domains. Part of this protection is monitoring for *domain reputation*. Domain reputation monitoring, which also includes IP monitoring, provides useful threat intelligence that helps an organization understand its own domain and also protect against external malicious domains. Understanding what domains have been deemed malicious can help with incident response and blacklisting controls. Even nonmalicious domains could wind up with low reputation as a result of being compromised and used to attack others. For this reason, an organization needs to also understand the reputation of its own domain. The following sections take a closer look at three common DNS attacks you need to be familiar with:

▶ Domain hijacking

▶ URL redirection

▶ DNS poisoning

Domain Hijacking

Domain hijacking occurs when a domain is taken over without the original owner's knowledge or consent. This can occur opportunistically when the domain ownership expires, but direct attacks are usually the result of security issues with the domain registrar or direct attacks via social engineering or through the administration portal of the domain owner. Domain registrars now include optional privacy controls and countermeasures to help thwart such attacks. Once an attacker has hijacked a domain, several opportunities exist to cause harm. The attacker may post embarrassing or malicious content from the domain on the web or may redirect the domain to another domain. The attacker might even sell the domain to another party.

Universal Resource Locator (URL) Redirection

URL redirection is a common technique that is often employed for legitimate purposes, but it can also be abused. First, let's look at a common example of

a useful redirect you have likely experienced. Imagine that you're logged in to your bank, and you create a bookmark for the page where you can transfer money. After logging out, you decide to revisit that bookmark. Because you aren't logged in, the bank implements a redirect function to send you back to the login page. How can an attacker take advantage of this process? If you trust http://www.example.com and see a link beginning with http://example.com/bank/example.php, you might feel confident that you are visiting the legitimate site. The attacker, however, actually sends a different link for you to click: http://example.com/banktransfer/example.php?url=http://malicious-web-site.example.com. This type of attack works when the original example.php page contains code like the following that has the intended useful purpose of redirecting you:

```
$redirect_url = $_GET['url'];
```

This code takes the parameter given to it and redirects the user. So if an attacker gives a malicious website URL as the parameter, the code instead redirects the user there. While redirection is a useful feature, organizations need to ensure that this function can't be abused. The following are a couple examples to prevent such abuse:

▶ Prevent offsite redirects by validating the input of URLs passed to ensure that all URLs passed use relative paths only.

▶ If you need to pass to other sites, use whitelisting.

DNS Poisoning

DNS poisoning enables a perpetrator to redirect traffic by changing the IP record for a specific domain, thus permitting attackers to send legitimate traffic anywhere they choose. The attacker not only sends a requestor to a different website but also caches this information for a short period, distributing the attack's effect to the server users. DNS poisoning is also referred to as *DNS cache poisoning* because it affects cached information.

Every Internet page request starts with a DNS query. If the IP address is not known locally, the request is sent to a DNS server. Two types of DNS servers are used: authoritative and recursive. Whereas DNS servers share information, recursive servers maintain information in cache. This means a caching or recursive server can answer queries for resource records even if it cannot resolve a request directly. A flaw in the resolution algorithm allows the poisoning of DNS records on a server. All an attacker has to do is delegate a false name to the domain server and provide a false address for the server. For example, imagine that an attacker creates the hostname hack.example.com. After that, the attacker queries your DNS server to resolve the host example.com. The DNS

server resolves the name and stores this information in its cache. Until the zone expiration, any further requests for example.com do not result in lookups but are answered by the server from its cache. It is now possible for the attacker to set your DNS server as the authoritative server for his or her zone with the domain registrar. If the attacker conducts malicious activity, the attacker can make it appear that your DNS server is being used for these malicious activities.

DNS poisoning can result in many different issues. Domain name servers can be used for DDoS attacks. Malware can be downloaded to an unsuspecting user's computer from the rogue site, and all future requests by that computer will be redirected to the fake IP address. This process could be used to build an effective botnet. This method of poisoning can also allow for code injection exploits, especially because content can be pulled from multiple websites at the same time.

To minimize the effects of DNS poisoning, check the DNS setup if you are hosting your own DNS server. Be sure the DNS server is not open recursive. An open-recursive DNS server responds to any lookup request without check-ing where it originates. Disable recursive access for other networks to resolve names that are not in your zone files. You can also use different servers for authoritative and recursive lookups and require that caches discard information except from the com servers and the root servers. From the user perspective, education works best. However, it is becoming more difficult to spot a prob-lem by watching the address bar on the Internet browser. Therefore, operating system vendors are adding more protection. Microsoft Windows User Account Control (UAC) notifies the user that a program is attempting to change the system's DNS settings, thus preventing the DNS cache from being poisoned.

Denial of Service

The purpose of a denial-of-service (DoS) attack is to disrupt the resources or services that a user would expect to have access to. These types of attacks are executed by manipulating protocols and can happen without the need to be validated by the network. An attack typically involves flooding a listening port on a user's machine with packets. The idea is to make that system so busy pro-cessing the new connections that it cannot process legitimate service requests.

Many of the tools used to produce DoS attacks are readily available on the Internet. Administrators use them to test connectivity and troubleshoot prob-lems on the network, and malicious users use them to cause connectivity issues.

Consider some examples of DoS attacks:

- ▶ **Smurf/smurfing:** This attack is based on the Internet Control Message Protocol (ICMP) echo reply function, also known as ping, which is the command-line tool used to invoke this function. In a smurf attack, the attacker sends ping packets to the broadcast address of the network but replaces the original source address in the ping packets with the source address of the victim. This causes a flood of traffic to be sent to the unsuspecting network device.

- ▶ **Fraggle:** This attack is similar to a smurf attack, but it uses UDP instead of ICMP. The attacker sends spoofed UDP packets to broadcast addresses, as in a smurf attack. These UDP packets are directed to port 7 (Echo) or port 19 (Chargen).

- ▶ **Ping flood:** A ping flood attempts to block service or reduce activity on a host by sending ping requests directly to the victim. A variation of this type of attack is the ping of death, in which the packet size is so large that the system does not know how to handle the packets.

- ▶ **SYN flood:** This attack takes advantage of the TCP three-way handshake. The source system sends a flood of SYN requests but never sends the final ACK, thus creating half-open TCP sessions. The TCP stack waits before resetting the port, and in the meantime, the attack overflows the destination computer's connection buffer, making it impossible to service connection requests from valid users.

- ▶ **Land:** In this attack, the attacker exploits a behavior in the operating systems of several versions of Windows, Linux, macOS, and Cisco IOS with respect to their TCP/IP stacks. The attacker spoofs a TCP/IP SYN packet to the victim system with the same source and destination IP address and the same source and destination ports. This confuses the system as it tries to respond to the packet.

- ▶ **Teardrop:** This form of attack targets a known behavior of UDP in the TCP/IP stack of some operating systems. An attacker sends fragmented UDP packets to the victim with odd offset values in subsequent packets. When the operating system attempts to rebuild the original packets from the fragments, the fragments overwrite each other, causing confusion. Because some operating systems cannot gracefully handle this type of error, the system is likely to crash or reboot.

DoS attacks come in many shapes and sizes. The first step in protecting yourself from such an attack is to understand the nature of the attacks in this list. Although various security solutions are designed specifically to help prevent

such attacks, you might consider other measures in your organization. Fundamentally, organizations should ensure that they have well-defined processes related to auditing, standard operating procedures, and documented configurations. Finally, being well versed in the nature of the different types of attacks can help you make better decisions when it comes to attack recognition and implementing controls such as packet filtering and rights management.

Distributed DoS

Another simple expansion of a DoS attack is referred to as a *distributed denial-of-service (DDoS) attack*. In this type of attack, masters are computers that run the client software, and zombies run software. The attacker creates master handlers or command-and-control servers, which, in turn, create many zombies, forming a botnet. The software running on the zombies can launch multiple types of attacks, such as UDP or SYN floods on a target. Figure 4.1 shows an example of a DDoS attack.

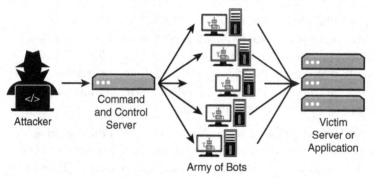

FIGURE 4.1 **Example of a DDoS attack**

Basically, the attacker distributes zombie software or infects multiple hosts (or even thousands of hosts), providing the attacker partial or full control of the infected computer system through one or more command-and-control servers. Finally, the army of bots or compromised machines attacks the victim by overwhelming it, making it slow or unable to respond to legitimate requests.

ExamAlert

When attackers compromise enough systems with the installed zombie software, they can initiate an attack against a victim from a wide variety of hosts. The attacks come in the form of the standard DoS attacks, but the effects are multiplied by the total number of zombie machines under the control of the attacker, resulting in distributed denial of service.

Often DoS and DDoS attacks involve reflection; that is, the attacker takes advantage of legitimate third-party services and spoofs the source address to be that of the victim. As a result, any replies from the service are directed at the victim, hiding the attacker's identity. Network time servers and DNS servers are common examples of third-party services used to execute such attacks. These attacks can further take advantage of amplification: An attack is magnified, increasing the amount of traffic sent to the victim, which is fundamental to a DoS attack. Requests to an NTP time server, for example, are amplified back by a factor of more than 500%. Because these attacks use UDP, a connection is not required, and the source is not verified.

Although DDoS attacks generally come from outside the network to deny services, you must also consider the effect of DDoS attacks mounted from inside the network. Disgruntled or malicious internal users may use DDoS attacks to disrupt services without any outside influence.

Many of the denial-of-service attacks discussed earlier are network-based attacks based on TCP, UDP, or ICMP. More modern attacks use Layer 7 application-based attacks, often against web servers. Such an attack generates a high number of requests each second against the application, often using a flood of GET and POST traffic via HTTP. Recently, DDoS attacks against *operational technology* (*OT*) have become more prevalent. These attacks are possible because operational technology is now being interconnected and exposed to the outside world, whereas, in the past, this technology was isolated in businesses and factories. Just consider how many devices and applications are being connected around the world outside information technology—in electrical grids, smart cities, automobiles, and IP-based video surveillance and in more common Internet of Things (IoT) devices like doorbells, smart thermostats, and lighting automation.

DDoS attacks can have a wide operational impact across an organization and the customers it serves. DDoS attacks aren't quiet, however; fortunately, they are easy to detect. Unfortunately, the impacts from an attack are felt immediately, and, if not quickly mitigated, can cause extended loss of operations, including lost revenue and even loss of lives. The following symptoms may indicate that a DDoS attack has been launched:

▶ Users report slow response from applications and services.

▶ Applications and services are not available outside of known maintenance windows or other failures.

▶ Anomalous spikes occur in requests coming in within a short time span, many of them from the same IP address or range of addresses.

> **ExamAlert**
>
> Denial-of-service attacks can be launched from the network layer or the application layer, and they can impact these layers as well. Networking devices, applications, and even operational technology can be impacted by DoS and DDoS attacks.

To help protect your network, you can set up filters on external routers to drop packets involved in these types of attacks. You should also set up another filter that denies traffic originating from the Internet that shows an internal network address. When you do this, you give up the ability to use ping and some other services and utilities for testing network connectivity, but this is a small price to pay for network protection. If the operating system allows it, reduce the amount of time before the reset of an unfinished TCP connection. Doing so makes it harder to keep resources unavailable for extended periods of time.

Subscribing to security emails and checking security websites daily ensures that you keep up with the latest attacks and exploits. Applying the manufacturer's latest operating system patches or fixes can also help prevent attacks.

Malicious Code and Script Execution

As you learned in Chapter 2, "Attack Basics," office applications provide a power function to automate tasks through the use of macros. *Malicious script execution* takes advantage of this power to create macro viruses. In addition, fileless viruses have used other automation tools and scripting languages, such as Windows PowerShell, to do their work. Scripts aid system administrators in efficiently performing operations and automating actions that otherwise would require multiple steps and manual interaction. An attacker can take advantage of the same benefits but for nefarious purposes. These scripting languages can be used as part of malware and can also be used inside a network to further the malicious work. Examples of these scripting languages include the following:

▶ **PowerShell:** PowerShell is a command-line scripting language from Microsoft for task automation and configuration management.

▶ **Python:** This common scripting language is included with most Linux distributions and has wide use in application development, including exploits.

▶ **Bash:** Commonly referred to as the Unix shell, Bash is the environment and command-line language for many versions of Apple's macOS and most Linux distributions.

▶ **Visual Basic for Applications (VBA):** Based on the Visual Basic programming language from Microsoft, VBA helps drive specific events or actions. Microsoft macros for Office documents are written or recorded using VBA.

Cram Quiz

Answer these questions. The answers follow the last question. If you cannot answer these questions correctly, consider reading this chapter again until you can.

1. The sales team reports that when it was traveling recently, team members received unsolicited photos to their mobile devices at the airport. Which of the following occurred?

   ○ **A.** Bluesnarfing

   ○ **B.** Bluejacking

   ○ **C.** On-path attack

   ○ **D.** Deauthentication

2. Which of the following is an attack that affects data availability?

   ○ **A.** Rogue AP

   ○ **B.** MAC address

   ○ **C.** On-path attack

   ○ **D.** DDoS attack

3. Before leaving for the day, one of the security administrators sends an email to the director of security, informing him that an evil twin had been found and removed from the network. The director forwards the email to you and asks what this means. Which of the following is the best reply?

   ○ **A.** A rogue wireless access point was found connected to the network.

   ○ **B.** A user's laptop was discovered to have had a spoofed MAC address.

   ○ **C.** Two identical antennas were lying in the hallway.

   ○ **D.** A network sniffer had been downloaded but not yet installed to a user's laptop.

4. Which specific type of attack occurs when a perpetrator redirects traffic by changing the IP record for a specific domain in order to be able to send legitimate traffic anywhere he chooses?

   ○ **A.** DNS poisoning

   ○ **B.** Domain hijacking

   ○ **C.** On-path browser attack

   ○ **D.** Port stealing

5. How would you mitigate ARP poisoning on a small network?

○ **A.** Implement whitelisting

○ **B.** Validate the input of URLs passed

○ **C.** Use a three-way handshake

○ **D.** Use static mappings for IP addresses

Cram Quiz Answers

Answer 1: B. Bluejacking involves the receipt of unsolicited photos or messages on a Bluetooth-enabled device from a nearby device. Bluesnarfing is also a Bluetooth attack, but it involves unauthorized pairing and access to the device, so answer A is incorrect. Answer C is incorrect. An on-path attack occurs when an attacker intercepts traffic between two parties. Answer D is incorrect as deauthentication refers to a frame being received when access points are disconnected.

Answer 2: D. A distributed denial-of-service (DDoS) attack is an attack from multiple infected systems that seeks to disrupt the victim, often affecting the ability of the system to respond and making the services and data unavailable. Answers A and C are incorrect, as a rogue access point and an on-path attack would still provide for availability but would compromise confidentiality. Answer B is incorrect as a MAC address is not an attack but a factory-assigned address for a network interface.

Answer 3: A. An evil twin is a rogue wireless access point and is the most accurate choice here. Answers B and C are both incorrect answers. Answer D is also incorrect. However, an attacker can use a network sniffer in conjunction with a rogue wireless access point. In addition, a wireless network sniffer can be used to help locate rogue access points.

Answer 4: A. Domain Name System (DNS) poisoning enables a perpetrator to redirect traffic by changing the IP record for a specific domain, thus permitting attackers to send legitimate traffic anywhere they choose. DNS poisoning sends a requestor to a different website and also caches this information for a short period, distributing the attack's effect to the server users. Answer B is incorrect. Domain hijacking, the act of changing domain name registration, occurs when an entire domain is taken over without the original owner's knowledge or consent. Answer C is incorrect. An on-path browser attack is a Trojan that infects web browser components such as browser plug-ins and other browser helper objects. Answer D is incorrect because port stealing is an on-path attack that exploits the binding between a port and a MAC address.

Answer 5: D. To mitigate Address Resolution Protocol (ARP) poisoning on a small network, you can use static or script-based mappings for IP addresses and ARP tables. Answers A and B are incorrect because validating the input of URLs passed and using whitelists applies to mitigating URL redirection in the context of this chapter. Answer C is incorrect and applies to a SYN flood attack, which takes advantage of the TCP three-way handshake.

What Next?

If you want more practice on this chapter's exam objective before you move on, remember that you can access all of the Cram Quiz questions on the Pearson Test Prep software online. You can also create a custom exam by objective with the Online Practice Test. Note any objective you struggle with and go to that objective's material in this chapter.

CHAPTER 5

Threat Actors, Vectors, and Intelligence Sources

This chapter covers the following official Security+ exam objective:

▶ 1.5 Explain different threat actors, vectors, and intelligence sources.

Essential Terms and Components

▶ advanced persistent threat (APT)

▶ threat actor

▶ threat vector

▶ threat actor attribute

▶ threat intelligence source

▶ open-source intelligence (OSINT)

▶ dark web

▶ indicator of compromise (IOC)

▶ automated indicator sharing (AIS)

▶ Structured Threat Information eXpression (STIX)

▶ Trusted Automated eXchange of Indicator Information (TAXII)

When examining attacks, threats, and vulnerabilities, understanding threat actors is important. Specifically, a *threat actor* is an individual, a group, or an entity that contributes to an incident—or, more simply, a person or an entity that executes a given threat. This is not a difficult concept, but it is often overlooked, particularly when deciding how to balance an organization's security against its capabilities. For example, the security mechanisms that protect your personal vehicle differ significantly from those that guard an armored truck. You might lock

your doors when you leave your car, but of course, someone could still quite easily break in to it. The threat to your car likely comes from a casual passerby looking for spare change or belongings you have left behind. The armored truck, on the other hand, faces a different kind of threat actor because it transports valuables and large sums of money.

This chapter discusses the types of threat actors and their common attributes, as well as *threat intelligence sources* and other research sources. Understanding these components enables organizations to make better decisions regarding risk and manage their vulnerabilities. You should be able to explain these threat actors, *threat vectors*, and information sources.

Threat Actor Attributes

When examining various threat actors, you must consider their attributes. Organizations that do so can build better threat profiles and classification systems to deploy more relevant and proactive defenses. Common *threat actor attributes* include the following:

▶ **Relationship:** Threats can be internal or external to an organization, and they might even come from a partner.

▶ **Motive:** Some incidents are accidental, but others are driven by financial gain or ideological differences.

▶ **Intent:** A threat could be malicious, with the aim to destroy data or steal information or tangible property.

▶ **Capability:** Several components must be considered here, including technical ability, financial means, access, political and social support, and persistence.

The relationship of a threat actor is most easily characterized as either internal or external. Script kiddies, hacktivists, organized crime, and nation-state actors are all examples of external threat actors. Internal threat actors work on the inside; for example, they might be system administrators or end users.

When examining threat actor capability, you must consider the level of sophistication and both the available resources and funds. For example, some threat actors operate as businesses, with well-established roles, responsibilities, and governance. Their capabilities are often enhanced by their technical resources and access to money for funding operations.

> **Note**
>
> When considering threat types and attributes, you might find it helpful to think about common personal situations. For example, consider your reasons for locking your personal belongings in a vehicle. What threat actors are you mitigating against? What are their attributes? How does a casual passerby differ from someone who has the tools and knowledge of a locksmith?

With insiders and end users there may not be a motive or any intention of causing harm. While this is a threat to be concerned with, the actions are often accidental. Other times, threat actors have a specific malicious or competitive intent. Of course, motives can vary in these cases. Consider a competitive threat. The motive could be a desire to gain a competitive advantage through espionage or malicious destruction to the business. Financial gain is another common motive that can include directly extorting money from victims through ransomware or stealing data to sell in a criminal ecosystem for subsequent attacks. Threat actors also can be driven by ideological and political motives.

> **ExamAlert**
>
> Assessing threat actors begins with identifying their relationship to the organization—internal or external.

Threat Actor Types

Depending on the particular threat, a threat actor can be an individual, a group, or an entity that acts to perpetrate a particular scenario. The following sections look at the most common threat actors:

▶ Script kiddies

▶ Insiders

▶ Hacktivists

▶ Criminal syndicates

▶ Competitors

▶ Nation-state actors

Notice that these threat actor types relate to threats from humans, not the environment. For example, the threat of a flood in a data center might stem from an impending hurricane, not from a particular individual or entity.

Generally speaking, throughout the media, and even in this book, we refer to threat actors as hackers. The term *hacker*, however, can also be used for someone who isn't inherently bad or doesn't have malicious intent. Fundamentally, a security hacker is someone who uses his or her knowledge of and skills with computer system hardware, software, networks, and systems to break them down, tamper, or gain unauthorized access. Hackers may be unauthorized, authorized or semi-authorized. In the security industry, the color of the hat worn is a metaphor used in the past to traditionaly describe the type of hacker:

▶ **Black hat (unauthorized):** This category is used to describe hackers involved with criminal activities or malicious intent. Black hat hackers may have a wide range of skills.

▶ **White hat (authorized):** White hat hackers, also known as ethical hackers, use their powers for good. They are much like the Jedi Knights from *Star Wars*, fighting the dark side. White hat hackers are often hired as penetration testers with permission to "attack" or test system security.

▶ **Gray hat (semi-authorized):** Gray naturally falls somewhere in the middle of black and white. These hackers can be a complicated group to positively identify, but generally they don't have malicious intent, although they often run afoul of ethical standards and principles. Often, they don't have permissions to attack a system but stop after discovering a vulnerability and try not to exploit it.

As you review the threat actors in the following sections, keep in mind that organizations need to consider how these different actors could be interrelated. For example, a terrorist group works much like hacktivists: The terrorists are driven by ideology, and hacktivists operate within the framework of organized crime. Or those involved in organized crime might exploit script kiddies within their ecosystem to distance themselves while achieving specific goals. Similarly, some nation-states might have close ties to organized crime. Finally, keep in mind that any of these threat actors can be further enabled through the compromise of an insider.

Script Kiddies

Script kiddies do not have to possess great talent. Even with few skills, they can run exploits that others have developed. Usually script kiddies cannot write sophisticated code; they might not even know how to program. Still, script

kiddies can undoubtedly have a huge negative impact on an organization. What makes them particularly dangerous is that they are often unaware themselves of the potential consequences of their actions. Of course, because they lack sophisticated skill, script kiddies often cannot adequately cover their tracks. Tracing their attacks is thus easier than tracing the attacks of more sophisticated threat actors.

Script kiddies might lack sophistication and financial means, but they are empowered by the number of readily available exploits and information available to them. They are often associated with website defacement attacks, but they have also been known to use DoS attacks to take down websites and even to plant Trojans and remote access tools within an organization.

Insiders

Attacks are often assumed to come from malicious outside hackers, but insider threats lead to many breaches. In many cases, insiders are employees who have the right intentions but either are unaware of an organization's security policy or simply ignore it. A common example is a well-intentioned employee who uses a personal web-based email account to send home sensitive files to work on later in the evening. In doing so, the employee sends these sensitive files in unencrypted form outside the organizational network. In another common scenario, a user brings in a USB thumb drive that has—unbeknownst to the user—been infected with malware. Proper training and education are key to preventing such nonmalicious insider threats.

Deliberate malicious insider threats also can be attack sources. These threats are typically motivated by financial gain, sabotage, and theft to gain competitive advantage. Consider the case of ex-National Security Agency (NSA) contractor Edward Snowden. Formerly an insider, Snowden circulated various documents and secrets about the NSA's surveillance program. Protecting against malicious insiders is a daunting and difficult task, but organizations must have policies in place to help identify risky personnel (for example, employees who have been terminated). Perhaps most importantly, organizations need mechanisms for proactively monitoring network and system activities.

ExamAlert

Insider threat actors can be malicious, as in the case of a disgruntled employee, or simply careless.

Hacktivists

Hacktivism can have a positive or negative connotation, just as the word *hack* does, depending on how it is used. In the case of threat actors, hacktivism involves using digital tools for malicious intent, based on political, social, or ideological reasoning. Hacktivists often are perceived as doing good because of their motives. For example, in early 2017, the group Anonymous took down thousands of sites related to child porn. This might be seen as a form of vigilantism, or at least a way of targeting illegal activity. On the other hand, an animal-rights hacktivist group could target an organization that launches a perfectly legal line of fur coats.

Criminal Syndicates

Criminal syndicates and organized crime tend to follow the money, so it should come as no surprise that organized crime is involved in networking systems today. The U.S. Organized Crime Control Act of 1970 states that organized crime "is a highly sophisticated, diversified, and widespread activity that annually drains billions of dollars from America's economy by unlawful conduct and the illegal use of force, fraud, and corruption." Clearly, this threat actor is sophisticated and has adequate financial means. In fact, organized crime itself has established its own complete economy, including a system within the underworld that affects information security. The Organized Crime Control Act identifies that funding comes from such illegal activities as gambling, loan sharking, property theft, distribution of drugs, and other forms of social exploitation. Organized criminals have simply adapted to become organized cybercriminals.

The challenges of defeating organized crime are the same today as they have been for decades, particularly given the vast resources and ecosystem involved. Consider a street-level drug dealer, part of the criminal ecosystem yet with no real connection to the organized crime network. More relevant are money mules, who are often recruited online and tasked with helping to either knowingly or unknowingly launder money.

Competitors

Competitors are generally expected to compete fairly and legally, but they do not always do so. Anticompetitive practices and industrial espionage are not new. However, the rise of the Internet and interconnected networking systems has given malicious competition a new channel of opportunity. For example, a competitor might seek to launch a DoS attack that keeps an organization from

conducting business and potentially drives business to the competitor because of the downtime. Often, however, competitive threat actors are looking for information to gain an edge or even to pilfer trade secrets and other intellectual property.

State Actors

A *state actor* is arguably the most sophisticated threat actor with the most resources. Nation-state threat actors are government sponsored, although those ties might not always be acknowledged. This threat actor is not necessarily relevant only to government organizations: Foreign companies are often targets as well. For example, corporations might possess intellectual property that another foreign entity can use to advance its goals and objectives. This type of threat actor is also patient and targets a wide attack surface that might include partner and even customer organizations. In 2011, RSA Security, a provider of two-factor authentication tokens, was hacked. Circumstances indicated that the attack was likely targeting at least one of the company's large customers, defense contractor Lockheed Martin. Naturally, a foreign nation could gain valuable resources and intellectual property from such a contractor.

State actor attacks have become more prevalent in recent years. Stuxnet, discovered in 2010, highlighted the sophistication and threat of nation-state attacks. This costly and highly sophisticated computer worm (see Chapter 1, "Social Engineering Techniques") is believed to be a cyberweapon that the United States and Israel allegedly developed to intentionally cause damage to Iran's nuclear facilities.

Advanced persistent threats (*APTs*) are often associated with nation-state threat actors. The name alone suggests sophistication. These certainly are not "smash and grab" attacks; rather, they are generally described as "low and slow." The goal of an APT is usually to infiltrate a network and remain inside, undetected. Such access often provides a more strategic target or defined objective, including the capability to exfiltrate information over a long period of time.

ExamAlert

The assets or goals of an organization relate to and influence the threat actor types that present the most significant risk.

Vectors

Now that you understand the different types of threat actors, you need to be familiar with the path they take to execute attacks. These paths are known as *attack vectors*, and understanding them is important to doing proper risk analysis and to better understanding countermeasures that may be required for defense. The following are attack vectors that hackers commonly use in order to uncover vulnerabilities and try to exploit systems:

- ▶ Direct access
- ▶ Wireless
- ▶ Removable media
- ▶ Cloud
- ▶ Email
- ▶ Improper usage
- ▶ Equipment damage, loss, or theft
- ▶ Supply chain

As you become familiar with these vectors, think about each one and how an attacker could use it to try to attack systems. A great exercise is to think about your own personal circumstances. Many households today have multiple devices connected to the Internet. Who has physical access to your systems? Do you have wireless home networking that extends outside the house or perhaps Bluetooth- or NFC-enabled devices? Have you borrowed removable media such as jump drives that you plug into your systems? What online applications and services do you use (for example, file conversion, file storage, collaboration, video conferencing)? How many phishing attempts do you get in your personal email (or your junk-mail folder)? Do you have young children or other family members who are not very computer savvy or do not understand the risks? What if your home succumbed to flooding, fire, or a burglary? Finally, even the supply chain attack vector can be applied to these examples. Consider the wireless access point, video camera, or smart assistant–enabled device you purchased online. Anyone from the manufacturer to the online store from which you purchased it to the mail carrier and anyone in between in theory has had opportunity to compromise that system before it arrived in your hands.

The criticality of these vectors varies. If you live alone, for example, perhaps you won't be so concerned about improper usage. If you have no reason to believe you are under government surveillance, perhaps the supply-chain vector

doesn't concern you. As you will see in Chapter 34, "Risk Management," many factors must be considered together. For example, perhaps the impact of an attack would be minor if you are only protecting a collection of humorous memes; on the other hand, if you had worked hard on a book manuscript, you might be more concerned about protecting your assets.

Threat Intelligence and Research Sources

Organizations today increasingly rely on threat intelligence data. This valuable data can be fed into systems and models to help organizations understand their overall risk. Further, this data is core to modern organizational security operations centers (SOCs). The data is used both for preventive and response measures.

This section explores a number of sources of threat intelligence, many of which are open and available to the public. This section provides a number of links for you to explorer further. *Open-source intelligence (OSINT)* is the term used for such information that is available for collection from publicly available information sources. On the other hand, some threat intelligence and research sources are closed-source, or proprietary; typically organizations can subscribe to these commercial solutions for a cost. Often this threat intelligence encompasses the security solutions provided by the commercial entity. Symantec, for example, offers one of the world's largest civilian threat intelligence networks. The intelligence includes telemetry data from billions of devices and sensors around the world.

Sharing Centers

Some organization, as they uncover threats—perhaps even realized against their own environments—choose not to share the data they've collected. However, the sharing of threat intelligence has increased over the years. This has been evident particularly across public and private commercial sectors, where governments, universities, health care, and commercial companies have collaborated together to share threat intelligence especially around specific types of threats. For example, protecting critical infrastructure is important to governments, and commercial organizations often manufacture, provide, and run much of the infrastructure. Such collaborations require public/private information sharing, and sharing centers have sprung up.

The U.S. government's Information Sharing and Analysis Organizations (ISAOs) was an initiative to promote threat information sharing across different industry sectors. Prior to that, Information Sharing and Analysis Centers (ISACs) were established to promote industry-specific sharing of threat intelligence. The first ISAC established was meant to enable private and public groups involved in critical infrastructure to share best practices and threat intelligence. Today, the National Council of ISACs has more than 20 member ISACs in multiple industries, such as automotive, aviation, elections infrastructure, and real estate.

Open-Source Intelligence

Recall that open-source intelligence (OSINT) is the term given to information available for collection from publicly available information sources. OSINT is available from varying sources and, of course, the Internet provides a treasure trove of such information. While OSINT provides a valuable resource to help identify and understand threats and how vulnerabilities are being exploited, it can also be used for malicious purposes. Attackers may use OSINT to advance their attacks as well as identify and explore their targets.

A number of popular OSINT sources are used to collect data through the use of threat intelligence platforms, which aggregate and correlate data from across various feeds. Predictive analysis can be used to combine this data with machine learning and statistical techniques to identify patterns to make predictions. OSINT sources can also be used ad hoc, without a platform or further active intelligence.

The following are some of the most common OSINT sources:

▶ **Vulnerability databases:** These databases provide data for publicly known vulnerabilities known as common vulnerabilities and exposures (CVEs). The following are three examples of databases that provide such information:

  ▶ **MITRE:** https://cve.mitre.org
  ▶ **CVE Details:** https://cvedetails.com
  ▶ **VulnDB:** https://vulndb.cyberriskanalytics.com

▶ **Adversary Tactics, Techniques, and Procedures (TTP):** MITRE ATT&CK provides attack methods and activities associated with specific threat actors; its huge knowledge base is based upon real-world observations. See https://attack.mitre.org.

▶ **Dark web:** The *dark web* can't be accessed the same way as regular websites but requires the use of special software that provides secure communications. Yes, this is often where attackers live and where operations of questionable legal status occur. Anyone can access the dark web, though, and many third parties provide dark web monitoring and intelligence services for a cost.

▶ **Indicators of compromise (IOC):** *Indicators of compromise (IOCs)* provide evidence or components that point to security breaches or events. IOCs can include items such as malware signatures, IP addresses, domain names, and file hash values, for example.

▶ **Automated indicator sharing (AIS):** *Automated indicator sharing (AIS)* is an initiative of the U.S. Department of Homeland Security (DHS) that enables the exchange of cybersecurity threat indicators. AIS uses two important standards:

    ▶ **Structured Threat Information eXpression (STIX):** *Structured Threat Information eXpression (STIX)* is a standardized and structured language that represents threat information in a flexible, automatable, and easy-to-use manner.

    ▶ **Trusted Automated eXchange of Indicator Information (TAXII):** *Trusted Automated eXchange of Indicator Information (TAXII)* is a specification for machine-to-machine communication that enables organizations to share security information with others as desired.

▶ **Threat maps:** Many threat maps are freely available from commercial software vendors. These maps provide a real-time look at cyberattacks occurring around the globe. The Kaspersky cyberthreat map provides an amazing visual look at different attacks, including reconnaissance, malware attacks, intrusions, and botnet activity. To take a look, see https://cybermap.kaspersky.com. Figure 5.1 shows an example of the information this site provides.

▶ **File/code repositories:** Software developers are increasingly using online code repositories (*repos*) such as GitHub for the private management of code or for collaboration with other developers regardless of location and to share code. Many of these repositories are publicly available. These repos provide opportunities to obtain not just open-source code but code specific to threat research and information gathering.

ExamAlert

Be familiar with these OSINT sources. Specifically, you need to know the acronyms TTP, IOC, and AIS, as they tie into other security processes and solutions.

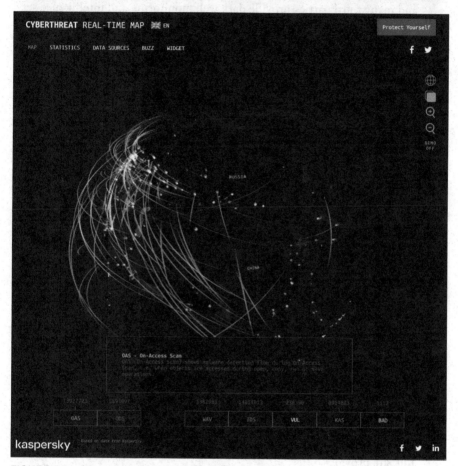

FIGURE 5.1 **An example of an interactive threat map**

Other publicly accessible sources that are particularly useful for further research include the following:

▶ Television

▶ Newspapers and magazines

▶ Professional publications

▶ Academic publications

▶ Photos

▶ Geospatial information

▶ Vendor websites

▶ Conferences

▶ Requests for comments (RFCs)

▶ Social media

In addition, certain tools and applications aggregate OSINT data or provide specific utilities for extracting it. Many resources are also readily available online. As a simple example, consider personal and professional social media web applications. An attacker can easily do reconnaissance and gather information on employees in an organization from these easily available online sites.

Despite the fact that threat actors use OSINT to discover data that helps them more easily attack a target, OSINT remains a valuable resource for organizations to defend against such attacks and also to identify and prioritize potential threat actors.

Understanding threat actors' motives, capabilities, and possible actions is particularly valuable. Organizations launching a new product, sponsoring an event, or penetrating a new foreign market, for example, can use OSINT to mitigate risk by identifying potentially new threat actors and associated attributes. Without prioritizing the threats, organizations run the risk of suffering one of the main drawbacks of OSINT: information overload.

> **ExamAlert**
>
> Do not confuse *open-source intelligence* with *open-source software*. OSINT refers to overtly gathered intelligence.

Cram Quiz

Answer these questions. The answers follow the last question. If you cannot answer these questions correctly, consider reading this chapter again until you can.

1. How do relationship and capability pertain to understanding specific threat actors?

   ○ **A.** They indicate the likelihood of vulnerabilities being discovered.

   ○ **B.** They are characteristics associated with building a threat profile.

   ○ **C.** They describe attributes that apply equally to all threats.

   ○ **D.** They are the two most important attributes when analyzing threat actors.

2. With which of the following is a "low and slow" attack most associated?

○ **A.** APT

○ **B.** Ransomware

○ **C.** OSINT

○ **D.** Script kiddies

3. Which one of the following best describes an ISAC?

○ **A.** A private information security database for attack countermeasures

○ **B.** A standardized language for the exchange of cybersecurity threat indicators

○ **C.** A center or group that promotes threat information sharing within a specific sector

○ **D.** A specification for machine-to-machine communications to share security information

4. Which threat actor is considered the most sophisticated and has the most resources?

○ **A.** Unathorized hacker

○ **B.** Authorized hacker

○ **C.** Semi-authorized hacker

○ **D.** State actor

5. You are analyzing pieces of forensic data found in log entries to identify malicious activities. Which of the following is a collection of evidence or components that points to a security breach or event?

○ **A.** Indicators of compromise

○ **B.** Automatic indicator sharing

○ **C.** Requests for comments

○ **D.** Adversary tactics, techniques, and procedures

Cram Quiz Answers

Answer 1: B. Relationship and capability are characteristics that can be attributed to threat actors. Other common attributes are motive and intent. Answer A is incorrect because these do not pertain to the discovery of vulnerabilities. Answer C is incorrect because attributes vary, depending on the specific threat actor. Answer D is incorrect because threat actors and overall risk are unique to each organization.

Answer 2: A. An advanced persistent threat (APT) is a "low and slow" style of attack executed to infiltrate a network and remain inside while going undetected. Answer B is incorrect because ransomware is obvious and sends a clear message to the end user in

an attempt to extort compensation from the victim. Answer C is incorrect. OSINT stands for open-source intelligence, which is the term given to information available for collection from publicly available sources. Answer D is incorrect because script kiddies, unlike APTs, are usually not sophisticated in their methods and are usually easily detected.

Answer 3: C. Information Sharing and Analysis Centers (ISACs) promote industry-specific sharing of threat intelligence. Answer A is incorrect. Answer B is also incorrect as it describes Structured Threat Information eXpression (STIX). Answer D is incorrect as this describes Trusted Automated eXchange of Indicator Information (TAXII).

Answer 4: D. A state actor is arguably the most sophisticated threat actor with the most resources. Answers A, B, and C are incorrect. Unauthorized hacker (black hat) describes malicious hackers who may be involved with criminal activities and have a wide range of skill. An authorized hacker (white hat), also known as an ethical hacker, uses his or her powers for good. A semi-authorized hacker (gray hat) falls somewhere in the middle of unauthorized and authorized hackers; they don't typically have malicious intent but often run afoul of ethical standards and principles.

Answer 5: A. The best answer here is indicators of compromise (IOC), which provide evidence or components that point to a security breach or event. IOCs can include items such as malware signatures, IP addresses, domain names, and file hash values. Answer B is incorrect. Automated indicator sharing (AIS) is an initiative from the U.S. DHS that enables the exchange of cybersecurity threat indicators. Answer C is incorrect. A request for comments (RFC) is a type of document that describes behaviors, methods, research, or innovations that have to do with technologies and the working of the Internet and systems connected to the Internet. Answer D in incorrect. Adversary tactics, techniques, and procedures (TTP) provide attack methods and activities associated with specific threat actors.

What Next?

If you want more practice on this chapter's exam objective before you move on, remember that you can access all of the Cram Quiz questions on the Pearson Test Prep software online. You can also create a custom exam by objective with the Online Practice Test. Note any objective you struggle with and go to that objective's material in this chapter.

CHAPTER 6

Vulnerabilities

This chapter covers the following official Security+ exam objective:

▶ 1.6 Explain the security concerns associated with various types of vulnerabilities.

Essential Terms and Components

▶ cloud-based vs. on-premises

▶ zero-day attack

▶ weak configuration

▶ third-party risk

▶ patch management

▶ impact

Vulnerability scanners are capable of prioritizing vulnerabilities based on accepted criteria that reflect the severity of various weaknesses. However, each organization is unique and has varying degrees of resources to fix vulnerabilities. Keep in mind that the mere act of patching a vulnerability introduces risk because the application of the patch might negatively affect the systems. Furthermore, most organizations require resources to ensure that such fixes are properly tested.

Organizations need to consider vulnerabilities across various factors, including existing security controls, the threat likelihood, the goals of the business, and the impact on the systems and on the business if the vulnerability is exploited. This chapter examines the impacts associated with many common vulnerability types. Identifying vulnerabilities gives an organization the opportunity to consider their impact and criticality and to evaluate approaches to remediate the weaknesses.

Zero-day vulnerabilities are particularly concerning because vulnerability scanners cannot initially detect them. Attackers who know about

these otherwise unknown vulnerabilities can take advantage of the situation. When vendors learn of such a vulnerability, they immediately work on a patch. In some cases, organizations may be pressured into immediately deploying patches without adequate testing.

Cloud-Based vs. On-Premises

Organizations continue to move to cloud-based computing rather than developing and maintaining systems on-premises, where they are responsible for everything from the physical elements up through the application. Organizations face varying considerations when considering *cloud-based vs. on-premises systems.* When the systems are moved into the cloud, an organization no longer has responsibility for the physical aspects. In fact, in most scenarios, the customer is responsible for the elements above the hypervisor in a virtualized environment. This means, however, that organizations still have a lot of responsibility and should be concerned about vulnerabilities. Many of the same vulnerabilities that affect on-premises systems also affect cloud-based systems. In addition, cloud-based systems bring new vulnerabilities and exposures. Almost everything in the cloud is accessible from behind a single console, and small misconfigurations can have huge impacts across the environment.

Zero-Day

A *zero-day* (or zero-hour or day-zero) *attack* or threat is a computer threat that tries to exploit computer application vulnerabilities that are unknown to others—even the software developer. (Those weaknesses are also called zero-day vulnerabilities.) Zero-day exploits involve using software to exploit security holes to carry out attacks; attackers carry out these exploits or share information about them before the developer of the target software knows about the vulnerability.

A zero-day attack differs from other attacks and vulnerabilities. Most attacks on vulnerable systems involve known vulnerabilities. In some cases, developers know about the vulnerabilities, but patches have not yet been issued. In most cases, however, attacks target known vulnerabilities for which fixes or controls exist but have not been implemented. In the case of zero-day attacks, the software developer does not know about the vulnerability and so has not created or distributed a fix for the software.

ExamAlert

Remember that for a zero-day vulnerability, a patch is not yet available. Keep this in mind when evaluating techniques to protect your organization. Effective security policies, training, and mitigations are most effective—even compared to the most aggressive patch management strategies—when it comes to zero-day exploits.

Weak Configurations

Improper and *weak configurations* across the architecture and systems and software can contribute to continued vulnerabilities. Most organizations follow standard good practices and use well-established frameworks, development life cycles, and governing principles for secure design and architecture. Consider the following examples, however, of configuration weaknesses that increase the likelihood of vulnerabilities:

▶ Software that allows users to perform tasks with unnecessary privileges, violating the principle of least privilege.

▶ Systems that fail open instead of failing securely. Such a system failure would allow an attacker to access resources.

▶ Security through obscurity, to prevent against only relatively insignificant threat actors.

▶ Unnecessary complexity, which makes systems management more difficult to understand and control.

The last point is particularly important as it relates to system sprawl and undocumented assets. Clear oversight of the design and architecture of systems is vital to operations and security. The design and architecture of systems can easily become poorly documented over time, often because of personnel changes, rapidly evolving needs, and disjointed operations. System sprawl and lack of clear documentation can then result in a loss of visibility and control, which can have negative impacts on an organization and lead to weak configurations.

Systems need to be managed to ensure operational efficiency and effective security practices. Organizations cannot really manage what they do not know about. Organizations therefore require sound information systems governance programs and often use automated tools to constantly monitor the network to identify assets and ensure that they have been properly provisioned and

documented. Otherwise, weak and improper configurations manifest in many ways, including the following:

▶ Errors

▶ Open permissions

▶ Unsecured root accounts

▶ Weak encryption

▶ Unsecure protocols

▶ Default settings

▶ Open ports and services

> **Note**
>
> Be able to explain security concerns associated with weak configurations, including open permissions, unsecured root accounts, errors, weak encryption, unsecured protocols, default settings, and open ports and services.

Configuration errors are common sources of data breaches. Configuration errors typically result when default configurations are not modified and when systems are not configured to align with standards or best practices.

Many vendors ship their systems for ease of use and entrust the customers with applying proper configurations. For example, systems that ship with a default password are open to a simple exploit that can have grave consequences. Many home routers used to ship with a default password that was common to all models of that particular router. Left unchanged, it provided simple access for any malicious attacker who knew the make and model of the device.

Most systems provide cryptographic methods that are based on strong standards. These should be used, and careful attention should be given to managing the cryptographic keys. It is not unusual, however, for these cryptographic standards to become outdated or deprecated due to flaws in design or improvements in technology that make their strength obsolete. It's important to implement encryption based on strong standards and ensure that the encryption continues to remain strong. An organization should never try to create its own cryptographic algorithms within systems. Such attempts tend to lack the peer review and scrutiny of standard algorithms.

Another example of weak configuration is the presence of unneeded applications and services. Such services provide additional avenues for attackers,

especially if default accounts aren't removed or changed. They also leave open ports, providing more vectors for reconnaissance and attack. An application running an unneeded web server is open to denial-of-service attacks against that HTTP port. In addition, each additional service could carry additional flaws that might go unnoticed. Many web servers, for example, can be configured to reveal directory contents and allow unauthorized users to download sensitive data. These situations themselves can be harmful, but an attacker can also use them to pivot within the environment to cause even more harm.

> **Note**
>
> A denial-of-service (DoS) attack against an unneeded web service is one example of how a nonessential service can potentially cause problems for an otherwise functional system.

One of the most common types of misconfigurations is improperly configured accounts. For example, accounts, along with the associated authentication and authorization mechanisms, may be configured in such a way that they do not restrict access to people who shouldn't have access. Misconfigured accounts can impact organizations in several ways, including allowing escalated privileges that then harm systems and allowing attackers to exfiltrate data. An unsecured administrator or root account can have serious implications for the entire system and anything it's connected to.

Devices are often left with default passwords set or with default accounts enabled. Certain accounts are installed by default. Administrators should know what these accounts are so they can determine which ones are really needed and which ones should be disabled to make the system more secure. It is also important for administrators to know which accounts, if any, are installed with blank passwords. The security settings in many of the newer operating systems do not allow blank passwords, but older operating systems might and legacy platforms might allow such vulnerabilities to exist.

Renaming or disabling the administrator account and guest account in each domain is advisable to prevent attacks on domains. Default credentials and unmonitored accounts such as the guest or admin accounts commonly established in older equipment and software soften security because they give attackers one component of access credentials. Attempts to compromise both an account and its associated password are more difficult if the account has been renamed or disabled or had its password changed.

Similar principles apply to routers and other network devices. Equipment manufacturers typically use a simple default password on their equipment, with the expectation that the purchaser will change the password. Default logins and passwords are freely available on the Internet, and leaving them in place on a live network poses a huge security risk.

> **ExamAlert**
>
> When you are presented with a scenario on the exam, you might be tempted to keep all services enabled to cover all requirements. Be wary of this option as it might mean you would be installing unnecessary services or protocols.

Improper or Weak Patch Management

Security begins at the hardware level. When a device is attacked at the hardware or firmware level, the root cause might not be detected for an extended period of time simply because people tend to implicitly trust hardware and firmware. In today's environment, however, hardware and firmware are no longer trustworthy and need to be secured. As the Internet of Things (IoT) grows, firmware- and hardware-based exploits will become more common. Just as software gets updated and patched, so does firmware. Organizations have always needed to ensure that firmware is up to date. Hardware manufacturers provide updates and software to perform these updates.

Improperly programmed software can be exploited. Software exploitation takes advantage of a program's flawed code and involves searching for specific problems, weaknesses, or security holes in software code. The most effective ways to prevent an attacker from exploiting software bugs is to ensure proper *patch management*. This includes the process of evaluating, testing, and deploying the latest manufacturer patches and updates, and to monitor appropriate resources for new vulnerabilities.

Because of the emergence of blended-threat malware, which targets multiple vulnerabilities in a single attack, all major operating systems and application solutions must be considered in system-hardening plans. Automated reverse engineering of newly released patches has significantly reduced the time from the initial release of an update until its first exploits are seen in the wild. Whereas unpatched applications previously could be targeted in a matter of months, now threats can materialize in only hours.

You should be familiar with the following types of updates:

▶ **Hotfix:** A hotfix is a small, specific-purpose update that alters the behavior of installed applications in a limited manner. Hotfixes are the most common type of update.

▶ **Service pack:** A service pack is a tested, cumulative set of all hotfixes, security updates, critical updates, and updates.

▶ **Update:** An update addresses a noncritical, non-security-related bug and is usually a fix for a specific problem. Although the term *update* is often used in a generic manner, this category can consist of various types of updates that can address critical issues. For example, Microsoft divides its update categories into critical, definition, and security types. A security update addresses a fix for a product-specific security-related vulnerability, and a critical update addresses a fix for a specific problem that is a critical non-security-related bug.

ExamAlert

To make the patching process easier, Microsoft releases its security-only updates, or monthly rollup, on a regular schedule. Any system running Microsoft products in an enterprise should be evaluated for the release requirements.

Updates for most systems are released on a schedule, which makes it easier to put a sensible plan into place. If an attacker learns of a vulnerability and releases an exploit for it before the update date, the security updates are posted ahead of schedule if the situation warrants.

Third-Party Risks

Every organization interfaces one way or another with a third party for management of systems or at least for the supply of systems and services. This creates what's known as *third-party risk*. Third parties may introduce into an organization vulnerabilities that need to be considered. The following are some examples of third-party relationships:

▶ Vendor management

▶ Supply chain

▶ Outsourced code development

▶ Data storage

Many systems are provided by third parties, and organizations need adequate processes in place to manage the vendor relationships and the software, hardware, and services these third parties provide. One important factor related to vendor management is ensuring systems operability between vendors. This is particularly important when multiple vendors' products must be integrated together and are expected to be interoperable without introducing new vulnerabilities. In addition, vendors tend to provide support for the systems only until a particular time. Most systems are at some point no longer supported by the vendor—either because there is a required upgrade or the product has been abandoned or discontinued. Unsupported software means more than just a lack of technical support or poor reliability: As systems a vendor once supported go end-of-life (EOL), the vendor no longer provides patches for newly discovered vulnerabilities. For example, attackers looking for Windows XP or Windows 7 systems might not find many of them, but when they do, they have easy targets. Such a system may potentially open the door to an attacker seeking to impact an organization in many ways, including establishing a foothold inside.

Maintaining proper governance is key when dealing with areas that are often out of sight, such as the supply chain, outsourced code development, and data storage. An organization may, for example, contract with a third party for off-site backups. Governance, policies, and due diligence will go a long way toward ensuring that expectations and requirements around data security and potential vulnerabilities are understood and addressed with third parties.

> **ExamAlert**
>
> If patches and system updates are no longer available because a system has gone end-of-life, attackers have an easy way to exploit the system.

Impacts

As you will see in Chapter 34, "Risk Management," an organization should do an analysis based on *impacts* it is likely to face. A breach, loss of a business process, or loss of information will likely result in some sort of impact, which needs to be measured to understand the severity. A more complex analysis considers the different types of impacts that result from the loss of a functional business process. Consider, for example, the importance of availability to an e-commerce site. An obvious impact is the loss of sales and income that occurs if web servers are not available. You likely can imagine other potential consequences. When

measuring impact, an organization should consider potential consequences across a broad set of categories, including the following:

- ▶ Data loss
- ▶ Data breaches and exfiltration
- ▶ Identity theft
- ▶ Financial
- ▶ Reputation
- ▶ Availability loss
- ▶ Life and safety

The example of the loss of web servers for an e-commerce site clearly illustrates a potentially severe impact on finances. In addition, the company's reputation would be impacted. The loss of web servers might not impact personal life and safety, but the loss of emergency management systems might. Subsequently, the loss of fire suppression systems could certainly have a significant impact on the availability of facilities, physical property, and related systems. Taken as a whole, all these factors could impact an organization financially.

Cram Quiz

Answer these questions. The answers follow the last question. If you cannot answer these questions correctly, consider reading this chapter again until you can.

1. Your company provides outsourced information security services and has a static web presence as most business is conducted over the phone and in person. Your website was hacked due to a vulnerability in the Apache web server. The attacker ended up modifying your home page with a message disparaging the company. Which one of the following impacts to the organization is most likely?

   ○ **A.** Data loss

   ○ **B.** Financial loss

   ○ **C.** Reputation loss

   ○ **D.** Data exfiltration

2. Which of the following threats is unknown to others and does not yet have a patch available?

   ○ **A.** Unsecured root accounts

   ○ **B.** Weak encryption

   ○ **C.** Unsecure protocols

   ○ **D.** Zero-day attack

3. Which of the following will go a long way toward ensuring that expectations and requirements around data security and potential vulnerabilities are understood and addressed with third parties? (Select three.)

- ○ **A.** Governance
- ○ **B.** Policies
- ○ **C.** Due diligence
- ○ **D.** DoS

Cram Quiz Answers

Answer 1: C. Often an attack on a vulnerability has multiple consequences. The best choice in this case is that an impact on the reputation of the company is the most likely consequence—particularly given that the company doesn't conduct business online, and the company that was hacked is a security company. Answers A, B, and D are incorrect.

Answer 2: D. A zero-day attack is an attack that tries to exploit computer application vulnerabilities that are unknown to others—even the software developer—and so there is not yet a patch available for them. Effective security policies, training, and mitigation are the most effective ways to deal with zero-day vulnerabilities. Although they all represent weak or improper configurations, answers choices A, B, and C are incorrect.

Answer 3: A, B, and C. Maintaining proper governance is key when dealing with areas that are often out of sight, such as the supply chain, outsourced code development, and data storage. Governance, policies, and due diligence will go a long way toward ensuring that expectations and requirements around data security and potential vulnerabilities are understood and addressed with third parties. Answer D is incorrect. A denial-of-service (DoS) attack against an unneeded web service is an example of how a nonessential service can potentially cause problems for an otherwise functional system.

What Next?

If you want more practice on this chapter's exam objective before you move on, remember that you can access all of the Cram Quiz questions on the Pearson Test Prep software online. You can also create a custom exam by objective with the Online Practice Test. Note any objective you struggle with and go to that objective's material in this chapter.

CHAPTER 7

Security Assessment Techniques

This chapter covers the following official Security+ exam objective:

▶ 1.7 Summarize the techniques used in security assessments.

Essential Terms and Components

▶ threat hunting

▶ vulnerability scan

▶ CVE/CVSS

▶ security information and event management (SIEM)

▶ security orchestration, automation, and response (SOAR)

A number of tools and techniques are available to help organizations conduct security assessment. Identifying vulnerabilities and threats is key to maintaining organizational security. In addition to identifying vulnerabilities, organizations need an approach to assess threats against their systems. A myriad of solutions are available. In the past, an organization first needed to move beyond simple log management and find a method to efficiently store and analyze log data across all of its networks, devices, and applications. Security information management (SIM) was the solution. Then, in addition, the data needed to be analyzed in real time to provide correlation across events and enable alerts and reporting. Security event management (SEM) was the solution in this case. SIM and SEM were eventually combined into what's known today as security information and event management (SIEM). This chapter looks at security assessment techniques, including how they are combined and continue to evolve.

Vulnerability Scans

Many network scanners are designed to be passive and non-intrusive to the target systems. Passive scanning poses minimal risk to the assessed environment because it is designed to avoid interfering with normal activity or degrading performance. However, tests against the system can affect network and system performance. A comprehensive *vulnerability scan* helps an organization identify vulnerabilities, uncover common misconfigurations, and understand where further security controls are required. The following points briefly summarize these three goals:

▶ **Identify vulnerability:** Vulnerabilities include outdated software versions that contain flaws or are missing patches.

▶ **Identify common misconfigurations:** Vulnerability scanners can identify many common misconfigurations. Some scanners are even capable of remediation. Checking for misconfigurations is most beneficial when deployed configurations are compared against an organization's security policies and standards.

▶ **Identify lack of security controls:** Identifying vulnerabilities provides an opportunity to remediate weaknesses. In some cases, organizations may find that they need to implement more security controls to mitigate the risk.

Vulnerability scanners fall into three broad categories, based on the devices they evaluate:

▶ **Network scanners:** This type of scanner probes hosts for open ports, enumerates information about users and groups, and proactively looks for known vulnerabilities.

▶ **Application scanners:** This type of scanner requires access to application source code or binaries but does not need to actually execute the application. Thus, this type of scanner tests an application from the inside. Application scanning supports all types of applications and is also known as static application security testing (SAST).

▶ **Web application scanners:** This type of scanner applies specifically to web applications and identifies vulnerabilities such as cross-site scripting, SQL injection, and path traversal. This type of scan executes an application and tests from the outside in. This type of scanning is known as dynamic application security testing (DAST).

A network vulnerability scanner, for example, is a software utility that scans a range of IP addresses, testing for the presence of known vulnerabilities in software configuration and accessible services. A traditional vulnerability scanner relies on a database of known vulnerabilities. It is an automated tool that can be directed at a targeted system or systems. Unlike systems that test for open ports, which test only for the availability of services, vulnerability scanners can check for the version or patch level of a service to determine its level of vulnerability.

Keep in mind that a vulnerability does not necessarily indicate an issue that needs to be immediately remediated—or even remediated at all. Using an analogy, consider a home as a subject for a vulnerability assessment. A broken deadbolt lock certainly seems like a vulnerability. Ideally, the homeowner would replace it; however, in some parts of the world, residents do not lock their doors anyway. A smashed window is a vulnerability as well. In some cases, it might make sense to mitigate a broken window simply by covering it with plastic to protect against the elements. Even a perfectly functioning window is a vulnerability, however. The benefit a window offers typically outweighs the benefits gained by living without windows. What is counted as a vulnerability typically depends on what you are trying to protect.

Upon completion of a vulnerability scan, an organization can generally choose to take one of three approaches:

▶ **Remediation:** The organization can patch the vulnerability.

▶ **Mitigation:** The organization can introduce a control to reduce the likelihood of the vulnerability being exploited or the impact if it is exploited.

▶ **Acceptance:** The organization can take no action if the risk is low, especially compared with the cost or operational impact of addressing the vulnerability.

There isn't necessarily a quick method for determining risk based on the output of a vulnerability scanner. Relevancy to the business, trade-offs, and identified threats and likelihoods need to be considered to accurately interpret the results.

Vulnerability scanners rely heavily on catalogs of known vulnerabilities. Two standards are commonly used, both of which are open industry standards:

▶ Common Vulnerabilities and Exposures (CVE)

▶ Common Vulnerability Scoring System (CVSS)

CVE is a standard for identifying vulnerabilities. It is designed to allow vulnerability databases to be linked together and does not contain attributes such as risk, impact, remediation steps, or detailed technical information. It primarily includes a description and a unique identifier assigned by the vendor where a patch has been provided to fix the vulnerability. CVE also includes related references, such as vulnerability reports and advisories.

On the other hand, CVSS is a framework for communicating the characteristics and severity scores of vulnerabilities. A CVSS score is a rating from 0 to 10. Calculation of the score is complex and takes various components into consideration, such as how easy it would be to exploit the vulnerability. CVSS scoring seeks to address the following questions:

▶ What is the attack vector? Does it require physical access, or can it be exploited over the network?

▶ What is the attack complexity?

▶ Are elevated privileges required?

▶ Is user interaction required?

ExamAlert

CVE is a list of publicly known vulnerabilities containing an ID number, description, and reference. CVSS provides a score from 0 to 10 that indicates the severity of a vulnerability.

Note

In U.S. government agencies, vulnerability is discussed using the Open Vulnerability Assessment Language (OVAL), sponsored by the Department of Homeland Security's National Cyber Security Division (NCSD). OVAL is intended to be an international language for representing vulnerability information. It uses an Extensible Markup Language (XML) schema for expression, allowing tools to be developed to test for identified vulnerabilities in the OVAL repository. OVAL vulnerabilities are based on CVE data.

Intrusive vs. Non-Intrusive

Vulnerability tests seldom disrupt systems. However, an initial port scan can cause a system to fail, particularly if the implementation of a particular service does not follow proper standards. Intrusive scans aim to verify vulnerabilities

by trying to exploit them. Organizations should take care before initiating such intrusive tests.

> **ExamAlert**
>
> Non-intrusive or non-invasive testing helps an organization minimize disruptions related to vulnerability assessment.

Credentialed vs. Non-Credentialed

Credentials such as usernames and passwords enable authorized access to a system. Scanners can be configured to run in either credentialed or non-credentialed mode. *Non-credentialed scans* are less invasive and provide an outsider's point of view. With *credentialed scans*, however, the system can ascertain more information, which results in a more complete vulnerability status with greater certainty. Both credentialed and non-credentialed scans can mistakenly identify a vulnerability when none exists; this is known as a *false positive*. Confirming a large number of false positives can be time-consuming and places a burden on IT resources. Credentialed scans tend to reduce false positives and can also reduce the opposite effect: *false negatives*. False negatives are more difficult to see than false positives. A false negative is a lack of result when there should be one. A false negative may occur, for example, when a vulnerability is new, and a check has not been developed yet to look for the vulnerability.

> **ExamAlert**
>
> With a false positive, a security scanner detects or flags a vulnerability when one does not exist. A false negative is the opposite: It is a lack of alert about a vulnerability when one actually exists.

Threat Assessment

Since evolving from SIM and SEM, SIEM has for years played a vital role in identifying threats and detecting security incidents. Now organizations are looking for ways to combine threat intelligence with SIEM as the intelligence gained can provide enriched data with greater context through correlation with external information. One trend that has emerged in recent years is that organizations now tend to assume that they have already been breached. Rather than be reactive, security teams look for ways to be proactive rather than simply

respond to incidents. Targeted threat hunting assessments have gained popularity as a result, and the programs and tools continue to evolve.

Security Information and Event Management (SIEM)

A *security information and event management* (*SIEM*) system provides the technological means to accomplish a number of goals related to security monitoring, including the following:

▶ Identifying internal and external threats

▶ Monitoring activity and resource usage

▶ Conducting compliance reporting for internal and external audits

▶ Supporting incident response

SIEM tools collect and correlate and subsequently provide alerts and information dashboards based upon that data. SIEM output can be used proactively to detect emerging threats and improve overall security by defining events of interest (EOI) and resulting actions. SIEM systems are the main element in compliance regulations such as SOX, GLBA, PCI, FISMA, and HIPAA. SIEM systems provide a plethora of fine-grained details to support incident response programs. The purpose of SIEM is to store and turn a large amount of data into knowledge that can be acted upon. SIEM systems are generally part of the overall security operations center (SOC) and have three basic functions:

▶ Centrally managing security events

▶ Correlating and normalizing events for context and alerting

▶ Reporting on data gathered from various applications

> **ExamAlert**
>
> Individual log data sources can generate more than 100,000 events each day, so answering critical questions about how much data to log from critical systems is important when deciding to use a SIEM system.

Consider, for example, that just one intrusion detection sensor or log data source can generate more than 100,000 events each day. SIEM systems rely on *log collectors*, which are responsible for aggregating and ingesting the log

data from the various sources such as security devices, network devices, servers, and applications. *Log aggregation* is the process by which SIEM systems combine similar events to reduce event volume. SIEM systems aggregate data from many network sources and consolidate the data so that crucial events are not missed. By default, events are usually aggregated based on the source IP address, destination IP address, and event ID. The purposes of aggregation are to reduce the event data load and improve efficiency. Conversely, if aggregation is incorrectly configured, important information could be lost. Confidence in this aggregated data is enhanced through techniques such as correlation, automated data filtering, and deduplication within the SIEM system.

Event aggregation alone is not enough to provide useful information in an expeditious manner. A common best practice is to use a correlation engine to automate threat detection and log analysis. The main goal of correlation is to build EOIs that can be flagged by other criteria or that allow for the creation of incident identification. To create EOIs, the correlation engine uses data aggregated by using the following techniques:

▶ Pattern matching

▶ Anomaly detection

▶ Boolean logic

▶ A combination of Boolean logic and context-relevant data

Finding the correct balance in correlation rules is often difficult. Correlation rules that try to catch all possible attacks generate too many alerts and can produce too many false-positive alerts.

A SIEM facilitates and automates alert triage to notify analysts about immediate issues. Alerts can be sent via email but are most often sent to a dashboard. To help with the large volume of alerts and notifications that SIEM systems generate, these systems typically provide data visualization tools. From a business perspective, reporting and alerting provide verification of continuous monitoring, auditing, and compliance. Event deduplication improves confidence in aggregated data, data throughput, and storage capacity. Event deduplication is also important because it provides the capability to audit and collect forensic data. The centralized log management and storage in SIEM systems provide validation for regulatory compliance storage or retention requirements. Regarding forensic data and regulatory compliance, WORM (write once read many) drives keep log data protected so that evidence cannot be altered. WORM drives permanently protect administrative data. This security measure should be implemented when an administrator with access to logs is under investigation or when an organization is discussing regulatory compliance.

Some SIEM systems are good at ingesting and querying flow data both in real time and retrospectively. However, significant issues are associated with time, including time synchronization, time stamping, and report time lag. For example, if a report takes 45 minutes to run, the analyst is already that far behind real time, and then time is also needed to read and analyze the results.

When designing a SIEM system, the volume of data generated for a single incident must be considered. SIEM systems must aggregate, correlate, and report output from devices such as firewalls, intrusion detection/prevention systems (IDSs/IPSs), access controls, and myriad network devices. How much data to log from critical systems is an important consideration when deciding to use a SIEM system.

SIEM systems have high acquisition and maintenance costs. If the daily events number in the millions per day and events are gathered from network devices, endpoints, servers, identity and access control systems, and application servers, a SIEM might be cost-effective. For smaller daily event occurrences, free or more cost-effective tools should be considered.

> **Note**
>
> SIEM systems can aggregate syslog data. Syslog is a decades-old standard for message logging. It is available on most network devices (such as routers, switches, and firewalls), as well as printers and Unix/Linux-based systems. Over a network, a syslog server listens for and then logs data messages coming from the syslog client.

SIEM systems continue to evolve to capture more and more use cases and to be combined with other solution sets. SIEM systems, for example, continue to help secure organizations against threats. Consider user behavior analysis, for example. A SIEM system can establish a baseline for user activity and identify anomalous behavior that deviates from that baseline. This often involves advanced techniques such as machine learning, and the SIEM system needs to be capable of comparing data across time horizons and across groups, such as the department the user works in. More recently, this data has been combined to perform *sentiment analysis*: Data can be tracked and analyzed to look for patterns that rely on human sentiment. In this way, systems are able to recognize threats before they become threats. This type of analysis should leverage external data sources, including those from the public domain. As discussed in the next section, SIEM systems are now being combined with other functions to perform security assessments.

ExamAlert

Know that sentiment analysis studies human emotions present within data—for example, negative, neutral, or positive opinions or attitudes. This data can be tracked and analyzed to look for patterns that rely on human sentiment.

Threat Hunting

Threat hunting is a proactive approach to finding an attacker before alerts are triggered. It is not reactive or detective. A reactive approach requires data such as the data a SIEM system provides; a detective approach relies on the use of various algorithms and rules. Threat hunting has the following key attributes:

▶ **Hypothesis:** Threat hunting starts with a hunch, often based on clues. Drivers may include analytics such as user behavior analytics, situational awareness (for example, based on internal risk assessment, trends, or high-value targets), and intelligence based on intelligence bulletins, intelligence feeds, or vulnerability scans.

▶ **People:** While many sources—such as those discussed in Chapter 5, "Threat Actors, Vectors, and Intelligence Sources," and earlier in this chapter—are used, threat hunting is centered around the security analyst, who has deep expertise and knowledge of the organization's environment.

▶ **Assumptive:** Threat hunting does not take a breach-preventive approach but rather assumes that the organization has already been breached.

▶ **Iterative:** Much like a penetration tester, a threat hunter must pivot frequently in order to continue lateral movement while seeking further evidence.

Throughout the process, a threat hunter is looking to disrupt the attacker during any phase of what's known as the *cyber kill chain*, which is a framework developed to track the steps or phases that an attacker goes through as part of an intrusion. (We examine the cyber kill chain more closely in Chapter 27, "Incident Response.") The threat hunting process combined with knowledge of the cyber kill chain allows a security analyst to quickly outmaneuver an attacker. The goal of the security team is to completely disrupt the attacker or quickly impede the attacker's ability to move across the attack chain.

A threat hunter relies on a number of intelligence sources, such as a SIEM system and external sources. Recall that in Chapter 5, we discussed various open and closed sources of threat intelligence and research. All the gathered data

may be intelligently pulled together using commercially available software and services. This bringing together of internal and external threat feeds is known as *intelligence fusion*, and it enables an organization to establish a more accurate threat profile. Internal and external sources are defined as follows:

▶ **Internal threat data:** Internal threat data consists of alert and event data from the SIEM system and any other raw log sources. It includes previous knowledge about prior attacks, including vulnerabilities exploited, previous indicators of compromise, details about the attacker, and packet captures. Baseline data on network traffic also makes it possible to understand what's expected and aid in identifying anomalies.

▶ **External threat data:** External threat data consists of structured threat information such as STIX, as well as unstructured data from security advisories, bulletins, and other OSINT tools. External threat feeds from security organizations providing such data as a service can also be used as data sources. Attacks across organizations are often similar in their techniques. Chances are good that your organization isn't the first to see an attacker and his or her methods, and external threat data can give you a warning about what is happening elsewhere.

Fusion analysis can aid in processing data and yielding more meaningful insights to provide a comprehensive look at the threats to an organization. This analysis can even compare internal telemetry data with external data to provide prioritized insight. A threat hunter with good threat data can more quickly identify indicators of compromise and indicators of attacks. Some intelligence platforms integrate with and can also provide capabilities to automate and orchestrate the actions required by security.

Security Orchestration, Automation, and Response (SOAR)

Security orchestration, automation, and response (SOAR) tools can aggregate intelligence from internal and external sources to provide fusion analysis and other insights. SOAR combines data and also provides for case management and automated workflow. Gartner, a leading technology research company, came up with the idea of SOAR. According to Gartner, SOAR primarily does three things:

▶ Threat and vulnerability management

▶ Security incident response

▶ Security operations automation

You can see that, as a combined platform, a SOAR solution combines security orchestration and automation (SOA) with threat intelligence platforms (TIP) and incident response platforms (IRP). SOAR works with and augments SIEM. Gartner expects that in the future these capabilities will merge.

> **ExamAlert**
>
> SOAR integrates all the security tools available in an organization and then automates incident responses.

Cram Quiz

Answer these questions. The answers follow the last question. If you cannot answer these questions correctly, consider reading this chapter again until you can.

1. After conducting a vulnerability assessment, which of the following is the best action to perform?

   O **A.** Disable all vulnerable systems until mitigating controls can be implemented.

   O **B.** Contact the network team to shut down all identified open ports.

   O **C.** Immediately conduct a penetration test against identified vulnerabilities.

   O **D.** Organize and document the results based on severity.

2. Your team is tasked with conducting a vulnerability assessment and reports back with a high number of false positives. Which of the following might you recommend to reduce the number of false positives?

   O **A.** Have the team run a vulnerability scan using non-credentialed access.

   O **B.** Have the team run a vulnerability scan using credentialed access.

   O **C.** Have the team run a port scan across all common ports.

   O **D.** Have the team run a port scan across all ports.

3. SOAR combines functions from which of the following? (Select three.)

   O **A.** Security orchestration and automation

   O **B.** Incident response platforms

   O **C.** Threat intelligence platforms

   O **D.** Penetration tests

4. Which of the following studies human emotions in data to detect patterns such as negative, positive, or neutral opinions or attitudes?

  ○ **A.** False positive

  ○ **B.** False negative

  ○ **C.** Sentiment analysis

  ○ **D.** Log aggregation

Cram Quiz Answers

Answer 1: D. After an assessment, the results should be organized based on the severity of risk to the organization. Answer A is incorrect because it is generally an extreme response, except in rare situations. Answer B is incorrect because many open ports are required for a network to function. Answer C is incorrect because, although a penetration test often does follow a vulnerability scan, it is not an immediate necessity and certainly is not required for all identified vulnerabilities.

Answer 2: B. Non-credentialed vulnerability scans result in a greater number of false positives. This type of scan provides an outsider point of view, and although it might indicate what an outsider is more likely to see, it does not show as effectively the full extent of vulnerabilities. A credentialed vulnerability scan provides access to systems that might otherwise not be accessible, making it possible to further determine legitimate vulnerabilities. As a result, answer A is incorrect. Answers C and D are incorrect because vulnerability scans initially do scan specified ports as part of the process.

Answer 3: A, B, and C. Security orchestration, automation, and response (SOAR) combines functions from security orchestration and automation, incident response platforms, and threat intelligence platforms either as a complete solution or as an integrated solution. Penetration tests are not part of the SOAR platform, so answer D is incorrect.

Answer 4: C. Sentiment analysis studies human emotions present within data, such as negative, neutral, or positive opinions or attitudes. The data can be tracked and analyzed to look for patterns that rely on human sentiment. Answers A and B are incorrect because a false positive occurs when a security scanner detects or flags a vulnerability when one does not exist and a false negative says you don't have a vulnerability when in fact you do. Answer D is incorrect. Log aggregation is the process by which SIEM systems combine similar events to reduce event volume. SIEM systems aggregate data from many network sources and consolidate the data so that crucial events are not missed.

What Next?

If you want more practice on this chapter's exam objective before you move on, remember that you can access all of the Cram Quiz questions on the Pearson Test Prep software online. You can also create a custom exam by objective with the Online Practice Test. Note any objective you struggle with and go to that objective's material in this chapter.

CHAPTER 8

Penetration Testing Techniques

> **This chapter covers the following official Security+ exam objective:**
>
> ▶ 1.8 Explain the techniques used in penetration testing.

> **Essential Terms and Components**
>
> ▶ white box
> ▶ black box
> ▶ gray box
> ▶ rules of engagement
> ▶ lateral movement
> ▶ privilege escalation
> ▶ persistence
> ▶ pivoting
> ▶ bug bounty program
> ▶ war flying
> ▶ war driving
> ▶ footprinting
> ▶ OSINT
> ▶ teaming (red, blue, white, purple)

Penetration testing differs from vulnerability scanning, which you just read about in Chapter 7, "Security Assessment Techniques." Vulnerability scanning seeks to merely programmatically identify vulnerabilities. A penetration test takes testing further by trying to exploit the vulnerabilities to gain access. As a result, penetration testing might be preceded by an attempt to assess vulnerabilities. Both vulnerability scanning and penetration testing present risk to an organization, but

penetration testing is considered a much higher risk. Mimicking real-world attacks can have real-world consequences for systems, so an organization conducting penetration testing must follow a carefully planned program and properly understand the potential trade-offs and risks.

Testing Methodology

Penetration testing, also commonly known as *pen testing*, is sometimes used as part of an organization's information security program to better understand the systems. Pen tests often incorporate real-world attacks to identify methods and weaknesses in the systems, with the aim of gaining deeper access or gaining access to specific targets. Penetration test results can be valuable. For example, they help organizations better understand how their systems tolerate real-world attacks. Identifying the required level of sophistication and the potential threats can help an organization allocate resources properly. Where required, penetration tests can also help quickly identify areas of weakness that need to be strengthened. Organizations can then quantify the adequacy of security measures that are in place and provide meaningful insight into specific threats against the environment. Based on its penetration test program, an organization can also measure its responses, including how quickly it can identify and mitigate attempts.

Systems administrators who perform amateur or ad hoc pen tests against networks to prove a particular vulnerability or evaluate the overall security exposure of a network do so at their peril. This is a bad practice because it generates false intrusion data, can weaken the network's security level, and can even violate privacy laws, regulatory mandates, or business entity guidelines. Certainly, regularly conducted penetration tests can help assess the effectiveness of an organization's controls, but these tests should always be performed within a defined program of governance that involves senior management.

Bug bounty programs, which are a form of penetration testing, have gained a lot of traction in recent years. *A bug bounty program* is a formalized program to identify the bugs that lead to a vulnerability or an exploit. While bug bounties can be public or private, they have gained widespread appeal as they are often open to the public for externally facing applications and services delivered from the web. Unlike a penetration test, a bug bounty program is offered only on externally facing applications and is not performed on internal applications unless the program is internal to employees, for example. Bug bounty programs have the advantage of providing continuous security testing. Further, the company running the program is free to set not just its own terms but also the dollar amount to be paid. Many bug bounty hunters are mostly seeking recognition.

Like a penetration test, a bug bounty program is well defined. Governance, terms, and the *rules of engagement* are critical and must be made very clear to those who might want to participate. The participants in a bug bounty program also have no understanding of the inner workings of the systems, which have traditionally been known as black boxes because the systems are opaque to the participants.

Penetration testing can be conducted using various techniques, classified as follows:

▶ **Black box (unknown environment):** In a *black box* test, the assessor has no knowledge of the inner workings of the system or the source code. The assessor simply tests the application for functionality as if he or she were a regular user of the system. An easy way to think about this is to imagine that you cannot see through or inside a black box.

▶ **White box (known environment):** *White box* testing, also called clear box or glass box testing, provides more transparency than black box testing. In white box testing, the assessor has knowledge of the inner workings of either the system or the source code. This can be thought of as testing from the perspective of the developer.

▶ **Gray box (partially known environment):** *Gray box* testing combines white and black box techniques. Think of this approach as translucent: The tester has some understanding or a limited knowledge of the inner workings.

As you can see, the categories refer to varying degrees of knowledge about the systems or applications being tested. Black box testing consumes less time and is less exhaustive than white box testing, and gray box testing falls in between. Figure 8.1 provides a comparison of the three testing types.

FIGURE 8.1 **Comparison between unknown, known and partially known penetration testing environments.**

ExamAlert

The industry is moving away from the use of boxes as metaphors. The exam will likely refer to each type by their environment state. A black box or unknown environment hides the contents (no knowledge). A white box or known environment is see-through (complete knowledge of inner workings). A gray box or partially known environment combines the two (limited knowledge).

Penetration testing includes the following components:

▶ **Verifying that a threat exists:** A penetration test seeks to exploit vulnerabilities. Before you can exploit a vulnerability, you must first understand the threat and its extent. As an analogy, a sheep farmer in an isolated location might be less concerned about locking his front door than about losing his sheep to wolves.

▶ **Bypassing security controls:** Penetration tests should seek to bypass security controls, just as a real attacker would. Verifying that a battering ram cannot penetrate a stone wall is worthless if a back gate is left wide open. Similarly, network firewalls might be protecting the pathways into the network, but an attacker might find an easier method of entry through a rogue wireless access point or modem. Another common method of bypassing security controls is to render them ineffective. For example, a DoS attack can be mounted on security controls to overload the controls, possibly enabling potentially easier access.

▶ **Actively testing security controls:** Active techniques include direct interaction with a specific target. Passive techniques seek to identify gaps that could lead to missing or misconfigured security controls. Active techniques, on the other hand, seek to identify whether controls are implemented properly. Consider a lock on a door. Passive testing might uncover documentation and policies indicating that locks are installed, whereas an active test would involve trying to open the door.

▶ **Exploiting vulnerabilities:** Unlike vulnerability scanning, penetration testing does not just check for the existence of a potential vulnerability but attempts to exploit it. A resulting exploit verifies the vulnerability and should lead to mitigation techniques and controls to deal with the security exposure. Most exploited vulnerabilities are likely to result from misconfigurations, kernel flaws, buffer overflows, input validation errors, and incorrect permissions.

Careful planning is required before conducting penetration testing. A penetration test involves four primary phases: planning, discovery, attack, and reporting (see Figure 8.2). Keep in mind that planning provides major input into the final reporting phase. In addition, the attack phase can lead to a loop for further discovery and subsequent attack.

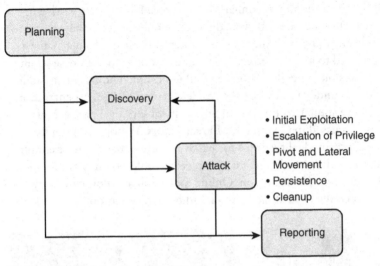

FIGURE 8.2 **Phases of a penetration test**

Planning

The planning phase does not involve actual testing. Its purpose is to set expectations and provide clarity regarding the plan and goals. This phase is an important part of the overall process because of the risks of penetration tests. The planning phase is the time to clearly define the rules of engagement—specifically, how the testing will be conducted, including expectations, and how potential situations should be handled (if, for example, sensitive data is revealed). An important output of this phase is a documented plan that includes the rules and expectations.

Discovery

With planning complete, the discovery phase of penetration testing begins. Discovery consists of two fundamental areas: information gathering and scanning and vulnerability analysis.

Information gathering and scanning involve conducting *reconnaissance* on the target through observation and other outside discovery tools. Many techniques and tools are available for potentially gaining important information; those resources will later serve as the intelligence needed for executing the attack, which is the next phase in the penetration test.

While gathering information, reconnaissance is considered either passive or active. Passive techniques are less risky than active ones because they do not require actively engaging with the targeted systems. Passive reconnaissance is often aptly referred to as *footprinting*. This phase is similar to the phase when a burglar first stakes out a neighborhood to find unoccupied homes or surveilling a specific home to understand when the residents come and go. A penetration test could well use similar techniques in physically observing a data center. OSINT tools, discussed in Chapter 5, "Threat Actors, Vectors, and Intelligence Sources," are an ideal resource for passive reconnaissance. For example, an organization's website and public user directory could potentially provide a great deal of pertinent information. Online tools such as whois can easily gather technical contacts, hostname, and IP address information.

> **ExamAlert**
>
> Remember that footprinting is part of the reconnaissance process. It is used to gather as much information about a target as possible in order to penetrate it.

> **Note**
>
> Whois is a free and publicly accessible directory from which domain names can be queried to discover contact and technical information behind registered domain names. Lookups can easily be performed at https://whois.icann.org.

Active reconnaissance, on the other hand, requires engaging with a target. Examples include port scanning and service identification. At a minimum, port scanners identify one of two states for a port on a host system: open or closed. These scanners also identify the associated service and, potentially, the application name being run. For example, this can include the specific FTP application name running on port 21 on a specific host. Such information reveals potential targets for penetration testing.

Given the ubiquity of wireless networks, two common reconnaissance missions may employ either active or passive methods to look for wireless attack vectors:

▶ **War driving:** War driving is the act of searching for wireless networks by using a portable computer or other mobile device from a moving vehicle on the ground.

▶ **War flying:** War flying is the act of searching for wireless networks by using a portable computer or other mobile device from an aircraft, such as a *drone* or another *unmanned aerial vehicle (UAV)*.

The next step involves vulnerability identification and analysis. Databases of publicly known vulnerabilities are available. Vulnerabilities can be manually identified, or automated scanners can be used, as discussed in Chapter 7.

Attack

During the attack phase, the tester tries to gain access or penetrate the system, often as a result of exploiting an identified vulnerability during the previous phase. The idea is to at least perform an initial exploitation, even if it does not reveal the ultimate goal or data of value. During this initial exploitation, the tester commonly has only regular user access and does not have access to high-value areas. However, this initial exploit provides the opportunity for the penetration tester to execute *privilege escalation*. The tester can then gain access at a higher authorization and conduct more advanced commands and routines. From there, the tester can likely begin to gain further access deeper into the network, in a process known as *lateral movement*. Moving laterally requires *pivoting*, often through multiple systems and in different directions in order to continue moving more deeply into the system. Throughout these pivots, the tester might try to install additional tools. This process, known as *persistence*, enables the tester to gain additional compromising information once an objective has been achieved or to ensure continuance despite temporary opposition. Achieving persistence may also involve, for example, planting backdoors to allow continued remote access into the systems.

Finally, the last step is *cleanup*. Attackers usually want to remove any mess or signs left behind that they have been in the systems, particularly if they expect to remain persistent. During penetration testing, cleanup is important to ensure that systems are back to their original state and that no new vulnerabilities have been introduced.

ExamAlert

The following are the progressive steps you should remember during the attack phase:

1. Initial exploitation
2. Escalation of privilege
3. Pivoting and lateral movement
4. Persistence
5. Cleanup

Reporting

Reporting is an important component of a penetration test. Specifically, as activity is documented, and depending on the plan, reporting might be required in the discovery and attack phases. After any penetration test, a comprehensive report should be delivered that includes, at a minimum, vulnerabilities identified, actions taken, and the results, mitigation techniques, and some sort of quantification of the risk.

Team Exercises

Organizations with mature security programs may find that assessments around *teaming* are beneficial. An assessment that is similar to a traditional penetration test but is more targeted is known as a *red team* assessment. Such exercises have a specific goal and may last longer than a scoped-out penetration test. A red team assessment is concerned specifically with vulnerabilities that will help accomplish a goal. The red team acts as the adversary, attacking and trying to remain unnoticed. Teaming exercises are fun, though, because they include additional teams. The *blue team* is the defenders. Their job is to counter the red team and keep the red team from accomplishing its mission. Teaming has an additional advantage as it makes it possible for an organization to measure and improve alerting and responses.

Recently, the idea of purple teams has become common. With *purple teaming*, the red and blue teams work together, often sitting down side-by-side to identify vulnerabilities, test controls, and explore ways to defeat and improve the controls. An additional team, known as the *white team*, should be involved as a neutral team. This team defines the goals and the rules and adjudicates the exercise. White teams tend to not be as technical as the red and blue teams; the members of the white team drive an exercises through their knowledge and involvement across governance and compliance. The white team, as a result, is the team that steers the exercise with its knowledge of overall risk strategy, including the goals and requirements of the business. Figure 8.3 provides a brief summary of these team.

ExamAlert

Know that the red team attacks, the blue team defends, and the white team referees. The purple team combines the skills and knowledge of the red and blue teams to achieve maximum effectiveness.

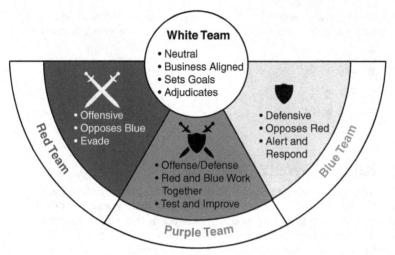

FIGURE 8.3 **A summary of red, blue, purple, and white teams**

Cram Quiz

Answer these questions. The answers follow the last question. If you cannot answer these questions correctly, consider reading this chapter again until you can.

1. You are conducting a penetration test on a software application for a client. The development team has provided you with complete details around the source code and development process. What type of test will you likely be conducting?

   ○ **A.** Black box

   ○ **B.** Vulnerability

   ○ **C.** White box

   ○ **D.** Answers A and B

2. A _____ team is _____, and a _____ team is _____.

   ○ **A.** blue, offensive, red, defensive

   ○ **B.** red, offensive, blue, defensive

   ○ **C.** red, offensive, white, defensive

   ○ **D.** white offensive, blue defensive

3. Place the following steps in the correct order for the attack phase: a. Persistence, b. Cleanup, c. Lateral movement, d. Privilege escalation, e. Initial exploitation.

   ○ **A.** a, b, c, d, e

   ○ **B.** e, d, c, a, b

   ○ **C.** e, a, c, d, b

   ○ **D.** a, e, d, b, c

4. Which of the following is part of a passive reconnaissance process and is used to gather as much information about a target as possible in order to penetrate it?

   ○ **A.** Footprinting

   ○ **B.** War driving

   ○ **C.** War flying

   ○ **D.** Bug bounty

Cram Quiz Answers

Answer 1: C. White box testing (known environment) is transparent. Because you are provided with source code, you have more knowledge about the system before you begin your penetration testing. Answer A is incorrect because black box testing (unknown environment) assumes no prior knowledge. Answer B is incorrect because this refers to a weakness. Therefore, answer D is also incorrect.

Answer 2: B. In teaming exercises, red teams are offensive, and blue teams are defensive. Answer A is incorrect. Answers C and D are also incorrect, as white teams are neutral.

Answer 3: B. The steps during the attack phase of a penetration test are 1. Initial exploration, 2. Privilege escalation, 3. Pivoting and lateral movement, 4. Persistence, and 5. Cleanup. Answers A, C, and D are incorrect as they are not ordered correctly.

Answer 4: A. Footprinting is part of a reconnaissance process. This process is used to gather as much information about a target as possible in order to penetrate it. This is similar to a burglar first staking out a neighborhood to find unoccupied homes or surveilling a specific home to understand when the residents come and go. Answer B is incorrect. War driving is the act of searching for wireless networks using a portable computer or other mobile device from a moving vehicle on the ground. Answer C is incorrect. War flying is the act of searching for wireless networks by using a portable computer or other mobile device from an aircraft, such as a drone or another unmanned aerial vehicles. Answer D is incorrect because a bug bounty is a form of penetration testing; it is a formalized program to identify bugs that lead to a vulnerability or an exploit.

What Next?

If you want more practice on this chapter's exam objective before you move on, remember that you can access all of the Cram Quiz questions on the Pearson Test Prep software online. You can also create a custom exam by objective with the Online Practice Test. Note any objective you struggle with and go to that objective's material in this chapter.

PART II

Architecture and Design

This part covers the following official Security+ SYO-601 exam objectives for Domain 2.0, "Architecture and Design":

▶ 2.1 Explain the importance of security concepts in an enterprise environment.

▶ 2.2 Summarize virtualization and cloud computing concepts.

▶ 2.3 Summarize secure application development, deployment, and automation concepts.

▶ 2.4 Summarize authentication and authorization design concepts.

▶ 2.5 Given a scenario, implement cybersecurity resilience.

▶ 2.6 Explain the security implications of embedded and specialized systems.

▶ 2.7 Explain the importance of physical security controls.

▶ 2.8 Summarize the basics of cryptographic concepts.

For more information on the official CompTIA Security+ SY0-601 exam topics, see the section "Exam Objectives" in the Introduction.

To properly secure computers, networks, and applications, you must understand the principles of secure design. This part of the book covers important security and system concepts, implementation of cybersecurity resilience, and secure application development and deployment, along with the security implications of embedded systems, virtualization, and cloud environments.

Planning a secure architecture and design is critical to ensure that proper controls are in place to meet organization goals and reduce risk. Secure architecture and systems design are based on frameworks, best practices, and guides. Secure design is holistic, encompassing physical security controls, logical controls, and additional internal and external systems. This part covers how architecture and design fit into an organization's security posture.

CHAPTER 9

Enterprise Security Concepts

This chapter covers the following official Security+ exam objective:

▶ 2.1 Explain the importance of security concepts in an enterprise environment.

Essential Terms and Components

▶ configuration management
▶ data sovereignty
▶ data protection
▶ data loss prevention (DLP)
▶ data masking
▶ data encryption
▶ data at rest
▶ data in motion
▶ data in processing
▶ tokenization
▶ hashing
▶ rights management
▶ hardware security module (HSM)
▶ cloud access security broker (CASB)
▶ Secure Sockets Layer (SSL)
▶ Transport Layer Security (TLS)
▶ hot site
▶ cold site
▶ warm site
▶ deception
▶ disruption

> ▶ honeypot
>
> ▶ honeyfile
>
> ▶ honeynet
>
> ▶ DNS sinkhole

Enterprise security requires architecture and design around a number of important concepts to ensure the security of data and defend against threats—from foundationally ensuring baselined systems that process data; to ensuring the confidentiality, integrity, and availability (CIA) of the data; to defending against threats that could compromise the data.

Configuration Management

Configuration management is its own discipline that can be broken into subdisciplines. Configuration management has been around for decades and, while it has roots in technical management, it has evolved to incorporate many different concepts across multiple domains. As related to information and cybersecurity, *configuration management* is the process of identifying, controlling, and auditing the deployment and changes made to an established baseline. Benefits include the ability to do things more efficiently and effectively while providing strong security controls and best practice. Examples of these benefits are realized in the following processes:

▶ Provisioning new systems

▶ Replicating environments

▶ Recovering from disasters

▶ Onboarding and training employees

▶ Ensuring stability through change management

▶ Ensuring hardened and secure systems

It is important to understand how configuration management contributes to secure configurations. A *baseline configuration* is based on a component or a system and includes the configurations and settings that are set as the foundation for all similar systems. This way, for example, when a Windows desktop is deployed to a user, the Windows desktop deployed to another user is set up the

same way, based on a well-documented baseline configuration. While having a baseline configuration may seem unnecessary for just two systems, you can imagine how useful it is in an organization with thousands or tens of thousands of systems. Without such configurations and the proper management of these configurations, an organization would be more susceptible to errors, malfunctions, and security breaches. Further, ongoing management and support of these systems would be overwhelming. It is therefore important that the configuration management process as well as all the baselines and standards be well documented. Consider, for example, the following:

▶ **Baseline configuration:** A baseline configuration should be documented such that another person could easily replicate the configuration, much like following a recipe. This standardization also helps in facilitating audit activities.

▶ **Diagrams:** Diagrams are particularly important for networks and interconnected complex systems. Examples include network maps, cabling and wiring diagrams, and application configuration and connections.

▶ **Standard naming convention:** An agreed-upon method of naming assets is valuable for everyday management and especially in the event of an emergency. For example, a computer could be named Therese-SF-Sales to indicate a computer assigned to Therese out of San Francisco in the Sales division. Computer names can indicate a number of physical properties, including building number, room number, and floor, or logical properties, such as owner, cost center, or function (such as email or web).

▶ **Internet Protocol (IP) schema:** As components and systems are added to IP-based networks, each is usually assigned an IP address. A small organization, for example, might designate systems by type according to the last octet of the IP address (for example, switches and routers could be numbered x.x.x.1 through x.x.x.10 and client computers x.x.x.11 through x.x.x.50).

ExamAlert

Remember that configuration management documentation often includes diagrams, baseline configurations, standard naming conventions, and IP schemas.

Security baseline configurations can be built atop baseline configurations in a layered approach, or multiple baseline configurations can be created. For example, a different approach might be taken for the computer of a regular user and that of a power user. While most baseline configurations include hardened

standards, a security baseline configuration can be more specific to the role of the specific system. An Active Directory (AD) domain controller, for example, may not need web server components installed on it, and a web server will likely be configured very differently from a database server.

Creating a hardened operating system is a large part of making sure that systems have secure configurations. Hardening the operating system includes planning against both accidental data deletion and directed attacks, such as by using fault-tolerant hardware and software solutions. In addition, an organization must implement an effective system for file-level security, including encrypted file support and secured file system selection that allows the proper level of access control. For example, NTFS allows file-level access control and encryption, whereas most FAT-based file systems allow only share-level access control, without encryption.

Organizations also must conduct regular update reviews for all deployed operating systems to address newly identified exploits and apply security updates and hotfixes. Many automated attacks take advantage of common vulnerabilities, often those for which patches and hotfixes are already available but not yet applied. Failure to update applications on a regular basis or perform regular auditing can result in an insecure solution that gives an attacker access to additional resources throughout an organization's network.

Operating system hardening includes configuring log files and auditing, changing default administrator account names and default passwords, and instituting account lockout and password policies to guarantee strong passwords that can resist brute-force attacks. File-level security and access control mechanisms can be used to isolate access attempts in the operating system environment.

Data Confidentiality

Maintaining the confidentiality of data is an important component of ensuring *data protection*. Confidentiality is about protecting data and ensuring privacy so that only those who should be authorized to view data are allowed to do so. Data protection involves preventing theft or disclosure of data—both intentional and unintentional.

Most enterprises implement a variety of tools to provide for data confidentiality. This section covers these technologies and tools, including data loss prevention, cloud access security brokers, data obfuscation techniques, rights management, hardware security modules, and encrypted traffic management.

Data Loss Prevention

Data loss prevention (*DLP*) products identify confidential or sensitive information through content analysis. Content analysis techniques include rule-based, database, exact file or data matching, partial document matching, and statistical analysis.

Data loss is a problem that all organizations face, and it can be especially challenging for global organizations that store a large volume of personally identifiable information (PII) in different legal jurisdictions. Privacy issues differ by country, region, and state. Naturally, organizations implement data loss prevention tools as a way to prevent data loss. Data loss prevention is a way of detecting and preventing confidential data from being exfiltrated physically or logically from an organization by accident or on purpose. DLP systems are basically designed to detect and prevent unauthorized use and transmission of confidential information, based on one of the three states of data: in use, in motion/transit, or at rest. DLP systems offer a way to enforce data security policies by providing centralized management for detecting and preventing the unauthorized use and transmission of data that the organization deems confidential. A well-designed DLP strategy allows control over sensitive data, reduces costs by preventing data breaches, and makes possible greater insight into organizational data use. International organizations should ensure that they are in compliance with local privacy regulations as they implement DLP tools and processes.

Data can exist in different states: in use, in transit, and at rest. Protection of data in use is considered to be an endpoint solution. With data in use, an application is run on end-user workstations or servers in the organization. Endpoint systems also can monitor and control access to physical devices such as mobile devices and tablets. Protection of data in transit is considered to be a network solution, and either a hardware or software solution can be installed near the network perimeter to monitor and flag policy violations. Protection of data at rest is considered to be a storage solution and is generally a software solution that monitors how confidential data is stored.

With a DLP solution, a user can be alerted about security policy violations to keep sensitive information from leaving the user's desktop. The following are some examples of actions for which an organization might want to alert users:

- ▶ Inadvertently emailing a confidential internal document to external recipients

- ▶ Forwarding an email containing sensitive information to unauthorized recipients inside or outside the organization

▶ Sending attachments such as spreadsheets with PII to an external personal email account

▶ Accidentally selecting Reply All and emailing a sensitive document to unauthorized recipients

USB flash drives and other portable storage devices are pervasive in the workplace and pose a real threat. They can introduce viruses or malicious code to the network and can store sensitive corporate information. In addition, sensitive information is often stored on thumb drives and external hard drives, which may be lost or stolen. DLP solutions allow policies for USB blocking, such as policies for blocking the copying of any network information to removable media or for blocking the use of unapproved USB devices.

Cloud Access Security Brokers

In recent years, many large organizations have embraced cloud services and begun storing data in the cloud. DLP solutions have expanded from email and local devices to include corporate data stored in the cloud. An organization must know how the cloud is being utilized before making decisions on a DLP solution:

▶ What files are being shared outside the organization?

▶ What files contain sensitive data?

▶ What abnormal events indicate threat or compromise?

Cloud service providers (CSPs) have introduced a variety of cloud storage services, such as Google Drive and Dropbox. These services represent new usage models for how we interact with data. For example, cloud storage enables collaboration and typically makes it possible to share data with a simple link. *Cloud access security brokers* (*CASBs*) have introduced innovative ways to gain visibility and control of these services. One of the primary use cases for a CASB is DLP for cloud applications and services such as Office 365, Salesforce, Google Suite, Dropbox, and Box.

Different DLP policies apply for different cloud services. Some are general cloud policies, such as a general policy for device access control. A specific policy for Box, for example, might focus on file sharing. Some concepts are a bit different in the cloud than on premises, such as how a file is shared (whether internally with the entire organization or externally and with whom), and whether data is shared publicly. CASBs are designed to understand these situations and provide dynamic policies to control and respond to various

circumstances. As CASBs have matured and been acquired by larger security vendors, in some of the better integrations, they work as part of the enterprise DLP program and serve as another extension to other use cases solved by DLP (for example, across the endpoint, network, data center, and now cloud services).

> **ExamAlert**
>
> Cloud access security brokers (CASBs) help organizations extend on-premises security solutions to the cloud. They are hardware or software solutions that act as intermediaries between users and cloud service providers (CSPs).

Encryption and Data Obfuscation

According to best practices, sensitive data should be encrypted at all times whenever possible. Data exposure can occur in applications when sensitive data—such as credit card numbers, personal health information (PHI), and authentication credentials—is not protected while it is being stored or transmitted.

When employees must use removable drives, finding a way to secure data that is taken outside a managed environment is part of doing business. *Data encryption* is essential. Some disk encryption products protect only the local drive and not USB devices. Other encryption products automatically encrypt data that is copied or written to removable media.

Protecting data through encryption and yet maintaining the capability for decryption can be broadly categorized into three high-level areas (similar to DLP), based on the state of the data:

▶ **Data at rest:** *Data at rest* is data in its stored or resting state, which is typically on some type of persistent storage such as a hard drive or tape. Symmetric encryption is used in this case.

▶ **Data in transit:** Data in transit is data moving across a network or from one system to another. Data in transit is also commonly known as *data in motion*. Transport layer encryption such as SSL/TLS is used in this case.

▶ **Data in processing:** *Data in processing* is data being processed in memory or cache. It includes the presentation of data, such as on a monitor. Homomorphic and other emerging techniques are used in this case.

The distinctions can be blurred, particularly when talking about data in processing. This is why the term *data in processing* is used rather than the term *data in use*, as it is with DLP. With DLP, data in use is specific to a user interacting with data on the endpoint, such as copying data from the file and other interactions. Data in processing, on the other hand, requires encryption techniques that can perform calculations upon encrypted data without the requirement to first decrypt the data.

ExamAlert

Remember that DLP solutions can incorporate one or all three methods of protecting data in various states: data in use (for example, data on laptop being moved to a USB drive), data in transit (for example, data going across the network), and data at rest (for example, data sitting on a file server or database). Encryption also can protect data at rest and data in transit. Encrypting data being used is more appropriately referred to as *data in processing* than *data in use*.

Encryption of data in processing is difficult to achieve, and it is typically done only for specific situations to meet certain requirements. For example, data in processing encryption is best suited to structured data, such as fields within a database. Certainly, adhering to field size limits or maintaining the referential integrity that a database requires is not trivial, but there are methods (often involving other security or usability trade-offs) to encrypt data or protect data through a means other than encryption, particularly where encryption makes it impossible to do needed work with data or makes it difficult to analyze data while encrypted.

ExamAlert

Encryption supports the confidentiality and integrity of data across three states: at rest, in transit, and in processing.

In situations like this and across other use cases, other methods of obscuring data besides encryption may be more suitable—or even required. The following are three methods that often accomplish the goals of confidentiality and privacy without the use of encryption:

▶ **Tokenization:** *Tokenization* involves assigning a random surrogate value with no mathematical relationship that can be reversed by linking the token back to the original data. Outside the system, a token has no value; it is just meaningless data. Tokenization can also preserve the format

of data (such as maintaining the type or length of data), which makes it suitable for databases and card payment processing.

▶ **Data masking:** *Data masking* involves desensitizing or removing sensitive or personal data but enabling the data to remain usable. False data that appears real is substituted for the real data. Masking is commonly required for application development, particularly where realistic test data is required. Like tokenization, data masking can preserve the data format and referential integrity.

▶ **Redaction:** Redaction involves obscuring data by replacing all or part of the content for security or privacy purposes. Redaction in physical documents typically means blacking out some text; redaction in information systems often uses the asterisk character. For example, a travel agent might need to see only the last four digits of a credit card number, and the preceding digits may be redacted and replaced with asterisks.

Figure 9.1 provides an example of applying encryption along with tokenization, masking, and redaction to credit card information.

Encrypted Values	Token Values
O/Mw+qmQITMzIZSz/ V5cje5rCwIWU8hMzM+=	6389 7207 2518 0518 Tbr Tfeilsia

Redacted Values	Masked Values
**** **** **** 9313 Eli *****	2223 0167 2837 2736 John Andreadis

FIGURE 9.1   **A comparison of different methods to obfuscate credit card data**

In Figure 9.1, the encrypted values are scrambled using a cryptographic algorithm, and the size of the output is larger than the original fields. Neither type nor length is preserved, and the data is of no use without first being decrypted.

With the tokenized values, you can see that both type and length are maintained, and the tokens can be alphabetic or numeric. In addition, a tokenized value can also be alphanumeric. A token value can include a prefix such as t to assure the viewer that it is a token surrogate value. Tokens are also useful in credit card applications as the check to ensure validity of a valid card number (that is, the Luhn check) can be maintained. And while not shown in the example, non-sensitive components such as the last four digits of the credit card number can be maintained while other parts are tokenized.

The redacted values provide only the required data. For example, on a credit card receipt, you are likely to see a series of asterisks with only the last four digits of your card number. The last four digits are enough to allow the store personnel to do their jobs, and the redaction maintains your security and privacy as the four digits are not enough to reverse the data back to the original data.

Finally, the masked values generally only need to seem realistic. In this example, an application being developed using credit card information doesn't necessarily need real data, and it certainly does not need data that has any requirement to ever be reversed. Note, however, that the masked credit card value in this example does include the first six digits of the credit card. This is a non-sensitive component known as the bank identification number (BIN), which the application may require to adequately test a related function. While the masked values look similar to token values, consider the potential differences based on the options described. Also remember that masked values cannot and should not ever have a reason to be reversed. The token value is mathematically not reversible and has no value outside this system to which it can be securely looked up or mapped back to the original number.

Rights Management

Rights managements can include digital rights management (DRM) and information rights management (IRM). Both DRM and IRM serve the purpose of protecting data from unauthorized access through encryption. DRM is primarily used for the protection of copyrighted material. An early use of DRM technology was with CDs and DVDs. When the contents of a disc are encrypted, the media cannot be copied without the decryption key, and only licensed players have that key; this process prevents such duplication. The same technology is often applied to books as well. Some textbooks from Pearson, for example, are protected by DRM. A DRM-protected book is encrypted and requires a third-party reader such as Adobe Digital Editions, which authorizes the use of the book and prevents copying. DRM protection is different from watermarking,

in which a book includes an overlaid watermark that makes the book uniquely yours and discourages copying.

IRM is a technology that is mostly used in organizations to protect sensitive information from unauthorized access. IRM provides for data security while also fostering collaboration within the organization and with external parties. IRM is commonly applied to email, engineering documents, and other business-related files that often need to be distributed and shared with other parties. IRM gives the owner the ability to protect these documents using encryption and also enables the owner to control and manage access to the documents, such as what the user can do with the document (for example, preventing copying and pasting, taking screenshots, and printing). IRM can even allow an owner to revoke a user's access even after a document has been distributed. IRM goes beyond the requirements of DRM by providing flexibility in the type of data to be protected and control mechanisms. IRM allows you to control the following:

▶ **Who:** Control who can and cannot access documents—by individual, by group, or based on email domains.

▶ **What:** Control what documents can be accessed by allowing access to specific documents or a specific set of documents based on various attributes.

▶ **When:** Control when and for how long documents can be accessed. Time limits can be set, and access can be removed on demand.

▶ **Where:** Control from where a document can be accessed. Access may be allowed based on the location of the user or based on various attributes, or access may be allowed only on the internal network.

▶ **How:** Control how users are able to interact with the document. Features within a document may be limited, if desired. A user might, for example, be unable to forward an email or might be prevented from saving or printing the document.

Hardware Security Module (HSM)

You should consider the use of a *hardware security module* (*HSM*) when data security through cryptographic functions is required and the keys used to protect the data are of high value. An HSM is a device used to protect and manage the keys required as part of an encryption or decryption operation. HSMs are

special-purpose devices with tamper-preventive secure cryptoprocessors. An HSM provides the following benefits:

▶ Generates secure cryptographic keys

▶ Provides secure key storage

▶ Provides key management capabilities

▶ Performs cryptographic functions, including digital signing and encryption/decryption operations

▶ Offers increased performance through cryptographic acceleration

ExamAlert

Know that an HSM is a physical security device that manages and safeguards digital keys and performs encryption and decryption for cryptographic functions. An HSM includes a cryptoprocessor that generates, stores, and manages digital keys and can perform performance-optimized cryptographic operations.

Encrypted Traffic Management

The use of encryption continues to grow within and across organizations. Specifically, transport layer encryption—through the use of *Secure Sockets Layer (SSL)* or *Transport Layer Security (TLS)*—is now used by default. It is applied to systems residing within organizational boundaries as well as to mobile and cloud applications. The world is going "dark," to use a phrase from intelligence organizations. While this has a positive impact on data confidentiality, it is challenging for organizations that are required to monitor and ensure the safe use of their employees. Encryption can be used, for example, to hide malicious activity and malware, and it can also be used to ensure that data isn't confidentially shared with someone with whom it shouldn't be shared.

To overcome these blind spots and allow security administrators to enforce acceptable use policies and stop encrypted threats, organizations look to systems that provide visibility into encrypted traffic flows. SSL/TLS decryption appliances and services are used for the following reasons:

▶ Monitoring of application performance

▶ Cloud services monitoring

▶ Malware detection

► DLP

► Forensic analysis

Solutions to manage encrypted traffic typically provide policy-based traffic direction and can improve performance.

Decrypting SSL traffic is only part of the equation. After decryption, the data has to be forwarded to the appropriate device for inspection. Analysis of the decrypted content is a joint effort and includes devices such as IDSs/IPSs, firewalls, secure web gateways, and DLP solutions. What device the packets go to depends on the policies in place. Much like SSL/TLS acceleration, SSL/TLS decryption can be offloaded to encrypted traffic management solutions. Further, network devices or systems beyond just DLP might require access to the decrypted traffic, and decrypted traffic can be forwarded to the appropriate device based on policies.

Data Integrity

Maintaining the integrity of data is an important part of ensuring data protection. The previous sections have shown many of the ways in which confidentiality can be applied to data, but what happens where the integrity of the document is critical? For example, a military commander might want to ensure the confidentiality of a message that says "Attack at dawn!" Protecting the integrity of that message is also critical. Imagine if the message were manipulated in transit to instead read "Attack at noon!" In fact, in many use cases, only data integrity and not confidentiality may be needed.

Data integrity is provided through a cryptographic method known as *hashing*, which is a cryptographic checksum, or through file integrity monitoring (FIM) solutions that employ hashing. Hashing with data integrity works much as it works in protecting passwords, as discussed earlier in Part I, "Attacks, Threats, and Vulnerabilities." How hashing works is also covered in greater detail in Chapter 16, "Cryptographic Concepts." Essentially, an algorithm is applied to a file to derive a checksum, and a checksum outputs a simple block of data. If the original document is modified, even slightly, a different checksum is produced. The electronic version of this book, for example, can be hashed to produce a simple output. The following example shows how I hash this chapter and the resulting output:

```
MW@MacBook ~ % md5 Chapter09-601-ExamCram.docx

MD5 (Chapter9-Security+ExamCram.docx)
=8ac9675d805a2d23f473684c4254c426
```

As long as the hashed .docx file does not change, every time it's hashed with the same MD5 algorithm, it will produce the same hashed output shown here (8ac9675d805a2d23f473684c4254c426). Renaming the file or even changing one letter will produce different output. In fact, now that I have added just these few lines of text, the hashed value I get changes as shown here:

```
MW@MacBook ~ % md5 Chapter09-601-ExamCram.docx

MD5 (Chapter9-Security+ExamCram.docx)
=8d15e340300307be5a0c3d2f14dc6a80
```

You can see that hashing is instrumental to ensuring the integrity of data within an organization. It has many applications, from documents to email communication to maintaining the integrity of system files. With system files, for example, hashing would reveal if a critical system file was subverted by malware.

Data Availability

In addition to confidentiality and integrity, availability is the final core piece of data protection.

Ensuring availability starts with analysis of business impacts and strong planning. Chapter 34, "Risk Management," goes into the details of the planning processes. Controls are required to ensure adequate response and recovery for organizations in case of breaches and disasters. For example, it is important to provide for regular backups of key information, including user file and email storage, database stores, event logs, and security details, such as user logons, passwords, and group membership assignments. A regular backup process helps ensure that loss of data through accidents or directed attacks does not severely impair an organization. In addition, an organization needs to plan detailed system restoration procedures, particularly in complex clustered, virtualized, and hybrid environments. This planning should explain any general or specific configuration details, such as those discussed earlier in this chapter, that might be required to restore access and ensure data availability.

Contingency planning to recover systems and data is needed in case of personnel loss or lack of availability. A contingency plan should address, for example, the procedures to follow when a disgruntled employee changes an administrative password before leaving. Another contingency plan might consider what to do when backups are unrecoverable.

> **Note**
>
> More and more application programming interfaces (APIs) are being made available across organizations and for use with external integrations to enable data flows across disparate systems and traditional boundaries. As a result, it is important to ensure confidentiality, integrity, and availability (CIA) of these APIs:
>
> ▶ **API confidentiality:** APIs, especially those accessing sensitive data, need to be protected using strong transport layer encryption. Controls should be in place to enforce appropriate authentication and access-based controls, depending on the intended use.
>
> ▶ **API integrity:** Protections to ensure the integrity of data should be in place based on unauthorized alterations to the data via the API.
>
> ▶ **API availability:** APIs can incur downtime and suffer from performance impacts, and they should be monitored to ensure proper function and availability.

Site Resiliency

In the event of a massive disaster or emergency, it might be necessary to operate at alternate site locations. Cloud infrastructure in recent years has helped tremendously with regard to site resiliency. Cloud infrastructure service providers offer options to choose from globally available physical locations that can be remotely provisioned to establish sites for recovery. The type of recovery site an organization chooses depends on the criticality of recovery and budget allocations. Three types of recovery sites exist:

▶ Hot site

▶ Warm site

▶ Cold site

Hot, warm, and cold sites can provide a means for recovery in the event that an event renders the original building unusable.

A *hot site* is a location that is already running and available 7 days a week, 24 hours a day. Such a site enables a company to continue normal business operations, usually within a minimal period after the loss of a facility. This type of site functions like the original site and is equipped with all the necessary hardware, software, network, and Internet connectivity fully installed, configured, and operational. Data is regularly backed up or replicated to the hot site so that it can be made fully operational in a minimal amount of time if a disaster occurs at the original site. If a catastrophe occurs, people simply need to drive to the site, log on, and begin working—without significant delay. Hot sites are

the most expensive to operate and are most common in businesses that operate in real time and for which any downtime might mean financial ruin.

A *warm site* is a scaled-down version of a hot site that is generally configured with power, phone, and network jacks. The site might have computers and other resources, but they are not configured and ready to go. In a warm site, the data is replicated elsewhere for easy retrieval. However, you still must do something to be able to access the data; this "something" might include setting up systems so that you can access the data or taking special equipment to the warm site for data retrieval. It is assumed that the organization itself will configure the devices, install applications, and activate resources or that it will contract with a third party for these services. Because a warm site is generally office space or warehouse space, such a site can serve multiple clients simultaneously. It take more time and cost to get a warm site operational than it takes to begin using a hot site.

A *cold site* is the weakest of the recovery plan options but also the least expensive—at least in the short term. Keep in mind that obtaining equipment for a cold site after a disaster occurs might be difficult, and the price might be high. A cold site is merely a prearranged request to use facilities, if needed. Electricity, bathrooms, and space are about the only facilities a cold site contract provides, and the organization is responsible for providing and installing all the necessary equipment. With a cold site, it takes time to secure equipment, install operating systems and applications, and contract services such as Internet connectivity.

> **ExamAlert**
>
> Be familiar with the various types of sites. Understand different scenarios for which you would choose a hot, warm, or cold site solution. Remember that a hot backup site includes a full duplicate of the source data center and has the fastest recovery time and highest cost. On the other hand, a cold backup site is the opposite and has a longer recovery window with a lower cost.

Geographic Considerations

Consideration of geography is critical for recovery and response. Think about alternate site planning, for example. The site should be located far enough from the original facility that it would be unlikely for the same disaster to strike both facilities. For example, the range of a flood depends on its category and other factors, such as wind and the amount of rain that follows. A torrential flood might wash away buildings and damage property such as electrical facilities. If

the hot site is within the same flood range as the main site, the hot site will be affected, too.

Cloud infrastructure service providers may be used in lieu of or as complements to physical recovery sites. In fact, cloud providers themselves have data centers all over the world and provide various regions from which infrastructure can be deployed.

Finally, legal implications such as *data sovereignty* laws might dictate the extent to which geographies are considered. Data sovereignty applies to data that is subject to the laws of the geography (most often a specific country) where the data resides. For example, if an organization is legally bound to specific data within its country's borders, offshore processing or backups would not be feasible.

Deception and Disruption

The honeypot may be the original deception technology. A honeypot can be used to identify the level of aggressive attention directed at a network and may be used to study an attacker's common methods of attack. A *honeypot* is a system configured to simulate one or more services in an organization's network. It is basically a decoy that is left exposed to network access. When an attacker accesses a honeypot system, the attacker's activities are logged and monitored by other processes so that those actions and methods can be later reviewed in detail. In the meantime, the honeypot distracts the attacker from valid network resources. A honeypot might be a simple target exposed to identify vulnerability exposure. Alternatively, a honeypot might interact with an attacker to build a better attack profile by tracking and logging the attacker's activities. Similarly, *honeyfiles* serve as bait on servers; these dummy files appear attractive to an attacker but do not contain any important information.

A *honeynet*, which is a collection of honeypots, creates a functional-appearing network that can be used to study an attacker's behavior. Honeynets use specialized software agents to create seemingly normal network traffic. Honeynets and honeypots can distract attackers from valid network content and help an organization obtain valuable information on attackers' methods. They also provide early warning of attack attempts that might later be waged against more secure portions of the network.

The deception provided by honeypots has evolved to be known generally as just *deception*. Honeypots required a lot of manual maintenance, didn't scale well, and often weren't believable; modern deception technologies overcome these problems and challenges. Many endpoint solutions, like those from

Symantec, now incorporate deception. Complete platforms around deception, like those from TrapX Security, are available to assist with threat detection while providing for more advanced use cases. A deception platform provides a full solution for creating and managing a deceptive environment and deploying artifacts across networks, user endpoint devices, servers, and applications. These elements or artifacts are used to attract and engage an attacker. In order of increasing deployment complexity, these artifacts include the following:

▶ Decoy (including bogus networks)

▶ Lure (including fake laptops, workstations, and servers)

▶ Honeytoken (including fake data, folders, files, users, and other network elements)

As attackers move across the various phases of a penetration, the idea is that that they will interact with these artifacts, starting with their reconnaissance of the environment. A huge advantage that deception technologies provide is low false positives. The artifacts typically sit still doing nothing, and no alarms are generated until an attacker does something against them. Deception involves two important considerations:

▶ **Believability:** A deception technique should be believable, or it might not entice attackers. For some organizations that don't have the resources to monitor and respond, this deterrence may be beneficial. However, for mature organizations with strong response capabilities or those that perhaps want to develop indicators of compromise, if an item is too believable, an attacker may ignore it. Striking the right balance in regard to believability is important.

▶ **Interaction:** The level of interaction with an artifact has an impact on its cost of operation. Low-interaction artifacts are less costly and simpler to deploy and manage. They are often more ideal for basic use cases related to threat detection. While high interaction artifacts are more costly, they provide greater insight and data for threat intelligence.

Modern deception technologies improve greatly over previous types, such as honeypots, primarily through automation. Automation improves ongoing maintenance of a system and decreases the requirement for specialized skills to manually create bogus artifacts. Today's deception technologies provide the following:

▶ Automated discovery of networks and resources to learn what the environment looks like

▶ Automated creation, deployment, and updating of decoys, lures, and honeytokens

▶ Automated responses and alerts for the security teams

> **ExamAlert**
>
> Think of honeypots, honeyfiles, honeynets, and deception technologies as traps that make it possible to fight unauthorized system access. They distract attackers from valid network content, enable you to study and learn an attacker's methods, and provide early warning of attack attempts that might later be waged against more secure portions of the network. Traditional honeypots are rarely used today and have been replaced by more modern deception technologies that provide high levels of automation.

Deception technologies work not only against individual human attackers but also against malware. Beyond using deception, another way to disrupt malware is by using sandboxing. Sandboxing allows malware to be detonated and run within a virtual environment, where it can cause no real harm. This way, the malware can be analyzed and tested across a number of different operating systems. A DNS sinkhole is another example of *disruption*. A *DNS sinkhole* prevents the resolution of hostnames for specified URLs and can help steer users away from malicious resources. This technique was used to diffuse the WannaCry ransomware attack in 2017.

> **ExamAlert**
>
> Remember that a DNS sinkhole protects users by preventing them from connecting to known malicious websites.

Cram Quiz

Answer these questions. The answers follow the last question. If you cannot answer these questions correctly, consider reading this chapter again until you can.

1. You are responsible for a critical business system. In case of disaster, this system needs to be operational within a minimal period of time at another site, regardless of cost. Which of the following recovery sites is most appropriate in this scenario?

    ○ **A.** Hot site

    ○ **B.** Warm site

    ○ **C.** Cold site

    ○ **D.** Resilient site

2. You decided to implement TLS encryption between two servers to protect the data being transferred between them. Which of the following states of data best represents what you are putting in place?

- ○ **A.** Data at rest
- ○ **B.** Data in transit
- ○ **C.** Data in processing
- ○ **D.** Data in use

3. Which of the following should be part of the configuration management process? (Select three.)

- ○ **A.** HSM
- ○ **B.** Diagrams
- ○ **C.** Standard naming conventions
- ○ **D.** IP schema

4. Which of the following helps an organization extend on-premises security solutions to the cloud?

- ○ **A.** CASB
- ○ **B.** Honeynet
- ○ **C.** Honeyfile
- ○ **D.** DNS sinkhole

Cram Quiz Answers

Answer 1: A. A hot site is a location that is already running and available 7 days a week, 24 hours a day. Such a site allows a company to continue normal business operations usually within a minimal period after the loss of a facility. Answer B is incorrect as a warm site is a scaled-down version of a hot site. Answer C is incorrect as a cold site would be the cheapest and the weakest in terms of resiliency after a disaster. Answer D is incorrect. While all sites represent site resiliency, only a hot site provides the most resiliency.

Answer 2: B. Data in transit (or motion) represents data moving across a network or from one system to another, and it is what transport layer encryption protocols like TLS protect. Answers A and C are both incorrect. Data at rest represents data in its stored or resting state, which is typically on some type of persistent storage, such as a hard drive or tape. Data in processing represents data being processed in memory or cache. Answer D is also incorrect as this is often associated with data in processing, particularly as it pertains to DLP systems.

Answer 3: B, C, and D. Diagrams, standard naming conventions, IP schema, and baseline configurations should all be part of the configuration management process. Answer A is incorrect as a hardware security module is a device used to protect and manage the keys required as part of an encryption or decryption operation.

Answer 4: A. A cloud access security broker (CASB) helps an organization extend on-premises security solutions to the cloud. It is a solution that acts as an intermediary between users and cloud service providers (CSPs). Answers B, C, and D are incorrect as they are all deception technologies.

What Next?

If you want more practice on this chapter's exam objective before you move on, remember that you can access all of the Cram Quiz questions on the Pearson Test Prep software online. You can also create a custom exam by objective with the Online Practice Test. Note any objective you struggle with and go to that objective's material in this chapter.

CHAPTER 10
Virtualization and Cloud Computing

This chapter covers the following official Security+ exam objective:

▶ 2.2 Summarize virtualization and cloud computing concepts.

Essential Terms and Components

▶ infrastructure as a service (IaaS)
▶ platform as a service (PaaS)
▶ software as a service (SaaS)
▶ cloud service provider (CSP)
▶ managed service provider (MSP)
▶ managed security service provider (MSSP)
▶ fog computing
▶ edge computing
▶ container
▶ microservice/API
▶ software-defined networking (SDN)
▶ software-defined visibility (SDV)
▶ serverless architecture
▶ virtualization

Virtualization

With power becoming more expensive and society placing more emphasis on becoming environmentally friendly, *virtualization* offers attractive cost benefits by decreasing the number of physical machines—both servers and desktops—required in an environment. On the client side, the capability to run multiple operating

environments enables a machine to support applications and services for an operating environment other than the primary environment. Currently, many implementations of virtual environments are available to run on just about everything from servers and routers to USB thumb drives.

The security concerns of virtual environments begin on the guest operating system. If a virtual machine is compromised, an intruder can gain control of all the guest operating systems. In addition, because hardware is shared, most virtual machines run with very high privileges. Therefore, an intruder who compromises a virtual machine may be able to compromise the host machine, too. Just as with regular host-installed environments, vulnerabilities also come into play with virtualization. (The section "VM Escape Protection," later in this chapter, covers the VENOM vulnerability.) Virtual machine environments need to be patched just like host environments, and they are susceptible to the same issues. You should be cognizant of sharing files among guest and host operating systems. While this capability provides for ease-of-use between the two systems, it also makes obtaining data from an attacker's point of view easier as well should one of the systems be compromised.

> **ExamAlert**
>
> If compromised, virtualized environments can provide access to not only the network but also any virtualization infrastructure. This means a lot of data is at risk.

Hypervisors

An important component of virtualization is the hypervisor. A hypervisor is a software- or hardware-layer program that permits the use of many instances of an operating system or instances of different operating systems on the same machine, independent of each other. This section discusses virtualization methods.

Type I Hypervisors

A Type I native hypervisor, or bare-metal hypervisor, is software that runs directly on a hardware platform. The guest operating system runs at the second level above the hardware. These hardware-bound virtual machine emulators rely on the real, underlying CPU to execute nonsensitive instructions at native speed. In hardware virtualization, a guest operating system is run under the control of a host system, where the guest has been ported to a virtual architecture that is almost like the hardware it is actually running on. The guest OS is not aware that it is being virtualized and requires no modification. The hypervisor translates all operating system instructions on the fly and caches the results for future use, and user-level instructions run unmodified at native speed.

Type II Hypervisors

A Type II hypervisor, or hosted hypervisor, is software that runs in an operating system environment where the guest operating system runs at the third level above the hardware. A Type II hypervisor runs as an application or a shell on another operating system that is already running. Operating systems running on the hypervisor are then called *guest* or *virtual* operating systems. This type of virtual machine consists entirely of software and contains no hardware components. Thus, the host can boot to completion and launch any number of applications as usual, with one of them being the virtual machine emulator. That emulator sets up CPU-specific control structures and uses a CPU instruction to place the operating system into a virtualized state.

A virtual machine monitor (VMM) provides a layer of software between the operating system(s) and the hardware of a machine to create the illusion of one or more virtual machines (VMs) on a single physical platform. A virtual machine entirely encapsulates the state of the guest operating system running inside it. Because virtual machines consist entirely of software and contain no hardware components, VMs offer distinct advantages over physical hardware.

Type I vs. Type II Hypervisors

Figure 10.1 shows the difference between a Type I hypervisor and a Type II hypervisor.

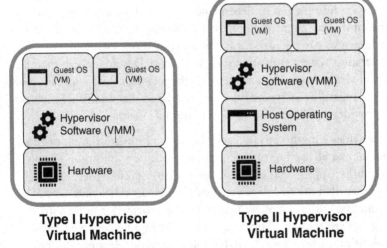

**Type I Hypervisor
Virtual Machine**

**Type II Hypervisor
Virtual Machine**

FIGURE 10.1   Comparing Type I and Type II virtual machine hypervisors

The distinction between Type I and Type II hypervisors has to do with whether an underlying operating system is present:

▶ **Type I:** Runs directly on the hardware, with VM resources provided by the hypervisor. VMware ESXi and Citrix XenServer are Type I hypervisors.

▶ **Type II:** Runs on a host operating system to provide virtualization services. VirtualBox, VMware Server, and Microsoft Virtual PC are Type II hypervisors.

Hyper-V standalone or integrated Windows servers are considered Type I hypervisors. Type II hypervisors tend to have better hardware compatibility because they use software-based virtualization.

> **ExamAlert**
>
> Type I hypervisors offer better management tools and performance and are used in larger environments. Type II hypervisors present more security implications because of their reliance on the underlying OS.

Containers and Microservices

For years, virtual machines have been used to allow a single server to run multiple operating systems and applications that are isolated from each other. As a result, organizations don't need to fire up a new physical server every time they need to run an important application. Unlike a virtual machine, a *container* consists of only the application and its dependencies. Then the containers, which are virtualized runtimes, can be piled on top of a single operating system. Whereas a virtual machine uses a hypervisor for hardware emulation, a container uses an engine for operating system emulation such as Docker. Developers can therefore easily move containers around and can have confidence that their application or service will run, regardless of where it is deployed. Specialized software such as Kubernetes provides a platform for managing multiple containers.

A container provides a method to package, deploy, and run a program or process. A container can be used to run an entire monolithic application. However, the monolithic approach is often broken up into reusable parts of loosely coupled services, called microservices, that can be managed by containers. This has several benefits. For example, *microservices/APIs* provide for more automated testing and are resilient. Microservices can be rapidly deployed across multiple applications, which speeds up development as developers can work on their particular services without worrying around how other applications or

services could misfunction. Each application only needs to be aware of the APIs or methods used to call the other service. Whereas microservices are about the software development technique, containers provide a viable method to package and run microservices.

> **Note**
>
> While containers are a huge enabler of microservices, microservices can be deployed on physical servers or virtualized servers.

Containers contain only applications and follow the minimal requirements to run an application in a container package. Containers do not require a hypervisor or separate OS instances because they share the same OS kernel as the host. This makes them more efficient and permits the host to run many containers simultaneously. Double to triple the number of applications generally can run on a single server with containers than can run with full VMs. Figure 10.2 provides an example of containers running on top of a container architecture.

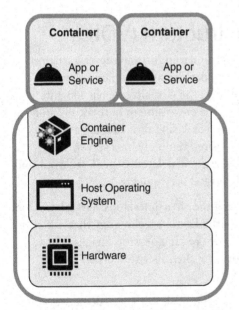

Container Architecture

FIGURE 10.2 **Two containers deployed in a container architecture**

The downside of containers is that because they use the same OS host kernel, the underlying operating system can theoretically be compromised if a user or

an application has elevated privileges within the container. The same quality assurance problem exists with containers as with VM marketplaces. Unless it properly vets a container, an organization can open itself to malware infection.

Virtualization is now used with handheld devices as well. Application cells are individual VM cells used to stage and run applications. This environment is most commonly found in Android mobile applications. Each application runs in its own Java virtual machine (JVM) to prevent the applications from affecting each other. The security problem with this design is that when apps are installed, they often ask for access to other apps or information. If access is granted, exfiltration of data can take place between the apps.

Entire virtual smartphones and tablets can be run simultaneously on the same physical device using an open-source virtualization architecture called Cells. Another way virtualization is affecting handheld devices is through cellular technology virtualization, which is based on the cloud radio access network (C-RAN) architecture. C-RAN centralizes the base station function for many radios into a single location. C-RAN works similarly to network functions virtualization (NFV) but provides more flexibility and efficiency.

Virtual Desktop Infrastructure (VDI)

Virtual desktop environments (VDEs) are similar in form to server virtualization but with some differences in usage and performance demands. Desktop virtualization is often the most dynamic of all the virtualized environments because far more changes are made inside the environment both locally and over the network than with a virtualized server. Using thin clients or virtual desktops, user desktop environments are stored remotely on a server. This makes it possible for configurations to be created, deleted, copied, archived, and downloaded over a network or remotely hosted very quickly.

Most VDEs include software for managing the virtual desktops. Virtual desktop infrastructure (VDI) is the server-based virtualization technology that hosts and manages virtual desktops. Functions include creating desktop images, managing the desktops on the servers, and providing client network access for the desktop.

Managing and deploying a VDI requires different skills than basic network management. Desktop virtualization requires high availability and storage capacity for a multitude of desktop clients and applications. If designed properly, resource utilization can be maximized and management costs can be reduced. Improper management can result in security risks and loss of productivity.

Virtual Machine (VM) Sprawl Avoidance

One drawback associated with virtual environments is *VM sprawl*. With VM sprawl, which is mainly associated with servers, multiple underutilized virtualized servers take up more space and consume more resources than are justified by their workload. VM sprawl can be confined to a single server room, or it can spread across multiple facilities in different geographic locations, especially where one company has acquired another or where two companies have merged.

VM sprawl occurs mainly because VMs are omitted from the change/life cycle management processes. IT can be mitigated with the following actions:

▶ Following the change control process

▶ Enforcing automatic deployment and configuration

▶ Decommissioning, archiving, or deleting virtual machines

▶ Using management agents

> **ExamAlert**
>
> VM sprawl can be prevented by implementing policies, automated reporting, and life cycle management tools.

VM sprawl control is necessary to reduce hardware and licensing costs, enhance security, and conserve resource consumption. This control can be accomplished by reallocating and better provisioning existing resources and formulating a strategy to address existing virtual machine sprawl and prevent its reoccurrence.

VM Escape Protection

The idea of VM guest escape has been discussed for many years. A VM is essentially a virtualized and isolated guest operating system that runs independently on an operating system. *VM escape* happens when the virtual machine breaks out of, or escapes from, isolation and becomes able to interact with the host operating system. VM escape does not affect bare-metal platforms; it affects only hosted platforms. A full VM escape happened with the Virtualized Environment Neglected Operations Manipulation (VENOM) exploit, which used malformed commands sent to the virtual floppy drives in VMs to create a buffer overflow that subsequently allowed a guest to escape. The exploit

demonstrated that attackers inside a guest VM can execute instructions in the memory space of the host operating system. In another instance, a virtual machine escape at the Pwn2Own hacking contest used a combination of three separate exploits.

The most obvious ways to prevent VM escape are to keep up to date on VM CVEs and immediately apply patches and to contact cloud service providers to inquire about patching affected products.

Virtual environment security is concerned with anything that directly or indirectly touches the hypervisor, so securing the hypervisor is critical. Organizations can approach hypervisor security through either architectural options or configuration choices.

Software-Defined Networking (SDN)

Software-defined networking (SDN) enables organizations to manage network services through a decoupled underlying infrastructure that allows for quick adjustments to changing business requirements. As the name implies, SDN differs from traditional networking in that it is software based rather than hardware based. In the SDN architecture, the control and data planes are decoupled, which provides a lot of flexibility. The system that makes decisions about where traffic is sent is the control plane. The underlying system that forwards the traffic is the data plane. Separating control of the network from the elements involved in forwarding the packets provides a more complete view of the network.

The SDN layer sits between the applications and the infrastructure. The network appears as one logical switch to applications because all network intelligence is centralized in software-based SDN controllers. Network devices do not need to understand a multitude of protocol standards because instructions come from the SDN controllers. With SDN, instead of configuring an array of devices in various locations, an administrator can instead configure the SDN layer.

> **ExamAlert**
>
> SDN encompasses multiple types of network technologies, making it possible to build highly scalable, adaptable, and flexible networks that can easily handle changing business requirements.

SDN architecture supports APIs that allow common network services and policy management to be specifically tailored to meet the changing business

objectives of the organization. An SDN approach fosters network virtualization, enabling IT staff to manage their servers, applications, storage, and networks with a common approach and tool set. Whether in a carrier environment or an enterprise data center and campus, SDN adoption can improve network manageability, scalability, and agility. Additional tooling can be paired with SDN to provide for the visualization of operations. In particular, this visualization combined with the capability to dynamically respond to events is known as *software-defined visibility (SDV)*.

Infrastructure as Code (IaC)

Infrastructure as code (IaC), also known as *programmable infrastructure*, enables infrastructure configuration to be incorporated into application code. IaC enables DevOps teams to test applications in production-like environments from the beginning of the development cycle. Validation and testing can then prevent common deployment issues.

> **Note**
>
> DevOps is a set of practices that combines software development (Dev) and information-technology operations (Ops) with a goal of shortening the systems development life cycle and providing continuous delivery with high software quality.

Automation frameworks such as Chef and Puppet, along with tools such as Ansible and Docker, make it possible to automatically configure the infrastructure and operating system layers through scripts or code. Developers write into a program the virtual infrastructure that the application code runs on. Basically, all configurations are written into the script or code, eliminating the need for a full environment. IaC provides the following benefits:

▶ Acts as a documentation reference point for the application infrastructure

▶ Provides a consistent starting point for deployments

▶ Supports infrastructure independence

▶ Prevents infrastructure inconsistencies

IaC is based on using proven coding techniques that encompass infrastructure.

On-Premises vs. Off-Premises

Network, compute, and storage functions have traditionally operated largely using a customer-managed, on-premises model, where everything is hosted onsite, often in corporate data centers. In the 1990s, application service providers (ASPs) such as web hosting companies and email providers—precursors to many of today's cloud companies—became popular. Organizations then found advantages in outsourcing some or even all of their information technology services to *managed service providers* (*MSPs*), which provided subscription service models supported by service-level agreements for the defined services. MSP services aren't limited to information technology services. The model applies to many categories, including power, transportation, media, and marketing, for example. In fact, businesses are now looking to *managed security service providers* (*MSSPs*) for their security needs. The services of MSSPs vary, but common use cases are for management of the network perimeter, day-to-day monitoring, and penetration testing and vulnerability assessment.

MSPs and MSSPs are not being replaced by the cloud; rather, the cloud is opening further opportunities for MSPs and MSSPs. In the past several years, many organizations have started migrating their physical infrastructures and virtualized infrastructures to varying cloud service models.

When an organization decides on a service and deployment model, it must consider certain factors, such as regulations, accessibility, and security. These considerations can be deciding factors in whether the organization maintains traditional customer-managed systems in its own data centers, chooses a hosting service, or opts for a large cloud environment via a cloud service provider (CSP) such as Amazon Web Services (AWS), Google Cloud Platform (GCP), or Microsoft Azure.

The primary benefit of an on-premises solution is control. When an organization chooses this model, it can be confident that all critical business infrastructure is protected and that the organization does not have to depend on someone else to be sure that its data is secure and its operations are running smoothly. The organization has complete control over who accesses its data and resources.

On-premises solutions tend to be costly due to the hardware and software required. An organization might have difficulty keeping up storage requirements, implementing new product features, or detecting insider breaches.

In a hosted environment, the organization employs the services of a data center provider. This model frees up internal resources for other uses, reduces

infrastructure costs, and taps the expertise of the service provider for security, availability, and maintenance. A hosted environment offers additional benefits as well:

▶ Secure rack cabinets

▶ Higher bandwidth

▶ Controlled cooling

▶ Tight physical security

▶ Continual monitoring and support at all hours

▶ Offsite backups

▶ Lower latency

The disadvantages of using a hosted environment include increased reliance on the data center provider for proper security, due diligence issues that the service-level agreement might not address, and inability to recover quickly in the event of a natural disaster because of the size of the environment.

Most cloud providers offer pay-as-you-go pricing so that the organization pays only for what it uses. Business productivity is enhanced because cloud-based applications can be accessed from a browser anywhere in the world. With cloud-based services, an environment can be rapidly provisioned, increasing speed. Environments also can be as rapidly deprovisioned, which means increased scalability. This scalability is particularly attractive to organizations that experience seasonal surges in business. Cloud services also provide dashboard and reporting functions, which frees up internal staff and enables the organization to focus more on innovating than managing resources.

Cloud Models

The term *cloud computing* arose from the cloud symbol that commonly represents the Internet in network diagrams. Although cloud computing has come to the forefront over the past couple years, its concept can be traced back to mainframe computing, where multiple users were given small slices of the computer's time to run whatever program they needed at that time. Today a cloud computing provider typically delivers computing power, storage, and common applications online to users who access them from a web browser or portal. In essence, cloud computing blends virtualization, distributed computing, and prevalent high-speed bandwidth.

As it is used today, *cloud computing* is a very general term that basically describes anything that involves delivering hosted computing services over the Internet. Cloud computing and virtualization are different. Virtualization separates physical infrastructure to create various dedicated resources to make one resource appear as many. Cloud computing provides access to a pool of scalable and automated services. Virtualization and the technologies discussed so far in this chapter are enabling technologies for cloud computing. The following are key characteristics of cloud computing:

▶ **On-demand self-service:** Capabilities can be provisioned as needed via a web browser or even automatically on demand without human intervention.

▶ **Broad access:** Cloud services are delivered over a network that can easily be accessed through common methods, such as using a desktop client and the Internet.

▶ **Elasticity:** Capabilities can be provisioned and released, which means resources can be allocated only as needed, and it is possible to both scale up and scale down.

▶ **Resource pooling:** Resources are brought together in a pooled (multi-tenant) model to provide services to many customers. The cloud provider uses a combination of physical and virtualized environments to dynamically allocate and release resources to customers.

▶ **Pay-as-you-go:** Cloud service providers automatically measure and meter usage, which enables flexible models for payment. For example, in the pay-as-you-go model, an organization is charged only for its actual usage or the time of its subscription.

Service Models

Cloud computing has a layered architecture of cloud infrastructures that uses both deployment and service models. The three cloud service models are the well-recognized models infrastructure as a service (IaaS), platform as a service (PaaS), and software as a service (SaaS).

One of the most important things to understand about security in the cloud is that it depends on shared responsibility between the consumer and the cloud service provider. Top-tier providers have invested a lot in providing strong security controls. However, the customer is not free of responsibility. It is important to understand what a provider is responsible for and what

your company is responsible for. To make the distinction clear, we consider several analogies of physical services you are familiar with. For example, when renting a car, you don't need to worry about the maintenance of the vehicle; the rental agency does that, and you are responsible for driving safely and fueling the tank. As another example, say that you want pizza for dinner. You could make pizza from scratch at home, in which case you would be responsible for everything, from buying ingredients to creating and baking the pizza to providing the plates and the seating. Alternatively, you could buy a frozen pizza and cook it at home, in which case you would be responsible for baking it and providing the plates and the seating. As another option, you could get takeout pizza, in which case you would be responsible for providing the plates and the seating. Finally, you could dine in at a pizza restaurant, in which case you would be responsible for obeying the rules of the establishment and ensuring that the bill is paid correctly. Figure 10.3 provides an outline of the shared responsibilities in the various cloud service models. The following sections discuss each of these service models.

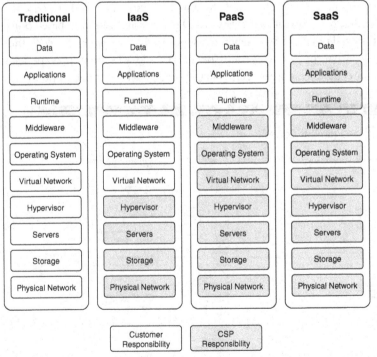

FIGURE 10.3   **The shared responsibility model**

IaaS

Infrastructure as a service (IaaS) delivers the computer infrastructure in a hosted service model over the Internet. This method of cloud computing allows the client to outsource everything that would normally be found in a typical IT department. Data center space, servers, networking equipment, and software can all be purchased as services. IaaS follows the same model as power and water: You're billed for how much you use. Thus, it falls under the category of utility computing. IaaS implementations typically have Internet connectivity, computer networking, servers or grid computing, and hardware virtualization.

By using IaaS, a server, a globally delivered application, or even an entire company can be run with just a web browser. The IaaS provider provides access to the services and interfaces the organization needs to interact with, build, and manage. Figure 10.4 shows a screenshot of the initial AWS Management Console, which provides a jumping-off point for configuring and managing the many services provided, including security, compute, storage, database, mobile, and machine learning services. Fundamental to these services is proper user identity and access management and policies. The EC2 (Elastic Compute Cloud) service under Compute, for example, makes it possible to launch a Linux- or Windows-based server in minutes. AWS provides identity-based policies and resource-based policies. Identity-based policies are attached to users, groups, or roles and specify the permissions for what those users, groups, or roles can do. Resource-based policies are assigned directly to resources such as data storage buckets or encryption keys.

FIGURE 10.4   **The AWS Management Console**

PaaS

Platform as a service (*PaaS*) delivers a platform to develop and manage applications over the Internet, without downloads or installation. PaaS systems are often development platforms designed to operate specifically in the cloud environment, and with them, developers do not need to worry about any servers. PaaS provides a unique advantage, making it possible to develop applications quickly for a wide audience. PaaS implementations typically have integrated development environment services, interface creation tools, and web and database integration. Facebook is actually an example of a PaaS, as developers are able to create applications for Facebook by using the APIs and tools provided to them by Facebook.

The lines between the IaaS and PaaS models can get blurry as some of the top PaaS providers are also IaaS providers (for example, Microsoft Azure, Amazon Web Services). AWS, for example, provides a solution called Elastic Beanstalk, which gives developers an easy way to deploy services. Even well-known SaaS providers offer PaaS (for example, Google via App Engine, Salesforce, ServiceNow).

Similar to PaaS is a more recent category known as function as a service (FaaS), which provides on-demand capabilities without the need for any server process to be running. The purpose of FaaS is to run application logic without the need to store any data. FaaS is part of what's known as *serverless architecture* or serverless computing, and it provides cost advantages because compute resources such as servers aren't required to be running. AWS Lambda is a popular example of FaaS.

SaaS

Software as a service (*SaaS*) delivers a licensed application to customers over the Web for use as a service on demand. The online services are delivered from the Web, and only a web browser is required to interact with them. Most SaaS solutions are built on IaaS. A SaaS vendor hosts an application and allows a customer to use the application, usually for a set subscription period, after which the application becomes inactive if not renewed.

The SaaS model is useful for giving individuals and businesses the right to access a certain application without having to purchase a full license. This on-demand licensing environment provides all the benefits of the full application without the up-front costs and maintenance associated with traditional software purchases. Documents and spreadsheets can be created and managed using SaaS clouds. Movies can be edited using SaaS clouds. Expense reports can be submitted using SaaS clouds. All of this is possible without anything more than a subscription and a web browser. In the past, separate software typically needed to be installed, and organizations need to maintain their own

infrastructure. Today, almost everyone using the Web takes advantage of SaaS services. Common examples include Evernote, Box, Dropbox, Office 365, G Suite, Salesforce, and Slack.

> **Note**
>
> IaaS, PaaS, SaaS, and so on are collectively known as *XaaS*, or *anything as a service*. This term covers the wide variety of products and services that may be implemented as services over the Internet.

The XaaS service models have done a lot to democratize computing. Imagine what it would have been like to start a business before the cloud and then think about what it's like today. Say you want to start selling widgets online. In the past, you would have had little choice but to commit up-front capital to buying servers or building out a data center. As a startup, you might have bought just a single server to manage the website and shopping cart. During the holiday traffic spikes, if your business boomed, you would need to quickly purchase additional servers to manage the load. But what would happen after the holiday? Sales would drop, and those extras servers would sit idle. Cloud computing solves this issue, allowing you to use only the compute power you need, in an elastic manner. The infrastructure needed to run your business can contract and expand on demand. Today, if your business continues to grow, and you start hiring, you are going to need HR systems, email, collaboration software, expense management, office suite applications, and so on. Not too long ago, organizations had to build and manage such systems themselves or purchase software to install and maintain. Today a thriving startup can subscribe to any one of these solutions through the cloud.

> **Note**
>
> The explosion of connected devices, such as those connected to the Internet of Things (IoT), has led to what's known as *fog computing*. Cloud and fog computing are similar, with fog computing being closer to the edge, near the end user or device. *Fog computing* typically complements cloud computing as it distributes the computing between the device and the cloud data center. Fog computing is particularly valuable for latency-sensitive devices and applications. This is critical where milliseconds matter, such as with autonomous vehicles, airlines, railroads, and various manufacturing and sensor-related use cases. Computations and analytics for time-sensitive decisions are brought closer to the device, and big data analytics, historical logging, and other resource-intensive computations can be transferred to the cloud and processed.

The terms *edge computing* and *fog computing* are often used interchangeably. Specifically, though, edge computing is the computing that happens near the edge, while fog computing encompasses this as well as the distribution and communication from the device through to the cloud. Perhaps it helps to consider that fog computing requires edge computing, but it's possible to have edge computing without fog computing.

Deployment Models

In addition to the service models discussed previously, cloud computing can be further classified based on how the service models are deployed. Four types of deployments are common in the industry to describe how cloud technologies are deployed and consumed: private, public, hybrid, and community.

Private

A private cloud is a hosted infrastructure on a private platform. It is sometimes referred to as an internal, corporate, or enterprise cloud. Because it is hosted on a private platform, this type of cloud affords organizations more control over the infrastructure and is usually restricted to organizational employees and business partners. A private cloud offers the capability to add applications and services on demand, much like a public cloud.

The advantages of using a private cloud design include better control over organizational data, higher levels of security and customization (due to flexibility in design specifications), better performance (due to a private cloud being deployed separately), and easier access to compliance data (because the information is readily available). The disadvantages of a private cloud include building capacity limitations and higher costs for infrastructure, maintenance, and administration. A private cloud is the best choice for an organization that needs strict control of business-critical data or highly regulated businesses, such as financial institutions.

Public

A public cloud is an environment in which the services and infrastructure are hosted at a service provider's offsite facility and can be accessed over the Internet for a monthly or yearly usage fee. Many organizations share the main infrastructure, but their data is logically separated from that of other organizations; this is referred to as *multitenancy*.

The advantages of using a public cloud include lower infrastructure, maintenance, and administrative costs; greater hardware efficiency; reduced implementation time; and availability of short-term usage. The disadvantages of a public cloud include greater vulnerability (because of multitenancy), diminished control of organizational data and the environment (because the environment is hosted at a service provider's facility), and reduced bandwidth (because data transfer capability is limited to that of the Internet service provider). A public cloud is the best choice when an organization requires scalability, wants reduced costs, lacks in-house administrative personnel, or has a high-maintenance, distributed network.

Hybrid

A hybrid cloud is a combination of public and private customer-managed infrastructure on premises. A private cloud ensures control of data, and other functions are hosted using a public cloud. This approach allows an organization to leverage the advantages of both environment types.

A hybrid cloud environment is the best choice when an organization offers services that need to be configured for diverse vertical markets or has varying needs. Hybrid clouds are also ideal for organizations migrating to public clouds, as they can ensure interoperability and efficiencies across the different environments. The hybrid approach is easily enabled by connecting through gateway services. AWS, for example, offers the AWS Transit Gateway, which allows customers to connect their networks in AWS to their on-premises networks. This gateway acts as a hub, providing a single connection point from the on-premises environment to the many virtual cloud networks provided by the CSP.

Community

Community clouds are designed to accommodate the mutual needs of a particular business community. A community cloud is generally industry specific, such as with healthcare or energy companies or in the public sector. Community clouds provide collaborative business processes in a cloud environment while maintaining a higher level of security using a hybrid cloud.

The community cloud option is best suited for organizations that want to increase cross-organizational or collaborative processes when in-house implementation is not possible due to conditions such as geographically distributed participants, fluctuating resource requirements, or resource limitations. An example of a community cloud is Google's implementation of Google Apps for U.S. government agencies.

Cram Quiz

ExamAlert

Make sure you understand the differences between the IaaS, PaaS, and SaaS service models and watch for scenarios asking you to identify the best cloud choice based on public, private, hybrid, or community features.

Cram Quiz

Answer these questions. The answers follow the last question. If you cannot answer these questions correctly, consider reading this chapter again until you can.

1. As part of its digital transformation strategy, your company no longer wants to be responsible for hosting the email system on premises or even in the cloud. Which of the following service models might you recommend?

   ○ **A.** IaaS

   ○ **B.** PaaS

   ○ **C.** SaaS

   ○ **D.** Either IaaS or PaaS

2. Which of the following are core services provided by cloud computing? (Select three.)

   ○ **A.** Self-service capability

   ○ **B.** Elasticity

   ○ **C.** Pay as you go

   ○ **D.** Perpetual licensing

3. You have been asked to provide a virtualized environment. Which of the following makes it possible for many instances of an operating system to be run on the same machine?

   ○ **A.** API

   ○ **B.** Virtual machine

   ○ **C.** Hypervisor

   ○ **D.** Container

4. Your company is expanding, and your boss asks for your recommendation regarding assistance with security management of the network perimeter, day-to-day monitoring, and penetration testing and vulnerability assessments. What should you propose?

   ○ **A.** Virtual sprawl avoidance

   ○ **B.** A transit gateway

   ○ **C.** A thin client

   ○ **D.** An MSSP

Cram Quiz Answers

Answer 1: C. SaaS delivers a licensed application to customers over the Internet for use as a service on demand. An example would be email like that provided by Google or Microsoft in the cloud. Answer A is incorrect. IaaS delivers computer infrastructure in a hosted service model over the Internet. IaaS would be appropriate for an organization that wants to manage its own mail server in the cloud, for example. Answer B is incorrect. PaaS delivers a computing platform—such as an operating system with associated services—over the Internet without downloads or installation. Neither IaaS nor PaaS would be appropriate, and so answer D is incorrect.

Answer 2: A, B, and C. Cloud computing delivers the following key services: self-service capability, elasticity, automated management, scalability, and a pay-as-you-go model. Perpetual licensing is a payment and licensing method for on-premises hardware and software, and so answer D is incorrect.

Answer 3: C. An important component of virtualization is the hypervisor. A hypervisor is a software- or hardware-layer program that permits the use of many instances of an operating system or instances of different operating systems on the same machine, independent of each other. Answer A is incorrect. An API is a set of functions that provides services across an application or operating system. Answer B is incorrect. A virtual machine is a hosted virtual system part of the hypervisor. Answer D is incorrect. Containers only contain the core applications and libraries required to run and talk directly to the host operating system on which they are placed.

Answer 4: D. Today, many businesses are looking to managed security service providers (MSSP) for their security needs. The services vary but include management of the network perimeter, day-to-day monitoring, and penetration testing and vulnerability assessment. Answer A is incorrect because VM sprawl happens when the number of virtual machines in a network grows to a point that is no longer manageable. Answer B is incorrect. A transit gateway acts as a hub, providing a single connection point from the on-premises environment to the many virtual cloud networks provided by the CSP. Answer C is incorrect. When using thin clients or virtual desktops, user desktop environments are stored remotely on a server. This facilitates configurations that can be created, deleted, copied, archived, and downloaded over a network or that can be remotely hosted very quickly.

What Next?

If you want more practice on this chapter's exam objective before you move on, remember that you can access all of the Cram Quiz questions on the Pearson Test Prep software online. You can also create a custom exam by objective with the Online Practice Test. Note any objective you struggle with and go to that objective's material in this chapter.

Secure Application Development, Deployment, and Automation

This chapter covers the following official Security+ exam objective:

▶ 2.3 Summarize secure application development, deployment, and automation concepts.

Essential Terms and Components

▶ application environment
▶ provisioning
▶ deprovisioning
▶ integrity measurement
▶ secure coding
▶ normalization
▶ stored procedure
▶ obfuscation
▶ camouflage
▶ code reuse
▶ dead code
▶ server-side validation
▶ client-side validation
▶ data exposure
▶ memory management
▶ automation
▶ scripting
▶ continuous integration and continuous delivery (CI/CD)

- ▶ Open Web Application Security Project (OWASP)
- ▶ elasticity
- ▶ scalability

Application Environment

Organizations that develop software tend to separate the process into various phases or *application environments*. Separate environments can also be used as a way to implement software application and operating system updates, especially in the test, staging, and production phases. For example, many organizations that have an application deployment life cycle test applications before deploying them. Separate environments are required because when applications are developed in production environments, programming mistakes can disable features, cause errors, or crash the application. Smaller organizations commonly use three environments, whereas larger organizations typically use four: development, testing, staging, and production.

Development and Testing

Organizations generally implement physical isolation or VLAN segmentation between the different environments. In the software development phase, the environment tends to be less restrictive than the testing environment for local rights because deeper levels of access might be required during development. When several developers are working on the same project, it is often advisable to have them work in a sandboxed or virtual environment so that code is not overwritten as it is developed. Versioning control software helps keep track of the software. Code gets checked out of a version control repository so that the system maintains a record of the code changes that occur. The development environment consolidates and validates the project team's work so that it can be tested.

The test environment should be isolated from development. During the testing phase, the code is tested to determine how it interacts with a normal environment. The testing environment is a clean copy of the development environment used for integration testing. The testing environment also measures the performance characteristics of the software.

In a physical isolation environment, a firewall normally separates the environments from each other and the outside world. In VLAN segmentation, VLANs

are often mapped into security zones. Traffic between zones must pass through a firewall that enforces the segmentation rules between the environments.

Testing and development environments often have lower security levels than do staging and production environments. Keeping these environments separate or isolated from each other provides segregation and prevents untested code from accidently being deployed. Development and testing environments often are deployed using a public cloud provider, and staging and production environments are deployed within an organization's private network.

Quality assurance (QA) and testing processes directly affect code quality. The earlier defects in software are found, the easier and cheaper they are to fix. The benefits of implementing a sound QA and testing process far outweigh the associated costs. Providing quality software also builds a positive reputation for the organization and provides customers confidence in the products they are purchasing.

Staging and Production

A *staging* environment is often implemented to reduce the risk of introducing issues upon deployment in the production environment. A staging environment is primarily used to unit test the deployment of code. The staging environment should closely match the production environment, and it can also verify that the software runs under security settings. Although the staging environment should be closely matched to the production environment, using virtual machines (VMs) in the staging environment might be acceptable as long as the VMs are not measuring performance. The staging environment can also be used as a demonstration or training environment.

Developers should be able to deploy code to the staging environment. Care must be taken to be sure that version control is employed and that the proper version of the software is ported over. Staging basically provides one last opportunity to find and remove flaws or features that are not intended for production.

After code has been thoroughly tested and run through the staging environment, it can be deployed to production. The *production* environment is the final stage in the process and the actual "live" environment that will be running the code. The production environment should contain only applications that have already been developed, tested, and staged in the other environments. All pertinent security settings should apply, and access to the production environment should be limited to a few experienced developers.

Provisioning and Deprovisioning

Provisioning is the creation or updating of a resource. *Deprovisioning* is the removal of a resource. Provisioning and deprovisioning are part of organizational life cycle management and can affect a number of assets. Software provisioning and deprovisioning are generally automated processes in which software packages are made available to computers and users through a self-service portal. Provisioning can be integrated with other technologies as well, especially in cloud-based environments. For example, in one particular implementation, VMware used a private cloud based on a software-defined data center architecture to automate the provisioning process. The results included reduced application environment provisioning time, increased developer productivity, improved capacity, and significant cost savings.

> ## ExamAlert
>
> Remember that provisioning is the creation or updating of a resource, and deprovisioning is the removal of a resource.

Integrity Measurement

When a program is run on a system, there is no indicator that shows how the code has affected the system on which the program is run. You do not know for sure that, after the program is run, the system is still exactly the same as it was beforehand. Because malware can infiltrate systems at a very low level, organizations need to be able to securely identify the software running on a system.

The way in which data about a system's hardware, configuration settings, or software is collected is referred to as *measurement*. *Integrity measurement* uses attestation challenges from computed hashes of system or application information to obtain confidence in the trustworthiness and identity of a platform or software. The purpose of attestation is to gain confidence in the trustworthiness and identity of a platform or software. Integrity measurement uses attestation challenges to query the integrity status of software.

Integrity measurement is done through the Trusted Platform Module (TPM) at load time. When an executable loads, a hash function is used to fingerprint information. This information could be the executable itself, the executable along with its input data, or a sequence of related files. The hash values are then used to establish code identity to verifiers through attestation. In addition, these hash values can be used along with a feature called *sealed storage*, which uses cryptographically secure secrets so that only a specific application can open data files.

Linux-based systems have the capability to implement the Integrity Measurement Architecture (IMA) through a kernel module. The IMA maintains a kernel trust chain. The IMA subsystem calculates the hash of a program before loading the program and validates the hash to a predefined list. When the system has a hardware TPM, the IMA maintains both a runtime measurement list and an aggregate integrity value over the list. This helps prevent undetectable software attacks.

Integrity measurement mechanisms that have been proposed and developed include those from the Trusted Computing Group (TCG). As noted in Chapter 15, "Physical Security Controls," the TCG is responsible for publishing the transitive trust concept with hardware root of trust for TPM. The TCG has also defined the Core Root of Trust for Measurement (CRTM), which is the first action executed when booting. The CRTM measures the bootloader and sends the hash value to the TPM for storage in one of the Platform Configuration Registers (PCRs) before execution. After bootloader execution and before OS execution, the OS image is measured, and the value is stored in a PCR extension. This process continues for all loaded applications. When an attestation challenge occurs, the TPM signs a set of PCR values with an attestation identity key (AIK). The challenger decides on the integrity and trust status of the platform by comparing the returned result against known-good values.

Change Management and Version Control

The software change management process is similar to the IT change management process. The primary function of change management is to control project or product changes so they meet both the defined scope and customer expectations. The capability to manage changes is a necessary component for quality in software products.

In organizations that closely align development and operations (for example, with DevOps), change management has a strong focus on responsiveness to requests for change and swift implementation of approved change requests. This is accomplished by using advanced automation and control tools to streamline the change- and release-management process. Different types of management are often consolidated into one pipeline.

Change management goes hand in hand with version control, and change management tools often are used to handle version control. *Version control*, or source control, is part of software configuration or change management that involves managing changes to collections of information. Version control involves tracking changes in the source code and providing software integrity during the development stages of the software development life cycle (SDLC). Strict version control prevents tampering with source code or executables.

Version control is done though a system, software tools, or applications that track software file changes and provide a way to manage changes to source code over time. Most version control systems use some form of distributed storage. For example, one tool might use one master server, and another tool might use a network of distributed servers.

Benefits of version control include the following:

▶ Historical data on changes to files

▶ Branching and merging capabilities

▶ Traceability

In a DevOps environment, version control is generally used as a predictor of performance because it can provide metrics for process improvement.

Secure Coding Techniques

Attacks against software vulnerabilities are becoming more sophisticated. Many times, a vendor misses a vulnerability and then, when it is discovered, does not address it for quite some time. The vendor decides how and when to patch a vulnerability. As a result, users have become increasingly concerned about the integrity, security, and reliability of commercial software. Software assurance describes vendor efforts to reduce vulnerabilities, improve resistance to attack, and protect the integrity of products. Software assurance is especially important in organizations where users require a high level of confidence that commercial software is as secure as possible. Secure software is achieved when it is created using best practices for secure software development.

The security of software code has come to the forefront in recent years, and coalitions have been formed to improve it. In addition, the industry offers certifications in software security. The Software Assurance Forum for Excellence in Code (SAFECode) works to identify and promote best practices for developing and delivering more secure and reliable software, hardware, and services. It was founded by EMC, Juniper Networks, Microsoft, SAP, and Symantec. Organizations such as (ISC)^2 offer certifications specifically geared toward *secure coding*, such as the Certified Secure Software Lifecycle Professional (CSSLP). Secure software requires a number of stages, including design, coding, source code handling, and testing.

Given the ubiquity of web applications today, a notable organization is the *Open Web Application Security Project* (*OWASP*). Since its founding, the organization has annually published the OWASP Top 10 list of web application security risks, and now it also publishes an annual list for API security. (Refer to Chapter 3, "Application Attacks," to review the top 10 security risks for web applications.) OWASP is a nonprofit organization that provides a number of great resources for improving the security of software, and it hosts local chapters around the globe. See https://owasp.org for more information.

Security must be implemented in software from the very beginning. In the early design phase, potential threats to the application must be identified and addressed. Organizations must take into consideration ways to reduce the associated risks. These objectives can be accomplished in a variety of ways, such as through threat modeling and mitigation planning, which involves analyzing potential vulnerabilities and attack vectors from an attacker's point of view. When the design is complete, the secure programming practices must be implemented. Secure coding involves inspecting an application's source code to identify vulnerabilities created by coding errors.

ExamAlert

Organizations should implement secure programming practices that reduce the frequency and severity of errors. Source code review should combine manual analysis and automated analysis tools.

Using automated tools along with manual review can reduce the vulnerabilities that might be missed by using only one method.

When the coding is done and the code has been reviewed, you must carefully handle the source code. Procedures for the secure handling of code include strict change management, tracking, and confidentiality protection of the code. To prevent malicious insiders from introducing vulnerabilities, only authorized

persons should be permitted to view or modify the code. An additional measure for the protection of code is to protect systems and code repositories from unauthorized access. When development is outsourced, you should conduct internal design and code reviews to prevent malicious code from being introduced.

The final step in secure code development is testing. In the testing phase, particular attention should be given to validating that the security requirements were met and the design and coding specifications were followed. Testing processes can include applying testing techniques such as fuzzing and using a variety of inputs to identify possible buffer overflows or other vulnerabilities. Some software vendors submit their products for external testing in addition to doing internal testing because an unbiased independent test might uncover vulnerabilities that would not be detectable using internal processes. The secure code testing phase can include the black box, white box, or gray box testing methods discussed in Chapter 8, "Penetration Testing Techniques."

> **Note**
>
> Fuzzing is software testing that provides invalid or unexpected testing data as an input to identify software exceptions, crashes, or other undesirable behavior.

Normalization

Applications often accept untrusted input strings and use techniques such as validation methods and input filtering. These methods are based on the strings' character data and are similar to using a block list to explicitly prevent the characters from being submitted. Although they are not really sufficient for complete input validation and sanitization, these methods do provide some level of security. For example, an application might be programmed to forbid certain tags in input in order to mitigate cross-site scripting (XSS) vulnerabilities. When an application uses this type of method, after it is accepted, the input should be normalized before it is validated. *Normalization* is the conversion of data to its anticipated simplest known form. It provides assurance that all equivalent strings have unique *binary* representations. This is necessary because, in Unicode, the same string can have many different representations.

If software accepts data merely because strings can have different representations, then the application can accept malicious code. With normalization, when the input is validated, the malicious input is correctly identified.

> **ExamAlert**
>
> Validating input before normalization allows attackers to bypass security mechanisms and execute malicious code.

Stored Procedures

Stored procedures are most often associated with databases and database queries. A *stored procedure* is a combination of precompiled SQL statements, stored in the database, that execute some task. The purpose of a stored procedure is to allow the acceptance of input parameters so that one procedure can be used by many clients using varied input data. This produces faster results and reduces network traffic.

Stored procedures can be used for security by encapsulating certain logic in server-side persistent modules. Client or user database communication is then restricted to use only server-side stored procedures. To increase security and reduce SQL injection vulnerabilities, data manipulation statements such as SELECT or DELETE have to go through the stored procedures before returning data. SQL injection vulnerabilities are reduced because stored procedures can be written so that the stored procedure has execute rights, without the client or user needing to have read/write permission on the underlying tables. Using stored procedures does not necessarily eliminate SQL injections, however: When dynamic SQL is allowed to be created inside a stored procedure, SQL injection can still occur.

Encryption, Obfuscation, and Camouflage

Encryption tends to be a catchall solution. When in doubt, encrypt. Encryption, obfuscation, and camouflage are used in the software development process to prevent software from being reverse engineered. These practices protect the trade secrets and intellectual property of organizations.

Encoding technologies have been developed to effectively hide executable program code in plain sight so the code does not have to be decrypted before it is run. This allows the software to run but not be reverse engineered.

Obfuscation, which has been used for a long time in interpreted languages, often involves shortening function and variable names and removing whitespace. The best way to see the prevalence of this technique is to view the source code of a

web home page such as Google's. When used in a malicious manner, obfuscation usually goes a step further and encrypts the underlying source code, which is then decrypted on the fly when the code is run.

> **ExamAlert**
>
> Whereas obfuscation uses the process of hiding original data with random characters or data, camouflage replaces sensitive data with realistic fictional data.

Camouflage can also protect software from reverse engineering. Fake source code is created by modifying a piece of original source code. When an attacker analyzes the program, the attacker sees the fake code, but the program executes the original code when it is run.

Use of these techniques can affect the functionality of the software and programs. For example, if SQL Server objects, procedures, or functions are encrypted, the source cannot be retrieved from the SQL Server database.

Code Reuse and Dead Code

Code reuse is the practice of using existing software to build new software. A great deal of the code used in software development is reused to save time and development costs. Although code reuse is beneficial because much of the work has already been done, it can introduce security flaws and vulnerabilities into a product. Developers sometimes use vulnerable or non-patched versions of reused components even after vulnerabilities are made public and more secure versions are available. Much of this code comes from third parties and enables attackers to target one component vulnerability that many applications might have used. For example, with the OpenSSL Heartbleed and GNU Bash Shellshock attacks, libraries and frameworks that contained unpatched vulnerabilities were used in applications. Either the development team lacked due diligence in these cases, or a vulnerability was discovered in code that had previously been considered reliable.

To mitigate the effects of introducing vulnerabilities through code reuse, organizations must exercise due diligence, keep components patched, and continually strive to find reliable sources of code when creating new products.

Dead code is code contained in a program that can be executed but no longer provides a useful resulting action. Dead code often occurs when software requirements change, and developers have not taken the time to clean up the old code. As a common programming practice, dead code should be deleted or removed.

The execution of dead code can exhaust resources such as computation time
and memory. In addition, an organization might face millions of dollars in costs
if dead code is awakened. For example, in one organization, reuse of a flag that
hadn't been used in eight years triggered the execution of a version of the code
that still had a dependency on the old flag. This misstep actually ended up
bankrupting the organization.

Use of Third-Party Libraries and SDKs

As mentioned previously, much of the code used to create applications comes
from third-party libraries. When using third-party libraries, an organization
must exercise due diligence by keeping track of and implementing library
updates and security measures. Most critical vulnerabilities in third-party
libraries are disclosed in the Common Vulnerabilities and Exposures (CVE)
system, making them quite visible for organizations to locate and track.

A *software development kit* (*SDK*) is a set of tools for creating applications using a
certain software package. For example, if you are creating an Android application, you use the Android SDK. SDKs present the same security issues as third-
party libraries. Known vulnerabilities in SDKs are also published via CVE. The
biggest problem with vulnerabilities in third-party libraries and SDKs is that
they can potentially affect millions of applications. This is why attackers have
recently shifted efforts to this area.

Server-Side vs. Client-Side Execution and Validation

Client-side validation occurs when the data entered into a form is validated
through a web page script via the user's browser before the form is posted back
to the originating server. Client-side validation is often used for convenience
because it gives immediate feedback to the user if incorrect data is input.
Client-side validation is an insecure form of validation in web applications
because it places trust in the browser. This form of validation allows the client
to execute validation and can be easily bypassed or altered; in addition, it allows
the user to view the page code by using built-in browser capabilities. When an

application accepts input from the client, the input should be validated on the server for type, length, and range.

Server-side validation occurs on the server where the application resides. Server-side validation helps protect against malicious attempts by a user to bypass validation or submit unsafe input information to the server. Server-side checks are more difficult to bypass than client-side checks and are a more secure form of input validation. Several techniques on the server side can improve validation, including identifying the acceptable data input type that is being passed from the client, defining the input format and type, building a validator routine for each input type, and situating the validator routines at the trust boundary of the application. A recommended approach is to initially perform client-side validation and then, after the input form has posted to the server, perform the validation a second time by using server-side validation.

Data Exposure

According to best practices, sensitive data should be encrypted at all times, including while in transit and at rest. *Data exposure* often occurs in applications because sensitive data such as credit card numbers, personal health information, and authentication credentials are not protected during transit. Other times, sensitive application data is stored unprotected, exposing the data.

Mitigation of data exposure should be addressed using an SDLC framework along with best practices. Addressing data exposure in both the requirements and design phases permits an organization to take a holistic approach to mitigation. Security best practices dictate that the following methods be included when building applications:

- ▶ Data validation
- ▶ Authentication and authorization
- ▶ Encryption

In particular, organizations should address the following three areas: exposed data that might be mistakenly uploaded, weak cryptography, and browser caching controls.

Proper Error Handling

Many of the software exploits that have emerged in the past few years have directly resulted from poor or incorrect input validation or mishandled exceptions. Common programming flaws include trusting input when designing an

application and not performing proper exception checking in code. These practices allow attacks such as buffer overflows, format string vulnerabilities, and utilization of shell escape codes. To reduce these programming flaws, organizations should review practices related to authentication, authorization, logging and auditing, code dependencies, error message, and code commenting.

Authentication strength is vital to the security of an application. Instead of hard-coding credentials into an application or storing them in plaintext, it is a good practice to encrypt authentication credentials. This is especially important for a web application that uses cookies to store session and authentication information. In web applications or multilayered systems in which the identity is often propagated to other contexts, authorization control should form a strong link to the identity through the life cycle of the authenticated session. Logging and auditing should be designed to include configurable logging and auditing capabilities. This facilitates the flexibility of collecting detailed information when necessary. Using libraries from established vendors minimizes the risk of unknown vulnerabilities, especially when using object-oriented programming that relies on the use of third-party libraries.

Take care when programming error messages. Although error messages are important in identifying problems, they should not divulge specific system or application information. Attackers usually gather information before they try to break in to an application, and detailed error messages can give an attacker the information necessary to escalate an attack. Information output in error messages should be on a need-to-know basis. Exception handling should log an error and provide the user with a standard message. It is best practice to avoid using comments in public-viewable code that could reveal valuable information about the application or system, especially in web applications where the code and associated comments reside on the browser.

Proper Input Validation

Input validation tests whether an application properly handles input from a source outside the application that is destined for internal processing.

ExamAlert

The most common result of improper input validation is buffer overflow exploitation. Additional types of input validation errors are format string and denial-of-service (DoS) exploits.

Application field input should always include a default value and character limitations to avoid these types of exploits. Software developers may overlook input validation, but it is very important. Testing code by sending varying amounts of both properly and improperly formatted data into the application helps determine whether the application is potentially vulnerable to exploits. Various methods can be used to test input validation, including automated testing, session management validation, race condition analysis, cryptographic analysis, and code coverage analysis.

An automated program can randomly perform input validation against the target, based on the program's capability to handle input without any established criteria for external interfaces of the application. This means that any component of the application can be tested with randomly generated data without a set order or reason. Testing an application for session management vulnerabilities consists of attempting to modify any session state variables to evoke undesirable results from the application. Access can be gained to other communication channels through modified variables, leading to privilege escalation, loss of data confidentiality, and unauthorized access to resources. When time elapses between a security operation and the general function it applies to, a window of opportunity is created that might allow an attacker to circumvent security measures. This is known as a *race condition*. Testing for race conditions involves attempting to access the file between the time the application creates the file and when the application actually applies the security.

Sensitive data such as passwords and credit card information is frequently protected using cryptographic methods. Knowing what algorithm an application uses might make it possible to exploit its weaknesses. In addition, if strong encryption is used but the vendor implementation is incorrect, the data might not be properly protected; this could result in errors such as improper creation or storage of the cryptographic keys and key management. Code coverage analysis verifies that proper security measures are taken on all possible paths of code execution to ensure that no paths enable security to be bypassed and leave the system in a vulnerable state. This type of analysis can be resource intensive and should be done in stages during application development.

Code Signing

The most common example of code signing is drivers. For example, by default, Microsoft operating systems block the installation of unsigned drivers. Code signing consists of signing executables using a certificate-based digital signature. This is done to provide trustworthiness in the executable. Code signing

proves the author's identity and provides reasonable assurance that the code has not been tampered with since it was signed.

The two types of code signing certificates are organizational code signing certificates, which are issued to organizations, and individual code signing certificates, which identify independent developers. A certificate is issued by a certificate authority (CA) that validates the legitimacy of the issuer. If a nefarious person steals a legitimate certificate, that certificate can be used to sign malware and makes the program seem legitimate to unsuspecting users. For this reason, many cybercriminals and cybercriminal groups such as Suckfly are stealing certificates and using them in malicious attacks.

Memory Management

Memory management optimizes performance by assigning blocks of memory to various processes and programs. It ensures that sufficient memory is available for any currently running program or process. Memory management is used in all computing functions and plays an integral part in programming applications. Application memory management is based on allocation and recycling. Programs are written to request blocks of memory, and the allocator is used to assign a block to the program. When the program no longer needs the data in the assigned allocated memory blocks, the blocks can be reassigned.

Proper memory management in software development is imperative because many vulnerabilities take advantage of improper memory management techniques. For example, buffer overflow vulnerabilities are based on the capability to overflow the memory allocated for a variable. Suggestions for mitigating vulnerabilities such as buffer overflows include the following:

▶ Verify that the buffer is as large as specified.

▶ Use input and output control for data that is untrusted.

▶ Properly free allocated memory upon completion of the functions.

▶ Do not use known vulnerable functions.

▶ Clear sensitive information stored in memory to avoid unintentional disclosure.

Automation and Scripting

Resiliency and automation strategies help mitigate organizational risk. *Resilience* is the organizational capacity to continue acceptable levels of service when disruption to vital processes or systems occurs. *Automation* can range from basic scripting to automated collective action systems. It includes functions such as courses of action, continuous monitoring, and configuration validation.

Automation greatly increases an organization's capability to detect and respond to threats. Automation systems or frameworks are used for courses of action and require the following:

▶ Interoperability and extensibility

▶ Built-in privacy protections

▶ Based on industry standards and international technical standards

▶ Capability to deal with system attack attempts

▶ Capability to effectively identify false positives (such as incorrectly identifying a vulnerability)

Automation systems combine machine learning with automation to respond to threats and maintain critical operations. Automated collection systems are meant to be resilient and secure because devices work together in near real time to anticipate and prevent attacks. These systems can be considered an extension of continuous monitoring, described in the next section.

Organizations have the option to automate individual areas as part of a holistic approach to automation. For example, an organization can automate infrastructure buildout to reduce the chance of security mistakes or can include automated security monitoring in system deployments as part of the configuration process.

ExamAlert

Automation makes managing and securing the environment easier. However, when done incorrectly, automation breaks more than it fixes.

On a smaller scale, organizations can use *scripting* and vendor-provided tools for automated courses of action such as security and network tasks. Automation scripts for management and provisioning are run through command-line interfaces (CLIs) and APIs. Automated configuration and provisioning capabilities are already built in to devices from most major vendors. For example,

Cisco IOS software provides embedded automation capabilities, and Windows PowerShell scripting is used to automate Windows administration and security tasks.

The purpose of continuous monitoring is to ensure that the processes are followed and enforced in order to detect organizational compliance and risk. In certain instances, such as to comply with industry regulations, continuous monitoring is required. For example, Payment Card Industry Data Security Standard (PCI DSS) compliance requires that an organization have well-defined processes in place to review and reassess security practices, even in highly dynamic business environments. FedRAMP, which focuses on cloud service providers (CSPs), requires that CSPs continuously monitor a cloud service offering to detect changes in the security posture of the system.

Tools often provide scripts to help with continuous monitoring. For example, Solar Winds maintains more than 100 predefined automation scripts in its script library. PowerShell can be used to implement continuous monitoring as well.

Configuration validation for organizations can be done through the Security Content Automation Protocol (SCAP), developed by the National Institute of Standards and Technology (NIST) to enable automated vulnerability management and policy compliance. Configuration Assessment as a Service (COAS) is a method developed in the European Union (EU) for automated validation and assessment of configuration settings over distributed environments. Configuration validation scripts can be written, depending on the target, and PowerShell can be used for configuration validation as well. For Windows machines, the Security Configuration and Analysis (SCA) snap-in works to validate configurations.

In addition, scripting languages such as Python can be used either alone or in combination with other scripts or tools. For example, Cisco DevNet has readily available scripts that leverage Cisco-provided Python libraries for device automation.

Secure DevOps

Development and operations (DevOps) originated in the recognition that organizational infrastructure should support development of the SDLC along with production capacity. Secure DevOps includes security in the SDLC, which was not always a major concern in developing software applications. When the topic was initially introduced, software developers had a negative reaction because it meant greater programming effort and delays in development and

release cycles. The evolution of secure DevOps has produced some best practices for increased security of developed applications, including the following:

▶ Address security concerns at the beginning of a project.

▶ Reduce faults by standardizing the integration cycle.

▶ Add automated security testing techniques.

From a secure DevOps perspective, software should be secure and resilient. Developers should be proficient with tools and thought processes to develop software that can withstand attacks and continue to function instead of ones that only seek to prevent attacks. These tools offer more flexibility in mitigating attack risks. A secure SDLC requires an organization to focus on practices such as security automation, continuous integration, and infrastructure as code. DevOps offers the following benefits:

▶ Speed

▶ Rapid delivery

▶ Reliability

▶ Scalability

▶ Increased collaboration

▶ Built-in security

A main DevOps concept is *continuous integration and continuous delivery (CI/CD)*. This process, which is similar to the SDLC, is shown in Figure 11.1.

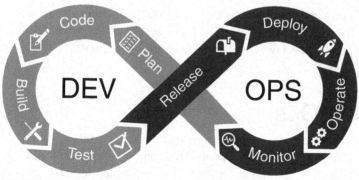

FIGURE 11.1 **The DevOps life cycle**

The CI/CD process is based on automated configuration and deployment scripts. Automated processes are critical to ensure that software operates as intended.

Continuous integration is the process in which the source code updates from all developers working on the same project are continually monitored and merged from a central repository. The repository is updated when a new commit or permanent change is detected. Software builds are triggered by every commit to the repository. CI helps avoid code merging conflicts that can arise when developers keep a working local copy of a software project for a long period of time.

The CI process is automated. A centralized server continually pulls in new source code changes as they are committed by developers. It then builds the software application and runs unit test suites for the project. When a process fails, the CI server fails the build and immediately notifies the project team of the failure.

ExamAlert

CI servers are also called *build servers* because of their main function. A CI server compiles, builds, and tests each new version of code committed to the central repository without user interaction.

All members of the team are notified when code in the repository fails. This prevents team productivity loss by limiting the chance of merge issues and rework due to a broken codebase.

Continuous delivery automates code changes and testing and prepares the code to be delivered or deployed into test or production after the build stage. CD is associated with the test and release stages, and it allows the code to be manually triggered for release as desired or to be automatically deployed once the code has passed all tests.

While CD ensures that new secure applications and features are released efficiently and quickly, the operation and monitoring stages provide for continuous feedback. This feedback helps provide continuous validation of existing code and ensures that a better product is developed more quickly.

DevOps includes extra rigor and testing in order to foster a more secure environment. Automation frameworks such as Chef and Puppet are already used for IT infrastructure. Continuous delivery for secure code using security automation is similar to the automation of IT infrastructure.

Scripting and automation are a large part of DevOps, especially security. Security testing can be automated so that security concerns are designed into systems at the beginning of the process and then are continually checked as part

of the software development process. These are the primary benefits of security automation:

► A more holistic approach to security because it is part of the build process

► Proactive scanning for common vulnerabilities throughout the entire process

► An available list of version control security checks with deployments

Security automation in the life cycle provides more secure, higher-quality code, at a faster rate.

Scalability and Elasticity

Although they are somewhat related, scalability and elasticity are two different concepts. *Scalability* is the capacity to expand the amount of production from the current infrastructure without negatively impacting performance. Scalability issues can cause failures in many areas, such as systems, applications, networks, and businesses.

Scalability can refer to systems or software applications and can be vertical or horizontal. Vertical scalability refers to the capability to scale up within a system; horizontal scalability refers to scaling linearly or scaling out to multiple systems. Applications are generally built with the capability to scale either vertically or horizontally so that lack of resources does not affect performance.

ExamAlert

Scalability can involve the capacity to decrease as well as increase services or resources.

Elasticity is the capacity to dynamically expand or reduce infrastructure resources by autonomously adjusting to workload changes to maximize resources. Elasticity involves the capability for rapid, automatic, and elastic provisioning of resources to quickly scale out as well as the capability to be rapidly released to quickly scale in. Because elasticity is used in scale-out solutions, allowing resources to be dynamically added or removed, it results in infrastructure costs savings. This is particularly useful when dealing with virtualized environments, where host availability is a concern. With elasticity, resources can be purchased as needed based on timeframe, platform, or operating system.

ExamAlert

Elasticity is most often found in cloud environments, where resources can be purchased for a short period of time based on demand and then deleted when no longer needed.

Organizations that have cyclical business periods often choose elastic options to reduce costs and administrative overhead. Security challenges in an elastic model include enforcing proper configuration, change management, and adequate administrative separation between virtual customer environments.

The main difference between elasticity and scalability has to do with resources. Scalability is based on the capability to handle the changing needs of a system, process, or application within the confines of the current resources. Elasticity is the capability to expand and reduce resources as needed at any given point in time.

Cram Quiz

Answer these questions. The answers follow the last question. If you cannot answer these questions correctly, consider reading this chapter again until you can.

1. Your team wants to use automation in the development process to help identify vulnerabilities that have been incorrectly identified before now. Which of the following best describes this type of mistaken identification?

   ○ **A.** Identity theft

   ○ **B.** False positive

   ○ **C.** False negative

   ○ **D.** Identity provider

2. Your organization's compute needs are relatively the same throughout the year except for the two months leading up to a holiday. The board of directors is interested in how the organization can handle this additional capacity for this time period without incurring unnecessary costs the rest of the year. Which of the following best describes the board's request?

   ○ **A.** Elasticity

   ○ **B.** Scripting

   ○ **C.** Continuous integration

   ○ **D.** Scalability

3. Your organization has been moving new applications from the testing environment directly to production, but lately there have been many issues. You have been asked to help mitigate these issues. Which of the following are the most appropriate? (Select two.)

   ○ **A.** Move the code to both production environments to troubleshoot on one in case the other fails.

   ○ **B.** Set up a parallel production environment.

   ○ **C.** Set up a staging environment to closely match the production environment.

   ○ **D.** Move the code to staging prior to moving it to production.

4. Your organization's development team wants to protect trade secrets and intellectual property. What should the team implement during the software development process to prevent software from being reverse engineered?

   ○ **A.** Normalization

   ○ **B.** Stored procedures

   ○ **C.** Obfuscation and camouflage

   ○ **D.** Automation and scripting

Cram Quiz Answers

Answer 1: B. A false positive is a result that incorrectly indicates that a particular condition, such as a vulnerability, is present. Answer C is incorrect as a false negative is not identified but is missed. Answers A and D are incorrect and refer to the use of someone else's identity and a system that manages identity information, respectively.

Answer 2: A. Elasticity is the capacity to dynamically expand or reduce infrastructure resources by adjusting workloads to maximize resources. Answer B is incorrect as this is not the most specific answer. Scripting refers to automation, which elastic capabilities are likely to require. Answer C is incorrect. Continuous integration refers to the development process of continuous monitoring and merging. Answer D, while closely related to elasticity, is incorrect, as scalability refers to the ability to expand the amount of production from the current infrastructure without negatively impacting performance.

Answer 3: C and D. A staging environment is often implemented to reduce the risk of introducing issues upon deployment into the production environment. The code will be moved to production after being moved to staging. Answers A and B are incorrect. This would not be done in the application development process and is more akin to providing for redundancy.

Answer 4: C. Obfuscation, camouflage, and encryption are all often used in the software development process to prevent software from being reverse engineered. These practices protect the trade secrets and intellectual property of an organization. Answer A is incorrect. Normalization is the conversion of data to its anticipated, or "normal," value. Answer B is incorrect because stored procedures are combinations of precompiled SQL statements, stored in a database, that execute some task. Answer D is incorrect

because automation and scripting greatly increase an organization's capability to detect and respond to threats. They combine machine learning with automation to respond to threats and maintain critical operations.

What Next?

If you want more practice on this chapter's exam objective before you move on, remember that you can access all of the Cram Quiz questions on the Pearson Test Prep software online. You can also create a custom exam by objective with the Online Practice Test. Note any objective you struggle with and go to that objective's material in this chapter.

CHAPTER 12

Authentication and Authorization Design

This chapter covers the following official Security+ exam objective:

▶ 2.4 Summarize authentication and authorization design concepts.

Essential Terms and Components

▶ authentication

▶ federation

▶ time-based one-time password (TOTP)

▶ HMAC-based one-time password (HOTP)

▶ false acceptance rate (FAR)

▶ false rejection rate (FRR)

▶ crossover error rate (CER)

▶ biometrics

▶ multifactor authentication (MFA)

▶ authentication, authorization, and accounting (AAA)

Identification and Authentication, Authorization, and Accounting (AAA)

It is necessary to discern the differences between the actions *identification* and *authentication, authorization, and accounting (AAA)* because you will be tested on all these concepts. *Identification* occurs when a user or device presents information such as a username, a process ID, a smart card, or another unique identifier and claims an identity. *Authentication*

is the process of validating an identity. It occurs when the user provides appropriate credentials, such as the correct password with a username. When identification through the presentation and acceptance of credentials is accomplished, the credentials must be measured against a list of all known credentials by the authentication service to determine *authorization* of the request before access rights during the session can be established. Authorization is based on security policy.

Accounting keeps track of the resources a user accesses by keeping a record of authentication and authorization actions. Accounting functions log session statistics and usage information, which can then be used for management tasks such as access control and resource utilization. Additional capabilities include billing, trend analysis, and capacity planning. Implementing the accounting component of AAA requires special server considerations.

These are the core components of AAA:

▶ The device that wants to access the network is known as the client.

▶ The policy enforcement point (PEP) is the authenticator. The PEP enforces the conditions of the client's access.

▶ The policy information point (PIP) holds data relevant to the decision on whether to grant access to the client.

▶ The policy decision point (PDP) is the crux of the AAA decision and is responsible for making the final decision about whether to grant access to the client.

▶ The accounting and reporting system tracks the client network usage and reports the "who, what, where, when, and why."

▶ Core AAA components are logical functions that can be combined and are not necessarily physical devices.

Multifactor Authentication

A method for authenticating users must be designed and implemented properly for an organization to achieve established business goals and security control objectives. Several common factors are used for authentication: something you know, something you have, something you are, something you do, and somewhere you are. Authentication factors provide a means of implementing multifactor authentication. *Multifactor authentication* provides additional security because account access requires more than a password.

ExamAlert

Forms of authentication credentials can be generally broken into three basic categories, or factors, depending on what is required to identify the access requester:

▶ Something you know (passwords, account logon identifiers)

▶ Something you have (smart cards, synchronized shifting keys)

▶ Something you are (fingerprints, retinal patterns, hand geometry)

Additional categories, more appropriately known as attributes, include the following:

▶ Something you can do

▶ Somewhere you are

▶ Something you exhibit

▶ Someone you know

The most common form of authentication combines two "something you know" forms of authentication: a username and a password or passphrase. This form is easily implemented across many types of interfaces, including standard keyboards and assistive technology interfaces. If both values match the credentials associated within the authorization system's database, the credentials can be authenticated and authorized for a connection.

An organization's authentication needs are relative to the value assigned to a particular resource's security. Additional authentication layers required for access increase both the administrative overhead necessary for management and the difficulty users have trying to reach needed resources. Consider, for example, the differences in authentication requirements for access to a high-security solution such as the Department of Energy's power grid control network and those needed to access an unprivileged local account at a public kiosk. In the first scenario, to establish authentication for rightful access, the use of a combination of multiple biometric, token-based, and password form authentication credentials might be mandatory. You can also use these access methods with more complex forms of authentication, such as dedicated lines of communication, time-of-day restrictions, synchronized shifting-key hardware encryption devices, and redundant-path comparison. You use these to ensure that each account attempting to make an access request is properly identified. In the second scenario, authentication might be as simple as an automatic anonymous guest logon that all visitors share.

Different mechanisms for authentication provide different levels of identification, different security of data during the authentication exchange, and suitability to different authentication methods, such as wireless or dial-up network access requests.

Multiple authentication factors can be combined to improve the overall strength of the access control mechanism.

A common example of a multifactor authentication system is an automated teller machine (ATM), which requires both a "something you have" physical key (your ATM card) and a "something you know" personal identification number (PIN). Issues with payment card systems have arisen following public attacks on vendors such as Target, resulting in expanded efforts to enable two-factor authentication using electronic chips in the cards (something you have) and a PIN (something you know). Combining two or more types of authentication improves access security above a single-factor authentication such as your "something you have" car key, which can be used alone without any additional credentials beyond simply possessing the physical key or its duplicate.

The difficulty involved in gaining unauthorized access increases as more types of authentication are used, although the difficulty also increases for users who want to authenticate themselves. Administrative overhead and cost of support also increase with the complexity of the authentication scheme, so a solution should be reasonable based on the sensitivity of the data being secured.

> **ExamAlert**
>
> The exam might ask you to distinguish between single-factor and multifactor authentication solutions. A multifactor authentication scenario involves two or more types of authentication (something you know, have, or are), not simply multiple credentials or keys of the same type. The common logon/password combination is single-factor authentication using your identity and something you know.

Single Sign-on

The proper identification of a person, device, or group is important to protect and maintain the confidentiality, integrity, and availability (CIA) of an organization's assets and infrastructure. Based on business policies, identification and access controls can be created to authenticate users and devices. Various methodologies are used to validate identification and grant resource access. Federation, single sign-on, and transitive trust are the three most popular methods of object identification and access validation.

Distributed enterprise networks often include many different resources, each of which might require a different mechanism or protocol for authentication and

access control. To reduce user support and authentication complexity, a single sign-on (SSO) capable of granting access across multiple services might be desirable. SSO solutions can use a central metadirectory service or can sequester services behind a series of proxy applications, as with the service-oriented architecture (SOA) approach. In the SOA network environment, the client-facing proxy application provides a standard mechanism for interacting with each service (called a wrapper), handling specialized logon, authentication, and access control functions behind the scenes and out of sight of the consuming user or service.

> **ExamAlert**
>
> With SSO, a user can log in to multiple applications during a session after authenticating only once. Access to cloud-based applications has ushered in widespread use of SSO technology in large enterprises.

All applications still require a password for login, but the software stores the password. When an application requires a login, the software automatically retrieves the password and provides it to the application on the user's behalf, resulting in an automatic login. The user still has a password for each system and must change it regularly, based on organizational policy.

Federation

Federation, which is related to SSO, makes it possible to connect identity management systems by allowing identities to cross multiple jurisdictions. A political federation involves myriad equal participants, collaborating through agreements and agreed-upon rules or mediators that can represent a particular political agenda. In the United Nations, for example, each governmental body assigns its own ambassador to speak for the country's interests. A federated identity management solution transfers this idea into technology by assigning an administrative account capable of enumerating local security principals and resources. Based on a preestablished trust relationship, a third party accepts the *attestation* from the original authenticating party. The federation system is accessible from each domain. Thus, accounts in one area can be granted access rights to any other resource, whether local or remote within the communicating domains. This enables enterprises to exchange identity information securely across Internet domains and integrate access to applications across distinct business units within a single organization.

> **ExamAlert**
>
> In a federated identity system, the user does not supply credentials directly to any application or service except the originating identity provider. The user's credentials are always stored with the originating organization or identity provider.

When the user logs in to a service, the service provider trusts the identity provider to validate the credentials instead of providing credentials to the service provider. This type of enterprise solution provides flexibility for organizations when acquisitions happen or when individual business units maintain independent authentication mechanisms across applications.

Federation and SSO are often used together but are two distinct and different concepts. Many federated identity management solutions provide some form of SSO, and many SSO systems are implemented using federated identity management. The two don't have to be intertwined; they can be used entirely separately from each other. The main difference is that federation eliminates the requirement to use a password. The federation server stores the username in each application and presents that application with a token that is then used for authentication.

Transitive Trust

In addition to the mechanisms described so far for provisioning identification and access control, transitive trust relationships can be configured for directory services to allow users to traverse domains. Transitive trust provides access across an enterprise or multiple enterprises, connecting resources and users across multiple resource pools. Two domains can be configured to share trust through configuration of an administrative connection between two resource pools.

> **ExamAlert**
>
> A one-way trust—in which, for example, Domain A trusts Domain B—allows resources in Domain A to be accessed by security principals (users, services, and so on) in Domain B. A two-way trust allows each domain to trust members of either domain. For example, with two-way trust, Domain A and Domain B resources can be accessed by authorized requests from user accounts in either Domain A or Domain B.

In compatible domains, a limited form of interoperation can be assigned directly between two resource pools through administrative actions within each

to specifically designate the other as a trusted resource pool and allow enumeration of accounts and available resources. Access control over any resource can then be granted or denied to any account in either domain. This connection is termed a *trust*, which is like a direct agreement between allied countries. If the trust is configured so that any domain trusting Domain A will then trust all other domains that Domain A trusts, this connection is called a *transitive trust*. This is like having your siblings trust a friend of your father, and the arrangement turns transitive if you and your siblings agree to trust everyone your father trusts.

Authentication Technologies

Employees should have access to facilities based on their roles or functions. This includes visitor control and access control to software programs for testing and revision. Access list restrictions specifically align a person's access to information with his or her role or function in the organization. Functional or role-based access control determines which persons should have access to certain locations within the facility. Access can be granted via cards, tokens, or biometrics.

Most modern access control systems use proximity cards that enable users to gain access to restricted areas. Proximity cards store details of the holder's identity much as chip and PIN bank cards do. The difference is that proximity readers can read the information using radio frequency communication, making actual contact with the card unnecessary. Simply holding the card close to the reader enables its details to be read and checked quickly.

Security tokens can be used to grant access to computers and devices. A security token is a small, easy-to-carry, tamper-resistant physical object. A token may be used in addition to a PIN or password so that if the token falls into the wrong hands, it is useless without the corresponding information. One of the most common physical security tokens is a key fob.

Tokens

One of the best methods of "something you have" authentication involves using a token, which can be either a physical device or a one-time password issued to the user seeking access. In the case of credit cards, this is an embedded chip in the card itself that must be paired with a "something you know" PIN code to avoid the $18.5 million exploit Target suffered in 2013. Tokens include solutions such as a chip-integrated smart card or a digital token (such as RSA

Security's SecurID token) that provides a numeric key that every few minutes and is synchronized with the authentication server. Without the proper key or physical token, access is denied. Because the token is unique and granted only to the user, pretending to be the properly authorized user (through spoofing) is more difficult. A digital token is typically used only one time or is valid for a very short period of time to prevent capture and later reuse. Most token-based access control systems pair the token with a PIN or another form of authentication to protect against unauthorized access using a lost or stolen token.

Telecommuters might use an electronic device known as a key fob that provides one part of a three-way match to use an insecure network connection to log in to a secure network. The key fob might include a keypad on which the user must enter a PIN to retrieve an access code, or it could be a display-only device such as a VPN token that algorithmically generates security codes as part of a challenge/response authentication system.

A one-time password (OTP) is a password that can be used only one time. An OTP is considered safer than a regular password because the password keeps changing, providing protection against replay attacks. The two main standards for generating OTPs are TOTP and HOTP. Both of these standards are governed by the Initiative for Open Authentication (OATH).

The *time-based one-time password* (*TOTP*) algorithm relies on a shared secret and a moving factor or counter, which is the current time. The moving factor constantly changes based on the time that has passed since an epoch.

The *HMAC-based one-time password* (*HOTP*) algorithm relies on a shared secret and a moving factor or counter. When a new OTP is generated, the moving factor is incremented, so a different password is generated each time.

The main difference between HOTP and TOTP is that HOTP passwords can be valid for an unknown amount of time. In contrast, TOTP passwords keep changing and are valid for only a short period of time. Because of this difference, TOTP is considered more secure. While traditionally many TOTP solutions were hardware based, TOTP solutions are commonly implemented via authentication applications on mobile devices.

ExamAlert

Remember that the main difference between HOTP and TOTP is that HOTP passwords can be valid for an unknown amount of time. TOTP passwords keep changing and are valid for only a short period of time and are more secure.

Mobile devices can used as authentication device. Many vendors offer OTPs via authentication applications for mobile devices such Apple IOS and Android. Figure 12.1 shows a screenshot of one authentication application, Google Authenticator. The figure shows the application maintaining one-time-use token codes across several different cloud-based logons. In addition to providing the username, the user would need to provide the password and the one-time-use code, which changes every 30 seconds, as indicated by the decreasing pie icon on the right-hand side.

FIGURE 12.1 Google's Authenticator mobile authentication application for delivering one-time token codes

An application might require an OTP for performing highly sensitive operations such as fund transfers. OTPs can be either *Short Message Service (SMS)* generated or device generated. Device-generated OTPs are better than SMS-generated OTPs because they eliminate the sniffing and delivery time issues associated with SMS-generated OTPs. Another feature of mobile software applications delivering OTPs is that the user can receive push notifications. With these notifications, the user doesn't need to manually enter a code but rather needs to accept the push notification, usually with a single tap. Table 12.1 briefly describes the common authentication methods.

TABLE 12.1 **Common Token and Similar Authentication Technologies**

Method	Description
Time-based one-time password	A one-time-use code from a hardware device or software application that provides a new code, usually every 30 or 60 seconds.
HMAC-based one-time password	A one-time-use code from a hardware device or software application that provides a new code after each use.
Short Message Service (SMS)–generated one-time password	A one-time-use code sent via SMS, typically to a mobile phone.
Token key	A token device that typically plugs in to a USB port.
Static codes	An issued set of one-time-use codes. Sometimes implemented on a static card, which uses a set of axes for cross-reference, much like a bingo card.
Phone callback	A telephone number that requires you to press a number (sometimes implemented to provide the one-time code).

ExamAlert

Be able to distinguish the authentication technologies listed in Table 12.1 for the exam!

Biometrics

In theory, the strongest security is offered by combining biometric (body-measuring) keys that are unique to a particular user's physical characteristics (such as fingerprints and retinal or iris patterns) with other authentication methods that involve either access passwords or token-based security requiring the possession of a physical smart card key.

The most unique qualities of an individual can be obtained by measuring and identifying the person's unique physical characteristics in "something you are" forms of biometric measurement authentication—called *biometrics*—such as fingerprints, retinal patterns, iris patterns, blood vessel patterns, bone structure, and other forms of physiological qualities unique to each person. Other "something you do" values can be measured, such as voice pattern recognition, movement kinematics, or high-resolution cardiac patterns. However, because these can change based on illness, injury, or exertion, they suffer high rates of false rejection (that is, valid attempts at authentication that are returned as failures).

Many systems are available to authenticate users by their body measurements (biometrics). Those measures are compared to values stored within an authorization system's database and provide authentication only if the new biometric values

match those previously stored. Another alternative is to store biometric data on smart card tokens, which the localized authentication service can pair with the requisite physical measurement without requiring a centralized database for comparison. When transactions against a central server storing large and complex biometric values might be difficult, users must be authenticated in a widely distributed scheme. Table 12.2 describes some of the most common biometric methods.

TABLE 12.2 **Common Biometric Measures for Authentication**

Method	Description	Issues
Fingerprint	Scans and identifies the swirls and loops of a fingerprint	Injury, scars, or loss of a finger might create false rejection results. The pattern alone can easily be counterfeited, so it is best to pair this method with at least one other measure.
Hand geometry	Measures the length and width of a hand's profile, including hand and bone measures	Loss of fingers or significant injury might create false rejection results.
Voiceprint	Measures the tonal and pacing patterns of a spoken phrase or passage	Allergies, illnesses, and exhaustion can distort vocal patterns and create false rejection results.
Facial recognition	Identifies and measures facial characteristics, including eye spacing, bone patterns, chin shape, and forehead size and shape	This method is subject to false rejection results if the scanner is not aligned precisely with the scanned face.
Retina	Scans and identifies the unique blood vessel and tissue patterns at the back of the eye	Illness or inaccurate placement of the eye against the scanner's cuff can result in false rejection results.
Veins/blood vessels	Identifies and measures unique patterns of blood vessels in the hand or face	Environmental conditions, clothing, and some illnesses can lead to false rejection results due to measurement inaccuracies.
Signature	Records and measures the speed, shape, and kinematics of a signature provided to an electronic pad	Attitude, environment, injury, and use of alcohol or medication can create variations in personal signature and might render false rejection results.
Gait	Records and measures the unique patterns of weight shift and leg kinematics while walking	Variations in gait due to attitude, environment, injury, and alcohol or medication use might render false rejection results.

> **ExamAlert**
>
> The exam might include questions about the various biometric methods, so be sure you are familiar with the categories in Table 12.2 and their issues. Remember that combinations of biometric solutions, such as readers for both hand geometry and blood vessel patterns, remain a single-factor "something you are" authentication solution unless they are also paired with something else, such as a "something you have" key card.

The success of using biometrics comes down to two key elements. First is the *efficacy rate* in uniquely identifying an individual along with how difficult it is for an attacker to trick the system. To understand this balance, it's important to understand that biometric devices are susceptible to false acceptance and false rejection rates. A *false acceptance rate (FAR)* measures the likelihood that the access system will wrongly accept an access attempt (in other words, allow access to an unauthorized user). The *false rejection rate (FRR)* is the percentage of identification instances in which false rejection occurs. In false rejection, the system fails to recognize an authorized person and rejects that person as unauthorized. The *crossover error rate (CER)* is the percentage of times the FAR and FRR are equal. The CER increases if routine maintenance procedures on biometric devices are not performed. Generally, the lower the CER, the higher the accuracy of the biometric system. The lower the FAR and FRR, the better the system.

Biometric data is basically information stored in a database that is used for comparison functions to protect the database against compromise. Forgery of biometric mechanisms can be an issue, especially where fingerprint technology is concerned.

> **ExamAlert**
>
> False acceptance rate (FAR) involves allowing access to an unauthorized user. False rejection rate (FRR) is the failure to recognize an authorized user.

Card Authentication

Strengthening an authentication system involves making it difficult to falsify or circumvent its process. Anonymous or open access is the weakest possible form of authentication, and a requirement for both a logon identifier and a password might be considered the simplest form of actual account verification. The highest levels of authentication might involve not only account logon but also criteria measuring whether the logon is occurring from specific network addresses or perhaps whether some type of additional physical security measure is present.

Proximity cards are a basic form of physical access controls. Such a card has an embedded microchip that holds very little information. The main purpose of the card is to determine access by matching the card identification number to information in a database. If the number is in the database, access is granted. The most common use of a proximity card is for door access. Proximity cards are also used for applications that require quick processing, such as toll booths and parking garages.

Smart card authentication is a form of "something you have" authentication that uses a standard wallet card with an embedded chip that can automatically provide an authenticating cryptographic key to a smart card reader. A smart card typically displays a picture of the cardholder and has a programmable chip that provides identification and authentication. Communication between the card and reader occurs either through direct physical contact or with a remote contactless electromagnetic field. Implementing smart cards into a physical security solution improves overall security by allowing additional identification methods such as biometrics to be used for authentication.

Certificate-Based Authentication

Certificate-based authentication involves using a digital certificate to identify a user or device before granting access to a resource. Certificate-based authentication is based on "something you have," which is the user's private key, and "something you know," which is the password that protects the private key.

IEEE 802.1X authentication allows only authorized devices to connect to a network. The most secure form of IEEE 802.1X authentication is certificate-based authentication. When this authentication model is used, every client must have a certificate to validate its identity. When implementing 802.1X with wired networks, using a public key infrastructure (PKI) to deploy certificates is recommended. PKI infrastructure is covered in depth in Chapter 25, "Public Key Infrastructure."

A personal identity verification (PIV) card is a contactless smart card used to identify federal employees and contractors. NIST developed the standard "Personal Identity Verification (PIV) of Federal Employees and Contractors," published as Federal Information Processing Standards (FIPS) Publication 201. A PIV card contains the data needed for the cardholder to be granted access to federal facilities and information systems, including separation of roles and strong biometric binding. A smart card used by the U.S. Department of Defense is known as a Common Access Card (CAC). Most civilian users who work for the federal government use PIV cards.

A CAC is a credit card–sized smart card used as an identification card for active duty uniformed service personnel, selected reserve personnel, DoD civilian employees, and eligible contractor personnel. It is also the principal card used to enable physical access to buildings and controlled spaces, and it provides access to DoD computer networks and systems. Homeland Security Presidential Directive 12 (HSPD 12) established the policies for a common identification standard for federal employees and contractors. DoD Instruction (DoDI) 1000.13 says that a CAC serves as the federal PIV card for DoD implementation of HSPD 12, which requires PIV cards to have secure components, including PKI digital certificates and biometrics. When a CAC is inserted into a smart card reader and the associated PIN is entered, the information on the card's chip is compared with data on a government server. Access is then either granted or denied.

ExamAlert

The exam might include questions about two relatively new forms of smart card required for U.S. federal service identity verification under the Homeland Security Presidential Directive 12 (HSPD 12):

▶ **Common access card (CAC):** A smart card used in military, reserve officer, and military contractor identity authentication systems

▶ **Personal identity verification (PIV) card:** A smart card used for federal employees and contractors

Cram Quiz

Answer these questions. The answers follow the last question. If you cannot answer these questions correctly, consider reading this chapter again until you can.

1. Which one of the following is provided to an AAA system for identification?

   ○ **A.** Passcode

   ○ **B.** Username

   ○ **C.** Password

   ○ **D.** One-time token code

2. Which of the following is an example of two-factor authentication?

   ○ **A.** Website requiring username and password

   ○ **B.** ATM requiring credit card and PIN

   ○ **C.** Website requiring a one-time token code to log in

   ○ **D.** ATM requiring facial recognition

3. The business units you represent are complaining that there are too many applications for which they need to remember unique complex passwords. This is leading many to write down their passwords. Which of the following should you implement?

- ○ **A.** TOTP
- ○ **B.** HOTP
- ○ **C.** MFA
- ○ **D.** SSO

4. Which of the following measures the likelihood that an access system will wrongly accept an access attempt and allow access to an unauthorized user?

- ○ **A.** FRR
- ○ **B.** FAR
- ○ **C.** CER
- ○ **D.** CAC

Cram Quiz Answers

Answer 1: B. A username is the most common factor used for identification. Answers A, C, and D are all incorrect as they represent forms of authentication and not identification.

Answer 2: B. A credit card is something you have, and the PIN is something you know. Answer A is incorrect as the username and password are both something you know (and the username is really just something to identify you). Answer C is incorrect, as this is just a single factor. (However, a one-time token code is commonly used as a second factor when used with a password, for example.) Answer D, like answer C, is just a single factor and is incorrect.

Answer 3: D. SSO refers to single sign-on capabilities. With SSO, a user can log in to multiple applications during a session after authenticating only once. Answers A, B, and C are incorrect. These all refer to multifactor authentication and the use of one-time passwords.

Answer 4: B. The false acceptance rate (FAR) measures the likelihood that an access system will wrongly accept an access attempt (in other words, allow access to an unauthorized user). Answer A is incorrect because the false rejection rate (FRR) is the percentage of identification instances in which false rejection occurs. Answer C is incorrect. The crossover error rate (CER) is the percentage of times the FAR and FRR are equal. Answer D is incorrect because a Common Access Card (CAC) is a smart card used in military, reserve officer, and military contractor identity authentication systems.

What Next?

If you want more practice on this chapter's exam objective before you move on, remember that you can access all of the Cram Quiz questions on the Pearson Test Prep software online. You can also create a custom exam by objective with the Online Practice Test. Note any objective you struggle with and go to that objective's material in this chapter.

Cybersecurity Resilience

Essential Terms and Components

▶ redundancy

▶ redundant array of inexpensive disks (RAID)

▶ dual power supply unit (PSU)

▶ uninterruptible power supply (UPS)

▶ generator

▶ managed power distribution unit (PDU)

▶ full backup

▶ differential backup

▶ incremental backup

▶ snapshot

▶ network load balancers

▶ network interface card (NIC) teaming

▶ high availability

▶ replication

▶ non-persistence

▶ defense in depth

Redundancy

Equipment will fail; as one movie character has suggested, "The world is an imperfect place." When a single drive crashes, sometimes the only

way to sustain operations is to have another copy of all the data. Redundancy and diversity are commonly applied principles for fault tolerance against accidental faults. Fault tolerance allows a system to continue functioning even when one of the components has failed. One way to ensure fault tolerance is to implement RAID solutions, which maintain duplicated data across multiple disks so that the loss of one disk does not cause the loss of data. Many RAID solutions can also support hot-swapping of failed drives and redundant power supplies so that replacement hardware can be installed without ever taking the server offline.

Diversity refers to having multiple versions of software packages in which redundant software versions are different. *Redundancy* is *replication* of a component in identical copies to compensate for random hardware failures. Multiple versions are used to protect against software failures. Maintaining multiple diverse versions will hopefully cover any individual software faults. Redundancy and diversity should be designed into critical facilities and applications. For example, *storage area networks* (*SANs*) are used to provide servers accessibility to storage devices and disks that contain critical data. To ensure redundancy, the data on a SAN is duplicated using SAN-to-SAN replication. Unlike with a backup, this occurs as changes are made. If one SAN fails, the other is available to provide the data. VM replication provides the same function for virtual machines. When replication occurs, the VM replicas are updated. In the event of a disaster, the VM can simply be powered on. Chapter 9, "Enterprise Security Concepts," discusses additional redundancy planning options around site resilience, such as hot, warm, and cold sites.

In addition to people, one of the most important assets to an organization is its data. Planning for every server setup should involve consideration of how to salvage data in the event that a component fails. Decisions about how to store and protect data depend on how the organization uses its data. The main goal of preventing and effectively dealing with any type of disruption is to ensure availability. This is often accomplished through redundancy. Redundancy is usually dispersed geographically, as well as through backup equipment and databases or hot sparing of system components. Of course, you can use RAID and clustering to accomplish and ensure availability as well, but neglecting single points of failure can be disastrous. A single point of failure is any piece of equipment that can bring down your operation if it stops working. To determine the number of single points of failure in an organization, start with a good map of everything the organization uses to operate. Pay special attention to items such as the Internet connection, routers, switches, and proprietary business equipment.

After you identify the single points of failure, perform a risk analysis. In other words, compare the consequences of the device failing to the cost of redundancy. For example, if all your business is web based, it is a good idea to have

some redundancy in case the Internet connection goes down. However, if the majority of your business is telephone based, you might look for redundancy in the phone system instead of with the ISP. In some cases, the ISP might supply both Internet and phone services. The point here is to be aware of where your organization is vulnerable and understand the risks so you can devise an appropriate backup plan.

In disaster recovery planning, you might need to consider redundant connections between branches or sites. Internally, for total redundancy, you might need two network cards in computers connected to different switches. With redundant connections, all devices are connected to each other more than once to create fault tolerance. Then, a single device or cable failure does not affect performance because the devices are connected by more than one means. This extra hardware and cabling make this a relatively expensive solution. This type of topology can also be found in enterprise-wide networks, with routers connected to other routers for fault tolerance.

Almost everything in IT depends primarily on electricity. Power is critical for redundancy. Without redundant power, it might not matter what other steps you've taken. When it comes to providing for power redundancy, the following are key considerations:

▶ **Dual supply:** Computers and networking equipment contain power supply units (PSUs), which provide power conversion to properly power the equipment. *Dual PSUs* or redundant power supplies are common for servers and enterprise networking equipment. Each provides half the power that's needed, and if one fails, the other takes over at 100%.

▶ **UPS:** An *uninterruptible power supply* (*UPS*) is used to protect electronic equipment and provide immediate emergency power in case of failure. A UPS typically stores energy via battery and serves as a short-term solution to power down equipment properly (for example, in small and home offices) or until emergency generators kick in for larger organizations.

▶ **Generator:** When power fails and the needs are beyond what a UPS can provide, *generators* can provide power. Generators range from the gasoline-powered versions homeowners are familiar with to fuel-powered, room-size generators capable of delivering massive amounts of electricity to power entire data centers.

▶ **Managed PDU:** For a home office user, a *managed power distribution unit* (*PDU*) is much like a power strip. For data centers, however, PDUs distribute power to the critical equipment. Many PDUs come with advance functions to improve the power quality and provide load balancing as well as remote monitoring.

> **ExamAlert**
>
> Remember that the key options for power redundancy include UPSs, generators, dual supplies, and managed PDUs.

Along with power and equipment loss, telephone and Internet communications might be out of service for a while when disaster strikes. Organizations must consider this factor when formulating a disaster recovery plan. Relying on a single Internet connection for critical business functions could prove disastrous to your business. With a redundant ISP, a backup ISP could be standing by in case an outage occurs at the main ISP. Traffic could then be switched over to the redundant ISP, and the organization could continue to do business without any interruptions.

In addition to helping with disaster recovery, using multiple ISPs can also relieve network traffic congestion and provide network isolation for applications. As organizations become global, dealing with natural disasters will become more common. Organizations might consider using solutions such as wireless ISPs in conjunction with VoIP to quickly restore phone and data services. Organizations might look to ISP redundancy to prevent application performance failure and supplier diversity. For example, businesses that transfer large files can use multiple ISPs to segregate voice and file transfer traffic to a specific ISP. More organizations are implementing technologies such as VoIP. When planning deployment, using multiple ISPs can improve network traffic performance, aid in disaster recovery, and ensure quality of service.

For risk mitigation, redundancy and diversity controls that can be implemented against threats include replication to different data centers, replication to different geographic areas, redundant components, replication software systems, distinct security zones, different administrative control, and different organizational control.

High Availability

One way to increase availability or provide *high availability* is to use server clustering. A server cluster is the combination of two or more servers that appear as one. Clustering increases availability by ensuring that if a server is out of commission because of failure or planned downtime, another server in the cluster takes over the workload. To provide load balancing to avoid functionality loss because of directed attacks meant to prevent valid access, continuity planning might include clustering solutions that allow multiple nodes to perform support while transparently acting as a single host to the user. High-availability clustering might also be used to ensure that automatic failover occurs in case hardware failure renders the primary node incapable of providing normal service.

Load balancing is the primary reason to implement server clustering. Load balancing provides high availability by distributing workloads across multiple computing resources. Load balancing aims to optimize the use of resources, maximize throughput, minimize response time, and avoid overload of any single resource. Load balancing is especially useful when traffic volume is high and it prevents one server from being overloaded while another sits idle. Load balancing can be implemented with hardware, software, or a combination of both. Typically, load balancing occurs in organizations with high website traffic, as well as in cloud-based environments.

You might need to set up redundant servers so that the business can still function in case of hardware or software failure. If a single server hosts vital applications, a simple equipment failure could result in days of downtime as the problem is repaired. In addition, some manufacturers provide redundant power supplies in mission-critical servers.

To ensure high availability and reliability, server redundancy is implemented. This means multiple servers are used to perform the same task. For example, if you have a web-based business with more than one server hosting your site, when one of the servers crashes, the requests can be redirected to another server. This provides a highly available website. If you do not host your own website, confirm whether the vendor you are using provides high availability and reliability.

> **ExamAlert**
>
> Mission-critical businesses today demand 100% uptime 24 hours a day, 7 days a week. Availability is vital, and many businesses cannot function without redundancy. Redundancy can take several forms, including automatic failover, failback, and virtualization. Perhaps the most notable advantage of server redundancy is load balancing.

Cross-site replication might be included in high-availability solutions that also require high levels of fault tolerance. In addition, individual servers can be configured to allow for the continued function of key services even in the event of hardware failure.

Load Balancers

Network load balancers are reverse proxy servers configured in a cluster to provide scalability and high availability.

Load balancing distributes IP traffic to multiple copies of a TCP/IP service, such as a web server, each running on a host within the cluster. Load balancing

is important for enterprise-wide services, such as Internet sites with high traffic requirements, web, FTP, media streaming, and content delivery networks or hosted applications that use thin-client architectures, such as Windows Terminal Services or Remote Desktop Services.

ExamAlert

Network load balancing distributes the workload among multiple servers while providing a mechanism for server availability by health-checking each server. From the client's point of view, the cluster appears to be a single server.

As enterprise traffic increases, network administrators can simply plug another server into a cluster. If server or application failure occurs, a load balancer can provide automatic failover to ensure continuous availability.

Load-balancing strategies involve scheduling via algorithms. Scheduling strategies are based on which tasks can be executed in parallel and where to execute these tasks. Several common algorithms are used:

▶ **Round-robin:** Traffic is sent in a sequential, circular pattern to each node of a load balancer.

▶ **Random:** Traffic is sent to randomly selected nodes.

▶ **Least connections:** Traffic is sent to the node with the fewest open connections.

▶ **Weighted round-robin:** Traffic is sent in a circular pattern to each node of a load balancer, based on the assigned weight number.

▶ **Weighted least connections:** Traffic is sent to the node with the fewest open connections, based on the assigned weight number.

Each method works best in different situations. When servers that have identical equipment and capacity are used, the round-robin, random, and least connections algorithms work well. When the load-balancing servers have disproportionate components such as processing power, size, or RAM, a weighted algorithm allows the servers with the maximum resources to be utilized properly.

Session affinity is a method in which all requests in a session are sent to a specific application server by overriding the load-balancing algorithm. Session affinity, also called a *sticky session*, ensures that all requests from the user during the session are sent to the same instance. Session affinity enhances application performance by using in-memory caching and cookies to track session information.

Some load balancers integrate IP load balancing and network intrusion prevention into one appliance. This provides failover capabilities in case of server failure, distribution of traffic across multiple servers, and integrated protection from network intrusions. Performance is also optimized for other IP services, such as Simple Mail Transfer Protocol (SMTP), Domain Name System (DNS), Remote Authentication Dial-In User Service (RADIUS), and Trivial File Transfer Protocol (TFTP).

To mitigate risks associated with failures of the load balancers, you can deploy two servers in what is called an active/passive or active/active configuration. In active/passive configuration, all traffic is sent to the active server. The passive server is promoted to active if the active server fails or is taken down for maintenance. In active/active configuration, two or more servers work together to distribute the load to network servers. Because all load balancers are active, they run almost at full capacity. If one of the load balancers fails, network traffic runs slowly, and user sessions time out. Virtual IP (VIP) addresses are often implemented in the active/active configuration. In this case, at least one physical server has more than one virtual IP address assigned, usually through a TCP or UDP port number. Using VIP addresses spreads traffic among the load-balancing servers. VIP addresses provide a connection-based workload balancing solution, so if the interface cannot handle the load, traffic bottlenecks and becomes slow.

NIC Teaming

Network interface card (NIC) teaming allows a NIC to be grouped with multiple physical NICs to form a logical network device known as a *bond*. This provides for fault tolerance and load balancing. When it is configured properly, the system sees the multiple NICs as a single network interface. NIC teaming is used in virtualized environments where a virtualized software NIC interacts with the physical NICs. In a fault-tolerance scenario, one of the physical NICs can be configured to take over for a failed NIC, eliminating the network interface as a single point of failure. Alternatively, NIC teaming can provide for load balancing. Incoming traffic requires a switch to appropriately balance the load between multiple NICs. Outgoing traffic, however, is balanced across the NICs.

RAID

The most common approach to data availability and redundancy is *redundant array of inexpensive disks (RAID)*. RAID organizes multiple disks into a large, high-performance logical disk. In other words, if you have three hard drives,

you can configure them to look like one large drive. Disk arrays are created to stripe data across multiple disks and access them in parallel, which allows the following:

▶ Higher data transfer rates on large data accesses

▶ Higher I/O rates on small data accesses

▶ Uniform load balancing across all the disks

Large disk arrays are highly vulnerable to disk failures. To address this issue, you can use redundancy in the form of error-correcting codes to tolerate disk failures. This method enables a redundant disk array to retain data for a much longer time than could an unprotected single disk. With multiple disks and a RAID scheme, a system can stay up and running when a disk fails, as well as during the time the replacement disk is being installed and data is being restored. Figure 13.1 shows common types of RAID configurations.

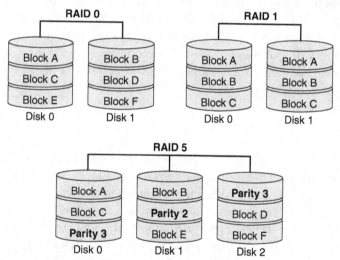

FIGURE 13.1 **Common RAID configurations**

The two major goals when implementing disk arrays are data striping for better performance and redundancy for better reliability. RAID comes in many flavors, and following are the more common ones:

▶ **RAID Level 0: Striped disk array without fault tolerance:** RAID 0 implements a striped disk array. The data is broken into blocks, and each block is written to a separate disk drive. Implementing RAID 0 requires a minimum of two disks.

▶ **RAID Level 1: Mirroring and duplexing:** This solution, called mirroring and duplexing, requires a minimum of two disks and offers 100% redundancy because all data is written to both disks. The difference between mirroring and duplexing is the number of controllers. Mirroring uses one controller, whereas duplexing uses one controller for each disk. In RAID 1, disk usage is 50%; the other 50% is for redundancy.

▶ **RAID Level 2: Hamming code error-correcting code (ECC):** In RAID 2, each bit of a data word is written to a disk. RAID 2 requires the use of extra disks to store an error-correcting code. A typical setup requires 10 data disks and 4 ECC disks. All modern disk drives incorporate ECC, so RAID 2 offers little additional protection. No commercial implementations of RAID 2 exist today. The controller required is complex, specialized, and expensive, and the performance is not very good.

▶ **RAID Level 3: Parallel transfer with parity:** In RAID 3, the data block is striped and written on the data disks. Implementing RAID 3 requires a minimum of three drives. In a parallel transfer with parity, data is interleaved bit-wise over the data disks, and a single parity disk is added to tolerate any single disk failure.

▶ **RAID Level 4: Independent data disks with shared parity disk:** With this level of RAID, entire blocks are written onto a data disk. Implementing RAID 4 requires a minimum of three drives. RAID 4 is similar to RAID 3, except that data is interleaved across disks of arbitrary size instead of in bits.

▶ **RAID Level 5: Independent data disks with distributed parity blocks:** In RAID 5, each entire block of the data and the parity are striped. RAID 5 requires a minimum of three disks. Because it writes both the data and the parity over all the disks, it has the best small read/large write performance of any redundancy disk array.

▶ **RAID Level 6: Independent data disks with two independent parity schemes:** This extension of RAID 5 allows for additional fault tolerance by using two-dimensional parity. RAID 6 uses Reed–Solomon codes to protect against up to two disk failures using the bare minimum of two redundant disk arrays.

▶ **RAID Level 10 (also called 1+0): High reliability combined with high performance:** RAID 10 combines RAID 1 and RAID 0 and requires a minimum of four disks. A variant of RAID 10 is called 0+1. This solution is a striped array that has RAID 1 arrays. Disks are mirrored in pairs for redundancy and improved performance, and data is striped across multiple disks. Both versions provide fault tolerance and increased performance.

> **ExamAlert**
>
> Know the different levels of RAID and the number of disks required to implement each one. The following are the most common forms of RAID:
>
> ▶ **RAID 0:** Spanned volume, no redundancy, highest write speed, highest performance. Requires a minimum of two drives.
>
> ▶ **RAID 1:** Mirroring, 100% duplication of data across all drives, lowest performance. Requires a minimum of two drives.
>
> ▶ **RAID 3:** Parallel transfer with parity bit, data written to all drives simultaneously while parity is calculated and written to its own nonredundant drive. Requires a minimum of three drives.
>
> ▶ **RAID 5:** Parallel transfer with distributed parity, data written to all drives simultaneously, parity written in segments across all drives for redundancy of parity as well as data segments, highest read rates. Requires a minimum of three drives.
>
> ▶ **RAID 10:** (Also called 1+0.) Combines RAID 1 and RAID 0. A variant exists, called 0+1. Both provide fault tolerance and increased performance. Requires a minimum of three drives.

When choosing a method of redundancy, opt for a level of RAID that the operating system supports. Not all operating systems support all versions of RAID. For example, Microsoft Windows Server supports RAID levels 0, 1, and 5. Additional fault tolerance may be considered for the path between the CPU and the RAID systems. This is known as *multipath*. In addition to hardware RAID, you can use software RAID. Software RAID is the best option when an organization does not have the budget for additional drives and when an organization is using older servers. Software RAID can provide more flexibility, but it requires more CPU cycles and power. It operates on a partition-by-partition basis and tends to be slightly more complicated than hardware RAID.

Another point to remember is that even if you set up a server for redundancy, you must still back up your data. RAID does not protect you from multiple disk failures. Regular backups enable you to recover from data loss that results from errors unrelated to disk failure (such as human, hardware, and software errors).

Backups

Data can be backed up on many media. Cloud backups are common, even for desktop environments. Many organizations choose to back up data to a cloud environment using one of the many services available. Cloud services offer continuous backup options so that you can easily recover your files without losing data associated with normal backup procedures and without having offsite

storage that is not immediately available. Enterprise solutions have options for protecting physical and virtual environments that include software, appliance, and offsite replication. In addition to the cloud, organizations typically rely on various media. Tape traditionally has provided a viable long-term archival option. Other options include disks, network attached storage (NAS), and SANs.

The backup procedures in use can also affect what is recovered following a disaster. Disaster recovery plans should identify the type and regularity of the backup process.

The following types of backups are used:

▶ Full

▶ Differential

▶ Incremental

▶ Copies and snapshots

When choosing a backup strategy, a company should consider the following factors:

▶ How often will data need to be restored? As a matter of convenience, if files are restored regularly, a full backup might be chosen because it can be done with one tape.

▶ How quickly does the data need to be restored? If large amounts of data are backed up, the incremental backup method might work best.

▶ How long does the data need to be kept before it is overwritten? In a development arena where data is constantly changing, a differential backup method might be the best choice.

> **Note**
>
> Snapshots and copies are appropriate for certain use cases but should not be considered formal backup options, especially for transactional systems.

When backups are complete, they must be clearly marked or labeled so that they can be properly safeguarded. In addition to these backup strategies, organizations employ tape rotation and retention policies. The various methods of tape rotation include the following:

► **Grandfather-father-son backup:** This is the most common rotation scheme for rotating backup media. The basic method is to define three sets of backups. The first set, the son, represents daily backups. A second set, the father, is used to perform full backups. The final set of three tapes, the grandfather, is used to perform full backups on the last day of each month.

► **Tower of Hanoi:** Based on the mathematics of the Tower of Hanoi puzzle, this is a recursive method in which every tape is associated with a disk in the puzzle. The disk movement to a different peg corresponds with a backup to a tape.

► **Ten-tape rotation:** This simple and cost-effective method for small businesses provides a data history of up to two weeks. Friday backups are full backups. Monday through Thursday backups are incremental.

All tape-rotation schemes can protect your data, but each one has different cost considerations. For example, the Tower of Hanoi is more difficult to implement and manage but costs less than the grandfather-father-son method. In some instances, it might be beneficial to copy, or *image*, a hard drive for backup purposes. For example, in a development office, where large amounts of data change constantly, spending money on a complex backup system to back up all the developers' data might not be the best plan. The company might find it less expensive and more efficient to buy another hard drive for each developer and have the developers back up data that way. If the drive is imaged, then a machine that suffers a hard drive failure can be swiftly returned to good running order.

Recovery planning documentation and backup media contain many details that an attacker can exploit when seeking access to an organization's network or data. Therefore, planning documentation, backup scheduling, and backup media must include protections against unauthorized access or potential damage. The data should be protected by at least a password and, ideally, encryption. When backups are complete, they must be clearly labeled so that they can be properly safeguarded. Imagine having to perform a restore for an organization that stores its backup tapes unlabeled in a plastic bin in the server room. The rotation is supposed to be on a two-week basis. When you go to get the needed tape, you discover that the tapes are not marked, and they are not in any particular order. How much time will you spend just trying to find the proper tape? Also, is it really a good practice to keep backup tapes in the same room with the servers? What happens if a fire occurs?

Considering how backup media is handled is just as important as determining how it should be marked. You certainly don't want to store optical media in a place where it can easily be scratched or store tapes in a high-temperature area. Make sure that you also have offsite copies of your backups stored where they are protected from unauthorized access, as well as fire, flood, and other environmental hazards that might affect the main facility. Normal backups should include all data that cannot be easily reproduced. Secure recovery services are another method of offsite storage and security for organizations to consider. In military environments, a common practice is to have removable storage media locked in a proper safe or container at the end of the day.

Distance must be considered when storing backups offsite. Think about your own personal home computer. Assuming that you have made backups, where are those backups? Sure, a copy that exists on the same computer might protect you if the original is deleted. But what if the hard drive crashes? Perhaps you considered this and moved a backup to a remote disk that resides in another room. If your house is consumed by fire, though, both will be lost. This is why many organizations must consider offsite backups. This option involves offsite tape storage through trusted third parties. Vendors offer a wide range of offsite tape-vaulting services, highly secure facilities that can include secure transportation services, chain of custody control for tapes in transit, and environmentally controlled storage vaults.

Full Backups

A *full backup* is a complete backup of all data. This is the most time- and resource-intensive form of backup, requiring the largest amount of data storage. In the event of a total loss of data, restoration from a complete backup is faster than other methods. A full backup copies all selected files and resets the archive bit, a file attribute used to track incremental changes to files for the purpose of the backup. The operating system sets the archive bit any time changes occur, such as when a file is created, moved, or renamed. This method enables you to restore using just one tape. Therefore, order of restoration doesn't matter: It is just a single restore. Theft poses the most risk because all data resides on one tape; only encryption can protect the data at that point.

Differential Backups

A *differential backup* is incomplete for full recovery without a valid full backup. For example, if the server dies on Thursday, two tapes are needed: the full backup from Friday and the differential from Wednesday. Differential backups require a variable amount of storage, depending on the regularity of normal

backups and the number of changes that occur during the period between full backups. Theft of a differential tape is riskier than with an incremental tape because larger chunks of sequential data can be stored on the tape the further away in time it is made from the last full backup.

> **ExamAlert**
>
> A differential backup includes all data that has changed since the last full backup, regardless of whether or when the last differential backup was made, because this backup does not reset the archive bit.

Incremental Backups

An *incremental backup* is incomplete for full recovery without a valid full backup and all incremental backups since the last full backup. For example, if the server dies on Thursday, four tapes are needed: the full backup from Friday and the incremental tapes from Monday, Tuesday, and Wednesday. Incremental backups require the smallest amount of data storage and require the least amount of backup time, but they typically require the most time for restoration. If an incremental tape is stolen, it might not be valuable to the offender, but it still represents risk to the company.

> **ExamAlert**
>
> An incremental backup includes all the data that has changed since the last incremental backup. This type of backup resets the archive bit. Be prepared to know how many backup tapes will be required to restore the system, given the date of a full backup and the date of either an incremental or differential backup.

Copies and Snapshots

A copy, or *snapshot*, is like a full backup in that it copies all selected files. However, it doesn't reset the archive bit. From a security perspective, losing a tape with a snapshot is the same as losing a tape with a full backup. Some important considerations separate these types of backups from the others. First, a snapshot often resides on the same system from which it was taken. Certainly, this can be useful if, for example, a snapshot was taken from a virtual machine image, and you now need to revert to that image. Or consider a simpler example of a copy of a document being stored on the same computer in case the original gets

corrupted. Neither of these situations helps if disaster strikes the entire primary hard drive of the system, though.

Traditional backup solutions are integrated within the operating system. It is important for such a solution to be able to interact with other transactional applications, such as databases, where data might be processing and residing only in memory. Therefore, a copy is only a very specific point-in-time capture at the storage level and thus might not be enough to perform a restoration.

A snapshot preserves the entire state and data of the virtual machine at the time it is taken. A snapshot includes the virtual machine settings and the state of the machine's virtual drives. The contents of the virtual machine's memory can also be included in the snapshot, but this is not recommended and rarely needed.

> **ExamAlert**
>
> Snapshots can capture sensitive data that is present on the system at a point in time and can inadvertently put personal information at risk.

Snapshots eliminate the need to create multiple VMs if an organization repeatedly needs to return a machine to the same state. In an environment that uses VM templates, using disk-based snapshots is a quick way to make a new VM from the template for provisioning.

A snapshot can also be used as a restore point when testing software or configuration changes. When you take a snapshot of a virtual machine, a new child disk is created for each attached disk. Keep in mind that, for a snapshot to work, the base disk is needed. Therefore, snapshots should not be used as a backup solution. Best practice for performance is to keep only two or three snapshots—and only for a short period of time. Inherent changes occur in the VM, and the snapshot file can grow quickly, filling up space in the datastore. Restoring a snapshot is often done using software automation.

Although VMware is the most popular product for VMs, Microsoft also offers a virtualized solution in Hyper-V. The Microsoft Hyper-V term for a snapshot is a *checkpoint*. Checkpoints work the same way as snapshots in VMware, with certain limitations. For example, they cannot be used in a VM designated as an Active Directory Domain Services role, such as a domain controller.

Non-persistence

A persistent system is one that is generally removable in the event of a failure. For example, if a CPU dies, the system information and data are generally

recoverable when the system is restored. In a non-persistent system, if a failure occurs, the information is lost. This is similar to what happens to memory contents when a system is shut down. Cloud environments tend to be fluid and work differently than physical desktop environments. Persistent cloud environments tend to be more difficult to support than non-persistent environments, especially with data storage or volumes.

Sometimes persistence is not desired. *Non-persistence* is related to the concept of elasticity. Because cloud environments are fluid, snapshots actually provide a way to capture persistence.

The primary purpose of a snapshot is to allow the user to revert to an earlier state if something causes the VM to not work properly. The parent snapshot of a virtual machine is the snapshot on which the current state is based. When the first snapshot is taken, that stored state becomes the parent snapshot of the VM.

Revert to Known State or Good Configuration

When you revert to a known state in a VM, you can revert to an earlier snapshot. Reverting is used to go to the parent snapshot of the VM. When you do this, you immediately discard the current disk and memory states and then revert to the disk and memory states of the parent snapshot. Some VM products have an option to use a "go to" feature that allows the user to choose any snapshot, not just the parent one. This can be helpful in a software development environment where several snapshots are used to test changes to a program or product. Options also can enable you to automatically revert to the parent snapshot whenever the machine is powered off.

> **ExamAlert**
>
> When a system reverts to an earlier snapshot, the reverted snapshot becomes the parent snapshot of the virtual machine.

In a non-persistent or cloud environment, sometimes virtual networking components change or are misconfigured. Rollback is used to prevent loss of connectivity to a host by rolling back to a previous valid or known configuration. This is similar to the Windows Roll Back Driver option except that it relates to the network instead of to individual machine drivers. Networking events that can cause rollbacks include host networking changes and modifications to distributed switches. Invalid host networking configuration changes cause host networking rollbacks. Network change that disconnects a host, such as when

updating DNS and routing settings, also triggers a rollback. Invalid updates to distributed switches can cause rollbacks to occur as well. For example, VLAN changes in a distributed port group can cause one or more hosts to be out of synchronization with the distributed switch. If the situation cannot be fixed manually, you can roll back the switch or port group to a previous configuration.

Similarly, operating systems may provide support during the boot process to revert to a previously working configuration. This option provides for further troubleshooting in case of a failure due to a failed update, malware, or a system conflict. Some versions of Windows, for example, have included the boot recovery option Last Known Good Configuration. This option was removed from Windows 10, which instead provides a recovery environment with a Safe Mode option that provides similar functions.

Live Boot Media

Live boot media is considered non-persistent because actions that occur between reboots do not persist. With live boot media, system RAM acts as a disk. When the media is removed and the system reboots, the RAM is cleared. Live boot media keeps the original media configuration. USB drives can be created with persistent storage through a persistent overlay file. Although there is some room for persistence, it has limitations and might not work with all OS distributions.

A saved VM such as a virtual disk can be booted using a CD-ROM, USB, or other similar storage device. Live boot media is often used in instances when an organization needs a very secure environment in an unsecure location. For example, bootable media is a live device that creates a secure, non-persistent environment on a personal or public computer. This live media provides a trusted environment for remotely accessing sensitive government services on nongovernment equipment.

Defense in Depth

Defense in depth is based on the premise that implementing security at different levels or layers to form a complete security strategy provides better protection and greater resiliency than implementing an individual security defense. Each component provides a different type of security protection, and when they are implemented together, they help improve the overall security posture of the organization.

ExamAlert

Defense in depth is a comprehensive security approach for protecting the integrity of organizational information assets. Vendor and control diversity contributes to a strong defense-in-depth strategy.

Defense in depth is rooted in military strategy and requires a balanced emphasis on people, technology, and operations to maintain information assurance (IA). Defense in depth stems from the philosophy that complete security against threats can never be achieved; the components that comprise a layered security strategy only impede threat progress until either the attacker gives up or the organization can respond to the threat.

Defense in depth relies on diversity across key areas such as controls, technologies, cryptography, and vendors. The idea is to create rational security layers within the environment for improved security. Control diversity, for example, involves layers of different categorical controls that are physical, technical, and administrative. (Chapter 31, "Control Types," explores each of these types of controls further.) Diversity is important across technology and vendors. Many organizations, for example, check files for malware against malware protection from two competing vendors, thus increasing the odds of catching what one vendor may have missed. Vendor diversity requires a variety of suppliers for the purchase of goods and services for the organization. This approach keeps an organization from relying on a small number of vendors or possibly only one particular vendor for its technology needs.

ExamAlert

It is a common misconception that the smaller number of vendors the organization uses, the less risk the organization faces.

Dependence on a small number of vendors can create a number of risks for an organization, including the following:

▶ Technological inefficiency

▶ High equipment and service costs

▶ Supply-chain rigidity

▶ Lack of innovation

▶ Increased risk

Having a larger, more diversified list of vendors helps mitigate risk and provides greater resiliency, reducing single points of failure and the likelihood of unnecessary or unplanned expenditures.

Cram Quiz

Answer these questions. The answers follow the last question. If you cannot answer these questions correctly, consider reading this chapter again until you can.

1. Which of the following RAID configurations can be configured with only two drives? (Select all that apply.)

   ○ **A.** Raid 0

   ○ **B.** Raid 1

   ○ **C.** Raid 3

   ○ **D.** Raid 5

2. Data loss occurs after the Wednesday differential backup, and the system is restored on Wednesday at 3 p.m. How many of the individual backups are required to completely restore the system?

   ○ **A.** 1

   ○ **B.** 2

   ○ **C.** 3

   ○ **D.** 4

3. Which one of the following best describes an outcome of vendor diversity?

   ○ **A.** Lack of innovation

   ○ **B.** Rigidity

   ○ **C.** Resiliency

   ○ **D.** Greater risk

4. Which solution gives you enough time to safely power down equipment until power is fully restored?

   ○ **A.** NIC teaming

   ○ **B.** Load balancer

   ○ **C.** PDU

   ○ **D.** UPS

Cram Quiz Answers

Answer 1: A and B. RAID 0 and RAID 1 both have a two-drive minimum. The other two choices, C and D, are incorrect as RAID 3 and RAID 5 have a three-drive minimum.

Answer 2: B. A differential backup will require two tapes to completely restore the system: the full tape backup from Sunday and the differential tape backup from Wednesday. Answer A is incorrect. If you use only the tape from Sunday, you will still be missing the data between that tape and the differential tape from Wednesday. Answers C and D are also incorrect.

Answer 3: C. Vendor diversity provides an organization with resiliency. Answers A, B, and D are associated with a lack of vendor diversity and not with having a diverse set of vendors to rely on.

Answer 4: D. An uninterruptible power supply (UPS) gives you enough time to safely power down equipment until power is fully restored. UPSs are used to protect electronic equipment and provide immediate emergency power in case of failure. Answer A is incorrect because NIC teaming allows a NIC to be grouped with multiple physical NICs to form a logical network device known as a bond. This provides for fault tolerance and load balancing. B is incorrect because network load balancers are reverse proxy servers configured in a cluster to provide scalability and high availability. Answer C is incorrect because a power distribution unit (PDU) is like a power strip that distributes power to the critical equipment. Many PDUs have advanced functions to improve power quality and provide load balancing as well as remote monitoring.

What Next?

If you want more practice on this chapter's exam objective before you move on, remember that you can access all of the Cram Quiz questions on the Pearson Test Prep software online. You can also create a custom exam by objective with the Online Practice Test. Note any objective you struggle with and go to that objective's material in this chapter.

CHAPTER 14

Embedded and Specialized Systems

This chapter covers the following official Security+ exam objective:

▶ 2.6 Explain the security implications of embedded and specialized systems.

Essential Terms and Components

▶ embedded system

▶ field-programmable gate array (FPGA)

▶ supervisory control and data acquisition (SCADA)

▶ industrial control system (ICS)

▶ Internet of Things (IoT)

▶ heating, ventilation, air conditioning (HVAC)

▶ multifunction printer (MFP)

▶ real-time operation system (RTOS)

▶ system on chip (SoC)

Embedded Systems

Embedded systems that are used to capture, store, and access data of a sensitive nature pose some unique and interesting security challenges. Embedded systems are found in printers, smart TVs, and HVAC control systems, among other devices.

Security protocols and encryption address security considerations from a functional perspective, but most embedded systems are constrained by the environments in which they operate and the resources they use. Attacks against embedded systems rely on exploiting security

vulnerabilities in the software and hardware components of the implementation and are susceptible to timing and side-channel attacks. Nonvolatile memory chips are found in many hardware devices, including TV tuners, fax machines, cameras, radios, antilock brakes, keyless entry systems, printers and copiers, modems, HVAC controls, satellite receivers, barcode readers, point-of-sale terminals, medical devices, smart cards, lockboxes, and garage door openers. The best protections for maintaining embedded device security include requiring software and hardware vendors to provide evidence that the software has no security weaknesses, perform remote attestation to verify that firmware has not been modified, and maintain secure configuration management processes when servicing field devices or updating firmware. In addition, organizations must provide proper security oversight and monitor the contractors and vendors that perform work on installed systems.

SoC and RTOS

System on chip (*SoC*) technology is basically a hardware module in a small form factor. SoC devices have good processing power, and the small footprint makes this technology ideal for reduced power consumption, lower cost, and better performance than are available with larger components. Some examples of developing technologies that take advantage of this are nanorobots, video devices for the visually impaired, and wireless antennas.

SoC involves integration between a microcontroller, an application or microprocessor, and peripherals. The peripherals could be a graphics processing unit (GPU), a Wi-Fi module, or a coprocessor. The processor is usually powerful enough to run an OS such as Windows, Linux, or Android. Intel's Curie module is about the size of a shirt button and contains all the components required to provide power for wearable devices.

A *real-time operating system* (*RTOS*) is a small operating system used in embedded systems and IoT applications that are typically run in a SoC environment. The primary purpose of an RTOS is to allow the rapid switching of tasks, with a focus on timing instead of throughput. An RTOS allows applications to run with precise timing and high reliability. RTOS technology is used in microcontrollers and implemented in wearable and medical devices and in in-vehicle systems and home automation devices.

Vulnerabilities associated with RTOS include the following:

▶ Exploitation of shared memory

▶ Priority inversion

- ▶ Interprocess communication (IPC) attacks

- ▶ Code injection

- ▶ DoS attacks

SoC designs integrate intellectual property (IP) blocks, which are often acquired from untrusted third-party vendors. Although the design of SoC requires a security architecture, it relies on third-party vendors and little standardization of the security architecture in the design. An IP that contains a security vulnerability can make an entire SoC untrustworthy, and the lack of standardization allows for actions such as device jailbreaking and DRM overriding.

It is possible to make a SoC design more secure following several ways:

- ▶ The device should be shielded from electromagnetic interference at the maximum level.

- ▶ Sensitive data should not be stored in the register or cache after processing.

- ▶ A separate security verification tool should be used to check the design.

The level of security built into SoC devices should take into consideration how easily a known vulnerability can be exploited and the amount of damage that can occur if the security of the device is compromised.

SoCs can also be implemented using a *field-programmable gate array* (*FPGA*). An FPGA is an integrated circuit that can be programmed or modified in the field. This means it is possible to make changes even after the FPGA has been deployed.

Working with or prototyping embedded systems today is incredibly simple and inexpensive, thanks to recent innovations such as the Arduino and Raspberry Pi. These low-priced, single-board computers are great for teaching, hobbies, and prototyping. The Raspberry PI contains a Broadcom SoC complete with integrated peripherals and an integrated CPU and GPU. These types of systems are now available with onboard FPGAs, combining the board's ease of use with reprogrammable chips.

SCADA and ICS

An organization might be able to exert better control over the management of security risks in environments that are considered static or less fluid than a cloud or virtualized environment. Environments such as SCADA systems, some

embedded systems, and mainframe systems are considered static because the technology behind them has been around for a long time. Thanks to business needs and vendor access, many of these systems that previously were on their own secure networks have become targets because they are connected to the Internet.

Supervisory control and data acquisition (SCADA) systems and *industrial control systems (ICSs)* include critical infrastructure systems across a number of sectors, such as infrastructure, facilities, industrial, logistics, and energy. Some common relatable examples include automation, monitoring, and control of the following:

▶ Electrical, nuclear, and other power generation, transmission, and distribution

▶ Just-in-time manufacturing and robotics

▶ Water distribution, water and wastewater treatment centers, reservoirs, and pipes

▶ Mass transit systems such as trains, subways, and buses, as well as traffic lights and traffic flow

▶ Airports, shipping, and space stations

SCADA is a subset of ICS. An ICS is managed via a SCADA system that provides a human–machine interface (HMI) for operators to monitor the status of a system. Other ICSs include industrial automation and control systems (IACSs), distributed control systems (DCSs), programmable logic controllers (PLCs), and remote terminal units (RTUs).

A targeted terrorist attack against an ICS poses a threat to the infrastructure. Ideally, two separate security and IT groups should manage the network infrastructure and the ICS or SCADA network. Because ICS security requirements differ, IT architects and managers who do not have previous experience on this type of system need to be trained specifically in ICS security and must be familiar with guidance documents. Otherwise, the stronger security controls required for an ICS might be inadvertently missed, putting both the organization and the community at increased risk. In addressing SCADA security concerns, one of the first lines of defense against attacks is to implement physical segregation of internal and external networks to reduce the attack surface by segregating the SCADA network from the corporate LAN. The SCADA LAN can be further segregated from the field device network containing the RTUs and PLCs by establishing an electronic security perimeter.

Guidance for proper security and established best practices for SCADA systems is available in ISA99: *Industrial Automation and Control Systems Security*, North American Electric Reliability Corporation (NERC): *Critical Infrastructure Protection (CIP)*, and NIST Special Publication 800-82: *Guide to Industrial Control Systems (ICS) Security*.

> **ExamAlert**
>
> A key control against attacks on SCADA systems is to implement physical segregation of internal and external networks to reduce the attack surface by segregating the SCADA network from the corporate LAN.

Smart Devices and IoT

Thanks to the *Internet of Things* (*IoT*), your smartphone can control household devices, and your voice can instruct devices to find information or perform certain functions. The IoT enables embedded system devices or components to interact with physical devices for the collection and exchange of data. While manufacturers continue to improve the built-in security of IoT devices, you need to be aware that some of them lack security controls or are configured with weak default settings.

The previous edition of this book said that Gartner predicted that 8.4 billion IoT devices would be connected in 2017, increasing to 25 billion by 2020. These numbers are about right, given the average estimates today, and the numbers are expected to grow!

Wearable technology has been around since the 1980s in the form of wearable heart rate monitors for athletes. The Fitbit debuted in 2011, and wearable technology came to the forefront with the release of the Apple Watch in 2015. Since then, other manufacturers have released devices such as smartwatches, wearable GPS trackers for pets, and the body-mounted cameras that many police departments now require.

Device manufacturers are being pushed to strengthen user data protection and implement security in designs in order to secure wearable technology. For organizations that use wearable technology in their everyday business, many devices can be controlled through policy. For example, organizations that use wearables to capture video and audio can create an acceptable use policy outlining parameters for use. Policy enforcement controls should also

be put in place. Other areas of concern related to wearable devices include the following:

▶ Bluetooth and Wi-Fi communication between wearable devices and smartphones

▶ Sale of sensitive information tracked by wearable devices

▶ Wearable device information stored in a public cloud

Organizations can restrict wearable device capabilities by disabling certain features through mobile device management (MDM) and restricting locations where wearable technology is allowed through geofencing.

Home automation is a rapidly growing field. The first widely used home automation device was the Roomba robot vacuum, which can be scheduled to automatically start whether or not the owner is near. One of the most popular home automation devices is the Amazon Echo. The Echo technically is a Bluetooth speaker, but it uses a digital assistant that can perform a variety of functions. This technology has even found its way into court cases. For example, recently Amazon handed over data from an Echo pertaining to a 2015 murder case.

Other home automation devices include smart thermostats, smart lighting, and smart locks. Interestingly, many of the home automation devices involve kitchen appliances such as refrigerators, coffee makers, garbage cans, and slow cookers. Smart forks can even track what you eat.

Home automation devices need to be protected. If an attacker can compromise your smart lock, house entry is possible without lock picking. Even without the inherent dangers of compromise, an unsecured device could be taken over with malware and used to participate in DDoS attacks. In addition, consider that the IoT goes well beyond the consumer. There are now commercial, industrial, infrastructure, and military IoT applications.

ExamAlert

An easy way to tell whether any home automation devices are susceptible to public attack is to use an Internet of Things scanner.

Several IoT scanners are available. The most widely used is Shodan, which is basically a search engine that looks for publicly accessible devices. It's critical to understand the communication methods, which may be short range, medium range, or long range. Examples include cellular (for example, 4G,

5G), radio, and Zigbee. Zigbee is a wireless set of protocols for wireless personal area networks (WPANs).

Consider these tips for securing such devices and, especially, home IoT devices:

- ▶ Secure the wireless network.

- ▶ Know what devices are communicating on the network and what they do.

- ▶ Install security software on devices that offer that option.

- ▶ Secure the smartphones and mobile apps that communicate with IoT devices.

Heating, Ventilation, Air Conditioning (HVAC)

Heating, ventilation, air conditioning (*HVAC*) devices use embedded systems to efficiently run environmental systems and reduce wasted energy. These devices switch on only when necessary through the control of individual circuits. Circuits are switched off when no guests, visitors, or employees are present.

In a large-scale system, an embedded system controls work through PC-based SoC boxes located near the HVAC elements they control. The boxes are usually rugged enough to function reliably in extreme-temperature locations and have extensive communication capabilities.

ExamAlert

Some HVAC monitoring software is not well updated or runs on older vulnerable versions of software. In addition, organizations often connect their HVAC equipment to the rest of their network, which leaves the network vulnerable.

The Target intrusion case is a great example. The initial intrusion into Target's systems was traced back to network credentials that were stolen from a third-party vendor. Target had given the HVAC subcontractor remote access to perform energy-consumption monitoring for regulating store temperatures.

Multifunction Devices

Most organizations have a multitude of printers and *multifunction devices* (*MFDs*) connected to their networks. These devices are just as susceptible to attacks as the PCs and devices that send print jobs to them, but they are often overlooked when it comes to security and employee security awareness training. The following security issues arise from use of printers and MFDs:

▶ Improper IP addressing

▶ Unsecured wireless printers

▶ Unattended sensitive information printouts

▶ Unpatched OSs

▶ Unnecessary services running

▶ Exclusion from data destruction policies

▶ Unchanged default logins and passwords

Enterprise printers and MFDs need to be included in security policies and protected just like any other network devices. Often security tools neglect to block access from a printer running old, vulnerable firmware. In addition to addressing the listed vulnerabilities, an organization should use encrypted connections for printing and accessing administrative control panels. If the budget allows, an organization should replace outdated models that have known vulnerabilities with newer models that provide better security options.

Embedded applications such as Follow Me Print extend single sign-on capabilities to allow users to log in to MFDs with their network password and print to virtually any printer. The embedded enabled MFD integrates with the directory services of all major OS vendors. The embedded copier interface, for example, allows users to immediately see the cost of print jobs.

Organizations must realize that an MFD is a computer that has storage, runs an embedded operating system, and provides network services. These devices are subject to the same attacks as other network devices and embedded systems, including information leakage and buffer overflows.

Protections for these devices include the following:

▶ Proper access control to the device and functions

▶ Inclusion of printers and MFDs in security planning and policies

▶ Implementation of protections for data in transit/motion and data at rest

Surveillance Systems

The use of camera surveillance systems has grown significantly in the past few years. The current market for smart cameras and camera systems is expected to grow rapidly. These systems will be used more and more for video surveillance, traffic monitoring, human interaction, and industrial automation.

Camera systems use smart cameras, which are basically video cameras that use embedded systems. Camera systems can contain embedded lighting, lenses, sensors, and processors.

Because these systems collect, store, and transmit data, they require the same security considerations as any other devices that hold sensitive data.

Noted camera system vulnerabilities include the following:

▶ Buffer overflows

▶ Disconnection of the camera from the Wi-Fi network

▶ Backdoors that allow Telnet or SSH to be remotely enabled

Vulnerabilities can be exploited through hard-coded weak default credentials or default usernames and passwords that have not been changed. In addition, the camera firmware and software should be regularly updated, just as in any other networked device.

Special-Purpose Devices

The embedded systems discussed so far work in a variety of industries. A special-purpose embedded system is devised for one industry in particular. The architecture is often based on a single-purpose processor and is designed to execute exactly one program. Special-purpose embedded devices are common in the medical, automotive, and aviation fields.

Medical Devices

Perhaps one of the fastest-growing IoT implementation industries is the healthcare sector. Medical devices have the capability for wireless connectivity, remote monitoring, and near-field communication (NFC). Medical advancements have enabled hospitals to deploy more IoT devices. One such advancement uses a neural–machine interface (NMI) for artificial legs that can decode an amputee's intended movement in real time. The attacker community has also taken notice, and more incidents in recent years have taken place in the healthcare sector than in the financial sector.

In 2013, concerns arose that Vice President Dick Cheney's pacemaker could be hacked, causing his death. In another instance, Johnson & Johnson publicly released a warning in 2016 to diabetic patients about an insulin pump security vulnerability. Shortly afterward, a team of researchers found several potentially fatal security flaws in various medical implants and defibrillators.

> **ExamAlert**
>
> Vulnerabilities in embedded medical devices present not only patient safety issues but also the risk of lateral movement within the network, which allows the attacker to move progressively through the network in search of a target.

If an attacker were able to exploit a vulnerability in a medical device and laterally move within the network, sensitive medical records could be at risk. According to industry professionals, U.S. hospitals currently average 10 to 15 connected devices per bed, amounting to 10 million to 15 million medical devices. A recent quick Internet search using Shodan revealed more than 36,000 publicly discoverable healthcare-related devices in the United States.

Government regulators such as the Food and Drug Administration (FDA) have responded to recent incidents with a fact sheet on cybersecurity. They offer the following recommendations for the mitigation and management of cybersecurity threats to medical devices:

▶ Medical device manufacturers and healthcare facilities should apply appropriate device safeguards and risk mitigation.

▶ Hospitals and healthcare facilities should evaluate network security and protect their hospital systems.

Like all other embedded devices, medical devices require security and updates. Because this area relies on third-party components that could be vulnerable, robust security protections must be implemented from the start.

Vehicles

Automobile in-vehicle computing systems have in the past been inaccessible to attackers. But the landscape is changing, thanks to the integration of wireless networks such as Global System for Mobile Communications (GSM) and Bluetooth into automobiles. Even parking meters have been upgraded, and connected systems *smart meters* may soon be able to directly communicate with vehicles. Current in-vehicle systems are capable of producing and storing data necessary for vehicle operation and maintenance, safety protection, and

emergency contact transmission. An in-vehicle system typically has a wireless interface that connects to the Internet and an on-board diagnostics interface for physical access. Many vehicles have data recorders that record vehicle speed, location, and braking maneuvers. Many insurance companies make use of such systems to offer discounts for safe driving. A device inserted into the on-board diagnostics (OBD) port of the vehicle sends the collected data to the insurance company for analysis.

All communication between controllers is done in plaintext. Because in-vehicle communications do not follow basic security practices, risks include unauthorized tracking, wireless jamming, and spoofing. A lot has been published regarding the capability to override a vehicle's controller area network (CAN) bus communications. For example, researchers Charlie Miller and Chris Valasek remotely attached to a Jeep Cherokee and were able to disable both the transmission and the brakes.

Risk mitigation recommendations include secure system software design practices, basic encryption, authentication of incoming data, and implementation of a firewall on the wireless gateway.

Aircraft and UAV

An aircraft has many embedded control systems, ranging from the flight control system to the galley microwave. A highly publicized article in 2016 highlighted a security researcher that used a flaw in an in-flight entertainment system to access a plane's controls. (Aviation experts asserted that this was technically impossible because the design isolates the infotainment system from the other systems performing critical functions.) Another vulnerability found in aviation control equipment is the use of hard-coded logon credentials that grant access to a plane's communications system using a single username and password. Other security issues are similar to those of medical embedded systems: use of undocumented or insecure protocols, weak credential protections, and the use of backdoors.

The technology associated with unmanned aerial vehicles (UAVs), or drones, has been widely used in military, agriculture, and cartography applications, among others. Drones are most often used for aerial photography, surveillance, and surveying. They have become mainstream and now are being used for delivery services such as Amazon. The first drone service delivery occurred in New Zealand in 2016, with a Domino's pizza. The Federal Aviation Administration (FAA) manages rules for drone delivery and other advanced drone operations. This includes a certification process for package delivery via drone.

Drones are subject to many of the same vulnerabilities as other embedded systems and lack strong security. They are susceptible to hijacking, Wi-Fi attacks, GPS spoofing attacks, jamming, and deauthentication attacks. These attacks can allow an attacker to intercept or disable a drone and access its data.

Resource Constraints

Security systems often require trade-offs. Already we've seen instances in which IoT devices couldn't be upgraded or even patched after a vulnerability was discovered. Many systems have poor authentication, and only recently are we starting to see widespread use of two-factor strong authentication for such devices. Because of the black-box nature of many of these devices, a level of *implied trust* is necessary. Whereas large organizations have governance and programs in place to verify security controls with vendors, for consumers, this can be difficult to verify. Other constraints include network, computer, power, and cryptographic capabilities. Cryptography, for example, carries a cost that needs to be considered along with our other factors particularly with devices containing limited resources.

ExamAlert

Embedded and specialized systems are particularly subject to resource constraints. First, consumers of such systems often need to accept a level of implied trust. Further, these systems must deal with limited resources that may affect power, computer, networking, cryptography, and authentication and the inability to fix vulnerabilities.

Particularly with the advent of the IoT, an increasing number of smart objects now require low power, including devices using radio-frequency tags. These devices require the same security demands but are at odds with strong cryptography and usually require significant amounts of resources. Or consider embedded cryptography, such as chips with integrated circuits on smart cards and credit cards. Essentially, these are tiny computers, capable of performing limited cryptographic functions. Research in these areas and the evolution of secure ciphers will continue to seek to sustain high levels of security while minimizing latency and meeting power and surface area requirements.

Cram Quiz

Answer these questions. The answers follow the last question. If you cannot answer these questions correctly, consider reading this chapter again until you can.

1. Which of the following are the most important constraints that need to be considered when implementing cryptography, particularly for embedded devices? (Select three.)

   ○ **A.** Security

   ○ **B.** Time

   ○ **C.** Performance

   ○ **D.** Power

2. Which of the following are associated with critical infrastructure systems where segmentation from public networks should be strongly considered? (Select two.)

   ○ **A.** SCADA

   ○ **B.** IoT

   ○ **C.** ICS

   ○ **D.** NIST

3. Your organization manufactures SoC technology. You have been tasked with ensuring secure design for these systems on chip. Which of the following suggestions are most appropriate? (Select two.)

   ○ **A.** Sensitive data should not be stored in the register after processing.

   ○ **B.** The device should be shielded from electromagnetic interference at the minimum level.

   ○ **C.** A separate security verification tool should be used to store sensitive data.

   ○ **D.** A separate security verification tool should be used to check the design.

4. Which of the following is a small operating system used in embedded systems and IoT applications that allows applications to run with precise timing and high reliability?

   ○ **A.** RTOS

   ○ **B.** FPGA

   ○ **C.** NERC

   ○ **D.** UAV

Cram Quiz Answers

Answer 1: A, C, and D. With smaller and lower-power devices, trade-offs and resource constraints need to be considered when implementing cryptography. These constraints include, for example, security, performance, and power. As a result, answer B is incorrect.

Answer 2: A and C. Supervisory control and data acquisition (SCADA) systems and industrial control systems (ICSs) include critical infrastructure systems such as networks related to manufacturing, logistics and transportation, energy and utilities, telecommunication services, agriculture, and food production. Answer B is incorrect. Internet of Things (IoT) devices are connected to public networks. This does not necessarily mean they aren't important, however, and IoT devices should be secured properly. Answer D is incorrect. The National Institute of Standards and Technology (NIST) publishes various papers, including guidance for protecting critical infrastructure.

Answer 3: A and D. System on chip (SoC) design should ensure that the device is shielded from electromagnetic interference (EMI) at the maximum level (not a minimum level); sensitive data should not be stored in the register or cache after processing; and a separate security verification tool should be used to check the design. Answers B and C are incorrect.

Answer 4: A. A real-time operating system (RTOS) is a small operating system used in embedded systems and IoT applications that allows applications to run with precise timing and high reliability. Answer B is incorrect because a field-programmable gate array (FPGA) is an integrated circuit that can be programmed or modified in the field. Answer C is incorrect because North American Electric Reliability Corporation (NERC) develops reliability standards that are overseen by the Federal Energy Regulatory Commission (FERC). Answer D is incorrect because a UAV is an unmanned aerial vehicle, such as a drone.

What Next?

If you want more practice on this chapter's exam objective before you move on, remember that you can access all of the Cram Quiz questions on the Pearson Test Prep software online. You can also create a custom exam by objective with the Online Practice Test. Note any objective you struggle with and go to that objective's material in this chapter.

CHAPTER 15

Physical Security Controls

This chapter covers the following official Security+ exam objective:

▶ 2.7 Explain the importance of physical security controls.

Essential Terms and Components

▶ bollard

▶ access control vestibule

▶ closed-circuit television (CCTV)

▶ Faraday cage

▶ air gap

▶ protected cable distribution

▶ hot aisle

▶ cold aisle

▶ secure data destruction

Perimeter Security

When planning security for network scenarios, many organizations overlook physical security. In many smaller organizations, the placement of servers, switches, routers, and patch panels is determined based on space restrictions, and equipment often ends up in odd places, such as in the coat closet by the receptionist's desk in the lobby, in the room with the copy machine, or in a storage room with a backdoor exit that is unlocked most of the time. Securing physical access and ensuring that access requires proper authentication are necessary to avoid

accidental exposure of sensitive data to attackers performing physical profiling of a target organization.

ExamAlert

Be familiar with physical security descriptions that indicate potential security flaws. Watch for descriptions that include physical details or organizational processes. Be particularly careful when exam questions address processes that use the same physical area for both common business traffic and data transport media or when data resources are placed in publicly accessible areas.

Physical access to a system creates many avenues for a breach in security. Unsecured equipment is also vulnerable to social engineering attacks. It is much easier for an attacker to walk into a reception area, say he or she is there to do some work on the server, and get access to the server in an unsecured area than it is for the attacker to get into a physically secured area with a guest sign-in/ sign-out sheet. In a secure design, physical security controls parallel data controls. When it comes to physical security, the most obvious element to control is physical access to systems and resources. Your goal is to allow only trusted use of these resources via positive identification that the entity accessing the systems is someone or something that has permission to do so, based on the security model you have chosen. The following section briefly describes physical security components used to protect the perimeter.

Signs, Fencing, and Gates

Some organizations are bound by regulations to warn employees and visitors about workplace hazards. One of the most common ways to accomplish this warning is to use signs. Warning signs can be both informative and deterring. For example, if an organization deals in caustic chemicals, signs warning of the chemicals can inform visitors while also deterring intruders. Agencies such as the Occupational Safety and Health Administration (OSHA), American National Standards Institute (ANSI), and the National Electrical Manufacturers Association (NEMA) have established specifications for safety signs.

A common deterrent is a fence or similar device that surrounds an entire building. A fence keeps out unwanted vehicles and people. One factor to consider in fencing is the height. The higher the fence, the harder it is to get over. To deter intruders, fence height should be 6 to 7 feet. For areas that need to be more secure, or to provide protection against a determined intruder, the fence should be 8 feet tall, with barbed wire on top.

Another factor to consider is the fence material. Removing wooden slats or cutting a chain-link fence with bolt cutters is much easier than drilling through concrete or block. Keep in mind that if the fence is not maintained or the area around it is not well lit, a fence can easily be compromised.

Another form of fencing is data center cage fencing, a secure cage that provides an additional physical security layer.

Where fences are used, gates usually control access through the fencing. They can be staffed or unstaffed. One of the main advantages of using automatic gates is the capability to use keycard readers and touchpad systems to control entry and exit. Unstaffed gates allow entry only to people who have clearance to enter an area. An additional benefit of using an automatic gate with keycard readers is that the system maintains a log of all area entries and exits. Hybrid staffed and automatic systems use a feature that checks entry via intercom; the gate can be opened when verification is complete. This type of system is often used for visitors and outside vendors.

Lighting

From a safety perspective, too little light can provide opportunities for criminals, and too much light can create glare and blind spots, resulting in potential risks. Protective lighting improves visibility for checking badges and people at entrances, inspecting vehicles, and detecting intruders both outside and inside buildings and grounds. Protective lighting should be located where it will illuminate dark areas and be directed at probable routes of intrusion.

Proper placement and positioning of fixtures can dramatically reduce glare. In areas where crime is a concern, install lamps with a higher color rendering index. Bright lighting and cameras reduce the likelihood that an area will experience unauthorized access attempts. A good design provides uniform lighting, minimizes glare, is compatible with CCTV, and complies with local light pollution and light trespassing ordinances. Regular maintenance ensures that the safety and security of both people and property are not compromised. Twice annually, conduct an audit of all exterior lighting.

Barricades and Bollards

To enhance the security of critical or vulnerable facilities, physical access control structures or barricades can be used to protect against unauthorized people, vehicles, explosives, and other threats. *Barricades* provide a high level of protection and can withstand direct-impact forces. Vehicle barricades often are used

in restricted areas to stop a vehicle from entering without proper authorization. A common barricade in many environments is a *bollard*, a short post that prevents vehicles from entering an area. Crash-rated barriers and bollards provide the best security but can be costly. Other examples of vehicle barricades include drop-arm gates, active bollard systems, planters, and crash barrier gates.

Cameras

Cameras and *closed-circuit television* (*CCTV*) are commonly used for perimeter surveillance. The video signal is processed and then transmitted for viewing at a central monitoring point. Traditionally, CCTV has been analog; however, recent technologies have taken advantage of the digital format, including IP video surveillance that uses TCP/IP for remote or wireless recording and monitoring. CCTV is a critical component of a comprehensive security program. It is important to appropriately plan and set clear and measurable objectives for a CCTV system. Failing to do so from the outset can be costly.

Many types of CCTV systems are available. Organizations should take into account technical, administrative, and legal considerations (including privacy) before and during the implementation of a CCTV system. Modern systems include a number of advanced features, including the ability to detect motion as well as identify and even alert upon specific recognition of objects. For example, camera systems have been combined with advanced intelligence to be able to detect weapons and other threats.

Security Guards

The presence of security guards can be reassuring to employees and can discourage intruders. Security guards are often armed, and they must be trained properly. The range of duties for guards can include staffing security gates, checking credentials, conducting active patrols, and monitoring CCTV feeds. *Guards* tend to be a greater visual deterrent than cameras alone and are often used in combination with other measures, such as deterrent signs.

> **ExamAlert**
>
> The exam might include questions about the various physical barrier techniques. Be sure you are familiar with the methods previously listed.

Perimeter security deterrents do not necessarily have to be designed to stop unauthorized access. As the name implies, they need to help deter access. That

is, a potential attacker might think twice about an attempt if he or she sees security deterrents; even an attacker considers the concept of risk/reward. Common examples include a sign indicating that the property is protected by a dog or an alarm system. Lighting, locks, dog, cleared zones around the perimeter, and even life-size cutouts of law enforcement officers can make a location appear less inviting to potential attackers.

In high-security environments, or when dealing with controls of grave importance, two-person integrity controls are sometimes used. This mechanism, known as the two-person rule, ensures that two people are required to authorize any access or operation. A relatively well-known example you may be familiar with involves the launching of weapons systems. In the United States, it's common practice for two people to verify and go through specific procedures before missiles are launched. Such a procedure helps prevent a single rogue guard from having significant negative impact, and it also provides greater certainty that mistakes will not occur.

Recent advances in camera systems and robotic technology have been combined to create robot security guards. These systems are most often seen in malls and parking lots. In addition to serving as visual deterrents, these robots have the capability to capture massive amounts of data that can later be used for investigations.

Internal Security

Mandatory physical access controls are common in government facilities and military installations, where users are closely monitored and very restricted. Because they are being monitored by security personnel and devices, users cannot modify entry methods or let others in. Discretionary physical control to a building or room is delegated to parties responsible for that building or room.

In role-based access methods for physical control, groups of people who have common access needs are predetermined, and access to different locations is allowed with the same key or swipe card. In this model, users generally have some security training and are often allowed to grant access to others by serving as escorts or by issuing guest badges. The security department coordinates the secure setup of the facility and surrounding areas, identifies the groups allowed to enter various areas, and grants access based on group membership.

> **Note**
>
> See Chapter 24, "Authentication and Authorization Solutions," for information about mandatory and role-based access controls.

Internally, security guards, surveillance cameras, motion detectors, limited access zones, token-based and biometric access requirements for restricted areas, and many other considerations could be involved in physical security planning. In addition, users must be educated about each measure taken to prevent circumvention and improve ease of normal access. The following sections briefly describe physical security components used to protect an organization when a person gets past the perimeter of the property.

Alarms

Alarm systems detect intrusions and monitor or record intruders. Electronic alarm systems are designed to detect, determine, and deter criminal activity or other threatening situations. An alarm system can detect an event such as an invasion, a fire, a gas leak, or an environmental change; determine whether an event poses a threat; then send a notification about the event. Alarm systems can also be combined with CCTV surveillance systems to automatically record the activities of intruders. Alarm systems can also interface with access control systems to electrically lock doors, for example.

Motion and Infrared Detection

The main purpose of a motion detector is to provide security against intruders by alerting security personnel to an unexpected presence or suspicious activity on the company's premises. A motion detector contains a sensor that is integrated with other technologies to trigger an alert when a moving object is in the sensor's field of view. Motion detectors can be based on light, sound, infrared, or ultrasonic technology. In addition to motion sensors, other sensors are available—for detection of motion, noise, proximity, moisture, temperature, sound, fire, steam, vibration, tilt, and touch. Even inexpensive off-the-shelf computer technology such as the Raspberry Pi can easily integrate with different types of sensors.

Infrared detection is based on an electrical signal that uses infrared light beams connected to a detector. It can be either active or passive. In active infrared detection, an alarm goes off when a constant light beam is interrupted. In passive infrared detection, a heat source event must trigger the alarm. Because infrared detectors pick up movement, they are useful when a high level of security must be maintained, such as in banks and restricted military facilities. These devices must be properly configured because they are extremely sensitive and can issue false alarms if they are set too stringently.

Access Control Vestibules

An access control vestibule is a holding area between two entry points that gives security personnel time to view a person before allowing him or her into the internal building. One door of a access control vestibule cannot be unlocked and opened until the opposite door has been closed and locked. In the most basic implementation of a mantrap, one door connects to the non-secured area, and the other door connects the portal to the secure area. Access control vestibules are often used to prevent tailgating and used in areas such as data centers. Mantrap doors are operated mainly via radio-frequency identification (RFID) cards and can be sophisticated enough to record a person's weight coming in and out—for example, to trigger an alarm if the person might be taking equipment from the data center.

> **ExamAlert**
>
> An access control vestibule is a physical access control system consisting of a small area and two interlocking doors. One door must close before the other door can be opened, creating a temporary "trapped" space. Access control vestibules were formerly known as mantraps.

Locks and Lock Types

Locks must be easy to operate yet deter intruders. Beyond the normal key locks, several different types can be considered. A cipher lock has a punch-code entry system. A wireless lock is opened by a receiver mechanism that reads a card that is held close to the receiver. A swipe card lock, such as those in hotels, requires a card to be inserted into the lock. Factors to consider related to locks are strength, material, and cost.

Access can be controlled by physically securing a system within a locked room or cabinet; attaching the system to fixed, unmovable furniture using cable locks or restraints; or locking a case to prevent the removal of key components. Non-standard case screws add another layer of security for publicly accessible terminals. Securing an area also involves ensuring that air ducts, dropped ceilings, and raised floors do not provide unauthorized avenues for physical access.

You can have the most secure lock on a door and use biometric devices for identification, but if the walls don't go up all the way and ceiling tiles can be removed to access rooms with sensitive equipment in them, someone can easily walk off with equipment and sensitive data. Be sure to consider all areas of a room.

Equipment Security

The next layer of physical security is the security of equipment. Physical access to a system creates avenues for security breaches. Many tools can be used to extract password and account information that can then be used to access secured network resources. Given the capability to reboot a system and load software from a USB drive, attackers might be able to access data or implant Trojan horses and other applications intended to weaken or compromise network security.

A more serious threat is theft or loss. Laptops and handheld devices are easy targets for thieves. Theft of laptops and handheld devices in an office setting is nearly as high as theft in cars and other forms of transportation. To prevent theft or loss, you must safeguard the equipment in your organization.

Cable Locks

To protect organization resources and minimize liability costs, each employee should take responsibility for securing office equipment. Laptops should never be left in an area where anyone can easily access them. Laptops, Apple iMacs, and any other easily transportable office computers should be physically secured. Security cables with combination locks can provide such security and are easy to use. The cable is used to attach the computer to an immovable object. Computers have one and sometimes two security cable slots. The security cable slots allow you to attach a commercially available antitheft device to the computer.

Computer locks commonly use steel cables to secure the PC to a desk; they are often found in computer labs and Internet cafes. A laptop lock is meant to protect both privacy and the computer. These locks come in different types: cable locks, case locks, and twist locks. The most common type of antitheft devices for portable computers usually include a length of metal stranded cable with an attached locking device and associated key. The cable is looped around an immovable object, and the locking device is inserted into a security cable slot.

Antitheft devices differ in design, so be sure yours is compatible with the security cable slot on the computer. Never leave a laptop unsecured. If an area is not safe, do not leave a laptop even if it is secured by a cable-locking device. Thieves have driven off with whole ATMs, with a goal of finding a way to bypass the lock later.

Cages and Safes

Tower-style computers can be targets for thieves not only because they have a higher resale value than laptops but also because of the data they might hold. For example, financial businesses have been hit hard by theft of desktop

computers that hold a lot of personal data. Secure computer towers and server cages that are bolted to the floor can improve physical security and prevent theft. In machines that are bolted to the floor, drive access can be either completely restricted or left available for ease of use. Server cages are most often found in data centers to protect server equipment and separate customer equipment. Colocation data centers can host the information of multiple customers, and a standard data center cage made of rigid metal is typically used. Cages can be modified based on customer specifications, such as stronger locks, restricted backside access, or military-grade requirements.

Some laptop security cases have special features to protect an organization's computers and data out in the field. For example, vendors make a safe that is designed for people who take their laptop computers home from work. In addition, high-security laptop safes store laptops in a manner similar to bank vault storage. Individual storage accommodates laptops in locking compartments, and those compartments can then be additionally secured behind the high-security main safe door when required. The open compartment version offers open shelves (usually one laptop per shelf) for storage that can be secured by the safe's main door. Other computer safe options include types made to securely store laptops and carry cases, plus other valuable equipment in reception areas, mobile car safes made to prevent smash-and-grab attacks, and home computer safes with electronic locks similar to the safes provided in hotel rooms.

Locking Cabinets and Enclosures

A locked cabinet may be used to hold equipment that is not in use or that does not have to be physically accessed on a regular daily basis. Enclosures are a common form of locking device more appropriate for data centers, where the systems are still active but can be locked away in an area that is adequately cooled. Vendors provide solutions such as a security cabinet enclosure that secures CPU towers and server blades. The housing is made of durable, heavy-duty steel for strength that lasts. The sides and door are ventilated to reduce the risk of overheating.

Another option is a wood laminate security computer cabinet that provides a computer workstation that can be locked away into a cabinet for space as well as security concerns. A computer cabinet includes a keyboard drawer and an adjustable top shelf. A slide-out bottom shelf accommodates a CPU and printer. It has built-in cable management grommets. Depending on what needs to be secured, some computer enclosures can hold everything from LCD/LED flat screens to entire systems. This type of security is often used for training

rooms, where the computers can be secured without having to be removed after each training session.

Screen Filters

A computer privacy screen filter might be a requirement, depending on the type of business an organization conducts. For example, HIPAA has stringent standards for patient privacy protection and requires medical, insurance, and other healthcare businesses and practitioners to protect the privacy and security of medical information, including information that is visible on computer screens. A computer screen filter limits the reading radius of the screen so that someone looking at the screen from the side cannot read what is onscreen. Many organizations require screen filters to shield important documents. In addition, privacy screen filters are often used by employees while traveling to protect information while sitting in airports, using public transportation, or working from other public places.

ExamAlert
Privacy screen filters can help prevent shoulder surfing.

Air Gaps

An *air gap* is a physical isolation gap between a system or network and the outside world. With an air gap, no system is connected to the Internet or connected to any other system that has Internet access. In a true air-gapped system, data is transferred to the system via removable media or a direct connection to another computer. Air gaps prevent unauthorized access and keep malware away from the systems. Air gaps are often used in industrial control systems (ICS), military classified networks, and credit and debit card payment networks. Air gaps are used for highly secure systems. However, they can be and have been compromised in the past, even though these systems are not connected to the Internet. Perhaps the most high-profile case involving the infection of an air-gapped system is Stuxnet.

ExamAlert
Remember that an air gap is a physical isolation gap between a system or network and the outside world. It prevents unauthorized access and keeps malware away from the systems.

Environmental Controls

Not all incidents arise from attacks, illegal activities, or other forms of directed threats to an enterprise. Many threats emerge from physical and environmental factors that require additional consideration in planning for security controls. The location of everything from a building to wireless antennas affects security. When picking a location for a building, an organization should investigate the type of neighborhood, population, crime rate, and emergency response times. This information helps in planning the physical barriers needed, such as fencing, lighting, and security personnel. An organization must also analyze the potential dangers from natural disasters and plan to reduce their effects when possible.

When protecting computers, wiring closets, and other devices from physical damage from either natural or human-caused disasters, you must select locations carefully. Proper placement of the equipment might cost a company a little money upfront, but it will provide significant protection from possible loss of data due to electrical damage, flooding, or fire.

Protected Cabling, Protected Distribution, and Faraday Cages

It is important to take shielding into consideration when choosing cable types and placement of cable. Coaxial cable was the first type of cable used in network computers. Coaxial cables are made of a thick copper core with an outer metallic shield to reduce interference. Coaxial cables have no physical transmission security and are simple to tap without anyone noticing and without interrupting regular transmissions. The electric signal, conducted by a single core wire, can easily be tapped by piercing the sheath. An attacker can then eavesdrop on the conversations of all hosts attached to the segment because coaxial cabling implements broadband transmission technology and assumes that many hosts are connected to the same wire. Another security concern with coaxial cable is reliability. No focal point, such as a switch or hub, is involved, and a single faulty cable can bring down the whole network. Missing terminators or improperly functioning transceivers can cause poor network performance and transmission errors.

Twisted-pair cable is used in most of today's network topologies. Twisted-pair cabling is either unshielded (UTP) or shielded (STP). UTP is popular because it is inexpensive and easy to install. UTP consists of eight wires twisted into four pairs. The design cancels much of the overflow and interference from one wire to the next, but UTP is subject to interference from outside

electromagnetic sources and is prone to radio-frequency interference (RFI) and electromagnetic interference (EMI), as well as crosstalk. Longer cable lengths transfer a more significant environmental measure of noise because wires can inadvertently act as antennas for broadcast emanations.

STP is different from UTP in that it has shielding surrounding the cable's wires. Some STP has shielding around the individual wires, which helps prevent crosstalk. STP is more resistant to EMI and is considered a bit more secure because the shielding makes wiretapping more difficult.

> **ExamAlert**
>
> Both UTP and STP are possible to tap, although it is physically a little trickier to do so than tapping coaxial cable because of the physical structure of STP and UTP cable.

With UTP and STP, adding devices to the network via open ports is easy on unsecured hubs and switches. As a result, hubs and switches should be secured from unauthorized access, and cables should be clearly marked so a visual inspection can quickly pinpoint whether something is awry. Software programs also can help detect unauthorized devices and the ports on which they will accept attempts at connection.

The plenum is the space between the ceiling and the floor of a building's next level. It is commonly used to run network cables. The cables in this part of a building must be plenum grade to comply with fire codes. The outer casing of this type of cable is more fire resistant than in regular twisted-pair cable.

Fiber-optic cable was designed for transmissions at higher speeds over longer distances, such as in underwater intercontinental telecommunications applications. Fiber uses light pulses for signal transmission, making it immune to RFI, EMI, and eavesdropping without specialized equipment capable of detecting transient optical emission at a fiber join or bend. Fiber-optic wire has a plastic or glass center, surrounded by another layer of plastic or glass with a protective outer coating. On the downside, fiber is still quite expensive compared to more traditional cable, it is more difficult to install, and fixing breaks can be time-intensive and costly as there may be hundreds or thousands of individual fibers in a single bundle. As far as security is concerned, fiber cabling eliminates the signal tapping that is possible with coaxial cabling. Tapping fiber is impossible without interrupting the service and using specially constructed equipment. This makes it more difficult for an attacker to eavesdrop or steal service.

Secure Internet Protocol Router Network (SIPRNET) and Non-Classified but Sensitive Internet Protocol Router Network (NIPRNET) are private government-run networks used for exchanging sensitive information in a secure manner. SIPRNET carries classified information up to the secret level. These systems use a *protected cable distribution* system called a protected distribution system (PDS). A PDS consists of copper or optical cables that are protected from unauthorized physical or electronic access. The purpose of a PDS is to deter, detect, and make it difficult to physically access the communication lines carrying national security information.

A more efficient way to protect a large amount of equipment from electronic eavesdropping is to place the equipment in a well-grounded metal box of conductive material, called a *Faraday cage*. Named after its inventor, Dr. Michael Faraday, this type of box can be small enough for a cell phone or can encompass an entire building. The idea behind it is to protect the contents from electromagnetic fields. The cage surrounds an object with interconnected and well-grounded metal, typically a copper mesh that is attached to the walls and covered with plaster or drywall. The wire mesh acts as a net for stray electrical signals either inside or outside the box. New forms of wall treatment (wallpaper) can be used to embed a Faraday mesh atop existing structural materials, retrofitting older buildings with Faraday-style protections to create cell phone-free zones in restaurants and theaters.

> **ExamAlert**
>
> Using a Faraday cage is an efficient way to protect a large amount of equipment from electronic eavesdropping.

HVAC

When doing facilities planning, you need to take into consideration the cooling requirements of computer data centers and server rooms. The amount of heat generated by some of this equipment is extreme and highly variable. Depending on the size of the space and the age and type of equipment the room contains, energy consumption typically ranges from 20 to 100 watts per square foot. Despite being smaller and more powerful, newer servers might consume even more energy than older ones. Some high-end facilities with state-of-the-art technology can require up to 400 watts per square foot. These spaces consume many times more energy than office facilities of equivalent size and must be planned for accordingly. Smaller, more powerful IT equipment is considerably hotter than older systems, making heat management a major challenge.

Monitor the area for hot spots and cold spots, ensuring that you don't have one exchange that is frigid cold under a vent and hot elsewhere. When water or drainpipes are located above facilities, it is important to ensure that upper-floor drains do not clog. One solution is to use rubberized floors above the data center or server room. Above all else, timely air conditioning maintenance is required.

Fire Suppression

Fire is a danger common to all business environments and must be planned for well in advance of any possible occurrence. The first step in a fire safety program is fire prevention.

The best way to prevent fires is to train employees to recognize dangerous situations and report them immediately. Knowing where a fire extinguisher is and how to use it can stop a small fire from becoming a major catastrophe. Many of the newer motion and ultrasonic-detection systems also include heat and smoke detection for fire prevention. These systems alert the monitoring station of smoke or a rapid increase in temperature. If a fire does break out somewhere in the facility, a proper fire-suppression system can help the organization avoid major damage. Keep in mind that laws and ordinances apply to the deployment and monitoring of a fire-suppression system. An organization has the responsibility to ensure that these codes are properly met. In addition, the organization should have safe evacuation procedures and periodic fire drills to protect its most important investment: human life.

Fire requires three main components to exist: heat, oxygen, and fuel. If you eliminate any of these components, the fire goes out. A common way to fight fire is with water in an attempt to take away oxygen and heat. A wet-pipe fire-suppression system is the type of system most people think of when they think of indoor sprinkler systems. The term *wet* describes the state of the pipe during normal operations. The *pipe* in the wet-pipe system contains water under pressure at all times. The pipes are interconnected and have sprinkler heads attached at regularly spaced intervals. The sprinkler heads have a stopper held in place with a bonding agent designed to melt at an appropriate temperature. When the stopper melts, it opens the valve and allows water to flow from the

sprinkler head to extinguish the fire. Keep in mind that electronic equipment and water don't get along well. Fires that start outside electrical areas are well served by water-based sprinkler systems, but all these systems should have both manual activation and manual shutoff capabilities. You want to be able to turn off a sprinkler system to prevent potential water damage. Most sprinkler systems are designed to activate only one head at a time. This works effectively to put out fires in the early stages.

Dry-pipe systems work in exactly the same way as wet-pipe systems, except that the pipes are filled with pressurized air instead of water. The stoppers work on the same principle. When a stopper melts, the air pressure is released and a valve in the system opens. One reason for using a dry-pipe system is that, when the outside temperature drops below freezing, any water in the pipes can freeze, and the pipes might burst. Another reason for justifying a dry-pipe system is the delay associated between the system activation and the actual water deployment. Some laws require a sprinkler system even in areas of a building that house electrical equipment, and there should be some delay so that someone can manually deactivate the system before water starts to flow. In such a case, a company could deploy a dry-pipe system and a chemical system together. The delay in the dry-pipe system could be used to deploy the chemical system first and avoid serious damage to the running equipment that would occur with a water-based sprinkler system.

Fire suppression systems are rated according to class:

▶ **Class A:** For Class A fires (trash, wood, and paper), water decreases the fire's temperature and extinguishes its flames.

▶ **Class B:** For Class B fires, foam extinguishes flames fueled by flammable liquids, gases, and greases. Liquid foam mixes with air while passing through the hose.

▶ **Class C:** Class C fires (energized electrical equipment, electrical fires, and burning wires) are put out using extinguishers based on carbon dioxide or halon. Halon was once used as a reliable, effective, and safe fire-protection tool, but in 1987, an international agreement known as the Montreal Protocol mandated the phase-out of environmentally damaging halons in developed countries due to emissions concerns. Therefore, carbon dioxide extinguishers have replaced halon extinguishers in all but a few locations. Carbon dioxide extinguishers do not leave a harmful residue, and exposure can be tolerated for a while without extreme protective measures, making them a good choice for an electrical fire in a data center or in other electronic devices.

▶ **Class D:** Class D fires are fires that involve combustible metals such as magnesium, titanium, and sodium. The two types of extinguishing agents for Class D fires are sodium chloride and a copper-based dry powder.

ExamAlert

Know the classes of fire and what is used to extinguish each type:

▶ **Class A:** Combustible materials; extinguish with water
▶ **Class B:** Liquids and gases; extinguish with foam
▶ **Class C:** Energized electronics; extinguish with carbon dioxide
▶ **Class D:** Combustible metals; extinguish with sodium chloride or copper-based dry powder

---

Hot and Cold Aisles

Data centers and server farms can have server racks be arranged with alternating rows facing opposing directions. Fan intakes draw in cool air vented to racks facing the *cold aisle*, and the fan output, which is hot air, is vented to the alternating *hot aisles* for removal from the data center (see Figure 15.1). This data center organization provides efficiency in thermal management by allowing supply ducts to serve all cold aisles and exhaust ducts to collect and draw away heated air.

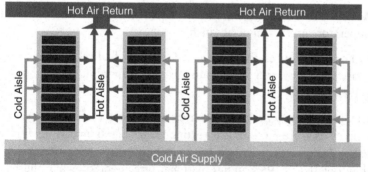

FIGURE 15.1 Simplified side view of hot aisles/cold aisles in a data center

Overcooling causes condensation on equipment, and too-dry environments lead to excessive static. In addition to monitoring temperature, organizations should monitor humidity. Humidity is a measure of moisture content in the air. A high level of humidity can cause components to rust and degrade electrical resistance or thermal conductivity. A low level of humidity can subject components to electrostatic discharge (ESD), causing damage; at extremely low levels,

components might be affected by the air itself. The American Society of Heating, Refrigerating and Air-Conditioning Engineers (ASHRAE) recommends optimal humidity levels in the range of 40% to 55%.

Environmental monitoring solutions can raise alerts or trigger automated responses, as needed. Alerting systems must be capable of sustaining operations during the event, and a water-sensing monitor should be able to function and raise an alert even when the environment is filled with water.

Monitoring systems must also be able to communicate in the event of service disruption so that alerts can be passed to responders even if the email server cluster has shut down due to thermal overload conditions. If a monitoring solution relies on networking for sensor measurement or raising alerts, environmental issues that degrade or prevent network communications might go unnoticed, or alerts might not reach responders in a timely manner.

Secure Data Destruction

Sensitive and privacy-related data (including log files, physical records, security evaluations, and other operational documentation) should be managed in an organization's retention and disposal policies. These policies should include specifications for access authorization, term of retention, and requirements for disposal. Depending on the relative level of data sensitivity, retention and disposal requirements can become extensive and detailed.

Clear policies and procedures should be put into place for *secure data destruction*, which is the proper disposal of data and associated hardware. Such practices should dictate that equipment the organization uses should be disposed of only in accordance with approved procedures, including independent verification that the relevant security risks have been mitigated. Procedures should be in place when disposing of old computer hardware, whether for recycling, disposal, donation, or resale.

The most prominent example of a security risk is a hard drive inside a computer that has not been completely or properly wiped. Some concerns about data erasure sufficiency in newer solid-state drives (SSDs) might require organizations to destroy drives instead of simply erasing them for normal disposal channels.

With the secure disposal of equipment, a wide range of scenarios needs to be considered:

▶ Breaches of health and safety requirements

▶ Inadequate disposal planning that results in severe business loss

▶ Remnants of legacy data from old systems that might still be accessible

▶ Disposal of old equipment that is necessary to read archived data

▶ Theft of equipment in use during cleanup of unwanted equipment

Proper disposal of removable media is also important. An organization must properly handle removable media when the data should be overwritten or is no longer useful or pertinent to the organization. Generally, all electronic storage media should be sanitized or purged when it is no longer necessary for business use, as well as before its sale, donation, or transfer of ownership. Sanitization and purging is the process of removing the contents from the media as fully as possible, making restoration of the data extremely difficult (or close to impossible). The following methods are acceptable for some forms of media sanitation:

▶ **Declassification:** This is a formal process of assessing the risk involved in discarding information.

▶ **Degaussing:** This method involves using a tool to reduce or remove the magnetic field of the storage media.

▶ **Wiping:** This method, which applies to magnetic storage devices, writes over all data on the media (often multiple times) and destroys what was originally recorded.

▶ **Encryption:** This method requires a strong key, effectively making the data unrecoverable without the key. This process can be combined with crypto shredding by purposely purging the key used to encrypt the data.

▶ **Destruction:** This process physically destroys both the media and the information stored on it. For USB flash drives and other solid-state non-ferric removable storage, this might be the only solution acceptable for certain controls and legal mandates. For paper records, destruction is the only viable option.

ExamAlert

An organization's information sensitivity policy defines the requirements for the classification and security of data and hardware resources, based on their relative level of sensitivity. Some resources, such as hard drives, might require extensive preparation before they can be discarded.

Paper records that contain sensitive information need to be destroyed. In addition to organizational requirements, regulations often include specific rules and recommendations. For example, in addition to requiring electronic PHI

to be destroyed, HIPAA requires that PHI in paper records be properly disposed. Many large organizations now depend on third-party vendors to collect and properly dispose of records on their behalf. Methods of media and paper destruction that organizations or third-party organizations may engage in include the following:

▶ **Burning:** Government organizations commonly use this method. Sensitive data is temporarily contained in burn bags and then incinerated.

▶ **Shredding:** This commonly used method involves destruction using blades, with varying degrees of effectiveness. Simple, low-cost solutions present problems because shredded documents sometimes can be reassembled.

▶ **Pulping:** This process involves dissolving paper, reducing it to its cellulose fibers. Organizations that provide shredding services often later pulp the shredded material before recycling it.

▶ **Pulverizing:** Special systems that contain rotating hammers crush materials at high speed before passing them through a sizing screen to turn them into tiny particles (or even dust).

Cram Quiz

Answer these questions. The answers follow the last question. If you cannot answer these questions correctly, consider reading this chapter again until you can.

1. The aerospace company you work for is developing a highly secret new component. The computers to develop the component need to be isolated to prevent connections to the outside world. Which of the following should you put in place to provide the most secure setup?

   ○ **A.** Firewall

   ○ **B.** Air gap

   ○ **C.** Hot and cold aisles

   ○ **D.** Pulverized network

2. Your training director has an unsupervised room that he wants to use as a training lab for the next few months. The lab will hold 20 laptops and confidential training manuals. Which of the following controls are most appropriate in this situation? (Select two.)

   ○ **A.** Cable locks

   ○ **B.** Locking cabinets

   ○ **C.** Mantrap

   ○ **D.** Biometric reader

3. Employees in your data center have notified you that they are receiving minor electrical shocks when they touch the metal enclosures and are worried about handling equipment such as servers and hard drives. Which of the following should you consider doing?

- ○ **A.** Decrease the humidity
- ○ **B.** Increase the humidity
- ○ **C.** Increase the temperature
- ○ **D.** Decrease the temperature

4. Which of the following is a type of barricade used to prevent unauthorized vehicles from entering an area?

- ○ **A.** Screened subnet
- ○ **B.** Faraday cage
- ○ **C.** SIPRNET
- ○ **D.** Bollard

Cram Quiz Answers

Answer 1: B. An air-gapped network provides the most secure setup. The computers inside the air gap may be interconnected but have no external access. Answer A is incorrect because a firewall may be required to be connected to the outside; although it could possibly secure the network, this setup would not provide the security of a completely closed network. Answer C is incorrect because hot and cold aisles are for data center HVAC. Answer D is incorrect because pulverizing is related to the secure destruction of materials.

Answer 2: A and B. The unsupervised training lab will benefit from cable locks and locking cabinets. The laptops can be secured to prevent theft. The locking cabinets can potentially be used to store the laptops and can also be used to protect the confidential documents. Answer C is incorrect. A mantrap is a holding area between two doors. Answer D is incorrect. Because this is an unsupervised lab where many people may have open access, the focus should be on protecting equipment and material from being taken. Biometric readers do not prevent this.

Answer 3: B. Humidity is a measure of moisture content in the air. A low level of humidity can subject components to electrostatic discharge (ESD), which can cause damage; at extremely low humidity levels, components might be affected by the air itself. Answer A is incorrect given the circumstance, although a high level of humidity can cause components to rust and degrade electrical resistance or thermal conductivity. Adjusting the temperature is incorrect, so both C and D are incorrect.

Answer 4: D. A barricade used in many environments is a bollard, a short post that prevents vehicles from entering an area. Answer A is incorrect because a screened subnet is an isolated network that sits between the public Internet and a private internal network. Answer B is incorrect because a Faraday cage is a well-grounded metal box of conductive material used to protect electronic equipment from eavesdropping. Answer C is incorrect because Secure Internet Protocol Router Network (SIPRNET) is a private government-run network used for exchanging sensitive information in a secure manner.

What Next?

If you want more practice on this chapter's exam objective before you move on, remember that you can access all of the Cram Quiz questions on the Pearson Test Prep software online. You can also create a custom exam by objective with the Online Practice Test. Note any objective you struggle with and go to that objective's material in this chapter.

CHAPTER 16

Cryptographic Concepts

This chapter covers the following official Security+ exam objective:

▶ 2.8 Summarize the basics of cryptographic concepts.

Essential Terms and Components

▶ digital signature

▶ key length

▶ key stretching

▶ salting

▶ hashing

▶ key exchange

▶ elliptical curve cryptography (ECC)

▶ perfect forward secrecy (PFS)

▶ quantum cryptography

▶ ephemeral

▶ blockchain

▶ mode of operation

▶ stream cipher

▶ block cipher

▶ symmetric cryptography

▶ asymmetric cryptography

▶ steganography

▶ homomorphic encryption

Cryptosystems

A cryptosystem or cipher system provides a method for protecting information by disguising it in a format that only authorized systems or individuals can read. The use and creation of such systems is called *cryptography*. Cryptography involves turning plaintext into ciphertext (encryption) and then turning ciphertext into plaintext (decryption). Specifically, encryption protects confidentiality and safeguards data integrity.

Related to cryptography, an *algorithm* is a mathematical procedure or sequence of steps taken to perform encryption and decryption. You can think of an algorithm as a cooking recipe, with the ingredients needed and step-by-step instructions. Algorithms are used in conjunction with a key for encryption and decryption. The process of encryption is based on two important principles:

▶ **Confusion:** The plaintext input should be significantly changed in the resulting ciphertext. More technically, each bit of the resulting ciphertext should depend on numerous parts of the key to hide any connection between the two, making it difficult to reverse from ciphertext to plaintext without the key.

▶ **Diffusion:** If the plaintext is changed, no matter how minor the change, at least half of the ciphertext should also change—and vice versa. Like confusion, diffusion makes things more difficult for an attacker. Specifically, diffusion mitigates the capability to identify patterns that might help break the cipher.

Keys

Cryptographic algorithms and keys work together. A key determines the output of a cryptographic algorithm and consists of a random string of bits. Keys used in cryptography provide for secrecy. In fact, a principle known as Kerckhoffs's principle (from the nineteenth century) states that "only secrecy of the key provides security." This is particularly important in relationship to the associated algorithms. An algorithm itself does not need to be (and should not be) kept secret. Depending on the type of algorithm used, either the same key is used for both encryption and decryption or else different yet mathematically related keys are used.

Keys also need to be of an appropriate *key strength* or *key length* to prevent brute-force attacks. Key size is expressed as the number of bits in the key used by the algorithm. The longer the key, the more difficult it is to crack. When

keys are generated, it needs to be done in such a way that they key contains enough *entropy*, or randomness. Modern cryptography relies on random numbers. However, *pseudo-random numbers* are also commonly used so that the numbers appear to be random, at least statistically, but are not truly so. An *initialization vector* (*IV*) is a fixed-size input of a random or pseudo-random value. In cryptography, an IV, for example, helps ensure that each message is encrypted differently. You would not want the same message, encrypted with the same key, to have the same resulting ciphertext. A *nonce* can also be used as an IV. A nonce is a random or pseudo-random number that is used only once and is associated with a time stamp. Nonces are commonly used with authentication protocols to ensure that older authentication messages cannot be reused.

Passwords are often thought of as keys because they act as such. For example, a password might be needed before a document can be encrypted. At least in reliable cryptographic systems, the password is used as an input to a key derivation function (KDF), which is used to derive the actual key based on the password as the origin point. Additional random data can be applied, or a key-stretching technique can be used. An eight-character password contains only 64 bits. *Key stretching* runs a password through an algorithm to produce an enhanced key that is usually at least 128 bits long.

In most instances, keys are static and used repeatedly for up to a year or even longer. In other cases, a key is used for only a single session. This type of key is known as an *ephemeral key*. Ephemeral keys are common to ephemeral key agreement protocols, covered in Chapter 17, "Secure Protocols." The term *ephemeral* is increasingly being used in computer technology in relationship to keys as well as computing systems and communication ports—to describe something of a temporary or short duration.

> **ExamAlert**
>
> Know that a static key is designed for long-term use, and an ephemeral key is designed to be used for a single transaction or session.

Key Exchange

An important concept in any discussion of encryption is *key exchange*. Historically, the challenge has been that to get a secret, you must share a secret. Consider a simple analogy of a password as the key. Imagine that you are friends with a kid who requires the secret password to gain secret access. Perhaps that password is "open sesame." The problem is that, at some point, the secret

password has to be shared with you. This process is likely not going to be secure and will be subject to eavesdropping. Even if the password were whispered to you, it would still be overheard. Another challenge is that you and the kid have to meet face to face, so you will likely receive the key "out of band" instead of when you are waiting at the door to gain entry.

Modern cryptography solves the age-old challenges of key exchange. Exchanging keys in many applications happens securely "in band" when you need to establish a secure session. Any type of out-of-band key exchange relies on sharing in advance, which means the key is delivered outside the network or process from which it will actually be used.

Symmetric Algorithms

Symmetric cryptography is a system that uses a common shared key between the sender and receiver. The primary advantages of such a system are that it is easier to implement than an asymmetric system and also typically is faster. However, the two parties must first somehow exchange the key securely. Assume, for example, that you have a friend located thousands of miles away from you. To exchange secure messages, you send messages back and forth in a secure lockbox; you both have a copy of the key to the lockbox. This works, but how do you securely deliver the key to your friend? Somehow the key must have been communicated or delivered to your friend, which introduces additional challenges of logistics and ways to ensure that the key is not compromised in the process. *Asymmetric cryptography* helps overcome these challenges.

Now imagine a system in which more than two parties are involved. In this scenario, every party participating in communications must have exactly the same key to compare the information. If the key is compromised at any point, guaranteeing a secure connection is impossible.

> **Note**
>
> Symmetric key algorithms are often referred to as secret key algorithms, private key algorithms, and shared secret algorithms.

Even given the possible risks involved with symmetric key encryption, the method is used often today mainly because of its simplicity and easy deployment. In addition, this is generally considered a strong encryption method if the source and destination that house the key information are kept secure.

> **ExamAlert**
>
> A symmetric key is a single cryptographic key used with a secret key (symmetric) algorithm. The symmetric key algorithm uses the same private key for both encryption and decryption operations. It is easier to implement than an asymmetric system and also typically is faster.

Symmetric encryption uses two primary types of methods for encrypting plaintext data:

▶ **Stream cipher:** With a *stream cipher*, plaintext bits are encrypted a single bit at a time. These bits are also combined with a stream of pseudo-random characters. Stream ciphers are known for their speed and simplicity.

▶ **Block cipher:** With a *block cipher*, plaintext is encrypted in blocks, which are fixed-length groups of bits. A block of plaintext is encrypted into a corresponding block of ciphertext. For example, a 64-bit block of plaintext would output as a 64-bit block of ciphertext. Because most plaintext does not fit within the precise block size, leftover text is padded to complete the block.

Block ciphers can be further described by their *mode of operation*. Because block ciphers encrypt based on the specified block size, the mode of operation defines how a cipher is continually applied to encrypt data larger than the specific block size.

Most block cipher modes require an initialization vector (IV), a fixed-size input of a random or pseudo-random value. In cryptography, an IV helps ensure that each message is encrypted differently. You do not want the same message, encrypted with the same key to have the same resulting ciphertext. Table 16.1 outlines the differences between block ciphers and stream ciphers.

TABLE 16.1 **A Comparison of Block Ciphers and Stream Ciphers**

Block Cipher	Stream Cipher
Encryption performed on a fixed-length block of plaintext (for example, 128 bits)	Encryption performed bit by bit
More complex and not as fast	High performance, requiring fewer resources
Requires padding to complete a block	Does not require padding because each bit is processed and is the smallest unit
High diffusion	Low diffusion
Less susceptible to malicious insertions	Susceptible to malicious insertions
Most symmetric algorithms are block ciphers	Block ciphers can operate in modes, essentially making them stream ciphers
A single error can corrupt an entire block	A single error in a bit is not likely to affect subsequent bits

Asymmetric Algorithms

An *asymmetric* encryption algorithm has two keys: a public key and a private key. The public key is made available to whomever will encrypt the data sent to the holder of the private key. The private key is maintained on the host system or application. Often the public encryption key is made available in a number of ways, such as through email or on centralized servers that host a pseudo-address book of published public encryption keys. One challenge, however, is ensuring the authenticity of a public key. To address this, a public key infrastructure (PKI) is often used. A PKI uses trusted third parties that certify or provide proof of key ownership (see Chapter 25, "Public Key Infrastructure"). Figure 16.1 illustrates the asymmetric encryption process.

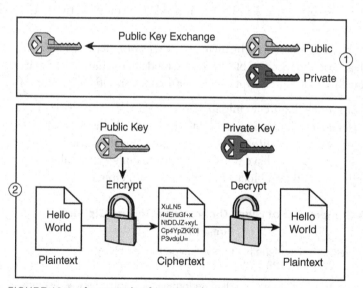

FIGURE 16.1   An example of asymmetric cryptography

Asymmetric algorithms are often referred to as *public key algorithms* because they use the public key as the focal point for the algorithm.

As an example of asymmetric encryption, think about the secure exchange of an email message. When someone wants to send a secure email to someone else, he or she obtains the target user's public encryption key and encrypts the message using this key. Because the message can be unencrypted only with the

private key, only the target user can read the information held within. Ideally, for this system to work well, everyone should have access to everyone else's public keys. Refer again to Figure 16.1. Note that the public key and the private key shown both belong to the recipient, yet the public key is provided through a key exchange. Anyone with the public key can use it to encrypt; only that person with the private key (that is, the recipient) can decrypt.

Imagine a postal mailbox that enables the letter carrier to insert your mail via an open slot, but only you have the key to get the mail out. This is analogous to an asymmetric system. The open slot is the public key. If you are concerned about the security of your mail, needing a single key only to get the mail out is much easier than ensuring that every letter carrier has a copy of your mailbox key. The letter carrier is also thankful he or she is not required to carry hundreds of different keys to complete mail delivery.

Keep the following points in mind regarding keys in asymmetric encryption:

▶ **Public keys encrypt, and private keys decrypt:** For example, Alice can encrypt a message with Bob's public key. Bob decrypts the message with his private key, which only he has.

▶ **Private keys sign, and public keys verify signatures:** For example, Alice signs a message with her private key. Bob verifies the message's signature with Alice's public key.

ExamAlert

Some general rules for asymmetric algorithms include the following:

▶ The public key can never decrypt a message that it was used to encrypt.

▶ With proper design, public keys should never be able to determine private keys.

▶ Each key should be capable of decrypting a message made with the other. For instance, if a message is encrypted with the private key, the public key should be able to decrypt it.

Public key encryption has proven useful on networks such as the Internet—primarily because the public key is all that needs to be distributed. Because nothing harmful can be done with the public key, it is useful over unsecured networks where data can pass through many hands and is vulnerable to interception and abuse. Symmetric encryption works fine over the Internet, too, but the limitations on securely providing the key to everyone who requires it can pose difficulties. In addition, asymmetric key systems can verify digital signatures, which provide assurance that communications have not been altered and that the communication arrived from an authorized source.

> **ExamAlert**
>
> In an asymmetric key system, each user has a pair of keys: a private key and a public key. To send an encrypted message, you must encrypt the message with the recipient's public key. The recipient then decrypts the message with his or her private key.

Elliptic Curve and Emerging Cryptography

Two other cryptosystems are *elliptic curve cryptography* (*ECC*) and (still emerging) quantum cryptography. ECC is a public key cryptosystem based on complex mathematical structures. ECC uses smaller key sizes than traditional public key cryptosystems. As a result, it is faster and consumes fewer resources, which makes it more ideal for mobile and wireless devices.

Unlike elliptic curves and other cryptosystems, *quantum cryptography* does not rely on mathematics. Instead, it relies on physics. Although this cryptosystem is slower, its primary advantage is increased security. Quantum mechanics protects against data disturbance because no one can measure the quantum state of the photons. The mere observation of a quantum system changes the system.

> **ExamAlert**
>
> Elliptic curve cryptography is an example of an asymmetric public key cryptosystem. It is often used for mobile and wireless devices.

Session Keys

Session keys, sometimes called *symmetric keys*, are randomly generated keys for performing both encryption and decryption during the communication of a session between two parties. Such a key is described as being symmetric because it is used for both encryption and decryption. When a session key is generated, the key is valid only during that one communication session. As a result, you can think of a session key as being temporary, for one-time use.

A session key is deleted after the communication ends, but the key exchange mechanism used to establish session keys (most notably, RSA) often relies on a private key. This can be the web server's private key, which is used to establish a secure session with the client. Although this is efficient, the challenge is that gaining access to the server's private key allows an adversary to decrypt the

communications. The benefit, however, is that organizations can use this private key so that security systems (for example, IDSs and web application firewalls) have visibility into the traffic.

This method of obtaining a symmetric key for a session completely depends on the secrecy of the private key. Because of this, *perfect forward secrecy* (*PFS*), or just *forward secrecy*, provides a mechanism to prevent the compromise of a private key used to create new session keys from past session keys that were compromised. As a result, PFS eliminates the vulnerability in which a compromised private key can be used to go back and decrypt all previous key exchange conversations. This is important because with a decrypted key exchange, previously used encryption keys could be retrieved to reveal entire transactions or messages.

PFS gained popularity in 2013, as revelations about government monitoring became public. Mainstream news reported on Twitter announcing that it would adopt forward secrecy to protect recorded traffic from potentially being decrypted later.

Nonrepudiation and Digital Signatures

Nonrepudiation is intended to provide, through encryption, a method of accountability that makes it impossible to refute the origin of data. It guarantees that the sender cannot later deny being the sender and that the recipient cannot deny receiving the data. This definition, however, does not factor into the possible compromise of the workstation or system used to create the private key and the encrypted digital signature. The following list outlines four key elements that nonrepudiation services provide on a typical client/server connection:

- ▶ **Proof of origin:** The host gets proof that the client is the originator of particular data or an authentication request from a particular time and location.

- ▶ **Proof of submission:** The client gets proof that the data (or authentication, in this case) has been sent.

- ▶ **Proof of delivery:** The client gets proof that the data (or authentication, in this case) has been received.

- ▶ **Proof of receipt:** The client gets proof that the data (or authentication, in this case) has been received correctly.

Digital signatures provide integrity and authentication. In addition, digital signatures provide nonrepudiation with proof of origin. Although authentication and nonrepudiation might appear to be similar, the difference is that, with nonrepudiation, proof can be demonstrated to a third party.

ExamAlert

Nonrepudiation is the assurance that something can't be denied by someone.

A sender of a message signs the message using his or her private key. This provides unforgeable proof that the sender did indeed generate the message. Nonrepudiation is unique to asymmetric systems because the private (secret) key is not shared. Remember that, in a symmetric system, both parties involved share the secret key; therefore, any party can deny sending a message by claiming that the other party originated the message.

Digital signatures attempt to guarantee the identity of the person sending the data from one point to another. The digital signature acts as an electronic signature used to authenticate the identity of the sender and to ensure the integrity of the original content (to make sure it has not been changed).

Note

Do not confuse the terms *digital signature* and *digital certificate*. (Chapter 25 provides further details.) In addition, do not confuse *digital signatures* with *encryption*. Digital signatures and encryption are related concepts, but their intentions and operations differ significantly. Finally, do not confuse a digital signature with the block of identification information that is often appended to an email, such as the sender's name and telephone number or digitally created image.

Digital signatures can easily be transported and are designed so that no one else can copy them. This ensures that something that is signed cannot be repudiated.

A digital signature does not have to accompany an encrypted message. It can simply be used to assure the receiver of the sender's identity and confirm that the integrity of the message was maintained. The digital signature contains the digital signature of the certificate authority (CA) that issued the certificate for verification.

The point of this verification is to prevent or alert the recipient to any data tampering. Ideally, if a packet of data is digitally signed, it can bear only the original mark of the sender. If this mark differs, the receiver knows that the

packet differs from what it is supposed to be, and either the packet is not unencrypted, or it is dropped altogether. This works based on the encryption algorithm principles discussed previously. If you cannot determine what the original data was in the encrypted data (in this case, the signature), faking the data and convincing the receiver that it is legitimate data is much harder.

Suppose, for example, that you need to digitally sign a document sent to your stockbroker. You need to ensure the integrity of the message and assure the stockbroker that the message is really from you. The exchange looks like this:

1. You type the email.

2. Using software built into your email client, you obtain a hash (which you can think of as digital fingerprint) of the message.

3. You use your private key to encrypt the hash. This encrypted hash is your digital signature for the message.

4. You send the message to your stockbroker.

5. Your stockbroker receives the message. Using software, he makes a hash of the received message.

6. The stockbroker uses your public key to decrypt the message hash.

7. A match of the hashes proves that the message is valid.

Hashing

A hash is a generated summary from a mathematical rule or algorithm that is commonly used as a "digital fingerprint" to verify the integrity of files and messages. *Hashing* ensures message integrity and provides authentication verification. In other words, hashing algorithms are not encryption methods, but they offer additional system security via a "signature" for data to confirm the original content.

A hash function works by taking a string (for example, a password or an email) of any length and producing a fixed-length string for output. Keep in mind that hashing works one-way. Although you can create a hash from a document, you cannot re-create the document from the hash. If this all sounds confusing, the following example should help clear things up. Suppose that you want to send an email to a friend, and you also want to ensure that, during transit, the message cannot be read or altered. You use software that generates a hash value of the message to accompany the email and then encrypts both the hash and the message. When the email is received, the recipient's software decrypts the message and the hash and then produces another hash from the received email.

The two hashes are compared, and a match indicates that the message was not tampered with (because any change in the original message would produce a change in the hash).

A password hash can use a salt, which is an additional input of random data to a function that hashes a password. This process, known as *salting*, helps defend against specific attacks in which hashed values are precomputed (for example, rainbow table attacks). Some of the attacks mentioned here work because users who have the same password would also have the same resulting hash. This problem can be overcome by making the hashes more random. Salting involves using a prefix consisting of a random string of characters added to passwords before they are hashed. Such a countermeasure makes it more difficult or impractical to attack passwords unless the attacker knows the value of the salt that needs to be removed.

Cryptographic hashes are susceptible to collisions and, thus, collision attacks. Recall the example in Chapter 2, "Attack Basics," about the birthday attack used to find collisions within hash functions. Such an attack tries to find two input strings of a hash function that have the same output. Although collisions are not likely, they can occur because hash functions produce a predefined output length, despite taking in an infinite input length.

> **ExamAlert**
>
> Remember that hashing data does not provide for confidentiality (or encryption) but rather provides verification of integrity (that the data hasn't been modified).

Use of Proven Technologies and Implementation

Because of the sensitive nature of cryptography, using well-known, proven technologies is crucial. Backdoors and flaws, for example, can undermine any encryption algorithm. Vendors might have their own encryption solutions, and most of them depend on well-known, time-tested algorithms; you should be skeptical of any vendor using a proprietary unproven algorithm.

Recall from earlier that Kerckhoffs's principle states that a cryptosystem should be secure even if everything about the system is known except for the key. Proven technologies are well-designed cryptosystems. Systems that require keeping the algorithms secret introduce additional measures related to what needs to be protected, and they often provide *security through obscurity*.

In addition to avoiding secret algorithms, or "snake oil" cryptography, be sure to steer clear of weak or deprecated algorithms. Even once-proven technologies can weaken over time. Only algorithms that are public and have been thoroughly reviewed and approved should be used. The National Institute of Standards and Technology (NIST) maintains publications and guidance for the use of approved cryptographic and hashing algorithms. The following is a summary of this and other good practices:

▶ Use well-known and approved cryptographic algorithms.

▶ Adhere to required minimum key guidance for the chosen algorithm.

▶ Use approved cryptographic modes.

▶ Use strong random number generators.

NIST's Federal Information Publication Standard 140-2 (FIPS 140-2) covers the secure design and implementation of cryptographic modules, and NIST provides a program to validate such modules to this standard. Cryptographic modules, or cryptographic service providers (CSPs), are the hardware, software, or firmware that implements cryptographic functions such as encryption, decryption, digital signature, random number generation, authentication, and key management.

Applications and systems can interface with these secure cryptographic modules, helping to ensure sound implementation based on vetted and sound cryptographic modules. However, modules provide varying security levels and options, particularly because different algorithms can be encapsulated within a module. Thus, consideration must be given to algorithm selection and the application to ensure an appropriate level of security. For example, a cryptography algorithm based on factoring and prime numbers uses more bits for keys than cryptography based on the algebraic structure of elliptic curves. As a result, the former requires compute resources, which makes the latter more ideal for mobile devices.

Steganography

A method commonly used for obfuscating data—particularly in media types such as audio, video, image files, and other documents—is steganography.

Steganography is a word of Greek origin that means "hidden writing." It involves hiding messages so that unintended recipients are not aware that there is any message. Compare this to cryptography, which does not seek to hide the fact that a message exists but just makes the message unreadable by anyone other than the intended recipients. Writing a letter using plaintext but in invisible ink is an example of steganography. The content is not scrambled in any way; it is

just hidden. Another interesting example, albeit a bit cumbersome, is the historical use of writing a secret message on the scalp of one's shaved head, allowing the hair to grow back, and then ultimately having it shaved again upon arrival at the intended recipient.

> **ExamAlert**
>
> Steganography is not cryptography. Whereas steganography hides the presence of a message, the purpose of cryptography is to transform a message from its readable plaintext into an unreadable form known as ciphertext.

Of course, steganography is useless if someone other than the intended recipient knows where to look. Therefore, steganography is best used when combined with encryption. If attackers do not even know that a message exists in the first place, they cannot attempt to crack it. As a result, steganography is not just the stuff of child's play or far-fetched spy movies.

Steganography actually entered mainstream media after the terrorist attacks of 9/11. Various reports indicated that the terrorists were (and others still are) using this practice to secretly hide messages. Modern uses include hiding messages in digital media and using digital watermarking. In addition, printers have used steganography, using tiny dots that reveal serial numbers and time stamps.

Cryptography Use Cases

Cryptography has many potential use cases. The following are common examples:

▶ **Confidentiality:** Ensures the privacy of data. This is the most common use case—or at least the one that many tend to think of during discussions on cryptography.

▶ **Integrity:** Ensures the accuracy of the data. Hashing, discussed earlier, is a common mechanism to ensure integrity. Assurance of message integrity, for example, might apply regardless of whether a message was encrypted.

▶ **Nonrepudiation:** Ensures accountability so that the origin of the data cannot be refuted. Nonrepudiation is needed to affirm the authenticity of a digital signature and verify that a message was indeed sent by the originator.

▶ **Authentication:** Ensures the secure transfer of authentication data between two entities or systems. Cryptographic authentication protocols are required for authentication. In addition, encryption and authentication work together. Both have their own responsibilities when it comes to securing communications and data.

> **Note**
>
> These days, it's easy to confuse the "crypto" ideas cryptography and cryptocurrency. Bitcoin, a leading cryptocurrency, is a decentralized currency for which balances are maintained on a public digital ledger known as a *blockchain*. Transactions are grouped into blocks shared with the network. Each block is linked to the previous block through a cryptographic hash. Part of what makes bitcoin so successful is its use of cryptography. A bitcoin wallet consists of two keys: a public key and a private key. Bitcoin can be sent to me by using my public key as the address; using my private key, I can spend bitcoin. Addresses are long alphanumeric numbers and may be represented as QR codes, which can be scanned or photographed with a mobile device for quick access and entry.

Recall from Chapter 9, "Enterprise Security Concepts," that protecting data through encryption and yet maintaining the capability for decryption can be broadly categorized into three high-level areas, based on the state of the data: data at rest, data in transit, or data in processing.

Emerging solutions like *homomorphic encryption* are attempts at providing alternatives to working with data in processing and would allow operations such as searching and sorting to be performed on ciphertext as if it were plaintext.

Other specific use cases and needs continue to exist. Although it is considered insecure on its own, obfuscation is commonly used with encryption. This includes, for example, first encrypting the obfuscated data. A primary use case for obfuscation without encryption involves trying to protect source code from reverse engineering. Research in combining obfuscation and encryption to protect source code continues.

Strong cryptographic implementations demonstrate *resiliency* to leakage and subsequent attacks, and research and development into highly resilient cryptography or leakage-resilient cryptography is continuing. For example, the physical implementation of cryptographic algorithms could leak information (for example, electromagnetic and power consumption), which can be leveraged to break the system.

Cryptography Constraints

Security systems often require trade-offs. Cryptography, for example, consumes resources in a system and carries a cost; security, performance, and power all need to be factored in. Modern computer systems and algorithms work well together. Furthermore, cryptographic implementations have made management easier. In fact, more than half of the web is now encrypted using HTTPS. When it comes to modern cryptography, performance and security have always been two important factors. How is it possible to increase the security robustness of an algorithm or a system without sacrificing speed and introducing more latency? Recently, especially with small and low-power devices, the trade-offs and resource constraints are continually being considered in the search for lighter-weight cryptography.

Cram Quiz

Answer these questions. The answers follow the last question. If you cannot answer these questions correctly, consider reading this chapter again until you can.

1. Which of the following attacks would be rendered ineffective by the use of salting?

   ○ **A.** Hash

   ○ **B.** Brute force

   ○ **C.** Dictionary

   ○ **D.** Rainbow table

2. You are exchanging secure emails with another user. You use a key to encrypt your outbound email, but then you are unable to decrypt the email you receive in return by using the same key you used to encrypt the outbound email. Which best explains what's happening?

   ○ **A.** Email clients do not support cryptography.

   ○ **B.** Asymmetric cryptography is being used.

   ○ **C.** You are using a stream cipher.

   ○ **D.** You are using a block cipher.

3. Which of the following is true regarding block and stream ciphers? (Select three.)

   ○ **A.** Block ciphers are more complex than and not as fast as stream ciphers.

   ○ **B.** Stream ciphers, unlike block ciphers, require padding.

   ○ **C.** Block ciphers have higher diffusion than stream ciphers.

   ○ **D.** Stream ciphers perform encryption bit by bit.

4. Which statement is false?

○ **A.** Symmetric key algorithms use the same private key to encrypt and decrypt.

○ **B.** Symmetric key algorithms are often referred to as public key algorithms.

○ **C.** ECC is an example of an asymmetric public key cryptosystem.

○ **D.** Symmetric key algorithms are typically faster than asymmetric systems.

Cram Quiz Answers

Answer 1: D. A rainbow table attack can be rendered ineffective by salting, which defends against precomputed hash values. Dictionary and brute-force attacks don't necessarily rely on precomputed hash values. Thus, answers B and C are incorrect. Answer A is incorrect because a hash is not a type of attack but instead describes a function.

Answer 2: B. In asymmetric cryptography, key pairs are used: one key to encrypt and the other to decrypt. The email you received would have been encrypted with your public key, and you would need to decrypt the email with your private key. This private key would not have been the key used to encrypt the original outgoing email. You would have used the recipient's public key for that. Answers A, C, and D are incorrect because you were able to originally encrypt an email outbound. Further, most email clients do support cryptography, and stream and block ciphers are methods for encrypting plaintext in symmetric algorithms.

Answer 3: A, C, and D. Stream ciphers do not require padding because each bit is processed and is the smallest unit; thus answer B is incorrect. All the other choices are true statements comparing block ciphers and stream ciphers.

Answer 4: B. Symmetric key algorithms are often referred to as secret key algorithms, private key algorithms, and shared secret algorithms. Asymmetric algorithms are often referred to as public key algorithms because they use the public key as the focal point for the algorithm. Answers A, C, and D are all true statements and are therefore incorrect answer choices.

What Next?

If you want more practice on this chapter's exam objective before you move on, remember that you can access all of the Cram Quiz questions on the Pearson Test Prep software online. You can also create a custom exam by objective with the Online Practice Test. Note any objective you struggle with and go to that objective's material in this chapter.

PART III

Implementation

This part covers the following official Security+ SYO-601 exam objectives for Domain 3.0, "Implementation":

▶ 3.1 Given a scenario, implement secure protocols.

▶ 3.2 Given a scenario, implement host or application security solutions.

▶ 3.3 Given a scenario, implement secure network designs.

▶ 3.4 Given a scenario, install and configure wireless security settings.

▶ 3.5 Given a scenario, implement secure mobile solutions.

▶ 3.6 Given a scenario, apply cybersecurity solutions to the cloud.

▶ 3.7 Given a scenario, implement identity and account management controls.

▶ 3.8 Given a scenario, implement authentication and authorization solutions.

▶ 3.9 Given a scenario, implement public key infrastructure.

For more information on the official CompTIA Security+ SYO-601 exam topics, see the section "Exam Objectives" in the Introduction.

To properly secure a network, you must understand the principles of secure design. This part covers secure protocols, application security, network design, wireless, mobile, cloud, identity, authentication, authorization, and public key infrastructure.

Implementing a secure architecture and design is critical to ensuring that proper controls are in place to meet organizational goals and reduce risk. This part of the book explains how architecture, design, and implementation fit into an organization's security posture.

CHAPTER 17

Secure Protocols

This chapter covers the following official Security+ exam objective:

▶ 3.1 Given a scenario, implement secure protocols.

Essential Terms and Components

▶ Domain Name System Security Extensions (DNSSEC)

▶ Secure Shell (SSH)

▶ Secure/Multipurpose Internet Mail Extensions (S/MIME)

▶ Secure Real-Time Transport Protocol (SRTP)

▶ LDAP over SSL (LDAPS)

▶ File Transfer Protocol, Secure (FTPS)

▶ SSH File Transfer Protocol (SFTP)

▶ Simple Network Management Protocol, version 3 (SNMPv3)

▶ Hypertext Transfer Protocol over SSL (HTTPS)

▶ Internet Protocol Security (IPsec)

▶ Authentication Header (AH)

▶ Encapsulated Security Payload (ESP)

▶ Secure Post Office Protocol, version 3 (POP3)

▶ Internet Message Access Protocol (IMAP)

The network infrastructure is subject to myriad internal and external attacks through services, protocols, and open ports. Older protocols that are still in use might leave a network vulnerable. Protocols such as Simple Network Management Protocol (SNMP) and Domain Name System (DNS) that were developed a long time ago and have been widely deployed can pose security risks, too. You must understand how to properly secure these protocols, especially if the network has been in existence for a while and newer or more secure protocols or versions have been developed. This chapter helps you understand how to use the proper network implementation of secure protocols to protect and mitigate threats against network infrastructure.

Secure Web Protocols

Basic web connectivity using Hypertext Transfer Protocol (HTTP) occurs over TCP port 80. No security is provided against the interception of transacted data sent in plaintext. Web protocol security is usually implemented at two layers: the transport layer and the application layer.

> **ExamAlert**
>
> To secure against web communication interception, transport layer security protocols such as Secure Sockets Layer (SSL) and Transport Layer Security (TLS) are used.

A more secure way to conduct web communication involves using SSL transport protocols operating on port 443, which creates an encrypted pipe through which HTTP traffic can be conducted securely. To differentiate a call to port 80 (http://*servername/*), *HTTP over SSL* calls on port 443, using HTTPS as the URL port designator (https://*servername/*).

HTTPS was originally created by Netscape Corporation. It used a 40-bit RC4 stream encryption algorithm to establish a secure connection encapsulating data transferred between the client and the web server. However, it can also support the use of X.509 digital certificates to allow the user to authenticate the sender. Now 256-bit encryption keys have become the accepted level of secure connectivity for online banking and electronic commerce transactions.

> **ExamAlert**
>
> An alternative to HTTPS is Secure Hypertext Transfer Protocol (S-HTTP), which was developed to support connectivity for banking transactions and other secure web communications. S-HTTP supports DES, 3DES, RC2, and RSA2 encryption, along with CHAP authentication; however, the early web browser developers (for example, Netscape and Microsoft) did not adopt it, so it remains less common than the HTTPS standard.

Although HTTPS encrypts communication between the client and the server, it doesn't guarantee that the merchant is trustworthy or that the merchant's server is secure. SSL/TLS is designed to positively identify the merchant's server and encrypt communication between the client and the server. When organizations use OpenSSL, they need to use version 1.0.1g or newer to avoid being vulnerable to the Heartbleed bug. Secure Sockets Layer (SSL) protocol communications occur between the HTTP (application) and TCP (transport) layers of Internet communications.

Millions of websites use SSL to protect their online transactions with their customers. SSL is a public key–based security protocol that Internet services and clients use for authentication, message integrity, and confidentiality. The SSL process uses certificates for authentication and encryption for message integrity and confidentiality. SSL establishes a stateful connection, in which both ends set up and maintain information about a session during its existence. In contrast, in a stateless connection, no prior connection has been set up. An SSL stateful connection is negotiated through a handshaking procedure between client and server. During this handshake, the client and server exchange the specifications for the cipher that will be used for that session. SSL communicates using an asymmetric key with a cipher strength of 40 bits or 128 bits.

SSL works by establishing a secure channel using public key infrastructure (PKI). This can eliminate the vast majority of attacks, such as session hijacking and information theft. As a general rule, SSL is not as flexible as IPsec (discussed next) from an application perspective, but it is more flexible for access from any location. Organizations must determine the usage requirements for each class of user and then decide on the best approach.

> **Note**
>
> The terms SSL and TLS are often used interchangeably and are denoted as SSL/TLS except when there is a need to refer to one of the protocols separately. Although the SSL protocol was deprecated with the release of TLS 1.0 in 1999, it is still common to refer to these related technologies as "SSL" or "SSL/TLS." The current version is TLS 1.3, defined in RFC 8446.

Another asymmetric key encapsulation (currently considered the successor to SSL) is the Transport Layer Security (TLS) protocol, based on Netscape's Secure Sockets Layer 3.0 (SSL3) transport protocol. TLS provides encryption using stronger encryption methods, such as AES. It can work without encryption altogether if it is desired for authentication only. SSL and TLS transport protocols are similar but not entirely interoperable. TLS also provides confidentiality and data integrity.

TLS has two layers of operation:

- ▶ **TLS Record protocol:** Allows the client and server to communicate using some form of encryption algorithm (or without encryption, if desired).

- ▶ **TLS Handshake protocol:** Allows the client and server to authenticate one another and exchange encryption keys to be used during the session.

Domain Name System (DNS) was originally designed as an open protocol. DNS servers are organized in a hierarchy. At the top level of the hierarchy, root servers store the complete database of Internet domain names and their corresponding IP addresses. Different types of DNS servers exist. The most common types follow:

▶ **Authoritative servers:** These servers are definitive for particular domains and provide information about only those domains. An authoritative-only name server returns answers to queries about just the domain names that have been specifically configured.

▶ **Caching or recursive servers:** These servers use recursion to resolve a given name, from the DNS root through to the authoritative name servers of the queried domain.

DNS does not check for credentials before accepting an answer, and attackers exploit this basic vulnerability. An attacker can cause DNS poisoning by delegating a false name to the domain server and providing a false address for the server. To prevent this from happening, the *Domain Name System Security Extensions (DNSSEC)* protocol was developed. DNSSEC protects against such attacks by providing a validation path for records.

With DNSSEC, validation is done through the use of a key and a signature. To properly validate the path, DNSSEC must be implemented at each domain level. The higher organization level signs the key of the lower domain level. For example, with the domain www.example.com, the root level signs the .com key, and the .com level signs the example.com key. DNSSEC follows the chain of trust from the lowest-level domain to the top-level domain, validating the keys at each level along the way.

> **ExamAlert**
>
> DNSSEC was developed to strengthen DNS through the use of digital signatures and public key cryptography.

Internet Protocol Security (IPsec)

The *Internet Protocol Security (IPsec)* authentication and encapsulation standard is widely used to establish secure VPN communications. IPsec can secure transmissions between critical servers and clients. This helps prevent network-based attacks from taking place. Unlike most security systems that function within the application layer of the OSI model, IPsec functions within the network layer.

IPsec provides authentication services and encapsulation of data through support of the Internet Key Exchange (IKE) protocol.

IPsec can be run in either tunnel mode or transport mode. Transport mode is used between endpoints such as a client and a server. It can also be used between a gateway and an endpoint when the gateway is being treated as an endpoint, such as in a Remote Desktop (RDP) session.

IPsec's default mode is tunnel mode. Tunnel mode is most often used between gateways such as a router and a firewall. When tunnel mode is used, the gateway acts as a proxy for the hosts. In tunnel mode, an AH or ESP header is used. The asymmetric key standard defining IPsec provides two primary security services:

▶ **AH:** *Authentication Header (AH)* provides authentication of the data's sender, along with integrity and nonrepudiation. RFC 2402 states that AH provides authentication for as much of the IP header as possible, as well as for upper-level protocol data. However, some IP header fields might change in transit, and when the packet arrives at the receiver, the value of these fields might not be predictable for the sender. AH cannot protect the values of such fields, so the protection it provides to the IP header is somewhat piecemeal.

▶ **ESP:** *Encapsulating Security Payload* (*ESP*) supports authentication of the data's sender and encryption of the data being transferred, along with confidentiality and integrity protection. ESP is used to provide confidentiality, data origin authentication, connectionless integrity, an antireplay service (a form of partial sequence integrity), and limited traffic-flow confidentiality. The set of services provided depends on options selected at the time of security association establishment and on the placement of the implementation. Confidentiality can be selected independently of all other services. However, the use of confidentiality without integrity/authentication (either in ESP or separately in AH) might make the traffic subject to certain forms of active attacks that could undermine the confidentiality service.

Protocols 51 and 50 are the AH and ESP components of the IPsec protocol. IPsec inserts ESP or AH (or both) as protocol headers into an IP datagram that immediately follows an IP header.

The protocol field of the IP header is 50 for ESP or 51 for AH. If IPsec is configured to do authentication instead of encryption, you must configure an IP filter to let protocol 51 traffic pass. If IPsec uses nested AH and ESP, you can configure an IP filter to let only protocol 51 (AH) traffic pass.

IPsec supports the Internet Key Exchange (IKE) protocol, which is a key management standard used to allow separate key protocols to be specified for use during data encryption. IKE functions within Internet Security Association and Key Management Protocol (ISAKMP), which defines the payloads used to exchange key and authentication data appended to each packet.

> **ExamAlert**
>
> IPsec provides secure VPN and Internet communications by authenticating and encrypting network data packets.

Secure File Transfer Protocols

File Transfer Protocol (FTP) passes a username and password in a plaintext form. Attackers can thus use packet sniffing on the network traffic to read these values and possibly use them to gain unauthorized access to the server. *File Transfer Protocol Secure (FTPS*, also called FTP-SSL), is an FTP extension that adds support for TLS and SSL. FTPS supports channel encryption, as defined in RFC 2228.

With FTPS, data transfers take place so that the parties can authenticate each other. It prevents eavesdropping, tampering, and forgery on the messages exchanged. FTPS includes full support for the TLS and SSL cryptographic protocols, including the use of server-side public key authentication certificates and client-side authorization certificates. In addition, FTPS supports compatible ciphers, including AES, RC4, RC2, Triple DES, and DES. It supports the hash functions SHA1, MD5, MD4, and MD2.

Secure variations of FTP ensure that data cannot be intercepted during transfer and allow the use of more secure transfer of user access credentials during FTP logon. SSH File Transfer Protocol (SFTP) uses Secure Shell (SSH) to transfer files. Unlike standard FTP, it encrypts both commands and data, preventing passwords and sensitive information from being transmitted in plaintext over the network. It is functionally similar to FTP but uses a different protocol. Therefore, a standard FTP client cannot talk to an SFTP server, nor can an FTP server connect to a client that supports only SFTP. SFTP is similar to the secure copy protocol (SCP) in that they both securely transfer files between hosts using SSH. While SCP is more efficient, it does not provide the remote function capabilities of SFTP such as the ability to remove files or perform a directory listing.

Do not confuse SFTP (SSH File Transfer Protocol) with FTPS (FTP Secure). FTPS uses more than one port and can be either implicit or explicit. FTPS (Implicit) uses TCP port 990 for commands and uses passive ports for data. FTPS (Explicit) uses TCP port 21 for commands and uses passive ports for data. Either SFTP or FTPS can be used in an enterprise network.

Secure Email Protocols

The Multipurpose Internet Mail Extensions (MIME) protocol extended the capability of the original Simple Mail Transfer Protocol (SMTP) to allow the inclusion of non-textual data within an email message. Embedding data within an email message is an easy way to send images, audio and video files, and many other types of non-ASCII text. To provide a secure method of transmission, the *Secure/Multipurpose Internet Mail Extensions* (*S/MIME*) protocol was developed. S/MIME is a widely accepted technology for sending digitally signed and encrypted messages that provides authentication, message integrity, and nonrepudiation. S/MIME is based on the following standards:

▶ Asymmetric cryptography, using the algorithms RSA, DSA, or elliptic curve

▶ Symmetric cryptography, using Advanced Encryption Standard (AES)

▶ Cryptographic Message Syntax, which provides the underlying key security

(For more detailed information on how asymmetric and symmetric cryptography works, refer to Chapter 16, "Cryptographic Concepts.") When S/MIME is used to secure email, the technology behind it increases security and verifies that the message received is the exact message sent.

Other email protocols, such as *Post Office Protocol, version 3* (*POP3*) and *Internet Message Access Protocol* (*IMAP*), can also be used in a more secure way. One of the biggest security issues with POP and IMAP is that login credentials are transmitted in plaintext over unencrypted connections. Keep in mind that POP3 and IMAP are used for retrieving email, whereas SMTP, over port 25, is used for

sending email. In secure POP3 or IMAP mail, the communication occurs over an SSL/TLS session, which mitigates this insecurity. Encrypting mail during transmission protects the communication and makes reading the email more difficult for an attacker. Because a certificate is used to verify the identity of the server to the client, the connection fails if a valid certificate is not present.

> **ExamAlert**
>
> Using POP3S (port 995) or IMAPS (port 993) allows the incoming data from the client to be encrypted because these protocols use an SSL/TLS session. SMTP is for outgoing email.

The ports used by secure versions of protocols differ from the ports used by insecure protocols. POP3 communicates over port 110, while POP3S uses port 995. IMAP communicates over port 143, while IMAPS uses port 993. Many sites disable IMAP and POP3 completely, forcing the use of an SSL/TLS-encrypted connection.

Secure Internet Protocols

The web, email, and file transfer are three of the most common applications used over the Internet. In addition to the protocols discussed earlier in this chapter, this section covers several other general Internet protocols you should be familiar with.

As a more secure replacement for the common command-line terminal utility Telnet, the *Secure Shell (SSH)* utility establishes a session between a client and host computers, using an authenticated and encrypted connection. SSH requires encryption of all data, including the login portion. SSH uses the asymmetric (public key) RSA cryptography method to provide both connection and authentication.

Data encryption is accomplished using one of the following algorithms:

▶ **International Data Encryption Algorithm (IDEA):** The default encryption algorithm used by SSH, which uses a 128-bit symmetric key block cipher.

▶ **Blowfish:** A symmetric (private key) encryption algorithm that uses a variable 32- to 448-bit secret key.

▶ **Data Encryption Standard (DES):** A symmetric key encryption algorithm using a random key selected from a large number of shared

keys. Most forms of this algorithm cannot be used in products meant for export from the United States.

▶ **Triple Data Encryption Standard (3DES):** A symmetric key encryption algorithm that dramatically improves upon the DES by using the DES algorithm three times with three distinct keys.

Using SSH helps guard against attacks such as eavesdropping, man-in-the-middle attacks, and spoofing. Attempts to spoof the identity of either side of a communication can be thwarted because each packet is encrypted using a key known only by the local and remote systems.

ExamAlert

Some versions of SSH, including Secure Shell for Windows Server, provide a secure version of File Transfer Protocol (SFTP) along with the other common SSH utilities.

Lightweight Directory Access Protocol (LDAP)

Lightweight Directory Access Protocol (LDAP) is a directory services protocol used on IP networks. By default, LDAP traffic is unsecured; that is, attackers can use network-monitoring programs to view LDAP traffic, including Active Directory (AD)–associated services that use LDAP for authentication. Encryption is recommended when LDAP is used over a network that is not secure.

ExamAlert

LDAP over SSL (LDAPS) is used to secure Lightweight Directory Access Protocol (LDAP) by enabling communication over SSL/TLS.

As with web, mail, and FTP protocols, LDAPS uses SSL/TLS to establish an encrypted tunnel to prevent traffic from being read. With LDAPS, the encrypted tunnel occurs between an LDAP client and a Windows AD domain controller. This is the process used for LDAPS communication:

1. An LDAP session is started between a client and the LDAP server, commonly referred to as the Directory System Agent (DSA) on default port 636. The Global Catalog is accessed via port 3269.

2. The server sends a client operation request response. The various requests a client can make include bind, search, and entry editing.

The DSA is the database that stores information hierarchically for easy retrieval. Information is encoded pursuant to the Basic Encoding Rules (BER) used by X.500 directories and is specified in RFC 4522.

Secure Real-Time Transport Protocol (SRTP)

Real-Time Transport Protocol (RTP) is used for video and audio communications on IP networks. As with many of the other protocols discussed previously, the design is inherently insecure, allowing for eavesdropping and communication interception. Support for RTP encryption in service provider gateways is lacking because of the inherent design. It is not possible to provide privacy and security for calls that go over the public switched telephone network (PSTN). The most common use of RTP is for VoIP. VoIP network communications are subject to the same attacks as other Internet communication methods.

Secure Real-Time Transport Protocol (SRTP or Secure RTP) is an extension to RTP that incorporates enhanced security features. As with RTP, it is intended particularly for voice over IP (VoIP) or video network communications.

SRTP adds confidentiality, message authentication, and replay protection to the communication exchange. UDP is still used as the RTP transport protocol, but keys are exchanged to enable encryption; this is similar to the HTTPS process used for secure web mail.

Simple Network Management Protocol (SNMP)

SNMP is an application layer protocol whose purpose is to collect statistics from TCP/IP devices. SNMP is used to monitor the health of network equipment, computer equipment, and devices such as uninterruptible power supplies (UPSs).

Simple Network Management Protocol, version 3 (SNMPv3) is the current standard, but some devices still use SNMPv1 or SNMPv2. The SNMP management infrastructure consists of three components:

▶ SNMP managed node

▶ SNMP agent

▶ SNMP network management station

The device loads the agent, which collects the information and forwards it to the management station. Network management stations collect a massive amount of critical network information and are likely to be targets of intruders. Using SNMP can help malicious users learn a lot about a system.

Many of the vulnerabilities associated with SNMP stem from using SNMPv1. Although these vulnerabilities were discovered many years ago, vulnerabilities are still being reported with current SNMP components. The only security measure SNMPv1 has in place is its community name, which is similar to a password. By default, the community name is public and often is not changed, thus leaving the information wide open to intruders.

SNMPv2 focused on performance more than security. One improvement was the implementation of Message Digest Algorithm 5 (MD5) for authentication between the server and the agent. SNMPv2 did not provide a way to authenticate the source of a management message, nor did it provide encryption. The plaintext password could still be sniffed from network traffic and was subject to replay attacks. SNMPv3 attempted to address the deficiencies in SNMPv2 by defining an overall SNMP architecture that included a set of security capabilities. SNMPv3 changed the structure to include access control, authentication, and privacy as a result of adding cryptographic security—specifically, support for AES and 3DES encryption.

SNMPv3 uses the same ports as SNMPv1 and SNMPv2. UDP port 161 is required for polling, and port 162 is required for notifications. SNMPv3 can also run over TCP. Figure 17.1 shows the layout of SNMPv3.

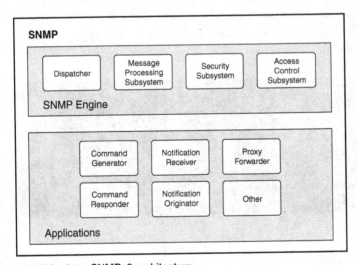

FIGURE 17.1 **SNMPv3 architecture**

RFC 2271 defines these components of an SNMP entity (refer to Figure 17.1):

▶ **Dispatcher:** Allows for concurrent support of multiple versions of SNMP messages

▶ **SNMP message processing subsystem:** Prepares messages for sending and extracts data from received messages

▶ **SNMP security subsystem:** Provides message security services

▶ **SNMP access control subsystem:** Provides authorization services

▶ **SNMP command generator:** Initiates request PDUs and processes the responses

▶ **SNMP command responder:** Receives request PDUs destined for the local system

▶ **SNMP notification originator:** Monitors a system and generates trap messages

▶ **SNMP notification receiver:** Listens for notification messages and generates response messages

▶ **SNMP proxy forwarder:** Forwards SNMP messages

With this improved architecture, the authentication mechanism provides a check to ensure that the received message was transmitted by the principal in the header, that no alteration occurred during transit, and that there was no purposeful delay or replay. The Data Encryption Standard (DES) algorithm is used to maintain privacy between a principal and a remote engine. The capability to allow different access levels in the agent configuration provides more granular access control.

ExamAlert

SNMPv3 introduces cryptographic security:

▶ **Confidentiality:** Provides encryption to prevent eavesdropping by an unauthorized source.

▶ **Integrity:** Ensures that data has not been tampered with while in transit and includes a packet replay protection mechanism.

▶ **Authentication:** Establishes that the message is from a valid source.

Secure Protocol Use Cases

Use cases for secure protocols can be either business or system focused. Business use cases look less at technology and more at how the business can help users get the end result they are seeking. In a system user case, technology is used to help users get the end result they are seeking. This section discusses system use cases. Use cases vary in terms of levels of complexity and difficulty, but they primarily explain the interaction of systems and environments. The use cases presented here are examples of how many of the secure protocols described previously in this chapter are applied.

Secure Web Communication

Because much of our daily activity is conducted via the Internet, web communication security is paramount in any organization. Depending on the protocol used, web communication security can involve one or more of the following: authentication, authorization, and message protection.

Using HTTPS for Web Communications

Use cases for deploying HTTPS in web communications are numerous. Whenever a website has any kind of nonpublic information, such as logins, HTTPS should be used. Some basic uses follow:

▶ A website that includes logins used only by administrators, such as an internal WordPress website

▶ User credentials that are required in a transaction, such as on bank websites, on sites that accept credit card payments, and with medical information access (One of the most well-known examples is PayPal.)

▶ Session cookies in which user credentials are stored

▶ Cloud-based environment communications

▶ Media streaming to protect privacy and to keep third-party analytics from collecting viewer data (Perhaps the most well-known implementation example is Netflix.)

▶ A method to prevent man-in-the-middle content hijacking

▶ A way to prohibit phishing websites and protect brand identity

By far the most common use case for HTTPS is secure communication for sites that collect sensitive data. Generally, use of HTTPS has become the norm. According to Google's Transparency Report, more than 50% of web pages loaded by desktop users are over HTTPS. In January 2017, Google began flagging HTTP pages that collect sensitive data as insecure.

Using SSL/TLS for Remote Access

Most devices inherently support SSL/TLS, so organizations do not need to install client-side software. The main purpose of SSL/TLS is to secure data in transit. SSL/TLS can be used in many different ways. The following use cases are particular to securing remote access communications:

▶ Virtual environment application access

▶ Remote administrative functions

▶ SSL VPN

▶ Connection to an internal application over HTTPS

The most common use case for using SSL/TLS for remote access is an SSL VPN. SSL VPNs, which work at Layers 5 and 6 of the OSI model, are the preferred choice for remote access. Because SSL/TLS VPN access can be initiated via a web browser, organizations can take advantage of an IT cost reduction benefit.

Using DNSSEC for Domain Name Resolution

As discussed previously in this chapter, DNS is inherently unsecure. The principle behind DNSSEC is that it functions as a way to provide a new PKI for authenticating Internet services. As DNSSEC becomes the foundation for secure Internet communication, use cases will continue to grow. Consider the most common DNSSEC use cases:

▶ Protection from DNS cache poisoning

▶ PKI usage within DNS

▶ DNS-Based Authentication of Named Entities (DANE), which enables the validation of X.509 certificates tied to TLS using DNSSEC lookups

▶ SSH host fingerprint posting (SSHFP) in DNS

The most common use case for DNSSEC for DNS is protection from DNS poisoning. The Internet Society maintains ongoing statistics regarding the adoption of DNSSEC. Recent reports indicate that a majority of top-level domain (TLD) zones are signed.

Secure File Transfer Communication

FTP is not considered a secure protocol because it does not provide for any type of encryption during data transfer. In March 2017, the FBI issued a Private Industry Notification to healthcare providers outlining how cybercriminals were gaining access to personally identifiable information (PII) patient data via anonymous access on FTP servers.

Using FTPS and SFTP for File Transfer

SFTP and FTPS are more secure file transfer options than FTP, with strong authentication capabilities. Organizations should use FTPS when they need to transfer sensitive or confidential data between a client and a server that is configured to use SSL for secure transactions.

SFTP is easier to implement in regard to firewalls because only port 22 needs to be opened. FTPS, on the other hand, uses multiple port numbers because it uses a control channel and opens new connections for the data transfer. Here are some of the most common use cases for FTPS and SFTP:

▶ Publishing files on an internal web portal

▶ Performing transparent FTP tunneling

▶ Downloading files from servers that are located on the Internet through a DMZ

▶ Reducing risks during data exchanges

▶ Meeting compliance requirements

▶ Performing server-to-server file transfer

▶ Conducting large or bulk file transfers

One of the most common use cases for the implementation of FTPS and SFTP is compliance. Laws such as HIPAA, PCI DSS, SOX, and GLBA require secure file transfers to protect confidential data. Failing to implement proper protections can result in penalties and reputation damage.

Some organizations opt for using a managed file transfer (MFT) service or application to secure FTP communications. Using this type of solution provides secure internal, external, and ad hoc file transfers. Industries including healthcare, accounting, engineering, insurance, legal, and manufacturing commonly use MFT solutions.

Secure Email Communications

Like file transfer protocols, email protocols were not built with security in mind. Unprotected email leaves an organization vulnerable to attacks and disclosure of confidential data. Email can be secured via S/MIME, POP3S, and IMAPS.

Using S/MIME, POP3S, and IMAPS for Email

S/MIME requires a PKI infrastructure so that clients can be issued certificates. S/MIME is used for confidentiality and integrity. POP3S and IMAPS use SSL as a method to secure emails in transit between a POP server or an IMAP server and the client. Because no control governs how the message is transferred between external servers, end-to-end message protection is not guaranteed. Here are some common use cases for secure email:

▶ Protecting confidential user information such as credit card numbers

▶ Encrypting messages to prevent identity theft

▶ Securing internal client messages

▶ Protecting email passwords from easily being read by someone intercepting the traffic between a client computer and an email server

Because S/MIME is a client-based protocol, the most common use case for this protocol is securing internal client messages. The client side is responsible for protecting the message. The message is protected until the authorized recipient opens it. Organizations choose S/MIME when they want to secure messages from client to client because it is a cost-effective way to implement encryption and digital signing of email.

> **ExamAlert**
>
> POP3S and IMAPS are mainly used to secure connections between client machines and their associated servers.

For example, Microsoft strongly recommends using TLS and SSL to secure communications between POP3 and IMAP clients and the Microsoft Exchange Client Access server. This use case is associated with protecting email passwords from easily being read by someone intercepting the traffic between a client computer and an email server.

Mail servers can also use DNSSEC verification to ensure that the server responsible for accepting email messages for the domain name is authentic and then retrieve the certificate fingerprint using secure mechanisms that bind the certificate to the domain.

Securing Internal Communications

Internal communications need to be secured not only from external threats but from internal threats as well. When business partners and vendors are able to access the same network and organizational users, additional measures to secure communication must be implemented. According to a recent Kaspersky report, 52% of businesses admit that the careless actions of employees put IT security at risk.

Using SRTP for Voice and Video

SRTP can secure voice and video. RFC 7201 lists several use cases in which SRTP can be implemented to secure voice and video:

▶ **Media security for SIP-established sessions:** This framework uses SIP with SDP procedures to exchange network addresses when the server endpoint has an SRTP-enabled server running.

▶ **Media security for WebRTC sessions:** In this implementation, JavaScript web application real-time media is transported using RTP and protected using a mandatory application of SRTP.

▶ **IP Multimedia Subsystem (IMS) security:** IMS media security uses end-to-access-edge security. SRTP is terminated in the first node in the core network.

▶ **Real-Time Streaming Protocol:** Using TLS-protected signaling, the client and server agree on the secure media transport of SRTP over UDP when doing the setup request and response.

Perhaps the most common use case for securing voice and video with SRTP is the first use case: security for SIP-established sessions. Cisco has published an extensive white paper on securing Internet telephony media with SRTP

and SDP. It is a guide for applying SRTP to voice, fax, and other IP telephony media for engineers and network administrators.

An everyday use case for SRTP is videoconferencing with Skype Connect, which uses TLS and SRTP to encrypt SIP messages and media streams between Skype and the organization's communication platform.

Using LDAPS for Directory Services

Much of organization communication is not restricted to the internal infrastructure, so encryption is recommended when LDAP is used over an insecure network. LDAPS works by using TLS to authenticate the connection between the LDAP client and the LDAP server. The data exchanges are then encrypted by a TLS-supported cipher suite. The following are some common use cases for LDAPS:

▶ Establishing an encrypted tunnel between an LDAP client and a Windows domain controller (DC)

▶ Securing LDAP subprotocols such as LDAP bind

▶ Preventing attackers from using network-monitoring software to read LDAP traffic between clients and DCs

▶ Using an application that integrates with AD and thus requires LDAP communication to be encrypted

---

ExamAlert

Organizations generally use LDAPS to protect the authentication session when an application authenticates with Active Directory Domain Services (AD DS).

A well-documented use case for using LDAPS with AD-integrated applications is Oracle PeopleSoft. An SSL connection is established between PeopleSoft and LDAP. For this to work correctly, SSL must be configured in both PeopleSoft and on the directory server.

Using SNMPv3 with Routing and Switching

SNMPv3 is designed to provide added security to earlier versions of the SNMP protocol. For a network that is publicly accessible, it is best to use SNMPv3, which provides more secure access and encryption. Keep in mind that added

security features on routers and switches result in reduced performance. Consider some use cases for SNMPv3 with routing and switching devices:

▶ Verifying that a message originated from a trusted source

▶ Validating that a packet has not been modified in transit

▶ Eliminating plaintext SNMP data on the network

▶ Securely monitoring interface counters, bandwidth usage, CPU load, and traps

▶ Securely backing up configuration files

The most common use case for SNMPv3 with routing and switching is to eliminate plaintext SNMP data on the network. SNMPv3 allows for granular control and advanced security mechanisms. It also does away with having to use the default read/write public community string that is accessible from anywhere. When SNMPv3 is used with routing and switching, common configurations include enforcing an SNMP view that restricts the download of full IP routing and ARP tables, using the maximum security level supported by SNMP managers, and using encrypted communication wherever possible.

Using Network Address Allocation

It is important to approach network address allocation with security in mind. Proper planning of IP address space across all layers of an organization network is critical to good traffic flow and adequate protection. Planning network address allocation entails dividing the network into subnets. Subnetting can be done for several reasons. If you have an IPv4 Class C address and 1,000 clients, you need to subnet the network or use a custom subnet mask to accommodate all the hosts.

Use cases for subnetting include the following:

▶ Network traffic control

▶ Improved network security

▶ Hosts arranged into different logical groups that isolate each subnet into its own mini-network

▶ Divisions based on business goals and security policy objectives

▶ Separation of branch offices

▶ Separation of intranets and extranets

The most common use case for network subnetting is to control network traffic. Splitting one network into two or more and using routers to connect the subnets means that broadcasts can be limited to each subnet. However, often networks are subnetted to improve network security, not just performance. Subnet divisions can be based on business goals and security policy objectives. For example, perhaps you use contract workers and want to keep them separated from the organization employees. Organizations with branches often use subnets to keep the branches separate. Other instances of subnetting include intranets and extranets.

When subnetting for IPv4 is done, an IP address usually originates from one of the IP address classes and default subnet masks listed in Table 17.1.

TABLE 17.1 **IPv4 Address Class, IP Range, and Default Subnet Mask**

Address Class	IP Address Range	Default Subnet Mask
Class A	0.0.0.0 to 126.255.255.255	255.0.0.0
Class B	128.0.0.0 to 191.255.255.255	255.255.0.0
Class C	192.0.0.0 to 223.255.255.255	255.255.255.0

Notice that the 127 network address is missing. Although the 127.0.0.0 network is technically in the Class A area, using addresses in this range causes the protocol software to return data without sending traffic across a network. For example, the address 127.0.0.1 is used for TCP/IPv4 loopback testing, and the address 127.0.0.2 is used for testing purposes.

Special ranges in each IP address class are used specifically for private addressing. These addresses are not considered routable on the Internet.

Take a look at the private address ranges:

▶ **Class A:** 10.0.0.0 network. Valid host IDs are from 10.0.0.1 to 10.255.255.254.

▶ **Class B:** 172.16.0.0 through 172.31.0.0 networks. Valid host IDs are from 172.16.0.1 through 172.31.255.254.

▶ **Class C:** 192.168.0.0 network. Valid host IDs are from 192.168.0.1 to 192.168.255.254.

To denote the network prefix for a subnet mask, the number of bits in the prefix is appended to the address with a slash (/) separator. This type of notation is called *classless interdomain routing (CIDR)*. Consider an example: A Class C internal address 192.168.0.0 with subnet mask 255.255.255.0 is written as 192.168.0.0/24.

IPv6 is designed to replace IPv4. IPv6 addresses are 128 bits instead of the 32 bits used in IPv4. IPv6 addresses are represented in hexadecimal. In IPv6, subnets use IPv6 addresses with 64 bits for the host portion. These addresses can be further subnetted, just as in IPv4. IPv6 is based on the concepts of variable-length subnet masking (VLSM) and CIDR. VLSM allocates IP addresses to subnets based on individual need instead of as a general network-wide rule. An example of CIDR notation for IPv6 is 2001:db8::/32, designating the address 2001:db8:: with a network prefix that consists of the most significant 32 bits. Just as in IPv4, blocks of addresses are set aside in IPv6 for private addresses. In IPv6, internal addresses are called unique local addresses (ULAs). Addresses starting with fe80: are called link-local addresses and are routable only in the local link area.

Figure 17.2 shows an internal network with two different subnets. This is an example of securing internal client messages. Notice the IP addresses, subnet masks, and default gateway.

ExamAlert

Watch for scenarios or examples similar to Figure 17.2, which ask you to identify a correct or incorrect subnet mask, default gateway address, or router.

IP Address: 192.168.1.15
Subnet Mask: 255.255.255.0
Default Gateway: 192.168.1.1

IP Address: 192.168.2.15
Subnet Mask: 255.255.255.0
Default Gateway: 192.168.2.1

Subnet
192.168.1.0  Subnet
192.168.2.0

IP Address: 192.168.1.25
Subnet Mask: 255.255.255.0
Default Gateway: 192.168.1.1

IP Address: 192.168.2.25
Subnet Mask: 255.255.255.0
Default Gateway: 192.168.2.1

FIGURE 17.2 **A segmented network**

Notice in Figure 17.2 that the subnets 192.168.1.0 and 192.168.2.0 are identified next to the router. These are not valid IP addresses for a network router; they are used to identify the 192.168.1.x and 192.168.2.x networks in routing tables.

Allocating network addresses can be done either statically or dynamically. Often client addresses are assigned via Dynamic Host Configuration Protocol (DHCP). This method is much easier than manual configuration, and DHCP has the capability to push out DNS configuration changes. DHCP servers face many of the same security problems associated with other network services, such as DNS servers.

Using Time Synchronization

Network Time Protocol (NTP) is a UDP communication protocol used to synchronize devices with a network time server. NTP time servers are arranged in a hierarchy, much like domain name servers. Accurate time is necessary for many network operations. Here are some use cases for time synchronization:

► Time-synchronized encryption and protocols such as Kerberos

► Time stamps in logs to track security breaches

► The modification times in shared filesystems

► Billing services and applications

► Regulatory mandates that require accurate time stamping

► Channel-based audio

► Surgical operations that are run simultaneously

► Digital certificates

Like many other older protocols, NTP has weaknesses. Exploitation of NTP weaknesses can result in time alterations and DoS attacks that shut down the server. In 2007, the Internet Engineering Task Force (IETF) began work on Network Time Security (NTS), a mechanism for using Transport Layer Security (TLS) and Authenticated Encryption with Associated Data (AEAD) to provide cryptographic security for NTP. NTS was submitted for review several years ago, and as of 2020, it was an approved draft RFC awaiting publication as a standard.

Using Subscription Services

Technology is advancing at a very fast rate, and organizations often have a hard time keeping up. We now have *anything as a service (XaaS)* to help. With this business model, companies offer services that are delivered via the Internet. Subscription services are part of XaaS, and they enable organizations to avoid the expense of upgrading hardware and software. The organization pays a monthly fee for a certain number of users or devices, and the service provider takes care of the software or hardware requirements. One of the most prominent subscription services is Microsoft Office 365, which bundles Office 365 with Windows 10. Consider some additional use cases for subscription services:

▶ Gateway antivirus and antispyware

▶ Web and application filtering

▶ IPSs/IDSs

▶ Network automation and data analytics

▶ Malware detection and quarantining

▶ Desktop and server hardware

Using a subscription model for IT offers direct benefits. For example, subscription services might be good for smaller organizations that would not be able to afford the outright purchase of hardware or software. Subscription services can also benefit larger organizations, especially with hardware.

ExamAlert

Remember that *anything as a service* (XaaS) refers primarily to the vast array of services available over the Internet via cloud computing technologies.

For example, take a look at the Microsoft 365 use case. If an organization has to replace thousands of PCs to meet the hardware requirements of Windows 10, it must provide the cost of the new machines and then deal with all the old hardware. Under a subscription service, Microsoft takes care of having equipment to run the OS; the user merely needs a browser.

Regarding security and subscription services, organizations choose a provider they can trust. Uptime, level of service, and security are all spelled out in a service-level agreement (SLA).

Cram Quiz

Answer these questions. The answers follow the last question. If you cannot answer these questions correctly, consider reading this chapter again until you can.

1. Which one of the following ports would block outgoing email?

   - ○ **A.** 25
   - ○ **B.** 110
   - ○ **C.** 443
   - ○ **D.** 22

2. Which of the following protocols use SSH? (Select two.)

   - ○ **A.** SCP
   - ○ **B.** FTPS
   - ○ **C.** SFTP
   - ○ **D.** SSL

3. What two primary security services does the asymmetric key standard defining IPsec provide?

   - ○ **A.** DNSSEC and S/MIME
   - ○ **B.** SRTP and LDAPS
   - ○ **C.** SMTP and SNMPv3
   - ○ **D.** AH and ESP

Cram Quiz Answers

Answer 1: A. Port 25 would block outgoing email. This is the unsecured port for SMTP, which sends mail. Answer B is incorrect as this is the port for POP3, which is used to retrieve email. Answer C is incorrect, as this is the port for secure web access over HTTPS. Answer D is incorrect, as this is the port used for SSH and SFTP.

Answer 2: A and C. Both SCP and SFTP use SSH. Do not get confused here. SSH FTP (SFTP) uses SSH, whereas FTP Secure (FTPS) uses SSL. SSL does not use SSH either. Therefore, answers B and D are incorrect.

Answer 3: D. The asymmetric key standard defining IPsec provides two primary security services: Authentication Header (AH), which provides authentication of the data's sender, along with integrity and nonrepudiation, and Encapsulating Security Payload (ESP), which supports authentication of the data's sender and encryption of the data being transferred, along with confidentiality and integrity protection. Answers A, B, and C are incorrect because DNSSEC was developed to strengthen DNS through the use of

digital signatures and public key cryptography. S/MIME is a widely accepted technology for sending digitally signed messages. SRTP is used to secure VoIP or video network communications. LDAPS protects the authentication session when an application authenticates with Active Directory. SMTP, over port 25, is used for sending email. SNMPv3 is used to collect statistics from TCP/IP devices.

What Next?

If you want more practice on this chapter's exam objective before you move on, remember that you can access all of the Cram Quiz questions on the Pearson Test Prep software online. You can also create a custom exam by objective with the Online Practice Test. Note any objective you struggle with and go to that objective's material in this chapter.

CHAPTER 18

Host and Application Security Solutions

This chapter covers the following official Security+ exam objective:

▶ 3.2 Given a scenario, implement host or application security solutions.

Essential Terms and Components

▶ antivirus

▶ anti-malware

▶ endpoint detection and response (EDR)

▶ data loss prevention (DLP)

▶ host-based intrusion prevention system (HIPS)

▶ host-based intrusion detection system (HIDS)

▶ host-based firewall

▶ boot integrity

▶ database tokenization

▶ secure cookie

▶ code signing

▶ allow list

▶ block list/deny list

▶ static code analysis

▶ dynamic code analysis

▶ fuzzing

▶ system hardening

▶ self-encrypting drive (SED)

▶ full disk encryption (FDE)

▶ hardware root of trust

▶ Trusted Platform Module (TPM)

▶ sandboxing

Endpoint Protection

Organizational attacks are likely to continue increasing in complexity, and all host devices must have some type of malware protection. Malicious code authors are using the dark parts of the Internet to create smarter, shadier, and stealthier threats. Worse, those authors can adeptly camouflage their work.

Firewalls and HIPS/HIDS Solutions

Desktops and laptops need to have layered security, just as servers do. However, many organizations stop this protection at antivirus software. In today's environment, that might not be enough to ward off malware, phishing, and rootkits. One of the most common ways to protect desktops and laptops is to use a host firewall. A firewall can consist of hardware, software, or a combination of both. For the purposes of this chapter, the discussion focuses on software firewalls, or *host-based firewalls* that can be implemented in the user environment.

The potential for hackers to access data through a user's machine has grown substantially as hacking tools have become more sophisticated and difficult to spot. This is especially true for telecommuters' machines. Always-connected computers, typically with cable modems, give attackers plenty of time to discover and exploit system vulnerabilities. Many software firewalls are available, and most operating systems come with them. Users can opt for the OS vendor firewall or can install a separate host-based firewall.

Firewalls have strengths and weaknesses. By design, firewalls close off systems to scanning and entry by blocking ports or nontrusted services and applications. However, firewalls must be properly configured. Typically, the first time a program tries to access the Internet, a software firewall asks whether it should permit the communication. Some users might find this annoying and, consequently, either disable the firewall or else allow all communications because they do not understand what the software is asking. Another caveat is that some firewalls monitor only for incoming connections, not outgoing ones. Monitoring outbound connections is important in the case of malware that "phones home." Without this type of protection, the environment is not properly protected. Remember that even a good firewall cannot protect you if users do not think before downloading and do not exercise a proper level of caution. No system is foolproof, but software firewalls installed on user systems can help make the computing environment safer.

Host-based intrusion detection system (HIDS) solutions involve processes running on a host monitoring event, application logs, port access, and other running processes to identify signatures or behaviors that indicate an attack or

unauthorized access attempt. Some HIDS solutions involve deploying on each host individual client applications that relay their findings to a central IDS server, which is responsible for compiling the data to identify distributed trends. Table 18.1 details some strengths of host-based IDS solutions.

TABLE 18.1 **Strengths of Host-Based IDS Solutions**

Strength	Description
Low number of false positives	Because HIDS solutions analyze logged events, both success and failure events can be monitored, with alerts generated only after passing a proper threshold.
Change monitoring auditing	HIDS solutions can monitor individual processes on each host, including changes to the auditing process.
Non-network attack detection	HIDS solutions can be used to monitor events on standalone systems, including access from the keyboard.
Encrypted communication monitoring	Some attacks make use of encrypted or encapsulated data communications, bypassing network-based IDS.
Cost savings by directed monitoring	Unlike network-based IDS systems, which must monitor all data traffic across the monitored network, host-based solutions require no additional hardware purchasing and can be deployed on systems that require only an IDS.
Single-point monitoring	In large switched networks, network-based IDS solutions can be inadvertently or purposefully bypassed by using a secondary access route. HIDS solutions are not limited to a particular communications path for detection.

Host-based intrusion prevention system (HIPS) solutions are a necessity in any enterprise environment. HIPS solutions protect hosts against known and unknown malicious attacks from the network layer up through the application layer. HIPS technologies can be categorized based on what they scan for, how they recognize an attack, and at what layer they attempt to detect the attack. HIPS systems encompass many technologies to protect servers, desktops, and laptops. A HIPS may be used as an all-in-one solution that includes everything from traditional signature-based antivirus technology to behavior analysis.

ExamAlert

The exam might use two different acronyms in intrusion detection questions: NIDS and NIPS. A network-based intrusion detection system (NIDS) examines data traffic to identify unauthorized access attempts and generate alerts. Network-based intrusion prevention system (NIPS) solutions are intended to provide direct protection against identified attacks. A NIDS solution might be configured to automatically drop connections from a range of IP addresses during a DoS attack, for example.

When using HIDS/HIPS solutions, you leave the security decisions up to the user. When a program runs with elevated privileges or for the first time, it gives the user the option to either allow or block the action. The system is only as good as the user's response. Most users choose the Allow option, inadvertently allowing the system to be infected.

In analyzing the output from HIDS and HIPS solutions, the biggest issue is false positives. For example, a HIPS monitors changes that other software programs attempt to make on the local system. Registry keys are problematic because a legitimate program is likely to add a key upon installation, and a HIPS may flag this as a malicious action.

Often a file integrity checker is included as part of an IDS. For example, Advanced Intrusion Detection Environment (AIDE) is a file and directory integrity checker for use on Linux-based systems.

> **ExamAlert**
>
> A file integrity checker tool computes a cryptographic hash such as SHA-1 or MD5 for all selected files and creates a database of the hashes. The hashes are periodically recalculated and compared to the hashes in the database to check for modification.

The primary purpose of a file integrity checker is to detect when a file has been improperly modified. As with HIDS/HIPS solutions, the biggest issue is false positives. Files often make changes when an application is updated or OS updates are applied. Keeping the hash database current is challenging, especially if it does not run in real time or is not run on a regular basis. File checkers serve a good purpose, of course, and even if the file integrity checker is run only once, the database information can provide a baseline record to let you know whether a file has been modified. This brings us to another problem with file integrity checkers: File integrity checkers should be run when a system is first installed, to create a clean database. If they are run after the system hits the Internet and a user starts downloading or installing files, the system might already be compromised. It is also a good security practice to store the hash database on a server offline so that attackers cannot alter it.

Anti-Malware and Other Host Protections

Antivirus software is a necessary software program for protecting the user environment. *Antivirus* software scans for malicious code in email and downloaded files. Antivirus software, in a way, works backward. Virus writers release a virus, it is reported, and then antivirus vendors reverse-engineer the code to find a

solution. After the virus has been analyzed, the antivirus software can look for specific characteristics of the virus. Remember that, for a virus to be successful, it must replicate its code.

The most common method used in an antivirus program is scanning. Scanning involves searching files in memory, the boot sector, and the hard drive and removable media for identifiable virus code. Scanning identifies virus code based on a unique string of characters known as a signature. When the virus software detects the signature, it isolates the file. Then, depending on the software settings, the antivirus software either quarantines the virus or permanently deletes it. Interception software detects virus-like behavior and pops up a warning to the user; however, because the software looks only at file changes, it might also detect legitimate files.

In the past, antivirus software used a heuristic engine to detect virus structures or used integrity checking as a method of file comparison. A false positive occurs when the software classifies an action as a possible intrusion when it is actually a nonthreatening action.

ExamAlert

Heuristic scanning looks for instructions or commands that are not typically found in application programs. However, these methods are susceptible to false positives and cannot identify new viruses until the database is updated.

Antivirus software vendors update their virus signatures on a regular basis. Most antivirus software connects to the vendor website to check the software database for updates and then automatically downloads and installs them as they become available. Besides setting your antivirus software for automatic updates, you should set the machine to automatically scan at least once a week. If a machine does become infected, it needs to be removed from the network as quickly as possible so that it cannot damage other machines.

The best defense against virus infection is user education. Most antivirus software used today is fairly effective, but only if it is kept updated and the user practices safe computing habits, such as not opening unfamiliar documents or programs. However, antivirus software cannot protect against brand-new viruses. Furthermore, users often do not take the necessary precautions and might even disable antivirus software if it interferes with programs that are currently installed on the machine. Be sure to guard against this type of incident through a combination of education and enabling tamperproof controls if available.

Especially in large enterprises, antivirus software has expanded to what is now generally known as *anti-malware*, given the range of the threats detected.

Advanced malware, such as ransomware, is complex malware that includes components such as command and control, data exfiltration, and payload execution. Traditional antivirus programs are ineffective against such malware because the malware uses a variety of techniques to obscure and avoid detection.

> **ExamAlert**
>
> Advanced malware tools use behavior-based and context-based detection methods instead of signature-based methods.

Advanced malware tools employ various methods to detect malware, including sandboxing and indicator of compromise (IoC) capabilities. Characteristics include continuous analysis and big data analytics. The main point to remember about advanced malware tools is that they tend to be complex enterprise solutions that are built to protect organizations before, during, and after a malware attack. For example, Cisco's Advanced Malware Protection uses real-time threat intelligence and dynamic malware analytics, along with continuous analysis. This tool can be deployed on endpoints, networks, and firewalls, as well as in cloud-based environments.

Antispam software is often part of antivirus software or a host security suite. Antispam software can add another layer of defense to the infrastructure. The most common installation locations are at the email server or email client. When the software and updates are installed on a central server and pushed out to the client machines, this is a centralized solution. When the updates are left up to the individual users, it is a decentralized environment. The main component of antispam software is heuristic filtering, which compares incoming email information against a predefined rule set. The software reads the contents of each message and compares the words in that message against the words in typical spam messages. Each rule assigns a numeric score to the probability that the message is spam. This score is then used to determine whether the message meets the acceptable level set. If many of the same words from the rule set are in the message being examined, the message is marked as spam. Specific spam filtering levels can be set on the user's email account. If the setting is high, more spam will be filtered, but this can also trigger false positives and lead to legitimate email being filtered as spam.

> **ExamAlert**
>
> Naturally, software cannot assign meaning to the words it examines. It simply tracks and compares the words used.

Additional settings can be used in a rule set. An email address that you add to the approved list—the allow list—is never considered spam. Using an allow list gives you flexibility in the type of email you receive. For example, adding the addresses of your relatives or friends to your allow list permits you to receive any type of content from them. Conversely, an email address that you add to a blocked list—known as a block or deny list—is always considered spam. Other factors might affect the ability to receive email on a allow list. For example, if attachments are not allowed and the email has an attachment, the message might be filtered even if the address is on the approved list.

For additional host protection, many antispyware programs are available. These programs scan a machine, much as antivirus software scans for viruses. As with antivirus software, it is important to keep antispyware programs updated and regularly run scans. Configuration options on antispyware software allow the program to check for updates on a regularly scheduled basis. Antispyware software should be set to load upon startup and to automatically update spyware definitions.

Most online toolbars come with pop-up blockers. In addition, various downloadable pop-up blocking software programs are available; the browsers included with some operating systems, such as Windows, can block pop-ups. As with much of the other defensive software discussed so far, pop-up blockers have settings that you can adjust. Try setting the software to a medium level so that it will block most automatic pop-ups but still allow functionality. Keep in mind that you can adjust the settings on pop-up blockers to meet organizational policy or to best protect the user environment.

Several caveats apply when using pop-up blockers. Remember that some pop-ups are helpful, and some web-based programmed application installers actually use pop-ups to install software.

ExamAlert

If all pop-ups are blocked, the user might not be able to install certain applications or programs.

It is possible to circumvent pop-up blockers in various ways. Most pop-up blockers block only JavaScript and do not block other technologies, such as Flash. On some Internet browsers, holding down the Ctrl key while clicking a link allows the browser to bypass the pop-up filter.

Endpoint Detection and Response (EDR)

Many of the solutions discussed previously now are available with *endpoint detection and response (EDR)* solutions. EDR isn't necessarily focused on prevention. The idea is to provide a layered solution that assumes something may not have been prevented. As a result, the goal of EDR is to detect and respond. EDR technology often uses a combination of machine learning and behavioral analytics to detect suspicious activity. Today EDR plays a predominant role as part of an overall endpoint security strategy. EDR solutions generally provide the following capabilities beyond anti-malware and antispyware:

▶ Application allow list

▶ Data loss prevention

▶ Full disk encryption

▶ Application control

▶ Host-based firewall

▶ Targeted attack analytics and behavioral forensics

▶ Intrusion detection and intrusion prevention

Data Execution Prevention (DEP)

Data execution prevention (DEP) is a security technology that can prevent security threats from executing code on a system.

> **ExamAlert**
>
> DEP works by preventing malware from executing in memory space that is reserved for operating system processes. DEP can be either hardware or software based.

Hardware-based DEP prevents code from being executed by using processor hardware to set a memory attribute designating that code should not run in that memory space. Both AMD and Intel platforms have DEP hardware capabilities for Windows-based systems. Software-based DEP prevents malicious code from taking advantage of exception-handling mechanisms in Windows by throwing an exception when the injected code attempts to run. This essentially blocks the malware from running the injected code.

Software-based DEP works even if hardware DEP is not available but is more limited. Its main function is to block malicious programs that use exception-handling mechanisms in Windows for execution. Sometimes older, nonmalicious programs trigger DEP due to faulty coding.

Data Loss Prevention (DLP)

Data loss is a problem that all organizations face, and it can be especially challenging for global organizations that store a large volume of PII in different legal jurisdictions. Privacy issues differ by country, region, and state. Organizations implement data loss prevention tools as a way to prevent data loss. *Data loss prevention* (*DLP*) tools can detect and prevent confidential data from being exfiltrated physically or logically from an organization by accident or on purpose. DLP systems are basically designed to detect and prevent unauthorized use and transmission of confidential information, based on one of the three states of data: in use, in motion, or at rest.

DLP systems offer a way to enforce data security policies by providing centralized management for detecting and preventing the unauthorized use and transmission of data that the organization deems confidential. A well-designed DLP strategy allows control over sensitive data, reduces the cost of data breaches, and achieves greater insight into organizational data use. International organizations should ensure that they are in compliance with local privacy regulations before implementing DLP tools and processes.

Protection of data in use is considered an endpoint solution. In this case, the application is run on end-user workstations or servers in the organization. Endpoint systems also can monitor and control access to physical devices such as mobile devices and tablets. Protection of data in transit is considered a network solution, and either a hardware or software solution is installed near the network perimeter to monitor and flag policy violations. Protection of data at rest is considered a storage solution and is generally a software solution that monitors how confidential data is stored.

When evaluating DLP solutions, key content-filtering capabilities to look for are high performance, scalability, and the capability to accurately scan nearly anything. High performance is necessary to keep the end user from experiencing lag time and delays. The solution must readily scale as both the volume of traffic and bandwidth needs increase. The tool should also be capable of accurately scanning nearly anything.

Here are some examples of security policy violations an endpoint solution would flag and alert a user about in order to prevent sensitive information from leaving the user's desktop:

▶ Inadvertently emailing a confidential internal document to external recipients

▶ Forwarding an email with sensitive information to unauthorized recipients inside or outside the organization

▶ Sending attachments such as spreadsheets with PII to an external personal email account

▶ Accidentally selecting Reply All and emailing a sensitive document to unauthorized recipients

USB flash drives and other portable storage devices are pervasive in the workplace and pose a real threat. They can introduce viruses or malicious code to the network and can store sensitive corporate information. Sensitive information is often stored on thumb and external hard drives, which then may be lost or stolen. DLP solutions allow policies for USB blocking, such as a policy to block the copying of any network information to removable media or a policy to block the use of unapproved USB devices.

> **ExamAlert**
>
> Although some DLP solutions provide remediation processes, an incident generally means that data has been lost. Be sure the proper protections are put in place.

Removable Media Control

Most DLP solutions have the capability to control or manage removable media such as USB devices, mobile devices, email, and storage media. In many instances, banning USB and not permitting copying to devices is not an acceptable solution. For example, thumb drives were banned after malicious software infected thousands of military computers and networks. The ban was a major inconvenience for those who relied on thumb drives. Aircraft and vehicle technicians stored manuals on thumb drives. Medical records of wounded troops were sometimes stored on thumb drives and accompanied patients from field hospitals in foreign countries to their final U.S.-based hospitals. Pilots used thumb drives to transfer mission plans from operations rooms to aircraft computers.

When employees must use removable drives, finding a way to secure data that is taken outside a managed environment is part of doing business. Encryption is essential. Some disk encryption products protect only the local drive, not USB devices. Other encryption products automatically encrypt data that is copied or written to removable media. Other solutions include antivirus software that actively scans removable media and grants access to only approved devices. In a Windows environment, group policy objects (GPOs) offer another solution.

Application Allow/Block Lists

Organizations control application installations by using either an *allow list* or a *block list/deny list*. Placing applications on an block or deny list involves listing all applications that the organization deems undesirable or banned and then preventing those applications from being installed. The concept of a block/deny list for applications is similar to the way antivirus software works. A block/deny list is generally done to reduce security-related issues, but organizations also can block time-wasting or bandwidth-intensive applications.

> **ExamAlert**
>
> An allow list for applications tends to make an environment more closed by allowing only approved applications to be installed. You may be already familiar with an allow list being known as a whitelist, and a block/deny list being known as a blacklist. Remember the industry is moving away from the use of the whitelist/blacklist terms.

An allow list approach uses a list of approved applications. If an application is not on the approved list of software, the application installation is denied or restricted. An allow list is the preferred method of restricting applications because the approved apps can be allowed to run using numerous methods of trust. This decreases the risk of infection and improves system stability.

Web Application Firewall

In response to the onslaught of web-based attacks, many organizations have implemented web application firewalls in addition to network firewalls. Put simply, a *web application firewall* is software or a hardware appliance used to protect an organization's web server from attack. A web application firewall can be an appliance, a server plug-in, or a filter that is used specifically for preventing execution of common web-based attacks such as Cross-Site Scripting (XSS) and SQL injection on a web server. Web application firewalls can be either signature based or anomaly based. Some look for particular attack signatures to try to identify an attack, whereas others look for abnormal behavior outside the website's normal traffic patterns. The device sits between a web client and a web server and analyzes communication at the application layer, much like a network stateful-inspection firewall. A web application firewall is placed in front of a web server in an effort to shield it from incoming attacks. Web application firewalls are sometimes referred to as *deep packet inspection (DPI) firewalls* because they can look at every request and response within web service layers.

Application Security

Application security begins with secure coding practices. Chapter 11, "Secure Application Development, Deployment, and Automation," covers many application security techniques in detail. Validating all data that can be provided to an application is one of the most important controls you should be familiar with. Lack of proper validation also leads to many of the top application security risks. Applications that take input from a source such as a user should be able to properly and safely handle that data before it is passed along for further processing. Special characters, markup, and other formatted code might be filtered out. At the least, you don't want that data to be interpreted so that it performs an unexpected or authorized task. Such input could also cause errors and other unexpected results.

After initial development, most executables designed to install and run on a device are digitally signed in a process known as *code signing*. Code signing provides validation of the author's identity and provides assurance that the software code has not been tampered with since it was signed. Many operating systems block or alert the installation of software that has not been signed by a trusted certificate authority (CA).

Cloud-based applications or applications designed for delivery over a network using a web browser depend on many of the same secure coding techniques as traditional applications. The use of *secure cookies* is a unique requirement you should be familiar with. When a client interacts with the server, the server provides a response in the Hypertext Transfer Protocol (HTTP) header that instructs the client's web browser to create one or more cookies, which are used to store data. This data is used with future requests when interacting with the associated sites.

Although websites are increasingly defaulting to being secure HTTPS sites, web application developers should only allow cookies to be used with HTTPS through the use of the Secure attribute. This attribute prohibits cookies from being transmitted over unencrypted HTTP to prevent the contents of the cookie from being read by a malicious actor.

During the development process—and certainly before code is released into production—code should be analyzed for mistakes and vulnerabilities. One method of analysis is manual secure code review, which is a laborious process of going line by line through the code to ensure that it is ready. While the software belonging to many organizations may never reach the 50 million lines of code in Microsoft Windows 10 or the 2 billion lines of code across Google services, modern software and web applications are too large to rely on manual

code review only. Therefore, automated tools are used and often integrated into the development process. The following sections discuss some of these tools.

Code Analyzers

Quality assurance and testing processes directly affect code quality. The earlier defects in software are found, the easier and cheaper they are to fix. The benefits of implementing a sound QA and testing process far outweigh the associated costs. The SDLC must include quality code and testing: Reports of website vulnerabilities and data breaches are reported in the news almost daily. Providing quality software also builds a positive reputation for an organization and gives customers confidence in the products they are purchasing.

Static Code Analyzers

Static code analysis is performed in a non-runtime environment. Typically, a static analysis tool inspects the code for all possible runtime behaviors and looks for problematic code such as backdoors or malicious code.

> **ExamAlert**
>
> Static analysis is a white-box software testing process for detecting bugs. The idea behind static analysis is to take a thorough approach to bug detection in the early stages of program development.

The same kind of compiler is used in static code analyzers that is used to compile code. Integrating a source code analyzer into a compiler makes the best use of the compiler and reduces complexity. The code analyzer can use preexisting compiler data flow algorithms to perform analysis. The analysis is a complete program analysis that checks complex code interactions. Static code analyzers can detect a wide array of vulnerabilities, including memory leaks.

Dynamic Analysis

As noted in the previous section, static code analysis is performed without executing any code. *Dynamic code analysis* is based on observing how the code behaves during execution. Dynamic analysis is done while a program is in operation and monitors functional behavior and overall performance. Dynamic analysis uses a technique called *fuzzing*, which enables an attacker to inject random-looking data into a program to see if it can cause the program to crash.

> **ExamAlert**
>
> Fuzzing is a black-box software-testing process in which semi-random data is injected into a program or protocol stack to detect bugs.

A systematic discovery approach should find application bugs sooner or later. The data generation part consists of generators. Generators typically use combinations of static fuzzing vectors or totally random data. Vulnerability identification relies on debugging tools. Most fuzzers are either protocol/file format dependent or data type dependent. New-generation fuzzers use genetic algorithms to link injected data and observed impact. OWASP provides a web page on fuzz vector resources, which is a great source for fuzzing methodology and real-life fuzzing vector examples.

Several different types of fuzzing exist:

▶ **Application fuzzing:** Attack vectors are within an application's inputs and outputs—for example, the user interface, the command-line options, URLs, forms, user-generated content, and RPC requests.

▶ **Protocol fuzzing:** Forged packets are sent to the tested application, which can act as a proxy and modify requests on the fly and then replay them.

▶ **File format fuzzing:** Multiple malformed samples are generated and then opened sequentially. When the program crashes, debugging information is kept for further investigation.

An advantage of fuzzing is that the test design is generally very simple, without any presumptions about system behavior. This approach makes it possible to find bugs that human testing would miss. With a closed application, fuzzing might be the only means of reviewing the security quality of the program.

The simplicity of fuzzing can be a disadvantage because it may not find more advanced bugs. In addition, a fuzzer that is very protocol aware tends to miss odd errors.

While fuzzers may generate data using known dangerous values, the use of random data is still a good idea for best results. Fuzzing can add another dimension to normal software-testing techniques.

Stress Testing

Stress testing measures how much stress an application or program can withstand before it breaks. Stress testing uses methods to overload the existing resources in an attempt to break the application. The primary purpose of stress testing is to assess the behavior of the application beyond normal conditions. It serves the following purposes:

▶ Offers a method of nonfunctional testing

▶ Identifies the breaking point of the application

▶ Determines application stability

▶ Provides statistics on application availability and error handling under high usage

▶ Produces information on crash conditions under lack of resources

▶ Provides a reference point for application robustness and stability

Application Sandboxing

Sandboxing allows programs and processes to be run in an isolated environment, to limit access to files and the host system. Running a program or file in a sandbox contains it so that it can be tested, and this reduces some security issues because the program or file cannot harm the host or make any changes to the host. In software development, especially when Agile methods are used, common best practice is to ensure that each developer works in his or her own sandbox. A sandbox is basically a technical environment whose scope is well defined and respected. Sandboxing reduces the risk of programming errors adversely affecting an entire team. In software development, the following types of sandboxes can be used:

▶ Development

▶ Project integration

▶ Demo

▶ Preproduction test or QA

▶ Production

Organizations that use development sandboxes have the distinct advantage of being able to scan applications more frequently and early in the SDLC. Their development teams are cognizant of application security, detect issues early in the process, and reduce risk to the organization.

Hardware and Firmware Security

Security begins at the hardware level. When a device is infected at the hardware or firmware level, the root cause might evade detection for an extended period of time simply because people tend to implicitly trust hardware and firmware. In today's environment, however, hardware and firmware are no longer trustworthy and need to be secured. As the Internet of Things (IoT) grows, firmware- and hardware-based exploits will become more common in the very near future.

FDE and SED

Full disk encryption (FDE), also called *whole disk encryption*, is commonly used to mitigate the risks associated with lost or stolen mobile devices and accompanying disclosure laws.

> **ExamAlert**
>
> FDE can be either hardware or software based. Unlike file- or folder-level encryption, FDE is meant to encrypt the entire contents of a drive—even temporary files and memory.

FDE involves encrypting the operating system partition on a computer and then booting and running with the system drive encrypted at all times. If the device is stolen or lost, the OS and all the data on the drive become unreadable without the decryption key.

Unlike selective file encryption, which might require the end user to take responsibility for encrypting files, encryption of the contents of an entire drive takes the onus off individual users.

As an example of full disk encryption, BitLocker is an FDE feature included with Microsoft Windows OSs. It is designed to protect data by providing encryption for entire volumes. By default, BitLocker uses the Advanced Encryption Standard (AES) encryption algorithm.

Encrypting File System (EFS) is a feature of Microsoft Windows OSs that provides filesystem-level encryption. EFS enables files to be transparently encrypted to protect confidential data from attackers who gain physical access to the computer. By default, no files are encrypted, so the encryption must be enabled. The user encrypts files on a per-file, per-directory, or per-drive basis.

Some EFS settings can be implemented through Group Policy in Windows domain environments, which gives the organization a bit more control.

It is not unusual for end users to sacrifice security for convenience, especially when they do not fully understand the associated risks. Nevertheless, along with the benefits of whole disk encryption come certain trade-offs. For example, key management becomes increasingly important as loss of the decryption keys could render the data unrecoverable. In addition, although FDE might make it easier for an organization to deal with a stolen or lost device, the fact that the entire drive is encrypted could present management challenges, including the inability to effectively control who has unauthorized access to sensitive data.

> **ExamAlert**
>
> After a device with FDE is booted and running, it is just as vulnerable as a drive that has no encryption on it.

The term *self-encrypting drive* (*SED*) is often used when referring to FDE on hard disks. The Trusted Computing Group (TCG) security subsystem storage standard *Opal* provides industry-accepted standardization SEDs. SEDs automatically encrypt all data in the drive, preventing attackers from accessing the data through the operating system. SED vendors include Seagate Technology, Hitachi, Western Digital, Samsung, and Toshiba.

Firmware and hardware implement common cryptographic functions. Disk encryption that is embedded in the hard drive provides performance that is very close to that of unencrypted disk drives; the user sees no noticeable difference from using an unencrypted disk. Advantages of hardware drive encryption include faster setup time, enhanced scalability, improved portability, and better system performance. Disadvantages include lack of management software and weak authentication components. Coupled with hardware-based technologies, a SED can achieve strong authentication. You can use hardware drive encryption to protect data at rest because all the data—even the OS—is encrypted with a secure mode of AES.

> **ExamAlert**
>
> With hardware drive encryption, authentication happens on drive power-up either through a software preboot authentication environment or with a BIOS password. Enhanced firmware and special-purpose cryptographic hardware are built into the hard drive.

To effectively use FDE products, you should also use a preboot authentication mechanism. That is, the user attempting to log on must provide authentication before the operating system boots. Thus, the encryption key is decrypted only after another key is input into this preboot environment. Vendors offer a variety of preboot authentication options, such as the following:

▶ **Username and password:** This is typically the least secure option.

▶ **Smart card or smart card–enabled USB token along with a PIN:** This option provides two-factor functionality, and the smart card can often be the same token or smart card currently used for access elsewhere.

▶ **Trusted Platform Module (TPM):** TPM can be used to store the decryption key (as discussed later in this chapter).

Full disk encryption is especially useful for devices taken on the road by people such as traveling executives, sales managers, or insurance agents. For example, on Windows-based laptops, FDE implementations could include combining technologies such as a TPM and BitLocker. Because encryption adds overhead, FDE is typically not appropriate for a computer in a fixed location with strong physical access control unless the data is extremely sensitive and must be protected at all costs.

TPM and HSM

Some organizations use hardware-based encryption devices because of factors such as the need for a highly secure environment, the unreliability of software, and increases in complex attacks. Hardware-based encryption basically allows IT administrators to move certificate authentication software components to hardware. For authentication, a user provides a credential to the hardware on the machine. Such a hardware-based authentication solution can be used with wireless networks and virtual private networks (VPNs) and eliminates the possibility of users sharing keys.

The Trusted Computing Group is responsible for the *Trusted Platform Module (TPM)* specification. At the most basic level, TPM provides for the secure storage of keys, passwords, and digital certificates. A TPM chip is hardware that is typically attached to the circuit board of a system. In addition, TPM can ensure that a system is authenticated and has not been altered or breached.

> **ExamAlert**
>
> A TPM chip is a secure cryptoprocessor that is used to authenticate hardware devices such as PCs, laptops, and tablets.

TPM consists of various components, and you should be familiar with key concepts such as the following:

▶ **Endorsement key (EK):** A 2,048-bit asymmetric key pair is created at the time of manufacturing. It cannot be changed.

▶ **Storage root key (SRK):** A 2,048-bit asymmetric key pair is generated within a TPM chip and used to provide encrypted storage.

▶ **Sealed storage:** TPM protects information by binding it to the system. This means that the information can be read only by the same system in a particular described state.

▶ **Attestation:** TPM vouches for the accuracy of the system.

A computer that uses a TPM chip has the capability to create and encrypt cryptographic keys through a process called *wrapping*. Each TPM chip has a root wrapping key, called the *storage root key* (*SRK*), that is stored within the TPM chip. In addition, TPM-enabled computers can create and tie a key to certain platform measurements. This type of key can be unwrapped only when the platform measurements have the same values that they had when the key was created. This process is called *sealing* the key to the TPM; decrypting it is called *unsealing*. Attestation and other TPM functions do not transmit users' personal information.

The idea behind TPM is to allow any encryption-enabled application to take advantage of the chip. Therefore, TPM has many possible applications, such as network access control (NAC), secure remote access, secure transmission of data, whole disk encryption, software license enforcement, digital rights management (DRM), and credential protection. Interestingly, part of what makes TPM effective is that the TPM module is given a unique ID and master key that even the owner of the system neither controls nor has knowledge of.

Critics of TPM argue that this security architecture puts too much control into the hands of the people who design the related systems and software. Concerns thus arise about several issues, including DRM, loss of end-user control, loss of anonymity, and interoperability. If standards and shared specifications do not exist, components of the trusted environment cannot interoperate, and trusted computing applications cannot be implemented to work on all platforms. It is also important to understand that TPM can store pre-runtime configuration parameters but does not control the software running on a device. If something happens to the TPM chip or the motherboard, you need a separate recovery key to access your data when simply connecting the hard drive to another computer.

> **ExamAlert**
>
> A TPM module can offer increased security protection for processes such as digital signing, mission-critical applications, and businesses that require high security. Trusted modules can also be used in mobile phones and network equipment.

Hardware-based cryptography ensures that the information stored in hardware is better protected from external software attacks. Newer Windows systems incorporate a TPM Management console. The TPM Management console and an API called TPM Base Services (TBS) can be used for administration of TPM security hardware.

Whereas a TPM module is an embedded chip, a *hardware security module* (*HSM*) is a removable or external device used in asymmetric encryption. An HSM can be described as a black-box combination of hardware and software and/or firmware that is attached or contained inside a computer used to provide cryptographic functions for tamper protection and increased performance. The main goals of HSMs are performance and key storage space. HSMs can also enforce separation of duties for key management by separating database administration from security administration. For example, HSMs support payment processing and cardholder authentication applications for PCI DSS compliance under FIPS 140-2.

Hardware can protect encryption keys better than software because it stores the cryptographic keys inside a hardened, tamper-resistant device. Some additional reasons hardware is better at protecting encryption keys are that the application does not directly handle the key; the key does not leave the device; and, because the host OS is not storing the key, it cannot be compromised on the host system.

Boot Integrity

Boot integrity ensures that the system is trusted and has not been altered during the boot process while the operating systems loads. The basic input/output system (BIOS) consists of firmware or software instructions about basic computer functions, stored on a small memory chip on the motherboard. BIOS is the first program that runs when a computer is turned on. *Unified Extensible Firmware Interface (UEFI)* is a newer version of BIOS. A computer equipped with UEFI runs it first when turned on.

UEFI is an industry-wide standard managed by the Unified Extended Firmware Interface Forum. UEFI defines a standard interface between an OS,

firmware, and external devices. The UEFI firmware enables OS boot loaders and UEFI applications to be called from the UEFI preboot environment.

UEFI is compatible with today's PCs, and the majority of computers use UEFI instead of BIOS. UEFI supports security features, larger-capacity hard drives, and faster boot times. UEFI-enabled OSs are preferred over BIOS-enabled OSs because they can run in 64-bit mode and provide better support for external devices and boot targets. Sophisticated attacks can occur with traditional boot processes.

> **ExamAlert**
>
> Remember that combining UEFI with a TPM establishes certainty that the system is trusted when the OS loads.

Boot drive encryption solutions require a secure boot or preboot authentication component. Today's PCs ship with a feature called Secure Boot, which UEFI supports. With Secure Boot enabled, a PC boots using only trusted software from the PC manufacturer. Secure Boot is basically an extension of UEFI. It was added to the UEFI specification in Version 2.2 as an optional component.

Most PC manufacturers that install current Windows OSs are required by Microsoft to enable Secure Boot. Secure Boot uses a series of sequential image verification steps in the boot sequence to prevent unauthorized code from running. Software images are authenticated by previously verified software before they are executed. This sequence is the beginning of what is called the *chain* or *root* of trust. It starts with the software that is executed from read-only memory (ROM). The ROM bootloader cryptographically verifies the signature of the next bootloader. That bootloader cryptographically verifies the signature of the next software image, and so on, until the full OS is loaded. This level of trust provides an authentication chain and validates the integrity of the rest of the system.

Windows 8 introduced a new feature called *Measured Boot* that can provide stronger validation than Secure Boot alone. Measured Boot measures each component, from firmware up through the boot start drivers, stores those measurements in the TPM chip on the machine, and then makes available a log that can be tested remotely to verify the boot state of the client. Microsoft's Measured Boot provides a number of advantages, including identifying and fixing errors automatically as well as stopping and mitigating malware attacks. Measured Boot can identify early untrusted applications trying to load and allows anti-malware solutions to load earlier for better protection.

Boot Attestation

The trustworthiness of a platform is based on *attestation*. Secure Boot permits a platform to record evidence that can be presented to a remote party in a platform attestation. The purpose of attestation is to give you confidence in the identity and trustworthiness of a target device before you interact with the device. Consider the following examples of when attestation is used:

▶ A device can access a network only if it is up-to-date and contains all OS patches.

▶ A laptop is allowed to access an enterprise environment only if it is running authorized software.

▶ A gaming machine can join the gaming network only if its game client is unmodified.

Think about how TPM chips are used in the attestation process. Recall from earlier in this chapter that the first component of a TPM chip is an endorsement key (EK). The EK is created at the time of manufacture. It cannot be changed and is used for attestation. An attestation identity key (AIK) is also created the time of manufacture. The AIK is a private key known only by the TPM chip. In addition, a set of special-purpose platform configuration registers (PCRs) participate in attestation by recording the aggregate platform state.

To perform attestation, the attesting platform's TPM chip signs new challenge and PCR values with the AIK. The challenger then verifies information before deciding whether to trust the attesting platform. Here are the actual steps in attestation:

1. The requesting party sends a message to the attesting platform, asking for evidence of authenticity.

2. A platform agent gathers the requested information.

3. The platform agent returns the information and credentials to the challenger.

4. The relying party verifies and validates the returned information, establishing identity and configuration of the platform.

5. If the relying party trusts the information provided to vouch for the attesting platform, it compares the attested configuration to configuration information that is already deemed trustworthy.

ExamAlert

Attestation is merely disclosure about the trustworthiness of a platform at a given point in time. It does not provide validation about the running state of a system.

> **Note**
>
> Original equipment manufacturers (OEMs) rely on global operations in their supply chains for manufacturing and shipping. The end product may cross several international borders and storage facilities along the way. This becomes problematic because it provides opportunities for product tampering before the equipment reaches the end user.
>
> During manufacturing, it is critical to ensure that any root of trust device is programmed securely. To mitigate supply-chain threats and risks, manufacturers often implement root of trust measures to be sure their products boot only authenticated code. One approach is to tie Secure Boot to the system by loading a component with Secure Boot logic and making it CPU independent. Control of the system is more reliable because the approach uses existing components. The likelihood that an attacker would remove and replace components to defeat Secure Boot capabilities is greatly reduced. A system approach that supports key revocation with in-band or out-of-band management can be implemented as well.
>
> Creating a key hierarchy to secure supply chains starts by building a root of trust at the very beginning level of the system and then using the Secure Boot process to validate the integrity of all software that executes on the platform. Secure boot has been proven to reduce the risks associated with global manufacturing operations and remote deployment.

Hardware Root of Trust

So far in this chapter, we have discussed roots of trust in regard to hardware such as TPM chips and software such as UEFI, which supports Secure Boot. Roots of trust are basically hardware or software components that are inherently trusted. Secure Boot is considered a root of trust. Roots of trust are inherently trusted and must be secure by design, which is why many roots of trust are implemented in hardware. Malware can embed itself at a level lower than the OS or can be disguised as an OS loader or *third-party update* or boot driver; a software root of trust would not be effective against such malware, but a hardware root of trust would.

TPMs and HSMs are good examples of *hardware roots of trust*. TPM is now embedded in all types of devices from most major vendors. Consider two implementation examples of how organizations are using hardware roots of trust:

- ▶ The Google Chromebook uses TPM to find and correct corruption in firmware.

- ▶ PricewaterhouseCoopers uses a TPM-aware cryptographic service provider (CSP) installed under a Microsoft cryptography API in its PCs to import identity certificates.

> **ExamAlert**
>
> Examples of hardware roots of trust include SEDs, TPMs, virtual TPMs, and HSMs.

> **Note**
>
> Hardware roots of trust are used extensively in virtual environments. According to NIST, hardware roots of trust are preferred over software roots of trust because they are less susceptible to change, have smaller attack surfaces, and exhibit more reliable behavior.

Operating System Security

Operating systems come in various shapes and forms and are essential in the computing environment. Many exploits occur due to vulnerabilities in operating system code that allow attackers to steal information and damage the system. Operating system security is of utmost importance because it involves the main platform of the computer. In addition, several areas must be secured because the OS communicates with the hardware, performs common required application tasks, and serves as an interface with programs and applications. The following are some of the most common operating system spaces to be secured:

▶ **Network:** A network supports local area network (LAN) connections for workstations, personal computers, and sometimes legacy terminals.

▶ **Server:** Servers are specialized machines that operate in a client/server architecture and used specifically for responding to network client requests.

▶ **Workstation:** A workstation is computer hardware that runs applications for a single end user.

▶ **Appliance:** An appliance is either industry-standard hardware or a virtual machine that contains software and/or an operating system.

▶ **Kiosk:** A kiosk consists of specialized hardware and software and provides access to information and applications in a locked-down environment to protect the kiosk.

▶ **Mobile OS:** A mobile operating system runs applications for a single end user on a mobile device.

Security planning and protection cover all devices connected to a network. Each OS is configured differently and has its own security considerations. For example, securing a web server involves different security considerations than securing an airport ticket kiosk.

Patch Management

Improperly programmed software can be exploited. Software exploitation involves searching for specific problems, weaknesses, or security holes in software code and taking advantage of a program's flawed code. The most effective ways to prevent an attacker from exploiting software bugs are to ensure that the latest manufacturer patches and service packs are applied and to monitor the web for new vulnerabilities.

ExamAlert

Before applying patches to systems, you should verify the integrity of any patch you download. Most publishers provide MD5 hash values, which you can use for comparison after you hash your downloaded file.

Applications and operating systems include a function for auto-updates. Usually this is a viable solution for workstations, laptops, and mobile devices; however, for critical servers, it is still typically best to go through proper patch testing to make sure the system is updated to a working state. Large organizations tend to rely upon patch management tools.

The patch management infrastructure of an organization includes all tools and technologies that are used to assess, test, deploy, and install software updates. This infrastructure is essential for keeping the entire environment secure and reliable, and it must be managed and maintained properly. When it comes to managing your infrastructure, chances are good that your network includes many types of clients, which might have different needs regarding updates and hotfixes.

ExamAlert

The most efficient way to update client machines is to use automated processes and products. Many vendors provide regular updates for installed products, managed through automated deployment tools or by manual update procedures that a system user carries out.

Regular maintenance is required to meet emerging security threats, whether you are applying an updated RPM (Red Hat Package Manager, a file format used to distribute Linux applications and update packages) by hand or using fully automated "call home for updates" options, such as those in many commercial operating systems and applications.

Various vendors provide solutions to assist in security patch management by scanning computers remotely throughout a network and reporting the results to a central repository. The results can then be assessed and compared to determine which computers need additional patches. One common example is Microsoft Endpoint Configuration Manager, formerly known as Microsoft System Center Configuration Manager.

Microsoft maintains an Automatic Updates website, which contains all the latest security updates. Starting with Windows 10, the user configuration options have changed so that, by default, updates are automatically downloaded and installed. Unless the update setting is changed manually or through Group Policy, all client computers will receive updates as soon as they come out.

Disabling Unnecessary Ports and Services

In security terms, *system hardening* refers to reducing the security exposure of a system and strengthening its defenses against unauthorized access attempts and other forms of malicious attention. A "soft" system is one that is installed with default configurations or unnecessary services or one that is not maintained to include emerging security updates. No completely safe system exists; the process of hardening simply reflects attention to security thresholds.

Systems installed in default configurations often include many unnecessary services that are configured automatically. These services are potential avenues for unauthorized access to a system or network. Many services have known vulnerabilities, and specific actions must be taken to make them more secure; some services could actually impair system function by causing additional processing overhead. Default configurations also allow for unauthorized access and exploitation.

> **Note**
>
> A denial-of-service (DoS) attack could be conducted against an unneeded web service; this is one example of how a nonessential service can potentially cause problems for an otherwise functional system.

Common default configuration exploits include both services (such as anonymous-access FTP servers) and network protocols (such as Simple Network Management Protocol). Others exploit vendor-supplied default logon/password combinations.

> **ExamAlert**
>
> When you are presented with a scenario on the exam, you might be tempted to keep all services enabled to cover all requirements. Be wary of this option as it might mean installing unnecessary services or protocols.

A computer can communicate through 65,535 TCP and UDP ports. The port numbers are divided into three ranges:

▶ **Well-known ports:** The well-known ports are 0 through 1,023.

▶ **Registered ports:** The registered ports are 1,024 through 49,151.

▶ **Dynamic/private ports:** The dynamic/private ports are 49,152 through 65,535.

Often these ports are not secured and, as a result, may be used for exploitation. Table 18.2 lists some of the most commonly used ports and the services and protocols that use them. Many of these ports and services have associated vulnerabilities. You should know what common ports are used by network protocols and how to securely implement services on these ports.

> **ExamAlert**
>
> Know the differences in the various ports that are used for network services and protocols.

TABLE 18.2 **Commonly Used Ports**

Port	Service/Protocol
15	Netstat
20	FTP data transfer
21	FTP control (command)
22	SSH/SFTP/SCP
23	Telnet
25	SMTP
53	DNS

Port	Service/Protocol
67, 68	DHCP
69	TFTP
80	HTTP
110	POP3
123	NTP
137, 138, 139	NetBIOS
143	IMAP
161/162	SNMP
389	LDAP
443	HTTPS
445	SMB
636	LDAPS
989/990	FTPS
1812	RADIUS
3389	RDP

The protocols listed in Table 18.2 might be currently in use on a network. These protocols, along with some older or antiquated protocols, could be configured open by default by the machine manufacturer or when an operating system is installed. Every operating system requires different services in order to operate properly. If ports are open for manufacturer-installed tools, the manufacturer should have the services listed in the documentation. Ports for older protocols such as Chargen (port 19) and Telnet (port 23) might still be accessible. For example, Finger, which uses port 79, was widely used during the early days of the Internet, but today's sites no longer offer the service. However, you might still find some old implementations of Eudora mail that use the Finger protocol. Worse, a mail client may have long since been upgraded, but the port used 10 years ago may have somehow been left open. The quickest way to tell which ports are open and which services are running is to do a Netstat scan on the machine. You can also run local or online port scans.

The best way to protect the network infrastructure from attacks aimed at antiquated or unused ports and protocols is to remove any unnecessary protocols and create access control lists to allow traffic on necessary ports only. By doing so, you eliminate the possibility of exploiting unused and antiquated protocols and minimize the threat of attack.

Least Functionality

Least functionality is based on the principle that, by default, systems provide a wide variety of functions and services, some of which are not necessary to support the essential operation of the organization. Least functionality prevents an organization from using a single system to provide multiple services, which would increase risk. Where feasible, organizations must limit component functionality to a single function per device and must disable any unnecessary protocols, ports, or services. Any functionality that does not support a business need should be removed or disabled.

The term *least functionality* comes from configuration management 7 (CM-7) in NIST 800-53, which states that an organization must configure an information system to provide only essential capabilities and must specifically prohibit or restrict the use of certain ports, protocols, or services. Network scanning tools can be used to identify prohibited functions, ports, protocols, and services. Enforcement can be accomplished through IPSs, firewalls, and endpoint protections.

Secure Configurations

Secure configurations are imperative to prevent malware from infiltrating a network. Hardening an operating system is a large part of making sure that systems have secure configurations. Hardening an operating system includes using fault-tolerant hardware and software solutions to prevent both accidental data deletion and directed attacks. In addition, an organization must implement an effective system for file-level security, including encrypted file support and secured filesystem selection that allows the proper level of access control. For example, NTFS allows file-level access control and encryption, whereas most FAT-based filesystems allow only share-level access control, without encryption.

Organizations also must conduct regular update reviews for all deployed operating systems to address newly identified exploits and apply security updates and hotfixes. Many automated attacks make use of common vulnerabilities for which patches and hotfixes are available but have not been applied. Failure to update applications on a regular basis or perform regular auditing can result in an insecure solution that gives an attacker access to additional resources throughout an organization's network.

IP Security (IPsec) and public key infrastructure (PKI) implementations must also be properly configured and updated to maintain key and ticket stores. Some systems can be hardened to include specific levels of access, gaining the

C2 security rating that many government deployment scenarios require. The Trusted Computer System Evaluation Criteria (TCSEC) rating C2 indicates a discretionary access control (DAC) environment with additional requirements such as individual logon accounts and access logging.

Operating system hardening includes configuring log files and auditing, changing default administrator account names and default passwords, and instituting account lockout and password policies to guarantee strong passwords that can resist brute-force attacks. File-level security and access control mechanisms isolate access attempts in the operating system environment.

Trusted Operating System

The trusted operating system concept was developed in the early 1980s and is based on technical standards of the TCSEC. Trusted operating systems are security-enhanced versions of operating systems that have access segmented through compartmentalization and role, least-privilege, and kernel-level enforcement. Individual components are locked down to protect memory and files, restrict object access, and enforce user authentication. Some applications cannot work on a trusted OS because of the strict security settings.

An operating system is considered a trusted OS if it meets specified security requirements. A certain level of trust can be assigned to an operating system depending on the degree to which it meets a specific set of requirements. A trusted operating system is designed from the beginning with security in mind. Evaluating the level of trust depends on security policy enforcement and the sufficiency of the operating system's measures and mechanisms.

Cram Quiz

Answer these questions. The answers follow the last question. If you cannot answer these questions correctly, consider reading this chapter again until you can.

1. Why do vendors provide MD5 values for their software patches?

  - ○ **A.** To provide the necessary key for patch activation
  - ○ **B.** To allow the downloader to verify the authenticity of the site providing the patch
  - ○ **C.** To ensure that auto-updates are enabled for subsequent patch releases
  - ○ **D.** To allow the recipient to verify the integrity of the patch prior to installation

2. Your developers made certain that any input to a search function they developed would result in commas, quotes, and other certain special characters being stripped out. Which of the following is likely their reasoning?

○ **A.** They are paranoid, and they should allow the original input term to process as is.

○ **B.** They want to prevent SQL injection by validating the input.

○ **C.** They want to prevent privilege escalation by providing proper exception handling.

○ **D.** They are lazy and didn't want to have to refactor their search algorithm.

3. You are a security administrator and learn that a user has been emailing files containing credit card number data from the corporate domain to his personal email account. This data is typically required to go to a third-party business partner. Which of the following solutions could you implement to prevent these emails or attachments from being sent to personal email accounts?

○ **A.** Implement a DLP solution to prevent employees from emailing sensitive data.

○ **B.** Implement a mail solution that requires TLS connections to encrypt the emails.

○ **C.** Implement a mail solution that employs encryption and that will prevent email from being sent externally.

○ **D.** Implement a DLP solution to prevent sensitive data from being emailed to non-business accounts.

4. Which of the following correctly matches each protocol to its default port?

○ **A.** SSH:22; SMTP:25; DNS:53; HTTP:80; LDAPS:389

○ **B.** SSH:21; SMTP:22; DNS:35; HTTP:110; LDAPS:636

○ **C.** SSH:22; SMTP:25; DNS:53; HTTP:80; LDAPS:636

○ **D.** SSH:22; SMTP:23; DNS:35; HTTP:69; LDAPS:389

5. Which of the following is a white-box testing process for detecting bugs in the early stages of program development?

○ **A.** Dynamic analysis

○ **B.** Static analysis

○ **C.** Fuzzing

○ **D.** Sandboxing

Cram Quiz Answers

Answer 1: D. MD5 is a hashing value used to verify integrity. Software developers provide these hash values so users can verify that nothing has changed. Answers A and B are incorrect. MD5 is for integrity checking, not authentication, and some patches may be downloaded from sites other than the original author's site. Answer C is incorrect.

Answer 2: B. The developers are following a best practice of input validation by preventing various types of negative impacts, such as SQL injection. Answers A, C, and D are all incorrect and are not directly related to the issue described here.

Answer 3: D. Implementing a DLP solution to prevent sensitive data from being emailed to non-business accounts is the best choice. Answer A is incorrect as this solution isn't necessarily needed to halt all email. Answer B is incorrect as transport encryption will still allow personal email accounts to receive the sensitive data. Answer C is incorrect because encryption will still allow the email to be sent externally.

Answer 4: C. Answer C maps the protocols with their correct default ports. The other answers, A, B, and D, are incorrect. Refer to Table 18.2 for a list of commonly used services and ports you should be familiar with.

Answer 5: B. Static analysis is a white-box software testing process for detecting bugs. Static analysis is a thorough approach to bug detection in the early stages of program development. Answers A and C are incorrect because dynamic analysis is done while a program is in operation. Dynamic analysis uses a technique called fuzzing, which is a black-box software-testing process in which semi-random data is injected into a program or protocol stack to detect bugs. Answer D is incorrect. Sandboxing allows programs and processes to be run in an isolated environment in order to limit access to files and the host system.

What Next?

If you want more practice on this chapter's exam objective before you move on, remember that you can access all of the Cram Quiz questions on the Pearson Test Prep software online. You can also create a custom exam by objective with the Online Practice Test. Note any objective you struggle with and go to that objective's material in this chapter.

CHAPTER 19

Secure Network Design

This chapter covers the following official Security+ exam objective:

▶ 3.3 Given a scenario, implement secure network designs.

Essential Terms and Components

▶ load balancing

▶ network segmentation

▶ screened subnet (previously known as demilitarized zone)

▶ east–west traffic

▶ Zero Trust

▶ virtual private network (VPN)

▶ network access control (NAC)

▶ port security

▶ jump server

▶ proxy server

▶ network-based intrusion detection system (NIDS)

▶ network-based intrusion prevention system (NIPS)

▶ web application firewall (WAF)

▶ next-generation firewalls (NGFW)

▶ unified threat management (UTM)

▶ network address translation (NAT) gateway

▶ access control list (ACL)

▶ IPv6

Network Devices and Segmentation

Secure network design depends on understanding the concepts of basic perimeter and internal network devices and devices that provide a myriad of additional services, such as acting as load balancers and as proxies that improve network functionality. Many of these devices were developed for faster connectivity and to eliminate traffic bottlenecks; others were developed for convenience. With all devices that touch a network, proper placement and security features are important implementation considerations.

Routers

Routers operate at the network layer of the OSI model. They receive information from a host and forward that information to its destination on the network or the Internet. Routers maintain tables that are checked each time a packet needs to be redirected from one interface to another. The tables inside the router help speed up request resolution so that packets can reach their destination more quickly. The routes can be added to the routing table manually or can be updated automatically using the following protocols:

- ▶ Routing Information Protocol (RIP/RIPv2)
- ▶ Interior Gateway Routing Protocol (IGRP)
- ▶ Enhanced Interior Gateway Routing Protocol (EIGRP)
- ▶ Open Shortest Path First (OSPF)
- ▶ Border Gateway Protocol (BGP)
- ▶ Exterior Gateway Protocol (EGP)
- ▶ Intermediate System-to-Intermediate System (IS-IS)

Although router placement is primarily determined based on the need to segment different networks or subnets, routers also have some good security features. One of the best features of a router is its capability to filter packets by source address, destination address, protocol, or port. *Access control lists (ACLs)* are used to do this filtering.

ExamAlert

In the broadest sense, an ACL is a rule that controls traffic to and from network resources.

Basic Internet routing is based on the destination IP address, and a router with a default configuration forwards packets based only on the destination IP address. In IP spoofing, an attacker gains unauthorized access to a network by making it appear (by faking the IP address) as if traffic has come from a trusted source.

ExamAlert

Routers can be configured to help prevent IP spoofing. Anti-spoofing techniques can include creating a set of access lists that deny access to private IP addresses and local host ranges from the Internet and also using strong protocol authentication.

Because routers are a crucial part of a network, it is important to properly secure them. The security that is configured when setting up and managing routers can be the difference between keeping data secure and providing an open invitation to an attacker. The following are general recommendations for router security:

▶ Create and maintain a written router security policy. The policy should identify who is allowed to log in to the router and who is allowed to configure and update it. The policy also should outline logging and management practices.

▶ Create and organize offline master editions of your router configuration files. Keep the offline copies of all router configurations in sync with the configurations that are actually running on the routers.

▶ Implement access lists that allow only the protocols, ports, and IP addresses that network users and services require. Deny everything else.

▶ Test the security of your routers regularly, especially after any major configuration changes.

Keep in mind that, no matter how secure your routing protocol, if you never change the default password on the router, you leave yourself wide open to attacks. At the opposite end of the spectrum, a router that is too tightly locked down can turn a functional network into a completely isolated network that does not allow access to anyone.

Network Address Translation (NAT)

A *network address translation (NAT) gateway* acts as a liaison between an internal network and the Internet. It allows multiple computers to connect to the

Internet using one IP address. An important security aspect of NAT is that it hides the internal network from the outside world because the internal network uses a private IP address.

Smaller companies can use Windows Internet Connection Sharing (ICS) to achieve NAT. With ICS, all machines share one Internet connection, such as a broadband modem. NAT can also be used for address translation among multiple protocols; it improves security and provides more interoperability in heterogeneous networks.

NAT is not generally used with secure protocols such as DNSSEC or IPsec because of its lack of support for TCP segment reassembly. IPsec uses cryptography to protect communications. NAT has to replace the headers of an incoming packet with its own headers before sending the packet. This might not be possible when IPsec is in use because IPsec information is encrypted.

IPv6 was developed before NAT was in general use. IPv6 is designed to replace IPv4. Addresses are 128 bits instead of the 32 bits used in IPv4. IPv6 addresses are represented in hexadecimal. Because IPv6 offers an almost infinite number of addresses, it makes NAT unnecessary. However, Network Address Translation—Protocol Translation (NAT-PT; RFC 2766) was developed as a means for hosts that run IPv6 to communicate with hosts that run IPv4.

Switches

Switches are the most common choice when it comes to connecting desktops to a wiring closet. Switches generally operate at the data link layer (Layer 2) of the OSI model. Their packet-forwarding decisions are based on Media Access Control (MAC) addresses. Switches allow LANs to be segmented, thus increasing the amount of bandwidth that goes to each device. Each segment is a separate collision domain, but all segments are in the same broadcast domain. Here are the basic functions of a switch:

- ▶ Filtering and forwarding frames
- ▶ Learning MAC addresses
- ▶ Preventing loops

Managed switches are configurable. You can implement sound security with switches much as you can configure security on a firewall or a router. Managed switches allow control over network traffic and who has access to the network. In general, you do not want to deploy managed switches using their default

configuration because the default configuration often does not provide the most secure network design.

A VLAN can be used to properly segment a network. A VLAN provides a way to limit broadcast traffic in a switched network, creating a boundary and, in essence, creating multiple, isolated LANs on one switch. A VLAN provides a logical separation of a physical network and often combines Layer 2 and Layer 3 switches. Layer 3 switches can best be described as routers with fast forwarding done through hardware. Layer 3 switches can perform some of the same functions as routers and offer more flexibility than Layer 2 switches.

Port Security

Port security is a Layer 2 traffic control feature on switches. It enables individual switch ports to be configured to allow only a specified number of source MAC addresses to come in through the port. The primary use of port security is to keep two or three users from sharing a single access port. You can use the port security feature to restrict input to an interface by limiting and identifying MAC addresses of the workstations that are allowed to access the port. When you assign secure MAC addresses to a secure port, the port does not forward packets with source addresses outside the group of defined addresses. If you limit the number of secure MAC addresses to one and assign a single secure MAC address, the workstation attached to that port is assured the full bandwidth of the port. By default, a port security violation forces the interface into the error-disabled state. Port security can be configured to enter one of three modes when a violation is detected: default shutdown mode, protect mode, or restrict mode. In protect mode, frames from MAC addresses other than the allowed addresses are dropped. Restrict mode is similar to protect mode, but it generates a syslog message and increases the violation counter.

The following security mechanisms provide port security:

▶ **Bridge Protocol Data Unit (BDPU) Guard:** A BDPU is used to exchange data to ensure the ideal path for the flow of data, but it can also be leveraged for an attack. BDPU Guard provides a mechanism to prevent receipt of a BDPU from a connected device such as a client and reflect the BPDU back to the switch.

▶ **Media Access Control (MAC) filtering:** This is a security control that authorizes access to only known network card addresses.

▶ **Loop detection:** This is a mechanism that prevents degraded network service when there are multiple paths carrying data from the same source to the same destination. Loop detection works by transmitting a special

loop packet that, when detected, prompts appropriately shutdown of ports. This helps prevent loops as well as broadcast storms, where data is forwarded by the switch from every port.

▶ **Dynamic Host Configuration Protocol (DHCP) snooping**: DHCP snooping prevents rogue DHCP servers from providing IP addresses to clients by validating messages from untrusted sources.

Designing a network properly from the start and implementing appropriate controls is important to ensure that the network is stable, reliable, and scalable. Physical and virtual security controls must be in place. Locate switches in a physically secure area, if possible. Be sure that strong authentication and password policies are in place to secure access to the operating system and configuration files.

> **ExamAlert**
>
> Various controls help maintain port security. Ensure that you are familiar with port security controls and keep in mind that even with filtering, MAC addresses can be spoofed, and multiple hosts can still easily be hidden behind a small router.

Virtual Local Area Network (VLAN)

A *virtual local area network* (*VLAN*) can be used to properly segment a network. The purpose of VLAN is to unite network nodes logically into the same broadcast domain, regardless of their physical attachment to the network. A VLAN provides a logical separation of a physical network. It is basically a software solution that supports the creation of unique tag identifiers that can be assigned to different ports on a switch.

A VLAN provides a way to limit broadcast traffic in a switched network, creating a boundary and, in essence, creating multiple, isolated LANs on one switch. When the hosts in one VLAN need to communicate with hosts in another VLAN, the traffic must be routed between them; this is called *inter-VLAN routing*. When a Layer 2 (data link layer) switch is used, a router is required to pass the traffic from one VLAN to another. When a Layer 3 (network layer) switch is used, inter-VLAN routing is done through Layer 3 interfaces.

> **ExamAlert**
>
> The purpose of a VLAN is to logically group network nodes, regardless of their physical location.

The most notable benefit of using a VLAN is that it can span multiple switches. Because users on the same VLAN do not have to be associated by physical location, they can be grouped logically. VLANs provide the following benefits:

▶ Users can be grouped by logical department instead of physical location.

▶ Moving and adding users is simplified. No matter where a user physically moves, changes are made to the software configuration in the switch.

▶ Grouping users with VLANs makes it easier to apply security policies.

Working with VLANs involves a variety of configurations and considerations. For example, when mapping VLANs onto a new hierarchical network design, it is important to check the subnetting scheme that has been applied to the network and associate a VLAN to each subnet. Allocating IP address spaces in contiguous blocks allows the switch blocks to be summarized into one large address block. In addition, different types of traffic might exist on the network, and organizations should consider this before they implement device placement and VLAN configuration.

Ideally, a VLAN should be limited to one access switch or switch stack. However, it might be necessary to extend a VLAN across multiple access switches within a switch block to support a capability such as wireless mobility. In such a situation, if you are using multiple switches from various vendors, you need to consider that some switch features might be supported on only one vendor's switches but not on other vendors' switches. You need to consider such points as VLAN Trunking Protocol (VTP) domain management and inter-VLAN routing when you have two or more switches in a network.

Keep in mind that use of a VLAN is not an absolute safeguard against security infringements. A VLAN does not provide the same level of security as a router. A VLAN is a software solution and cannot take the place of a well-subnetted or routed network. It is possible to make frames hop from one VLAN to another. This takes skill and knowledge on the part of an attacker, but it is possible.

Bridges

Bridges are often used when two different network types need to be accessed. Bridges provide some network layer functions, such as route discovery, as well as forwarding at the data link layer. They forward packets only between networks that are destined for the other network. Several types of bridges exist:

▶ **Transparent basic bridge:** Acts similarly to a repeater. It merely stores traffic until it can move on.

▶ **Source routing bridge:** Interprets the routing information field (RIF) in the LAN frame header.

▶ **Transparent learning bridge:** Pinpoints the routing location by using the source and destination addresses in its routing table. As new destination addresses are found, they are added to the routing table.

▶ **Transparent spanning bridge:** Contains a subnet of the full topology for creating loop-free operation.

Looping problems can occur when a site uses two or more bridges in parallel between two LANs to increase the reliability of the network. A major feature in Layer 2 devices is Spanning Tree Protocol (STP), a link-management protocol that provides path redundancy and prevents undesirable loops in the network. Multiple active paths between stations cause loops in the network. When loops occur, some devices see stations appear on both sides of the device. This condition confuses the forwarding algorithm and allows duplicate frames to be forwarded. This situation can occur in bridges as well as Layer 2 switches.

A *bridge loop* occurs when data units can travel from a first LAN segment to a second LAN segment through more than one path. To eliminate bridge loops, existing bridge devices typically employ a technique referred to as the *spanning tree algorithm*. The spanning tree algorithm is implemented by bridges interchanging special messages known as *bridge protocol data units* (*BPDUs*). The STP Loop Guard feature provides additional protection against STP loops.

> **ExamAlert**
>
> Spanning Tree Protocol is designed to detect and prevent loops. It also helps prevent loops on managed switches.

An STP loop is created when an STP blocking port in a redundant topology erroneously transitions to the forwarding state. This usually happens because one of the ports of a physically redundant topology no longer receives STP BPDUs. In its operation, STP relies on continuous reception or transmission of BPDUs, based on the port role. The Loop Guard feature makes additional checks. If BPDUs are not received on a non-designated port and Loop Guard is enabled, that port is moved into the STP loop-inconsistent blocking state instead of the listening/learning/forwarding state. Without the Loop Guard feature, the port assumes the designated port role. The port then moves to the STP forwarding state and creates a loop.

Security Devices and Boundaries

A firewall is a component placed on a computer or a network to help eliminate undesired access by the outside world. It can consist of hardware,
software, or a combination of both. A firewall is the first line of defense
for a network. The primary function of a firewall is to mitigate threats by
monitoring all traffic entering or leaving a network. How firewalls are configured is important, especially for large companies. A compromised firewall
might spell disaster in the form of bad publicity or a lawsuit—not only for
the company whose firewall is compromised but for the companies it does
business with. For smaller companies, a firewall is an excellent investment
because most small companies do not have a full-time technology staff, and
an intrusion could easily put them out of business. All things considered, a
firewall is an important part of your defense, but you should not rely on it
exclusively for network protection. Figure 19.1 shows an example of firewall
placement in a small network.

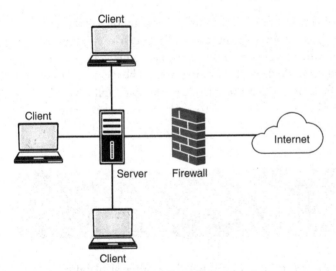

FIGURE 19.1   **A small network firewall placement**

Generally, a firewall can be described as being either stateful or stateless. A
stateless firewall tends to work as ACL filters. This type of firewall does not
inspect traffic. It merely observes the traffic coming into and going out of the
network and then allows or denies packets based on the information in the
ACL. Because this type of firewall does minimal filtering, it tends to be faster
than a stateful firewall and is best for heavy traffic loads.

> **ExamAlert**
>
> A stateless firewall tends to work as basic ACL filters. A stateful firewall is a deeper inspection firewall type that analyzes traffic patterns and data flows.

A *stateful firewall* is a deeper inspection firewall type that analyzes traffic patterns and data flows. This allows a more dynamic access control decision because the network state is not static. Stateful firewalls are better when it comes to identifying unauthorized communication attempts because they watch the state of the connection from beginning to end, including security functions such as tunnels and encryption.

Rules can be created for either inbound traffic or outbound traffic. Inbound rules explicitly allow or explicitly block inbound network traffic that matches the criteria in the rule. Outbound rules explicitly allow or explicitly block network traffic originating from the computer that matches the criteria in the rule.

In many firewalls, granular rules can be configured to specify the computers or users, programs, services, or ports and protocols. Rules can be configured so that they are applied when profiles are used. As soon as a network packet matches a rule, that rule is applied, and processing stops. The more restrictive rules should be listed first, and the least restrictive rules should follow; if a less restrictive rule is placed before a more restrictive rule, checking stops at the first rule.

> **ExamAlert**
>
> The order of firewall rules affects their application. When a less restrictive rule is placed before a more restrictive rule, checking stops at the first rule.

Implicit deny is an access control practice in which resource availability is restricted to only logins that are explicitly granted access. The resources remain unavailable even when logins are not explicitly denied access. This practice is commonly used in Cisco networks, where most ACLs have implicit deny as the default setting. By default, an implicit deny all clause appears at the end of every ACL, and based on this, anything that is not explicitly permitted is denied. Essentially, an implicit deny works the same as finishing an ACL with the statement deny ip any any. This ensures that when access is not explicitly granted, it is automatically denied by default.

ExamAlert

The implicit deny is generally used by default in firewall configurations. An access list has an implicit deny at the end of the list; unless you explicitly permit it, traffic cannot pass.

Designing a network properly from the start and implementing appropriate controls is important to ensure that the network is stable, reliable, and scalable. Physical and virtual security controls must be in place. Controls include segregation, segmentation, and isolation. The network should be segmented to separate information and infrastructure based on organizational security requirements.

Network segregation, isolation, and segmentation are some of the most effective controls an organization can implement to mitigate the effect of network intrusion. When properly implemented, these controls can be used as preventive measures to protect sensitive information. In sensitive systems such as supervisory control and data acquisition (SCADA) networks, applying *network segmentation* in layers, from the data link layer through the application layer, can go a long way toward protecting vital infrastructure services. Segmentation, isolation, and segregation entail more than just segmenting networks via firewalls. They also include restricting intersystem communication to specific ports or protocols.

ExamAlert

Some key considerations for implementing good network segmentation, segregation, and isolation are knowing how users and systems interact and communicate with each other, implementing least privilege and need-to-know principles, using whitelisting instead of blacklisting, and addressing all layers of the OSI model.

When your computers are on separate physical networks, you can divide your network into subnets that enable you to use one block of addresses on multiple physical networks. If an incident happens and you notice it quickly, you can usually contain the issue to the affected subnet.

In addition to securing internal connectivity, you should secure connections between interconnecting networks. This might be appropriate when an organization establishes network interconnections with partners, as in an extranet or with an actual connection between the involved organizations because of a merger, an acquisition, or a joint project. Business partners can include government agencies and commercial organizations. Although this type of

interconnection increases functionality and reduces costs, it can result in security risks, including compromise of all connected systems and any network connected to those systems, along with exposure of data the systems handle. With interconnected networks, the potential for damage greatly increases because a compromise of a system on one network can easily spread to other networks. Networks that partners, vendors, or departments share should have clear separation boundaries.

Air gaps are physically isolated machines or networks that do not have any connection to the Internet or any machine that connects to the Internet. Even when an organization implements an air gap, there are still risks to the environment. For example, files such as patches and updates must be exchanged with the outside world, employees connect personal devices to the network, and misconfigurations can cause vulnerabilities.

It is important not to neglect physical security. Place switches in a physically secure area, if possible. Make sure that network management stations are secure both physically and on the network. You might even consider using a separate management subnet and protecting it using a router with an access list.

As you create a network security policy, you must define procedures to defend your network and users against harm and loss. With this objective in mind, network design and its included components play an important role in implementing security for the organization. An overall security solution includes design elements such as zones and topologies that distinguish private networks, intranets, and the Internet. This section discusses these elements and helps you tell them apart and also understand their places in the security of the network.

Screened Subnet

A *screened subnet* or demilitarized zone (DMZ) is a small network between an internal network and the Internet that provides a layer of security and privacy. Both internal and external users might have limited access to the servers in the screened subnet. Figure 19.2 depicts a screened subnet. Firewalls play a huge role in managing both east–west traffic and north–south traffic. *East–west traffic* refers to traffic within a data center between servers, and *north–south* traffic refers to data transfers between the data center and outside of the network. The single firewall shown earlier in Figure 19.1 is an example of north–south traffic control. Screened subnets are a great example of controlling east–west traffic.

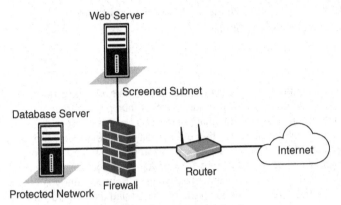

FIGURE 19.2   An example of a screened subnet

Web servers and mail servers are often placed in the screened subnet. Because these devices are exposed to the Internet, it is important that they be hardened and kept current with patches. The screened subnet allows external users to access information that the organization deems necessary but that will not compromise any internal organizational information. This configuration permits outside access yet prevents external users from directly accessing a server that holds internal organizational data.

> **ExamAlert**
>
> An exposed server or a segmented network that provides public access to a critical service, such as a web server or an email server, can be configured to be isolated from an organization's network but to report attack attempts to the network administrator. Such a network is called a screened subnet (formerly known as a demilitarized zone or DMZ).

In addition to a screened subnet, many organizations have intranets and extranets. An *intranet* is a subnet portion or segmented zone of an internal network that uses web-based technologies. The information is stored on web servers and accessed using browsers. The web servers don't necessarily have to be accessible to the outside world. This is possible because the IP addresses of the servers are reserved for private internal use. If the intranet can be accessed from public networks, this access should be accomplished through a virtual private network (VPN) for security reasons.

An *extranet* is a subnet or segmented zone of the public portion of a company's IT infrastructure that grants resource access to partners and resellers that have proper authorization and authentication. This type of arrangement is commonly used in business-to-business relationships. An extranet can open an

organization to liability, so care must be taken to properly configure VPNs and firewalls to strictly enforce security policies.

The main objectives in the placement of network firewalls are to allow only traffic that the organization deems necessary and provide notification of suspicious behavior. Most organizations deploy at least two firewalls. The first firewall is placed in front of the screened subnet to allow requests destined for servers in the screened subnet or to route requests to an authentication proxy. The second firewall is placed between the screened subnet and the internal network to allow outbound requests. All initial necessary connections are located on the screened subnet machines. For example, a RADIUS server might be running in the screened subnet for improved performance and enhanced security, even though its database resides inside the company intranet. Most organizations have many firewalls; the level of protection is strongest when a firewall is close to the outside edge of the environment. Figure 19.3 shows an example.

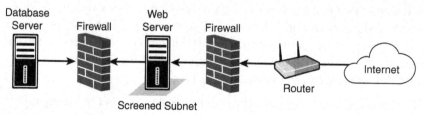

FIGURE 19.3   **A network with a screened subnet separated by two firewalls**

When deploying multiple firewalls, you might experience network latency. If you do, check the placement of the firewalls and possibly reconsider the topology to ensure that you get the most out of the firewalls. Another factor to think about is the use of a storage-area network (SAN) or network-attached storage (NAS) behind a firewall. Most storage environments span multiple networks, creating a virtual bridge that can counteract a firewall, providing a channel into the storage environment if a system is compromised in the screened subnet.

For better security, segment a wireless network by placing a firewall between the WLAN and the rest of the network. Because IPsec is a solution to securely authenticate and encrypt network IP packets, you can use IPsec to provide strong security between a Remote Authentication Dial-In User Service (RADIUS) server and a domain controller or to secure traffic to a partner organization's RADIUS servers. RADIUS provides authentication and access control within an enterprise network. Many VPN solutions use IPsec, which is an excellent solution in many circumstances. However, IPsec should not be a direct alternative for WLAN protection implemented at the network hardware layer.

> **Note**
>
> An important security concept common in managing screened subnets is a jump server or jump box. A *jump server* is a system used to access systems in different security zones, such as a screened subnet. It is an especially hardened system just for this purpose that provides a method to access resources in the screened subnet from the protected network via other trusted systems.

Web Application Firewalls

Web application firewalls (*WAFs*) can examine HTTP application traffic and identify threats through deep packet inspection techniques. Often we do not think in terms of application-level security when discussing devices such as firewalls, IPSs, IDSs, and proxies. However, most next-generation devices are capable of being application aware. To meet the changing ways organizations do business, *next-generation firewalls* (*NGFWs*) have been developed. NGFWs are considered application-aware. This means they go beyond the traditional port and IP address examination of stateless firewalls to inspect traffic at a deeper level. Application layer firewalls integrate the functions of other network devices, such as proxies, IDSs, and IPSs. Many application layer firewalls use an IPS engine to provide application support. As a result, various blended techniques are used to identify applications and formulate policies based on business rules.

Application layer firewalls are preferred to network layer firewalls because they have the capability to do deep packet inspection and function at Layer 7 of the OSI model. Network layer firewalls mainly function at Layer 3 of the OSI model and, as such, are basically limited to packet forwarding.

Proxies

A *proxy server* operates on the same principle as a proxy-level firewall: It is a go-between for the network and the Internet. Proxy servers are used for security, logging, and caching. Various types of proxy servers exist, including forward, reverse, and transparent proxy servers, as well as caching, multipurpose, and application proxy servers.

When a caching proxy server receives a request for an Internet service (usually on port 80 or 443), it passes the request through filtering requirements and checks its local cache for previously downloaded web pages. The web pages are stored locally, so response times for web pages are faster, and traffic to the Internet is substantially reduced.

The web cache can also be used to block content from websites that you do not want employees to access, such as pornography, social media, or peer-to-peer networks. You can use this type of server to rearrange web content to work for mobile devices. This strategy also provides better utilization of bandwidth because it stores all your results from requests for a period of time.

A caching server that does not require a client-side configuration is called a *transparent proxy server*. In this type of server, the client is unaware of a proxy server. Transparent proxies are also called *inline, intercepting,* or *forced prox-ies*. The proxy redirects client requests without modifying them. Transparent proxy servers are implemented primarily to reduce bandwidth usage and client configuration overhead in large networks. Transparent proxy servers are found in large enterprise organizations and ISPs. Because transparent proxies have no client overhead and can filter content, they are ideal for use in schools and libraries.

Most proxy servers today are web application proxies that support protocols such as HTTP and HTTPS. When clients and the server cannot directly connect because of some type of incompatibility issue, such as security authentication, an application proxy server is used. Application proxies must support the application for which they are performing the proxy function and do not typically encrypt data. On the other hand, multipurpose proxy servers, also known as universal application-level gateways, are capable of running various

operating systems (such as Linux, Windows, and macOS) and allowing multiple protocols to pass through (such as HTTP, FTP, NNTP, SMTP, IMAP, LDAP, and DNS). They also can convert between IPv4 and IPv6 addresses. These proxies can be used for caching, converting pass-through traffic, and handling access control. They are not restricted to a certain application or protocol.

Depending on the network size and content requirements, either a forward or reverse proxy is used. Forward and reverse proxies add a layer of security to the network by controlling traffic to and from the Internet. Both types of proxy servers are used as intermediaries for requests between source and destination hosts. A *forward proxy* controls traffic originating from clients on the internal network that is destined for hosts on the Internet. Because client requests are required to pass through the proxy before they are permitted to access Internet resources, forward proxy servers are primarily used to enforce security on internal client computers and are often used in conjunction with a firewall. Forward proxies can also be implemented for anonymity because they do not allow direct client access to the Internet.

Reverse proxy servers do just the opposite: A *reverse proxy server* operates on the server side to cache static HTTP content when the server accepts requests from external Internet clients. The primary purpose of a reverse proxy server is to increase the efficiency and scalability of the web server by providing load-balancing services. Full reverse proxies are capable of deep content inspection and often are implemented in order to enforce web application security and mitigate data leaks.

> **ExamAlert**
>
> Know the differences between forward and reverse proxy servers.

Proxy servers are used for a variety of reasons, and their placement depends on usage. You can place proxy servers between the private network and the Internet for Internet connectivity or internally for web content caching. If an organization is using a proxy server for both Internet connectivity and web content caching, you should place the proxy server between the internal network and the Internet, with access for users who are requesting the web content. In some proxy server designs, the proxy server is placed in parallel with IP routers. This design allows for network load balancing by forwarding all HTTP and FTP traffic through the proxy server and all other IP traffic through the router.

Proxies today play a huge role in filtering inappropriate or malicious content. Content filtering proxies control Internet content that is available for use in

the organizational environment. Internet content filters compare a collection of terms, words, and phrases to content from browsers and applications. This type of software can filter content from various Internet activities and applications, such as instant messaging, email, and Microsoft Office documents. Content filtering reports only on violations identified in the specified applications listed for the filtering application. In other words, if the application filters only Microsoft Office documents and a user chooses to use Office, the content is filtered. If the user chooses to use something other than Office, that content is not filtered.

Internet content filtering works by analyzing data against a database contained in the software. If a match occurs, the data can be addressed in one of several ways, including filtering, capturing, or blocking the content and closing the application. Operating system parental controls is an example of software that enables Internet content filtering.

Unlike antivirus and antispyware applications, content monitoring does not require daily updates to keep the database effective and current. On the downside, content filtering needs to be "trained."

> **ExamAlert**
>
> A misconfigured web content filter can either prevent legitimate content or allow prohibited content. For example, if the IP addresses or domains of customers are accidentally blocked, customers become blacklisted.

Accidentally blacklisting customers can have a very detrimental effect on business. The issue with most content filters is that they look at only HTTP traffic and filter based on a database of words.

Content filters can be bypassed by using HTTPS, a filter evasion application such as TOR, or a web proxy service. To prevent a content filter from being bypassed, select a solution that is used inline, has the capability to decrypt HTTPS, and uses real-time analysis to detect proxy website behavior.

Content filtering proxies can be hardware or software. Many network solutions use some combination of both. Configurations include deployment behind a firewall or in a screened subnet, with public addresses behind a packet-filtering router. Content filters and gateway appliances that filter are most often placed inline behind a corporate firewall. When a filter is placed directly inline, all network traffic to the Internet passes through the filter. This facilitates filtering and scanning of all Internet traffic requests, content filtering and scanning of

downloads for spyware and viruses, and application filtering. The following are also available modes for filters:

- ▶ One network interface, with the client configured in proxy mode
- ▶ One network interface in routed proxy mode
- ▶ Two network interfaces in pass-through mode
- ▶ Two network interfaces, with the client configured in proxy mode

Hardware appliances are usually connected to the same network segment as the users they monitor. These appliances use access control filtering software on the dedicated filtering appliance. The device monitors every packet of traffic that passes over a network. In a multisegmented network, the filter must be installed in a location where it can both receive and manage Internet requests from the filter and communicate with installed agents.

Every proxy server in a network must have at least one network interface. A proxy server with a single network interface can provide web content caching and IP gateway services. To provide Internet connectivity, you must specify two or more network interfaces for the proxy server.

Unified Threat Management (UTM)

Spyware, malware, worms, and viruses pose serious threats to both system integrity and user privacy. The prevalence of such malicious programs can also threaten the stability of critical systems and networks. Vendors have responded by offering converged *unified threat management* (*UTM*) security appliances that contain varying information security–related functions, including spam-filtering functions and antivirus protection. For example, the Barracuda Spam and Virus Firewall has antivirus protection built in. Another example is the Cisco Web Security Appliance.

A malware inspection filter is basically a web filter applied to traffic that uses HTTP. The body of each HTTP request and response is inspected. Malicious content is blocked, and legitimate content passes through unaltered. Passing files can be hashed and matched against the signatures stored in a malware signature database. Other approaches include caching files for running a heuristic scan later within the file cache. If the scan finds a malicious file in the file cache, the signature is inserted in the malware signature database so that it can be blocked in the future.

Other UTM features may include, for example, email filtering, DLP, content filtering, and an application layer firewall. In UTM devices, updates are posted hourly to ensure that the latest definitions are in place. As with any appliance that provides multiple functions, a UTM appliance is a single point of failure. To maintain availability, organizations might need to have two units deployed in automatic failover mode. Minimally, a UTM appliance provides a network firewall and IDS and IPS capabilities.

VPN Concentrators

Employees in today's mobile workforce require a secure method for accessing corporate resources while on the road or working from home. One of the most common methods implemented for this type of access is a *virtual private network (VPN)*. A *VPN concentrator* is used to allow multiple external users to access internal network resources using secure features that are built into the device. A VPN concentrator is deployed where a single device must handle a very large number of VPN tunnels. Remote-access VPN connectivity is provided using either Internet Protocol Security (IPsec) or Transport Layer Security (TLS/SSL). User authentication can be via RADIUS, Kerberos, Microsoft Active Directory, RSA SecurID, digital certificates, or the built-in authentication server.

In addition to IPsec VPNs, technologies such as TLS and its predecessor, SSL, can be used to secure network communications. These VPNs use the SSL and TLS protocols to provide a secure connection between internal network resources and remote users such as bring your own device (BYOD) users, vendors, and business partners. Because TLS is a point-to-point communication encryption technology, it can be used to secure traffic in a variety of applications, including web- and email-based communications. The main advantage of SSL and TLS VPNs over IPsec VPNs is simple end-user implementation because they function via a browser and an Internet connection.

In a typical scenario, the VPN concentrator allows users to utilize an encrypted tunnel to securely access a corporate network or other network via the Internet. Another use is internally, to encrypt WLAN or wired traffic when the security of login and password information is paramount for high-level users and sensitive information. You can implement a VPN concentrator to prevent login and password information from being captured. A VPN concentrator also allows ACLs to be applied to remote user sessions. These scenarios use various technologies that you need to comprehend to properly implement the correct VPN solution.

VPN concentrators come in various models and allow for customized options, such as the numbers of simultaneous users, amount of throughput needed, amount of protection required, and tunnel modes. For example, Cisco VPN concentrators include components that allow for split tunneling, increased capacity, and throughput.

ExamAlert

With an always-on VPN, the user is always on a trusted and secured network.

The workforce has become very mobile, allowing employees to work anytime and anywhere. This shift has led organizations to replace traditional IPsec VPNs with SSL/TLS VPNs that include an always-on solution. In addition, Zero Trust concepts are being applied to eliminate VPNs as resources become more and more distributed, and the paradigm of a single trusted network no longer exists.

Instead of depending on the user to establish a VPN connection, an always-on VPN client immediately and automatically establishes a VPN connection when an Internet connection is made. Network authentication occurs through certificates or other enterprise solutions, and the connection is transparent to the user. Examples of always-on VPN solutions include Microsoft DirectAccess and Cisco AnyConnect Secure Mobility.

So far, this section has mainly discussed the technologies used to secure VPN communications, but other modes and types of VPNs exist as well. When you think of VPNs, you likely think of remote-access VPNs that connect single hosts to organizational networks. However, site-to-site VPNs are also possible.

ExamAlert

Besides being configured to secure traffic between a remote user and the corporate network, a VPN can be configured as a site-to-site VPN.

A *site-to-site* VPN is implemented based on IPsec policies assigned to VPN topologies. These VPNs connect entire networks to each other. An example of this type of implementation might be a VPN connecting a bank branch office to a network and the main office. Individual hosts do not need VPN client software. They communicate using normal TCP/IP traffic via a VPN gateway, which is responsible for setting up and breaking down the encapsulation and encryption traffic.

The last item this section discusses is the mode in which the VPN operates. Two modes are available: full tunneling and split tunneling.

Full tunneling works exactly as it sounds like it would: All requests are routed and encrypted through the VPN. In split tunneling, the traffic is divided. Internal traffic requests are routed over the VPN, and other traffic, such as web and email traffic, directly accesses the Internet.

With split tunneling, the traffic is split after the VPN connection is made through the client configuration settings, such as the IP address range or specific protocols. Split tunneling is mainly used to reserve bandwidth while the users are on the Internet and to reduce the load on the VPN concentrator, especially when the organization has a large remote workforce. Split tunneling can also be useful when employees are treated as contractors on client sites and require access to both employer resources and client resources.

NIDS and NIPS

An *intrusion detection system* (*IDS*) is designed to analyze data, identify attacks, and respond to intrusions by sending alerts. IDSs differ from firewalls in that whereas a firewall controls the information that gets into and out of the network, an IDS can also identify unauthorized activity. IDSs are also designed to identify attacks in progress within the network, not just on the boundary between private and public networks. Intrusion detection is managed by two basic methods: knowledge-based and behavior-based detection.

IDSs identify attacks based on rule sets, and an IDS typically has a large number of rules. Rule writing is an important and difficult part of network security monitoring. Luckily, security vendors do a lot of the rule writing. For example, Proofpoint currently has more than 37,000 rules, in several popular formats, and also hosts a web page that provides a daily rule set summary. Of course, these rules might need to be modified to meet the needs of the organization.

The two basic types of IDSs are network-based and host-based IDSs. As the names suggest, *network-based IDSs* (*NIDSs*) look at the information exchanged between machines. *Host-based IDSs* (*HIDSs*) look at information that originates on individual machines. Consider the following differences between the two types:

- ▶ NIDSs monitor the packet flow and try to locate packets that got through the firewall but were not supposed to do so. They are best at detecting DoS attacks and unauthorized user access.

- ▶ HIDSs monitor communications on a host-by-host basis and try to filter malicious data. These types of IDSs are good at detecting unauthorized file modifications and user activity.

ExamAlert

NIDSs try to locate packets that the firewall missed and that are not actually allowed on the network. HIDSs collect and analyze data that originates on the local machine or a computer hosting a service. NIDSs tend to be more distributed than HIDSs.

NIDSs and HIDSs should be used together to ensure that an environment is truly secure. IDSs can be located anywhere on a network. You can place them internally or between firewalls. As with other network devices, the placement of a NIDS determines the effectiveness of the technology.

A typical NIDS consists of sensors to monitor packet traffic, a server for management functions, and a management console. A *sensor* collects information about a network and can really be anything from a network tap to a firewall log. Sensors in both NIDS and NIPS have real-time network awareness. Generally, sensor placement depends on what the organization wants to protect, the calculated risk, and traffic flows. Sensors should be placed closest to assets identified as high priority or most important. Other considerations with sensor placement include the following:

▶ Use or purpose of the sensor

▶ Bandwidth utilization

▶ Distance from protected assets

Sensors can be placed outside the perimeter of the firewall as an early detection system or can be used internally as an added layer of security. Using sensors outside the perimeter firewall generates a lot of noise. This is not typically the ideal placement, but it can occasionally work for fine-tuning security policy. Internally placed sensors that are near the local network switching nodes and near the access routers at the network boundary have reduced false alarm rates because the sensors do not have to monitor any traffic blocked by the firewall. Sensors should be placed in the screened subnet because compromise of a machine in this zone could lead to a compromise of the internal network.

Intrusion detection software and devices are reactive, or passive. This means that the system detects a potential security breach, logs the information, and signals an alert after the event occurs. By the time an alert has been issued, the attack has usually occurred and has damaged the network or desktop. A passive device is sometimes referred to as an *out-of-band device*.

ExamAlert

Out-of-band devices only listen passively. They do not change or affect the traffic.

Network-based intrusion prevention systems (*NIPSs*) are sometimes considered to be an extension of IDSs. NIPSs can be either hardware or software based, as with many other network protection devices. Intrusion prevention differs from intrusion detection in that it actually prevents attacks instead of only detecting the occurrence of attacks.

> **ExamAlert**
>
> NIPSs are designed to sit inline with traffic flows and prevent attacks in real time. An inline NIPS sits between the systems that need to be protected and the rest of the network.

NIPSs proactively protect machines against damage from attacks that signature-based technologies cannot detect because most NIPS solutions can look at application layer protocols such as HTTP, FTP, and SMTP. When implementing a NIPS, keep in mind that the sensors must be physically inline to function properly.

> **ExamAlert**
>
> An IDS detects and alerts. An IPS detects and prevents. Know the difference between the two concepts.

A NIPS is often referred to as an *in-band device*. Because the device is analyzing live network traffic, an in-band device acts as the enforcement point and can prevent an attack from reaching its target. In general, in-band systems are deployed at the network perimeter, but they also can be used internally to capture traffic flows at certain network points, such as into the data center.

Detection Methods

Behavior-based intrusion detection methods are rooted in the premise that an intrusion can be detected by comparing the normal activity of a network to current activity. Any abnormalities from normal or expected behavior of the network are reported via an alarm. Behavior-based methods can identify attempts to exploit new or undocumented vulnerabilities, can alert to elevation or abuse of privileges, and tend to be independent of operating system–specific processes. Behavior-based methods consider any activity that does not match a learned behavior to be intrusive. These methods are associated with a high false alarm rate. If a network is compromised before the learned behavior period, any malicious activity related to the compromise is not reported.

Signature-based detection methods are considered knowledge based because the underlying mechanism is a database of known vulnerabilities. Signature-based methods monitor a network to find a pattern or signature match. When they find a match, they generate an alert. Vendors provide signature updates, similar to antivirus software updates, but generally signatures can be created any time a particular behavior needs to be identified. Because pattern matching can be done quickly when the rule set is not extensive, the system or user notices very little intrusiveness or performance reduction.

> **ExamAlert**
>
> Signature-based methods only detect known signatures or patterns, so these events must be created for every suspicious activity. They are more reactive because an attack must be known before it can be added to the database.

Signature-based methods provide lower rates of false alarms compared to behavior-based methods because all suspicious activity is in a known database. Anomaly-based detection methods are similar to behavior-based intrusion detection methods. Both are based on the concept of using a baseline for network behavior. However, a slight variation exists between the two.

In anomaly-based detection methods, after the application is trained, the established profile is used on real data to detect deviations. Training an application entails inputting and defining data criteria in a database. In a behavior-based intrusion detection method, the established profile is compared to current activity, and monitoring seeks evidence of a compromise instead of the attack itself.

> **ExamAlert**
>
> Anomaly-based detection methods require the application engine to be able to decode and process all monitored protocols, which leads to high initial overhead. After the initial protocol behavior has been defined, scalability becomes more rapid and straightforward.

The rule development process for anomaly-based methods can become complicated because of the differences in vendor protocol implementations.

Heuristic intrusion detection methods are commonly known as anomaly-based methods because heuristic algorithms are used to identify anomalies.

> **ExamAlert**
>
> Much like anomaly-based methods, heuristic-based methods are typically rule based and look for abnormal behavior. Heuristic rules tend to categorize activity into one of the following types: benign, suspicious, or unknown. As an IDS learns network behavior, the activity category can change.

The slight difference between heuristic- and anomaly-based methods is that anomaly-based methods are less specific. Anomaly-based methods target behavior that is out of the ordinary instead of classifying all behavior.

Analytics

A *false positive* occurs when a typical or expected behavior is identified as being irregular or malicious. False positives generally occur when an IDS detects the presence of a newly installed application and the IDS has not yet been trained for this new behavior. Sometimes anomalous behavior in one area of an organization is acceptable, while in other areas it is suspicious.

False positives in IDS management are problematic because they can easily prevent legitimate IDS alerts from being identified quickly. Rule sets need to be tuned to reduce the number of false positives. A single rule that generates false positives can create thousands of alerts in a short period of time. In addition, the alerts for rules that cause repeated false positives are often ignored or disabled, which increases risk to the organization because legitimate attacks might eventually be ignored, increasing the probability that the system will be compromised by the type of attack the disabled or ignored rule was actually looking for.

A *false negative* occurs when an alert that should have been generated did not occur. In other words, an attack takes place, but the IDS doesn't detect it. False negatives most often happen because an IDS is reactive, and signature-based systems do not recognize new attacks. Sometimes in a signature-based system, a rule can be written to catch only a subset of an attack vector. Several risks are associated with false positives. When false positives occur, missed attacks are not mitigated, and the organization is likely to have a false sense of security. In addition, in an environment that relies on anomaly detection and in a host-based intrusion detection system (HIDS) that relies on file changes, if a system was compromised at the time of IDS training, false negatives will occur for any already exploited conditions.

ExamAlert

You should be familiar with the following terms for the exam:

▶ **False positive:** A typical or expected behavior is identified as being irregular or malicious.

▶ **False negative:** An alert that should have been generated did not occur.

Network Access Control (NAC)

One the most effective ways to protect a network from malicious hosts is to use *network access control* (*NAC*). NAC helps ensure that computers are properly configured. NAC systems are available as software packages or dedicated NAC appliances, although most are dedicated appliances that include both hardware and software. Some of the main uses for NAC follow:

▶ Guest network services

▶ Endpoint baselining

▶ Identity-aware networking

▶ Monitoring and containment

The idea with NAC is to secure the environment by examining the user's machine and then grant (or not grant) access based on the results. NAC is based on assessment and enforcement. For example, if a user's computer patches are not up to date and no desktop firewall software is installed, you might decide to limit access to network resources. Any host machine that does not comply with your defined policy could be relegated to a remediation server or put on a guest VLAN. The basic components of NAC products follow:

▶ **Access requestor (AR):** The AR is the device that requests access. Assessment of the device can be self-performed or delegated to another system.

▶ **Policy decision point (PDP):** The PDP is the system that assigns a policy based on the assessment. The PDP determines what access should be granted and can be the NAC's product-management system.

▶ **Policy enforcement point (PEP):** The PEP is the device that enforces the policy. This device can be a switch, a firewall, or a router.

NAC systems can be integrated into a network in four ways:

▶ **Inline:** An inline NAC system exists as an appliance inline, usually between the access point and the distribution switches.

▶ **Out of band:** An out-of-band NAC system intervenes and performs an assessment as hosts come online and then grants appropriate access.

▶ **Switch based:** Switch-based NAC works similarly to inline NAC, except that enforcement occurs on the switch itself.

▶ **Host or endpoint based:** Host- or endpoint-based NAC relies on an installed host agent to assess and enforce access policy.

NAC implementations require several design considerations such as whether to integrate with an agent or be agentless. For example, out-of-band designs might or might not use agents, and they can use 802.1X, VLAN steering, or IP subnets. In a NAC system that uses agents, devices are enrolled in the NAC system, and an agent is installed on the device. The agent reports to a NAC policy server. Agents provide detailed information about connected devices to enforce policies. An agent might permanently reside on an end device, or it might be dissolvable. If the agent is dissolvable, it provides one-time authentication, reports information to the NAC system, and then disappears. Because agents can be spoofed by malware, an organization needs to be vigilant about proper malware protection or should use an agentless NAC solution.

ExamAlert

Because the user clicks on a web link to download a dissolvable agent, this type of agent is also referred to as a portal-based agent.

Agents perform more granular health checks on endpoints to ensure a greater level of compliance. When a health check is on a computer or laptop, it is often called a *host health check*. Health checks monitor availability and performance for proper hardware and application functionality.

Agentless solutions are mainly implemented through embedded code within an Active Directory domain controller. The NAC code verifies that the end device complies with the access policy when a user joins the domain, logs on to, or logs out of the domain. Active Directory scans cannot be scheduled, and the device is scanned only during these three actions. Another instance in which an agentless solution is deployed is through an IPS.

Agentless solutions offer less functionality and require fewer resources than do agent-based solutions. A good solution for a large, diverse network or a network in which BYOD is prevalent is to combine both agent and agentless functionality and use the agentless solution as a fallback. Agents often do not work with all devices and operating systems. An alternative might be to use a downloadable, dissolvable agent; however, some device incompatibility might still arise.

In addition to providing the capability to enforce security policy, contain noncompliant users, and mitigate threats, NAC offers business benefits. These include compliance, a better security posture, and operational cost management.

Cram Quiz

Answer these questions. The answers follow the last question. If you cannot answer these questions correctly, consider reading this chapter again until you can.

1. Your company will have a new branch office. You need to seamlessly provide branch office users access to the corporate network resources as if they were at the corporate offices. Which of the following would best enable you to accomplish this goal?

   ◯ **A.** VLANs

   ◯ **B.** Site-to-site VPN

   ◯ **C.** Spanning Tree Protocol

   ◯ **D.** Screened subnet

2. You are consulting for an organization that has only ever required outbound Internet access. The organization now needs to deploy a web server for its customers (and it will maintain the web server) but is concerned about inbound access to the organization network. Which one of the following should you recommend?

   ◯ **A.** VLAN

   ◯ **B.** VPN

   ◯ **C.** Load balancer

   ◯ **D.** Screened subnet

3. Your company requires a switch feature that makes additional checks in Layer 2 networks to prevent STP issues. Which of the following safeguards should be implemented?

   ◯ **A.** Loop Guard

   ◯ **B.** Flood protections

   ◯ **C.** Implicit deny

   ◯ **D.** Port security

4. You are implementing server load balancing. In which configuration is the passive server promoted to active if the active server fails?

○ **A.** Active/active

○ **B.** Round-robin

○ **C.** Weighted round-robin

○ **D.** Active/passive

5. Your network IDS is reporting a high number of false positives. What does this mean?

○ **A.** Typical or expected behavior is being identified as irregular or malicious.

○ **B.** Alerts that should have been generated are not occurring.

○ **C.** The activity is being categorized into one of the following types: benign, suspicious, or unknown.

○ **D.** The IDS is preventing intrusions instead of detecting them.

Cram Quiz Answers

Answer 1: B. Besides being configured to secure traffic between a remote user and the corporate network, a VPN can be configured as a site-to-site VPN. Answer A is incorrect, as VLANs are logical separations of a physical network. Answer C is incorrect. Spanning Tree Protocol is a link-management protocol that provides path redundancy. Answer D is incorrect. A screened subnet is a subnetwork where an organization places externally facing servers.

Answer 2: D. A screened subnet is the best choice as it would allow the organization to expose a web server to the public yet have it isolated from the internal network via a logical subnetwork. Answers A and B are incorrect. VLANs are logical separations of a physical network. A VPN would provide for secure remote access into internal resources for the employees. Answer C is incorrect. While a load balancer can be used to manage the traffic to the organization's website and may be something the organization wants to consider, it does not meet the need to prevent inbound access to the network.

Answer 3: A. The Loop Guard feature makes additional checks in Layer 2 switched networks to prevent loops. Answer B is incorrect because flood protection is a firewall feature to control network activity associated with DoS attacks. Answer C is incorrect because implicit deny is an access control practice in which resource availability is restricted to only logons that are explicitly granted access. Answer D is incorrect because port security is a Layer 2 traffic control feature on Cisco Catalyst switches. It enables individual switch ports to be configured to allow only a specified number of source MAC addresses to come in through the port.

Answer 4: D. In an active/passive configuration, all traffic is sent to the active server. The passive server is promoted to active if the active server fails or is taken down for maintenance. Answer A is incorrect. In an active/active configuration, two or more servers work together to distribute the load to network servers. Answers B and C are incorrect because in a round-robin load-balancing strategy traffic is sent in a sequential, circular pattern to each node of a load balancer, and in a weighted round-robin strategy traffic is sent in a circular pattern to each node of a load balancer, based on the assigned weight number.

Answer 5: A. A false positive occurs when a typical or expected behavior is identified as irregular or malicious. Answer B is incorrect. A false negative occurs when an alert that should have been generated did not occur. Answer C is incorrect because this describes heuristic intrusion detection rules, which tend to categorize activity into one of the following types: benign, suspicious, or unknown. Answer D is incorrect. In fact, the opposite is true: An intrusion detection system (IDS) detects intrusions and sends alerts, whereas an intrusion prevention system (IPS) detects and prevents intrusions.

What Next?

If you want more practice on this chapter's exam objective before you move on, remember that you can access all of the Cram Quiz questions on the Pearson Test Prep software online. You can also create a custom exam by objective with the Online Practice Test. Note any objective you struggle with and go to that objective's material in this chapter.

CHAPTER 20

Wireless Security Settings

This chapter covers the following official Security+ exam objective:

▶ 3.4 Given a scenario, install and configure wireless security settings.

Essential Terms and Components

▶ Wi-Fi Protected Access Version 2 (WPA2)

▶ Wi-Fi Protected Access Version 3 (WPA3)

▶ Counter Mode Cipher Block Chaining Message Authentication Code Protocol (CCMP)

▶ Simultaneous Authentication of Equals (SAE)

▶ Extensible Authentication Protocol (EAP)

▶ Protected EAP (PEAP)

▶ EAP Flexible Authentication via Secure Tunneling (EAP-FAST)

▶ EAP-Transport Layer Security (EAP-TLS)

▶ EAP Tunneled Transport Layer Security (EAP-TTLS)

▶ IEEE 802.1X

▶ Remote Authentication Dial-In User Service (RADIUS)

▶ pre-shared key (PSK)

▶ Wi-Fi Protected Setup (WPS)

▶ captive portal

▶ site survey

▶ heat map

▶ Wi-Fi analyzer

Access Methods

As wireless technology has become nearly ubiquitous, the focus on wireless security has increased. Many improvements have been made over the years, in particular in terms of preventing unauthorized access to wireless networks. It is important to understand how access is provided to authorized clients, while ensuring that those who are not authorized are not allowed.

Authentication to wireless networks is typically accomplished through one of the following methods:

▶ Open authentication

▶ Shared authentication

▶ Extensible Authentication Protocol (EAP) authentication

Although it is not as common as it once was, the simplest option for many wireless networks is to forgo authentication and use an open network. An open network does not provide encryption; it does not even require a password to connect. In fact, an open network does not attempt to provide any security at all. Users simply select the network name or the service set identifier (SSID) for the network. Open configuration is not recommended.

Some open networks first require the user to connect through a *captive portal*, which is a web page that is launched first when connecting through a network. It usually requires some type of interaction before the user is allowed access to other networking or Internet sites. Open networks might use captive portals for advertising or to provide terms of use for the connecting user. Such portals are common in public places such as airports and coffee shops. The user simply clicks Accept, views an advertisement, provides an email address, or performs some other required action. The network then grants access to the user and no longer holds the user captive to the portal.

Shared authentication uses a *pre-shared key* (*PSK*). Essentially, the key on the wireless access device is the same key that each user can use to connect to the network.

Extensible Authentication Protocol (*EAP*) is commonly used in larger organizations. The authentication process is a bit more involved because an authentication server is required. EAP is an extension of Point-to-Point Protocol (PPP) and allows for flexibility in authentication, including authentication methods beyond just a username and a password. Instead of using PPP, however, the *IEEE 802.1X* standard defines using EAP over both wired Ethernet and wireless networks.

EAP is a challenge/response protocol that can be run over secured transport mechanisms. It is a flexible authentication technology and can be used with smart cards, one-time passwords, and public key encryption. EAP also provides support for public certificates that are deployed using auto-enrollment or smart cards. These security improvements enable access control to Ethernet networks in public places such as malls and airports.

Wireless Cryptographic Protocols

To properly manage the risk of wireless networks and prevent unauthorized access, you must understand the wireless cryptographic protocols available. Organizations of all sizes—even home users—need to be aware of the available technologies. The industry has done a lot to help make technology simple and easy to use, but it has also introduced vulnerable technologies to make the setup and configuration of wireless clients mindlessly simple.

Consider, for example, *Wi-Fi Protected Setup* (*WPS*), originally known as Wi-Fi Simple Config. WPS is an extension of the wireless standards whose purpose was to simplify for end users the process of establishing secure wireless home networks. As Wi-Fi devices entered the mainstream, setup was initially complex. Consequently, users often ran with default configurations, leaving their wireless networks wide open and easy to exploit. WPS was introduced as a better option.

WPS provides two certified modes of operation. The first requires the user to enter a PIN code when connecting devices. The second method requires the user to simply push a button on the AP and connect the wireless device. In 2011, however, a major security vulnerability was exposed; in fact, the vulnerability was so severe that the solution was to turn off WPS capabilities altogether. It turned out that the user's PIN could be recovered through brute-force attack in as few as 11,000 guesses, or within several hours. In some cases, disabling WPS was not even enough to prevent such attacks, and a firmware upgrade was required to completely disable the feature.

> **ExamAlert**
>
> Wi-Fi Protected Setup should not be used. At a minimum, it should be disabled.

Since WPS was determined to be insecure, several protocols have been developed to protect wireless networks. The primary goals of these cryptographic protocols are to protect the authentication and connection process and to also

ensure the confidentiality of data sent through the air. Four common protocols have worked to achieve these goals:

▶ **Wired Equivalent Privacy (WEP):** This original wireless encryption standard should not be used today, but it still occasionally is. Its goal was to provide security on par with that of wired networks, but WEP has many known security issues. It was superseded in 2003 by WPA.

▶ **Wi-Fi Protected Access (WPA):** WPA was developed in response to security concerns over WEP. WPA is implemented using a couple different options for encryption.

▶ **Wi-Fi Protected Access Version 2 (WPA2):** WPA2 further improved on WPA. Since 2006, it has been required for Wi-Fi-certified devices. WPA2 introduced the use of Advanced Encryption Standard (AES) for encryption.

▶ **Wi-Fi Protected Access Version 3 (WPA3):** WPA3 added more features and strengths to the widely adopted WPA2 protocol. Specifically, WPA3 maintains strong cryptographic algorithms while improving key exchange.

> **Note**
>
> The Wi-Fi Alliance is a consortium of companies that has a major impact on wireless technologies. It contributes to the standards process and is responsible for certifying wireless devices. The alliance coined the term *Wi-Fi* and still claims it as a registered trademark.

Wired Equivalent Privacy (WEP)

WEP is the most basic form of encryption that can be used on IEEE 802.11-based wireless networks to ensure that data sent between a wireless client and its access point remains private. Originally, wireless networks were typically based on the IEEE 802.11 standard, which had serious data transmission security shortcomings. When this standard was put into place, the 802.11 committee adopted the WEP cryptographic protocol.

To understand WEP's shortcomings, you need to know how it operates. WEP uses a stream cipher called RC4 for encryption. RC4 uses a shared secret key to generate a long sequence of bytes from a generator. This stream is then used to produce the encrypted ciphertext. Early 802.11b networks used 40-bit

encryption because of government restrictions. However, hackers can crack a 40-bit key in a few hours. Breaking RC4 encryption is much easier if an attacker can isolate a second instance of encryption with a single key. In other words, the weakness is that the same keys are used repeatedly.

> **Note**
>
> IEEE 802.11 is the family of standards for wireless networks maintained by the Institute of Electrical and Electronics Engineers (IEEE).

Wi-Fi Protected Access (WPA)

Much like WEP, *Wi-Fi Protected Access* (*WPA*) includes a method to encrypt wireless traffic between wireless clients and wireless access points. WPA has been included in 802.11-based products since WEP was deprecated in 2004. WPA includes a strategy for restricting network access and encrypting network traffic based on a shared key. The Wi-Fi Alliance developed WPA to replace WEP after security flaws were found in WEP. WPA protects networks by incorporating a set of enhanced security features. WPA-protected networks require users to enter a passkey to access the wireless network. WPA has two different modes:

▶ **WPA-Personal:** Known also as *WPA-PSK* (Pre-Shared Key), WPA-Personal requires a password consisting of 8 to 63 characters. All devices on the wireless network must use this password.

▶ **WPA-Enterprise:** Known also as *WPA-802.1X mode*, WPA-Enterprise requires security certificates and uses an authentication server from which the keys can be distributed.

WPA-Personal and WPA-Enterprise target different users and are applicable to both WPA and WPA2. WPA-Personal is designed for home and small office use; it uses a pre-shared key and does not require a separate authentication server. WPA-Enterprise, in contrast, is better suited for larger organizations because it provides increased security. This comes with a trade-off, of course. WPA-Enterprise requires a *Remote Authentication Dial-In User Service* (*RADIUS*) authentication server, which demands additional effort for setup and maintenance.

> **ExamAlert**
>
> Remember that WPA2 and WPA3 provide greater protection than WPA and WEP. Furthermore, WEP has been deprecated and is no longer considered secure.

Temporal Key Integrity Protocol

WPA adopted the *Temporal Key Integrity Protocol* (*TKIP*). Based on RC4, TKIP was designed to overcome many limitations of WEP and delivered huge improvements in message integrity and confidentiality. TKIP uses a unique key with each packet, unlike WEP, which used the same key. In addition, TKIP provides a more robust method of doing integrity checks to prevent man-in-the-middle attacks. WPA with TKIP is a huge improvement over WEP, but TKIP has been deprecated since 2012 and is no longer considered secure.

Counter Mode with Cipher Block Chaining Message Authentication Code Protocol

With the introduction of WPA2, TKIP was essentially replaced with *Counter Mode Cipher Block Chaining Message Authentication Code Protocol* (*CCMP*), based on the Advanced Encryption Standard (AES) encryption cipher. While CCMP is more resource-intensive than TKIP, it supports much longer keys and more advanced security for data confidentiality, user authentication, and user access control. CCMP is based on the AES encryption algorithm and provides significant security improvements over TKIP. WPA is usually associated with TKIP, and WPA2 is typically linked to AES, but this pairing isn't necessary.

Wi-Fi Protected Access Version 2 (WPA2)

Wi-Fi Protected Access Version 2 (*WPA2*), based on the IEEE 802.11i standard, provides government-grade security by implementing the AES block cipher encryption algorithm and 802.11-based authentication. WPA2 incorporates stricter security standards than WPA and is configurable in either the PSK or Enterprise mode. As with WPA, two versions of WPA2 exist: WPA2-Personal and WPA2-Enterprise. WPA2-Personal protects unauthorized network access via a password. WPA2-Enterprise verifies network users through a server. WPA2 is backward compatible with WPA and supports strong encryption and authentication for both infrastructure and ad-hoc networks. Additionally, as in WPA, WPA2 supports CCMP based on both AES and TKIP.

Wi-Fi Protected Access Version 3 (WPA3)

Wi-Fi Protected Access Version 3 (WPA3) was developed to replace WPA2. Like WPA2, WPA3 includes both Personal and Enterprise versions. WPA3 maintains equivalent cryptographic strength through the required use of 192-bit AES for the Enterprise version and optional 192-bit AES for the Personal version. With the Personal edition, key exchange is improved with WPA3. WPA2 uses pre-shared keys. WPA3 helps prevent offline password attacks by using *Simultaneous Authentication of Equals* (*SAE*), which allows users to choose easier-to-remember passwords and, through forward secrecy, does not compromise traffic that has already been transmitted even if the password becomes compromised.

Authentication Protocols

Four protocols are used with EAP and provide authentication for wireless networks (see Table 20.1):

▶ EAP-Transport Layer Security (EAP-TLS)

▶ Protected EAP (PEAP)

▶ EAP Tunneled Transport Layer Security (EAP-TTLS)

▶ EAP Flexible Authentication via Secure Tunneling (EAP-FAST)

EAP-Transport Layer Security (EAP-TLS) uses certificate-based mutual authentication, negotiation of the encryption method, and encrypted key determination between the client and the authenticating server.

EAP messages are encapsulated into 802.1X packets and are marked as EAP over LAN (EAPoL). After the client sends a connection request to a wireless access point, the authenticator marks all initial communication with the client as unauthorized. Only EAPoL messages are accepted while in this mode. All other types of communication are blocked until credentials are verified with an authentication server. Upon receiving an EAPoL request from a client, the wireless access point requests logon credentials and passes them to an authentication server. RADIUS is usually employed for authentication purposes; however, 802.1X does not make it mandatory. *RADIUS federation* allows a user's valid authentication to be shared across trusted entities. This trust must be established beforehand, and the RADIUS server makes assertions about the user identity and other attributes. This enables users to seamlessly roam across

different wireless networks without having to reauthenticate with unique credentials of another entity.

Protected EAP (PEAP) provides several additional benefits over EAP-TLS, including an encrypted authentication channel, dynamic keying material from TLS, a fast reconnect capability using cached session keys, and server authentication that guards against unauthorized access points. PEAP offers a means of protecting another EAP method within a TLS tunnel. PEAP is thus basically a secure wrapper around EAP; it is essential in preventing attacks on password-based EAP methods. As part of PEAP negotiation, the client establishes a TLS session with a RADIUS server. Using a TLS session as part of PEAP serves several purposes:

▶ The client can authenticate the RADIUS server; that is, the client establishes the session only with a server that holds a certificate trusted by the client.

▶ It protects the authentication protocol from packet snooping.

▶ Negotiation of the TLS session generates a key that the client and RADIUS server can use to establish common master keys. These keys then derive the keys used to encrypt the WLAN traffic.

Secured within the PEAP channel, the client authenticates itself to the RADIUS server using EAP. During this exchange, the traffic within the TLS tunnel is visible only to the client and the RADIUS server; it is never exposed to the wireless AP.

EAP Tunneled Transport Layer Security (EAP-TTLS) is similar to PEAP but further builds on TLS. With an established secure tunnel, the server authenticates the client using authentication attributes within the TLS wrapper.

EAP Flexible Authentication via Secure Tunneling (EAP-FAST) is a proposed replacement to the Lightweight Extensible Authentication Protocol (LEAP), which for years has been known to contain vulnerabilities. The goal of EAP-FAST is to provide a replacement that is also lightweight but secure. EAP-FAST also works like PEAP but does not require client or server certificates. Instead, it uses a Protected Access Credential (PAC), which is essentially a

shared secret between the client and the authentication server to establish a tunnel in which authentication is then performed. For many organizations that don't want to manage certificates, EAP-FAST might be an ideal alternative to LEAP.

Table 20.1 compares the various flavors of EAP authentication protocols.

TABLE 20.1 **Comparing EAP Authentication Protocols**

	EAP-TLS	PEAP	EAP-TTLS	EAP-FAST
Client certificate required	Yes	No	No	No
Server certificate required	Yes	Yes	Yes	No
Ease of deployment	Difficult	Moderate	Moderate	Easy
Security	High	Medium	Medium	Medium

Each protocol is developed and backed by specific vendors. An organization's choice of vendors might dictate the choice of solution. Organizations also need to consider their appetite for managing a certificate infrastructure and deploying certificates. Not having to worry about certificates greatly reduces the burden for many.

> **ExamAlert**
>
> EAP-TLS requires client and server certificates for mutual authentication. Both PEAP and EAP-TTLS eliminate the requirement to deploy client certificates. EAP-FAST does not require any certificates.

Wireless Access Installations

No network is complete without wireless access points. Most businesses provide wireless access for both employees and guests. With this expected convenience come security implications that must be addressed to keep the network safe from vulnerabilities and attacks. This section covers basic access point types, configurations, and preventive measures an organization can implement to mitigate risk and reduce its attack surface.

Wireless local area network (WLAN) controllers are physical devices that communicate with each access point (AP) simultaneously. A centralized access controller (AC) is capable of providing management, configuration, encryption, and policy settings for WLAN access points. A controller-based WLAN design

acts as a switch for wireless traffic and provides thin APs with configuration settings. Some ACs perform firewall, VPN, IDS/IPS, and monitoring functions.

The level of control and management options an AC needs to provide depend on the type of access points the organization implements. Three main types of wireless access points exist:

▶ **Fat:** Fat wireless access points are also sometimes called *intelligent access points* because they are all-inclusive: They contain everything needed to manage wireless clients, such as ACLs, quality of service (QoS) functions, VLAN support, and band steering. Fat APs can be used as standalone access points and do not need an AC. However, this capability makes them expensive because they are built on powerful hardware and require complex software.

▶ **Fit:** A fit AP is a scaled-down version of a fat AP and uses an AC for control and management functions.

▶ **Thin:** A thin access point is nothing more than a radio and antenna controlled by a wireless switch. Thin access points are sometimes called *intelligent antennas*. In some instances, APs do not perform WLAN encryption; they merely transmit or receive the encrypted wireless frames. A thin AP has minimal functionality, and a controller is required. Thin APs are simple and do not require complex hardware or software.

ExamAlert

A fat access point is also known as an intelligent or standalone access point. A thin access point is also known as an intelligent antenna and is managed by a WLAN controller.

Antenna Types, Placement, and Power

When designing wireless networks, it is important to configure antenna types, placement, and power output for maximum coverage and minimum interference. Four basic types of antennas are commonly used in 802.11 wireless networking applications: parabolic grid, Yagi, dipole, and vertical.

Wireless antennas are either omnidirectional or directional. An omnidirectional antenna provides a 360-degree radial pattern to provide the widest possible signal coverage. An example of an omnidirectional antenna is the type of antenna commonly found on an AP. Directional antennas concentrate the wireless signal

in a specific direction, limiting the coverage area. An example of a directional antenna is a Yagi antenna.

The need or use determines the type of antenna required. When an organization wants to connect one building to another building, for example, a directional antenna is used. If an organization is adding Wi-Fi internally to an office building or a warehouse, an omnidirectional antenna is used. If an organization wants to install Wi-Fi in an outdoor campus environment, a combination of the two antennas is used.

APs with factory-default omnidirectional antennas cover an area that is roughly circular and is affected by RF obstacles such as walls. When using this type of antenna, common practice is to place APs in central locations or divide an office into quadrants. Many APs use multiple-input, multiple-output (MIMO) or multiuser multiple-input, multiple-output (MU-MIMO) antennas. A MIMO antenna takes advantage of multipath signal reflections. Ideally, you should locate an AP as close as possible to an antenna. The farther the signal has to travel across the cabling between the AP and the antenna, the more signal loss occurs. Loss is an important factor when deploying a wireless network, especially at higher power levels. Loss occurs as a result of the signal traveling between the wireless base unit and the antenna.

APs that require external antennas need additional consideration. You need to configure the antennas properly, consider what role the AP serves (AP or bridge), and consider where the antennas are placed. When an antenna is mounted on the outside of the building or when the interface between the wired network and the transceiver is placed in a corner, it locates the network signal in an area where it can easily be intercepted. Antenna placement should not be used as a security mechanism.

Professional *site surveys* for wireless network installations and proper AP placement are sometimes used to address coverage area and security concerns. Upfront planning takes time and effort but can pay off in the long run, especially for large WLANs. Site surveys use *Wi-Fi analyzers* and other wireless analyzers to understand and map out the wireless infrastructure. One output is a wireless *heat map*, which provides a visual method for understanding coverage and signal strength. Figure 20.1 shows an example heat map of an office floor plan. In this example, the map indicates a strong signal near the placement of the wireless access point, and the signal fades toward the outside edges. These heat maps can help understand where signal interference may be an issue because of doors, building materials, microwaves, and neighboring wireless networks.

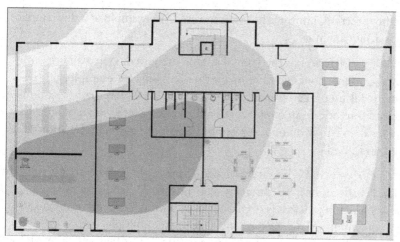

FIGURE 20.1   An example of a wireless coverage heat map

Site surveys and heat maps provide the following benefits:

▶ Identify dead zones where there is no wireless coverage

▶ Identify trouble areas to help eliminate slows speeds and poor performance

▶ Automate wireless network evaluation

▶ Help adequately build out an efficient network

ExamAlert

Physical placement and transmit power adjustments can make it harder for intruders to stay connected to your APs—but never count on physical placement alone to stop attackers.

One of the principal requirements for wireless communication is that the transmitted wave must reach the receiver with ample power to allow the receiver to distinguish the wave from the background noise. An antenna that is too strong raises security concerns. Strong omnidirectional Wi-Fi signals are radiated to a greater distance into neighboring areas, where the signals can be readily detected and viewed. Minimizing transmission power reduces the chances of data leaks. Companies such as Cisco and Nortel have implemented dynamic power controls in their products. The system dynamically adjusts the power output of individual access points to accommodate changing network conditions, helping ensure predictable wireless performance and availability.

> **ExamAlert**
>
> Reducing the energy consumption of wireless communication devices is an important issue in WLANs. Know the mechanisms that prevent interference and increase capacity.

Transmit power control is a mechanism that minimizes the unwanted interference between different wireless networks. Adaptive transmit power control in 802.11 WLANs on a per-link basis helps increase network capacity and improves the battery life of Wi-Fi-enabled mobile devices.

Band direction and selection are also important parts of wireless access control management. The 2.4-GHz band used for older standards such as 802.11a/b/g is crowded and subject to both interference from other wireless devices and co-channel overlays from other access points because of the limited number (three) of nonoverlapping channels. Standards such as 802.11n and 802.11ac use the 5-GHz band, which offers 23 nonoverlapping 20-MHz channels. The newest standard, 802.11ax (Wi-Fi 6), will eventually succeed the previous standards. 802.11ax will work over both the 2.4-GHz and 5-GHz bands and will also work with the 6-GHz band. 802.11ax will provide a number of performance benefits, including the capability to avoid interference with other nearby networks.

Cisco wireless LAN controllers can be configured for load balancing through band direction and band selection. Band direction allows client radios capable of operating on both 2.4-GHz and 5-GHz bands to move to a 5-GHz access point for faster throughput of network transfers. In a Cisco AP, clients receive a 2.4-GHz probe response and attempt to associate with the AP before receiving a 5-GHz probe response. Band selection works by delaying client 2.4-GHz radio probe responses, causing the client to be directed toward the 5-GHz channels. 802.11n can use 2.4 GHz or 5 GHz. The main purpose of band selection is to help the 802.11n-capable dual-band clients select 5-GHz access points. Band selection can cause roaming delays and dropped calls, so it is not recommended on voice-enabled WLANs.

MAC Filter

Most wireless network routers and access points can filter devices based on their MAC addresses. A MAC address is a unique identifier for network adapters. *MAC filtering* is a security access control method in which the MAC address is used to determine access to the network. When MAC address

filtering is used, only the devices with MAC addresses configured in the wireless router or access point are allowed to connect. MAC filtering permits and denies network access through the use of blacklists and whitelists. A *blacklist* is a list of MAC addresses that are denied access. A *whitelist* is a list of MAC addresses that are allowed access.

MAC addresses give a wireless network some additional protection, but they can be spoofed. An attacker can potentially capture details about a MAC address from the network and pretend to be that device in order to connect to the network. MAC filtering can be circumvented by scanning a valid MAC using a tool such as airodump-ng or Aircrack-ng Suite and then spoofing one's own MAC address into a validated MAC address. When an attacker knows a MAC address that is not in the blacklist or is in the whitelist, MAC filtering is almost useless.

Disabling SSID Broadcast

A *service set identifier* (*SSID*) is used to identify a wireless access point on a network. The SSID is transmitted so that wireless stations searching for a network connection can find it. By default, SSID broadcast is enabled. When you disable this feature, the SSID configured in the client must match the SSID of the AP; otherwise, the client cannot connect to the AP. Having SSID broadcast enabled essentially makes your AP visible to any device searching for a wireless connection.

To improve the security of your network, change the SSIDs on your APs. Using the default SSID poses a security risk even if the AP is not broadcasting it. When changing default SSIDs, do not change them to reflect your company's main names, divisions, products, or address. Using such guessable SSIDs would make you an easy target for attacks such as war driving, war flying, and war chalking. With war driving, a person in a moving vehicle searches for Wi-Fi wireless networks using a portable computer or another mobile device. War flying is similar but involves the use of aircraft or drone technology. War chalking involves drawing symbols in public places to advertise open Wi-Fi networks. Keep in mind that if an SSID name is enticing enough, it might attract hackers.

Turning off SSID broadcast does not effectively protect a network from attacks. Tools such as Kismet enable non-broadcasting networks to be discovered almost as easily as broadcasting networks. From a security standpoint, securing a wireless network using protocols that are designed specifically to address wireless network threats is better than disabling SSID broadcast.

Cram Quiz

ExamAlert

Turning off SSID broadcast does not effectively protect a network from attacks. It is much better to secure a wireless network using protocols that are designed specifically to address wireless network threats than to disable SSID broadcast.

Cram Quiz

Answer these questions. The answers follow the last question. If you cannot answer these questions correctly, consider reading this chapter again until you can.

1. A member of your team made changes to the configuration of the wireless network. Existing devices are still able to connect to the network, but you are unable to find the network to connect to when trying to deploy a new laptop. What change did the team member most likely make?

   ○ **A.** Disabled MAC filtering

   ○ **B.** Disabled SSID broadcasting

   ○ **C.** Enabled MAC filtering

   ○ **D.** Enabled SSID broadcasting

2. Your users are all connected to a wireless access point using WPA2-PSK. Your manager wants you to confirm what cryptographic standard is being used. Which of the following is most likely?

   ○ **A.** AES

   ○ **B.** DES

   ○ **C.** MD5

   ○ **D.** WEP

3. As you are deploying wireless authentication protocols, a request comes up to eliminate the need for client certificates. Which of the following requires a client certificate?

   ○ **A.** EAP-TLS

   ○ **B.** PEAP

   ○ **C.** EAP-TTLS

   ○ **D.** EAP-FAST

4. Your organization is conducting a wireless site survey for proper AP placement. Which of the following provides a visual method for understanding the coverage and signal strength and may help with this process?

- ○ **A.** MAC filtering
- ○ **B.** Yagi
- ○ **C.** MU-MIMO
- ○ **D.** Heat map

5. You want your users' valid authentication information to be shared across trusted entities so the users can seamlessly roam across different wireless networks without having to reauthenticate. Which of the following can allow this?

- ○ **A.** RADIUS federation
- ○ **B.** WPA3
- ○ **C.** CCMP
- ○ **D.** Captive portal

Cram Quiz Answers

Answer 1: B. The team member most likely disabled SSID broadcasting, as the network name can no longer be seen from the wireless clients. The network is still there, and existing clients can still connect as they have already been configured; however, the name of the network doesn't show. As a result, answer D is incorrect. Answers A and C are incorrect. MAC filtering would specifically deny the clients specified from joining, but they would still see the network name if SSID broadcasting were enabled.

Answer 2: A. The correct answer is AES. WPA2 introduced the use of Advanced Encryption Standard (AES) for encryption. Answer B is incorrect as DES is a deprecated algorithm. Answer C is incorrect as MD5 is a hashing algorithm. Answer D is incorrect as WEP is the original wireless encryption mechanism but is rarely used today due various security issues.

Answer 3: A. EAP-TLS requires a client certificate and provides the strongest security of the protocols listed here. PEAP, EAP-TTLS, and EAP-FAST do not require client certificates, so Answers B, C, and D are incorrect.

Answer 4: D. Site surveys use Wi-Fi and other wireless analyzers to understand and map out the wireless infrastructure. One output is a wireless heat map, which provides a visual method for understanding coverage and signal strength. Answer A is incorrect because MAC filtering is a security access control method in which the MAC address is used to determine access to the network. Answers B and C are incorrect because a Yagi antenna is an example of a directional antenna, and multiuser multiple-input, multiple-output (MU-MIMO) antennas take advantage of multipath signal reflections.

Answer 5: A. RADIUS federation allows a user's valid authentication to be shared across trusted entities. This enables users to seamlessly roam across different wireless networks without having to reauthenticate with the unique credentials of another entity. Answer B is incorrect because WPA3 is the latest Wi-Fi specification and offers greater wireless security for Wi-Fi-certified WPA3 devices. Answer C is incorrect. *Counter Mode Cipher Block Chaining Message Authentication Code Protocol* (*CCMP*) is based on the AES encryption algorithm and provides significant security improvements over TKIP. Answer D is incorrect because captive portals are common in public places such as airports and coffee shops. The user simply clicks Accept, views an advertisement, provides an email address, or performs some other required action. The network then grants access to the user and no longer holds the user captive to the portal.

What Next?

If you want more practice on this chapter's exam objective before you move on, remember that you can access all of the Cram Quiz questions on the Pearson Test Prep software online. You can also create a custom exam by objective with the Online Practice Test. Note any objective you struggle with and go to that objective's material in this chapter.

Secure Mobile Solutions

Essential Terms and Components

▶ mobile device management (MDM)

▶ MicroSD hardware security module (HSM)

▶ unified endpoint management (UEM)

▶ mobile application management (MAM)

▶ SEAndroid

▶ rooting/jailbreaking

▶ sideloading

▶ bring your own device (BYOD)

▶ corporate-owned, personally enabled (COPE)

▶ choose your own device (CYOD)

▶ virtual desktop infrastructure (VDI)

Communication Methods

Just about every technology magazine and article published mentions a new mobile device, operating system release, or service provider merger. We are just beginning to see the benefits of 5G (the fifth generation of cellular wireless standards) technology, which provides capabilities beyond 4G LTE mobile networks to accommodate real-time

applications across billions of interconnected devices. A mobile device contains a full filesystem, applications, and data. Mobile devices need to be protected in a similar manner to regular computers. The composition of a mobile device is different than that of a regular computer, though, because it is an embedded device, so security is a bit more challenging. Mobile devices can communicate using several methods, including cellular, Bluetooth, Wi-Fi, and near-field communication.

Cellular communications are the main mode that a mobile device uses to connect to a service provider network. A cellular network consists of the following components:

▶ Cellular layout (towers)

▶ Base station (which connects to the tower)

▶ Mobile switching office (the centerpiece of the operation)

▶ Public switched telephone network (PSTN)

Today wireless providers transmit voice calls over this traditional circuit-switched network design, and subscribers use the newer IP-based 4G and 5G LTE networks to access the Internet and other data services.

> **ExamAlert**
>
> Two cellular voice technologies are currently used: Code-Division Multiple Access (CDMA) and Global System for Mobile Communications (GSM). GSM is the dominant technology and is used in more than 100 countries, mostly in Asia and Europe.

GSM devices use a subscriber identity module (SIM) to communicate with the provider network. CDMA, which relies on a soft handoff, allows for fewer dropped calls and provides a more secure underlying technology than GSM. Currently, AT&T and T-Mobile run on GSM networks, while Sprint and Verizon Wireless use CDMA.

Long-Term Evolution (LTE) is used for faster data transfer and higher capacity. Different variations of LTE networks exist across carriers that use different frequencies. Sprint, T-Mobile, Verizon, and AT&T all have their own bands of LTE.

For users who lack traditional landline or cellular coverage, satellite communication (SATCOM) is an option for mobile device use. SATCOM uses an artificial satellite for telecommunication that transmits radio signals. It can cover

far more distance and wider areas than most other radio technologies. Because satellite phones do not rely on phone transmission lines or cellular towers, they function in remote locations. Most satellite phones have limited connectivity to the Internet, and data rates tend to be slow, but they come with GPS capabilities to indicate the user's position in real time.

The most common satellite phones are Inmarsat, Iridium, Globalstar, and Thuraya. Some satellite phones use SIM cards and others do not. For example, Globalstar does not use SIM cards, whereas Inmarsat and Iridium do.

Mobile devices also communicate via wireless signals. The most common are Wi-Fi and Bluetooth. Mobile Wi-Fi connectivity basically works just like connecting your laptop to a wireless router for Internet access. Through the device's Settings menu, you can access available Wi-Fi networks. Additional capabilities of Wi-Fi are described later in this chapter.

Mobile devices are equipped for Bluetooth, which is short-range wireless connectivity. A common cellular use for Bluetooth is listening to music. Users also can pair a cell phone with a car infotainment center so they can talk on the phone "hands free" while driving. In fact, drivers sometimes wear wireless headsets for the same purpose.

Bluetooth uses a spread-spectrum, frequency-hopping, full-duplex signal. An antenna-equipped chip in each device that wants to communicate sends and receives signals at a specific frequency range defined for short-range communication. For Bluetooth devices to communicate, they pair with each other to form a personal area network (PAN), also known as a *piconet*. This process is done through discovery, with one device making itself discoverable by the other device. Bluetooth is a common mobile connectivity method because it has low power consumption requirements and a short-range signal.

Near-field communication (NFC) is a set of standards for contactless communication between devices. NFC chips in mobile devices generate electromagnetic fields. This allows a device to communicate with other devices. Although NFC is considered contactless, in most practical uses, devices establish communication by being close or even touching. Contactless payment systems such

as those in coffee shops, train stations, and some supermarkets allow payment through the phone's NFC chip: The user simply holds the phone close to the payment terminal.

The NFC standard has three modes of operation:

▶ **Peer-to-peer mode:** Two mobile devices exchange data.

▶ **Read/write mode:** An active device receives data from a passive device.

▶ **Card emulation:** The device is used as a contactless credit card.

Most users are familiar with NFC as a feature of their smartphone. The NFC technology makes tap-and-go services such as Apple Pay and Google Pay work.

Many Android mobile devices natively support ANT+. ANT is a proprietary multicast wireless sensor technology developed by ANT Wireless.

ExamAlert

ANT technology enables you to view fitness and health monitoring data in real time on your mobile device. ANT is a wireless protocol for use over short distances that creates PANs and is similar to Bluetooth.

For example, the ANT+ heart rate belt has the capability to communicate with Garmin sports watches. The main difference between ANT and Bluetooth is that ANT tends to have a lower power consumption rate and is geared toward sensor usage.

Another wireless mobile technology used for device communication over a short range is infrared (IR). IR transceivers are relatively inexpensive and provide short-range communication solutions. IR communication is most commonly used in mobile technology with IR cameras. IR technologies are quickly advancing, and soon smartphones might have IR cameras built in. The FLIR One is an example of an infrared camera attachment for a smartphone or tablet. Recent Apple patents and design rumors indicate that future iPhones could use infrared technology to provide sophisticated cameras or embed a fingerprint scanner that uses infrared emitters and sensors. In 2015, Peel Technologies was granted a patent for IR technology that allows users to control their TV through their cell phone. Many vendors, such as Fluke, have developed IR cameras for night vision recording that can be used with a handheld device. In addition, fire and police departments use IR for thermal sensing to find people in burning buildings and locate suspects at night or in heavily wooded areas.

Another communication method mobile devices use is USB. USB communications allow a cell phone to be used for data or audio or a mass storage device. USB communication is commonly used to create a hotspot by connecting a laptop to a cell phone for Internet connectivity. Often this method is used for security reasons when Internet access is needed but only untrusted public Wi-Fi networks such as those in an airport, hotel, or coffee shop are available. USB connectivity also allows a mobile device to act as a modem, fax, or extension interface to plug in to other USB devices. In addition, the mobile USB port can be used for connecting to forensic acquisition devices when information needs to be gathered for an investigation.

Mobile Device Management Concepts

The commingling of personal and organizational data on mobile devices is inevitable unless some safeguards are in place, such as keeping sensitive data only on secure servers and accessing it remotely using secure communication techniques outlined in the security policy. Another option is to separate user data from organizational data on the device. This separation limits business risk associated with enterprise data on mobile devices by compartmentalizing the data. It leaves employees' private information untouched and makes it possible to enforce policies and compliance at the application level.

Device, Application, and Content Management

Managing mobile device access and usage in an organization is a challenging endeavor. Businesses take various approaches to dealing with handheld devices, and each business has different needs. Because handheld technology moves at a much faster pace than computer technology, administrative nightmares can happen quickly. While mobile device and mobile operating system manufacturers include security capabilities, many third parties provide a host of management solutions to augment and extend the options, which is particularly important for organizations. Android, for example, uses Security-Enhanced Linux (SELinux) to enable *SEAndroid*, which provides access control over the running processes.

Mobile management is necessary to protect organizational assets at various levels, including the device itself, applications, and content. This section discusses these three concepts.

Mobile Device Management

Mobile device management (*MDM*) and *unified endpoint management* (*EUM*) differ from *mobile application management* (*MAM*). MDM provides functionality and control over enterprise devices by allowing the enrollment of enterprise devices for management functions such as provisioning devices, tracking inventory, changing configurations, updating, managing applications, and enforcing policies. For example, VPN and passcode settings can be pushed out to users to save support a lot of time and effort.

> **ExamAlert**
>
> MAM focuses on application management. MDM solutions provide a more comprehensive level of device management, from managing applications and application data all the way down to device firmware and configuration settings. UEM expands on MDM by providing unified capabilities across MAM and MDM and also including content and threat management, identity and access management, and application containerization.

Both iOS and Android isolate applications and sensitive operating system features using a method called *sandboxing* or *containerization*. Android uses the SEAndroid capabilities mentioned previously. Sandboxing is a security method that keeps running applications separate. Although this design reduces the threat surface, malware or spyware can still potentially be installed. The mobile threat landscape increases with ambiguous applications, such as those that require excessive privileges or that access sensitive data. Too often, users click through permission requests when installing an application, giving full access to information on the device. Other advanced features of mobile endpoint solutions are discussed next. Many of these capabilities, including the capabilities already discussed, are brought together under UEM solutions.

> **ExamAlert**
>
> In a corporate environment, applications can be managed by provisioning and controlling access to available mobile applications. This process is called mobile application management (MAM).

Mobile Content Management

One of the biggest security risks involves applications that share data across environments such as Dropbox, Box, Google Drive, OneDrive, and iCloud. Organizations should carefully consider what apps to allow on their production networks.

When dealing with shared data, mobile content management (MCM) comes into play. MCM has several different definitions, but in the context of this discussion, it refers to access to content from mobile devices that are not managing content for a mobile-accessible website. An MCM system is used to control access to the file storage and sharing capabilities of services. These services can be cloud based, as with Office 365 and Box, or can function as middleware connecting the mobile device with existing data repositories. Many of these services are used for collaboration and better workflow by interfacing with other productivity applications. One such example is the capability for real-time coauthoring in Office Online through Box.

With MCM, several layers of access exist—not only for the mobile user but also for the applications and services. An MCM solution must incorporate identity management, so it offers control over what data end users are able to access. Many MCM products provide enhanced security features by using secure storage containers to secure organizational data downloaded to a mobile device.

Mobile Application Management

In addition to device security, you need to consider mobile application security. The primary attack points on mobile devices are data storage, key stores, the application file system, application databases, caches, and configuration files. Recommendations for application security include restricting which applications may be installed through whitelisting, digitally signing applications to ensure that only applications from trusted entities are installed on the device, and distributing the organization's applications from a dedicated mobile application store.

Access controls rely on credentials to validate the identities of users, applications, and devices. Application credentials such as usernames and passwords are stored in databases on a device, and often the credentials are not encrypted. MDM solutions allow organizations to manage application credentials in ways that reduce the risk of compromised credentials, protect data more effectively, reduce operational costs, and improve efficiency.

Security best practices require strong authentication credentials so that a device can be trusted both on the enterprise's network and with access to enterprise applications. Passwords are one of the primary methods of acquiring access. For applications that require authentication, passwords need to be sufficiently long and complex. However, although using strong passwords reduces the overall risk of a security breach, strong passwords do not replace the need for other effective security controls.

> **ExamAlert**
>
> Using static passwords for authentication is a flawed security practice because passwords can be guessed, forgotten, or written down.

Mobile phones that are capable of running Java applets are common, so a mobile phone can be used as an authentication token. Many vendors offer one-time passwords (OTPs) as an authentication solution for Java-capable mobile devices. An application might require an OTP for performing highly sensitive operations such as fund transfers. OTPs can be either Short Message Service (SMS) generated or device generated. Device-generated OTPs are better than SMS OTPs because they eliminate the sniffing and delivery time issues associated with SMS OTP.

Managing mobile applications is a top security concern for organizations. Applications can be managed through whitelisting or blacklisting. The general concept behind application whitelisting differs from that of blacklisting. Instead of attempting to block malicious files and activity, as blacklisting does, application whitelisting permits only known good apps.

> **ExamAlert**
>
> When security is a concern, whitelisting applications is a better option because it allows organizations to maintain strict control over the apps employees are approved to use.

Whitelisting of apps can be controlled through various MDM polices. One of the most effective techniques for managing a whitelist is to automatically trust certain publishers of software. Whitelisting increases administrative overhead but offers better control. In a highly secure environment, maintaining a whitelist also entails exerting strict device control, preventing pairing over USB, deploying only in-house enterprise apps, and removing user capability to install or delete apps.

The concept of transitive trust for mobile devices is similar to identity federation but can cross boundaries of authentication domains at the application layer. Identity federation defines a set of technologies used to provide authentication (sign-in) services for applications. Transitive trust enables decentralized authentication through trusted agents.

> **ExamAlert**
>
> Application transitive trust and authentication can be used to improve the availability of service access but can also present security issues. When applications interact with each other, restricting one application can create an environment for data to still leave the mobile device through the other application. An application with only local permissions could then send sensitive data through third-party applications to external destinations.

You might want to encrypt data from a mobile application for several reasons. Application data may be encrypted to make sure that files exported to shared storage, such as the device's SD card, are not easily accessible to other applications. Some applications store sensitive data on mobile devices and require encryption. Application encryption can also be used to encrypt sensitive information stored by the app or to limit content accessibility to users who have the appropriate access key. Some encryption options for encrypting applications are to use MDM to allow the device itself to encrypt the data, thus enabling the application to provide its own encryption scheme, or to use an MDM application-wrapping technology that wraps system calls and automatically performs encryption and decryption on the application data.

When data is encrypted, procedures for key management and key recovery must be in place. Encryption key management systems can be console-based software or hardware appliances.

> **ExamAlert**
>
> Key management is intended to provide a single point of management for keys and to enable users to both manage the life cycle of keys and store them securely. It also makes key distribution easier.

Some mobile operating systems have built-in application key management features. In iOS, keychains provide storage for encryption keys and certificates. After an application requests access to a keychain, it can store and retrieve sensitive data. Android has a similar keychain capability. On a mobile device, extracting a key and decrypting data is easy when the key is stored either with the encrypted data or as a file private to the application, especially if the device is rooted. This weakness could give unauthorized applications access to sensitive information. To better protect the keys, one solution is not to store keys but to derive them from user-entered passwords.

Protections

The risk areas associated with mobile devices are physical risk (including theft or loss), unauthorized access risk, operating system or application risk, network risk, and mobile device data storage risk. To mitigate these risks, many of the same protections that apply to computers apply to mobile devices. Safeguards include screen locks, encryption, remote wiping, GPS tracking, and proper access. This section discusses these protections.

Screen Locks, Passwords, and PINs

All mobile phones offer a locking capability. When locking is turned on, the user must input a PIN/passcode or password to access the phone and applications. A screen lock prevents access to the device by requiring the user to input a PIN/passcode before gaining access to the device content.

> **ExamAlert**
>
> PINs/passcodes and pattern locks are a basic form of security and a first line of defense. They should be required on all devices that access corporate resources.

The screen lock is similar to a password-protected screensaver on a computer. The lock code is usually a four-digit code or PIN. A pattern lock uses a pattern drawn on the screen instead of requiring a PIN/passcode. Android devices usually refer to this four-digit code as a PIN, whereas iOS devices refer to it as a passcode. A device should be configured to automatically lock the device screen after a brief period of inactivity.

The number of times a user can attempt to input a password or code depends on the OS or corporate policy. For example, by default, the vendor might allow seven failed attempts before the device is locked. If the user fails to enter the correct passcode or password on the screen after seven attempts, the phone prompts the user to wait 30 seconds before trying again. For a reset, the user is required to provide the original email account name and password used to set up the phone. Corporate policies might be more restrictive and tend to lean more toward five failed attempts before the phone becomes locked.

Biometrics and Context-Aware Authentication

Biometric authentication methods have been a part of security practices for a while. Biometric authentication is based on some type of physical characteristic that is unique to an individual. Biometric methods embedded in mobile phones

include fingerprint, face, iris, voice, and signature recognition. Most mobile devices today provide support for fingerprint or facial recognition. These are currently the most common biometric methods used in mobile devices.

Biometric methods are not foolproof. Some fingerprint recognition technologies can be fooled by a copy of a person's fingerprint, and facial recognition technologies can be defeated using a three-dimensional image of a user's social media photo. Still, biometric authentication is more secure than weak passwords. The best approach to mobile device security is to combine biometric authentication with a strong password or PIN.

A shift is taking place toward context-aware authentication for mobile devices. The idea behind *context-aware authentication* is to use machine learning to determine whether a user resource request is valid or whether the account was compromised. The access decision is based on what is considered learned normal behavior for the user. More technically, machine learning algorithms determine a confidence level regarding whether the access request is the real user and not a malicious actor. Context awareness is a preferred method for authentication because environments are fluid, and static methods do not have the capability to understand the context of a login attempt, calculate risk based on the context analysis, and change requirements appropriately.

The risks associated with cloud computing and BYOD have made context-aware security a more viable approach. Context-aware authentication more effectively protects against fraudulent and unauthorized access attempts because it assesses risk for resources that the user accesses. An extension of context-aware authentication is Google's Trust API, which uses proximity-based authentication on mobile devices. A trust score is calculated based on user-specific data points.

Remote Wiping

The data stored on a mobile device is worth a lot more than the device itself. Mobile devices carry a variety of personal and business information, and preventing them from getting into the wrong hands is critical. Many of today's smartphones support a mobile kill switch or remote wiping capability.

ExamAlert

Remote wiping allows a handheld device's data to be remotely deleted if the device is lost or stolen. All the major smartphone platforms have this capability. The most common ways to remotely wipe a device are using an application installed on the handset, working through an IT management console, and using a cloud-based service.

Via remote administration, any BlackBerry Enterprise Server (BES) handset can be erased, reset to factory default settings, or set to retain its previous IT policy. This is done via the Erase Data and Disable Handheld command over the wireless network. By default, the device deletes all data after ten bad password attempts.

Apple's iPhone offers a service that enables users to locate lost devices via GPS and erase their data remotely.

To enable remote wipe on enterprise Android phones, the phone must have the Google Apps Device Policy app installed. This is similar in functionality to the remote-control features for a BES. BlackBerry has extended its MDM capabilities to include Android and iOS within BES.

Remote wipes are not fail-safe. If someone finds a phone before the remote wipe occurs and either takes the device off the network or force-reboots and restores the device, that person can recover sensitive data. In the case of Black-Berry devices, if the device is turned off or taken outside the coverage area, the remote wipe command is queued on the BES until the device can be contacted. If a user is removed from the BES before the command has reached the smart-phone, data will not be erased from the device.

In addition to enterprise or built-in remote wiping tools, third-party products can be used to remove sensitive information. Some products are good solutions for a particular device type, whereas others cover all three major mobile device types. Most solutions can securely wipe media cards, be configured to wipe data remotely from a device that has been lost or stolen, automatically wipe the device clean when there is an attempt to insert another SIM card, or disable the phone functionality.

Several vendors offer services to Apple users that allow remote wiping on a lost or stolen iPhone. Other options can erase all data on the iPhone after a certain number of failed passcode attempts. iPhone since iOS 8 includes hardware encryption, and all data is encrypted on-the-fly. This means that, for newer iOS versions, you do not need to actually wipe the phone's entire contents; remotely wiping the encryption key is enough.

Geolocation, Geofencing, and Push Notifications

If a mobile device is lost, you can use geolocation to track it. Geolocation uses *Global Positioning System* (GPS) tracking to find the location of a device. In addition, employers sometimes use this feature to locate employees based on their device location.

> **ExamAlert**
>
> GPS tracking features can be used on company-issued devices as a deterrent to prevent the unauthorized personal use of vehicles and the practice of taking unauthorized unscheduled breaks.

GPS can also be used to deal with serious crimes. For example, GPS-enabled devices could help locate and recover a hijacked armored vehicle and possibly save the lives of the guards.

The location of a mobile phone is tracked primarily through GPS. In addition, applications provide a host of services based on GPS. Usually each application can be controlled with regard to its use of GPS for location services. Some applications use General Packet Radio Service (GPRS) and allow the GPS coordinates to be downloaded in a variety of formats. This makes it easy to import the coordinates into mapping software or create archives. For example, BlackBerry's push technology enables IT administrators to track devices through a web-based mapping platform, accessible from any computer or cell phone with an Internet connection. Applications such as Phone Tracker and Find My Device can reveal any geographic locations visited.

Services also provide GPS tracking for devices. For example, the AccuTracking online GPS cell phone tracking service provides real-time device locations for a monthly service charge. Software is installed on the phone, a PC is used to add the device to the vendor's web interface, the phone communicates with the server, and the device can be tracked through the vendor website.

Apps such as Foursquare that are installed on devices take advantage of geolocation. These apps report device location to other app users so they can find nearby friends. *Geofencing* takes geolocation a step further and uses GPS coordinates or *radio-frequency identification* (*RFID*) to define a geographic perimeter. When a device enters or exits the perimeter, an alert or notification is sent. The Apple Find My Friends app allows geofence-based notifications to inform users when someone enters or leaves a designated area. Geofencing is commonly used to alert local businesses to users' locations so they can use push advertising.

> **ExamAlert**
>
> Geofencing can be used on company-issued devices as a virtual time clock and can deter time theft.

Various geofencing applications provide automated employee time tracking. Some also integrate with third-party solutions such as QuickBooks so that employee time sheets can go directly into an accounting system for payroll.

With push technology, which began with BlackBerry, as soon as a device connects to the cellular network, new emails or updates can be automatically pushed to the device. When a mobile app is installed on a device today, a user can opt in to receive notifications whenever new content is available. A *push notification* is a brief message or alert that is sent through the installed application to the users who have opted in for notifications. Push notification services have three main components:

► Operating system push notification service (OSPNS)

► App publisher

► Client app

Push notification services are often used in conjunction with geolocation and geofencing. Advertisers target users according to location by setting up geofenced messages. As soon as the device enters the geofence, an advertisement is pushed to the user's device. Most airline apps use push notifications to remind customers when to check in. Other businesses use geotargeting and assess user histories for push notifications.

Push notifications have become popular in the business environment for internal communication as a way to engage employees and to notify them of important events or emergency situations. HR may use push notifications for onboarding, paperwork deadline reminders, recognition, training sessions, and benefits programs.

Storage Segmentation and Containerization

Malware and security risks such as data leakage have greatly increased in the past few years, putting at risk sensitive corporate information on user devices. *Storage segmentation* and *containerization* separate personal and business content on a device.

> **ExamAlert**
>
> Storage segmentation protects business content from security risks introduced by personal usage.

Security and data protection policies are applied to a segmented business container on a personal or company-owned device.

Segmentation and containerization are necessary when an organization has a BYOD environment. These approaches are used in conjunction with MAM as a way to apply policies to mobile devices. They provide an authenticated, encrypted area of the mobile device that can be used to separate sensitive corporate information from the user's personal use of the device. Additional benefits of containerization are capabilities to do the following:

▶ Isolate apps

▶ Control app functions

▶ Delete container information

▶ Remotely wipe the device

Applications provided by mobile technology vendors offer a security container that separates company and personal information. The enterprise container securely houses enterprise data and applications on the device, encrypting all data with strong Advanced Encryption Standard (AES) encryption. This solution also encrypts any data in transit between the device and servers behind the organization's firewall.

The downside to segmentation and containerization is that they are third-party solutions and tend to be costly if an organization lacks the infrastructure required. Secure containers also can limit the apps that employees can use, for compatibility issues, and some solutions do not provide adequate protection because they rely on device-level controls. This means that if a weak passcode is used and the device is compromised, the data is also compromised.

Full Device Encryption (FDE)

As with data on hard drives, data on mobile devices can be encrypted. However, this presents some challenges. For starters, entering complex passwords on small keyboards is difficult, and multifactor authentication is often infeasible. In addition, mobile devices have limited processing power, and the extra computation required for encryption could cause them to suffer performance issues. The always-on nature of these devices also means that encryption can easily break functionality. Another consideration is that because of the variety of devices, a company might have to implement multiple encryption methods. For example, BlackBerry Enterprise Server can be used to manage built-in data encryption, and Android mobile devices can use a third-party encryption solution.

Mobile voice encryption can allow executives and employees to discuss sensitive information without having to travel to secure company locations. A number of options are available for voice encryption. Vendors make *microSD hardware security module* (*HSM*) flash cards that fit into certain mobile devices. The software is installed on the phone when the card is first inserted into a device. This makes it possible to provide hardware-based authentication and cryptographic operations from the tiny slot in a mobile device.

Another hardware option is *embedded encryption*, which is offered in some solutions and consists of three main components:

▶ Embedded encryption software on the chip

▶ Linux-based management server

▶ TrustChip software development kit (SDK)

Third-party software applications can provide secure VoIP communication for iPhone and Android devices by using 256-bit AES military-grade encryption to encrypt calls between users. For added security, strong RSA encryption can be used during the symmetric key exchange. This type of application can provide VoIP connectivity for secure calls over several networks, including cellular and Wi-Fi.

When using voice encryption software, keep in mind that it must be installed on each mobile phone to create a secure connection. You cannot create a secure encrypted connection between a device that has software installed and one that does not. The same is true for hardware solutions. For example, an application encrypts voice only when the phone calls another phone using the same application. The user sees an icon on the display indicating that the call is encrypted.

As with many other solutions, using voice encryption is not an end-all solution. Many commercially available mobile voice encryption products can be intercepted and compromised using a little ingenuity and creativity. Some applications can be compromised in as little as a few minutes.

Enterprise-level encryption solutions are also available for various devices. For example, security vendors provide device protection on iOS and Android mobile devices. With such products, it is possible to secure mobile devices by centrally configuring security settings and enabling lockdown of unwanted features; furthermore, these products offer remote over-the-air locking or wiping features that can be used when a device is lost or stolen, and they have self-service portals that allow end users to register new devices and either lock or wipe lost or stolen phones.

Enforcement and Monitoring

Both enterprise administrators and users need to be aware of the growing risks associated with the convenience of having the Internet and the corporate network data in the palm of your hand. The most effective way to secure restricted data is not to store it on mobile devices. Of course, this is easier said than done.

MDM provides functionality and control over enterprise devices by allowing an organization to manage, secure, and monitor employee devices. MDM is one part of an overall enterprise mobility management (EMM) approach. EMM typically includes MDM, MAM, and identity management. This section covers these additional tools and technologies for mobile device enforcement and monitoring.

EMM allows an organization to perform advanced management of devices, including the following functions:

▶ Restricting changes to mobile network, Wi-Fi, or VPN access

▶ Controlling USB transfers, as well as transfers to external media

▶ Restricting users from sharing their locations in an app

▶ Preventing users from resetting devices by using a factory reset

Jailbreaking and Rooting

Jailbreaking and rooting are similar in that they alter the device capability. However, they have different functionality and apply to different mobile operating systems.

> **ExamAlert**
>
> Jailbreaking is associated with Apple devices. Rooting is associated with Android devices.

Apple controls iOS apps by using a private key for app authorization to protect devices from the risks associated with questionable apps. Users often want to run apps that they feel are safe but that Apple has not authorized. To run these apps, an iOS device must be jailbroken. Essentially, *jailbreaking* removes the restriction that the device must run only Apple-authorized apps. Jailbreaking is done by installing a custom kernel that allows root access to the device through

an application such as RedSn0w, which then uses a package manager such as Cydia to allow unauthorized application installation. Jailbreaking can be classified as either tethered or untethered. In tethered jailbreaking, the user must start the device from a software installation on a computer. In untethered jailbreaking, the device does not need to be connected to a computer in order to start; the device is altered so that it can start on its own.

With an Android device, if a user wants to run apps that are not available on the Google Play Store, the choices are either rooting the device or sideloading the app (as discussed in the next section). *Rooting* allows complete access to the device. Root-level access allows a user to configure the device to run unauthorized apps and set different permissions by circumventing Android's security architecture.

Rooted or jailbroken devices pose a risk to organizational data. In a BYOD environment, the organization might not know if or when users jailbreak or root devices. To mitigate this vulnerability, most EMM solutions have the capability to detect jailbroken and rooted devices. Detection is done by identifying indicators such as the existence of Cydia on iOS devices or having an alert sent when an app invokes the superuser APK in Android systems. The device is then marked as noncompliant and can be removed from the network or denied access to enterprise apps. The associated data authorized for the device can then be prohibited.

Custom Firmware, Carrier Unlocking, and OTA Updates

Technically, there is a difference between rooting or jailbreaking a device and loading custom firmware or unlocking a device. The most common scenario for installing custom firmware on a device is for forensic acquisition. Most forensic tools require a deep level of access to the device, and the acquisition process can sometimes involve the installation of custom firmware.

Users might want to load custom firmware on their devices so that they can use a different language, switch from the manufacturer-induced skin to a different look, or get rid of the unnecessary applications that are installed by default so they can free up space on the device. Installing custom ROM requires using a custom bootloader and a custom recovery manager. Root access is not necessarily required. Alternatively, the Replicant OS, a free Android distribution, can give users the flexibility they are looking for in custom firmware.

Carrier unlocking is the process by which users modify a device so that they do not have to use the original carrier or service provider. Carrier unlocking

is done mainly because most service providers require two-year contracts with customers. Many consumers complained about this practice. In 2014, President Obama signed the Unlocking Consumer Choice and Wireless Competition Act, which makes it legal for consumers to unlock their phones.

> **ExamAlert**
>
> Unlocking allows users to select any wireless provider they choose without having to purchase a new device.

When a device is unlocked, it can only use a service provider whose technology is compatible with the device hardware. For example, an original Verizon device using CMDA technology cannot necessarily be activated on an AT&T GSM network because the device might not have the required SIM slot.

Most U.S. carriers unlock a device upon request, as long as the contract is fully paid, so an organization might not be aware of changes, especially in a BYOD environment. EMM solutions allow the organization to look at device monitoring and usage thresholds that indicate a carrier switch. When an organization is reimbursing employees for associated costs, the organization can help the employee choose an appropriate option when switching carrier plans, as long as it is done legally instead of through jailbreaking or rooting the device.

Mobile devices have the capability to receive and install over-the-air (OTA) systems and application updates that are pushed over Wi-Fi to the device. Device users are notified that an update is available so that they can either install or postpone the update. OTA firmware updates are done through the device's recovery partition, which has the software required to unpack the update package and run it on the system.

OTA updates can be managed through EMM. For example, with Android OS, a device policy controller (DPC) app can be deployed to mobile devices. This gives the organization control over when the OTA updates are installed through a local OTA policy. When the OTA policy is set, the updates are installed according to the policy settings, and users have no control over when the updates are installed; users also are not notified of updates.

Third-Party App Stores and Sideloading

Less invasive processes than rooting or jailbreaking a device are also available to users who want to install apps that are not authorized by their OS vendor. For example, users can download from third-party app stores such as Amazon,

GetJar, AppBrain, and Appolicious. On Android devices, users can easily install third-party apps by changing the option in the device's security settings, even though it is disabled by default.

Third-party app stores are problematic for organizations because often the apps at these stores are not properly vetted. To prevent downloaded apps from third-party app stores, EMM solutions can be configured to not allow users to modify settings or to allow only whitelisted apps to be installed on the devices. Another option, albeit a more costly one, is for an organization to provide its own enterprise app store. The organization's store can host IT-approved apps and allow only apps from the enterprise app store to be installed on devices.

Sideloading is a process in which a user goes around the approved app marketplace and device settings to install unapproved apps. Before sideloading can be done on an Android device, users must enable the installation from unknown sources in the system security settings. Sideloading on an Android device can be done one of three ways:

▶ **Manual:** Using a USB connection and a file manager application

▶ **Android Debug Bridge (adb):** Using a command-line installation similar to Linux-based installs

▶ **AirDroid:** Using a drag-and-drop application installer

Sideloading on iOS devices can be done by using the Cydia Impactor tool. As with the installation of apps from third-party app stores, sideloading an app poses a risk to the organization because those apps have not been vetted and thus could introduce malicious software and compromise sensitive corporate data. The organizational protections are the same as for third-party apps. MAM configurations prevent the installation of apps from untrusted sources. EMM implementations can further lock down a device by applying policies that are capable of deleting apps and wiping a device.

Storage and USB OTG

Most mobile devices have an external media card used for storage. Most devices support USB Host Mode, also known as *USB on-the-go* (*OTG*). USB OTG is a standard that enables mobile devices to communicate with each other through a USB cable that users attach. Examples of USB and USB OTG functions include importing camera data from the device, copying files onto a USB drive, and attaching a full-size USB keyboard or mouse. To mitigate the vulnerability such a solution introduces, most EMM solutions can prevent users from accessing unauthorized sources such as USB storage or file-sharing sites.

The data on a media card needs to be encrypted. Full device encryption is an added feature that enables users to secure sensitive information on a mobile device's removable flash memory storage card. The data is accessible only when the card is installed in a particular mobile device. If the card is ever lost or stolen, the information remains secure because it is encrypted.

Enforcement for Normal Device Functions

Many organizations produce and store proprietary information. Because mobile devices can instantly share location, take pictures, text, and record video and audio, allowing these devices on a network poses security risks. Policies should cover the use of camera, video, texting, and audio recordings as they relate to the organizational work environment.

Geotagging location services, based on GPS positions and coordinates, also present security risks. *Geotagging* allows location data to be attached to images, videos, SMS messages, and website postings, providing permanent and searchable data. Geotagging can be limited by turning off features in social network accounts, disabling location services, and selectively using location features.

> **ExamAlert**
>
> Security risks associated with geotagging include unwanted advertising, spying, stalking, and theft. Some social networking sites and services show the location of logged use.

Texting and sending pictures via text (MMS) is a growing concern for most organizations. Excessive texting during work hours can interfere with employee productivity. Texting policies might be required in situations where personal information could be disclosed, such as health or financial services. The Final Omnibus Rule of March 2013 introduced a new HIPAA texting policy. The revisions apply not only to healthcare providers but also to third-party healthcare industry service providers and business associates. The HIPAA texting policy was written to address the risk associated with sending patient health information via SMS and placing patient health information on mobile devices. In environments where SMS/MMS communications contain sensitive information, encrypted messaging must be used to keep these communications secure and to comply with regulations. Employees should be made aware of policies on corporate texting and pictures sent via text (MMS). Rich Communication Services (RCS) is a protocol that has been in the works for many years and is currently used alongside SMS and MMS. RCS is slated to eventually replace both SMS and MMS.

Unused features on mobile devices should be disabled. Depending on the organizational needs, disabling other features on devices might be advisable as well. For example, if an employee works with highly confidential or trade secret information, the organization might require that the camera and microphone on corporate devices be disabled.

> **ExamAlert**
>
> A comprehensive mobile policy should clearly state restrictions on the use of cameras, video, audio, or location sharing and other applications and services.

Employees might be trustworthy, but if an employee's device contains organizational information and is lost or stolen, proprietary information might be compromised. In high-security areas, employees might have to surrender their mobile devices. In other situations, settings can be disabled or controlled through EMM implementations.

Wi-Fi Methods, Tethering, and Payments

Wi-Fi has been a mobile communication method for a while. A mobile device can use two different Wi-Fi methods to connect to another device: direct and ad hoc. Both allow multiple devices to directly connect without the use of a wireless access point.

The *Wi-Fi Direct* standard enables quick connections with effortless setup through peer-to-peer wireless networking. When Wi-Fi Direct is used, one device acts as a wireless access point, and other devices connect to it. The device acting as the access point is called the Group Owner (GO). Other devices connect to it as clients in station mode. Devices discover each other the same way a device finds a wireless network. Connected devices are not limited to Wi-Fi Direct, so devices that are not Wi-Fi Direct enabled can connect as well. Wi-Fi Direct uses the Wi-Fi Protected Setup (WPS) protocol to exchange credentials, which means users do not need to know a shared password. To connect, a user only needs to enter a PIN code or push a device button. Wi-Fi Direct can be used to perform tasks such as printing to a wireless printer, transferring photos between devices, or sending files to a computer. Wi-Fi Direct is meant for easily connecting a small number of devices for a short period of time.

Wi-Fi Direct device connections can happen anywhere and anytime and do not require access to a Wi-Fi network. However, the use of WPS is a major security concern because it has been proven insecure. The Wi-Fi Direct Alliance

recommends that, Wi-Fi Direct device connections be protected by WPA3 instead of WPS.

A mobile ad hoc network (MANET) is part of the IEEE 802.11 standard called Independent Basic Service Set (IBSS). No hierarchy governs IBSS devices, and all the devices are called *nodes*. IBSS nodes regularly send beacons to announce the existence of the network. IBSS networks have no security requirement, and security can range from no encryption to a supported Wi-Fi encryption protocol. The concept of MANET is simple, but because many configuration options are available, inexperienced users tend to find it hard to use.

MANET is most often used by the military and emergency services. It can also be used by education institutions for classrooms and labs.

Depending on the manufacturer of an organization's WLAN equipment, organizational policy might control the capability to use Wi-Fi Direct. For example, Cisco Wireless LAN controllers can be used to configure the Wi-Fi Direct Client Policy to disallow this type of connection or to allow the connection but not allow the setup of a peer-to-peer connection. In Windows networks, MANET can be controlled through group policy.

Tethering involves sharing a device's Internet connection with other devices through Wi-Fi, Bluetooth, or a USB cable. This technique basically allows a device to act as a modem. Tethering is used when no other method exists for connecting to the Internet. Tethering can be especially useful when traveling, but it has some downsides: Speed can be slow, the battery of the tethering device drains more quickly, and, depending on the carrier, additional data charges might apply.

Organizational policy on tethering might differ from restrictions on mobile device use in general. Unsecured public Wi-Fi networks are not considered safe. An organization might prefer to absorb the extra cost and keep data more secure by sending it directly through an employee's tethered mobile device. When this is the case, the additional cost must be monitored, especially when employees travel overseas. EMM solutions can help monitor costs associated with tethering and provide flexible tethering controls.

Users can also use mobile devices to make payments for meals and other expenses and to transfer money. Mobile payments can be made in several ways, including with mobile wallets, contactless payments, carrier billing, and card payments. Mobile payments generally fall into several categories:

▶ **Daily transactions:** Most often associated with a mobile wallet

▶ **Point-of-sale (POS) payments:** Goods and services vendors

► **Carrier payments:** Billed directly through the carrier, most often associated with charitable donations via text

► **Mobile card reader:** Often associated with small businesses that accept credit card payment via a tablet

Each type of payment has apps used for the payment processing. For example, POS systems often support Apple Pay, Samsung Pay, and Android Pay. The NFC reader in the POS terminal takes care of the payment details after a user merely holds a device near the POS. When organizations issue employees company credit cards and want to mitigate vulnerabilities associated with mobile payment systems, MDM or EMM systems can disable the services or apps associated with mobile payment systems.

Deployment Models

Employees are increasingly using personal devices for critical job functions, and organizations are therefore seeking better control over mobile devices and to implement solutions such as MDM and MAM. MDM, secure access to data, and application control all require a holistic security approach. Human factors combined with role-based management can help protect an organization against data loss and threats, as well as ensure that the organization is meeting compliance requirements. This section discusses the current mobile deployment models and considerations.

BYOD, CYOD, COPE, and Corporate-Owned Devices

Bring your own device (BYOD) focuses on reducing corporate costs and increasing productivity by allowing employees, partners, and guests to connect to the corporate network for access to resources. BYOD gives employees freedom to choose the device, applications, and services that best meet their needs. When employees can use their own personal devices, productivity usually increases. From a management perspective, BYOD has increased administrative overhead because many different devices are in use, and the organization has no control over the software or applications users have installed.

Employers sometimes offer reimbursement for business use of a personal device. In some states, the reimbursement is required by law. For example, California Labor Code Section 2802 states that employers are required to

reimburse employees for necessary expenses, including all reasonable costs. This translates to reimbursement for the percentage of the cost associated with business calls.

In *choose your own device* (*CYOD*), the organization controls which devices an employee can choose by providing a list of approved options. CYOD is more restrictive than BYOD and gives the organization greater control over which devices are allowed on the network. In most implementations of CYOD, the organization purchases an employee's device and pays the data usage costs. Device ownership thus rests with the organization, and employees must surrender their devices when they leave or are terminated. This method of managing user devices can reduce the hardware and management costs related to corporate-owned devices, but it cannot completely eliminate them.

With corporate-owned devices, organizations issue employees devices they can use. In this model, which is sometimes called use what you are told (UWYT), the mobile devices available for use are predetermined. Users are issued devices based on corporate policy and, often, their roles in the organization. Corporate-owned devices provide a clear separation between employees' personal and business lives. This is often inconvenient for users because they are required to carry two mobile devices, one for each function.

Corporate-owned, personally enabled (*COPE*), or company-issued business only (COBO), is similar in principle to corporate-owned devices but allows personal use of the device. With COPE, the devices are the organization's responsibility, so monitoring policies must be in place, and devices must be kept up to date. As with corporate-owned devices, this deployment model enables the organization to disconnect a device from the network in the event of a compromise or malware infection. Financial institutions and healthcare providers tend to choose COPE to meet regulatory compliance requirements. Because the organization has to supply, update, and monitor devices, the cost of this implementation method is much higher than the costs of BYOD or CYOD; COPE is generally not cost-effective for small businesses.

Virtual Desktop Infrastructure

Virtual desktop infrastructure (*VDI*) is a technology by which an organization hosts virtual desktops on a centralized server. Generally, employees use a client app to securely connect to the virtual infrastructure that hosts a user's desktop. VDI allows the organization to securely publish personalized desktops for each user through a managed infrastructure. Organizations are extending their VDI to mobile devices, in an implementation model referred to as virtual mobile infrastructure (VMI) or mobile VDI. With this technology, instead of using a

hosted desktop, the user receives a hosted mobile device OS. There are two different methods for setting up a client to access mobile VDI:

▶ **Client-based mobile VDI:** A mobile VDI client must be installed on each mobile device.

▶ **Browser-based mobile VDI:** A web browser is used to access a mobile VDI client.

Mobile VDI is especially useful in BYOD environments because it provides access to both organizational and personal data without the inherent risk of commingled data. Security for EMM and BYOD is already built in to mobile VDI because data and applications are stored on the organization's infrastructure, there is little to no data transfer to the mobile device, and users might have no need for client software on the mobile device. This can reduce the risk associated with lost devices and the need for remote wiping on those lost devices. However, if a mobile VDI experiences an infrastructure failure, users are not able to access resources.

Deployment Strategies

Implementing a mobile deployment program and associated policies requires consideration of general technical aspects, financial responsibility, technical support, and corporate liability. BYOD, CYOD, and COPE deployments vary among organizations.

> **ExamAlert**
>
> Formulating a BYOD, COPE, or CYOD program requires a security model that provides differentiated levels of access by device, user, application, and location.

Cost is one of the primary differences between BYOD, CYOD, and COPE deployments. For COPE and CYOD, all costs reside with the organization; BYOD users pay their own device costs but might receive reimbursement for associated business costs. In addition to the cost, organizations must address some overall challenges related to securing sensitive data in any deployment method in order to protect organizational resources.

Architecture/Infrastructure Considerations

Implementing a BYOD, CYOD, or COPE program requires planning and understanding the access methods and device management options for the

devices. In addition to looking at the 802.11 infrastructure, organizations should consider bandwidth, network saturation, and scalability. Devices might need to be manually provisioned, but the design architecture usually includes some type of MDM solution so that security, management of mobile endpoints, self-service for enterprise applications, and onboarding can be more easily managed. Most MDM solutions offer management capabilities through virtualization architecture, identity-based access and provisioning, device identification, authentication, authorization, single sign-on, and policy enforcement. When choosing a centralized MDM strategy, an organization can use a solution offered by a mobile device vendor or use a product from a third party. Both approaches are similar and use a typical client/server architecture.

Adherence to Corporate Policies and Acceptable Use

Many organizations use a self-service method through a preconfigured profile to minimize IT intervention. This method offers a simplified way to identify domain user groups that are permitted to onboard their devices. When an employee is terminated, retires, or quits, segregating and retrieving organizational data and applications might be difficult. The BYOD, CYOD, or COPE policy should address how data and corporate-owned applications will be retrieved in such a situation. In some instances, the organization might opt for a total device wipe.

When implementing a BYOD, CYOD, or COPE policy, employees need to be made aware of, understand, and accept this policy as it relates to the organization's other policies. Many organizations stipulate that they have the right to wipe a device at any time and will not assume responsibility for any loss of data if a device is wiped. Some organizations require employees to install software that provides additional security. Corporate policies might ban rooted or jailbroken devices, and they might prohibit the use of file-sharing sites such as Dropbox, Google Drive, OneDrive, or iCloud. Users who are part of a BYOD, CYOD, or COPE program are expected to adhere to all corporate policies.

In a BYOD, CYOD, or COPE environment, an organization might choose to have a personal device use policy in addition to the organizational acceptable use policy. A personal device use policy defines responsibilities, guidelines, and terms of use for employee-owned devices accessing the organizational network. Often a personal device use policy is created to address expense limitations as well as access to the Internet, applications, and peer-to-peer file sharing for personal purposes instead of corporate purposes.

Employee consent or user acceptance of a BYOD, CYOD, or COPE policy helps protect an organization in the event that security measures such as seizing a device and deleting all device data need to be implemented. Signed agreements should be kept on file in case the organization needs to take future action that pertains to a device.

> **ExamAlert**
>
> An organization should ensure that employees provide written consent to all terms and conditions of the BYOD, CYOD, or COPE policy so that it can easily refute any claim of policy unawareness.

Legal Concerns

Legal concerns for implementing a BYOD, CYOD, or COPE program and related policies include whether the policies will be enforceable, whether data privacy laws will restrict security controls and required user consent, whether laws and regulations could limit the ability to audit and monitor activity on personally owned devices, and consent to access the device for business purposes. Furthermore, some legal ramifications relate to determining the liability of the organization for application usage, licensing, removing sensitive data and organizational applications, and wiping data from a personal device. All legal concerns should be addressed prior to program implementation.

Privacy

Data privacy is a concern—for both individuals and the organization—when employees bring their own devices to the corporate network. This is especially important in organizations that are bound by legal requirements regarding the storage of private personal information, such as in the medical and financial industries. Privacy concerns should be addressed in BYOD, CYOD, or COPE policies. A BYOD, CYOD, or COPE policy might need to contain language prohibiting or limiting remote access for certain categories of sensitive data.

Employees should be notified of the organization's monitoring and personal data access capabilities. The BYOD, CYOD, or COPE policy should clearly disclose how the organization will access an employee's personal data. If the organization offers device data backup, the policy should also state whether personal data will be stored on backup media. An organizational BYOD, CYOD, or COPE policy may clearly indicate that the organization does not guarantee employee privacy when an employee chooses to be part of the BYOD, CYOD, or COPE workforce.

Data Ownership and Support

Data ownership on an employee-owned device used on a corporate network becomes tricky because of the combination of corporate data and personal data. Many organizations approach this issue by using either containerization or MDM solutions. When formulating a BYOD, CYOD, or COPE policy, an organization should clearly state who owns the data stored on the device and specifically address what data belongs to the organization. The policy should include language stipulating that the organization will remotely wipe data if the employee violates the BYOD, CYOD, or COPE policy; terminates employment; or purchases a new device. Some organizations also reiterate user responsibility for backing up any personal data stored on the device.

Many organizations save IT support costs by implementing BYOD programs, which reduce their device support obligations. Support time is minimal and mostly limited to helping employees initially get the devices up and running on the network. Most BYOD policies state that employees are responsible for voice and data plan billing and for maintenance of their devices. CYOD and COPE policies, on the other hand, establish what types of devices are permitted to access the network and what support is provided.

Patch and Antivirus Management

When corporate data resides on a personal device, it faces risk from viruses, malware, and OS-related vulnerabilities.

ExamAlert

In a BYOD environment, the organization sets minimum security requirements or mandates security as a condition for giving personal devices access to network resources.

Policy should clearly state the requirements for installing updates, patches, and antivirus software. Policy options might include the approval of updates and patches or specific antivirus software, as well as mandatory reporting of any suspected instances of malware infection. In addition, a policy might include material on policy compliance, state that IT may push updates as required, and detail the responsibility for antivirus software costs.

Forensics

A key issue in BYOD, CYOD, and COPE is how to handle device data when an investigation is required. Any captured data will likely include an employee's personal information along with corporate data. Although tools can be used to record WLAN data from capture points for forensics, many times a device itself requires imaging. Organizations can try to limit the scope of an investigation or perform data capture when a personal device is involved. However, prevailing litigation consequences for failing to preserve data might take precedence. Organizations need to ensure that proper BYOD, CYOD, and COPE incident response procedures are formulated and communicated to users.

ExamAlert

In a BYOD, CYOD, or COPE environment, legal requirements take precedence. In an investigation, employees might be temporarily unable to use their devices during the investigation period.

Cram Quiz

Answer these questions. The answers follow the last question. If you cannot answer these questions correctly, consider reading this chapter again until you can.

1. Which of the following enables the use of location services for applications on mobile devices?

   ○ **A.** BYOD

   ○ **B.** GPS

   ○ **C.** MMS

   ○ **D.** OTA

2. As more users are using mobile devices for work, you have been tasked with supporting the compliance team by ensuring that policies can be enforced. You also need remote management capabilities of the devices. Which of the following solutions should you consider?

   ○ **A.** GPS

   ○ **B.** MDM

   ○ **C.** OTP

   ○ **D.** PIN

3. Which of the following are deployment strategies for mobile devices? (Select three.)

   ○ **A.** BYOD

   ○ **B.** CYOD

   ○ **C.** COPE

   ○ **D.** BYOB

4. What device security methods can be implemented to protect business content from security risks associated with personal usage? (Select two.)

   ○ **A.** Jailbreaking

   ○ **B.** Storage segmentation

   ○ **C.** Containerization

   ○ **D.** Rooting

5. What feature enables users to secure sensitive information on a mobile device's removable flash memory storage card?

   ○ **A.** FDE

   ○ **B.** UEM

   ○ **C.** OTA updates

   ○ **D.** VDI

Cram Quiz Answers

Answer 1: B. GPS services built in to mobile devices provide a number of useful services related to the location of the device. Answer A is incorrect because bring your own device (BYOD) is a model for allowing users to use their own devices in the workplace. Answer C is incorrect because MMS is used to send multimedia via text. Answer D is incorrect because OTA is a mechanism for updating software over the air.

Answer 2: B. A mobile device management (MDM) solution helps with management of mobile devices, including remote management capabilities as well as policy enforcement. Answer A is incorrect because GPS relies on satellite technology to provide location services. Answers C and D are both incorrect but are important to ensuring authentication to the device and applications: OTP is a one-time password, usually for applications, and a PIN provides a means to authenticate into the device.

Answer 3: A, B, and C are correct. BYOD, COPE, and CYOD are all deployment strategies for mobile devices in organizations. Answer D is not a mobile device deployment strategy, and thus it is incorrect.

Answer 4: B and C are correct. Storage segmentation and containerization separate personal and business content on a device. They are necessary when an organization has a BYOD policy. These approaches are used in conjunction with MAM as a way to apply policies to mobile devices. Answers A and D are incorrect; illegally gaining administrative privileges on Apple iOS is called jailbreaking and on Android devices is called rooting.

Answer 5: A. Full device encryption (FDE) enables users to secure sensitive information on a mobile device's removable flash memory storage card. Answer B is incorrect because unified endpoint management (UEM) is a newer security approach that focuses on managing and securing all devices, including desktops, laptops, tablets, and smartphones, from a single location. Answer C is incorrect because mobile devices have the capability to receive and install over-the-air (OTA) systems and application updates that are pushed over Wi-Fi to devices. Answer D is incorrect because virtual desktop infrastructure (VDI) is the process by which an organization hosts virtual desktops on a centralized server.

What Next?

If you want more practice on this chapter's exam objective before you move on, remember that you can access all of the Cram Quiz questions on the Pearson Test Prep software online. You can also create a custom exam by objective with the Online Practice Test. Note any objective you struggle with and go to that objective's material in this chapter.

CHAPTER 22

Cloud Cybersecurity Solutions

This chapter covers the following official Security+ exam objective:

▶ 3.6 Given a scenario, apply cybersecurity solutions to the cloud.

Essential Terms and Components

▶ cloud security control

▶ security group

▶ dynamic resource allocation

▶ instance

▶ virtual private cloud (VPC) endpoint

▶ cloud access security broker (CASB)

▶ next-generation secure web gateway (SWG)

In Chapter 10, "Virtualization and Cloud Computing," you got an introduction to cloud computing concepts. This chapter looks more specifically at securing components across the different service models, such as infrastructure as a service (IaaS) and software as a service (SaaS). It's important to remember the shared responsibility model discussed Chapter 10. The focus of this chapter is on the responsibilities of the customers of IaaS and SaaS, and not on the responsibilities of the cloud service provider (CSP).

The share of responsibility changes as you get deeper into cloud services, particularly as IaaS and PaaS overlap. For example, the share of responsibility differs in Amazon Web Services (AWS) for infrastructure services, container services, and abstracted services. Keep in mind, however, that IaaS offers a great number of cloud-native controls. While they offer value-added solutions such as those

related to security and compliance, many of these controls are critical configuration components to the core services offered.

Cloud Workloads

IaaS providers make it simple to instantly launch computers and containers via web services either programmatically or through a graphical interface. These elastic compute capabilities make *dynamic resource allocation* viable. These computer *instances* can be launched on demand quickly, enabling organizations to scale capacity up and down quickly. Customers pay for only what they use. Further, automatic scaling capabilities make it possible to define the circumstances that will scale the systems up or down, based on defined criteria.

Dynamic resource allocation presents two important security concerns. The first security concern involves automatic scaling of capacity. Everything done in an IaaS environment needs the proper permissions after being authenticated. This includes programmatic requests to the application programming interface (API) to scale up or down computers. Within AWS, for example, an administrator can use roles to ensure that when new instances are launched, each instance automatically receives the specified role with the proper permissions. In addition, permissions can be assigned to users to grant them specific access to the APIs that control auto-scaling.

The second security concern is that ease of use combined with the rapid capability of provisioning and deprovisioning compute services can hamper visibility efforts. Organizations need to be aware of the resources deployed, such as computer instances. All of the major IaaS providers provide dashboards and tools to provide such awareness. In addition, third-party applications are available for maintaining awareness across different IaaS cloud service providers.

Cloud providers provide administrative access to the operating system of the container instances. As with instance workloads, the customer is responsible for the security of the operating system as well as the data and the access to these workload services. The infrastructure and workloads established, maintained, and secured by the customer can be deployed in worldwide locations established by the IaaS provider. Resources are usually deployed within a virtual private cloud (VPC), which is part of a logical availability zone. The availability zones are then contained within geographic regions.

Regions and Availability Zones

Regions are separate geographic locations where IaaS cloud service providers maintain their infrastructure. Regions are located around the world, and users typically pick the region from the management console that they are closest to in order to reduce latency. There are, however, other factors to consider. Not all regions provide all services. Regions may also differ in their costs. Finally, compliance regulations need to be taken into consideration. Certain regulations, for example, may have strict data residency requirements.

Within regions are availability zones. Availability zones are isolated locations in which cloud resources can be deployed. While resources aren't replicated across regions, they are replicated across availability zones. This, in essence, provides load-balancing capabilities. Your systems can be designed so that if they fail in one availability zone, they automatically continue to function in the others.

Virtual Private Cloud (VPC)

Rather than just launch computer resources with an assigned public IP address, an organization can deploy systems with private IP addresses within isolated spaces. This is known as a virtual private cloud (VPC), and it is essentially the networking layer in an IaaS environment. Multiple subnets may exist within a single VPC. A *VPC endpoint* enables a VPC to be connected with other services without the need for additional technologies such as a VPN connection or an Internet gateway. Resources in the VPC must make any requests, as the connected services are not able to initiate requests via the VPC endpoint.

A number of best practices should be followed for a VPC in a cloud environment:

- ▶ Ensure high availability of resources and cloud deployments through the use of availability zones
- ▶ Use security groups and network-based access control lists
- ▶ Use policies to control access
- ▶ Ensure central logging of API activity and use tools to monitor connections and capture traffic between your interfaces in the VPC

Security Groups

Compute instances in cloud environments typically require access to other resources, and other resources may require access to the provisioned instances.

Cloud provider *security groups* are essentially virtual firewalls that authorize traffic to and from the compute resources. AWS, for example, automatically creates a security group for you when you launch your first instance of a computer. The following are some key points to keep in mind about security groups, particularly in terms of how they are different from traditional firewalls:

▶ By default, a security group only allows inbound traffic on port 22 for SSH. All other inbound traffic is denied by default.

▶ Traffic cannot be explicitly blocked. Traffic can only be allowed.

▶ Traditionally, firewalls have allowed both source and destination ports. Security groups allow only destination ports.

▶ Security groups are stateful. Thus, if port 80 is allowed on the way in, it is also allowed on the way out.

As a best practice, security groups should only have required ports open and should allow access only from known IP addresses and ranges.

Cloud providers also provide network access control lists (ACLs). Network ACLs, unlike security groups, are not stateful and do support deny rules. A network ACL is beneficial when you need to control traffic between subnets.

> **ExamAlert**
>
> Security groups cannot explicitly block traffic. They can only allow traffic.

Policies

In the cloud, access to resources is governed by policies and their permissions. Polices are attached to an entity, which may be a user, a user group, or a role. Depending on the IaaS cloud, there may be various types of policies. Two basic policies that you should understand are identity-based policies and resource-based policies.

An identity-based policy defines the permissions regarding what a user, group, or role can do. For example, a user who needs to launch a computer instance would be assigned a policy that contains the specific permission to start a workload.

Resource-based policies, on the other hand, are attached to specific resources within the IaaS environment, and these policies define who has access and what activities they are allowed to perform.

Figure 22.1 illustrates the difference between identity-based policies and resource-based policies. Note that Oliver, Max, and Annie can perform some type of action on specific resources with the identity-based policies. The resource-based policies specify the particular users with access and what they can do. However, it's very important to understand where things aren't so clear or where there appear to be conflicts. Consider the following:

▶ Oliver's policies are straightforward. Both the identity-based and resource-based policies allow him to list and read on resource X.

▶ Although Max's identity-based policy only specifies list and read on resource Y and Z, his resource-based policy on resource Y policy also grants him the ability to write. The resource-based policy on Z denies him access. An explicit deny overrides any other allowance.

▶ Annie is able to list, read, and write on all three resources, based on her identity-based policy. Even though she isn't listed on any of the resource-based policies, she is allowed access to these resources and can perform the actions as she is not explicitly denied.

▶ Even though Trent doesn't have an identity-based policy assigned, he is able to access both resource Y and resource Z. The resource-based policy for resource Z grants Trent full access. Resource Y grants him list and read.

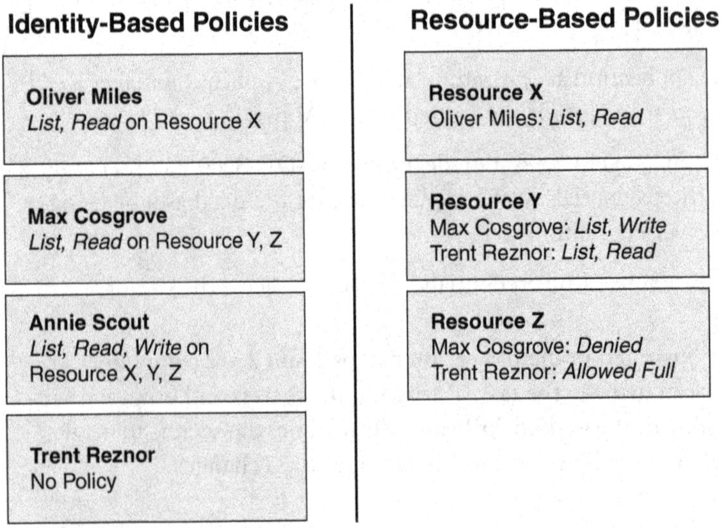

FIGURE 22.1 Evaluating identity-based and resource-based policies

> **ExamAlert**
>
> By default, all access is denied unless an explicit allow permission is granted in a policy. Any explicit deny in any policy overrides any allow.

Managing Secrets

Resources that require long-term credentials such as API keys, encryption keys, and database credentials should not be hard-coded into application configuration files or buried within the source code. Cloud providers and third parties provide systems for managing secrets. For example, AWS's secrets management service, Secrets Manager, works with the built-in AWS Identity and Access Management (IAM) policies that allows people and systems to retrieve passwords only when they need them and under the right circumstances. Secrets management protects and manages access to the applications and services. All secrets are encrypted at rest and in transit. Figure 22.2 illustrates a scenario in which a custom application requires access to a database. The credentials to access the database are stored in the secrets management service. Figure 22.2 illustrates the following steps:

1. The administrator creates the credentials on the database that the application will use.

2. The administrator stores the credentials in the secrets management system. The credentials are stored as a named secret (such as App-DB-Secret).

3. When the application accesses the database, the application makes a call to the secrets manager for the named secret (App-DB-Secret).

4. The secrets management system decrypts App-DB-Secret and securely transmits the credentials to the application (not the database) by using transport layer encryption.

5. The application uses the credentials received to access the database.

In the example illustrated in the figure, after steps 1 and 2 are complete, the secrets manager can manage the task of rotating the secrets and programmatically managing retrieval based on API calls. Meanwhile, the secrets manager provides audit details of all access and any configuration changes.

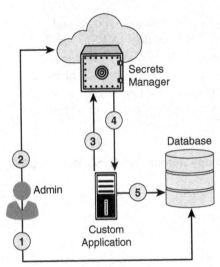

FIGURE 22.2 Using a secrets manager for application access to a database

Central Logging

Maintaining proper control and management over logging is important with security monitoring and auditing. Infrastructure, applications, and services deployed in cloud environments should be aggregated to a central logging facility. The major IaaS cloud providers provide logging for all activities, using their APIs as the services interact. These events should then be written to a storage location in the cloud service provider. These centralized logs can be used for further inspection and analysis in other IaaS-based security and monitoring systems or integrated with any SIEM solution or service, such as those offered by Sumo Logic. AWS provides AWS CloudTrail, which can be written to an S3 storage bucket designed as a log archive. CloudTrail and other similar services provide the ability to maintain a history of API calls across an IaaS account. This history includes when an API was called and what user called and the source IP address. At a minimum, you should log the following in a cloud environment:

▶ Privileged account actions taken on any and all resources

▶ Access to the audit trails and storage

▶ All authentication attempts both successful and unsuccessful

▶ Create and delete events for all resources and objects across the infrastructure

The three major IaaS cloud service providers are Amazon, Google, and Microsoft. Their platforms are known as Amazon Web Services (AWS), Google Cloud Platform (GCP), and Microsoft Azure. While AWS got a huge head start, the others have quickly caught up in terms of functionality. The three providers offer similar services, but the terminology differs slightly across the three providers. Table 22.1 compares the terminology used by these three vendors.

TABLE 22.1 A Comparison of Terminology Across the Three Major IaaS Providers

AWS	GCP	Azure
Instance	Compute engine	VM image
Availability zone	Availability zone	Availability zone
Virtual private cloud	Virtual private cloud	Virtual private cloud
Auto-scaling group	Compute engine autoscaler	VM scale sets
Region	Region	Region
CloudFront	Cloud CDN	Azure CDN
NAT gateway	Cloud routes	NAT gateway
Virtual private cloud	Virtual private cloud	Virtual network
S3 bucket	Cloud storage	Blob storage
Elastic load balancing	Cloud load balancing	Load balancing
Lambda function	Cloud functions	Function apps
Simple notification service	Cloud publish/subscribe	Event grid topics
Amazon Redshift	BigQuery	SQL Data Warehouse
AWS Glue	Cloud Composer	Azure Data Factory
Amazon RDS	Cloud SQL	Azure DB
DynamoDB	Cloud Datastore	Cosmos DB

Third-Party Cloud Security Solutions

While IaaS cloud service providers offer robust cloud-native security solutions, there are gaps. Third-party offerings can fill these gaps and complement IaaS security services. These solutions provide critical capabilities that are typically not provided by IaaS cloud service providers.

A *cloud access security broker* (*CASB*) traditionally provides security services for Software as a Service (SaaS) applications. However, CASBs along with *next-generation secure-web gateways* (*SWGs*) provide the capability to deliver

static and dynamic access to the management plane of IaaS providers, just as they do any SaaS app. Policies may, for example, simply deny access, or policies may dynamically prevent access based on other telemetry and attributes (for example, where the user is located and the user's current threat profile). Software-defined perimeter (SDP) solutions can also broker similar access beyond the management plane down to the specific applications running on cloud workloads. Many of these capabilities are being combined as a solution stack under the Secure Access Service Edge and Zero Trust monikers.

Each of the major IaaS cloud providers offers a marketplace or an app store, from which many of these and other security-related solutions can be deployed. AWS, for example, groups third-party solutions based on either structural or situational awareness. Structural awareness solutions help manage risk and apply protections to systems and data. They include the following:

- **Cloud compliance and best practices:** Visualization and continual assessment of the environment, including the ability to enforce known good standards

- **Instance and container visibility:** Monitoring and protection of containers through their life cycle

- **Virtual private network:** Secure access to applications running in a VPC for remote employees

- **Secure data:** Encryption and key management solutions to protect data and meet regulatory compliance standards

- **Vulnerability assessment and management:** Visibility into the attack surface to discover and resolve security issues

- **Software composition analysis:** Management and security for open-source licenses

- **Operational intelligence:** Aggregation and correlation for the analysis of data across security, performance, and availability

- **DevSecOps:** Automated and continuous process management for continual integration and delivery of secure applications

- **Cyber risk management:** Prioritized insight into the threats, vulnerabilities, and impacts of cloud assets

The situational awareness solutions detect security events and are capable of responding, recovering, and helping with continual improvement. They include the following:

▶ **Firewalls and proxies:** Provide fine-grained inspection of traffic for potential threats at both the network and application levels

▶ **Endpoint detection and response:** Protect endpoints, including cloud workloads from zero-day and other attacks

▶ **Intrusion detection systems:** Monitor networks and workloads for security events

▶ **Backup and restoration:** Protect data from errors, failures, and accidental deletion

▶ **Disaster recovery:** Provides additional flexibility to quickly recover from a disaster, ensuring that cloud workloads are available

▶ **Security information and event management:** Ingests, correlates, and prioritizes events for deeper visibility into anomalous behavior and threat mitigation

▶ **Workload isolation:** Provides dynamic security control for microservices, containers, and other workloads

Cram Quiz

Answer these questions. The answers follow the last question. If you cannot answer these questions correctly, consider reading this chapter again until you can.

1. A user does not have an identity-based policy and requires access to a storage resource but is denied access. Which of the following do you need to do in order to allow him access?

○ **A.** Assign an identity-based policy to the user to allow access

○ **B.** Assign an override for any deny attribute in the identity-based policy

○ **C.** Remove the deny from the resource-based policy

○ **D.** Change the deny to an allow permission on the resource-based policy

2. You need to block SSH inbound traffic on a virtual instance. Which of the following would accomplish this goal?

○ **A.** Assign an explicit inbound block rule for port 22 on the security group.

○ **B.** Assign a resource-based policy on the instance to block port 22.

○ **C.** Remove the inbound allow rule from the security group for port 22.

○ **D.** Remove the resource-based policy on the instance allowing port 22.

3. Which of the following allows a VPC to be connected with other services without the need for additional technologies such as a VPN connection or an Internet gateway?

- ○ **A.** CASB
- ○ **B.** SWG
- ○ **C.** VPC endpoint
- ○ **D.** DevSecOps

Cram Quiz Answers

Answer 1: D. An explicit deny prevents access and overrides any allow statement. The deny needs to be removed. Because the user doesn't have an identity-based policy, the allow permission on the resource also needs to be granted. Answer A is incorrect because the explicit deny still overrides the allow. Answer B is incorrect, as explicit denies take precedent and there is no such option for an override attribute. Answer C is incorrect, as by default without any policies assigned, the user does not have access.

Answer 2: C. Remove the inbound rule that allows port 22 from the security group. This rule is enabled by default. Security groups do not block traffic. They only allow specific traffic, so answer A is incorrect. Finally, resource-based policies do not pertain to network traffic, so answers B and D are incorrect.

Answer 3: C. A virtual private cloud (VPC) endpoint allows a VPC to be connected with other services without the need for additional technologies such as a VPN connection or an Internet gateway. Resources in the VPC must make any requests, as the connected services are not able to initiate requests via the VPC endpoint. Answers A and B are incorrect because cloud access security brokers (CASBs) along with next-generation secure-web gateways (SWGs) provide the capability to deliver static and dynamic access to the management plane of IaaS providers, just as they do any SaaS app. Answer D is incorrect because DevSecOps involves automated and continuous process management for continual integration and delivery of secure applications.

What Next?

If you want more practice on this chapter's exam objective before you move on, remember that you can access all of the Cram Quiz questions on the Pearson Test Prep software online. You can also create a custom exam by objective with the Online Practice Test. Note any objective you struggle with and go to that objective's material in this chapter.

CHAPTER 23

Identity and Account Management Controls

This chapter covers the following official Security+ exam objective:

▶ 3.7 Given a scenario, implement identity and account management controls.

Essential Terms and Components

▶ identity provider (IdP)
▶ account type
▶ account policy
▶ geofencing
▶ geotagging
▶ geolocation

Account Types

The accounts tied to a user's identity directly affect your organization's level of protection. You might find it strange to think that you need to protect a system from its own users. However, internal users have the greatest access to data and, therefore, the greatest opportunity to either deliberately sabotage it or accidentally delete it. A logon banner statement should tell users that network access is granted under certain conditions and that their activities might be monitored. This helps the organization cover itself legally and reminds users that they are expected to follow security policy protocols.

IT organizations often use shared accounts for privileged users, administrators, or applications. This practice presents security and compliance risks because use cannot be attributed to a particular user, and

determination of specific access rights and audit of access use is impossible. One of the first steps in providing a secure account access environment is to eliminate the use of shared accounts. Providing each set of access credentials to a single principal—either a user or a machine service—enables an organization to measure every use of data access to determine a baseline for expected and acceptable use. You can then monitor against the baseline to look for variations that indicate potential misuse of enterprise resources or data access.

A next step in providing a secure account access environment is to use a variety of *account types*. For example, users with administrative credentials should not rely on their privileged accounts for everyday activities such as using email because if they run into an unexpected piece of malware, the malware might gain access to those elevated privileges. Issuing an administrative user a common account for normal access and a separate administrative credential set to use when needed limits the span of control for the user's operational account. Linux users have been doing this for some time, using sudo (superuser do) to perform administrative functions from their session account.

Certain groups and accounts are installed by default. As an administrator, you should know what these are. For example, service accounts are often installed for interaction with the operating system, and local service accounts typically interact with the Windows OS and tend to have default passwords. By knowing which accounts are installed by default, you can determine which of them are really needed and which of them can be disabled to make the system more secure. You should also know which accounts, if any, are installed with blank or well-established passwords. Common machine accounts used in web-based access systems are often targets for unauthorized access attempts, particularly when left in default or well-known configuration states.

ExamAlert

The administrative account should be used only in administering the server. An individual using the administrative account would put a company's entire business in jeopardy if he or she accessed a malware-infected website or opened the wrong email. In addition, generic accounts used by multiple users must be prohibited.

The security settings in many of the newer operating systems do not allow blank passwords. However, accounts in older operating systems might still have a blank password or a well-known default. For example, older routers often came with the username admin and password admin configured, and sometimes these credentials were not changed. Anyone with this easily obtained knowledge could then simply try this username and password combination.

Default credentials and unmonitored accounts such as the guest or admin account commonly established in older equipment and software soften security because they provide one component of access credentials to potential attackers or their tools. Replacing a default administrative account named admin with one that uses a more generic or obscure name adds another obstacle. Attackers then must break both the account name and its associated authentication keys.

Account Management

Account management is fundamental to security practices. Following good practice is important as it's the foundation for how users and services gain access to other systems. The following sections provide general concepts around good practices as they relate to the account life cycle.

Onboarding and Offboarding

When an employee joins or leaves an organization, the process of onboarding/offboarding occurs. Onboarding is the process of creating an identity profile and the information required to describe that identity. Onboarding can also include registering the user's assets, such as a computer and mobile devices, and provisioning them so they can be used to access the corporate network. The organization creating and managing this identity is known as the *identity provider (IdP)* and is responsible for authenticating the identity.

Many organizations use a self-service method through a preconfigured profile to minimize IT intervention. As part of best-practice onboarding procedures, some solutions offer integration with Active Directory, which is a simplified way to identify domain user groups that are permitted to onboard their devices. Offboarding is the opposite process: User identities that no longer require access to the environment are disabled or deactivated and then deleted from the environment, based on organizational policy. When an employee is terminated, retires, or quits, segregating and retrieving organizational data and

applications can be difficult if the user's own devices were used. BYOD policies should address how data and corporate-owned applications will be retrieved during the offboarding process. In some instances, the organization might opt for a total device wipe.

Account provisioning policies for the creation, update, and removal of accounts must be integrated into an organization's HR process and regularly audited to ensure continued compliance. Legacy access groups should be similarly expired when they are no longer appropriate to the organization's operational structure to eliminate potential avenues of unauthorized access through normal line-of-business operations. During separation procedures, passwords and other security credentials should be automatically expired to prevent unauthorized access when those credentials are no longer appropriate. During termination proceedings, this is typically coordinated between managers and the IT department to protect against a terminated employee carrying out retributive or exploitive actions on organizational resources.

Least Privilege

Least privilege is an access control practice in which a logon is provided only the minimum access to the resources required to perform its tasks. Remember the phrase *less is more* when considering security principles: Grant no more access than is necessary to perform assigned tasks. When dealing with user access, there is often a fine line between sufficient access to get the job done and too much access. An organization can manage user access by using groups and group policies. Keep this least privilege practice in mind when comparing the access control options.

Access Auditing and Reviews

User access reviews allow you to identify misapplied changes or other access control adjustments through direct assignment or inherited nesting of role access rights. In these reviews, you can find and rectify accidents or malicious attempts to gain unauthorized access rights. Periodic access reviews for access management can help ensure that the necessary personnel have access to essential systems, and unauthorized employees do not. A more formal type of user access review is called *access recertification*. Access recertification is typically the responsibility of the organization's chief information security officer (CISO) because it involves stating that current access adheres to the organization's internal policies and compliance regulations.

A common good practice is that access to high-risk applications should be reviewed quarterly and that every application should have a review conducted at least annually. A baseline must be established to account for normal line-of-business operations and should be updated regularly to reflect changes in the organization's processes and software applications. Examples include identifying the business owners of every application and classifying the data in applications. With a baseline, you can identify unusual activity based on regular review of all accounts (including "permanent" machine and service accounts), and then disable and remove any unneeded credentials. Access reviews should also be conducted for group membership and role/group alignment for organization assignment. Based on these reviews, you can correct accidental access rights assignment through role and group membership. Users should also be notified of their access rights and the need to alert the IT staff if their access appears to be greater than allowed by their role.

Education and regular operational control reviews should be part of an organization's continuous improvement program to ensure that users comply with security protections and understand the requirements demanded by both their acceptance and use of data access credentials. An organization needs to understand requirements in any attempt to control data access in order to conform to those requirements. Technical controls must be continuously monitored to protect against violation of policy through purposeful or accidental access. An important best practice is to make sure separation of duties among developers, data custodians, and IT administration is well defined and documented.

The purpose of continuous monitoring is to ensure that the processes for user account provisioning, life cycle management, and termination are followed and enforced. Continuous monitoring begins with knowing what user account activity should be present. Continuously monitoring user access enables you to detect unauthorized access from attackers using system backdoors and avert widescale incidents. Industry regulations might require continuous monitoring. For example, Payment Card Industry Data Security Standard (PCI DSS) compliance requires that an organization have well-defined processes in place to review and reassess security practices, even in highly dynamic business environments.

Monitoring should involve a process to record and monitor significant changes to user accounts and groups to ensure that access is not granted outside a formal approval process. Activities that should be monitored and reviewed include the business need for each active account, reconciliation of existing active accounts with account access requests, and account and privilege updates. Close attention should be paid to administrative privilege updates, which may signify compromised accounts.

Time of Day and Location Restrictions

By default users can log in at any time when created with most systems. Many times, restricting logon hours is necessary for maintenance purposes. For example, say that a backup runs at 11:00 p.m. each day. In this case, you might want to be sure that everyone is off the system while the backup is occurring. As another example, say that databases get reindexed on a nightly basis. In this case, you might have to confirm that no one is changing information or locking records during the reindexing process.

Restricting logon hours is also a good way to be sure that an attacker is not logging in with stolen passwords during off-peak hours. You can restrict logon hours by days of the week, hours of the day, or both. You can also assign time-of-day restrictions to ensure that employees use computers only during specified hours. Such restrictions can be useful for organizations when users require supervision, when security certification requires it, or when employees are mainly temporary or shift workers.

> **ExamAlert**
>
> Each OS is different, and the effects of a restriction may depend on whether the user is currently logged on when the restriction time begins. In a Microsoft environment, the Automatically Log Off Users setting determines whether users are forced to log off when their logon hours expire. In other environments, the user might be allowed to stay logged on, but once logged off, the user cannot log back on. The logon schedule is enforced by the Kerberos group policy setting Enforce User Logon Restrictions, which is enabled by default in Windows Active Directory environments.

Because employees have become very mobile, organizations often implement BYOD policies. Location-based policies allow organizations to permit users to access resources in both organizational and personal location settings. Location-based policies are policies based on where a user or device is located. One example is a web filtering policy that prevents inappropriate surfing in the workplace but allows employees to have unrestricted access to web content when they are outside the corporate environment. In the past, organizations often restricted access from anywhere except the corporate headquarters where everybody works. Mobile devices have eliminated some of the traditional boundaries. Say that a specific user needs to access particular systems but should be allowed to do so only when in her home country. If she is outside the country, she should be prevented from authenticating. Attributes on the user's mobile devices can be set to protect the network and systems by allowing access only in the home country. These attributes are related to location, and many of

them are made possible through the use of location-based services. The following are three common location-based services:

▶ **Geofencing:** *Geofencing* is a location-based service that is used to trigger some type of action when a user exits or enters a geographic boundary. For example, a smart thermostat might turn on the air conditioning when a user's phone enters a 3-mile radius of the home.

▶ **Geolocation:** *Geolocation* identifies a device based on its current geographic coordinates.

▶ **Geotagging:** *Geotagging* adds an identifying tag to something based on the location. For example, every photo taken with a smartphone can be tagged with the geographic coordinates where the photograph was taken.

Geolocation can be used in account policy decision making, much like the network location of an IP address. Through the use of location awareness, organizations can more intelligently protect systems. For example, an organization can prevent impossible logins, as a way of protecting authentication credentials. Say that a user logs in to a system today first thing in the morning from his home office in New York City. Then three hours later, the same user logs in to a system from Los Angeles. The organization could have high confidence that this is not possible and could, via policy, prevent the second login from succeeding; it could even disable the account or force a password reset.

Logical Access Controls

A user account holds information about a specific user, such as name, password, and the level of permission the user has in the associated access control lists (ACLs). User accounts should follow standard naming conventions and can also contain more specific information, such as the department the user works in, a home phone number, and the days and hours the user is allowed to log on to specific workstations. Groups can be created to make the sharing of resources more manageable. A group contains users who share a common need for access to a particular resource; groups can be nested in other groups to better aggregate access permissions for multiple roles. Even though the particular terms might differ from one operating system to another, they all refer to the access that a user or group account is specifically granted or denied.

When working with logical controls, two models exist for assigning permissions and rights:

▶ **User-based model:** In the user-based model, permissions are uniquely assigned to each user account. For example, in a peer-to-peer network or

a workgroup, access may be granted based on individual needs. The user-based access type is also found in government and military situations and in private companies where patented processes and trademark products require protection. User-based privilege management is usually implemented for specific parts of the network or specific resources. This type of policy is time-consuming and difficult for administrators to handle, and it does not work well in large environments. You will find that creating groups and assigning users to those groups makes the administration process much easier.

▶ **Role- or group-based model:** When working with groups, remember that no matter what OS you are working with, if you give a user full access in one group and deny access in another group, the result is deny access. However, group permissions are cumulative. Therefore, if a user belongs to two groups and one of them has more liberal access, the user will have the more liberal access, except where the deny access permission is involved. If a user has difficulty accessing information after he or she has been added to a new group, the first item to check for is conflicting permissions.

ExamAlert

When assigning user permissions, remember that if one of the groups to which the user is assigned has liberal access and another group has no access, the result is no access.

Access control over large numbers of user accounts can be more easily accomplished by managing the access permissions on each group; those permissions are then inherited by the group's members. In this type of access, permissions are assigned to groups, and user accounts become members of the groups based on their organizational roles. Each user account has access based on the combined permissions inherited from its various group memberships. These groups often reflect divisions or departments of the company, such as human resources, sales, development, and management. In enterprise networks, groups can also be nested. Group nesting can simplify permission assignment if you know how to use hierarchical nesting. On the other hand, group nesting can complicate troubleshooting if you do not know what was set up for each level or why and, thus, do not know where a deny or allow permission is assigned.

Account Policy Enforcement

As the number of systems and users grows in an organization, *account policy* enforcement becomes critical. An organization should set account policies that define strong security for its systems. Account policies are a subset of the policies that are configurable in group policy.

Credentials must be assigned for specified time periods, with an automatic failover to access denial if they are not renewed to ensure that provisioned accounts are used and then cease to operate. This is often necessary in workforces of short-term or temporary workers, whose accounts could otherwise be left intact and unmonitored after the workers rotate to new positions. Such an account presents a target for brute-force types of attacks on logon passwords, whereby the login attempts can be spread over a long period of time to avoid detection of the potentially many failed logins.

> **ExamAlert**
>
> The Account Expires attribute specifies when an account expires and can be used to enhance security. For example, temporary or contract workers should have user accounts that are valid for only a certain amount of time. This way, when an account expires, it can no longer be used to log on to any service. Statistics show that many temporary accounts are never disabled. Limiting the time an account is active for such employees should be part of the policies and procedures. In addition, user accounts should be audited on a regular basis and deprovisioned or reprovisioned based on role changes.

Every credential, whether a simple logon password, certificate, token, or smart card, should carry a built-in lifetime that ensures termination of that credential, even if it is lost or forgotten. Auditing procedures need to reveal long-term inactive accounts and machine accounts that should be routinely expired and reestablished to protect against long-term attacks and limit exploitation if they are compromised during the normal period of use.

In Windows environments, Active Directory domains use Group Policy Objects (GPOs) to store a wide variety of configuration information, including password policy settings. Domain account policy settings control password settings. These settings are contained within the default domain GPO and applied at the domain level. The domain may contain Organizational Units (OUs) that have their own defined account policy. In these situations, the OU policy will be enforced but only when the user logs on locally to the machine (for example, not into the domain).

Of course, passwords are often used to gain access to services and resources, so password length, duration, history, and complexity requirements are all important to the security of a network. When setting up user accounts, it is important to carefully plan policies.

> **ExamAlert**
>
> In organizations that use Windows Active Directory Domain Services (AD DS) or a similar directory service architecture for enterprise management, group policy assignment of access controls can mandate that security configuration technical controls be applied based on organizational unit or domain membership to handle all accounts within an organization or to establish default configuration settings.

Password Complexity

Passwords that contain only alphanumeric characters are easy to compromise by using publicly available tools. Passwords should therefore contain additional characters and meet complexity requirements. Windows specifies the following criteria for a strong password:

▶ The password may not contain the user's account name or full name value.

▶ The password must contain three of the following: uppercase letters, lowercase letters, numbers, nonalphanumeric characters (special characters), and any Unicode character that is categorized as an alphabetic character but is not uppercase or lowercase.

Complexity requirements can be enforced when passwords are changed or created. These requirements, combined with a minimum password length of eight, ensure that there are at least 218,340,105,584,896 different possibilities for a single password, which means a brute-force attack would be difficult—though not impossible.

Account Expiration

In the normal course of business, you might sometimes create domain user accounts for a short duration. This type of account is useful for contractors or temporary employees, for example. With this kind of user, accounts should automatically expire after a specified date. When an account expires, the user then is no longer allowed to log on to the domain, and the operating system displays an error message, informing the user that the account has expired.

Forgotten Passwords

If a user forgets a password, administrators should not be able to recover the old password. Instead, they should verify the proper identity and issue new credentials. When a user forgets a password, the user will need to perform a password reset. Password resets are also performed when a new account is created to set an initial password. Password resets can take place in several ways, ranging from an in-person visit with an IT staff member to a fully automated self-service utility. If the identity of the user requesting a password reset is not properly verified, an attacker could easily pose as a user and gain access to that user's password. Reset mechanisms should first verify the user's identity. Common verification methods include using predetermined challenge/response questions set during account creation, emailing recovery information, or texting a code to the user's mobile phone.

Account Lockout

Account lockout policy settings help prevent attackers from guessing users' passwords and decrease the likelihood of successful attacks on a network. An account lockout policy disables a user account when an incorrect password is entered a specified number of times over a certain time period. Account lockout policy settings control the threshold for this response and the actions to be taken when the threshold is reached. Figure 23.1 shows the Windows local security policy settings for the account lockout policy and associated values.

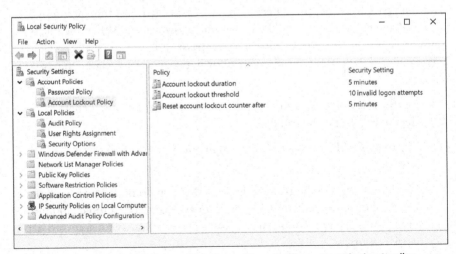

FIGURE 23.1 **Windows local security policy settings for the account lockout policy**

The Account Lockout Duration Policy setting determines the number of minutes that a locked-out account remains locked out before it is automatically unlocked. The available range is from 1 through 99,999 minutes. A lockout duration value of 0 specifies that the account will be locked out until an administrator explicitly unlocks it. The lockout threshold can be set to any value from 0 to 999. If the lockout threshold is set to 0, accounts will not be locked out due to invalid logon attempts. The Reset Account Lockout Counter After setting determines the number of minutes that must elapse from the time a user fails to log on before the failed logon attempt counter is reset to 0. If the account lockout threshold is set to a number greater than 0, this reset time must be less than or equal to the value of account lockout duration. A disadvantage of configuring these settings too restrictively is that users might have to make excessive help desk calls. General best practices dictate that you lock out user accounts after three to five failed login attempts to prevent programs from deciphering the passwords on locked accounts through repeated brute-force attempts.

Password Age and History

The Maximum Password Age setting determines the number of days that a password can be used before the system requires the user to change it. You can set passwords to expire after any number of days between 1 and 999, or you can specify that passwords never expire by setting the number of days to 0. Microsoft operating systems use both a maximum password age and a minimum password age. If the maximum password age is set, the minimum password age must be less than the maximum password age. When the maximum password age is set to 0, the minimum password age can be any value between 0 and 998 days. Consider the following suggestions related to password age:

▶ Set the maximum password age to a value between 30 and 90 days, depending on the environment.

▶ Try to expire the passwords between major business cycles to prevent work loss.

▶ Configure a minimum password age so that you do not allow passwords to be changed immediately. This way, an attacker has a limited amount of time in which to compromise a user's password and gain access to network resources.

Figure 23.2 shows the Windows Local security policy settings for the password policy and associated values.

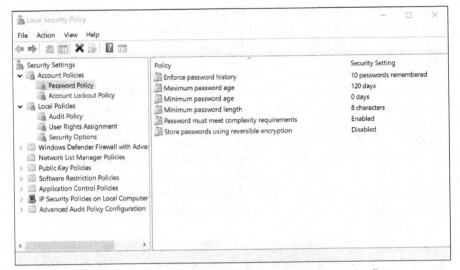

FIGURE 23.2   **Windows local security policy settings for the password policy**

Password history or reuse is an important concern in any organization. When allowed to do so, users tend to reuse the same password over a long period of time. The longer the same password is used for a particular account, the greater the chance that an attacker will be able to determine the password through brute-force attacks. Allowing users to reuse old passwords greatly reduces the effectiveness of a good password policy.

Most operating systems have settings that manage the password history and do not allow users to reuse a password for a certain length of time or before a certain number of password changes. The Enforce Password History setting in Windows operating systems determines the number of unique new passwords that must be associated with a user account before an old password can be reused. Specifying a low number for this setting allows users to continually use the same small number of passwords repeatedly. Configure the server to not allow users to use the same password this way. Setting Enforce Password History to 24 helps mitigate vulnerabilities caused by password reuse.

Password Length and Rotation

Making the password length at least 8 characters and requiring combinations of uppercase and lowercase letters, numbers, and special characters is good practice. In Windows operating systems, the Minimum Password Length

setting determines the least number of characters that can make up a password for a user account. You can set a value of between 1 and 14 characters, or you can establish that no password is required by setting the number of characters to 0.

In most environments, an 8-character password is recommended because this is long enough to provide adequate security but still short enough for users to easily remember. Adding complexity requirements helps reduce the possibility of a dictionary attack. Although longer passwords are more effective against attacks, requiring long passwords can lead to account lockouts due to mistyping and can actually decrease security because users might be more likely to write down their passwords. User education on the proper way to create long passwords that they can easily remember is the best solution.

> ## ExamAlert
>
> The key aspects of password control include required complexity, password length, and account lockout/expiration terms. Password policies help secure a network and define the responsibilities of users who have been given access to company resources. You can use the account lockout policy to secure a system against attacks by disabling the account after a certain number of attempts for a certain period of time.

Require users to change passwords every 30 to 90 days, depending on how secure the environment needs to be. Remember that the more often users are required to change passwords, the greater the chance that they will write them down, potentially exposing them to unauthorized use.

Cram Quiz

Answer these questions. The answers follow the last question. If you cannot answer these questions correctly, consider reading this chapter again until you can.

1. Your corporate policies require the use of passphrases rather than passwords. Which of the following technical controls could be put in place to best promote the use of passphrases? (Select two.)

   - ○ **A.** Lockout
   - ○ **B.** Length
   - ○ **C.** History
   - ○ **D.** Complexity

2. Your account policies require employees to change their passwords every 30 days. The employees, however, continue to create passwords that are susceptible to dictionary attacks, and they are just alternating between two passwords with each change. Which of the following policies would be the best choices for fixing this? (Select two.)

- ○ **A.** Lockout
- ○ **B.** Length
- ○ **C.** History
- ○ **D.** Complexity

3. What is the term for disabling, deactivating, or deleting a user identity from the environment based on company policy when the user leaves the company?

- ○ **A.** Least privilege
- ○ **B.** IdP
- ○ **C.** Onboarding
- ○ **D.** Offboarding

4. Every photo taken with a smartphone at an investigation firm includes data on the geographic coordinates where the photograph was taken. What term describes this action?

- ○ **A.** Geofencing
- ○ **B.** Geosynchronous
- ○ **C.** GPO
- ○ **D.** Geotagging

5. Ramone, a user in your organization, is a member of the accounting group, which has full access permission to a folder named Private Information Assigned. Ramone also belongs to the sales group, which has deny access permission assigned to the same private information folder. What can Ramone do to the private information folder?

- ○ **A.** Nothing
- ○ **B.** Everything
- ○ **C.** Save files to the folder
- ○ **D.** Save files to the folder and delete files in the folder

Cram Quiz Answers

Answer 1: B and D. Length would ensure longer choices, and complexity would ensure the use of special characters and mixed case. Answer A is incorrect as a lockout would lock the user out after a specified number of incorrect attempts. Answer C is incorrect as history would enforce the allowed number of times a new password must be used before an old password can be reused.

Answer 2: C and D. A history policy determines the number of times a user must create new passwords before being able to reuse a previous one, so it prevents a user from alternating between two passwords. For example, a history setting of 30 would mean the user could not reuse the same password until the 31st password change. Complexity would help prevent password cracking. Answers A and B are incorrect. While length seems viable, complexity is a better choice, given the dictionary attacks. Lockout is related to requiring an account reset (based on too many invalid passwords, for example).

Answer 3: D. *Offboarding* means that identities of users who no longer require access to the environment are disabled or deactivated and then deleted from the environment, based on organizational policy. Onboarding is the opposite process, so answer C is incorrect. Answer A is incorrect because *least privilege* is an access control practice in which a logon is provided only the minimum access to the resources required to perform its tasks. Answer B is incorrect because the organization creating and managing identity, known as the identity provider (IdP), is responsible for authenticating the identity.

Answer 4: D. Geotagging adds an identifying tag to something based on location. For example, every photo taken with a smartphone is tagged with the geographic coordinates of where the photograph was taken. Geolocation can be used in account policy decision making, much like the network location of an IP address. Answer A is incorrect because geofencing is used to trigger some type of action when the user exits or enters a geographic boundary. Answer B is incorrect because the term *geosynchronous* describes a satellite that follows the pattern of the earth's orbit. Answer C is incorrect because Active Directory (AD) domains use group policy objects (GPOs) to store a wide variety of configuration information, including password policy settings.

Answer 5: A. No matter what OS you are working with, if you give a user full access in one group and deny access in another group, the result is deny access. However, group permissions are cumulative. Therefore, if a user belongs to two groups, and one has more liberal access, the user will have the more liberal access, except where the deny access permission is involved. If a user has difficulty accessing information after he or she has been added to a new group, the first item to check for is conflicting permissions. Therefore, answers B, C, and D are incorrect.

What Next?

If you want more practice on this chapter's exam objective before you move on, remember that you can access all of the Cram Quiz questions on the Pearson Test Prep software online. You can also create a custom exam by objective with the Online Practice Test. Note any objective you struggle with and go to that objective's material in this chapter.

CHAPTER 24

Authentication and Authorization Solutions

This chapter covers the following official Security+ exam objective:

▶ 3.8 Given a scenario, implement authentication and authorization solutions.

Essential Terms and Components

▶ authentication management

▶ password vault

▶ Trusted Platform Module (TPM)

▶ hardware security module (HSM)

▶ knowledge-based authentication (KBA)

▶ Extensible Authentication Protocol (EAP)

▶ Challenge Handshake Authentication Protocol (CHAP)

▶ Password Authentication Protocol (PAP)

▶ 802.1X

▶ Remote Authentication Dial-In User Service (RADIUS)

▶ single sign-on (SSO)

▶ Security Assertion Markup Language (SAML)

▶ Terminal Access Controller Access Control System Plus (TACACS+)

▶ Open Authorization (OAuth)

▶ OpenID

▶ Kerberos

- ▶ attribute-based access control (ABAC)
- ▶ role-based access control (RBAC)
- ▶ rule-based access control
- ▶ mandatory access control (MAC)
- ▶ discretionary access control (DAC)
- ▶ conditional access
- ▶ privileged access management (PAM)

Authentication

Authentication and authorization issues such as unencrypted credentials, incorrect permissions, and access violations leave an organization vulnerable. Sometimes organizational configurations expose credentials. For example, the Starbucks iOS mobile app sent user passwords in plaintext for most of a year before the app was fixed. The vulnerability happened because of the way crash information data was produced. Because users often reuse personal passwords on their corporate and organizational accounts, a mobile app vulnerability like this could well lead to the compromise of organizational data.

Many of the protocols and services discussed in this chapter provide methods to help with various authentication issues, such as using strong underlying protections of the password itself and helping to ensure ease of use by allowing the user to remember one password to authenticate across multiple applications and services. Single-sign on (SSO) solutions provide this capability. Given the proliferation of applications, ensuring strong passwords while providing ease of use is especially critical for large organizations.

An alternative to SSO solutions, and still often a needed supplement, is the use of a password vault. A *password vault* can store all of user's credentials, protected with a single strong password. Forgetting passwords presents unique challenges. For example, a password reset process provides an avenue for an attacker to compromise an account. As a result, many organizations have implemented safety measures in the process, such as *knowledge-based authentication* (*KBA*). KBA is often also used to mitigate risk where further verification is required after initial authentication if there is any doubt. KBA is based on personal information that is known by the user or can be

something easily recalled, such as questions previously answered about the first street you grew up on or your first pet's name. KBA may also include publicly available information drawn from databases or credit reports, such as domain names registered or monthly mortgage payment. KBA should never be relied upon as the only mechanism but can be paired with other controls to mitigate risk.

KBA and, in particular, the need to facilitate password resets is often a function of authentication management. *Authentication management* involves the management of user credentials across their life cycle, from onboarding and ongoing management to offboarding. Authentication management has grown well beyond password synchronization and self-service password resets. Organizations have deployed hundreds of applications both on premises and in the cloud. Users are mobile. Users have a lot of devices, which means they have a lot of credentials to manage. In addition to passwords, there are smart cards, hardware and software multifactor tokens, biometrics, KBA security questions, digital certificates, and more.

> **Note**
>
> *Trusted Platform Module* (*TPM*) chips and *hardware security modules* (*HSMs*) provide strong hardware-based cryptographic solutions across a number of use cases, including password protection and device identification and authentication. Refer to Chapter 18, "Host and Application Security Solutions," for more on TPMs and HSMs.

Unencrypted Plaintext Credentials

Weak passwords are often discovered when using security tools such as those described in Chapter 23, "Identity and Account Management Controls." Recall the previous Starbucks example: An organization can mitigate this type of exposure in several ways. Authentication alone is typically not sufficient when weak passwords are used. When an application or a service stores or sends passwords in plaintext, risk to the organization can be reduced by sending the credentials via an encrypted channel such as HTTPS. This prevents malicious users from capturing the plaintext passwords.

Probably one of the most unintentional exposures of a password in plaintext occurs when a user logs in and types the password into the username field. In a Windows environment, failed logins record the plaintext password in the Security log. Most web applications log unsuccessful login attempts, so passwords

can similarly end up being logged with web-based applications. Although an attacker would need additional information to obtain the associated username, it could be possible. For example, when users log in incorrectly, they usually immediately attempt to log in again. Chances are pretty good that the next successful login is the username associated with the previous failed login. This method of association has a greater success rate in a small environment. The best defense against this type of exposure is to educate users about the vulnerability such a failed login presents and have them change the password after it happens.

Filesystem Permissions

When trying to access resources such as files, you have likely seen the message "Access Denied" at some point. This notification is a sign that filesystem permissions are set to deny access to the requested resource. These common user activities tend to be associated with permission issues:

▶ Reading, modifying, and deleting files

▶ Accessing shared folders on the network

▶ Using services such as remote access or remote desktop services

▶ Using devices such as printers

These activities can be restricted by design or because of misconfigured user account permissions. Keep in mind that the principle of least privilege is critical for proper security. Users should not have more permissions than they require to do their job. For example, a user could have access to employee records or customer data that should be restricted to a small group of upper management.

> **ExamAlert**
>
> The biggest security issue with incorrect user account permissions is that they could grant access to information that a user should not be able to access.

One of the best examples of misconfigured user access involves Chelsea (formerly Bradley) Manning, who was able to exfiltrate sensitive data because of misconfigured permissions. Misconfigured permissions leave a network vulnerable and can violate regulatory compliance.

Auditing user permissions is one way of identifying access violations and issues. Auditing user permissions is generally a two-step process that involves turning on auditing within the operating system and then specifying the resources to be audited. After you enable auditing, you also need to monitor the logs that are generated. Auditing should include both privilege and use. Access use and rights changes should be audited to prevent unauthorized or unintentional access or an escalation of privileges that, for example, might give a guest or restricted user account access to sensitive or protected resources.

When configuring an audit policy, it is important to monitor both successful and failed access attempts. Failure events enable you to identify unauthorized access attempts. Successful events can reveal accidental or intentional escalation of access rights.

In a Windows environment, user permissions are generally assigned via group policy. Group policies can get complex, leading to permission issues. The easiest way to determine what group policies have been applied is to use GPResult, a command-line utility that determines the policy for a given user or computer. Another helpful tool for troubleshooting permissions issues for users or groups is AccessChk. It shows the permissions that specific users and groups have for files, folders, registry keys, Windows services, and other objects. Using Access-Chk is a quick way to determine whether the proper level of security has been applied.

Permissions in Windows are relatively straightforward and self-explanatory. As shown in Figure 24.1, these are the standard Windows permissions:

▶ **Full Control:** Gives the user complete control, including the ability to modify permissions on files and folders.

▶ **Modify:** Gives the user the ability to read a file, write changes, and modify permissions.

▶ **Read & Execute:** Permits the user to see folder content, read files and attributes, and run programs.

▶ **List Folder Contents:** Permits the user to view the contents of a folder. This permission applies only to folders and not files.

▶ **Read:** Permits the user to read a file but not make changes to the file.

▶ **Write:** Permits the user to change the contents of files and folders and create new files.

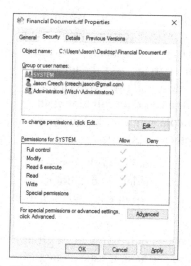

FIGURE 24.1 Standard Microsoft Windows file permissions

As shown in the figure, basic permissions are simple to apply and manage. These basic permissions can be combined into more advanced special permissions, which can be accessed by clicking the Advanced button on the Security tab (refer to Figure 24.1). Table 24.1 shows how the basic permissions are combined to form the advanced permissions.

TABLE 24.1 Windows Basic and Advanced Permissions

Advanced Permission	Full Control	Modify	Read & Execute	List Folder Contents	Read	Write
Traverse folder/ execute file	X	X	X	X		
List folder/read data	X	X	X	X		
Read attributes	X	X	X	X		
Read extended attributes	X	X	X	X		
Create files/write data	X	X				X
Create folders/ append data	X	X				X
Write attributes	X	X				X

Advanced Permission	Full Control	Modify	Read & Execute	List Folder Contents	Read	Write
Write extended attributes	X	X				X
Delete subfolders and files	X					
Delete	X	X				
Read permissions	X	X	X	X	X	X
Change permissions	X					
Take ownership	X					

ExamAlert

Review Table 24.1 and make sure you are familiar enough with this material that, when given a scenario, you can identify required permissions. Keep in mind that permissions are inherited from their containers, except where explicitly allowed or denied. An allowed permission will only ever override a denied permission when a member is part of multiple groups, and one group has an explicit allow while the other group has an inherited deny.

Linux provides for many of the same outcomes as Windows, but file permissions are implemented quite differently. In Linux, there are three basic permission types:

▶ **Read (represented as the letter r or the number 4):** When applied to a file, allows the user to view the contents of a file. When applied to a directory, allows the user to view the names of the files within the directory.

▶ **Write (represented as the letter w or the number 2):** When applied to a file, allows the user to modify and delete a file. When applied to a directory, allows the user to delete the directory; create, delete, and rename files; and modify the contents of any file that the user is allowed to read.

▶ **Execute (represented as the letter x or the number 1):** When applied to a file along with the read permission, allows the user to run a file such as an executable or a script.

Before we look at how these permissions are applied, you need to understand that Linux involves three different types of entities:

▶ **Owner:** The owner is usually provided all permissions as the owner of the file or folder.

▶ **Group:** The group is a named group to which users can belong.

▶ **Others:** Others includes everyone else and cannot override permissions given by the owner or group.

Permissions are represented in three groups of three, where read, write, and execute may apply across owner, group, and others. The permissions are commonly represented together, and a dash is used to denote no permission assigned. For example, the following represents a file that can be modified (and read) by everyone: -rw-rw-rw-. The first three characters are the owner, the second three are the group, and the final three characters are others.

> **Note**
>
> As noted earlier in this section, the permissions can also be represented by numbers rather than with r, w, and -. These numbers can be added together to set permissions. For example, 640 represents -rw-r-----. The 6 gives the user read and write (4+2=6). The 4 gives the group read, and the 0 provides no permissions.

Access Violations

You already know that too much access creates risk for an organization, and too little access slows productivity. Just as user access can be managed via auditing, access violations can be managed through enterprise-level software. In a Windows environment, Microsoft Operations Manager (MOM) has an Audit Collection Services (ACS) function that collects audit events in a database that can then be queried. ACS provides two preconfigured reports:

▶ Access Violation Account Locked report

▶ Access Violation Unsuccessful Logon Attempts report

In addition to the tools available in an OS, vendors provide software to manage access violations. For example, certain software and services allow organizations to automate the recognition and notification of access permission violations so that they can then calculate the financial impact of the violations.

Authentication Issues

Users are likely to have experienced authentication issues at some time or other. Perhaps the most annoying problem arises when a frequently visited site makes changes, and a user's password no longer works. When both the username and password are correct, other factors are causing the authentication issue. These are the most common authentication issues:

▶ Incorrect username

▶ Incorrect password

▶ Disabled or deleted account

▶ Restricted user rights

▶ Computer not in the domain

▶ Domain controller not available

To resolve these authentication issues, the first item to check as you begin the troubleshooting process is that the correct username and password have been entered. Then you need to verify that the user's password has not expired or that the account has not been disabled. Finally, check to be sure no basic connectivity issues exist between the client machine and the domain controller.

Even if no local machine and network issues are present, authentication issues can occur. For example, Microsoft had authentication issues that prevented access to related applications for anyone with a cloud-based account. In such a situation, only the service provider can resolve the authentication issue.

Authentication Protocols

This section discusses the various identity and access services and explores how they are used. It covers services that use tickets, such as Kerberos; services that use challenge mechanisms, such as Challenge Handshake Authentication Protocol (CHAP); remote access services, such as RADIUS; and federated services, such as OAuth.

Password Authentication Protocol (PAP) is a simple authentication protocol in which the username and password are sent to the remote access server in plaintext. PAP offers no protection from playback or trial-and-error attacks. The remote server is in control of the frequency and timing of the login attempts. Using PAP is strongly discouraged because user passwords are easily readable from the Point-to-Point Protocol (PPP) packets exchanged during the authentication process. PPP is a protocol for communicating between two points

using a serial interface, and it provides service at Layer 2 of the OSI model (the data link layer). The default status of any PPP link is to not require authentication of the remote host. PAP is typically used only when connecting to older Unix-based remote access servers that do not support more secure authentication protocols.

Challenge Handshake Authentication Protocol (*CHAP*) can be used to provide on-demand authentication in an ongoing data transmission. CHAP uses a one-way hashing function that first involves a service requesting a CHAP response from the client. The client creates a hashed value that is derived using the Message Digest (MD5) hashing algorithm and sends this value to the service, which also calculates the expected value. The server, referred to as the *authenticator*, compares these two values. If the values match, the transmission continues. This process is repeated at random intervals during a session of data transaction to help eliminate the possibility of a replay attack. The process of authenticating is called a *three-way process*. Actually, however, four steps are involved because the first step is establishing the connection, but the authentication process itself is a three-way process. CHAP is an improvement over PAP because it hashes the password but still sends the username in plaintext. CHAP functions over PPP connections.

Microsoft CHAP (*MSCHAP*) is an encrypted authentication mechanism that is similar to CHAP. It comes in two versions, MSCHAPv1 and MSCHAPv2. MSCHAPv1 is a one-way authentication method in which the server requires authentication from the client. This version should not be used. MSCHAPv2 provides stronger security because it uses a new string each time the authentication is challenged. In MSCHAPv2, the client and server mutually authenticate and use two encryption keys: one for sending data and one for receiving data.

PAP, CHAP, and MSCHAP are authentication protocols intended for use primarily by hosts and routers that connect to a PPP or PPP over Ethernet (PPPoE) network server via switched circuits or dial-up lines. These are all older, less secure protocols. In August 2012, Microsoft advised against using MSCHAPv2 and recommended using either MSCHAP with Protected Extensible Authentication Protocol (PEAP) or more secure alternatives, such as L2TP/IPsec.

When implementing security for a legacy protocol such as MSCHAPv2, *Extensible Authentication Protocol* (*EAP*) can be used. EAP is a password-based authentication framework. In this implementation, the client doesn't need to have a certificate, but the authentication server has one. Passwords from the clients are sent using hashes to the authentication server.

If the environment allows for a stronger authentication method, PEAP can be used. PEAP acts as a TLS/SSL tunnel and protects the authentication traffic. PEAP uses a certificate on the authentication server and optionally a certificate on the client.

802.1X

Devices that need to connect to a wireless network can also be controlled via the Institute of Electrical and Electronics Engineers (IEEE) *802.1X* standard. (Do not confuse this with 802.11.) 802.1X provides standards for port-based access control, whereas 802.11 is specific to wireless technology. 802.1X provides a method for authenticating a device to another system via an authentication server. 802.1X specifically provides for the encapsulation of EAP over the IEEE family of standards for packet-based networks. The standard essentially facilitates the use of various authentication methods, such as RADIUS, digital certificates, and one-time password devices.

AAA Protocols and Services

Two prominent security protocols used to control access in networks are TACACS+ and RADIUS. *Remote Authentication Dial-In User Service (RADIUS)* remote access control system provides authentication and access control in an enterprise network, using UDP transport to a central network access server. In turn, this provides credentials for client access to resources in the extended enterprise. RADIUS was originally developed for use in dial-up connectivity over telephony, and you might still find RADIUS servers in larger enterprises where logons must span resources located in multiple logon realms.

A protected network segment might implement a virtual private network (VPN) or remote access server (RAS) gateway connection to allow an authenticated external service request to reach a protected server by communicating with a RADIUS server. The requesting account must provide its credentials to the RADIUS server, which then authorizes the access request. A RADIUS server supports a variety of authentication methods, including PPP, PAP, CHAP, and Unix login authentication mechanisms.

> **ExamAlert**
>
> RADIUS provides authentication and authorization functions as well as network access accounting functions. However, it does not provide further access control.

RADIUS can forward authentication and authorization requests between authentication domains (called *realms*) and thus can facilitate cross-enterprise authentication, often as part of a *single sign-on* (*SSO*) solution.

Terminal Access Controller Access Control System Plus (*TACACS+*) is a protocol that was developed by Cisco and released as an open standard beginning in 1993. Although it derives from TACACS, TACACS+ is a separate protocol that handles authentication, authorization, and accounting (AAA) services. TACACS+ is similar to RADIUS but uses TCP as a transport method; it uses port 49 as the default port. TACACS+ takes a client/server model approach. The client first queries the server. The client is typically a router or a firewall that is used to determine whether the user has proper authorization to access the network. The server sends back a reply indicating whether the user passed authentication.

Both TACACS+ and RADIUS have an accounting function, so if a device were intentionally compromised, an audit trail would show the originating IP address and the user account logged in to the device. TACACS+ offers several advantages over RADIUS:

▶ TACACS+ tends to be more reliable because it uses TCP instead of UDP.

▶ TACACS+ encrypts the entire body of the packet in the original access request packet. RADIUS encrypts only the password, leaving information such as the username subject to the compromise.

▶ TACACS+ uses the AAA architecture. TACACS+ can therefore be used for authorization and accounting with separate authentication methods. RADIUS combines the authentication and authorization features of AAA, making it difficult to use the functions separately.

▶ TACACS+ provides methods to control the authorization of router commands. RADIUS is not as useful for router management or as flexible for terminal services because it does not allow users to control the commands that can be executed.

Consider an example of when TACACS+ should be used instead of RADIUS: An organization requires the use of Kerberos authentication but also needs authorization and accounting functions. In this instance, the network access server (NAS) informs the TACACS+ server that it has successfully authenticated on a Kerberos server. The server then provides authorization information without requiring reauthentication.

To minimize the chance of compromising the entire user/password database, a TACACS+ server should not run other applications. Proper access control lists

should be implemented, and additional security steps (such as using TCP wrappers) should be taken to prevent connection to the TACACS+ server in the event that an internal device is compromised.

Federated Services

Technologies used for federated identity include SAML, OAuth, OpenID, Simple Web Tokens, and JSON Web Tokens. These technologies use secure tokens. Token authentication is a good approach to authentication because it is stateless. Instead of authenticating with the username and password for each resource, the user authenticates once with the username and password and then receives a secure token. The token is then used for further authentication and expires after a set amount of time. This method prevents storage of user information on the server or in a session. Using tokens provides restrictive permissions to third-party applications such as Twitter and Facebook.

Security Assertion Markup Language (*SAML*) is an Extensible Markup Language (XML) framework for creating and exchanging security information between online partners. It is a product of the OASIS Security Services Technical Committee. Most cloud and Software as a Service (SaaS) service providers favor SAML because it provides authentication assertion, attribute assertion, and authorization assertion. Authentication assertion validates the user's identity. Attribute assertion contains information about the user, and authorization assertion identifies what the user is authorized to do.

The main purpose of SAML is to provide single sign-on for enterprise users. The SAML framework defines three main functions:

▶ The user seeking to verify its identity is the principal.

▶ The entity that can verify the identity of the end user is the identity provider.

▶ The entity that uses the identity provider to verify the identity of the end user is the service provider.

The following process occurs with single sign-on:

1. The user accesses a resource.

2. The service provider issues an authentication request.

3. The identity provider authenticates the user.

4. The identity provider issues an authentication response.

5. The service provider checks the authentication response.

6. When validation is complete, the resource returns the content.

The main difference between SAML and other identity mechanisms is that SAML relies on assertions about identities. The weakness in the SAML identity chain is the integrity of users. SAML uses SAM, XML, HTTP, and SOAP protocols. To mitigate risk, SAML systems need to use timed sessions, HTTPS, and SSL/TLS.

Open Authorization (*OAuth*) is a framework used for Internet token-based authorization. The main purpose of OAuth is API authorization between applications. Two versions are used; the most current is Version 2.0.

The OAuth framework consists of the following:

▶ The resource owner

▶ The OAuth provider, which is the hosting resource server

▶ The OAuth consumer, which is the resource consumer

OAuth 2.0 defines four roles: resource owner, authorization server, resource server, and client. It creates separate roles for the resource server and authorization server. OAuth 2.0 obtains authorization for the user via an access token and then uses that token to make user requests. Flows, which are called *grant types* in OAuth 2.0, make it possible to get access tokens. There are several grant types:

▶ *Authorization code:* This grant type is used for server-side applications. The user is prompted to authorize the application, the identity provider supplies an authorization code, and the application server exchanges the authorization code for an access token.

▶ *Implicit:* This grant type is used for client-side web applications. This grant type doesn't have a server-side component. It skips the authorization code generation step. Immediately after the user authorizes the application, an access token is returned.

▶ *Password credentials:* This grant type is used for first-class web applications or mobile applications. This grant type is to be used only for native web or mobile applications because it allows applications to collect the user's username and password and exchange them for an access token.

▶ *Client credentials:* This grant type is used for application code to allow an application to access its own resources. The application makes a request, using its own credentials, to receive an access token.

OAuth 2.0 uses the JSON and HTTP protocols. Because it only provides authorization services, it does not support secure methods such as client verification, encryption, or channel binding. OAuth 2.0 relies on underlying technologies, implementers, and other protocols to protect the exchange of data. SSL/TLS is recommended to prevent eavesdropping during the data exchange. If a user was not logged in to the server before the OAuth initiation request, resource providers should automatically log the user out after handling the third-party OAuth authorization flow to prevent session management exploits.

> **ExamAlert**
>
> OAuth does not provide authentication services. It is used exclusively for authorization services, which makes it different from OpenID and SAML.

OpenID Connect is an identity layer based on OAuth 2.0 specifications that is used for consumer single sign-on. OpenID Connect is similar to the open standard *OpenID*, sponsored by Facebook, Microsoft, Google, PayPal, Ping Identity, Symantec, and Yahoo!. In 2015, Google recommended switching from OpenID to OpenID Connect. OpenID Connect implements authentication as an extension to the OAuth 2.0 authorization process and provides additional mechanisms for signing, encryption of identity data, and session management.

The OpenID Connect protocol specifications guide states this process for validation:

1. The client sends a request to the OpenID provider (OP).

2. The OP authenticates the end user and obtains authorization.

3. The OP responds with an ID token and an access token.

4. The client sends a request with the access token to the UserInfo endpoint.

5. The UserInfo endpoint returns claims about the end user.

OpenID Connect uses an ID token structure that contains an authorization server's claims about the authentication of an end user via a JSON Web Token (JWT). A JWT is used to prove that the sent data was created by an authentic source. The flows determine how the ID token and access token are returned to the client. Authentication takes place through one of three flows:

▶ The authorization code flow returns an authorization code to the client, which then exchanges it for an ID token and an access token.

▶ The implicit flow eliminates the token endpoint. All tokens are returned from the authorization endpoint.

▶ The hybrid flow can have some tokens returned from the authorization endpoint and some returned from the token endpoint.

The OpenID Connect specification takes attacks into consideration and resolves many of the security issues with OAuth 2.0. However, if guidelines are not followed to implement it securely, broken end-user authentication can result.

Shibboleth is a SAML-base, open-source federated identity solution that provides SSO capabilities and federated services and is popular in research and educational institutions. Ongoing development, support, and maintenance are performed by the Shibboleth Consortium. Shibboleth works similarly to other SSO systems, and it supports services outside organizational boundaries. Shibboleth uses the following three elements:

▶ The identity provider (IdP), located in the home organization, authenticates the user.

▶ The service provider (SP), located at the resource organization, performs the SSO process for the protected resource.

▶ The discovery service (DS) is useful for finding the user's IdP. It can be located anywhere on the Web and is not a required component.

The functions that happen with Shibboleth SSO are the same as the functions described for SAML. Shibboleth is a flexible solution because it is based on standards. Some federated systems are designed to work only when the identity provider and the service provider are in the same organization, but Shibboleth works across organizations. This flexibility enlarges the attack surface. The Shibboleth Consortium maintains a current list of security advisories issued from incorrect configurations by service or identity providers.

Kerberos

To avoid sending the open plaintext logon information across an unsecured network, one solution is to use the symmetric key authentication protocol known as *Kerberos* (created by the Athena project at MIT and named for the three-headed dog Cerberus that guarded Hades). Kerberos is an authentication protocol that has been around for decades and is an open standard. *Symmetric key* means that the client and the server must agree to use a single key in the encryption and decryption processes.

In Kerberos authentication, a client sends its authentication details not to the target server but to a key distribution center (KDC), as follows:

1. The client first contacts a certificate authority (CA).

2. The CA creates a time-stamped session key with a limited duration (by default, 8 hours) by using the client's key and a randomly generated key that includes the identification of the target service.

3. This information is sent back to the client in the form of a ticket-granting ticket (TGT).

4. The client submits the TGT to a ticket-granting server (TGS).

5. This server generates a time-stamped key encrypted with the service's key and returns both to the client.

6. The client uses its key to decrypt its ticket, contacts the server, and offers the encrypted ticket to the service.

7. The service uses its key to decrypt the ticket and verify that the time stamps match and the ticket remains valid.

8. The service contacts the KDC and receives a time-stamped, session-keyed ticket that it returns to the client.

9. The client decrypts the keyed ticket by using its key. When each one agrees that the other is the proper account and that the keys are within their valid lifetime, communication is initiated.

Kerberos Version 5 includes support for a process known as *mutual authentication*, in which both client and server verify that the computer with which they are communicating is the proper system. This process helps prevent man-in-the-middle attacks, in which an unauthorized party intercepts communications between two systems and masquerades as the other system. The unauthorized party might pass some data intact, modify other data, or insert entirely new sets of values to accomplish desired tasks.

In mutual authentication, one system creates a challenge code based on a random number and then sends that code to the other system. The receiving system generates a response code using the original challenge code and creates a challenge code of its own; it sends both back to the originating system. The originating system verifies the response code as a value and returns its own response code to the second system, generated from the challenge code returned with the first response code. After the second system has verified its returned response code, it notifies the originating system. Both systems then consider themselves mutually authenticated.

The strength of Kerberos authentication comes from its time-synchronized connections and the use of registered client and service keys within the KDC. Kerberos also creates some challenges, such as the need to use a standard synchronized time base for all systems involved. Difficulties arise if the KDC is unavailable or if the cached client and service credentials were accessed directly from the granting servers. An important advantage of time-stamped credentials is that they help prevent spoofing and replay attacks.

> **ExamAlert**
>
> Not all authentication services provide the same functions, and aligning the proper service with the right environment requires knowledge of the basics of each service. Remember that Microsoft Active Directory networks rely on Kerberos for credentials exchange, so all systems must share a common time service to maintain synchronization.

Access Control

Access control generally refers to the process of making resources available to accounts that should have access, while limiting that access to only what is required. You need to know these forms of access control:

▶ Mandatory access control (MAC)

▶ Discretionary access control (DAC)

▶ Attribute-based access control (ABAC)

▶ Rule-based access control

▶ Role-based access control (RBAC)

The most basic form of access control involves assigning labels to resources and accounts (for example, SENSITIVE, SECRET, and PUBLIC). If the labels on an account and a resource do not match, the resource remains unavailable in a nondiscretionary manner. This type of access control, called *mandatory access control* (*MAC*, also referred to as *multilevel access control*), is often used within government systems, where resources and access are granted based on the categorical assignments such as classified, secret, or top secret. Mandatory access control applies to all resources within the network and does not allow users to extend access rights by proxy.

A slightly more complex system of access control involves restricting access for each resource in a discretionary manner. *Discretionary access control* (*DAC*) scenarios allow individual resources to be individually made available or secured against access. Access rights are configured at the discretion of the accounts that have the authority over each resource, including the capability to extend administrative rights through the same mechanism. In DAC, a security principal (account) has complete control over the objects that it creates or otherwise owns unless this is restricted through group or role membership. The owner assigns security levels based on objects and subjects and can make his or her own data available to others as desired. A common scenario for DAC is online social network users choosing who can access their data.

The Trusted Computer System Evaluation Criteria (TCSEC) specification that many government networks use explicitly specifies only the MAC and DAC forms of access control. The TCSEC specification is sometimes referred to as the Orange Book because of the original color of the printed manual's cover (DoD 5200.28-STD).

The designation RBAC is sometimes used to refer to rule-based access control in addition to role-based access control. *Rule-based access control* dynamically assigns roles to users based on criteria that the data custodian or system administrator defines. Rule-based access control includes controls such as the time of day, the day of the week, specific terminal access, and GPS coordinates of the requester, along with other factors that might overlay a legitimate account's access request. Implementation of rule-based access control might require that rules be programmed using code instead of allowing traditional access control by checking a box.

In a *role-based access control* (*RBAC*) scenario, access rights are first assigned to roles. Then accounts are associated with these roles, without the direct assignment of resource access rights. This solution provides the greatest level of scalability in large enterprise scenarios, where explicitly granting rights to each individual account could rapidly overwhelm administrative staff and increase the potential for accidentally granting unauthorized permissions.

RBAC combines some direct access aspects of mandatory access control and varying discretionary access rights based on role membership. Delegated administration over rights granted through RBAC is itself managed by specialized administration roles instead of through ownership or direct control over the individual resources, as in strictly DAC solutions.

> ### ExamAlert
>
> Remember that the exam might use the *RBAC* acronym to refer to *rule-based access control*. In a rule-based access control solution, access rights can vary by account, time of day, the trusted OS, or other forms of conditional testing. Exam items that deal with *conditional access* (for example, time-of-day controls) are examining rule-based access control. Items that involve assigning rights to groups for inheritance by group member accounts are focusing on role-based access control.

As the RBAC specification became popular and made possible central management of enterprise access control, the need for access control lists (ACLs) was reduced. RBAC does not easily support multifactor decisions and lacks the capability to associate roles with access control requirements. This makes long-term maintenance difficult.

Attribute-based access control (*ABAC*) is a logical access control model that the Federal Identity, Credential, and Access Management (FICAM) Roadmap recommends as the preferred access control model for information sharing among diverse organizations. ABAC is based on Extensible Access Control Markup Language (XACML). The reference architecture is similar to the core components of AAA. The ABAC authorization process is determined by evaluating rules and policies against attributes associated with an entity, such as the subject, object, operation, or environment condition. Attributes are characteristics that define specific aspects of the entity. When an access request is made, the access decision is based on the evaluation of attributes and access control rules by the attribute-based access control mechanism.

ABAC is a more dynamic access control method. When attribute values change, the access is changed based on the attribute changes. ABAC systems are capable of enforcing both DAC and MAC models. ABAC is well suited for large and federated enterprises, which makes it more complicated and costly to implement and maintain than simple access control models.

Privileged Access Management

In addition to authentication management, discussed earlier in the chapter, *privileged access management* (*PAM*) addresses the notion of ensuring least privilege and preventing attackers from using elevated privileges to cause disruption. PAM helps in regard to privileged access to sensitive data and critical business functions:

▶ **Privileged account discovery:** PAM identifies privileged accounts such as those that use administrative credentials to log on to workstations and even where privileged accounts are hard-coded into software and other communications.

▶ **Governing access:** PAM enables management through the account life cycle, including how accounts get access and what privileges are required.

▶ **Auditing activity:** PAM provides logging activity of privileged access use and attempts, as well as anomalous behavior tracking.

▶ **Automated task management:** PAM helps with automation of repeatable tasks, such as software installations, scheduled tasks, and service account interaction.

PAM is particularly important where access to backend systems is required. Another example is systems that communicate with each other, such as a server talking to a backend database server. Often there may be no human element involved but just one machine accessing another. The specific types of accounts for which you might consider a PAM solution include the following:

▶ Service accounts

▶ Administrator and root accounts

▶ Application accounts

▶ Network accounts

Cram Quiz

Answer these questions. The answers follow the last question. If you cannot answer these questions correctly, consider reading this chapter again until you can.

1. Which of the following use SAML? (Select two.)
   - ○ **A.** Secure token
   - ○ **B.** OpenID
   - ○ **C.** OAuth
   - ○ **D.** LDAP

2. Which of the following is a true statement regarding role-based access control?
   - ○ **A.** Access rights are first assigned to users. Roles are then associated with those access rights.
   - ○ **B.** Access rights are first assigned to roles. User accounts are then associated with those access rights.
   - ○ **C.** Access rights are first assigned to roles. User accounts are then associated with those roles.
   - ○ **D.** Access rights are first assigned to users. Roles are then associated with those users.

3. Which of the following statements are correct regarding Shibboleth SSO? (Select two.)
   - ○ **A.** The identity provider (IdP) authenticates the user.
   - ○ **B.** The service provider (SP) authenticates the user.
   - ○ **C.** The identity provider (IdP) performs the SSO process for the protected resource.
   - ○ **D.** The service provider (SP) performs the SSO process for the protected resource.

4. What type of access control is often used in government systems, where resources and access are granted based on categorical assignments such as classified, secret, or top secret?
   - ○ **A.** Mandatory access control (MAC)
   - ○ **B.** Discretionary access control (DAC)
   - ○ **C.** Attribute-based access control (ABAC)
   - ○ **D.** Role-based access control (RBAC)

5. Which of the following is a symmetric key–based authentication protocol that uses a key distribution center?
   - ○ **A.** TACACS+
   - ○ **B.** Kerberos

○ **C.** RADIUS

○ **D.** HSM

6. Based on the following permissions for a file, which one of the following statements is not true?

   `rwxr-----`

   ○ **A.** The owner has read, write, and execute permissions.

   ○ **B.** The group has read permissions.

   ○ **C.** Those other than the owner or group have no permissions.

   ○ **D.** Only the group has both read and write permissions.

Cram Quiz Answers

Answer 1: B and C. OpenID and OAuth are both federated services that use SAML
technology. These technologies do use secure tokens for authentication, but secure
tokens don't necessarily use SAML, so Answer A is incorrect. Answer D is incorrect as
this is a directory service that does not specifically use SAML.

Answer 2: C. In a role-based access control (RBAC) scenario, access rights are first
assigned to roles. Then user accounts are associated with those roles, without the direct
assignment of resource access rights. The other choices are all incorrect statements, so
Answers A, B, and D are incorrect.

Answer 3: A and D. Shibboleth works similarly to other SSO systems, and it supports
services outside organizational boundaries. The identity provider (IdP) authenticates the
user. The service provider (SP), performs the SSO process for the protected resource.
Answers B and C are incorrect.

Answer 4: A. This type of access control, called MAC, is often used in government
systems. Answer B is incorrect because DAC scenarios allow individual resources to
be individually made available or secured against access. Access rights are configured
at the discretion of the accounts that have the authority over each resource, including
the capability to extend administrative rights through the same mechanism. Answer C
is incorrect because ABAC is a logical access control model that the Federal Identity,
Credential, and Access Management (FICAM) Roadmap recommends as the preferred
access control model for information sharing among diverse organizations. ABAC is
based on Extensible Access Control Markup Language (XACML). Answer D is incorrect. In a role-based access control (RBAC) scenario, access rights are first assigned to
roles. Then accounts are associated with these roles, without the direct assignment of
resource access rights.

Answer 5: B. Kerberos is a symmetric key authentication protocol that has been around
for decades and is an open standard. With Kerberos authentication, a client sends its
authentication details not to the target server but to a key distribution center (KDC).
Answer A is incorrect. TACACS+ is a protocol that handles authentication, authorization, and accounting (AAA) services. It is similar to RADIUS but uses TCP as a transport method; it uses port 49 as the default port. TACACS+ takes a client/server model
approach. Answer C is incorrect. The Remote Authentication Dial-In User Service

(RADIUS) remote access control system provides authentication and access control in an enterprise network, using UDP transport, to a central network access server. In turn, this provides credentials for client access to resources in the extended enterprise. Answer D is incorrect because the main focuses of hardware security modules (HSMs) are performance and key storage space. HSMs can also enforce separation of duties for key management by separating database and security administration.

Answer 6: D. Based on the permissions shown, Answers A, B, and C are all true statements, while answer D is not. The first three permissions represent the owner, which has read, write, and execute permissions. The second three permissions represent the group, which only has read permissions. The third three permissions indicate that everyone else does not have any permissions.

What Next?

If you want more practice on this chapter's exam objective before you move on, remember that you can access all of the Cram Quiz questions on the Pearson Test Prep software online. You can also create a custom exam by objective with the Online Practice Test. Note any objective you struggle with and go to that objective's material in this chapter.

CHAPTER 25

Public Key Infrastructure

This chapter covers the following official Security+ exam objective:

▶ 3.9 Given a scenario, implement public key infrastructure.

Essential Terms and Components

▶ public key infrastructure (PKI)

▶ digital certificate

▶ key management

▶ certificate authority (CA)

▶ intermediate CA

▶ registration authority (RA)

▶ certificate revocation list (CRL)

▶ Online Certificate Status Protocol (OCSP)

▶ certificate signing request (CSR)

▶ distinguished encoding rules (DER)

▶ privacy enhanced mail (PEM)

▶ personal information exchange (PFX)

▶ stapling

▶ pinning

▶ trust model

▶ key escrow

▶ certificate chaining

PKI Components

To begin to understand the applications and deployment of a *public key infrastructure (PKI)*, you should understand the various pieces that make up a PKI. A PKI is a vast collection of varying technologies and policies for the creation and use of digital certificates. A PKI encompasses certificate authorities, digital certificates, and a variety of tools, systems, and processes. As previous chapters show, digital certificates are a critical component in providing secure systems. For example, in Chapter 24, "Authentication and Authorization Solutions," you learned that many implementations of EAP in wireless networks require digital certificates to verify the identity of the client or server. Digital signatures are digitally signed data blocks, and they provide several potential functions but most notably are used for identification and authentication purposes. The requirement for certificates adds complexity. This chapter discusses how these certificates are generated and managed.

The basic concepts of public and private keys that you learned about in Chapter 16, "Cryptographic Concepts," play an important role in PKI. This infrastructure makes use of both types of keys and lays a foundation for binding keys to an identity via a certificate authority (CA). This gives the system a way to securely exchange data over a network using an asymmetric key system. For the most part, this system consists of digital certificates and the CAs that issue the certificates. These certificates identify individuals, systems, and organizations that have been verified as authentic and trustworthy.

Recall that symmetric key cryptography requires a key to be shared. For example, suppose the password to get into the clubhouse is "open sesame." At some point in time, this key or password needs to be communicated to other participating parties before it can be implemented. PKI provides confidentiality, integrity, and authentication by overcoming this challenge. With PKI, it is not necessary to exchange the password, key, or secret information in advance. This is useful when involved parties have no prior contact or when exchanging a secure key is neither feasible nor secure.

PKI is widely used to provide secure infrastructure for applications and networks, including access control, resources from web browsers, and secure email. PKI protects information by providing the following:

▶ Identity authentication

▶ Integrity verification

▶ Privacy assurance

▶ Access authorization

▶ Transaction authorization

▶ Nonrepudiation support

ExamAlert

A public key infrastructure consists of technologies and policies for the creation and use of digital certificates.

Certificate Authority (CA)

Certificate authorities (*CAs*) are trusted entities and an important concept related to PKI. An organization can use third-party CAs, and it can also establish its own CA, typically for use only within the organization. A CA's job is to issue certificates, verify the holder of a digital certificate, and ensure that holders of certificates are who they claim to be. A common analogy for a CA is a passport-issuing authority. To obtain a passport, you need the assistance of someone else (for example, a customs office) to verify your identity. Passports are trusted because the issuing authority is trusted.

Registration authorities (*RAs*) provide authentication to the CA on the validity of a client's certificate request; in addition, an RA serves as an aggregator of information. For example, a user contacts an RA, which then verifies the user's identity before issuing the request of the CA to go ahead and issue a digital certificate.

ExamAlert

A CA is responsible for issuing certificates. Remember that an RA initially verifies a user's identity and then passes along to the CA the request to issue a certificate to the user.

CAs follow a chained hierarchy, or *certificate chain*, when verifying digital certificates, to form what's known as a chain of trust. Starting with a trust anchor, known as the root CA, certificates are trusted transitively through one or many certificates within the chain. Here is an example of *certificate chaining*:

1. The root certificate verifies certificate A.

2. Certificate A verifies certificate B.

3. Certificate B verifies certificate C.

This also works in reverse:

1. Certificate C references certificate B.

2. Certificate B references certificate A.

3. Certificate A references the root certificate.

Certification Practice Statement

A *certification practice statement* (*CPS*) is a legal document that a CA creates and publishes for the purpose of conveying information to those who depend on the CA's issued certificates. The information within a CPS provides for the general practices the CA follows in issuing certificates and customer-related information about certificates, responsibilities, and problem management. It is important to understand that these statements are described in the context of operating procedures and system architecture. Certificate policies, on the other hand, indicate the rules that apply to an issued certificate. A CPS includes the following items:

▶ Identification of the CA

▶ Types of certificates issued and applicable certificate policies

▶ Operating procedures for issuing, renewing, and revoking certificates

▶ Technical and physical security controls that the CA uses

Trust Models

Certificate authorities in a PKI follow several *trust models* or architectures. The simplest model is the single-CA architecture, in which only one CA exists to issue and maintain certificates. This model might benefit smaller organizations because of its administrative simplicity, but it can present many problems. For example, if the CA fails, no other CA can quickly take its place. Another problem can arise if the private key of the CA becomes compromised; in this scenario, all the issued certificates from that CA would be invalid. A new CA would have to be created, and the new CA would need to reissue all the certificates.

A more common model—and one that reduces the risks inherent with a single CA—is the hierarchical CA trust model. In this model, an initial root CA exists at the top of the hierarchy, and subordinate CAs, or *intermediate CAs*, reside beneath the root. The subordinate CAs provide redundancy and load balancing in the event that any of the other CAs fail or need to be taken offline. Because

of this model, you might hear PKI referred to as a *trust hierarchy*. An intermediate CA has a certificate that is issued by the trusted root. This certificate is issued so the intermediate CA can issue certificates for others. This results in a trust chain that begins at the trusted root CA, goes through the intermediate, and ends with the SSL certificate issued to a server with which you are interacting.

A root CA differs from subordinate CAs in that the root CA is usually offline. Remember that if the root CA is compromised, the entire architecture is compromised. If a subordinate CA is compromised, however, the root CA can revoke the subordinate CA.

An alternative to this hierarchical model is the cross-certification model, often referred to as a *web of trust*. In this model, CAs are considered peers to each other. Such a configuration, for example, might exist at a small company that started with a single CA. As the company grew, it continued to implement other single-CA models and then decided that each division of the company needed to communicate with the others. To achieve secure exchange of information across the company, each CA established a peer-to-peer trust relationship with the others. As you might imagine, such a configuration could become difficult to manage over time.

> **ExamAlert**
>
> The root CA should be taken offline to reduce the risk of key compromise. It should be made available only to create and revoke certificates for subordinate/intermediate CAs. A compromised root CA compromises the entire system.

A solution to the complexity of a large cross-certification model is to implement a *bridge CA model*. Remember that, in the cross-certification model, each CA must trust the others. By implementing bridging, however, you can have a single CA, known as the *bridge CA*, serve as the central point of trust.

> **ExamAlert**
>
> Certificates rely on a hierarchical chain of trust. If a CA's root key is compromised, any keys issued by that CA are compromised as well.

Key Escrow

Key escrow occurs when a CA or another entity maintains a copy of the private key associated with the public key signed by the CA. This scenario allows the

CA or escrow agent to have access to all information encrypted using the public key from a user's certificate and to create digital signatures on behalf of the user. Therefore, key escrow is a sensitive topic in the PKI community. Harmful results might occur if the private key is misused. Because of this issue, key escrow is not a favored PKI solution.

Despite public concerns about escrow for private use, key escrow is often considered a good idea in corporate PKI environments. In most cases, an employee of an organization is bound by the information security policies of that organization (which usually mandate that the organization has a right to access all intellectual property generated by a user and to any data that an employee generates). In addition, key escrow enables an organization to overcome the large problem of forgotten passwords. Instead of revoking and reissuing new keys, an organization can generate a new certificate using the private key stored in escrow.

> **ExamAlert**
>
> Key escrow is used for third-party custody of a private key.

Digital Certificate

A *digital certificate* is a digitally signed block of data that allows public key cryptography to be used for identification purposes. The most common types of certificates are the SSL or TLS certificates used on the Web. Essentially, these certificates ensure secure communications, which occur when a website uses https:// instead of just http:// in the browser address bar, accompanied by a closed padlock.

CAs issue these certificates, which are signed using the CA's private key. Most certificates are based on the X.509 standard. Although most certificates follow the X.509 Version 3 hierarchical PKI standard, the PGP key system uses its own certificate format. X.509 certificates to be signed contain the following fields:

▸ **Version Number:** This field identifies the version of the X.509 standard that the certificate complies with.

▸ **Serial Number:** The CA that creates the certificate is responsible for assigning a unique serial number.

▸ **Signature Algorithm Identifier:** This field identifies the cryptographic algorithm used by the CA to sign the certificate. An *object identifier* (*OID*) is used. An OID is a hierarchical globally unique identifier for an object.

▶ **Issuer Name:** This field identifies the directory name of the entity signing the certificate, which is typically a CA.

▶ **Period of Validity:** This field identifies the time frame for which the private key is valid, if the private key has not been compromised. This period is indicated with both a start time and an end time; it can be of any duration, but it is often set to 1 year.

▶ **Subject or owner name:** This field is the name of the entity that is identified in the public key associated with the certificate. This name uses the X.500 standard for globally unique naming and is often called the distinguished name (DN) (for example, CN=Sri Puthucode, OU=Sales, O=CompTIA, C=US).

▶ **Subject or Owner's Public Key:** This field includes the public key of the entity named in the certificate, in addition to a cryptographic algorithm identifier and optional key parameters associated with the key.

▶ **Extensions:** This field optionally provides methods in X.509 Version 3 certificates to associate additional attributes. This field must not be present in previous versions. Common extensions include specific key usage requirements, such as allowing the public key of the certificate to be used only for certificate signing.

▶ **Signature Value:** This value provides the computed digital signature from the signed certificate's body, used as an input. The signature ensures the validity of the certificate.

You likely have used the most common application of digital certificates: Websites that ask for personal information, especially credit card information, use digital certificates. (Not necessarily all of them use digital certificates, but they should.) The traffic from your computer to the website is secured using Secure Sockets Layer (SSL)/Transport Layer Security(TLS), and the web server uses a digital certificate for the secure exchange of information, as indicated by a small padlock located in the status bar or address bar of most browsers. By clicking this icon, you can view the digital certificate and its details.

ExamAlert

Remember the components of an X.509 certificate. You might be required to recognize the contents of a certificate.

Figure 25.1 provides an example of a digital certificate that appears when you click the lock icon in the browser address bar. Specifically, note that the

certificate applies to www.example.org, including any subdomains, and note that this certificate is chained to an intermediary CA's certificate (DigiCert SHA2 Secure Server CA), which is chained to the root CA's certificate (Digi-Cert Global Root CA). Next, note the different fields, many of which are described in the preceding list.

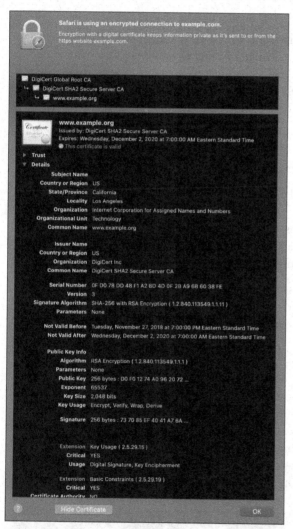

FIGURE 25.1   Details of a digital certificate

Public and Private Key Usage

Digital certificates and key pairs can be used for various purposes, including privacy and authentication. The security policy of an organization that is using a key or the CA defines the purposes and capabilities for the certificates issued.

To achieve privacy, users need the public key of the individual or entity they want to communicate with securely. This public key is used to encrypt the data that is transmitted, and the corresponding private key is used on the other end to decrypt the message.

> **ExamAlert**
>
> You can obtain another's public key (which is freely available to anyone) and use it to encrypt a message to that person. As a result, that person can use his or her private key, which no one else has, to decrypt the message. The public and private keys are mathematically related.

Authentication is achieved by digitally signing the message being transmitted. To digitally sign a message, the signing entity requires access to the private key.

In short, the key usage extension of the certificate specifies how the private key can be used—either to enable the exchange of sensitive information or to create digital signatures. In addition, the key usage extension can specify that an entity can use the key both for the exchange of sensitive information and for signature purposes.

In some circumstances, dual or multiple key pairs might be used to support distinct and separate services. For example, an individual in a corporate environment might require one key pair just for signing and another just for encrypting messages. Another example is a reorder associate who has one key pair to use for signing and sending encrypted messages and another one that is restricted to ordering equipment worth no more than a specific dollar amount. Multiple key pairs require multiple certificates because the X.509 certificate format does not support multiple keys.

Certificate Signing Request

To install a digital certificate, a specific request needs to be generated and submitted to the CA. The applicant applies to the CA for a digital certificate known as a *certificate signing request* (CSR). Included within the request is the applicant's public key, along with information about the applicant such as the following:

- ▶ Fully qualified domain name
- ▶ Legally incorporated name of the company
- ▶ Department name
- ▶ City, state, and country
- ▶ Email address

Before submitting a CSR, the applicant generates a key pair consisting of a public key and a private key. The public key is provided with the request, and the applicant signs the request with the private key. If all is successful, the CA returns a digital certificate that is signed with the CA's private key.

Certificate Policy

A *certificate policy* indicates specific uses applied to a digital certificate and other technical details. Not all certificates are created equal. Digital certificates that are issued often follow different practices and procedures and are issued for different purposes. The certificate policy provides the rules that indicate the purpose and use of an assigned digital certificate. For example, one certificate might have a policy indicating its use for electronic data interchange to conduct e-commerce, whereas another certificate might be issued to digitally sign documents.

Remember that a certificate policy identifies the purpose for which a certificate can be used. In addition, other types of information can be included within a certificate policy:

▶ Legal issues often used to protect the CA

▶ Mechanisms for how the CA will authenticate users

▶ Key management requirements

▶ Instructions for what to do if the private key is compromised

▶ Lifetime of the certificate

▶ Certificate enrollment and renewal

▶ Rules regarding exporting the private key

▶ Private and public key minimum lengths

ExamAlert

The applicant's public key is submitted along with the CSR.

Certificate Types

Three types of validated TLS certificates exist, each with its own level of trust:

▶ **Domain validation (DV):** This type of certificate includes only the domain name. DV certificates can easily be issued, just as a domain name lookup can easily be performed against whois, a database of registered

domains. DV certificates are inexpensive and can be acquired quickly, so if trust is important or if a public-facing website is desired, organizations should consider another type of validated certificate.

▶ **Organizational validation (OV):** This certificate type provides stronger assurance than a DV certificate as organizations are vetted against official government sources; the OV certificate is therefore a common certificate type for many public-facing websites. Unlike with a DV certificate, OV certificates verification requires a more manual review and verification process; this can take days to process.

▶ **Extended validation (EV):** This certificate type provides a high level of trust and security features. EV certificates are easily identified as the business name in the address bar is green. EV certificates are designed to provide assurance against phishing attacks. As the name implies, this certificate type requires a comprehensive validation of the business, which can take up to a couple weeks to acquire.

ExamAlert

DV certificates are the quickest and least expensive certificates to acquire. EV certificates can take a couple weeks and are the most expensive, but they also provide the highest level of trust.

You should also be familiar with the following special certificates:

▶ **Wildcard:** This certificate provides any number of subdomains for a single registered domain. The name for the certificate thus might look like *.example.com, which would be valid for www.example.com, sub.example.com, and so on.

▶ **SAN:** This type of certificate takes advantage of the subject alternate name (SAN) extension. It provides for the use of multiple domain names or even IP addresses within a single certificate. This certificate is also known as a unified communications (UC) certificate.

▶ **Code signing:** This type of certificate is required to digitally sign software packages. It provides assurance that the software is authentic and has not been tampered with.

▶ **Self-signed:** Self-signed certificates are often used for testing purposes or when trust is not a concern. Certificates are typically signed by another entity or CA. When a web browser recognizes that a certificate is a self-signed certificate, it provides an alert to the user that the connection is not trusted.

▶ **Email:** This type of certificate is also known as an S/MIME (Secure/Multipurpose Internet Mail Extensions) certificate. An email certificate is required to digitally sign or encrypt email messages.

▶ **Root signing:** A root signing certificate is usually provided by a recognized CA. Organizations with a root signing certificate thus can sign for themselves any number of certificates. These certificates, in turn, are trusted by those outside the organization because web browsers include, by default, many trusted certificates for recognized CAs. For example, an organization that wants to run its own CA in-house, particularly when trust needs to be extended outside the organization, should purchase a root signing certificate.

▶ **User:** Known also as a client certificate, a user certificate identifies an individual. Just as a website's TLS certificate authenticates the website to a particular user, a user certificate can authenticate a user to a remote server. This works much the way a password works.

▶ **Machine/computer:** Much like a user certificate, a machine/computer certificate authenticates a client system. This type is primarily used with machine-to-machine communications.

ExamAlert

Given a scenario, be able to identify the types of certificates.

Certificate Formats

Certificates can have various file extension types. Some, but not all, extension types are interchangeable. Be sure to determine whether a certificate is binary or Base64 ASCII encoded. Table 25.1 provides a brief comparison of common certificate formats.

The most common format and extension for certificates is *privacy enhanced mail* (*PEM*), which is mostly associated with Apache web servers. The PEM format is a Base64 ASCII-encoded text file, which makes copying the contents from one document to another simple. A PEM file might contain several certificates and private keys within a single file, although having each component (that is, each certificate and key) as its own file is common. A single certificate includes the header BEGIN CERTIFICATE, preceded and followed by five dashes, and the footer END CERTIFICATE, preceded and followed by five dashes. A single private key includes the header BEGIN ENCRYPTED PRIVATE KEY,

preceded and followed by five dashes, and the footer END ENCRYPTED PRIVATE KEY, preceded and followed by five dashes. In addition to the .pem file extension, .crt, .cer, and .key extensions can be used. However, .key is typically used when the file contains only the private key.

Another Base64-encoded certificate format is P7B, also known as PKCS#7. This format uses the .p7b or .p7c file extension, which is commonly supported on the Windows operating system and Java Tomcat. This format includes the header BEGIN PKCS7 and the footer END PKCS7, each of which is preceded and followed by five dashes.

The binary form of a PEM certificate is a *distinguished encoding rules* (DER) certificate. In addition to the .der extension, .cer and .crt extensions can be used for DER-encoded certificates. DER-encoded certificates are common on Java platforms.

Another binary certificate format is PFX, also known as PKCS#12. Extensions for *personal information exchange* (PFX)–encoded certificates include .pfx and .p12. This type of certificate is common to the Windows operating system for importing and exporting certificates and private keys. PFX supports a private key, and one or more certificates can be stored within a single binary file.

Table 25.1 provides an overview of the certificate formats.

TABLE 25.1 **Summary of Certificate Formats**

Certificate Format	Encoding	Systems	Extensions
DER	Binary	Java	.der
			.cers
			.crt
PEM	Base64 ASCII	Apache HTTP	.pem
			.cer
			.crt
PFX (PKCS#12)	Binary	Windows	.pfx
			.p12
P7B (PKCS#7)	Base64 ASCII	Windows and Java Tomcat	.p7b
			.p7c

ExamAlert

DER and PFX certificates are binary encoded and cannot be edited with a plaintext editor, as the Base64 ASCII–encoded PEM and P7B certificates can.

Certificate Revocation

Digital certificates can be revoked. Revoking a certificate invalidates a certificate before its expiration date. A digital certificate contains a field indicating the date until which the certificate is valid. This date is mandatory, and the validity period can vary from a short period of time up to several years. Revocation can occur for several reasons. For example, a private key might become compromised, the private key might be lost, or the identifying credentials might no longer be valid. Other reasons for revocation include fraudulently obtained certificates or a change in the holder's status, which could indicate less trustworthiness.

Revoking a certificate is just not enough. The community that trusts this certificate must be notified that the certificate is no longer valid. This is accomplished via either of the following mechanisms:

▶ **CRL:** The *certificate revocation list* (*CRL*) is a mechanism for distributing certificate revocation information. A CRL is used when verification of the digital certificate takes place to ensure the validity of the digital certificate. A limitation of CRLs is that they must be constantly updated at least every two weeks; otherwise, certificates might be accepted despite having been recently revoked.

▶ **OCSP:** *Online Certificate Status Protocol* (*OCSP*) is a newer mechanism for identifying revoked certificates. OCSP checks certificate status in real time online instead of relying on the end user to have a current copy of the CRL.

Both OCSP and CRLs are used to verify the status of a certificate. Three basic status levels exist in most PKI solutions: valid, suspended, and revoked. You can check the status of a certificate by going to the CA that issued the certificate or to an agreed-upon directory server that maintains a database indicating the status level for the set of certificates. In most cases, however, the application (such as a web browser) has a function available that initiates a check for certificates.

ExamAlert

When a certificate has expired, the client is likely to receive an error message saying that the website cannot be trusted. In some situations, users may not have the correct root certificates installed into their web browsers.

OCSP Stapling

Although OCSP provides for real-time status checking, it requires the CA to respond to every client request to validate a site's certificate. High-traffic websites burden the CA with these requests because they need to respond to a potentially overwhelming number of certificate validity requests. A mechanism known as OCSP *stapling* helps reduce this load by allowing the web server to instead "staple" a time-stamped OCSP response as part of the TLS handshake with the client. The web server is then responsible for handling OCSP requests (instead of the CA). The OCSP stapling process involves the following steps:

1. A TLS-encrypted web server presents its certificate to the CA to check the validity.

2. The CA responds with the certificate status, including a digitally signed time stamp.

3. The web server staples the CA's signed time stamp to the certificate when a client web browser connects.

4. The client web browser verifies the signed time stamp.

OCSP stapling provides several benefits. First, it improves the performance of the secure connection. Next, privacy concerns are reduced because the end user's browser does not need to potentially contact a third-party CA to verify the certificates and reveal the browsing history. Finally, reliability is improved. If the client were unable to connect to an overburdened CA, for example, the client would otherwise accept a potentially invalid certificate—or simply end the connection.

> **ExamAlert**
>
> Using CRLs is not as efficient as OCSP. The lists need to be frequently updated and are not reliable if they are outdated.

Before a certificate is revoked, it might be suspended. Certificate suspension occurs when a certificate is under investigation to determine whether it should be revoked. This mechanism allows a certificate to stay in place, although it is not valid for any type of use. Users and systems are notified of suspended certificates. New credentials do not need to be retrieved, however; it is only necessary to be notified that current credentials have had a change in status and are temporarily not valid for use.

Pinning

Certificate *pinning* extends beyond certificate validation (discussed earlier in this chapter) to thwart man-in-the-middle attacks. Hashes of public keys for popular web servers are built into applications such as web browsers. A similar (though now deprecated) variation, known as HTTP Public Key Pinning (HPKP), used public key pins, which are essentially hashed values of the public key communicated to the browser client from the server in the HTTP header. After obtaining the server certificate, the client verified the public key against the hash of the public key.

Cram Quiz

Answer these questions. The answers follow the last question. If you cannot answer these questions correctly, consider reading this chapter again until you can.

1. Your organization has established a hierarchical PKI and deployed several CAs in the process. Which one of the following steps should your organization be sure to take?

   ○ **A.** Take the root CA offline.

   ○ **B.** Take all subordinate CAs offline.

   ○ **C.** Take the root CA online.

   ○ **D.** Take all subordinate CAs online with the exception of the intermediates.

2. What type of key goes into key escrow?

   ○ **A.** Public

   ○ **B.** Shared

   ○ **C.** Private

   ○ **D.** Session

3. Your organization has developed a custom application that requires a check for the validity of digital certificates even when the Internet is not available. Which of the following meets this requirement?

   ○ **A.** CRL

   ○ **B.** OCSP

   ○ **C.** SAN

   ○ **D.** CPS

4. Which of the following types of certificates allows you to digitally sign and encrypt email messages and attachments?

- ○ **A.** DER
- ○ **B.** PFX
- ○ **C.** Self-signed
- ○ **D.** S/MIME

Cram Quiz Answers

Answer 1: A. Best practice is to take the root CA offline to reduce the risk of compromise of the entire PKI; thus, answer C is incorrect. Answer B is incorrect because the subordinate CAs are signed by the root CA and should not be taken offline as they need to manage requests. Although subordinate CAs should be online, Answer D is incorrect as it suggests taking the intermediates offline, which are the same as the subordinates.

Answer 2: C. Confidential secret or private keys go into key escrow. Public keys are known and have no need for escrow, so answer A is incorrect. A shared key or session key (for single use) is a key that performs both encryption and decryption and would not be usable if left in key escrow. Answers B and D are incorrect.

Answer 3: A. CRL provides a mechanism to ensure the validity of digital certificates by using a list that must be updated every two weeks. Answer B is incorrect. While OCSP also checks for certificate validity, it works in real time and requires Internet access. Answer C is incorrect because SAN is a type of certificate that takes advantage of the subject alternate name extension. A CPS is a legal document that a CA creates and publishes, so Answer D is incorrect.

Answer 4: D. S/MIME (Secure/Multipurpose Internet Mail Extensions) is a protocol that allows you to encrypt email messages and attachments and digitally sign them. Answers A and B are incorrect because distinguished encoding rules (DER) and personal information exchange (PFX) are certificate formats/extensions. Answer C is incorrect because self-signed certificates are often used for testing purposes or when trust is not a concern.

What Next?

If you want more practice on this chapter's exam objective before you move on, remember that you can access all of the Cram Quiz questions on the Pearson Test Prep software online. You can also create a custom exam by objective with the Online Practice Test. Note any objective you struggle with and go to that objective's material in this chapter.

PART IV

Operations and Incident Response

This part covers the following official Security+ SY0-601 exam objectives for Domain 4.0, "Operations and Incident Response":

▶ 4.1 Given a scenario, use the appropriate tool to assess organizational security.

▶ 4.2 Summarize the importance of policies, processes, and procedures for incident response.

▶ 4.3 Given an incident, utilize appropriate data sources to support an investigation.

▶ 4.4 Given an incident, apply mitigation techniques or controls to secure an environment.

▶ 4.5 Explain the key aspects of digital forensics.

For more information on the official CompTIA Security+ SY0-601 exam topics, see the section "Exam Objectives" in the Introduction.

This part covers assessment of organizational security as well as incident response based on policies and procedures and also gets into more specifics about the tools and data sources used as part of an incident response program. Incident response covers a life cycle of responsibilities from identification to investigation and mitigation. After an incident, forensics and restoration can take place.

CHAPTER 26

Organizational Security

This chapter covers the following official Security+ exam objective:

▶ 4.1 Given a scenario, use the appropriate tool to assess organizational security.

Essential Terms and Components

▶ tracert/traceroute
▶ nslookup/dig
▶ ipconfig/ifconfig
▶ Nmap
▶ ping
▶ hping
▶ netstat
▶ Netcat
▶ ARP
▶ route
▶ cURL
▶ theharvester
▶ sn1per
▶ scanless
▶ dnsenum
▶ Nessus
▶ Cuckoo
▶ head
▶ tail
▶ cat

▶ grep

▶ chmod

▶ logger

▶ Secure Shell (SSH)

▶ PowerShell

▶ Python

▶ OpenSSL

▶ tcpreplay

▶ Wireshark

▶ tcpdump

▶ dd

▶ Memdump

▶ WinHex

▶ FTK imager

▶ Autopsy

▶ exploitation framework

▶ password cracker

▶ data sanitization

Shell and Script Environments

Many of the tools covered in this chapter are executed from a text-based command-line interface (CLI), also known as a shell. The command line offers a powerful window into local and remote systems to perform and execute commands. In Windows environments, it is known as the Command Prompt. With Apple macOS and most other Linux-based systems, it is commonly known as the terminal and uses the Bash implementation of the Unix shell. When accessing remote computers, organizations use the *Secure Shell* (*SSH*) utility, which establishes a session between the client and host computers and uses an authenticated and encrypted connection. The following command launches SSH from the terminal (see Figure 26.1) and attempts to establish a connection to a remote SSH-enabled system:

```
ssh example.com
```

OpenSSH is a common implementation of the SSH protocol. It is based on capabilities provided by OpenSSL for cryptographic operations. *OpenSSL* provides for secure communications and is used by the majority of websites.

Applications and development environments may also include their own shell environments, which can also be initiated from the command line. For example, these two environments both provide powerful scripting capabilities for automation:

▶ **PowerShell:** *PowerShell* is a command-line shell and scripting interface for Microsoft Windows environments. PowerShell files use the file extension .ps1.

▶ **Python:** *Python* is a general-purpose programming language available on many Linux distributions and Apple's macOS. The Python file extension is .py.

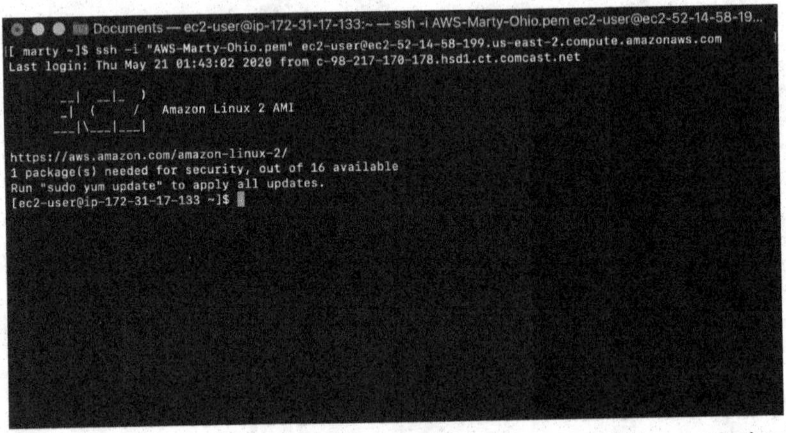

FIGURE 26.1 Using a command-line interface to access a remote computer by using SSH

It is important to be familiar with the basic file manipulation commands described in Table 26.1. These commands are often used in the context of security operations and other commands described in this chapter.

TABLE 26.1 **Command-Line File Manipulation Commands**

Program	Description	Common Syntax	Example and Description
head	Displays the beginning of a text file or a file fed to the command.	head [OPTION]. . . [FILE]. . .	head -n 3 letter.txt Returns the first three lines of the file, letter.txt.
tail	Displays the tail end of a text file or a file fed to the command.	tail [OPTION]. . . [FILE]. . .	tail letter.txt Returns the last 10 lines (default) of the file, letter.txt.

Program	Description	Common Syntax	Example and Description
cat	Reads files sequentially. Used to concatenate files.	`cat [OPTIONS]. . . [FILE]. . .`	`cat file1.text file.txt` Concatenates and displays the two files.
grep	Searches files for a pattern or regular expression.	`grep [OPTIONS] PATTERN [FILE. . .]`	`grep root /etc/passwd` Returns the results where the word root is found within the passwd file.
chmod	Changes access permissions for files and directories.	`chmod [OPTION]. . . MODE[,MODE]. . . FILE. . .`	`chmod 400 cert.pem` Changes the certificate file cert.pem to be publicly viewable.
logger	Adds logs to the local syslog file or a remote syslog server.	`logger [OPTIONS. . .] [MESSAGE. . .]`	`logger -n 192.168.1.100 "A short log line"` Adds the message in quotation marks to the log of the remote server at the given IP address.

ExamAlert

Given a scenario, be able to execute the proper file manipulation commands, including *head*, *tail*, *cat*, *grep*, *chmod*, and *logger*.

Network Reconnaissance and Discovery

Port scanners are often part of a comprehensive vulnerability assessment solution. However, a port scanner can also be a standalone utility. A port scanner simply scans a range of specific ports to determine what ports on a system are open. It can scan a single machine or a range of IP addresses and check for responses on service ports. A response on port 80, for example, might reveal the operation of an HTTP host. Port scanners are useful in creating an inventory of services hosted on networked systems. When they are applied to test ports on a single system, it is termed a *port scan*. A scan across multiple hosts is referred to as a *port sweep*.

Port scanner results are valuable to system administrators and attackers alike. Port scanners typically identify one of two states for a port: open or closed. In addition, some port scanners can provide other information, such as the type of operating system running on the targeted system and services running over the ports.

Network scanners identify active network hosts. One of the most common network scanning tools is a network mapper, which is a software utility that is used to conduct network assessments over a range of IP addresses. A network mapper compiles a list of all systems, devices, and network hardware present in a network segment. This information can be used to identify simple points of failure, conduct a network inventory, and create graphical details suitable for reporting on network configurations. Nmap and Nessus are two of the most common network mapping software utilities used in today's networks. These tools use Active Discovery to locate network hosts and open ports and identify operating systems.

Many network scanners can do a lot more than simply map a network. For example, they can identify rogue systems, which present a problem for organizations because they are set up or added to the network without approval. Most rogue systems are wireless, but a rogue system can technically be any type of unauthorized system, such as a test system, a voice over IP device, or a printer. Well-meaning insiders might use rogue access points with the best of intentions, so they are not necessarily malicious. Fortunately, detecting rogue access points is possible through the use of network scanners. For example, Nessus and tools from SolarWinds can be used to identify rogue systems. Many network reconnaissance and discovery tools are included with operating systems and can easily be operated from the command line.

The following utilities are network command-line diagnostic tools that are commonly used to assess the security posture of an organization:

▶ **ipconfig/ifconfig/ip:** ipconfig displays the TCP/IP settings on a Windows machine. It can display the IP address, subnet mask, default gateway, and Windows Internet Naming Service (WINS), DNS, and MAC information. It is useful for verifying that the Transmission Control Protocol/Internet Protocol (TCP/IP) configuration is correct if connectivity issues arise. *ipconfig* works on Windows-based systems; *ifconfig* works on Mac and other Linux-based systems. The newer ip command is used in a manner similar to ipconfig but has more functionality.

▶ **ping:** Packet Internet Groper (*ping*) is a utility that tests network connectivity by sending an Internet Control Message Protocol (ICMP) echo request to a host. It is a good troubleshooting tool for determining whether a route is available to a host.

▶ **ARP:** ARP provides information from a table that contains a mapping of known MAC addresses to the associated IP addresses. ARP is necessary because the underlying hardware cannot translate IP addresses. The ARP cache maintains a table of MAC-to-IP addresses, so using ARP is a quick way to find a machine's MAC address.

▶ **tracert/traceroute:** These utilities trace the route a packet takes and record the hops along the way. They are good tools to use to find out where a packet is getting hung up. The *tracert* utility works on Windows-based systems; *traceroute* works on Mac and other Linux-based systems.

▶ **nslookup/dig:** This command-line utility troubleshoots a Domain Name System (DNS) database. It queries the DNS server to check whether the correct information is in the zone database. *nslookup* is used on Windows-based systems; dig, which stands for Domain Information Groper, is used on Mac and other Linux-based systems.

▶ **netstat/nbtstat:** The *netstat* utility displays all the ports on which the computer is listening and is useful for quickly determining active connections. It can also display the routing table and pre-protocol statistics. nbtstat is a diagnostic tool for NetBIOS over TCP/IP that is primarily designed is to help troubleshoot NetBIOS name resolution problems in Windows operating systems.

▶ **Nmap:** Network Mapper (*Nmap*) is a network scanning tool used for locating network hosts, detecting operating systems, and identifying services. Nmap is most often used in security auditing but can also be useful for routine administrative tasks such as monitoring host uptime or host inventory.

▶ **Netcat:** *Netcat* is a network utility for gathering information from TCP and UDP network connections. It is a versatile tool that can be used for functions such as port scanning, monitoring, banner grabbing, and file copying. Netcat is Linux based, but versions are available for Windows machines.

▶ **hping:** *hping* is a TCP/IP packet assembler and analyzer that provides a number of security capabilities. Common uses include port scanning, path discovery, OS fingerprinting, and firewall testing.

▶ **route:** The *route* command provides the capability to view and make entries into network routing tables.

▶ **cURL:** *cURL* provides the ability to get and send data by using URLs. For example, when you type the curl command followed by any URL, the output returns the HTML source for the web page. Figure 26.2 shows this command against a domain and the results. cURL can also be used to grab banner information from websites.

▶ **dnsenum:** The *dnsenum* command enumerates DNS by finding DNS servers and DNS records such as mail exchange servers, domain name servers, and the address records for a domain.

▶ **theharvester:** *theharvester* gathers emails, domains, employee names, ports, banners (from sources such as search engines, Twitter, and Linked-In), and key servers. It can plug into Shodan, which is a searchable database of Internet-connected devices.

▶ **sn1per:** *sn1per* is an automated penetration testing recon scanner that enumerates and scans for vulnerabilities.

▶ **scanless:** *scanless* is a port scanning utility that uses websites to do scanning on your behalf, allowing you to remain anonymous.

▶ **Nessus:** *Nessus* is a well-known vulnerability scanner that has a wide range of capabilities.

▶ **Cuckoo:** Cuckoo is a malware analysis tool. Essentially, you provide Cuckoo with a file, and it returns results indicating what the file did when it was executed in an isolated environment.

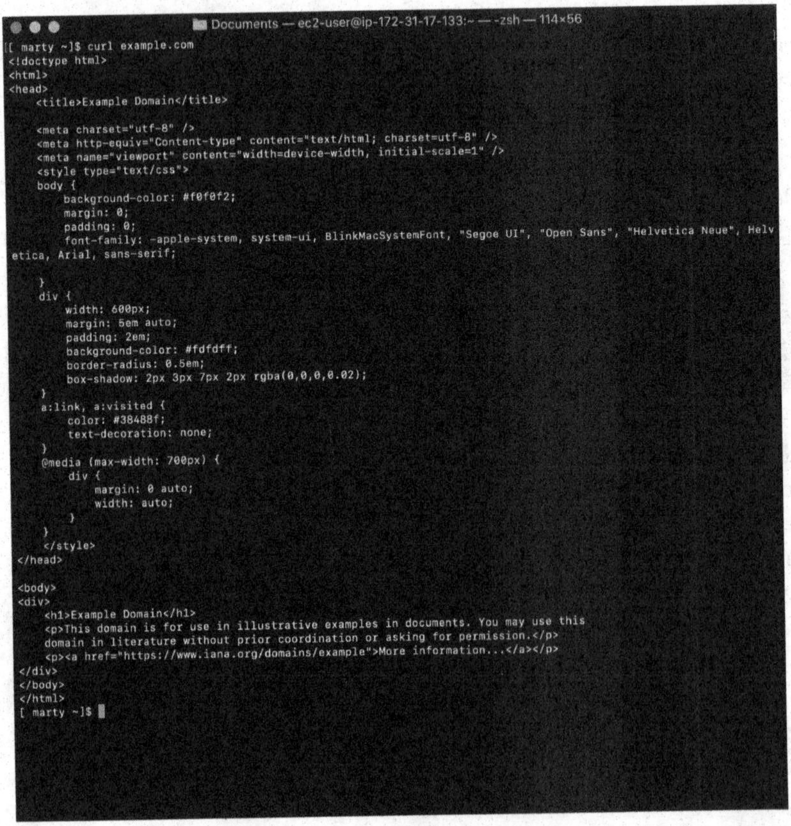

FIGURE 26.2 **Using the cURL command to return the source code of a web page**

Most of these utilities are useful for security operations, but they are also used by adversaries for reconnaissance and attacks. For example, banner grabbing is a technique used to identify what operating system is running on a machine and determine what services are running. Attackers and active vulnerability scanning solutions use banner grabbing to help identify the OS type and running services. This information helps them narrow the list of vulnerability signatures to scan for or footprint an organization. The more you understand about the specific operating systems, applications, and version information, the easier it is to identify vulnerable systems and conduct targeted attacks. Netcat is a tool that is commonly used for banner grabs. For example, you might type the following at a command shell:

```
nc www.example.com 80
```

Then you can simply press Enter to establish a connection, and then you just need to send a bad request. This could be as simple as typing any letter followed by pressing Enter. Depending on the system, the results will likely provide information about the host, including the type and version of web server running and the type and version of operating systems running. For a system administrator, this is a handy way to identify assets. Such information also makes vulnerability management tools more intelligent. Of course, this command can also help an attacker figure out what exploit to use against the system.

ExamAlert

Be familiar at a high level with all the tools covered in this chapter. You might want to consider opening the command-line interface on your personal computer and experimenting with the commands. Help documentation can often be reached by typing the command followed by a space and -h or by preceding the command with man (for manual).

Many of the command-line utilities in the preceding list rely on underlying technologies. For example, ping and traceroute rely on ICMP. Internet Control Message Protocol (ICMP) is meant to be an aid for other protocols (as well as system administrators) to test connectivity and search for configuration errors in a network. ping uses the ICMP echo function and is the lowest-level test of whether a remote host is alive. A small packet containing an ICMP echo message is sent through the network to a particular IP address. The computer that sent the packet waits for a return packet. If the connections are good and the target computer is up, the echo message return packet is received. Ping is one of the most useful network tools because it tests the most basic function of an IP network. It also shows the time to live (TTL) value and the amount of time it

takes for a packet to make the complete trip, also known as the round-trip time (RTT), in milliseconds (ms). Figure 26.3 shows an example of how ping is used.

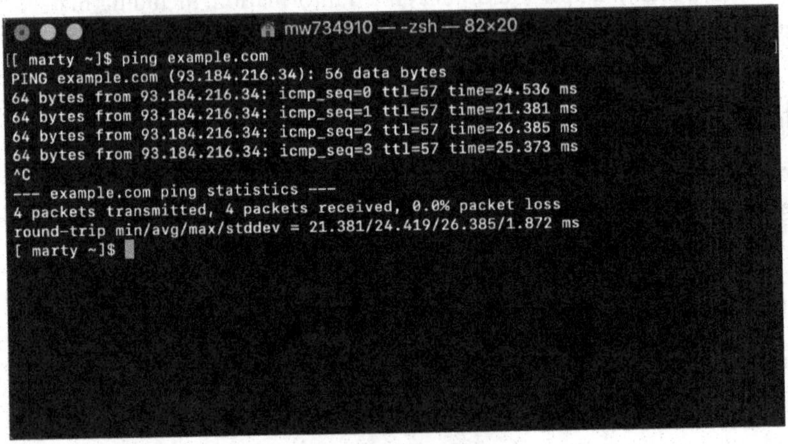

```
● ● ●                      🖾 mw734910 — -zsh — 82×20
[[ marty ~]$ ping example.com
PING example.com (93.184.216.34): 56 data bytes
64 bytes from 93.184.216.34: icmp_seq=0 ttl=57 time=24.536 ms
64 bytes from 93.184.216.34: icmp_seq=1 ttl=57 time=21.381 ms
64 bytes from 93.184.216.34: icmp_seq=2 ttl=57 time=26.385 ms
64 bytes from 93.184.216.34: icmp_seq=3 ttl=57 time=25.373 ms
^C
--- example.com ping statistics ---
4 packets transmitted, 4 packets received, 0.0% packet loss
round-trip min/avg/max/stddev = 21.381/24.419/26.385/1.872 ms
[ marty ~]$ ▌
```

FIGURE 26.3   Using the ping command-line utility

The traceroute tool uses an ICMP echo request packet to find the path. It sends an echo reply with the TTL value set to 1. When the first router sees the packet with TTL 1, it decreases it by one, to 0, and discards the packet. As a result, it sends an ICMP time exceeded message back to the source address. The source address of the ICMP error message is the first router address. Now the source knows the address of the first router. Generally, three packets are sent at each TTL, and the RTT is measured for each one. Most implementations of traceroute keep working until they have gone 30 hops, but this can be extended to up to 254 routers.

The utility ping relies on ARP to identify IP addresses because 48-bit MAC addresses must be mapped to an IP address in order for devices on different networks to communicate. The following are some of the Layer 3 protocols used to perform MAC-to-IP address mapping:

▶ Address Resolution Protocol (ARP)

▶ Reverse ARP (RARP)

▶ Serial Line ARP (SLARP)

▶ Inverse ARP

The output from command-line tools can be saved and imported into other tools. For example, the output from tcpdump is often saved and imported into Wireshark for easier interpretation. Command-line tools can also provide some of the same functionality as other tools—without all the overhead. For example,

Netcat can establish a TCP connection to a web server and then grab the banner to fingerprint the OS the server is running. Both dig and nslookup can map IP addresses to domain names and other related information, including mail exchanges and name servers.

Exploitation Frameworks

Exploitation frameworks are used often used for penetration testing and risk assessment. They can be used in conjunction with vulnerability scanners such as Nessus. Each exploitation framework contains a set of exploits for known vulnerabilities that are run against a host to determine whether the host is vulnerable to the exploit. Exploitation involves the following steps:

1. Select a target system.

2. Select an exploit.

3. If prior reconnaissance was conducted, determine whether the exploit might work on the target system.

4. Select and configure the exploit payload.

5. Select an encoding method for the payload so it can get through the IDS.

6. Run the exploit.

Some of the most well-known exploitation frameworks are Metasploit, Canvas, and Core Impact. Exploitation frameworks exist for systems as well as for specific web browsers. The Browser Exploitation Framework (BeEF) is a penetration testing tool that focuses on exploiting vulnerabilities in web browsers by using client-side attacks.

Packet Capture and Replay

Protocol analyzers, also known as packet sniffers, help you troubleshoot network issues by gathering packet-level information across the network. This type of software utility is used on a hub, on a switch supervisory port, or in line with network connectivity to enable the analysis of network communications. Protocol analyzers can identify individual protocols, specific endpoints, and sequential access attempts. These applications capture packets and can conduct protocol decoding, turning the information into readable data for analysis. Protocol analyzers can do more than just look at packets, though. They are useful in many other areas of network management, such as monitoring the network for unexpected, unwanted, and unnecessary traffic. For example, if a network is

running slowly, a protocol analyzer can tell you whether unnecessary protocols are running on the network. You can also filter specific port numbers and types of traffic so that you can keep an eye on indicators that might cause problems. Many protocol analyzers can be run on multiple platforms and do live traffic captures and offline analysis. Software USB protocol analyzers are also available for the development of USB devices and analysis of USB traffic.

You can place protocol analyzers inline or between the devices for which you want to capture the traffic. If you are analyzing storage-area network (SAN) traffic, you can place an analyzer outside the direct link with the use of an optical splitter. The analyzer then is placed to capture traffic between the host and the monitored device.

The following are the common protocol analyzer tools you should be familiar with:

- **tcpdump:** The *tcpdump* utility is a command-line packet analyzer tool that captures TCP/IP packets sent and received on a specific interface. The tcpdump tool is used on Mac and other Linux-based systems; Windump is used on Windows-based systems.

- **tcpreplay:** *tcpreplay* is a command-line tool used for replaying network traffic from files saved with tcpdump or other utilities that write packet capture library (.pcap) files.

- **Wireshark:** *Wireshark* is a well-known packet analyzer that is similar to tcpdump but provides a graphical user interface.

ExamAlert

Be familiar with the packet capture and replay tools tcpdump, tcprelay, and Wireshark.

Some operating systems have built-in protocol analyzers. Windows Server operating systems come with a protocol analyzer called Microsoft Message Analyzer. In the Unix environment, many administrators use tools such as ps and vmstat that come with the core operating system. Oracle Solaris has a popular utility called iostat that provides good information about I/O performance.

A sniffer and protocol analyzer are generally accepted as being the same tool. As software packages continue to add features, the lines between the two are blurring. However, a sniffer is a tool that is designed to "sniff" the network and capture packets. In the simplest sense, a sniffer relies on a user to conduct

further analysis and interpretation. On the other hand, a protocol analyzer is capable of providing further details and context on the captured packets.

> **ExamAlert**
>
> A protocol analyzer is used to capture network traffic and generate statistics for creating reports. After the packets have been captured, you can view the information.

Password Crackers

Weak passwords are easily compromised. Users must be educated about the importance of their access credentials and the potential impact of sharing their passwords and logons, using weak passwords, and using easily guessed passwords. They should also be instructed in how to create a strong password. Even when users are educated about the dangers of using the same password for multiple accounts and when to change passwords, they often don't follow good practices. As a result, it is imperative to test the passwords that employees use.

> **ExamAlert**
>
> *Password crackers* are software utilities that allow direct testing of user logon password strength. This type of tool conducts a brute-force password test by using dictionary terms, specialized lexicons, or mandatory complexity guidelines.

Chapter 2, "Attack Basics," covers various types of password attacks. In addition to using helpful software programs, you can look for online password-cracking tools that enable you to input the hash and get the password returned in plaintext. There is even an online password-cracking tool for WPA-protected Wi-Fi networks that cracks password hashes in a manner similar to other online cracking tools.

Common password-cracking tools include the following:

▶ Brutus

▶ Cain and Able

▶ John the Ripper

▶ THC Hydra

When used by an organization as an assessment tool, a password cracker should provide only the relative strength of a password and not the password itself to avoid weakening logon responsibility under evidentiary discovery actions.

Forensics and Data Sanitization

Organizations maintain data such as names, addresses, Social Security numbers, and personal health information. User training programs address legal or regulatory requirements for accessing, transporting, storing, and disposing of data and data storage devices. Most times an organization has a legal obligation to protect and dispose of data properly. This includes encryption systems for mobile and removable storage devices, data access logging requirements under laws such as HIPAA, and review of retention and destruction policy.

A data destruction policy spells out what happens when sensitive data contained on a device is no longer needed but the device is being repurposed. Often the device or media is sanitized.

> **ExamAlert**
>
> *Data sanitization* is the process of removing the contents from a device or media as fully as possible, in an attempt to make it extremely difficult to restore. Sanitization can be accomplished using either a software tool or a combination of a software tool and firmware.

Sanitization falls into one of the following categories:

▶ **Clear:** Standard read and write commands

▶ **Purge:** Physical or logical techniques that make recovery impossible

▶ **Destroy:** Physical or logical techniques that render the device useless

Examples of software used to wipe data stored on hard drives include DBAN and BCWipe. Organizations that use self-encrypting drives (SEDs) also use cryptographic erasure (CE). CE takes advantage of the encrypted data by sanitizing the encryption key. This is a quick and effective method that leaves only the ciphertext on the media.

After sanitization, a certificate of media disposition is completed. The certificate can be either a hard copy or an electronic copy stating the process and method used to sanitize the data. NIST Special Publication 800-88, "Guidelines for Media Sanitization," provides detailed information on how to sanitize media, based on the organization's categorization of information confidentiality.

Disk wiping capabilities are also provided as part of a number of data forensic utilities. Some basic forensic utilities you should be familiar with include the following:

▶ **dd:** *dd* is a command-line utility that converts and copies files and is useful for transferring data, modifying data, wiping disks, recovering data, generating random files, and benchmarking drive performance.

▶ **Memdump:** *Memdump* is a command-line utility that returns the contents of system memory.

▶ **WinHex:** *WinHex* is a hex editor that also provides data analysis, data recovery, data gathering, and disk wiping capabilities.

▶ **FTK Imager:** *FTK Imager* is a disk imaging tool that is used to save the image of a hard drive. FTK Imager is also part of a complete FTK computer forensics software solution.

▶ **Autopsy:** *Autopsy* is a software tool used to examine hard drives and mobile devices for evidence recovery.

Cram Quiz

Answer these questions. The answers follow the last question. If you cannot answer these questions correctly, consider reading this chapter again until you can.

1. A security analyst identifies malware that is traced back to the IP address 93.184.216.34. Which one of the following tools might the security analyst use to determine if an active connection to that IP address still resides on the infected system?

○ **A.** tracert

○ **B.** ping

○ **C.** netstat

○ **D.** nslookup

2. Which of the following commands would you use to look for failure or warning errors in /var/log/secure?

○ **A.** logger "failure or warning" /var/log/secure

○ **B.** grep 'failure\warning' /var/log/secure

○ **C.** head -n 15 errors

○ **D.** cat failure warning

3. Which of the following utilities would result in the following output:

```
HTTP/1.1 400 Bad Request
Date: Thu, 21 May 2020 04:17:05 GMT
Server: Apache/2.4.29 (Ubuntu)
Content-Length: 319
Connection: close
Content-Type: text/html; charset=iso-8859-1
```

- ○ **A.** Netcat
- ○ **B.** ping
- ○ **C.** nslookup
- ○ **D.** route

4. Which of the following is a software tool used to examine hard drives and mobile devices for evidence recovery?

- ○ **A.** tcpdump
- ○ **B.** Wireshark
- ○ **C.** John the Ripper
- ○ **D.** Autopsy

Cram Quiz Answers

Answer 1: C. netstat is a command-line utility that displays incoming and outgoing network connections. Answer A is incorrect because tracert would show the path or hops taken from the infected system to the IP address. Answer B is incorrect because ping would show the analyst if the remote IP address is potentially still alive and responding to requests. Answer D is incorrect because this is a tool for querying DNS servers.

Answer 2: B. grep searches in files, looking for desired data, based on patterns or regular expressions. In this example, grep is looking for either the word failure or the word warning in /var/log/secure. Answer A is incorrect because logger is used to write to the log file, and in this case it would write to the local log file the text contained between the quotes. Answer C is incorrect because head returns the beginning of a file, and this would return the first 15 lines in the file named errors. Answer D is incorrect because this command would concatenate the two files together.

Answer 3: A. Netcat can be used to grab website banners, and in this case, the website Netcat acquired on port 80 is running Apache web server 2.4.29 on Ubuntu. Answers B, C, and D are incorrect because ping, nslookup, and route would not return this information.

Answer 4: D. Autopsy is a forensics software tool used to examine hard drives and mobile devices for evidence recovery. Answer A is incorrect because the tcpdump utility is a command-line packet analyzer tool that captures TCP/IP packets sent and received. Answer B is incorrect because Wireshark is a well-known packet analyzer that is similar to tcpdump but that provides a graphical user interface. Answer C is incorrect because John the Ripper is a password-cracking tool.

What Next?

If you want more practice on this chapter's exam objective before you move on, remember that you can access all of the Cram Quiz questions on the Pearson Test Prep software online. You can also create a custom exam by objective with the Online Practice Test. Note any objective you struggle with and go to that objective's material in this chapter.

Incident Response

This chapter covers the following official Security+ exam objective:

▶ 4.2 Summarize the importance of policies, processes, and procedures for incident response.

Essential Terms and Components

▶ incident response plan

▶ incident response process

▶ tabletop exercise

▶ MITRE ATT&CK

▶ Diamond Model of Intrusion Analysis

▶ cyber kill chain

▶ disaster recovery planning (DRP)

▶ business continuity planning (BCP)

▶ continuity of operations planning (COOP)

▶ incident response team (IRT)

Attack Frameworks

Many incidents occur inadvertently, but others are malicious attacks (either internal or external). Such incidents happen in most organizations, no matter how strict their security policies and procedures. Planning for such events is vital to ensure effective incident handling and response when the time comes. Proper planning can mean the difference between quick recovery and ruin.

Cyber Kill Chain

Incident response requires an understanding of the process of an attack and how attacks are executed. This is particularly important where automation is desired as part of the incident response program. An intrusion kill chain is often used to describe the stages of a cyberattack. Lockheed Martin developed a framework to help defend its networks based on the chain of actions that an attacker takes. This model, which has since been adopted by the security industry, is known as the *cyber kill chain*.

The cyber kill chain shows the steps an attacker takes from beginning to end. The idea is that not all infiltrations are immediately thwarted, and it's necessary to disrupt or break the chain wherever the attacker is as early as possible. The chain can use different solutions, instruments, and response types. While there are variations on of the cyber kill chain, the Lockheed Martin cyber kill chain includes the following seven phases, from the attacker's perspective:

▶ **Reconnaissance:** Identifying and researching the target

▶ **Weaponization:** Preparing for and staging the attack

▶ **Delivery:** Launching the attack

▶ **Exploitation:** Gaining access by taking advantage of a vulnerability

▶ **Installation:** Establishing persistence

▶ **Command and control:** Enabling remote control for further manipulation

▶ **Actions on objectives:** With control, achieving the goals

In order to defend and respond in each of these phases, it's important to understand the attacker's actions. An intrusion kill chain can further describe the adversarial actions and what the corresponding defenders' actions should be. Ideally, an organization will break the chain before an attacker can achieve his or her ultimate goal.

MITRE ATT&CK

MITRE ATT&CK is another framework that is similar to a kill chain but focuses more on a knowledge base of different attack techniques in order to understand and defend against an attacker. MITRE ATT&CK defines the following 12 tactics:

▶ Initial access

▶ Execution

▶ Persistence

▶ Privilege escalation

▶ Defense evasion

▶ Credential access

▶ Discovery

▶ Lateral movement

▶ Collection

▶ Command and control

▶ Exfiltration

▶ Impact

MITRE ATT&CK also includes many different matrices for attack planning, mobile device attacks, and attacks across various operating system platforms. Further, a number of high-level tactics and corresponding lists of techniques are provided in the framework. MITRE ATT&CK can be used in a number of different scenarios across a security organization and provides a reference for incident response. Incident response teams can use the framework to plan ahead and also to mitigate attacks because the framework aids in understanding the specific threats.

Diamond Model of Intrusion Analysis

Another similar framework to be familiar with is the *Diamond Model of Intrusion Analysis*. This model places the basic components of malicious activity at one of the four points on a diamond shape: adversary, infrastructure, capability, and victim. The model provides for analysis of threats related to intrusion. While it appears simple, this model provides a flexible framework that is self-referential, providing much more intrusion analysis detail with varying analytics. It takes a more scientific approach to the process and even provides a mathematical framework for analysis and decision making.

ExamAlert

Be sure you are familiar with attack frameworks, including the cyber kill chain, MITRE ATT&CK, and the Diamond Model.

Incident Response Plan

An incident response plan needs to include preparation, roles, rules, and procedures. Incident response procedures should define how to maintain business continuity while defending against further attacks. An organization may have a specific team of technical and security investigators that respond to and investigate security incidents, but many do not. If an organization has no such explicitly defined team, first responders need to handle the scene and the response. Systems should be secured to prevent as many incidents as possible and should be monitored to detect security breaches as they occur.

> **Note**
>
> The National Institute of Standards and Technology (NIST) has issued a report on incident response guidelines that can help an organization spell out its own internal procedures. These guidelines serve as best practices and can be found at http://nvlpubs.nist.gov/nistpubs/SpecialPublications/NIST.SP.800-61r2.pdf.

Organizational policies and practices provide structural guidance to ensure quality and efficiency in the workplace. To properly preserve evidence, an organization must put together an *incident response team* (*IRT*) that knows how to handle incidents. Incident response plans help this team intelligently react to an intrusion. If a plan is not in place and duties are not clearly assigned, the organization could end up in a state of panic. An incident response plan provides a formal approach for how the organization will respond to incidents. Incident response methodologies typically emphasize preparation so that the organization is ready to not only respond to incidents but also prevent them by ensuring that systems, networks, and applications are sufficiently secure. The components of an incident response plan should include preparation, roles, rules, and procedures. Specifically, the "NIST Computer Security Incident Handling Guide" (SP 800-61) provides guidance on the important elements, which include the following:

▶ Mission, strategies, and goals of incident response

▶ Senior management approval

▶ Approach to incident response

▶ Response team communications

▶ Metrics for measuring response capabilities and effectiveness

- ▶ Roadmap for maturing response capability

- ▶ How the incident response program fits into the organization

The plan starts with the mission, strategies, and goals of incident response; this information lays the groundwork for the required capabilities. The plan can then be implemented immediately. Of course, the plan also should continually evolve to make sure it meets the defined mission, strategies, and goals. Occasionally revisiting the plan helps ensure that the program continues to mature based on the defined roadmap. Keep in mind, however, that an organization's mission and strategies can change. For this reason, companies should revisit the program at least annually to assess changes and adjust accordingly.

Documented Incident Type/Category Definitions

Planning for every conceivable type of incident is impractical. Still, incidents vary, and different types of response strategies are needed. Let's consider incidents that take place in the real world. Terrorism events might be classified based on attack vector, but focusing on and planning incident responses to every potential tactic is not feasible. Even at the airport, for example, security might face the threat of liquids one day, shoes the next, and so on. The following are common network attack vectors, each potentially meriting its own incident response procedures:

- ▶ **Web and cloud:** Attacks perpetrated through websites and cloud-based applications and infrastructure

- ▶ **Email:** Attacks through email, such as with phishing and dangerous attachments

- ▶ **Improper usage:** Incidents that violate acceptable use policies, Internet policies, and other organizational policies (see Chapter 33, "Organizational Security Policies")

- ▶ **Equipment damage, loss, or theft:** Incidents that involve computing equipment, including laptops and mobile devices, as well as other information systems

Roles and Responsibilities

An incident response program must include stakeholder management, which defines roles and responsibilities. Even with proper communication and

notification following an incident, plans will be less effective if any confusion surrounds what role people are supposed to play and what they must do. Formal definition also grants clear authority for actions to be taken during an incident. Consider who can perform the following actions:

▶ Confiscate computers and other information systems

▶ Disconnect data networks and other information systems

▶ Monitor systems for further analysis and activity

▶ Communicate with the press

Reporting Requirements and Escalation

An incident response plan should be clear about how an incident or a potential incident should be reported and escalated. This involves the use of a formal communication plan. Incident identification involves gathering events from various sources (such as log files, intrusion detection systems, and firewalls) to procure evidence on whether an event is an incident. When an incident is analyzed and prioritized, the incident response team needs to notify the appropriate individuals so that all people who need to be involved can play their roles.

The exact reporting requirements vary among organizations, but parties that are typically notified include the chief information officer (CIO), chief information security officer (CISO), other internal incident response team members, system owners, human resources officials, public affairs officers, legal department personnel, federal agencies, and law enforcement personnel, when necessary.

In 2013, a data breach incident at Target put some 110 million people at risk of credit fraud and identity theft. Companies such as Neiman Marcus, eBay, Home Depot, and Sony have also made headlines due to large-scale data breaches. One of the most important points about a data breach is that mitigation of further data loss is necessary. An organization needs to conduct a thorough investigation of a suspected or confirmed loss or theft of account information within 24 hours of the compromise. Incident notification is often a legal requirement in responding to a data breach. Data breach notification laws provide direction on steps to take following a data breach and might define both responsibilities and liabilities involved in a breach. A key challenge in responding to a data breach is determining whether and when notification is an appropriate response; the legal team often makes this determination. Data breach notification laws are continually changing, and businesses should

consider the statutes of all states in which they do business or where residents have personal information.

Cyber-Incident Response Teams

A cyber-incident response team (CIRT) has a key role that is defined as part of an incident response plan. The team should consist of technical and security investigators who respond to and look into security incidents. When a suspected or confirmed incident occurs, the CIRT should be notified to handle the situation and execute the *incident response process*.

> **Note**
>
> A CIRT is also referred to as a computer incident response team, a computer security incident response team (CSIRT), a cyber-security incident response team, or simply an incident response team (IRT).

Most large organizations have response teams that are made up of full-time employees. However, many of these same organizations also partially outsource some of the responsibilities, particularly for more serious incidents. Other organizations choose to outsource the entire team and process. Varying structures are used, depending on the team's makeup. Most structures fall within one of the three models described by NIST:

- ▶ **Central:** A single team is responsible for incidents. This model is common in smaller organizations, particularly companies that aren't geographically dispersed.

- ▶ **Distributed:** Multiple teams are involved. Each team might be assigned specific areas, based on different components of the organization or physical geography.

- ▶ **Coordinating:** As in the central model, a single team is established. However, this team only provides guidance for other teams. The coordinating model therefore also has attributes of the distributed model.

Regardless of the model, the CIRT needs to collaborate with others during an incident. Management, information security, physical security, support, legal, human resources, public affairs, privacy, and potentially other personnel are critical to the CIRT's success. These groups have specific expertise and responsibilities and can assist each other throughout the response process.

Training, Tests, and Exercises

An incident response plan should include requirements for training, tests, and simulated exercises. Mature incident response programs also likely have dedicated plans that focus on these activities. Executing these activities has two primary purposes: to ensure effectiveness during an incident and to identify any deficiencies that should be addressed or mitigated. For these activities to actually translate to better results in the future, however, they must be part of the lessons learned in the post-incident activities. (These activities are discussed in further detail later in this chapter.)

Proper training is critical to the success of any formal program. Specific to incident response, training starts with clear communication of the roles and responsibilities discussed earlier. Within each role, the specific set of skills needed to perform the corresponding responsibilities should be considered. Each role must get adequate training.

Tests, unlike exercises (discussed next), apply specifically to systems that are usually operational. For example, this might include the capability to recover a system from a backup. Where possible, tests should include the actual systems in operation. For example, if failover is to be tested, the system should be taken offline to determine whether it actually cuts over to the next system as expected.

Exercises tend to be simulations—that is, they don't affect operational systems. Exercises are scenario based. For example, an exercise might involve an attacker exfiltrating a database of customer data. The two primary types of exercises are tabletop and functional exercises. As the name implies, in a *tabletop exercise*, the appropriate individuals and teams are brought together (typically around a table) for a discussion. In an exercise on a customer data breach, for example, the group members would discuss their individual roles and how they would coordinate. In contrast, in a functional exercise, participants go through the motions of their response as they would during an actual emergency. Again, however, the response is simulated, so it does not affect systems in operation.

> **ExamAlert**
>
> Incident response exercises are either discussion oriented (as with tabletop exercises) or more focused on simulated response (as with functional exercises).

Consider the simple analogy of a fire alarm response. Children and staff members in school are trained on what to do when they hear the fire alarm. Tests are conducted to ensure that the fire alarms function. Exercises are performed to

ensure that the staff and students can execute what they have been trained for by actually exiting the building and congregating at a specified location.

Incident Response Process

A process generally consists of a series of steps or phases. The incident response life cycle includes four primary phases:

▶ Preparation

▶ Identification and analysis

▶ Containment, eradication, and recovery

▶ Post-incident events

Figure 27.1 illustrates the flow and loops of this process. As mentioned earlier, the key components of an incident response plan should include preparation, roles, rules, and procedures that are critical to the incident response process and life cycle.

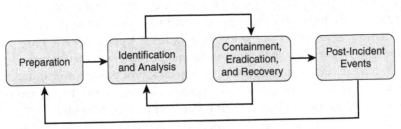

FIGURE 27.1   Incident response process

Preparation

Organizational policies and practices offer structural guidance designed to ensure quality and efficiency in the workplace. To properly preserve evidence, an organization should have an incident response team that knows how to handle incidents. Incident response methodologies typically emphasize preparation so that the organization is ready to not only respond to incidents but also prevent incidents by ensuring that systems, networks, and applications are sufficiently secure.

Various tools and resources are needed to handle an incident. Proper preparation starts with ensuring that these resources are defined and available. "NIST

Computer Security Incident Handling Guide" (SP 800-61) provides a wealth of information to use as a baseline and highlights specific tools and resources. The following list covers the broad categories of resources that incident handlers need, along with some examples:

▶ **Communications and facilities:** Contact information, encrypted communications, secure storage facility, and phones

▶ **Hardware and software for analysis and mitigation:** Forensics workstations, protocol analyzers, portable printer, cameras, and blank media

▶ **Ancillary analysis resources:** Port lists, documentation, network diagrams, and existing system baselines

An incident response team commonly has a jump kit. Much like a first-aid kit, a jump kit is pre-prepared and available for immediate use in case of an incident. The jump kit should contain tools and resources from the categories just listed.

Incident Identification and Analysis

Many risks to enterprise networks relate both to vulnerabilities present in system and service configurations and to network and user logon weaknesses. Signs of an incident are either precursors or indicators. A precursor is a sign that an incident might occur in the future. An indicator is a sign that an incident might have occurred or might be occurring now. Not every precursor or indicator is guaranteed to be accurate. For example, intrusion detection systems can produce false positives. Thousands or millions of indicators can be generated daily, and each indicator must be evaluated to determine its legitimacy. An accurate indicator does not necessarily mean that an incident has occurred, so determining whether an event is truly an incident is a matter of judgment.

The first step is to analyze and validate the incident or incidents. When the response team has determined that an incident has occurred, the next step involves taking a comprehensive look at the incident activity to determine its scope. Documentation is important for eliminating errors and ensuring an efficient process. A proper determination of the scope of an incident helps prioritize potential needs for deeper analysis, as well as the next step in the process for containment. To help with prioritization efforts, the response team should consider and categorize the impact and recoverability effort. This includes the following:

▶ **Functional impact of the incident:** A categorization that uses varying degrees of impact severity, from none (no effect) to high (unable to provide critical services).

- **Information impact of the incident:** The type of impact on information. For example, if personally identifiable information of individuals was accessed, this might be categorized as a privacy breach.

- **Recoverability from the incident:** The extent of the recoverability efforts. This can include a defined category, from simple, in which recovery is well understood and does not require additional resources, to severe, in which recovery is not possible.

Finally, the incident response team should notify the proper individuals and teams, according to procedures defined in the incident response program.

Containment, Eradication, and Recovery

The process by which evidence is handled at the scene is often much more important than the laboratory analysis work done later. First responders are the first ones to arrive at the incident scene. The success of data recovery and potential prosecution depends on the actions of the individual who initially discovers the computer incident. How the evidence scene is handled can strongly affect the organization's capability to successfully prosecute the perpetrator. Police officers are trained to have a good understanding of the limits of applicable laws, but many systems administrators and network security personnel are not. The entire work area—not just the computer involved—is a potential crime scene. Evidence might include removable media, voicemail messages, and handwritten notes. The work area should be secured and protected to maintain its integrity. Under no circumstances should anyone be allowed to remove items from the scene without proper authorization.

Isolating systems or devices involved in an incident gives a forensics team time to develop a tailored remediation strategy. The infected systems need to be isolated and quarantined. Quarantining involves finding each infected machine and disconnecting, removing, or blocking it from the network so that it cannot infect other unpatched machines on the network.

For example, when a malware-infected machine that regularly reports back to a designated host fails to report as expected, the malware might overwrite or encrypt all the data on the host's hard drive. Incident response personnel should not assume that they have prevented further damage to the host simply because they have disconnected a host from the network. In cases such as this, the organization can redirect the attacker to a sandbox, where the team can monitor the attacker's activity to gather additional evidence and more clearly understand the attack. This approach comes with additional risks, of course, including possible legal ramifications.

> **ExamAlert**
>
> Although removing an attacked device from a network is generally advisable, this process can cause additional damage when sophisticated malware is involved.

Incident response functions can take many forms, depending on the severity of the incident and the organizational policy. The response team might send out recommendations for mitigation, recovery, containment, and prevention to systems and network administrators, who then complete the response steps. Alternatively, team members might perform the mitigation actions themselves.

In keeping with the severity of the incident, the organization can mitigate the impact of the incident by containing it and eventually restoring operations to normal. Mitigation needs to occur before an incident damages resources. Because of the need to act quickly, mitigation is often based on judgment and fast decision making. Decisions are easier to make if strategies and procedures for incident mitigation are already in place. Organizations should define acceptable risks in dealing with incidents and develop strategies accordingly. The incident type determines the mitigation type. Organizations should create separate mitigation strategies for each major incident type, with criteria clearly documented.

> **ExamAlert**
>
> *Mitigation* refers to the action of minimizing the impact of an incident. Accurately determining the cause of each incident is important so that the team can fully contain the attack and any exploited vulnerabilities to prevent similar incidents from occurring in the future.

Depending on the nature of the incident, the organization might opt for destruction of physical property. In such a case, rebuilding or reconstituting the organization could be necessary. Reconstitution options include continuing to operate from the current alternate site, beginning an orderly phased return to the original site, and beginning to establish a reconstituted organization at another location. In recovery, administrators restore systems to normal operation and confirm that the systems are functioning normally.

Higher levels of system logging or network monitoring are often part of the recovery process. After a resource is successfully attacked, it is often attacked again, or other resources in the organization are attacked in a similar manner. Eradication and recovery should be done in a phased approach that prioritizes remediation steps. Eradication means removing elements of the incident, such as malware. Recovery is about restoring systems to normal, which often

includes restoring from backups or rebuilding systems. For large-scale incidents, recovery can take months.

> **ExamAlert**
>
> Not all incidents require eradication. Sometimes systems only need to be recovered. On the other hand, sometimes eradication goes hand-in-hand with recovery. For example, whereas eradication might include disabling breached user accounts, recovery would include changing passwords.

Post-Incident Activities

After mitigating an incident, an organization issues a report containing details about the incident, such as the cause, the cost, and recommendations for preventing future incidents. Incident reporting allows the organization to review and adjust its processes in order to reduce additional incidents and losses. Organizations might be subject to industry requirements for reporting certain types of incidents. Where they are, requirements and guidelines cover external communications and information sharing (what can be shared with whom, when, and over what channels) and identify the handoff and escalation points in the incident management process. In addition, forensic analysis of information might require further reporting to law enforcement or clients, depending on the findings and evidentiary data.

The follow-up response can involve sharing information and lessons learned with other response teams and appropriate organizations and sites. One of the most important parts of incident response is lessons learned. A lessons-learned meeting should be conducted within a few days of a major incident; alternatively, a lessons-learned report can be filed. A lessons-learned meeting or report provides incident closure by reviewing what occurred, describing the action taken to mitigate and contain the incident, and summarizing how well the mitigation worked. Lessons-learned reports provide valuable information for updating incident response policies and procedures. Postmortem analysis of incident handling often reveals missing steps or procedures.

Following a data breach, a company typically incurs costs related to notifying customers and processing claims for damages. Expenses related to the following may be incurred when a data breach results in the loss or theft of third-party information:

▶ A forensic examination to determine the severity and scope of the breach

▶ Notification of third parties

- ► Call center hotline support

- ► Credit or identity monitoring

- ► Public relations, for damage control

- ► Legal defense

- ► Regulatory proceedings, fines, and penalties

In addition, regulatory settlements might require the breached organization to produce or implement a comprehensive written information security program that is subject to periodic audits.

Continuity and Recovery Plans

Business continuity planning (BCP) and *continuity of operations planning (COOP)* ensure the restoration of organizational functions in the shortest possible time, even if services resume at a reduced level of effectiveness or availability. *Disaster recovery planning (DRP)* extends this process to ensure full recovery of operational capacity following a disaster (natural or human caused). Instructions and details for recovery should occur before an incident. Plans should be determined, and they also should be regularly updated and tested to ensure that the appropriate stakeholders are identified, communication plans can be implemented, and responders can properly execute response and recovery plans. These plans should address different scenarios for incident handling responses and notification procedures following identification, short-term recovery of key service and operational data access functions as part of continuity of operation preparedness, and long-term sustained recovery to full operational status in disaster recovery planning. A business recovery plan, business resumption plan, and contingency plan are also considered part of business continuity planning. If an incident occurs, an organization might also need to restore equipment (in addition to data) or personnel lost or rendered unavailable by the nature or scale of the disaster.

Disaster Recovery

Failure to recover from a disaster could destroy an organization. Many organizations realize the criticality of disaster recovery planning only after a catastrophic event (such as a hurricane, flood, or terrorist attack). However, disaster recovery is an important part of overall organization security planning for every organization. Natural disasters and terrorist activity can overcome even the

most rigorous physical security measures. Common hardware failures and even accidental deletions might require some form of recovery capability.

Disaster recovery involves many aspects, including the following:

▶ **Disaster recovery plan:** This plan is a written document that defines how the organization will recover from a disaster and how to restore business with minimal delay. The document also explains how to evaluate risks; how data backup and restoration procedures work; and the training required for managers, administrators, and users. A detailed disaster recovery plan should address various processes, including backup, data security, and recovery.

▶ **Disaster recovery policies:** These policies detail responsibilities and procedures to follow during disaster recovery events, including how to contact key employees, vendors, customers, and the press. They should also include instructions for situations in which bypassing the normal chain of command might be necessary to minimize damage or the effects of a disaster.

▶ **Service-level agreements:** SLAs are contracts with ISPs, utilities, facilities managers, and other types of suppliers that detail the minimum levels of support that must be provided (including during failure or disaster).

Fundamental to any disaster recovery plan is the need to provide for regular backups of key information, including user file and email storage; database stores; event logs; and security principal details such as user logons, passwords, and group membership assignments. Without a regular backup process, loss of data through accidents or directed attack could severely impair business processes.

Disaster recovery planning should include detailed system restoration procedures, particularly in complex clustered and virtualized environments. This planning should explain any general or specific configuration details that might be required to restore access and network function.

A restoration plan also should include contingency planning to recover systems and data in case of administration personnel loss or lack of availability. This plan should include procedures to follow if a disgruntled employee changes an administrative password before leaving. Statistics show that more damage to a network comes from inside than outside. Therefore, any key root-level account passwords and critical procedures should be properly documented so that another equally trained individual can manage the restoration process. This documentation must also include backout strategies to implement if the most

recent backup proves unrecoverable or if alternative capacity and equipment are all that remain available.

As part of redundancy and recovery planning, an organization can contract annually with a company that offers redundancy services (for a monthly service charge or a fee that is otherwise negotiated). When contracting services from a provider, be sure to carefully read the contract. Daily fees and other incidental fees might apply. In addition, in a large-scale incident, the facility could well become overextended.

In the beginning stages of the organizational security plan, the organization must decide how it will operate and how it will recover from any unfortunate incidents that affect its capability to conduct business. Redundancy planning encompasses the effects of both natural and human-caused catastrophes. Often these catastrophes result from unforeseen circumstances. Site planning for recovery is key.

Continuity of Operations Planning

Business continuity is mostly synonymous with continuity of operations planning (COOP). Specifically, COOP is an initiative that U.S. President George W. Bush implemented in 2007 to ensure that government departments and agencies can continue operation of their essential functions under circumstances involving natural, human-caused, and technological threats and national security emergencies. Continuity of operations is generally viewed as being the same as business continuity, but it primarily focuses on the government and public sectors. Policies and procedures are designed to ensure that an organization can recover from a potentially destructive incident and resume operations as quickly as possible following an event.

The main goal of preventing and effectively dealing with any type of disruption is to ensure availability. This primarily includes making sure of the following:

▶ Failover is available for required system redundancy. This can be automatic or manual.

▶ Alternate processing sites are available that are geographically different from the primary facilities.

▶ Alternate business practices are available in case systems or logistics prevent normal operating practices.

> **ExamAlert**
>
> A continuity of operations plan provides guidance to ensure that the organization can continue operation of its essential functions under emergencies. It should include details about relocation to alternate sites, if needed.

An organization should also consider contingencies for personnel replacement in the event of loss (death, injury, retirement, termination, and so on) or lack of availability. Succession planning is a process in which an organization ensures that it recruits and develops employees to fill each key role within the organization. Clear lines of succession and cross-training in critical functions are key. Organizations also need communications plans for alternative mechanisms of contact to alert individuals of the need for succession. Such considerations are imperative for meeting recovery time objectives (RTOs) and recovery point objectives (RPOs).

Proper continuity of operations planning should allow for training and tabletop exercises, similar to those discussed earlier in this chapter for incident response. Tabletop exercises involve key personnel participating in an informal, simulated scenario setting. The exercises are conducted to evaluate an organization's capability to execute one or more portions of a business continuity or disaster recovery plan. Tabletop exercises should be conducted on a regular basis to accomplish the following:

▶ Test and evaluate business continuity or disaster recovery policies, as well as procedures to identify plan weaknesses and resource gaps.

▶ Train personnel and clearly define roles and responsibilities to improve performance, communication, and coordination.

▶ Meet regulatory requirements.

A progressive exercise program is made up of gradually more complex exercises, with each one building on the previous one until the exercises are as close to reality as possible. When escalated to a full-scale exercise, this should involve a wide range of organizations, including fire, law enforcement, and emergency management personnel, as well as, when necessary, other entities such as local public health and public safety agencies.

Lessons learned play a key role after incident response. The same applies with continuity of operations. After training exercises and actual events, it is important to debrief and identify what went well and where improvement is needed. Some organizations, particularly government agencies, refer to these as *after-action reports*. In addition to identifying strengths and weaknesses, these reports should maintain a clear outline of what occurred.

Cram Quiz

Answer these questions. The answers follow the last question. If you cannot answer these questions correctly, consider reading this chapter again until you can.

1. Your rapid response team has been alerted about and identified a highly dangerous virus on a couple systems in one of your subnets. What step should your team take next?

    ○ **A.** Identification

    ○ **B.** Containment

    ○ **C.** Recovery

    ○ **D.** Eradication

2. Which of the following stakeholders are typically notified first when a confirmed incident has occurred? (Select two.)

    ○ **A.** Press

    ○ **B.** CISO

    ○ **C.** End users

    ○ **D.** Legal

3. What is the term given to a framework or model outlining the phases of attack to help security personnel defend their systems and respond to attacks?

    ○ **A.** Command and control

    ○ **B.** Intrusion kill chain

    ○ **C.** Cyber-incident response

    ○ **D.** CIRT

4. Which of the following is a written document that defines how an organization will recover from a disaster and how to restore business with minimal delay?

    ○ **A.** Tabletop agreement

    ○ **B.** Service-level agreement

    ○ **C.** Disaster recovery policy

    ○ **D.** Disaster recovery plan

Cram Quiz Answers

Answer 1: B. The team now knows that the virus has been identified and should seek to contain or isolate the virus to prevent its spread. If the team fails to contain the virus, it needs to take mitigating actions. Answer A is incorrect because the team has already identified the virus. As a result, answers C and D are incorrect. Eradication and then recovery would typically follow containment.

Answer 2: B and D. The exact reporting requirements vary among organizations, but parties that are typically notified include the chief information officer (CIO), chief information security officer (CISO), other internal incident response team members, human resources officers, public affairs personnel, the legal department, and law enforcement officers, when necessary. Answer A is incorrect because the press is not normally notified when an incident occurs. Answer C is incorrect because the end users are not normally notified initially when an incident occurs.

Answer 3: B. An intrusion kill chain is often used to describe the stages of a cyberattack; it also helps security teams defend their systems and helps incident response teams respond to attacks. Answers A, C, and D are incorrect. Command and control usually represents a stage of an attack in which the attacker tries to gain remote capabilities. Cyber-incident response would certainly respond to incidents but does not represent a framework or model attack phase. Similarly, CIRT is the acronym for cyber-incident response team.

Answer 4: D. A disaster recovery plan is a written document that defines how the organization will recover from a disaster and how to restore business with minimal delay. The document also explains how to evaluate risks; how data backup and restoration procedures work; and the training required for managers, administrators, and users. Answer A is incorrect and invalid. However, in tabletop exercises, the appropriate individuals and teams are brought together for a discussion. In an exercise on a customer data breach, for example, the group members would discuss their individual roles and how they would coordinate. Answer B is incorrect because service-level agreements (SLAs) are contracts with ISPs, utilities, facilities managers, and other suppliers that detail the minimum levels of support that must be provided during a failure or disaster. Answer C is incorrect because a disaster recovery policy details the responsibilities and procedures to follow during disaster recovery events, including how to contact key employees, vendors, customers, and the press.

What Next?

If you want more practice on this chapter's exam objective before you move on, remember that you can access all of the Cram Quiz questions on the Pearson Test Prep software online. You can also create a custom exam by objective with the Online Practice Test. Note any objective you struggle with and go to that objective's material in this chapter.

CHAPTER 28

Incident Investigation

This chapter covers the following official Security+ exam objective:

▶ 4.3 Given an incident, utilize appropriate data sources to support an investigation.

Essential Terms and Components

▶ SIEM dashboard

▶ log file

▶ syslog

▶ journalctl

▶ nxlog

▶ bandwidth monitoring

▶ metadata

▶ NetFlow/sFlow

Suspected incidents or indicators require analysis and validation. When the response team has determined that an incident has occurred, the next step is to take a comprehensive look at the incident activity to determine its scope. A proper determination of the scope of the incident helps the team prioritize potential needs for deeper analysis, as well as the next step in the process for containment. To help with prioritization efforts, the response team should consider and categorize the impact and recoverability effort. A number of tools are available to support these investigations.

SIEM Dashboards

Chapter 7, "Security Assessment Techniques," provided an overview of security information and event management (SIEM) solutions. Recall that SIEM solutions provide a number of useful purposes, one of which is supporting incident response. The primary function of a SIEM system is to aggregate data from various sources. Such a system can therefore be used to aggregate data on an incident, based on source IP, destination IP, and event ID. Having the raw data aggregated together in a single spot is valuable for incident investigation. Furthermore, the correlation engine part of a SIEM system can help uncover important information relevant to the investigation. It is important to consider the events of interest and other factors that led to the requirement for an investigation. Sensitivity is an important factor to consider as a SIEM system combines indicators with other techniques, such as pattern matching and anomaly detection. False positives waste investigative efforts.

A SIEM system supports an investigator by providing intelligent correlation. Unlike simple logging, a SIEM system can tie together individual benign events to reveal more details about what occurred and why it's of concern. For example, a proxy log might show that a user successfully authenticated and is currently making outbound web requests. At the same time, a physical security access log might show that the same user left the office some time ago. By themselves there isn't anything too concerning about either of these events. When taken together, however, they indicate an issue. As another example, say that you enter a password incorrectly the first time you try to log in to an application. That application logs the invalid login attempt, and the SIEM system sees it, too; by itself, the failed login is not a problem. If your user account also incorrectly tried to log in to 20 other applications around the same time, however, that is a problem, and the SIEM system can see it. These correlations a SIEM system can make become critical to creating meaningful alerts and helping incident investigators.

> **ExamAlert**
>
> Individual logs are useful for providing indicators of incidents and supporting security incident investigations. A SIEM system is able to correlate across these sources to help an investigator validate and further research an incident.

Dashboards and trending also provide meaningful and easy-to-visualize information based on correlated data. SIEM systems provide comprehensive charting capabilities to identify patterns and abnormal activities. Modern SIEM solutions also go beyond just static visualizations. A static image can certainly

help identify trends and potential incidents, but it's the ability to drill down that really helps an incident investigator. SIEM systems provide interactive dashboards with charts, sensors, graphs, and trends that can be easily explored by automatically filtering and exploring the data through interactive drilldowns. Figure 28.1 shows an example of a SIEM *dashboard*.

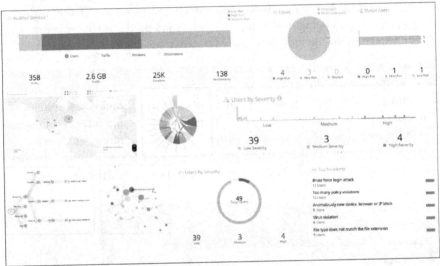

FIGURE 28.1   **An example of a SIEM system security dashboard**

Logging

Logging is the process of collecting data to be used for monitoring and auditing purposes. *Log files* are documentation, but how do you properly set up a log? You should develop standards for each platform, application, and server type to create a checklist or monitoring function. When choosing what to log, carefully consider your options. Logs take up disk space and use system resources. They also have to be read; if you log too much, the system bogs down, and weeding through the log files to determine what is important takes a long time. Be sure to mandate a common storage location for all logs. Documentation also should state the proper methods for archiving and reviewing logs.

All devices, operating systems, and applications have log files that generate important data, such as authentication attempts and errors. For example, application log files contain error messages, operational data, and usage information that can help manage applications and servers. Analyzing web application logs enables you to understand who visited the application, on what pages, and how

often, and it also provides information on errors and performance problems of the web application. Analysis of logs from web servers such as Apache, IIS, ISA, and Tomcat is automatic and can contribute important insight into website and web application quality and availability. Web server logs are usually access logs, common error logs, custom logs, and W3C logs. W3C logs are used mainly by web servers to log web-related events, including web logs. Operating systems can also generate dump files. Such a file provides a log of the different processes running and being loaded for the system at a particular point in time. These files may also include data related to what was loaded into memory.

Unlike a security log, the application and system logs are available for all users to view. You can use the application log to determine how well an application is running. The system log shows events that occur on an individual system. You can configure settings such as the size of the log file and filtering of events. Event logging is used for troubleshooting or notifying administrators of unusual circumstances. Be sure that you have the log file size set properly, that the size is monitored, and that the logs are periodically archived and cleared.

ExamAlert

Carefully consider where you store log files to keep intruders from gaining access to them. By doing so, you eliminate the ability for intruders to cover their tracks.

Table 28.1 lists and describes the fields and their descriptions for Windows events from the Windows Event Viewer.

TABLE 28.1 **Field Names and Associated Description for Windows Events**

Field Name	Field Description
Type	The type of the event, such as error, warning, or information
Time	The date and time on the local computer when the event occurred
Computer	The computer on which the event occurred
Provider Type	The type of event that generated the event, such as a Windows event log
Provider Name	The name of the event, such as Application or Security
Source	The application that logged the event, such as Microsoft SQL Server
Event ID	The Windows event number
Description	A description of the event

The Event ID and Description fields are especially important. The Event ID field makes it easy to research an event in the Microsoft Knowledge Base, and the Description text usually explains what happened in simple language.

Other operating systems also have built-in and downloadable tools that enable you to view statistics about the system, such as CPU usage, memory usage, hard drive space, bandwidth usage, temperature, fan speeds, battery usage, uptime, and the top five processes. In addition, third-party programs can monitor network health. These programs can monitor the entire network, including devices such as modems, printers, routers, switches, and hubs.

To monitor the health of all systems, you install agents on the machines and then monitor those agents from a central location. For example, Simple Network Management Protocol (SNMP) is an application layer protocol whose purpose is to collect statistics from TCP/IP devices.

The nuances of system logging and monitoring are varied and detailed, but system logs are broadly classified as follows:

▶ **System event logs:** These logs record the events that occur across the system and, most notably, that are related to the operating system. Keep in mind that these logs are specific to the system, not the user interacting with the system. Examples include hardware failures, drivers that do not load properly, and issues related to performance.

▶ **Audit logs:** Audit logs help ensure proper process and provide a useful record for auditors. Such logs provide security information such as data on successful and unsuccessful login attempts, user creation and deletion, log data deletion, user privilege modification, and file access. These logs also provide accountability and, in the case of an incident, give a record of what occurred for forensics and recovery purposes.

▶ **Security logs:** These logs contain events specific to systems and application security. Security solutions deployed within the network—for example, anti-malware software, intrusion detection systems, remote access software, vulnerability management software, authentication servers, network quarantine systems, routers, and firewalls—are a major source of such logs.

▶ **Access logs:** These logs provide information about requests and connections between systems. This can include, for example, connections between an LDAP client and a directory server (which might include details such as the IP address) and records related to the binding operation. Web servers are another common source of access logs. For example,

a web server logs access to each resource, such as a page or an image. Included in the log entry are details such as IP address, browser, operating system, referring page, and a date and time stamp.

> **ExamAlert**
>
> System logs vary. Be able to recognize event, audit, security, and access logs and be sure you understand when each would be used in specific scenarios.

Figure 28.2 shows an example of Windows Event Viewer, from which Windows logs can be viewed; this figure shows the Security log. Systems generate sizable logs. When dealing with a large volume of logs and events, anomalies occur, and it can be difficult to find or recognize the anomalies. Intrusion detection system logs tend to have better automatic processing to find anomalies in network traffic than system and event logs.

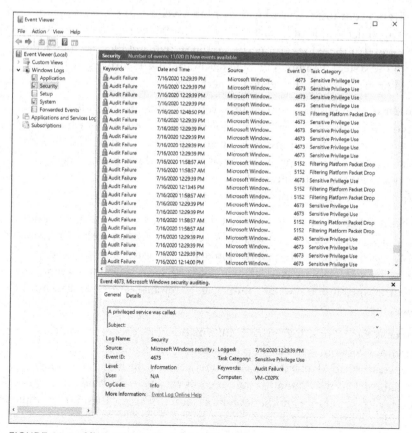

FIGURE 28.2   **Microsoft Windows Event Viewer Security log**

To detect log file anomalies, the data needs to be collected, cleaned, structured, and then analyzed. Anomaly detection deduces dynamic thresholds by learning a baseline or pattern of events. Data mining techniques are often used in the analysis phase. Because systems don't always stay static, dynamic rules can be combined with data mining techniques to produce valid anomalies.

The capability to correlate information across various data sources is paramount. Event correlation helps identify anomalies and behaviors that warrant additional investigation. Although anomaly-detection tools can automate anomaly detection in logs, it is important to understand the system. Sometimes manual analysis is required to detect anomalies.

The following are a few other tools related to logging that you should be familiar with:

▶ **Syslog:** *Syslog* is a decades-old standard for message logging. It is available on most network devices (such as routers, switches, and firewalls) as well as printers and Unix/Linux-based systems. Over a network, a syslog server listens for and then logs data messages coming from the syslog client, which can help in identification and detailed investigation of security incidents. Rsyslog and syslog-ng are similar but build on the capabilities of syslog by adding support for advanced filtering, configuration, and output.

▶ **journalctl:** *Journalctl* is a tool for querying journald, which is the logging service for Linux-based systems. Unlike syslog, journald can't log to remote locations, but it provides a mechanism to easily forward logs to syslog.

▶ **nxlog:** *nxlog* is used for centralized logging across various platforms, supporting myriad different log types and formats.

ExamAlert

The exam might ask a question regarding a log you aren't familiar with. Take your time to examine the sample log. Particularly note the source and destination IP addresses, which may be abbreviated SRC and DST. The terms *local* and *remote* might also be used. In addition, a log might show an IP address as a source pointing to the destination with the notation -> between the source and destination.

Network Activity

An incident investigator can take advantage of a number of tools related to monitoring network activity, which is usually required as part of incident analysis and investigation. Three common types of tools are bandwidth monitors, network flow data, and protocol analyzers.

A protocol analyzer is a good tactical tool for an investigator, but it lacks the ability to scale across an entire organization, given the need to target the implementation of probes in specific areas of the organization. For an investigation, however, this may not be an issue. Network flow activity, on the other hand, can complement direct packet capture.

> **Note**
>
> Network activity monitors essentially provide metadata about network communications. Metadata such as source and destination and protocol information are vital for investigations. Metadata may not in and of itself seem particularly valuable or sensitive, but it can provide valuable clues that help in piecing together details and activity. *Metadata* is simply data that provides information about other data. Metadata is very useful in regard to investigations, and practically everything digital contains metadata, including files and email. A digital photograph, for example, contains metadata on file type, size, and dates. In addition, a photograph taken with a mobile device may also contain the location where the photo was taken, what type of device was used, and all the camera settings.

Bandwidth monitoring tools are useful for identifying DDoS attacks, malicious host activity, data exfiltration, and other suspicious behavior. They help identify interfaces, applications, users, and protocols that are consuming bandwidth. Bandwidth monitoring tools can be as simple as those available as part of every operating system to more enterprise-oriented networking solutions, such as those that are part of a network flow solution. Figure 28.3 shows the Activity Monitor, which provides bandwidth monitoring for macOS. This utility can be useful, for example, for quickly understanding what applications or services are having a large impact on the network bandwidth. In Figure 28.3, you can see that the traffic is sorted by bytes received. This is not necessarily a security issue, but it indicates that someone is streaming music!

Process Name	Sent Bytes	Rcvd Bytes ∨	Sent Packets	Rcvd Packets	PID	Ports
mDNSResponder	2.4 MB	10.5 MB	8,145	39,507	290	79 _mo
Spotify Helper	60 KB	8.4 MB	107	6,161	41332	94 mw
Google Chrome Helper	1.1 MB	7.6 MB	5,708	21,260	872	194 mw
Spotify	766 KB	4.6 MB	2,339	10,799	41323	578 mw
wssa-ui	164 KB	4.4 MB	20,906	73,263	774	182 mw
biometrickitd	418 KB	1.1 MB	2,641	3,031	461	88 root
apsd	878 KB	1.1 MB	2,212	2,122	171	219 root
Google Drive File Stream	1.1 MB	514 KB	1,778	1,329	849	483 mw
dnscrypt-proxy	2.0 MB	397 KB	8,830	8,838	45801	21 nob
netbiosd	52 KB	263 KB	603	2,879	949	24 _net
mobileactivationd	320 KB	238 KB	1,734	1,708	460	69 root
UserEventAgent	300 KB	219 KB	2,735	2,708	128	748 root
GlobalProtect	3 KB	204 KB	9	35	761	340 mw
wssad	4.4 KB	164 KB	73,263	20,906	436	84 root
commerce	15 KB	90 KB	53	101	663	101 mw
syspolicyd	39 KB	85 KB	126	93	214	172 root
ClearPassOnGuard	1 KB	66 KB	11	1,842	772	183 mw
homed	2 KB	55 KB	10	54	652	171 mw
Safari Networking	43 KB	54 KB	165	367	1178	130 mw
parsecd	6 KB	51 KB	7	40	646	80 mw
Google Chrome	4 KB	47 KB	21	154	822	1,133 mw
OnGuardService	33 KB	34 KB	919	926	140	36 root
Microsoft Word	35 KB	29 KB	60	54	7040	2,202 mw
Privacy Dashboard (Safari)	6 KB	29 KB	50	51	1181	162 mw
dns-updater	3 KB	29 KB	78	78	169	70 root
appstoreagent	3 KB	23 KB	19	26	882	125 mw
Box	5 KB	22 KB	21	36	800	243 mw
SubmitDiagInfo	3 KB	16 KB	88	75	459	58 root
rapportd	12 KB	13 KB	58	81	639	153 mw
nxtcoordinator	2.5 MB	13 KB	2,939	243	181	47 root
Firefox	7 KB	11 KB	138	142	19876	1,955 mw
Active Trader Pro	914 bytes	10 KB	3	9	62141	250 mw
trustd	1 KB	6 KB	4	12	624	241 mw
LastPass	5 KB	6 KB	28	22	1200	298 mw
Rakuten Cash Back (Safari)	6 KB	4 KB	25	21	1186	166 mw

Packets in:	8,358,491	Data received:	4.57 GB
Packets out:	12,489,083	Data sent:	1.31 GB
Packets in/sec:	84	Data received/sec:	9.19 KB
Packets out/sec:	160	Data sent/sec:	17.9 KB

FIGURE 28.3 **Activity Monitor for macOS**

Protocol Analyzers

Protocol analyzers, also known as packet sniffers, help you troubleshoot network issues by directly capturing packet-level information across the network. These applications capture packets and can conduct protocol decoding by turning the information into readable data for analysis. Protocol analyzers can do more than just look at packets. They are useful in many other areas of network management, such as monitoring the network for unexpected, unwanted, and unnecessary traffic. Protocol analyzers can identify individual protocols, specific endpoints, and sequential access attempts. These applications capture packets and can conduct protocol decoding, which involves turning the information into readable data for analysis. Protocol analyzers are often used for network management and monitoring, and they are also valuable tools for security investigators. A network running slowly could indicate an attack, and a protocol

analyzer can be used to identify port information and traffic type, which may be useful in an investigation to understand malicious activity.

Network Flow

NetFlow was originally introduced by Cisco. The term has since become synonymous with any network flow monitoring utilities. *NetFlow* collects packets as they are entering or exiting a network, via a router interface. A flow is considered to be a set of packets in a specific period that share common characteristics, such as the same source, destination, and protocol. NetFlow collects the packets, which are then provided to a NetFlow collector. A NetFlow application can then analyze the data, which is useful for incident investigations for intrusion analysis. An alternative to NetFlow is sFlow (sampled flow), which is also used for network monitoring. *sFlow* samples packets and provides analysis to identify unauthorized network activity and investigate DDoS attacks. Network flow activity builds a summary of the communication between two points on a network. IPFIX (Internet Protocol Flow Information Export) is based on a NetFlow implementation and serves as an industry standard for the export of flow information from network devices.

Cram Quiz

Answer these questions. The answers follow the last question. If you cannot answer these questions correctly, consider reading this chapter again until you can.

1. What is the term for tying individual events together to provide meaningful alerts?
   - ○ **A.** Event correlation
   - ○ **B.** Alert respondence
   - ○ **C.** Event mutuality
   - ○ **D.** Alert aggregation

2. You have been tasked with setting up a remote logging facility to send logs from various applications and network devices. Which of the following is the best choice?
   - ○ **A.** sFlow
   - ○ **B.** journalctl
   - ○ **C.** Syslog
   - ○ **D.** NetFlow

3. Which of the following provides information about other data?

- ○ **A.** nxlog
- ○ **B.** SNMP
- ○ **C.** syslog-ng
- ○ **D.** Metadata

Cram Quiz Answers

Answer 1: A. Event correlation, often performed by security tools such as a SIEM systems, provides the ability to tie together individual log entries from across systems into meaningful and actionable alerts. Answers B, C, and D are incorrect.

Answer 2: C. A syslog server can listen for clients, thus acting as a remote logging facility. Answer B is incorrect as journalctl is only used to query journald. journald is a logging service, but it is not capable of logging to remote locations. Answers A and D are incorrect because these are both related to monitoring network flow packets.

Answer 3: D. Metadata is data that provides information about other data. Metadata is useful in regard to investigations, and practically everything digital contains metadata, including files and email. Answer A is incorrect because nxlog is used for centralized logging across various platforms and supports a myriad of different log types and formats. Answer B is incorrect because Simple Network Management Protocol (SNMP) is an application layer protocol whose purpose is to collect statistics from TCP/IP devices. Answer C is incorrect because syslog-ng is a log management solution that helps improve the performance of a SIEM system.

What Next?

If you want more practice on this chapter's exam objective before you move on, remember that you can access all of the Cram Quiz questions on the Pearson Test Prep software online. You can also create a custom exam by objective with the Online Practice Test. Note any objective you struggle with and go to that objective's material in this chapter.

CHAPTER 29

Incident Mitigation

This chapter covers the following official Security+ exam objective:

▶ 4.4 Given an incident, apply mitigation techniques or controls to secure an environment.

Essential Terms and Components

▶ application allow list

▶ application block list/deny list

▶ quarantine

▶ isolate

▶ containment

▶ segmentation

▶ secure orchestration, automation, and response (SOAR)

▶ runbook

▶ playbook

Applying techniques to mitigate an incident is a critical part of the incident response process. Recall from Chapter 27, "Incident Response," the primary phases of the incident response process. Applying mitigation techniques or controls in order to secure an environment is key to the containment, eradication, and recovery phases.

Containment and Eradication

Incident mitigation requires containment and eradication of the threat. *Containment* usually isn't a long-term solution. Where initial configuration errors exist, eradication may simply involve fixing those errors. On the other hand, eradication may also be short term. The primary purpose of incident response is to reduce or prevent further damage

from an incident. This usually involves reducing the attacker's access. While not always ideal, the most immediate way to stop an incident that is still in progress is to shut down the affected systems. Shutting down systems impacts operations and so isn't usually a viable solution, and it may not even be feasible because of the impact. It's important to find a balance between shutting things down completely and letting the attack run rampant. This balancing act usually has operational repercussions, but shutting down systems is usually a short-term means to stop the bleeding until longer-term solutions and remediation strategies can be put in place. It is usually more appropriate and often necessary to make immediate changes to security systems, such as implementing firewall, router, and endpoint configuration changes. There are a number of ways an incident can be mitigated, including the following:

► Blocking unauthorized access

► Quarantining, cleaning, and removing malware

► Blocking unauthorized access

► Blocking sources such as email, websites, and IP addresses

► Approving source IP addresses and services that should be allowed

► Blocking ports, services, and applications

► Modifying data loss prevention (DLP) scanning to look at outbound files for larger data sizes

► Redirecting URLs

► Isolating workstations and networked systems

The following sections cover various technologies that are useful in mitigating threats and how they can be used to help mitigate the impact of an incident.

ExamAlert

The exam requires you to draw on knowledge from multiple chapters for this objective. In addition to being familiar with the content covered in this chapter, you need to be familiar with related content covered in Part III, "Implementation."

Quarantining

Anti-malware endpoint solutions should be applied on endpoints, including servers. Ideally if a machine becomes infected, it should be *isolated* from the rest of the machines by being removed from the network. Most anti-malware

solutions used today are fairly effective. Even so, new malware types or zero-day threats may get through. In addition, users might disable security software if they are able to do so because it interferes with programs that are currently installed on the machine. As a result, it may be necessary to isolate a system and ensure that the machine is scanned. An important function provided by anti-malware solutions is the ability to *quarantine* infected files. Quarantining a file does not delete it or clean it. Rather, quarantining involves moving a file to a managed and safe location so that it does not affect anyone else or spread.

Malware usually seeks to exploit a vulnerability. This means there are three basic types of systems during such an incident:

▶ Infected systems

▶ Patched systems

▶ Unpatched systems

Whereas infected systems should be isolated and malicious files quarantined, unpatched systems should be attended to in parallel. You essentially need to inoculate them against the malware by ensuring that endpoint security solutions are updated and patching the systems if a patch is available.

Configuration Changes

When systems can't be shut down, the impact of an attack can often be mitigated through temporary configuration changes. In addition to firewall and application configuration changes, which are discussed shortly, the following changes can mitigate an incident:

▶ **Content filtering/URL filtering:** Content filtering is particularly useful for limiting email and web content from known sources. During an attack, filters may need to be adjusted to limit further damage. For example, emails with certain known characteristics can be blocked, based on the subject, the sender, the body, or the attachment.

▶ **Certificate revocation:** Certificates ensure trusted secure communication between clients and servers. However, to mitigate an attack in which the attacker has a trusted certificate or an upstream trusted authority has been compromised, revocation of the certificate or trust may be needed.

▶ **DLP:** Data loss prevention rules can be adjusted to prevent data from being exfiltrated.

Firewalls

Firewalls act as gatekeepers for hosts and networks. Firewalls are not implemented to completely isolate computers and networks. While they do block access, allowing proper access is a key function. As a result, firewalls provide a point of entry. During an incident, modifying the rules on a firewall can have a huge impact on ensuring that damage is mitigated. Firewalls can be configured to block, for example, certain locations and ports. They can also be very specific, such as blocking access from a particular host. Configuration changes on a firewall can be particularly helpful in mitigating several types of attacks, such as phishing attacks, session hijacking, and exposed hosts. General good practices should be followed on the initial configuration of a firewall rule set. However, mitigating an incident may require more precision or loosening of the rule set.

Keep in mind the following regarding firewall rules:

► Rules can be inbound, outbound, or both.

► Rules can include services, which specify the type of traffic or port number.

► Rules can be set to allow or deny.

► Rules can be wildcarded.

► Rules can be set based on priority.

Firewall configurations usually start by blocking all traffic by default and then allowing only specific traffic in and out. Over time, however, a firewall may become quite porous, despite efforts to have limited access. Correctly configuring a firewall can keep the firewall functioning well. A Layer 4 network firewall rule allows you to control the following components:

► Permission

► Traffic protocol

► Source IP address

► Destination IP address

► Destination port

You can be very specific with the rules, which makes mitigating incidents with firewall configuration changes effective. For example, consider malware in an environment that is communicating outbound on port 80 to a specific command and control server. On one hand, a simple firewall rule change to block

outbound port 80 would be effective, but it would also block all web traffic. A rule could be implemented, for example, to block port 80 traffic (or even all traffic) to the particular IP address of the command and control server or to a range of IP addresses.

Remember that firewalls also play an important role in *segmentation*, such as isolating the protected network from the public network through a DMZ. Depending on the incident, further configuration changes may be needed to limit access into or out of the DMZ or to deploy additional segmentation capabilities. A virtual local area network (VLAN) can also be created to limit access and reduce the attack surface. A VLAN logically unites network nodes into the same broadcast domain, regardless of their physical attachment to the network. VLANs provide logical separation of a physical network.

Application Control

Recall the difference between allow lists and block lists. *Application allow lists* don't attempt to block unwanted applications and servers as *application block/ deny lists* do. Applications allowed or approved lists permit only known good applications, allowing only specific programs to be executed; any program that is not specifically approved is blocked.

In application allow lists, an organization approves software applications that are permitted to be used on assets. Only those approved applications can be run. The primary purpose of allow lists is to protect resources from harmful applications. For example, in Microsoft environments, AppLocker can be used to allow applications based on the following three conditions:

- ▶ Publisher, for digitally signed files

- ▶ Path, which identifies an application by its location

- ▶ File hash, which uses a system-computed cryptographic hash

AppLocker rules merely allow or prevent an application from launching. They have no control over how an application behaves after it is launched.

> **ExamAlert**
>
> Application allow lists explicitly defines the applications allowed to be run and is useful in preventing users and attackers from executing unauthorized applications.

As with many other control technologies, false positives can result when applications are updated or new applications are installed. Application allow list

information thus needs to stay updated. The administrative and maintenance overhead associated with complex solutions is therefore higher, as is the overhead when a allow list is not automated.

> **ExamAlert**
>
> When security is a concern, application allow lists are a better option than block/deny lists because it allows organizations to maintain strict control over the apps employees are approved to use.

Block list/deny lists are generally done to reduce security-related issues, particularly where bad actors are known. During an incident, an otherwise allowable destination or application can be denied. Many mobile device management (MDM) systems employ the use of allow or deny lists. If an MDM system prohibits the use of a certain application, the end user will not be able to use it. This could be an effective approach, for example, if a previously allowed application now presents an attack vector.

Other configuration changes that may be required include application segmentation and containerization. These methods are often used in conjunction with mobile management as a way to apply policies to mobile devices. They provide an authenticated, encrypted area of the mobile device that can be used to separate sensitive corporate information from the user's personal use of the device. Additional benefits of containerization are capabilities to do the following:

- ▶ Isolate apps
- ▶ Control app functions
- ▶ Delete container information
- ▶ Remotely wipe the device

Secure Orchestration, Automation, and Response (SOAR)

Secure orchestration, automation, and response (SOAR) is a technology stack consisting of orchestration and automation along with threat intelligence and incident response. Essentially, the platform ingests data from various sources and then applies workflows that can be integrated across multiple systems into specific actions. Orchestration is the process of ingesting and combining the different sources of data and coordinating the workflows. Many workflows still

require manual steps, but many other steps can be automated. This automation allows systems to take specific actions without human interaction. SOAR systems combine data, people, technology, and process to do the following:

▶ Prioritize and manage security operations activities

▶ Formalize incident response steps for consistency to ensure that best practices are followed

▶ Automate responses for quick containment

SOAR systems can support a number of different use cases. As related to incident mitigation, SOAR systems can use incident-related data to map operational playbooks into a digital format to automate workflows and response.

The idea of automating playbooks is to provide efficient and consistent response to incidents. A *playbook* provides manual orchestration of incident response. For example, specific incidents and threats have their own playbooks. As a result, the response that an organization takes is formalized in a step-by-step procedure.

The incident response plans covered in Chapter 27 provide general governance over incident response, whereas playbooks provide more meaningful steps for specific incident types. An incident response playbook provides specific guidance based on the incident and is similar to a *runbook* used by IT operations for reference for routine procedures administrators perform.

> **ExamAlert**
>
> A SOAR platform is valuable for incident mitigation because it helps in automating data gathering and response. Specific technical response techniques can be automated for the most severe vulnerabilities and threats, such as automatically patching systems or making firewall rule configuration changes.

A SOAR system can assist with orchestration and automation in a number of ways, including the following:

▶ **Updating and revoking certificates:** Queries from a certificate management system can identify expiring certificates. This data can then be mapped to user information in a directory system. Then an email is automatically sent to the user to take the proper actions. Finally, the SOAR system can later check to ensure that proper action was taken and, if not, continue escalation automatically.

▶ **Dealing with malicious network traffic:** Aggregated threat alerts enriched with additional data can then take automated actions. This could include, for example, closing specific ports on specific host-based firewalls only. It could also include IP address or domain blocking at the network-based firewall or updating of content and URL filters.

▶ **Preventing data loss:** Based on specific DLP alerts, SOAR can help automate notifications and combine an alert with additional data to understand the threat. This can include, for example, isolating the host and blocking the data path or informing the cloud application security solution to remove a shared link to a sensitive file.

Cram Quiz

Answer these questions. The answers follow the last question. If you cannot answer these questions correctly, consider reading this chapter again until you can.

1. Your administrators remotely access web servers in the DMZ only from the internal network over SSH. However, these servers have come under attack via SSH from the IP address 93.184.216.34. Which of the following should you do to stop this attack?

   ○ **A.** Configure a rule to block outbound SSH requests to 93.184.216.34

   ○ **B.** Shut down the SSH service on all web servers

   ○ **C.** Add a rule to block inbound requests on port 22

   ○ **D.** Add a rule to block port 21 inbound requests from 93.184.216.34

2. Your organization was recently the victim of a large-scale phishing attack. Your manager has tasked you with automating response to quickly notify users and, if feasible, automatically block outbound requests to the attacker's web page. Which of the following will accomplish this goal?

   ○ **A.** Email the users to warn them of the phishing attack

   ○ **B.** Update URL filters to block the site the phishing attack points to

   ○ **C.** Email the users to warn them of the phishing attack and send an email to the security administrator to have him configure a URL filter to block the site that the phishing attack points to

   ○ **D.** Implement SOAR or workflows to trigger emails to users and to use threat intelligence to automatically configure URL filters to block the attacker's site

3. Which of the following are benefits of application allow lists? (Select two.)

○ **A.** Prevents users and attackers from executing unauthorized applications

○ **B.** Allows end users to freely use any application that has not been explicitly denied

○ **C.** Allows organizations to maintain strict control over applications employees can use

○ **D.** Blocks specific applications from being executed

Cram Quiz Answers

Answer 1: C. Because your administrators access the servers from the internal network, you don't need to worry about preventing valid access on SSH port 22 from the outside. As a result, you should just close all inbound requests. Answer B wouldn't allow the administrators to access the systems even internally. The port for SSH is 22 and not port 21, which is FTP. Answers A, B, and D are incorrect.

Answer 2: D. A SOAR platform provides orchestration and automation across systems and would accomplish the goal of automatically providing these functions when tied in with the other systems. Answers A and B are only partial solutions, and answer C doesn't achieve the goal of automation.

Answer 3: A and C. An application allow list describes what applications can be launched. It thus prevents the execution of unauthorized applications, which are all applications that are not explicitly allowed. Answers B and D describe the explicit block as a result of block/deny list and are incorrect answer choices.

What Next?

If you want more practice on this chapter's exam objective before you move on, remember that you can access all of the Cram Quiz questions on the Pearson Test Prep software online. You can also create a custom exam by objective with the Online Practice Test. Note any objective you struggle with and go to that objective's material in this chapter.

CHAPTER 30
Digital Forensics

This chapter covers the following official Security+ exam objective:

▶ 4.5 Explain the key aspects of digital forensics.

Essential Terms and Components

▶ legal hold

▶ chain of custody

▶ time offset

▶ order of volatility

▶ preservation

▶ e-discovery

▶ non-repudiation

▶ strategic intelligence/counterintelligence

Forensics is the process of preserving evidence and collecting data. During the process, the following actions should be performed:

▶ Document an investigation from initial notification through conclusion.

▶ Locate data and any devices of potential evidentiary value.

▶ Identify data of interest.

▶ Establish an order of volatility to identify the first level of data capture desired.

▶ Eliminate external mechanisms of modification.

▶ Collect all data of potential evidentiary value.

▶ Create forensic duplicates of data for review.

▶ Store original data and devices in a manner that preserves integrity.

▶ Perform forensic evaluation and document findings (or lack thereof).

▶ Report findings as appropriate.

With information systems, forensics relates to both e-discovery and data recovery. *E-discovery* concerns the discovery of electronically stored information. Data recovery involves retrieving lost or corrupted data from media when it is otherwise inaccessible by typical means. During the forensics process, many of the requirements and methods are related to e-discovery and data recovery. The former is particularly important because incidents are often a part of legal matters. Data recovery is commonly associated with common failures (such as hard drive crashes), and the forensics process also involves data recovery when data might have been deleted or encrypted.

> **ExamAlert**
>
> From a forensics standpoint, *preservation* is a common theme, especially preservation of evidence for use in legal proceedings.

Data Breach Notifications

A data breach is often the reason for a forensic investigation. As a result, it's important for an organization to understand regulatory laws. Furthermore, international regulations are increasingly important as a company does more business globally. Because outsourcing and the cloud are commonly used, companies of all sizes should be concerned about data breaches. Most violations are handled by management, the information technology team, and the human resources department. Civil and criminal violations aren't only a corporate or organizational matter; they are also a governmental matter outside the organization. Likewise, data breaches may also need to be governed outside the organization. A policy statement should include the jurisdiction and data residency requirements for an organization. Organizations partnering with third parties, such as those offering cloud services, need to understand their right to audit the service provider and what happens following a data breach.

The first data breach notification law in the United States was California's S.B. 1386, a bill that was enacted in August 2002 and put into effect in July 2003. Almost all U.S. states and territories now have enacted breach notification laws

that require organizations to notify consumers whose personal information has been compromised. Beyond state and federal data breach notification, organizations formed in the United States are also bound by laws related to the protection and proper disclosure of data (see Chapter 32, "Regulations, Standards, and Frameworks").

Organizations that operate on a multinational level generally must comply with both national and international regulations. For example, U.S. entities that have data transactions within the European Union (EU) need to meet General Data Protection Regulation (GDPR) requirements. Because some of the GDPR provisions are stricter than U.S. laws and regulations, initial organizational data protection standards might not be strong enough to comply with EU regulations. For example, U.S. organizations must be aware of these international privacy laws, among others:

▶ **Australia:** Privacy Act and Privacy Amendment Act

▶ **Canada:** Personal Information Protection and Electronics Document Act

▶ **United Kingdom:** Data Protection Act

▶ **EU:** Privacy Directive

▶ **Japan:** Computer Processed Personal Data Protection Act

▶ **Germany:** Federal Protection Act

Different countries have different approaches to notifying customers. This is especially important in a global economy. Notification of affected customers should be addressed in an organization's incident response plan. If an organization resides in an area that is not subject to a specific notification law, the organization should adhere to common law liability and treat each incident on a case-by-case basis. In addition, state and provincial laws might require compliance.

> **ExamAlert**
>
> National laws and federal regulations supersede state and provincial laws.

Regulations can affect many aspects of security planning, investigations, and forensics. For example, changes to the Federal Rules of Civil Procedure (FRCP) made requests for electronic data a standard part of the discovery process in federal lawsuits. This means that an organization needs to have a record-retention policy.

It is imperative to know the legal ramifications of any incident that occurs. Be sure to check the state laws concerning privacy, liability, and spam. Consider an example of what can happen. Imagine that your state has a strict antispam law. The company email server was misconfigured and has an open relay that allows it to be used for spamming purposes. A spammer sends email on the price of gasoline in Europe to 500,000 people. This could prove fatal to the company. First, all email would cease. Your ISP would put the company's IP address on the spammers' list. The open relay would have to be fixed and validated before you could send any email. You would be reported for spamming and fined $10 per email. This could put your company out of business. The company likely would have insurance, but there's a good chance the insurance company would not cover this type of incident.

Finally, compliance with laws and regulations comes into play during complex third-party relationships. As part of a comprehensive monitoring program, an organization should periodically conduct regular assessments of business relationships to verify that all third parties conform to laws, regulations, and established policies and procedures.

Strategic Intelligence/ Counterintelligence Gathering

The forensics process places heavy emphasis on proper preservation and collection. Incidents such as a breach might require further intelligence gathering and counterintelligence. Considering the complexity of computer systems, after a breach occurs, it is necessary to make sure that attackers do not still have footprints in the organization. For example, attackers could remain active within the environment or might have placed persistent threats for subsequent access. Active logging is a common intelligence gathering tool used during the forensics process. Active logging cannot tell you what happened in the past, however: It can only examine what has happened since it was put into operation.

Many organizations have *strategic intelligence* and *counterintelligence* capabilities in place already. Forensically, these capabilities are similar to those of a DVR system for video recording: Investigators can easily replay what happened across the computer networks. Considering counterintelligence is also important when using such tools. The forensics process might seek to keep adversaries from knowing they are being monitored.

Track Person-hours

The cost of a forensic investigation can run into thousands of dollars. As soon as the work proposal or court order is executed, person-hours tracking and administrative work begin. Costs are an important part of project planning. Calculating the number of person-hours and other related expenses provides a way to estimate that investigation costs are within the budgeted amount. The costs include the acquisition, investigation, and reporting of time and expenses. An organization needs to assess the costs of an investigation against the potential benefits to determine whether the investigation would be cost-effective and technically feasible.

Order of Volatility

When a potential security breach must be reviewed, the digital forensics process comes into play. Data of potential evidentiary value can be stored in many different forms in a subject system. Some storage locations preserve the data even when a system is powered off, whereas others hold data for only a brief interval before it is lost or overwritten. Even the process of evaluation can modify or overwrite these volatile storage areas. Shutting off a running system might completely wipe all data stored in active memory. In some cases, evidence that is relevant to a case might exist only temporarily.

Evidence collection should follow the order of volatility. Specifically, during the collection process, the forensics team should proceed from the most volatile evidence to the least volatile pieces. Evidence can be lost when a computer is powered down. If you can capture volatile data before you unplug the computer, you can get a snapshot of the system at the time you arrived on the scene. You should collect the following information:

▶ System date and time

▶ Current network connections

▶ Current open ports and applications listening on those ports

▶ Applications currently running

Data capture is highly dependent on the order of volatility, in which the capture and examination of more durable storage can eliminate data of potential evidentiary value at more volatile levels. Consider the *order of volatility* for a typical system:

1. **Registers and caches:** Data stored within the CPU's registers and cache levels. This data might remain for only nanoseconds before it is overwritten by normal system operations.

2. **Routing and process tables:** Data stored within networking and other active devices. Ongoing operations can modify this data externally.

3. **Kernel statistics:** Data regarding current kernel operations. This data can be in constant transit between cache and main memory.

4. **Main memory:** Data stored within the system's RAM storage.

5. **Temporary file systems:** Data stored within elements of system memory allocated as temporary file storage, such as a RAM disk, or within virtual system drives.

6. **Secondary memory:** Data stored in nonvolatile storage, such as a hard drive or other form of media that retains data values after a system shutdown.

7. **Removable media:** Nonvolatile removable media such as backup tape storage media.

8. **Write-once storage:** Nonvolatile media that is not subject to later overwriting or modification, such as CD-Rs, DVD-Rs, and printouts.

> **ExamAlert**
>
> Order of volatility demands that evidence be collected first from the most volatile systems (such as registers and caches) and later from the least volatile systems (such as archival media). Be sure that if you are presented with a list like the preceding one, you are able to put them in the correct order of volatility.

Chain of Custody

The *chain of custody* provides a clear record of the path evidence takes from acquisition to disposal. This concept establishes provenance and is critical to the integrity of the forensics process. Provenance marks an origin and records ownership even as possession changes. It provides for authenticity and *non-repudiation* by clearly establishing the origin and proof of custody.

> **Note**
>
> Cloud environments present great challenges to determining provenance, particularly as the infrastructure hardware is in physical locations unknown by and not managed by the end consumer. As a result, the data available within the cloud environment and the provenance of the data are crucial. In particular, metadata about the data objects and user interactions may provide origin and other historical clues for forensic investigations.

Key to any form of forensic investigation is adherence to standards for the identification, collection, storage, and review of evidence. It is important to create a log of all actions taken, including any inferences and causative details used to identify data of potential evidentiary value. This log should support the chain of custody for any evidentiary data, as well as track person-hours, expense, details of identification, and contact data for any witnesses and statements provided during an investigation. For evidence to be useful, it must have five properties:

▶ **Admissible:** Evidence must be usable in court or within an organization's practices. It must follow all appropriate legal requirements and guidelines for identification, acquisition, examination, and storage.

▶ **Authentic:** Evidence must be proven to relate to the incident, and any changes must be accounted for in evidence review logs.

▶ **Complete:** In addition to data of evidentiary value, evidentiary gathering must include both directly related data (for example, logging details of the suspect's login) and indirectly related data (for example, a list of all accounts logged into a server when an attack occurred).

▶ **Reliable:** Evidentiary identification, acquisition, review, and storage practices must ensure that the data remains authentic and unmodified to the best extent possible, based on the data's order of volatility.

▶ **Believable:** Evidence must be clear and easy to understand, and it also must be related to the original binary or encrypted data through a process that is clear, documented, and free of manipulation during transition. Raw hexadecimal data is difficult for juries to review, but a chart illustrating the same information must represent the evidentiary data in a manner that another forensic analyst can replicate with the same end result.

Forensics requires vast knowledge of computer hardware, software, and media to protect the chain of custody over the evidence, avoid accidental invalidation or destruction of evidence, and preserve the evidence for future analysis. Computer forensic review involves applying investigative and analytical techniques to acquire and protect potential legal evidence. Therefore, a professional in this field needs to have a detailed understanding of the local, regional, national, and international laws affecting the process of evidence collection and retention, especially in cases involving attacks waged from widely distributed systems located in separate regions.

The practice of forensic analysis is a detailed and exacting one; precise actions must be taken during an investigation. Investigative tasks must not be attempted without training in the hardware, software, network, and legal issues involved in forensic analysis. Consider the major concepts behind computer forensics:

▶ Identify the evidence.

▶ Determine how to preserve the evidence.

▶ Extract, process, and interpret the evidence.

▶ Ensure that the evidence is acceptable in a court of law.

Each state has its own laws that govern how cases can be prosecuted. For cases to be prosecuted, evidence must be properly collected, processed, and preserved. Whereas the corporate world tends to focus on prevention and detection, law enforcement focuses on investigation and prosecution.

Forensic analysis involves establishing a clear chain of custody over the evidence. This relates to the documentation of all transfers of evidence from one person to another, including the date, time, and reason for the transfer and the signatures of both parties involved in the transfer. In other words, it tells how the evidence made it from the crime scene to the courtroom, including documentation on how the evidence was collected, preserved, and analyzed. Every time data of possible evidentiary value is moved, accessed, manipulated, or reviewed, the chain of custody must be maintained, and actions must be logged. Forensic analysis of information might require further law enforcement action, depending on findings and evidentiary data of interest.

> **Note**
>
> As an organization places more data on infrastructures that the organization does not own, security and forensic processes and tools require revaluation to properly protect data and gather forensic evidence.

If you are asked to testify about data that has been recovered or preserved, it is critical that you, the investigating security administrator, be able to prove that no other individuals or agents could have tampered with or modified the evidence. This requires careful collection and preservation of all evidence,

including the detailed logging of investigative access and the scope of the investigation. Defining the scope is crucial to ensure that accidental privacy violations and unrelated exposure do not contaminate the evidence trail. After data is collected, you must secure it in such a manner that you, the investigating official, can state with certainty that the evidence could not have been accessed or modified during your custodial term.

> **ExamAlert**
>
> Proper chain of custody helps ensure that evidence is handled correctly and strictly secured. For evidence to be useful, it must be admissible, authentic, complete, reliable, and believable.

Data Acquisition

Prior to data acquisition, the *legal hold* process ensures that anything that might be relevant to a legal matter is not destroyed. An organization should have a legal hold process to perform e-discovery to preserve and gather such information. A legal hold is an important part of the forensics process during an information breach.

Data acquisition is an important concept that relates to the forensics process. Data acquisition involves gathering data or copying data to an image or other media. Special forensics systems can assist with the process and ensure that the original source media is not modified in any way. Proper data acquisition is vital to ensure completeness and accuracy. It also ensures that the process cannot be repudiated. The data acquisition process includes gathering and capturing the following:

- ▶ System images
- ▶ Network traffic and logs
- ▶ Video
- ▶ Time offset
- ▶ Hashes
- ▶ Screenshots
- ▶ Witnesses

The following sections look at these aspects of data acquisition in more detail.

Capture System Images

The capture of a system image is essentially the creating of a duplicate copy of the media being captured. This often includes capturing individual components such as a memory card, device firmware, or an entire disk drive that contains an operating system (OS), files, and other digital artifacts. These artifacts include items that are not readily available and that may provide clues to previous actions, including items such as those stored in volatile memory, running processes, open network sockets, cached data, and deleted and hidden data.

Drive imaging can be performed in several ways: from the disk to the disk image, from the disk to an image file, and from an image file to a disk. A *forensic image* is a snapshot of a system that is meant to be analyzed and preserved. On the other hand, a *duplicate copy*, also known as a *clone*, is created when the system may be modified in the course of a working investigation.

Regardless of whether direct device-to-device copies of the media or forensic evidence copies are created for examination, the process should be forensically sound. Examination of the media should be conducted in a forensically sound environment—that is, an environment over which the examiner has complete control. You can use a full system image to further examine data in an operational state, although you must put protections in place to prevent external communication through wired and wireless connectivity; it is important to guard against external manipulation and also against the risk that a suspect will be alerted. When available, use a write-blocking device to access the suspect media to capture a system image. You can use software or hardware write blockers. A software write blocker stops any operating system write operations from modifying the media. A hardware write blocker is a physical device that sits between a drive and a controller card.

Data storage should be duplicated using verified forensic utilities. Then only the duplicate should be reviewed in subsequent investigations to protect the original from modification or corruption. Virtual machine (VM) images are acquired either by using tools specifically designed to capture a VM environment or by using built-in vendor tools. System images can usually be easily validated from a forensics standpoint. Other environments are more challenging (for example, big data environments that contain unstructured data spread across diverse environments).

Capture Network Traffic and Logs

Analysts can use data from network traffic to reconstruct and analyze network-based attacks. When deciding what evidence to capture, first identify potential

sources where the breach might have occurred in the networking environment. These resources typically include network traffic and files. After identifying the resources, gather the log files that capture network traffic flows for management devices, servers, workstations, and wireless and mobile devices. Network traffic data is usually recorded to a log or stored in a packet capture file; an examiner can collect the logs along with the packet capture.

Remote access logging occurs on the remote access server or the application server, but in some cases, the client also logs information related to a connection. Each system has a unique method for tracking and logging access, so capturing all related log files is important. Keep in mind that collecting network traffic can pose legal issues, especially if you must capture information that involves privacy or security implications. If logs will be needed as court evidence, an organization might want to collect copies of the original log files, the centralized log files, and interpreted log data in case questions arise about the accuracy of the copying and interpretation processes.

Capture Video and Photographs

If at all possible, after an incident occurs, record video of the entry of all persons into the affected area. Recording the entrance of a forensics team into the area helps you refute claims that evidence was planted at the scene. You might also want to take photographs of the evidence and make notes at the scene. For example, in the event of an intrusion, you might want to take a photograph of a monitor. If the computer will be dissembled onsite for imaging, pictures of the computer should be taken from all angles to document the system hardware components and how they are connected. Carefully photograph the inside of the machine and note the serial number, internal drives, and peripheral components. Label the evidence and then photograph the evidence again after you attach the labels. It might be a good idea to use a 35 mm camera for your photographs. Digital images are easy to manipulate, and film negatives can validate the pictures if questions arise over whether the images were altered. Ideally, one person should handle the documentation while another person handles the evidence. You want to be able to prove that you did not alter any of the evidence.

You can find valuable evidence about physical access in recordings from closed-circuit television (CCTV) systems and other video systems. However, some organizations must deploy adequate signage to state whether camera systems are monitored or merely present for later prosecution of wrongdoing. For example, individuals expecting live monitoring of security cameras might signal to the cameras for assistance during an emergency; in the absence of proper signage, they might be able to later sue the organization. Some

CCTV systems might employ non-visible-spectrum cameras, such as thermal imaging systems that can spot heat blooms and body heat sources even when those sources are otherwise concealed. CCTV systems should be configured to observe access paths and location areas without displaying data, password entry, and similar details.

Record Time Offset

Records should be kept on all data and devices collected, including details such as system *time offset* from a verified time standard (for example, using NTP), nonstandard hardware or equipment configurations, and video codecs available for video manipulation and running services (if the system is in operation). Recording the time offset is critical to an accurate examination when dates and times are at issue, and it should be done at the beginning of any examination.

Keep in mind that just because a computer was seized in a particular time zone does not mean that it is configured for that time zone. Computers can be moved from one zone to another, can be incorrectly configured, and can be deliberately altered, so the time and time zone offset might not be accurate. When computers are examined, their date and time settings should be recorded and compared with the current time to calculate the difference between the two. This difference can then be used as an offset and applied to all the time evidence on the computer. For example, when a computer that is imaged in Mountain Standard Time is analyzed with a tool that is in Eastern Standard Time, the time zone is adjusted to accurately reflect the time of the imaged drive. To resolve these issues, you need to know the machine's BIOS time and the time zone offset for which it is configured so that you can apply the correct time zone offset to your case. The time zone offset in Windows operating systems is stored in the registry.

> **ExamAlert**
>
> Time offset adjustments cannot reveal anything about the accuracy of the events on a computer. The time offset adjustment establishes only the accuracy of the date and time record of the device when it was acquired.

Take Hashes

You should generate checksums or hashes of all data and applications before and after any in-depth analysis is performed to validate that the forensic analysis has not produced unexpected modifications of evidentiary data. After

a drive has been imaged, a hash value of the image should be taken and compared against the hash of the original drive. Matching hashes provide for nonrepudiation and ensure that you did not change anything.

The most common method of taking a hash of a drive is to calculate a hash of the entire drive. Most forensic tool sets include a utility to calculate either a cyclic redundancy check (CRC) or a Message Digest 5 (MD5) hash value. Other valid methods are available to generate a single value for a file or collection of files, but the CRC and MD5 hash values are the most common. Each of these algorithms examines the input and generates a single value. Any changes to the input result in a different value.

After you have ensured the physical integrity of the media, you can mount the media and access it in read-only mode. It is important that you explicitly separate the suspect media from other media during any access to the data. The only safe way to ensure that nothing changes the data on the drive is to use trusted tools to access the media only once. The only reason to directly access suspect media is to copy it for analysis.

Capture Screenshots

You should capture screenshots during the investigation and include them in forensic documentation for later reporting or testimony of the process and resulting findings. These screenshots should supplement photographs of the scene prior to evidence gathering and video of the collection and analysis process. Whenever possible, you should capture and preserve network traffic and logs to aid in the identification of related processes, remote virtual storage systems, and distributed computing functions that might relate to the investigation.

Collect Witness Interviews

Witnesses are an important part of any crime investigation. An investigator who interviews anyone as part of the investigation should create a list of the persons interviewed, including their names, email addresses, and what they saw (when, where, and how). The interviewer should minimize physical distractions such as noise or the presence of other persons. Witnesses should be encouraged to volunteer information without prompting. In cases such as the release of malware, denial-of-service (DoS) attacks, or theft of information, it is sometimes possible to obtain more information than expected just by asking. An interviewer may even end up with a confession if the threat came from an insider.

Cram Quiz

Answer these questions. The answers follow the last question. If you cannot answer these questions correctly, consider reading this chapter again until you can.

1. Organize the following items from the most volatile to the least volatile: removable media, main memory, hard drive, and cache.

   ○ **A.** Removable media, main memory, hard drive, cache

   ○ **B.** Main memory, hard drive, main memory, cache

   ○ **C.** Cache, main memory, hard drive, removable media

   ○ **D.** Cache, hard drive, main memory, removable media

2. What are the five properties required for evidence to be useful?

   ○ **A.** Objectionable, authentic, closed, mendacious, and genuine

   ○ **B.** Didactic, authentic, complete, reliable, and believable

   ○ **C.** Admissible, spurious, contrived, untried, and questionable

   ○ **D.** Admissible, authentic, complete, reliable, and believable

3. Evidence from a recent breach consists of marked tags that indicate who was in possession of evidence on a given date and time. Which of the following does this represent?

   ○ **A.** Chain of custody

   ○ **B.** Time offset

   ○ **C.** Data acquisition

   ○ **D.** Order of volatility

Cram Quiz Answers

Answer 1: C. The correct order, from most volatile to least volatile, is cache, main memory, hard drive, removable media. Keep in mind that a hard drive is considered secondary memory. Answers A, B, and D are incorrect.

Answer 2: D. For evidence to be useful, it must have five properties: admissible, authentic, complete, reliable, and believable. Answers A, B, and C list incorrect choices.

Answer 3: A. The chain of custody provides a clear record of the path evidence takes from acquisition to disposal. Answer B is incorrect because time offset is recorded against a verified time standard. Answer C is incorrect because data acquisition is specific to gathering data or copying data to an image or other media. Answer D is incorrect because the order of volatility has to do with first capturing the data that is most volatile.

What Next?

If you want more practice on this chapter's exam objective before you move on, remember that you can access all of the Cram Quiz questions on the Pearson Test Prep software online. You can also create a custom exam by objective with the Online Practice Test. Note any objective you struggle with and go to that objective's material in this chapter.

PART V

Governance, Risk, and Compliance

> **This part covers the following official Security+ SYO-601 exam objectives for Domain 5.0, "Governance, Risk, and Compliance":**
>
> ▶ 5.1 Compare and contrast various types of controls.
>
> ▶ 5.2 Explain the importance of applicable regulations, standards, or frameworks that impact organizational security posture.
>
> ▶ 5.3 Explain the importance of policies to organizational security.
>
> ▶ 5.4 Summarize risk management processes and concepts.
>
> ▶ 5.5 Explain privacy and sensitive data concepts in relation to security.

For more information on the official CompTIA Security+ SYO-601 exam topics, see the section "Exam Objectives" in the Introduction.

Avoiding risk is often difficult, and sometimes it is even impossible. Thus, effective risk management strategies must be applied to mitigate (reduce) the likelihood and impact of "bad risks" or to enhance (improve) the likelihood and results of "good risks." A good risk might be the chance of a windfall profit or some other beneficial outcome. Most risks that the exam addresses, however, are of the bad risk type. In these cases, an attacker seeks unauthorized access to data or services. This part covers important concepts related to risk management.

Managing risk requires strong governance with an understanding of the goals of the organization, an understanding of the critical functions performed within the organization, and a comprehensive assessment of the risk the organization faces. From this understanding, an organization can develop appropriate policies, plans, and procedures related to organizational security that are commensurate with the overall goals and acceptable risk tolerance and threshold of the organization.

CHAPTER 31

Control Types

This chapter covers the following official Security+ exam objective:

▶ 5.1 Compare and contrast various types of controls.

Essential Terms and Components

▶ managerial control

▶ operational control

▶ technical control

▶ preventive control

▶ detective control

▶ corrective control

▶ deterrent control

▶ compensating control

▶ physical control

To compare controls, it is helpful to understand the general taxonomy of controls. A control is simply a defense or countermeasure put in place to manage risk. If a risk cannot be completely avoided or transferred, but the organization is not willing to completely accept the risk, the most appropriate action is to mitigate the risk. Controls can be classified in several ways, and some controls can apply across various types. At a high level, controls are classified as technical, management, or operational. Controls can be further classified by their functional use or according to the time period during which they are acted upon. For example, functionally, they can be classified as deterrent, preventive, detective, or corrective controls.

Nature of Controls

You can apply three general classifications of controls to mitigate risks, typically by layering defensive controls to protect data with multiple control types. This technique is called a layered defensive strategy, or *defense in depth*. These are the three types of controls:

▶ **Technical:** *Technical controls* are security controls that are executed by technical systems. Technical controls include logical access control systems, security systems, encryption, and data classification solutions.

▶ **Managerial:** *Managerial controls* (or administrative controls) include business and organizational processes and procedures, such as security policies and procedures, personnel background checks, security awareness training, and formal change-management procedures. They are usually controlled by and promulgated with people.

▶ **Operational:** *Operational controls* include organizational culture and *physical controls* that form the outer line of defense against direct access to data, such as protecting backup media; securing output and mobile file storage devices; and paying attention to facility design details, including layout, doors, guards, locks, and surveillance systems.

Functional Use of Controls

The categories of controls just described can be further classified by their functional use or based on the time when they are in use. The following sections describe these controls and provide examples of each of them:

▶ Deterrent

▶ Preventive

▶ Detective

▶ Corrective

Consider the importance of having both detection controls and prevention controls. In a perfect world, we would need only prevention controls. Unfortunately, not all malicious activity can be prevented. As a result, it is important to make detection controls part of a layered security approach. For example, the best-protected banks use both detective controls and preventive controls.

In addition to the locks, bars, and security signs, the bank probably has various detective controls, such as motion detectors and cash register audits.

> **ExamAlert**
>
> Controls work together as a security system and provide layered defense mechanisms for defense in depth.

Deterrent Controls

Deterrent controls are intended to discourage individuals from intentionally violating information security policies or procedures. Deterrents do not necessarily have to be designed to stop unauthorized access. As the name implies, these controls need to help deter access. They usually take the form of a punishment or consequence that makes performing unauthorized activities undesirable. Deterrence involves detecting violations that are attached to some form of punishment that the intruder fears. Examples of deterrent controls are warnings indicating that systems are being monitored. Perhaps you have seen or know someone who has a "Beware of Dog" sign but doesn't actually have a dog.

Preventive Controls

Preventive controls attempt to prevent unwanted events by inhibiting the free use of computing resources. Preventive controls are often hard for users to accept because they restrict free use of resources. Examples of preventive administrative controls include security awareness, separation of duties, access control, security policies and procedures, intrusion prevention systems, firewalls, and anti-malware.

Detective Controls

Detective controls attempt to identify unwanted events after they have occurred. Common technical detective controls include audit trails, intrusion detection systems, system monitoring, checksums, and anti-malware. Common physical detective controls include motion detectors, CCTV monitors, and alarms. Administrative detective controls are used to determine compliance with security policies and procedures. They can include security reviews and audits, mandatory vacations, and rotation of duties.

Corrective Controls

Corrective controls are reactive and provide measures to reduce harmful effects or restore the system that is being affected. Examples of corrective controls include operating system upgrades, data backup restoration, vulnerability mitigation, and anti-malware.

> **Note**
>
> Did you notice that anti-malware is listed as an example for all three types of controls? Anti-malware is preventive because it can block certain potentially dangerous file types from being downloaded. It is detective because it can identify and alert administrators when a file is infected with malware. Finally, it is corrective because it can quarantine or fix infected files.

> **ExamAlert**
>
> Some controls can be multiple types. A visible camera, for example, serves as a detective control (if actively monitored) and also as a deterrent to a would-be attacker, which makes it preventive as well. Without active monitoring by a security guard, however, cameras are likely useful only for later analysis to identify the actor and means following an incident. Security guards, on the other hand, easily serve as both preventive and detective controls. In addition, a security guard can be a corrective control by initiating an immediate response to an incident and potentially alerting others about the identified threat.

Compensating Controls

Compensating controls are alternative controls that are intended to reduce the risk of an existing or potential control weakness. Compensating controls are not a shortcut to compliance or security. They come into play when a business or technological constraint exists and an effective alternate control is used in the current security threat landscape. For example, if separation of duties is required but duties cannot be separated because of company size, compensating controls should be in place. These can include audit trails and transaction logs that someone in a higher position reviews.

We need look no further than our daily lives to find examples and analogies of the various types of controls and compensating controls we encounter every day. In your digital life, you might have met someone who doesn't want to incur the cost (monetary and perceived technical) of running anti-malware software.

That person might compensate, for example, by being extra careful and navigating to only well-known, trusted websites. Or consider parents traveling with a baby but without the normal control of a crib's high rails. Perhaps you can already see the compensating control of the child sleeping in between the parents in bed or among pillows on the floor.

In another practical example, consider that most organizations have well-defined standards for controls that are commensurate with the risk. One such standard might require third-party web-based applications to enforce at least 12-character alphanumeric passwords. If the vendor does not support this, of course, an organization can try to demand it, but until it is a real possibility, the organization can decide not to use that vendor or perhaps consider a temporary measure, such as detailed logging and monitoring of session events or frequent password changes.

Cram Quiz

Answer these questions. The answers follow the last question. If you cannot answer these questions correctly, consider reading this chapter again until you can.

1. Which of the following are functional control types? (Select three.)

   ○ **A.** Deterrent

   ○ **B.** Preventive

   ○ **C.** Compensating

   ○ **D.** Detective

2. A recent audit revealed that most of the organization is not properly handling sensitive data correctly. To address this shortcoming, your organization is implementing computer security awareness training. What type of control is this?

   ○ **A.** Logical

   ○ **B.** Administrative

   ○ **C.** Detective

   ○ **D.** Physical

Cram Quiz Answers

Answer 1: A, B, and D. Functional controls can be deterrent, preventive, detective, and corrective controls. Compensating controls are alternative controls put in place to reduce the risk of an existing or potential control weakness. Thus, answer C is incorrect.

Answer 2: B. This is an example of a managerial or administrative control. Answers A, C, and D are incorrect. While technical controls such as data classification systems and DLP can help address this situation, security awareness training is not of a technical or

logical nature. Awareness training can serve a functional use (for example, deterrent, preventive, detective, or corrective), but given the situation, this was not a detective functional control.

What Next?

If you want more practice on this chapter's exam objective before you move on, remember that you can access all of the Cram Quiz questions on the Pearson Test Prep software online. You can also create a custom exam by objective with the Online Practice Test. Note any objective you struggle with and go to that objective's material in this chapter.

CHAPTER 32

Regulations, Standards, and Frameworks

This chapter covers the following official Security+ exam objective:

▶ 5.2 Explain the importance of applicable regulations, standards, or frameworks that impact organizational security posture.

Essential Terms and Components

▶ General Data Protection Regulation (GDPR)

▶ Payment Card Industry Data Security Standard (PCI DSS)

▶ Center for Internet Security (CIS)

▶ National Institute of Standards and Technology (NIST)

▶ NIST Cybersecurity Framework (CSF)

▶ NIST Risk Management Framework (RMF)

▶ International Organization for Standardization (ISO)

▶ Cloud Security Alliance (CSA)

Industry-Standard Frameworks and Reference Architectures

The security architecture of an organization is based on some type of security framework. If an organization is bound by regulations, it must base its security architecture on these regulations. An organization that is multinational or that does business in another country could be subject to additional restrictions, based on regulatory compliance in that country.

When designing an organizational security architecture, in addition to regulations, the components taken into consideration include standards, frameworks, and guides. *Standards* describe specific mandatory controls based on policies. *Guides*, or guidelines, provide recommendations or good practices. A *framework* generally includes more components than a guide and is used as a basis for the implementation and management of security controls.

Regulatory and Non-regulatory Requirements

Regulatory requirements are created by government agencies and are mandated by law. Regulation can exist on an international, national, or local level. Non-compliance with regulatory requirements can result in serious consequences for organizations, including financial implications such as fines or negative effects on stock values and investor relations. Examples of regulatory requirements for U.S. organizations include the following:

▶ The Health Insurance Portability and Accountability Act (HIPAA) of 1996 sets national standards for protecting health information.

▶ The Gramm–Leach–Bliley Act (GLBA) establishes privacy rules for the financial industry.

▶ The *Payment Card Industry Data Security Standard (PCI DSS)* is designed to reduce fraud and protect customer credit card information.

▶ The Sarbanes–Oxley Act (SOX) governs financial and accounting disclosure information.

The preceding list provides common requirements for U.S. organizations; however, multinational organizations are generally required to comply with both national and international regulations. The *General Data Protection Regulation (GDPR)* is a European Union (EU) law for data protection and privacy that many U.S. organizations comply with.

Non-regulatory requirements are developed by agencies that develop technology, metrics, and standards for the betterment of the science and technology industry. The *National Institute of Standards and Technology (NIST)* is an example of a U.S. non-regulatory organization. The European Union Agency for Network and Information Security (ENISA) is a similar organization that focuses on information security expertise for the EU.

> **ExamAlert**
>
> Many non-regulatory bodies assist organizations by offering guidance in implementing legislation and improving the overall security of critical information infrastructure and networks.

Industry-Specific Frameworks

A framework provides a foundation to strengthen an organization's security posture and guide regulation compliance. Organizations use frameworks to ensure legal compliance, demonstrate security posture, and reduce liability. An organization's decision to use a particular framework might depend on the industry, the organization's location, or the organization's size. Common security frameworks include the following:

▶ The *International Organization for Standardization* (*ISO*) and the International Electrotechnical Commission (IEC) 27002 provide best practice recommendations on information security management.

▶ The ISO/IEC 27001 is a standard for information security management, for which organizations may be certified if they meet the requirements.

▶ The ISO/IEC 27701 extends ISO 27001 with enhancements for privacy in order to establish and maintain information management systems specific to privacy.

▶ The ISO/IEC 31000 provides a framework for the risk management process.

▶ Service Organizational Control (SOC) 2 results in a report provided to service providers that attests to their practices around confidentiality, integrity, availability, and privacy. Organizations that do business with security service providers, including cloud service providers, should ensure that each of these vendors has a SOC 2 report. This report provides a mechanism for vendors to communicate their controls externally.

▶ The *National Institute of Standards and Technology* (*NIST*) is a U.S. government–based entity that provides a cybersecurity framework for government and various industries.

▶ Control Objectives for Information and Related Technology (COBIT) is a set of best practices for IT management.

▶ The Committee of Sponsoring Organizations (COSO) of the Treadway Commission is a widely accepted control framework for enterprise governance and risk management.

▶ The Health Information Trust Alliance Common Security Framework (HITRUST CSF) is a security framework developed specifically for healthcare information.

▶ *Cloud Security Alliance (CSA) Cloud Controls Matrix (CCM)* provides foundational security guidance for cloud vendors and helps customers with assessment of cloud service providers.

ExamAlert

The SOC 2 report helps organizations such as cloud service providers provide assurance of their controls to existing and prospective customers.

For example, the U.S. Department of Energy's Sandia National Laboratories is responsible for providing the framework for supervisory control and data acquisition (SCADA) security policy that is specific to SCADA systems. On the international front, the G7 finance ministers and central bank governors issued a set of fundamental elements of cybersecurity for the financial sector. This guidance was produced to help banks improve cybersecurity and promote the consistency of cybersecurity approaches among G7 partners. U.S. federal agencies are required to follow the *NIST Risk Management Framework (RMF)*. NIST recently introduced the *NIST Cybersecurity Framework (CSF)*, which resulted from a collaboration between the government and the private sector.

Of course, organizations have different regulatory compliance goals, so choosing the correct framework is important to the overall security posture of an organization. Some general observations about frameworks follow:

▶ ISO/IEC 27002 can be used for any industry but tends to be used by cloud providers that want to validate active security programs.

▶ NIST is specific to U.S. government agencies but can be and is often applied in just about any other industry.

▶ COBIT is most commonly used to attain compliance with the Sarbanes–Oxley Act (SOX).

A myriad of other frameworks work for different industries. For example, educational institutions might choose Operationally Critical Threat, Asset, and Vulnerability Evaluation (OCTAVE). OCTAVE was developed by Carnegie

Mellon University's Computer Emergency Response Team (CERT) and takes a strategic approach to information security.

Benchmarks and Secure Configuration Guides

Benchmarking typically determines how much of a load a system, device, or server can handle by comparing two or more systems or components of a system. The most common use of a benchmark is to measure performance. Applying that concept to security is the principle behind security benchmarks and secure configuration guides. Perhaps the most widely used resource for benchmarks is the *Center for Internet Security* (*CIS*). CIS is the main provider of more than 100 configuration guides and comprehensive checklists for various platforms that help organizations mitigate security vulnerabilities.

Benchmarks and guides are useful because they include desirable characteristics. For example, they are based on use cases in which security is paramount, and they take technology performance into consideration. CIS benchmarks and secure configuration guides are based on international best practices and are commended by industry vendors and governing bodies.

Platform- and Vendor-Specific Guides

CIS benchmarks provide guidance on creating a secure configuration posture for an organization. Each CIS benchmark undergoes two phases of consensus review by subject matter experts and allows for feedback from the community. Some of the benchmark categories follow:

▶ Desktops and web browsers

▶ Mobile devices

▶ Network devices

▶ Security metrics

▶ Servers

▶ Operating systems

▶ Virtualization platforms and cloud

In addition to the CIS benchmarks, many vendors provide platform- and product-specific guides that cover web and application servers, operating systems, and network infrastructure devices. For example, the Microsoft Security Response Center (MSRC) provides prescriptive guidance, and Cisco provides a wide library of documents and best practices on securing Cisco devices. In addition, NIST produces specific guides and documents such as *Guidelines on Securing Public Web Servers*.

General-Purpose Guides

General-purpose security guides are available as guidance for organizations that might just want some guidance on servers that are used for general purposes. For example, NIST publishes the *Guide to General Server Security*, which addresses general security issues related to typical servers. The guide addresses the underlying operating system, server software, and ways to maintain a secure configuration.

The *General-Purpose Operating System Security Requirements Guide (SRG)* and the *Operating System Security Requirements Guide* are informational tools for improving the security of Department of Defense (DoD) systems. The *General-Purpose Operating System Protection Profile (OSPP)* guide also is available. This guide was created as a joint effort between the National Information Assurance Partnership (NIAP) and the British Standards Institution (BSI) to develop a Common Criteria Protection Profile that is often used in the certification process in accordance with ISO/IEC 15408 and the Common Criteria.

Cram Quiz

Answer these questions. The answers follow the last question. If you cannot answer these questions correctly, consider reading this chapter again until you can.

1. Which of the following are the most compelling reasons that secure configuration baselines have been established? (Select three.)

   ○ **A.** Industry representatives

   ○ **B.** Organizational requests

   ○ **C.** Government mandates

   ○ **D.** Regulatory bodies

2. Your organization is looking to move the internally developed and managed HR system to a SaaS vendor. Which of the following should you request from the vendor?

○ **A.** SOX report

○ **B.** COBIT

○ **C.** SOC 2 report

○ **D.** Benchmark guides

Cram Quiz Answers

Answer 1: A, C, and D. Security baselines are often established by government mandates, regulatory bodies, or industry representatives. For example, think of the PCI DSS requirements established by the credit card industry for businesses that collect and transact using credit information. Answer B is incorrect because organizational requests are merely requests, and security baselines are often established to comply with some type of regulation or standard.

Answer 2: C. A SOC 2 report provides evidence to a third-party attestation around the service provider's security controls. Answer A is incorrect because SOX is a regulatory standard governing financial accounting. Answer B is incorrect because COBIT provides a set of best practices for IT management. Answer D is incorrect because benchmark guides are usually available to anyone and only serve as guides, though they still need to be followed.

What Next?

If you want more practice on this chapter's exam objective before you move on, remember that you can access all of the Cram Quiz questions on the Pearson Test Prep software online. You can also create a custom exam by objective with the Online Practice Test. Note any objective you struggle with and go to that objective's material in this chapter.

CHAPTER 33

Organizational Security Policies

This chapter covers the following official Security+ exam objective:

▶ 5.3 Explain the importance of policies to organizational security.

Essential Terms and Components

▶ acceptable use policy (AUP)

▶ job rotation

▶ separation of duties

▶ least privilege

▶ nondisclosure agreement (NDA)

▶ service-level agreement (SLA)

▶ memorandum of understanding (MOU)

▶ business partnership agreement (BPA)

▶ interconnection security agreement (ISA)

Policy Framework

To ensure that proper risk management is coordinated, updated, communicated, and maintained, it is important to establish clear and detailed security policies that are ratified by an organization's management and brought to the attention of its users through regular security-awareness training. Policies that users do not know about are rarely effective, and those that lack management support can be unenforceable. Several policies can support risk management within the organization, as described in the following sections.

To protect information and the organization, the risk management framework includes various components:

- **Policy:** Provides the foundation on which everything else is built. Policies are general management statements.

- **Standard:** Describes specific mandatory controls, based on a given policy.

- **Guideline:** Provides recommendations or good practices.

- **Procedure:** Provides instructions and greater specifics, detailing how a policy, standard, and guideline will be implemented.

Policies tend to be higher level and more descriptive, whereas procedures are prescriptive. A procedure is sometimes also known as a *standard operating procedure* (*SOP*), although SOPs tend to have a further level of specificity in providing step-by-step instructions to ensure a standardized and repeatable method for performing a task.

Human Resource Management Policies

Human resources (HR) policies and practices should reduce the risk of theft, fraud, or misuse of information facilities by employees, contractors, and third-party users. The primary legal and HR representatives should review all policies for privacy issues, legal issues, and HR enforcement language. Many, if not most, organizations require legal and HR review of policies.

Background Checks

Organizational policies often drive the need to hire trustworthy, competent employees. As a result, an organization might require background checks before offering employment. Background checks can be quite simple, requiring only reference checks, or can involve more stringent checks, such as verifying educational credentials, checking for criminal records, verifying employment history, and conducting drug testing.

Onboarding and Offboarding

The hiring process should include provisions for making new employees aware of acceptable use, data handling, and disposal policies, as well as sanctions that

could be enacted if violations occur. An organization should also institute a formal code of ethics to which all employees must subscribe, particularly privileged users and those with broad administrative rights. Likewise, procedures need to be in place to ensure that when employees leave the organization, in addition to having all access removed, they return equipment and data. The process should be clear regarding expectations, particularly those related to confidential or internal-use-only data.

Mandatory Vacations

The organization's security policy should require users to take vacations and rotate positions or functional duties. This policy should outline the way a user is associated with necessary information and system resources and the way access is rotated between individuals. Employees must be able to do each other's jobs to avoid corruption, validate cross-checks, and minimize the effect of personnel loss. All employees must be adequately cross-trained and should have only the minimal level of access necessary to perform their normal duties (*least privilege*). Another benefit of mandatory vacations is that they help identify gaps in employee capabilities.

Separation of Duties

Too much power can lead to corruption, whether in politics or network administration. Most governments and other organizations implement some type of balance of power through *separation of duties*. It is important to include a separation of duties when planning for security policy compliance. Without this separation, all areas of control and compliance could end up in the hands of a single individual. The idea of separation of duties hinges on the concept that a scenario in which multiple people conspire to corrupt a system is less likely than a scenario in which a single person seeks to corrupt it. For example, in financial institutions, to violate the security controls, all the participants in the process have to agree to compromise the system.

> **ExamAlert**
>
> For physical or operational security questions, avoid giving one individual complete control of a transaction or process from beginning to end. Also implement policies such as job rotation, mandatory vacations, and cross-training. These practices also protect against the loss of a critical skill set due to injury, death, or another form of personnel separation.

Job Rotation

As an extension of the separation of duties best practice, rotating administrative users between roles both improves awareness of the mandates of each role and ensures that fraudulent activity cannot be sustained. This is also the reason users with administrative access might be required to take mandatory vacations, allowing other administrators to review standard operating practices and protocols in place. You can easily remember the idea of *job rotation* by thinking of the English translation of the Latin phrase *Quis custodiet ipsos custodes?*: "Who will guard the guardians themselves?"

Clean Desk Policies

A clean desk policy is one of the top strategies for reducing the risk of security breaches in the workplace. Training should include details of the organization's clean desk policy, encouraging users to avoid jotting down hard-to-recall passphrases or details from electronic systems that might contain PII. A clean desk policy can also increase employee awareness about protecting sensitive information. Users should understand why taping a list of their logons and passwords under their keyboards is a bad idea.

> **ExamAlert**
>
> A clean desk policy can be a vital tool in protecting sensitive and confidential materials in the hands of end users. A clean desk policy requires that users remove sensitive and confidential materials from workspaces when they leave and lock away items they are not using.

Role-Based Awareness and Training

For organizations to protect the integrity, confidentiality, and availability of information in today's highly diverse network environments, each person involved needs to understand his or her roles and responsibilities. NIST Special Publication 800-16 outlines the advantages of role- and performance-based security training and presents models for the two training models. All employees need fundamental training in IT security concepts and procedures. Training can then be broken into three levels: beginning, intermediate, and advanced. Each of these levels is linked to roles and responsibilities, based on the skills and abilities necessary to perform the required responsibilities. Of course, an individual might perform more than one role within

the organization, and such employees might need intermediate or advanced IT security training in their primary job role but require only beginning training in their secondary role.

Awareness is different from training. The primary difference is that training is more active. Awareness deals with recognition, specifically helping employees recognize IT security concerns. A common example of security awareness might be distributing pens and posters with security slogans or exhortations. Training relates more specifically to the specific competencies required of the individual. Effective training requires an understanding of user types who interact across information systems. Specific training can be role based and tailored to specific roles and responsibilities.

Users can be the following types:

▶ **General user:** These users typically make up most of the user population. They have general nonprivileged access to use and transact across information systems.

▶ **Privileged user:** These users have access to otherwise restricted data and system functions.

▶ **System administrator:** This user is the custodian of the data and has responsibility for technical control over the systems that contain and process data.

▶ **Executive user:** These users are more likely to have privileged access to sensitive data but also nonprivileged access to systems. These users have overall accountability for the security efforts of the organization.

▶ **Data owner:** This user often is responsible for a specific information asset and many times is a senior person within a department or division. For example, the vice president of human resources might be the data owner for all employee data.

▶ **System owner:** This user is responsible for the systems that contain and process data. Typically, the system owner oversees the employees who are responsible for the technical control and operations of such systems. The system owner also works closely with the data owner to ensure that data is secure across its life cycle.

Executive users, data owners, and system owners are all responsible for drafting and promulgating security policies, standards, and procedures related to the information systems.

> **ExamAlert**
>
> You must understand the differences among the different user types. Specifically, be sure you understand that each role requires different training. Executive users, data owners, and system owners, in particular, are responsible for drafting and promulgating security policies.

Many organizations rely on computer-based training (CBT), which can be effectively delivered via computer and mobile devices and specifically tailored to the organization's needs. CBT also provides additional benefits, including the following:

▶ Continued engagement that can be revisited, which can help with efficacy and retention of knowledge

▶ Flexible deployment through the Internet with flexible scheduling

▶ Ability to track the learner's progress and use of analytics to provide for continual improvement

▶ Encouraging healthy competition while making learning fun through gamification, including the ability to earn badges, score points, or play against others

Continuing Education

User education and training are required to ensure that users are made aware of expectations, options, and requirements related to secure access in an organization's network. These programs should continue beyond the onboarding process and should occur regularly. Education can include many different forms of communication, including the following:

▶ New employees and contract agents should be educated in security requirements as part of the hiring process.

▶ Reminders and security-awareness newsletters, emails, and flyers should be provided to raise general security awareness.

▶ General security policies should be defined, documented, and distributed to employees.

▶ Regular focus group sessions and on-the-job training should be provided for users regarding changes to the user interface, application suites, and general policies.

▶ General online security-related resources should be made available to users through a simple, concise, and easily navigable interface.

ExamAlert

Combining security training during employee orientation with ongoing training is ideal to ensure that employees recognize and retain information and also gain necessary skills and understanding.

User training should ensure that operational guidelines, restrictions on data sharing, disaster recovery strategies, and operational mandates are clearly conveyed to users and refreshed regularly. Policies might also require refresher training during transfers between organizational components or between roles/job duties under the rotation policy. Details such as data classification (high, medium, low, confidential, private, public), sensitivity of data and handling guidelines, legal mandates related to data forms such as personally identifiable information (PII) in financial or healthcare settings, best practices, and consumption standards can vary widely among organizational units. The proper protocols for access, storage, and disposal should vary accordingly. In response to the continued expansion of electronic technology provided by users in bring your own device (BYOD) settings, security awareness training is key to managing user habits and expectations developed as a result of the prevalence of mobile devices and computing equipment in homes.

Acceptable Use Policy/Rules of Behavior

An organization's *acceptable use policy* (*AUP*) must provide details that specify what users can do with their network access. Such rules help protect the organization's data and guard against legal liability. This includes email and instant messaging usage for personal purposes, limitations on access times, and the storage space available to each user. Such policies generally also include rules of behavior or a code of conduct to ensure that users behave in a manner that is legal, ethical, and within the cultural expectations of the organization.

An acceptable use policy should be written in clear, specific language and should include the following main components:

▶ Detailed standards of behavior

▶ Detailed enforcement guidelines and standards

▶ Acceptable and unacceptable uses

▶ Consent forms

▶ Privacy statement

▶ Disclaimer of liability

An organization should be sure that its acceptable use policy complies with current state and federal legislation and does not create unnecessary business risk to the company due to employee misuse of resources. Upon logon, users should see a statement that network access is granted under certain conditions and that all activities could be monitored. This way, you can be sure to cover any legal ramifications. Acceptable use policies commonly also address use of the Internet, covered next.

Internet Usage

An organization should set expectations on appropriate use of the Internet through an acceptable use policy or an Internet use policy. In addition to protecting the organization's data, such policies help ensure employee productivity and discourage disruptive and illegal activities. Obvious examples include guidelines that prohibit accessing or transmitting threatening or illegal material. In the past, organizations commonly prohibited the use of personal email and disallowed other nonbusiness use of corporate systems and Internet access. Many policy statements today do provide for personal use but limit this use, especially when it is excessive. Internet usage policies also often govern the appropriate use of email and social media.

Email and social media provide open platforms that enable seamless data sharing, allowing organizations and partners to interface and extend network services and applications. An organization uses email for communication inside and outside the organization. Social media is often used beyond the organization to communicate externally and garner opinions about products and services. These technologies improve collaboration and communication within and across partners and also raise the level of productivity and interaction between workers. Although such tools enable instant collaboration and increase productivity, they pose serious privacy concerns. Organizations must be cautious because of potential negative impacts such as damage to brand recognition and liability for online defamation and libel claims.

> **ExamAlert**
>
> An organization must carefully consider risks vs. benefits when deciding on a social media strategy. The organization must evaluate the risks related to using social media as a business tool to communicate with affiliates, granting employee access to social media sites while on the corporate network, and allowing employee use of social media tools from corporate-issued mobile devices.

Strategies to address the risks of email and social media usage should focus on user behavior and should be supported by user training and awareness programs. Technical controls can assist in policy enforcement and in blocking, preventing, or identifying potential incidents. Examples of technical controls include mobile device management (MDM) and mobile application management (MAM). These are enterprise solutions that you can use in social media application security, protection, and asset management. To ensure secure email usage, many organizations today engage in phishing campaigns. These campaigns typically involve simulations that mimic phishing attempts and track when users inappropriately click links or open files that they otherwise should not. Users who fail such campaigns may be presented with immediate feedback or tasked with taking appropriate training.

Controls should be monitored to ensure that they are effective. In addition, an organization can engage a brand protection firm that scans the Internet and looks for misuse of the organization's brand. This approach maintains awareness of potential fraud and establishes clear guidelines about what information should be posted as part of a social media presence.

Nondisclosure Agreements

A *nondisclosure agreement* (*NDA*) is a legally binding document that organizations might require of both their own employees and anyone else who comes into contact with confidential information, including vendors, consultants, and contractors. The purpose of an NDA is to protect an organization's intellectual property and trade secrets. As a legally binding document, it protects the information from being improperly disclosed, even after the relationship is terminated, such as for employees who move to a competing organization or partners who work across competing organizations.

Disciplinary and Adverse Actions

Policies should specify consequences for violations. Policies often can be enforced through technical controls, such as content and web filters. The most common and simple example of a policy is a statement such as, "An employee found to be in violation of this policy may be subject to disciplinary action, including termination of employment." Again, policy awareness and training are required. In most cases, disciplinary actions depend on the nature of the violation and the status of the individual involved. Most violations are handled by management, the information technology team, and the human resources

department. However, civil and criminal violations need to be governed outside the organization. As a result, policy statements should include the jurisdiction responsible for interpreting applicable laws.

Exit Interviews

Exit interviews are a vital tool to help an organization identify workplace factors that lead employees to leave. These interviews provide a feedback loop to allow human resources personnel to improve the current situation and also adapt programs to ensure that the company can continue to recruit and hire the best talent. Other benefits include potentially learning more about competing organizations (for example, are other organizations paying more?) and ensuring that the employee has a positive exit experience. A member of the human resources department typically conducts an exit interview in a one-on-one setting with the exiting employee. Exit interviews are typically voluntary and confidential to help ensure candid responses from the employee.

Third-Party Risk Management

Integrating systems and data with third parties such as vendors or business partners can combine complexity and inefficiency, leading to increased risk for the organization. Risks in partnerships are usually analyzed only during the onboarding process; after a relationship is established, organizations often forget about associated risks. Security policies and procedures need to be followed, however, to identify risks and security controls that will be implemented to protect the confidentiality, integrity, and availability of any connected systems and the data that will pass between them or be accessed. Controls should be appropriate for the environment and should contain a centralized platform to monitor the range of assessments, tasks, and responsibilities of all parties. Policies should define ownership and accountability. Both organizations must maintain clear lines of regular communication. Risk assessments and audits should be conducted regularly, and a record of compliance should be established so that documentation pertains to the due diligence performed. In addition, the legal and regulatory environment should be monitored for changes that impact the partnership or third-party agreement.

Risks exist in the supply chain and should be considered and managed. Supply-chain risks include both hardware and software risks. For hardware, a simple example is personal computers purchased from a supplier or manufacturer in

your home country that relies on parts and components from foreign sources. Even commercial software from a particular vendor likely includes many different components from other vendors and open-source software. Hardware and software is also susceptible to varying risks, based on specific support agreements. Two important components include the end of life (EOL) date and the end of service life (EOSL) date. The EOL and EOSL dates are points within a product's life cycle that mark the end of production and may limit or end the vendor's liability. EOSL usually means that service and maintenance for the solution are no longer provided. For example, a software vendor may not sell or add features to a solution that has gone EOL but still provide security updates and fix vulnerabilities up to the EOSL date. It is common practice for vendors to announce an EOL date prior to the actual date to provide customers plenty of time to upgrade or plan for alternatives.

Interoperability Agreements

Third-party risk can vary greatly, depending on each individual third-party arrangement. Sometimes the risks are clear-cut. Other times, the risks seem unclear. To establish responsibilities in collaboration or the delivery of services, interoperability agreements are used. Agreements can be tailored to the circumstances and requirements of the participating parties, the various collaborative arrangements agreed upon, or the complexity of the service relationship. These agreements help create a common understanding about the agreement and each party's responsibilities. The following are several agreements that are commonly used in business:

▶ **Service-level agreement (SLA):** A *service-level agreement* (*SLA*) is a contract between a service provider and a customer that specifies the nature of the service to be provided and the level of service that the provider will offer to the customer. An SLA often contains technical and performance parameters, such as response time and uptime, but it generally does not include security measures.

▶ **Business partner agreement (BPA):** A *business partner agreement* (*BPA*) is a contract that establishes partner profit percentages, partner responsibilities, and exit strategies for partners. This is strictly a business arrangement that specifies partner financial and fiduciary responsibilities. It does not cover security measures.

▶ **Memorandum of understanding (MOU):** A *memorandum of understanding* (*MOU*), which is sometimes called a memorandum of

agreement (MOA), is a document that outlines the terms and details of an agreement between parties, including each party's requirements and responsibilities. An MOU that expresses mutual accord on an issue between two or more organizations does not need to contain legally enforceable promises; it can be legally enforceable based on the intent of the parties.

▶ **Interconnection security agreement (ISA):** An *interconnection security agreement* (*ISA*) is an agreement between organizations that have connected or shared IT systems. The purpose of an ISA is to document the technical requirements of the interconnection, such as identifying the basic components of the interconnection, methods and levels of interconnectivity, and potential security risks associated with an interconnection. An ISA also supports an MOU between the organizations.

Another agreement commonly encountered is a Health Insurance Portability and Accountability Act (HIPAA) business associate agreement (BAA). This contract is signed between a HIPAA-covered entity and a HIPAA business associate (BA) to protect personal health information (PHI) in accordance with HIPAA guidelines.

Organizations can take additional steps, such as the following, to ensure that they are meeting compliance and performance standards:

▶ Annually approve and review third-party arrangements and performance.

▶ Maintain an updated list of all third-party relationships and periodically review the list.

▶ Take appropriate action with any relationship that presents elevated risk.

▶ Review all contracts for compliance with expectations and obligations.

The organization might also consider requiring an annual attestation by the partner or third party, stating adherence to the contract and its established controls, policies, and procedures.

ExamAlert

Third-party risk includes determining expectations, which can be spelled out in SLAs, BPAs, MOUs, and ISAs. Depending on the situation, an SLA, an MOU, and an ISA might all be necessary. An ISA is the only document that specifically outlines any technical solution and addresses security requirements.

Cram Quiz

Answer these questions. The answers follow the last question. If you cannot answer these questions correctly, consider reading this chapter again until you can.

1. Say that you work for a cloud service provider. Prior to signing off on a purchase order for a new security cloud service, a prospective customer wants to understand the nature of what you are providing and what levels of service in regard to performance and uptime your service offers. What should you provide the prospective customer?

   O **A.** ISA

   O **B.** MOU

   O **C.** BPA

   O **D.** SLA

2. Which of the following legally binding controls should you consider in order to protect sensitive information from being improperly disclosed by a third-party vendor you are hiring for consulting work in the organization?

   O **A.** DLP

   O **B.** SOP

   O **C.** Separation of duties

   O **D.** NDA

3. Your organization currently runs an operating system for which software developed after the end of last month may no longer work or even be installable. Which of the following best describes this milestone for the operating system?

   O **A.** ISA

   O **B.** EOL

   O **C.** NDA

   O **D.** MOU

Cram Quiz Answers

Answer 1: D. A service-level agreement (SLA) is a contract between a service provider and a customer that specifies the nature of the service to be provided and the level of service that the provider will offer to the customer. An SLA often contains technical and performance parameters, such as response time and uptime, but it generally does not include security measures. Answers A, B, and C are also types of interoperability agreements, but they are not applicable in this case.

Answer 2: D. A nondisclosure agreement (NDA) is a legally binding document that organizations might require of both their own employees and anyone else who comes into contact with confidential information, including vendors, consultants, and contractors.

The purpose of an NDA is to protect an organization's intellectual property and trade secrets. While data loss prevention (DLP) can help protect an organization's data from being improperly disclosed, DLP is a program related to technical controls rather than a legally binding contract. Thus, answer A is incorrect. Answer B is incorrect as standard operating procedures (SOP) specify step-step-instructions for a task. Answer C is incorrect as this would help protect all areas of control being assigned to a single person.

Answer 3: B. End of life (EOL) marks the end of a product's life cycle that began with the product first being generally available. While security patches may still be offered, the vendor does not provide for new features or continued compatibility. Answer A is incorrect because an ISA is an agreement between organizations that have connected or shared IT systems. Answer C is incorrect because an NDA is a legally binding document that organizations might require of both their own employees and anyone else who comes into contact with confidential information. Answer D is incorrect because an MOU is a document that outlines the terms and details of an agreement between parties, including each party's requirements and responsibilities.

What Next?

If you want more practice on this chapter's exam objective before you move on, remember that you can access all of the Cram Quiz questions on the Pearson Test Prep software online. You can also create a custom exam by objective with the Online Practice Test. Note any objective you struggle with and go to that objective's material in this chapter.

Risk Management

This chapter covers the following official Security+ exam objective:

▶ 5.4 Summarize risk management processes and concepts.

Essential Terms and Components

▶ risk acceptance

▶ risk avoidance

▶ risk transference

▶ risk mitigation

▶ risk register

▶ risk matrix/risk heat map

▶ risk assessment

▶ risk awareness

▶ risk appetite

▶ qualitative risk assessment

▶ quantitative risk assessment

▶ single loss expectancy (SLE)

▶ annualized loss expectancy (ALE)

▶ annualized rate of occurrence (ARO)

▶ business impact analysis (BIA)

▶ recovery time objective (RTO)

▶ recovery point objective (RPO)

▶ mean time to repair (MTTR)

▶ mean time between failures (MTBF)

▶ single point of failure

Risk Analysis

Risk is the possibility of or exposure to loss or danger. *Risk management* is the process of identifying and reducing risk to a level that is acceptable and then implementing controls to maintain that level. Risk comes in various types. Risk can be internal, external, or multiparty. Banks provide a great example of multiparty risk: Because of the ripple effects, issues at banks have effects on other banks and financial systems.

Risk analysis helps align security objectives with business objectives. This involves dealing with how to calculate risk and return on investment. Risk analysis identifies risks, estimates the effect of potential threats, and identifies ways to reduce the risk without the cost of the prevention outweighing the risk. Risk is a function of threats, vulnerabilities, and potential impact. The level of risk is often assessed by using the following simple equation:

Risk = Threat × Vulnerability × Impact

To determine the relative danger of an individual threat or to measure the relative value across multiple threats to better allocate resources designated for risk mitigation, it is necessary to map the resources, identify threats to each, and establish a metric for comparison. A business impact analysis (BIA) helps identify services and technology assets as well as provide a process by which the relative value of each identified asset can be determined if it fails one or more of the CIA (confidentiality, integrity, and availability) requirements. The failure to meet one or more of the CIA requirements is often a sliding scale, with increased severity as time passes. Recovery point objectives (RPOs) and recovery time objectives (RTOs) in incident handling, business continuity, and disaster recovery must be considered when calculating risk.

Risk Register

Risk assessment should not be a one-time event. As an organization evolves, change is inevitable. Risk management needs to be part of a continual framework from which risk can easily be communicated and continually adapted.

A *risk register*, usually implemented as a specialized software program, cloud service, or master document, gives an organization a way to record information about identified risks. Risk registers often include enterprise- and IT-related risks. With threats and vulnerabilities identified, the organizations can then implement controls to manage the risk appropriately. (The next section discusses these techniques.) The risk register should contain specific details about the risks, especially any residual risks the organization faces as a result of

controls or mitigation techniques employed. Common contents of a risk register include the following:

▶ Risk categorization groupings

▶ Name and description of the risk

▶ A measure of the risk through a risk score

▶ The impact to the organization if the risk is realized

▶ The likelihood of the risk being realized

▶ Mitigating controls

▶ Residual risk

▶ Contingency plans that cover what happens if the risk is realized

The risk register is a strategic component for an organization. The register also helps ensure that an organization's risk tolerance and *risk appetite* are correctly aligned with the goals of the business. As a result, reporting from a risk register should be clear and understandable. The outputs should be available and visible across the business, including to management and senior executives responsible for strategy, budget, and operations.

> **ExamAlert**
>
> A risk register provides a single point of entry to record information about identified risks to the organization. An organization might have one risk register for information systems and another risk register for enterprise risks, but the two are increasingly being combined.

Risk Response Techniques

Risk management involves creating a risk register document that details all known risks and their related mitigation strategies. Creating the risk register involves mapping the enterprise's expected services and data sets, as well as identifying vulnerabilities in both implementation and procedures for each. Risk cannot be eliminated outright in many cases, but mitigation strategies can be integrated with policies for *risk awareness* training ahead of an incident. Formal risk management deals with the alignment of four potential responses to each identified risk:

▶ **Avoidance:** *Risk avoidance* seeks to eliminate the vulnerability that gives rise to a particular risk. This is the most effective solution, but it often is not possible due to organizational requirements. For example, eliminating

email to avoid the risk of email-borne viruses is an effective solution but is not likely a realistic approach.

▶ **Transference:** With *risk transference*, a risk or the effect of its exposure is transferred by moving to hosted providers that assume the responsibility for recovery and restoration. Alternatively, organizations can acquire insurance to cover the costs of equipment theft or data exposure. Insurance related to the consequences of online attacks is known as *cybersecurity insurance*.

▶ **Acceptance:** With *risk acceptance*, an organization recognizes a risk, identifies it, and accepts that it is sufficiently unlikely or of such limited impact that corrective controls are not warranted. Risk acceptance must be a conscious choice that is documented, approved by senior administration, and regularly reviewed.

▶ **Mitigation/deterrence:** *Risk mitigation* involves reducing the likelihood or impact of a risk's exposure. Risk deterrence involves putting into place systems and policies to mitigate a risk by protecting against the exploitation of vulnerabilities that cannot be eliminated. Most risk management decisions focus on mitigation and deterrence, balancing costs and resources against the level of risk and mitigation that will result.

Bruce Schneier, a well-known cryptographer and security expert, was asked after the tragic events of 9/11 if it would be possible to prevent such events from happening again. "Sure," he replied. "Simply ground all the aircraft." Schneier gave an example of risk avoidance, albeit one he acknowledged as impractical in today's society. Consider the simple example of an automobile and its associated risks. If you drive a car, you have likely considered those risks. The option to not drive deprives you of the many benefits the car provides that are strategic to your individual goals in life. As a result, you have come to appreciate mitigating controls such as seat belts and other safety features. You accept the residual risks and might even transfer some of the risk through a life insurance policy. Certainly, when it comes to the risks of the vehicle itself, insurance plays a vital role. Not carrying insurance even carries risk itself because insurance is often required by law. Examples abound of people who have even accepted that risk, making a conscious choice to drive without insurance.

Finally, the choices you make related to risk often result in residual risk. Living in a high-crime neighborhood might spur someone to put bars on a home's windows. That's one problem seemingly mitigated. However, in case of a fire, the bars would render common egress points in the home no longer accessible.

Threat Assessment

Before discussing risk assessment, you must consider threat assessment. Part I, "Attacks, Threats, and Vulnerabilities," discusses and compares the different types of attacks, threats, and vulnerabilities.

A *threat* can be thought of as the potential that a vulnerability will be identified and exploited. A threat vector is the method a threat uses to get to the target. Threat vectors, as discussed in Part I, include viruses, worms, botnets, malware, phishing attacks, and keyloggers. Analyzing threats can help an organization develop security policies and prioritize securing resources. Threat assessments are performed to determine the best approaches to securing the environment against a threat or class of threats. Threats might exist, but if an environment has no vulnerabilities, it faces little or no risk. Likewise, little or no risk affects environments that have vulnerability without threat. Consider the simple analogy of a hurricane. Few would argue that a hurricane represents a threat. However, consider a home on the coast in Florida and a home inland in the Midwest. The former is certainly vulnerable to a hurricane, whereas the latter is not.

Probability is the likelihood that an event will occur. In assessing risk, it is important to estimate the probability or likelihood that a threat will occur. Assessing the likelihood of occurrence of some types of threats is easier than assessing other types. For example, you can use frequency data to estimate the probability of natural disasters. You might also be able to use the mean time to failure (MTTF) and mean time before repair (MTBF), both covered later in this chapter, to estimate the probability of component problems. Determining the probability of attacks by human threat sources is difficult. Threat source likelihood is assessed using skill level, motive, opportunity, and size. Vulnerability likelihood is assessed using ease of discovery, ease of exploit, awareness, and intrusion detection.

Threat source types can be classified into four areas:

▶ **Adversarial:** Threats from individuals, groups, organizations, and nation-states that intend to do harm

▶ **Accidental:** Actions by regular and privileged users that are not of malicious intent but that occur inadvertently

▶ **Structural:** Equipment and software failures

▶ **Environmental:** Natural and human-caused disasters, such as fires, floods, hurricanes, infrastructure failures, and unusual events

Chapter 5, "Threat Actors, Vectors, and Intelligence Sources," covers these adversarial and accidental threat actors. It is particularly important to understand the difference and overlap between natural and human-caused disasters. Typically, a natural disaster such as a tornado is beyond an organization's control. Most often those types of disasters are an act of nature. A fire, on the other hand, could be an act of nature, caused by a lightning storm, or it could be arson.

Furthermore, consider the internal versus external components of a threat source. In fact, across all four of the categories just listed, the threat source can be either internal or external. The adversary might be an insider or an outsider looking to cause harm. Even accidental threats, which are typically internal, can be caused externally (by a customer, for example). Structural threats are commonly internal, but in today's interconnected world, organizations depend on the systems of many partners and third parties that are external to the organization. Finally, even environmental threats such as a fire or flood can be caused by an insider or an outsider.

> **ExamAlert**
>
> Threat assessments must consider internal and external categories of threats. Either of these can apply to environmental and human-caused threats.

Risk Assessment

Recall that assessing risk is largely a function of threat, vulnerability, and impact. However, an important factor must be considered between the threat and the vulnerability: the likelihood that a threat will occur to exploit a vulnerability. As a result, a risk assessment consists of the following five steps:

1. Identify threats.

2. Identify vulnerabilities.

3. Determine the likelihood of occurrence.

4. Determine the magnitude of the impact.

5. Determine the risk.

After performing a threat assessment and vulnerability assessment, you must consider the likelihood that the threats identified might actually occur. To most accurately gauge the probability of an event occurring, you need to use a combination of estimation and historical data. Most risk analyses use a fiscal year to set a time limit on probability and confine proposed expenditures, budget, and depreciation.

A common categorization resulting from likelihood assessment might be based on a qualitative probability rated as high, medium, or low. Be sure to consider the motivation and capability of the threat source, the nature of the vulnerability, and the existence and effectiveness of current controls to mitigate the threat. Often the three values are translated into numeric equivalents for use in quantitative analytical processes: high (1.0), medium (0.5), and low (0.1). The next section further compares qualitative and quantitative measures.

Responses must be coupled with the likelihood determined in the risk analysis. For example, the risk analysis might advocate putting corrective measures in place as soon as possible for all high-level threats. Medium-level threats might require an action plan for implementation as soon as is reasonable, and low-level threats might be dealt with as possible or might simply be accepted.

By nature, risk always has the potential for negative impact. Given a particular likelihood of occurrence, organizations must next determine the magnitude of the impact. A simple measure of impact can range from very low to very high or from negligible impact to catastrophic impact. The size of the impact varies in terms of cost and impact on critical factors. Considering both the impact assessment and the risk assessment together helps you assess the probabilities and consequences of risk events if they are realized. Table 34.1 provides a *risk matrix* that can help you understand the level of risk as either low, medium, or high for both likelihood and impact. When a risk matrix is color coded, it is referred to as a *risk heat map*.

Based on the risk matrix, you can prioritize risks to establish an importance ranking from most critical to least critical. Ranking risks in terms of their criticality or importance is an important business function because it provides insight into where resources might be needed to prevent or mitigate high-probability risk events.

> **ExamAlert**
>
> A risk map or risk heat map is a visual tool for communicating specific risks an organization faces. A heat map helps an organization identify and prioritize risks by using the level of risk based on likelihood and impact data.

TABLE 34.1 **Level of Risk Based on Likelihood and Impact**

Likelihood	Level of Impact				
	Very Low (1)	**Low (2)**	**Moderate (3)**	**High (4)**	**Very High (5)**
Very High (5)	5 (Medium)	10 (High)	15 (High)	20 (High)	25 (High)
High (4)	4 (Low)	8 (Medium)	12 (High)	16 (High)	20 (High)
Moderate (3)	3 (Low)	6 (Medium)	9 (Medium)	12 (High)	15 (High)
Low (2)	2 (Low)	4 (Low)	6 (Medium)	8 (Medium)	10 (High)
Very Low (1)	1 (Low)	2 (Low)	3 (Low)	4 (Low)	5 (Medium)

Qualitative vs. Quantitative Measures

The preceding discussions are largely qualitative because they do not attempt to assign dollar values to the risk analysis process. Quantitative measures give the clearest measure of relative risk and expected return on investment or risk reduction on investment. Not all risk can be measured quantitatively, though, so qualitative risk assessment strategies are needed. The culture of an organization greatly affects whether its risk assessments can be performed via quantitative (numeric) or qualitative (subjective/relative) measures.

Qualitative risk assessment can involve brainstorming, focus groups, surveys, and other similar processes to determine asset worth and valuation to the organization. Uncertainty is also estimated, allowing for a relative projection of qualitative risk for each threat, based on position in a risk matrix/heat map that plots the probability (very low to very high) and impact (very low to very high). Numeric values can be assigned to each state (very low = 1, low = 2, moderate = 3, and so on) to perform a quasi-quantitative analysis, but because the categories are subjectively assigned, the result remains qualitative.

Quantitative results are generally easier for senior management to understand, but intensive labor and time are required to gather all related measurements. Compared to quantitative measures, qualitative measures tend to be less precise, more subjective, and more difficult in assigning direct costs for measuring ROI/RROI (return on investment/rate of return on investment).

Because a quantitative assessment is less subjective than a qualitative one, the process requires that a value be assigned to each of the various components. To perform a *quantitative risk assessment*, an estimation of potential losses is calculated. Next, the likelihood of some unwanted event is quantified, based on the threat analysis. Finally, depending on the potential loss and likelihood, the quantitative process arrives at the degree of risk. Each step relies on the concepts of single loss expectancy, annual rate of occurrence, and annual loss expectancy.

> ### ExamAlert
>
> Remember the difference between quantitative (numeric) and qualitative (subjective/relative) measures. Quantitative (think quantity) measures are expressed numerically, whereas qualitative (think quality) measures are expressed as "good" or "bad."

Single Loss Expectancy

Single loss expectancy (*SLE*) is the expected monetary loss every time a risk occurs. SLE equals asset value multiplied by the threat exposure factor, which is the percentage of the asset lost in a successful attack. The formula looks like this:

Asset value × Exposure factor = SLE

Consider an example of SLE using denial-of-service (DoS) attacks. Firewall logs indicate that the organization was hit hard one time per month by DoS attacks in each of the past 6 months. You can use this historical data to estimate that you likely will be hit 12 times per year. This information helps you calculate the SLE and the ALE. (The ALE is explained in greater detail shortly.)

An asset is any resource that has value and must be protected. Determining an asset's value can most mean determining the cost to replace the asset if it is lost. Simple property examples fit well here, but figuring asset value is not always so straightforward. Other considerations could be necessary, including the value of the asset to adversaries, the value of the asset to the organization's mission, and the liability issues that would arise if the asset were compromised.

The exposure factor is the percentage of loss that a realized threat could have on a certain asset. In the DoS example, imagine that 25% of business would be lost if a DoS attack succeeded. The daily sales from the website are $100,000, so the SLE would be $25,000 (SLE = $100,000 × 0.25). The possibility of certain threats is greater than that of others. Historical data presents the best method of estimating these possibilities.

Annual Rate of Occurrence

The *annual rate of occurrence* (*ARO*) is the estimated possibility of a specific threat taking place in a one-year time frame. The possible range of frequency values is from 0.0 (the threat is not expected to occur) to some number whose magnitude depends on the type and population of threat sources. When the probability that a DoS attack will occur is 50%, the ARO is 0.5. After you calculate the SLE, you can calculate the ALE, which gives you the probability of an event happening over a single year.

Annual Loss Expectancy

The *annual loss expectancy* (*ALE*) is the expected monetary loss that can be expected for an asset from risk over a one-year period. ALE equals SLE times ARO:

SLE × ARO = ALE

ALE can be used directly in a cost/benefit analysis. Going back to our earlier example, if the SLE is estimated at $25,000 and the ARO is 0.5, the ALE is $12,500 ($25,000 × 0.5 = $12,500). In this case, spending more than $12,500 to mitigate risk might not be prudent because the cost would outweigh the risk.

> **ExamAlert**
>
> Calculating risk includes the following formulas:
>
> Risk = Threat × Vulnerability × Impact
>
> SLE = Asset value × Exposure factor
>
> ALE = SLE × ARO

Business Impact Analysis

Business impact analysis (*BIA*) is the process of determining the potential impacts resulting from the interruption of time-sensitive or critical business processes. IT contingency planning for both disaster recovery and operational continuity relies on conducting a BIA as part of the overall plan to ensure continued operations and the capability to recover from disaster. Whereas a risk assessment focuses on the relative likelihood of potential threats to an organization, a BIA focuses on the relative impact of the loss of operational capability on critical business functions. Conducting a business impact analysis involves identifying critical business functions and the services and technologies required for them, along with determining the associated costs and the maximum acceptable outage period.

For hardware-related outages, the assessment should also include the current age of existing solutions, along with standards for the expected average time between failures, based on vendor data or accepted industry standards. Planning strategies are intended to minimize this cost by arranging recovery actions to restore critical functions in the most effective manner based on cost, legal or statutory mandates, and calculations of the mean time to restore.

Critical Functions

A business impact analysis is a key component in ensuring continued operations. For that reason, it is a major part of a business continuity plan (BCP) or continuity of operations plan (COOP). The focus is ensuring the continued operation of key mission and business processes. U.S. government organizations commonly use the term *mission-essential functions* to refer to functions that need to be immediately functional at an alternate site until normal operations can be restored. Essential functions for any organization require resiliency. Organizations also must identify the dependent systems for both the functions and the process that are critical to the mission or business.

Identification of Critical Systems

A BCP must identify critical systems and components. If a disaster is widespread or targets an Internet service provider (ISP) or key routing hardware point, an organization's continuity plan should detail options for alternate network access. This should include dedicated administrative connections that might be required for recovery. Continuity planning should include considerations for recovery in case existing hardware and facilities are rendered inaccessible or unrecoverable. It should also consider the hardware configuration details, network requirements, and utilities agreements for alternate sites.

Single Points of Failure

A *single point of failure* is a potential risk posed by a flaw in business continuity planning that allows one fault or malfunction to take down an entire system or enterprise. Single points of failure are avoided with redundancy and various fault-tolerant protocols. For example, single points of failure can be eliminated by using server clustering technology, redundant switches, and redundant network connections.

Naturally, systems that support critical missions or business processes should not be subject to single points of failure. High availability describes the process for ensuring system redundancy and proper failover. Maintaining such systems requires more resources and is more expensive. As a result, high availability is ideal for mission-critical systems that cannot be unavailable.

> **ExamAlert**
>
> Ensuring the continued operation of critical functions, or mission-essential functions, is a major component of the risk management process. This task starts with identifying and understanding systems that are directly relevant to the mission or goals of the organization. Such systems should be designed for high availability and should not be subject to single points of failure.

Recovery Objectives

Recovery point objective (RPO) and *recovery time objective (RTO)* are crucial in risk mitigation planning. RPO, which specifically refers to data backup capabilities, is the amount of time that can elapse during a disruption before the quantity of data lost during that period exceeds business continuity planning's maximum allowable threshold. Simply put, RPO specifies the allowable data loss. It determines up to what point in time data recovery can happen before business is disrupted. For example, if an organization does a backup at 10:00 p.m. every day and an incident happens at 7:00 p.m. the following day, everything that changed since the last backup would be lost. The RPO in this context is the backup from the previous day. If the organization set the threshold at 24 hours, the RPO would be within the threshold because it is less than 24 hours.

The RTO is the amount of time within which a process must be restored after a disaster to meet business continuity requirements. The RTO is how long the organization can go without a specific application; it defines how much time is needed to recover after a notification of process disruption.

> **ExamAlert**
>
> Be certain that you understand the distinction between RPO and RTO. RPO designates the amount of data that will be lost or will have to be re-entered because of network downtime. RTO designates the amount of time that can pass before the disruption begins to seriously impede normal business operations.

MTTF, MTBF, and MTTR

When systems fail, one of the first questions asked is "How long will it take to get things back up?" It is better to know the answer to such a question *before* disaster strikes than try to find the answer afterward. Fortunately, established mechanisms can help you determine this answer. Understanding these mechanisms is a big part of the overall analysis of business impact.

Mean time to failure (MTTF) is the length of time a device or product is expected to last in operation. It represents how long a product can reasonably be expected to perform, based on specific testing. MTTF metrics supplied by vendors about their products or components might not have been collected by running one unit continuously until failure. Instead, MTTF data is often collected by running many units for a specific number of hours and then is calculated as an average based on when the components fail.

MTTF is one of many ways to evaluate the reliability of hardware or other technology and is extremely important when evaluating mission-critical systems hardware. Knowing the general reliability of hardware is vital, especially when it is part of a larger system. MTTF is used for nonrepairable products. When MTTF is used as a measure, repair is not an option.

Mean time between failures (*MTBF*) is the average amount of time that passes between hardware component failures, excluding time spent repairing components or waiting for repairs. MTBF is intended to measure only the time a component is available and operating. MTBF is similar to MTTF, but it is important to understand the difference. MTBF is used for products that can be repaired and returned to use. MTTF is used for nonrepairable products. MTBF is calculated as a ratio of the cumulative operating time to the number of failures for that item.

MTBF ratings can be predicted based on product experience or data supplied by the manufacturer. MTBF ratings are measured in hours and are often used to determine the durability of hard drives and printers. For example, typical hard drives for personal computers have MTBF ratings of about 500,000 hours.

These risk calculations help determine the life spans and failure rates of components. These calculations help an organization measure the reliability of a product.

One final calculation assists with understanding approximately how long a repair will take on a component that can be repaired. The *mean time to repair* (*MTTR*; also called mean time to recovery) is the average time required to fix a failed component or device and return it to production status. MTTR

is corrective maintenance. The calculation includes preparation time, active maintenance time, and delay time. Because of the uncertainty of these factors, MTTR is often difficult to calculate. In order to reduce the MTTR, some systems have redundancy built in so that when one subsystem fails, another takes its place and keeps the whole system running.

> **ExamAlert**
>
> Mean time between failures (MTBF) is the average time before a product requires repair. Mean time to repair (MTTR) is the average time required to fix a failed component or device and return it to production status. On the other hand, mean time to failure (MTTF) is the average time before a product fails and cannot be repaired. MTBF and MTTR consider a component that can be repaired, whereas MTTF considers a component that cannot be repaired.

Impact

As the name suggests, a businesses impact analysis (BIA) requires careful examination of the potential business impact. The loss of a business process or function is likely to result in some sort of impact, which is measured as part of a BIA to understand the severity. This can simply include an impact rating of low, medium, or high. A more complex analysis considers the different types of impacts that result from the loss of a functional business process. Consider, for example, the importance of availability to an e-commerce site. The most obvious consequence is the loss of sales and income if web servers are not available. You likely can imagine other potential consequences.

When measuring impact, an organization should consider potential consequences across a broad set of categories, including the following:

▶ Life and safety

▶ Facilities and physical property

▶ Intellectual property

▶ Finance

▶ Reputation

The preceding example of the loss of web servers for an e-commerce site clearly shows a potentially severe impact on finance. In addition, the company's reputation would be impacted. The loss of web servers might not impact personal life and safety, but the loss of emergency management systems might.

Subsequently, the loss of fire suppression systems could certainly have a significant impact on facilities and physical property. These factors together could further impact an organization financially.

Further assessing impact requires drilling down into the specifics and other calculations. How long can the web servers be down? How much money will be lost per hour? How long can the business remain viable as a result? If an entire facility is destroyed, do alternative sites exist from which to do business?

> **ExamAlert**
>
> Understanding the impact of an adverse event is a key component of risk management. Impact should consider life, property, safety, finance, and reputation.

Cram Quiz

Answer these questions. The answers follow the last question. If you cannot answer these questions correctly, consider reading this chapter again until you can.

1. Which of the following is the monetary loss that can be expected for an asset from risk over a year?

   ○ **A.** ALE

   ○ **B.** SLE

   ○ **C.** ARO

   ○ **D.** BIA

2. Your manager needs to know, for budgetary purposes, the average life span for each of the firewall appliances. Which of the following should you provide?

   ○ **A.** MTBF

   ○ **B.** RPO

   ○ **C.** RTO

   ○ **D.** MTTF

3. An organization is increasingly subject to compliance regulations and is making strong efforts to comply with them but is still concerned about issues that might occur. Management decides to buy insurance to help cover the costs of a potential breach. Which of the following risk response techniques is the organization using?

   ○ **A.** Avoidance

   ○ **B.** Transference

   ○ **C.** Acceptance

   ○ **D.** Mitigation

4. Which of the following equations best represents the proper assessment of exposure to danger?

- ○ **A.** Risk = Threat × Vulnerability × Impact
- ○ **B.** Impact = Risk × Threat × Vulnerability
- ○ **C.** Vulnerability = Threat × Risk × Impact
- ○ **D.** Threat = Risk × Impact × Vulnerability

Cram Quiz Answers

Answer 1: A. The annual loss expectancy (ALE) is the expected monetary loss that can be expected for an asset from risk over a one-year period. It is calculated by multiplying the single loss expectancy by the annual rate of occurrence (SLE × ARO). Therefore, answers B and C are incorrect. Answer D is incorrect because this is a business impact analysis, which is the process for determining potential impacts resulting from the interruption of business processes.

Answer 2: D. The mean time to failure is the length of time a device or product is expected to last in operation. It represents how long a product can reasonably be expected to perform, based on specific testing. Answer A is incorrect because the mean time between failures (MTBF) is the average amount of time that passes between hardware component failures, excluding time spent repairing components or waiting for repairs. Answers B and C are incorrect because RPO and RTO are used for risk-mitigation planning. The recovery point objective (RPO) specifies the allowable data loss. The recovery time objective (RTO) is the amount of time within which a process must be restored after a disaster to meet business continuity requirements.

Answer 3: B. Insurance is a classic example of transferring risk. Answers A, C, and D are incorrect because although these are all methods of transferring risk, none of them transfers the risk from one organization to another.

Answer 4: A. Risk is a function of threats, vulnerabilities, and potential impact. Assessing the level of risk is often portrayed through the simple equation Risk = Threat × Vulnerability × Impact. Answers B, C, and D are incorrect because threat, vulnerability, and impact are considered together to provide an appropriate measure of risk.

What Next?

If you want more practice on this chapter's exam objective before you move on, remember that you can access all of the Cram Quiz questions on the Pearson Test Prep software online. You can also create a custom exam by objective with the Online Practice Test. Note any objective you struggle with and go to that objective's material in this chapter.

Sensitive Data and Privacy

This chapter covers the following official Security+ exam objective:

▶ 5.5 Explain privacy and sensitive data concepts in relation to security.

Essential Terms and Components

▶ data type classification

▶ personally identifiable information (PII)

▶ data owner

▶ data controller

▶ data processor

▶ data custodian/steward

▶ data privacy officer (DPO)

▶ information life cycle

▶ privacy impact assessment (PIA)

▶ terms of agreement

▶ privacy notice

Sensitive Data Protection

Information systems today are part of almost everything an organization does. The loss of information and information systems has a material impact on various organizational processes and functions. Privacy therefore requires careful consideration.

Ensuring the confidentiality, integrity, and availability of data is at the core of an information security risk management program. Organizations are tasked with many data security and privacy practices that

need to be carried out, as defined in policies related to data handling and data management. Failure to ensure the confidentiality, integrity, and availability of data can result in the following:

▶ Reputational damage

▶ Identify theft

▶ Intellectual policy theft

▶ Regulatory fines and lawsuits

Data policies, which used to govern overall IT administrative tasks, need to be based on organizational requirements and regulatory compliance.

Policies for data protection should include how to classify, handle, store, and destroy data. It is important for an organization to document its security objectives. Later, it can change and adjust the policy when and as needed. An organization might have a reason to make new classifications as business goals change; when it does, it needs to make sure the changes are recorded in its documentation. Customers should also be provided with appropriate *privacy notices* and *terms of agreement*, particularly when an organization offers an electronic service and collects personal data. This is an ongoing, ever-changing process.

Data protection scenarios begin with proper classification of data, based on the impact of its loss or unauthorized access. Organizational data assets might also be subject to legal discovery mandates, and a careful accounting is vital to ensure that data can be located, if requested, and that it is protected against destruction or recycling. Proper data handling also ensures that data storage media can be properly processed for reuse or disposal when appropriate. Special requirements for sensitive data might require the outright destruction of a storage device and logging of its destruction in the inventory catalog.

Be sure to refer to Chapter 9, "Enterprise Security Concepts," for a refresher on privacy-enhancing technologies, such as tokenization, data masking, and redaction.

Data Sensitivity Labeling and Handling

Information must be classified according to its value and level of sensitivity so that the appropriate level of security can be used and access to data can be controlled. A system of classification should be effective and easy to administer and should be uniformly applied throughout the organization. Data classification is an important component of *information life cycle* management. This is the

process around the management of data from its creation to disposal. A common data classification scheme includes the following classifications:

▶ **Public:** Non-sensitive data that has the least, if any, negative impact on the organization. Press releases and marketing materials are two common examples.

▶ **Proprietary:** Data disclosed outside the organization on a limited basis. Proprietary data often includes information that is exchanged with prospective customers and business partners, for example. Such data is usually protected by a signed nondisclosure agreement (NDA).

▶ **Private:** Compartmental data used within a specific division, such as human resources. Typically, disclosure of private data does not cause the company much damage, but this data should be protected for confidentiality reasons. An example of this type of data is the year-end bonus payout for each employee.

▶ **Confidential:** Data that might cause damage to the organization if it were exposed. Confidential data might be widely distributed within an organization but is typically reserved for employees only and should not be shared outside. Examples might include competitive battle cards and employee training presentations.

▶ **Sensitive:** Data that would have a severe impact to an organization if it were exposed. Sensitive data typically should not be broadly shared internally or externally. Access to sensitive data should be limited and tightly controlled.

The U.S. government uses a classification system with Top Secret and Secret among the most sensitive classifications. If the information in these categories fell into the wrong hands, it could have grave or severe consequences for national security. Keep in mind that data does not necessarily always stay within one classification. Information about a project under consideration might be considered sensitive until the project plans are finalized. At that point, it might require a lesser classification. As another example, consider a publicly traded company's financial reports. Eventually, the company will publicly release its quarterly financial statements. However, while the reports are being gathered and prepared, such data is considered sensitive.

> **ExamAlert**
>
> An NDA should be in place to protect proprietary data that an organization needs to share with an outside entity.

The preceding discussion focuses mainly on the confidentiality of data. However, data classification should also consider the impact on integrity and availability. For example, data classified as public will likely have no confidentiality implications. However, such data is still subject to integrity and availability considerations. Financial reports available to the public could certainly have a significant impact on an organization if the integrity of that data were compromised. Furthermore, not properly making this information available could have consequences. Similarly, private data needs to be protected for integrity, availability, and confidentiality.

> **ExamAlert**
>
> Be sure to consider confidentiality, integrity, and availability in any scenario that involves data classification. Although public data does not require confidentiality, it might be important to consider its integrity and availability.

Understanding and documenting how classifications correlate to security objectives is important. When classifications are established, they should be adhered to and closely monitored, and employees should be trained so that they understand the information classifications. Data classifications can also help when submitting discoverable information that is subject to the Federal Rules of Civil Procedure, if the organization will be involved in a lawsuit.

Privacy Laws and Regulatory Compliance

Particularly in light of various privacy laws regarding sensitive data about individuals, organizations have implemented processes to identify and label data that may potentially be subject to such laws and regulations. Two of the most common examples are *personally identifiable information* (PII) and personal health information (PHI). PII is, broadly, any data that can be used to identify an individual. More specifically, the U.S. Office of Management and Budget defines PII as "information which can be used to distinguish or trace an individual's identity, such as their name, social security number, biometric records, etc. alone, or when combined with other personal or identifying information which is linked or linkable to a specific individual, such as date and place of birth, mother's maiden name, etc."

To be considered PII, information must be specifically associated with an individual person. Gender and state of residence, for example, don't by themselves identify an individual. Information that is either provided anonymously or not associated with its owner before collection is not considered

PII. Unique information, such as a personal profile, a unique identifier, biometric information, and an IP address that is associated with PII, can be considered PII. The definition of PII is not anchored to any single category of information or technology. An organization must train employees to recognize that non-PII data can become PII data whenever additional information is made publicly available (in any medium and from any source) so that, when combined with other available information, it could be used to identify an individual. Organizations should require all employees and contractors to complete privacy training annually, beginning within a set number of days after the start of employment.

> **ExamAlert**
>
> PII is information about a person that contains some unique identifier from which the identity of the person can be determined. Examples of PII include name, address, phone number, fax number, email address, financial profile, Social Security number, and credit card information. PII is not limited to these examples and includes any other personal information that is linked or linkable to an individual.

PHI applies to specific organizations that create and collect health information, as covered under the Privacy Rule of the Health Insurance Portability and Accountability Act (HIPAA). HIPAA's Privacy Rule regulates the use and disclosure of PHI for organizations. Organizations must understand their responsibilities regarding such data and must also know the practices they must abide by. For example, PHI must be protected for 50 years after an individual's death. In addition, the Privacy Rule specifically requires that the covered entities abide by the following regarding PHI:

▶ Organizations must disclose PHI to individuals within 30 days, upon request.

▶ Individuals must be notified of uses regarding their PHI.

▶ A patient's written authorization is required before PHI is disclosed for treatment or payment.

▶ Organizations must take reasonable steps to ensure the confidentiality of communications with individuals.

▶ Reasonable efforts must be made to disclose minimal information to achieve its purpose.

▶ Disclosures of PHI must be tracked, and privacy and policy procedures must be documented.

> **Note**
>
> Many other privacy and regulatory requirements affect the safeguarding and handling of personal information. In the United States, examples include the Gramm–Leach–Bliley Act, the Fair Credit Reporting Act, and the Children's Online Privacy Protection Act. Related examples include the General Data Protection Regulation (GDPR) and the Personal Information Protection and Electronic Documents Act (PIPEDA). As of May 2018, GDPR strengthens and unifies data protection for individuals within the European Union. Although GDPR is a law in the European Union, it has wide range globally because many organizations operate globally and have customers around the world. PIPEDA is a Canadian law that governs the collection and use of personal information.

For many organizations, privacy policies mandate detailed requirements to assure privacy and spell out significant legal penalties for noncompliance. As a result, organizational privacy policies will play a big role in helping to drive compliance.

A privacy policy must contain the following features:

▶ A list of the categories of PII the operator collects

▶ A list of the categories of third parties with which the operator might share such PII

▶ A description of the process by which consumers can review and request changes to their PII collected by the operator

▶ A description of the process by which the operator notifies consumers of material changes to the operator's privacy policy

Data Roles and Responsibilities

All data in your organization should have assigned data roles. This starts with data ownership. The data owner is responsible for determining how much risk to accept. On the surface, data ownership might seem to be a simple matter. However, one look at a transaction that involves third parties proves otherwise. When an employee purchases an airline ticket for business travel, processing intermediaries such as payment systems, ticket processors, and online booking tools assert a right to capture and distribute travel data. These intermediaries might also make data available to third-party aggregators. The question of rightful ownership remains murky. Depending on who you ask, the data being collected could belong to the organization, the booking agency, or the airline.

The organization must decide who will be permitted to access data and how those parties can use it. To protect organizational data, when the organization enters any third-party agreement, the topic of data ownership and data aggregation must be addressed.

Some cloud services offer data ownership agreements that specifically identify the data owner and outline ownership of relevant data. When assessing data ownership, especially when the organization is using a cloud provider, consider the following:

▶ A determination of what is relevant data

▶ Provisions for exercising rights of ownership over the data

▶ Access to the organization's environments

▶ Costs associated with exercising rights of ownership over the data

▶ Contract term and termination conditions

▶ Liability of the cloud provider

Data classification and appropriate data ownership are key elements in an organization's security policy. These concepts must be extended to third-party entities to properly protect data that belongs to the organization. A key component of any security program is clearly defined roles and responsibilities. Pertaining specifically to the data, you should be familiar with three primary roles:

▶ **Data owner:** The *data owner* often is responsible for a specific information asset and is often a senior person within a department or division. For example, the vice president of human resources could be the data owner for all employee data. The data owner is responsible for determining the classification level of the data.

▶ **Data custodian/steward:** The *data custodian* is responsible for implementing the data classification and security controls, given the classification determined by the data owner. The data custodian is also known as the data *steward*.

▶ **Data privacy officer:** The *data privacy officer* (*DPO*) is responsible for legal compliance with data privacy regulations and manages data protection risk that relates to ensuring the proper management of personal and protected information. For example, in addition to the requirements mentioned in the previous section, HIPAA also requires covered entities to designate a privacy officer.

The GDPR has further defined two additional roles: the data controller and the data processor. GDPR defines the *data controller* as "a natural or legal person, which alone or jointly with others, determines the purposes and means of personal data processing." This role is essentially the manager of personal data. An individual who process personal data on behalf of the data controller is known as a *data processor*.

> **ExamAlert**
>
> Data owners determine the level of classification for their data, and data custodians/stewards implement the classification and security controls for the data.

Data Retention and Disposal

Sensitive and privacy-related data (including log files, physical records, security evaluations, and other operational documentation) should be managed according to an organization's retention and disposal policies. These should include specifications for access authorization, term of retention, and requirements for disposal. Depending on the relative level of data sensitivity, retention and disposal requirements may become extensive and detailed.

Industry best practices and laws can also affect the retention and storage of data, log files, and audit logs. For example, in the United States, the Federal Rules of Civil Procedure (FRCP) have implications for data retention policies. They govern the conduct and procedure of all civil actions in federal district courts. Organizations can face issues related to the discovery, preservation, and production of digitally stored information. For example, if an organization is sued by a former employee for wrongful termination, the department might be compelled during the discovery phase of the suit to produce all documents related to that individual's work performance. This used to mean personnel records and copies of any written correspondence (such as memos and letters) concerning the performance of that employee. Previously, debate sometimes arose over what constitutes a document, given that most records now reside in electronic format. The FRCP establishes that electronic data is clearly subject to discovery. It goes further and says that all data is subject to discovery, regardless of storage format or location; email, instant messaging, mobile devices, and voice mail, for example, are all subject to discovery.

Consideration must be given to the burden placed on organizations when they are required to produce data, as well as the economics and advantage of data retained. Consider the Payment Card Industry Data Security Standard (PCI

DSS) requirements governing the use and storage of credit card data. An organization that processes and stores credit card data is likely to be subject to these regulations. However, choosing to forgo the burden by outsourcing credit card processing and not storing the data could impact personalized business and other value-added services the company could offer its clients.

By limiting the collection of personal information to the least amount necessary to conduct business, an organization limits potential negative consequences in case of a data breach involving PII. Organizations should consider the types, categories, and total amount of PII used, collected, and maintained. When PII is no longer relevant or necessary, it should be properly destroyed in accordance with any litigation holds and the Federal Records Act. Organizations should also ensure that retired hardware has been properly sanitized before disposal. When organizations choose to capture and retain sensitive data, privacy-enhancing technologies should be employed to protect the data and ensure privacy. This includes minimizing the types of data collected and stored to only that which is necessary. Otherwise, data should be protected by controls such as data masking, tokenization, and anonymization. Refer to Chapter 9 for details on these techniques.

Data retention policies should consider the requirements surrounding retention of data. In lieu of any requirements, the policies need to balance the needs for proper safeguarding and potential legal burdens against the value of retaining the data. At a minimum, these policies should clearly describe which data is retained and for how long. Proper disposal and disposal techniques are covered in depth in Chapter 15, "Physical Security Controls."

Privacy Impact Assessment

A *privacy impact assessment (PIA)* is needed for any organization that collects, uses, stores, or processes personal information. This includes, for example, the data of employees, partners, and customers. Specific types of sensitive data include PII and PHI. The PIA is an important first step in identifying such information assets. A *privacy threshold assessment* can determine whether a system contains such information. This assessment is required before an organization analyzes impact and determines how to best protect the information. A privacy threshold assessment can be as simple as distributing a questionnaire to system and application owners. The assessment might consist of an assortment of specific data fields for the owner to select. Examples could include name, Social Security number, gender, citizenship, place of birth, address, phone number, credit card number, driver's license number, race, income, and banking information.

As demonstrated earlier, an analysis of the impact of loss or disclosure is needed. A common consequence might be regulatory fines. In fact, all 50 states have laws requiring notification of breaches involving personally identifiable information. Consider, though, that other consequences might be worse. For example, imagine the consequences of the unauthorized disclosure of personnel information for operatives working undercover for a federal agency.

> **ExamAlert**
>
> Assessing threat actors begins with identifying their relationship to the organization as internal or external.

Cram Quiz

Answer these questions. The answers follow the last question. If you cannot answer these questions correctly, consider reading this chapter again until you can.

1. Your organization uses the *private* and *public* labels to classify data, as the internal security policy details how data should be protected based on the classification label. The decision was made to add an additional "proprietary" label. Which is the most likely reason this was done?

   ○ **A.** To create more searchable data

   ○ **B.** To provide better data classification

   ○ **C.** To clarify data that should not be shared outside the organization

   ○ **D.** To reduce costs

2. Which one of the following is responsible for implementing the data classification and security controls?

   ○ **A.** Data owner

   ○ **B.** Data custodian

   ○ **C.** Data privacy officer

   ○ **D.** Data controller

3. Which data classification type contains data that would have a severe impact to the organization were it exposed, that should not be broadly shared internally or externally, and that should be tightly controlled?

   ○ **A.** Public

   ○ **B.** Proprietary

   ○ **C.** Confidential

   ○ **D.** Sensitive

Cram Quiz Answers

Answer 1: B. This additional level of classification will help differentiate how data should be protected. While it could help make data more searchable, the question indicates that it's related to the policy for how data should be protected. Thus, answer A is incorrect. Answer C is incorrect because proprietary data may still be shared outside the organization. Answer D is also incorrect because there may arguably be an indirect cost reduction as a result, but this is not the most appropriate choice, given the question.

Answer 2: B. The data custodian is responsible for implementing the data classification and security controls, given the classification determined by the data owner. The data custodian is also known as the data steward. Answers A, C, and D are incorrect. The owner is responsible for determining the classification level of the data. The data privacy officer (DPO) is responsible for legal compliance with regulations. The controller is the manager of personal data according to General Data Protection Regulation (GDPR).

Answer 3: D. Data that is classified as sensitive would have a severe impact to an organization if it were exposed. It typically should not be broadly shared internally or externally. Access to sensitive data should be limited and tightly controlled. Answer A is incorrect. *Public data* is non-sensitive data that has the least, if any, negative impact on the organization. Answer B is incorrect. *Proprietary data* often includes information that is exchanged with prospective customers and business partners. Answer C is incorrect. *Confidential data* might cause damage to the organization if it were exposed. It might be widely distributed within an organization but is typically reserved for employees only and should not be shared outside.

What Next?

If you want more practice on this chapter's exam objective before you move on, remember that you can access all of the Cram Quiz questions on the Pearson Test Prep software online. You can also create a custom exam by objective with the Online Practice Test. Note any objective you struggle with and go to that objective's material in this chapter.

Glossary of Essential Terms and Components

A

acceptable use policy (AUP) An organization's policy that provides specific detail about what users may do with their network access, including email and instant messaging usage for personal purposes, limitations on access times, and the storage space available to each user.

access control list (ACL) In the broadest sense, the underlying data associated with a network resource that defines the access permissions. The most common privileges include the ability to read, write to, delete, and execute a file.

accounting The tracking, primarily for auditing purposes, of users' access to resources.

active logging A common intelligence gathering tool used during the forensics process.

active reconnaissance Reconnaissance that requires engaging with the target, such as through port scanning and service identification.

Address Resolution Protocol (ARP) A protocol that resolves a device's assigned IP address to its MAC hardware address.

administrative control A control based on business and organizational processes and procedures.

Advanced Encryption Standard (AES) A symmetrical 128-bit fixed-block encryption system that has a key size of 128, 192, or 256 bits and replaces the legacy DES standard.

advanced persistent threat (APT) A threat that is rooted in the capability to infiltrate a network and remain inside while going undetected. This access often provides the means for a more strategic target or defined objective, including the capability to exfiltrate information over a long period of time.

adversarial artificial intelligence (AI) Techniques such as machine learning used to solve a variety of problems and challenges used by an adversary.

Agile An SDLC model that breaks development into cycles. The Agile model combines iterative and incremental process models.

air gap A physical isolation gap between a system or network and the outside world.

annual loss expectancy (ALE) The expected cost per year arising from a risk's occurrence. It is calculated as the product of the single loss expectancy (SLE) and the annualized rate of occurrence (ARO).

annual rate of occurrence (ARO) The number of times a given risk will occur within a single year.

antispam A software program that can add another layer of defense to the infrastructure by filtering out undesirable email.

antivirus A software program used to protect the user environment that scans for email and downloadable malicious code.

Arduino A low-cost single-board computer used to create interactive projects.

armored virus A virus that is hard to detect and that seeks to make analyzing its functions difficult.

ARP poisoning An attack in which a perpetrator tricks a device into thinking any IP address is related to any MAC address. In addition, perpetrators can broadcast a fake or spoofed ARP reply to an entire network and poison all computers.

asymmetric keys A pair of key values (one public and the other private) used to encrypt and decrypt data, respectively. Only the holder of the private key can decrypt data encrypted with the public key; this means that anyone who obtains a copy of the public key can send data to the private key holder in confidence.

attribute-based access control (ABAC) A logical access control model recommended as the preferred access control model for information sharing among diverse organizations by the Federal Identity, Credential, and Access Management (FICAM) Roadmap.

auditing The tracking of user access to resources, primarily for security purposes.

authentication The process of identifying users.

Authentication Header (AH) A component of the IPsec protocol that provides integrity, authentication, and antireplay capabilities.

authorization The process of identifying what a given user is allowed to do.

automated indicator sharing (AIS) An initiative from the U.S. Department of Homeland Security that enables the exchange of cyber-security threat indicators.

B

banner grabbing A technique used to identify what operating system is running on a machine, as well as the services that are running.

baseline A measure of normal activity that is used to determine abnormal system and network behaviors.

Bcrypt A key-stretching algorithm based on the Blowfish cipher that provides an adaptive hash function.

behavior-based IDS A detection method in which a user notices an unusual pattern of behavior, such as a continually operating hard drive or a significantly slowed level of performance.

behavior-based monitoring The use of established patterns of base-line operations to identify variations that might identify unauthorized access attempts.

birthday attack An attack that finds collisions within hash functions, resulting in a more efficient method of brute-forcing one-way hashes.

black box (unknown environment) A test conducted when the assessor has no information or knowledge about the inner workings of the system or knowledge of the source code.

blockchain A digital ledger where transactions are grouped into blocks, each linked to the previous block through a cryptographic hash and shared with the network.

block cipher An algorithm that transforms a message from plaintext (unencrypted form) to ciphertext (encrypted form), one piece at a time. The block size represents a standard chunk of data that is transformed in a single operation.

Blowfish A block cipher that can encrypt using any size chunk of data and perform encryption with any length encryption key, up to 448 bits.

bluejacking An attack used to generate messages that appear to be from the device itself, leading users to follow obvious prompts and establish an open Bluetooth connection to the attacker's device.

bluesnarfing A Bluetooth attack that can expose or alter a user's information.

boot sector virus A type of virus that is placed into the first sector of a hard drive so that when the

computer boots, the virus loads into memory.

bot Short for robot, an automated computer program that needs no user interaction. Bots allow hackers to take control of a system. Many bots used together can form a botnet.

botnet A large number of computers (bots) that forward transmissions to other computers on the Internet. You might also hear a botnet referred to as a zombie army.

bring your own device (BYOD) A policy that allows employees to use personal mobile devices for access to enterprise data and systems.

brute-force attack An attack that relies on cryptanalysis or algorithms capable of performing exhaustive key searches.

buffer overflow An attack that occurs when the data presented to an application or a service exceeds the storage space allocation that has been reserved in memory for that application or service.

business continuity plan (BCP) A plan that describes a long-term systems and services replacement and recovery strategy, designed for when a complete loss of facilities occurs. A business continuity plan prepares for automatic failover of critical services to redundant offsite systems.

business impact analysis (BIA) The process of determining the impacts that might result from the interruption of time-sensitive or critical business processes.

business partner agreement (BPA) A type of contract that establishes the responsibilities of each partner.

C

captive portal A web page that is first launched when a user is connecting through a network and that usually requires some type of interaction before the user is allowed access to other networking or Internet sites.

cat A command-line file-manipulation command for reading files sequentially that is used to concatenate files.

.cer A common certificate extension.

certificate authority (CA) A system that issues, distributes, and maintains current information about digital certificates. Such authorities can be private (operated within a company or an organization for its own use) or public (operated on the Internet for general public access).

certificate policy A statement that governs the use of digital certificates.

certificate revocation list (CRL) A list generated by a CA that enumerates digital certificates that are no longer valid and the reasons they are no longer valid.

certificate signing request (CSR) A request to apply for a digital certificate.

certification practice statement (CPS) A document that defines the practices and procedures a CA uses

to manage the digital certificates it issues.

chain of custody The documentation of all transfers of evidence from one person to another, showing the date, time, reason for transfer, and signatures of both parties involved in the transfer. Chain of custody also refers to the process of tracking evidence from a crime scene to the courtroom.

Challenge Handshake Authentication Protocol (CHAP) A widely used authentication method in which a hashed version of a user's password is transmitted during the authentication process.

chmod A command-line tool used to change access permissions for files and directories.

choose your own device (CYOD) An option in which an organization controls the devices an employee can use by providing a list of approved devices.

cipher A method of encrypting text. The term *cipher* also refers to an encrypted message (although the term *ciphertext* is preferred).

cipher block chaining (CBC) A commonly used mode that provides for confidentiality only and not integrity.

clickjacking A hijacking attack that takes advantage of browser vulnerabilities and allows the attacker to redirect clicks or keystrokes to something the user does not expect.

cloud access security broker (CASB) A Gartner-created term that describes a cloud cybersecurity

layer focused on visibility, compliance, data security, and threat protection.

Cloud Security Alliance (CSA) A nonprofit organization that provides security best practices for cloud-based services and computing.

cold site A remote site that has electricity, plumbing, and heating installed, ready for use when enacting disaster recovery or business continuity plans. At a cold site, the company enacting the plan supplies all other equipment, systems, and configurations. Compare this with hot and warm sites.

common access card (CAC) A smart card used in military, reserve officer, and military contractor identity authentication systems.

compensating control An alternative control that is intended to reduce the risk of an existing or potential control weakness.

computer/cyber-incident response team (CIRT) A team of experts that responds to security incidents. Also referred to as a CSIRT (computer security incident response team).

confusion A method that involves hiding any connection between ciphertext and plaintext, making it difficult to reverse from ciphertext to plaintext without the key.

container A technology that packages applications and services together with their runtime environment, allowing them to be run anywhere.

continuity of operations plan (COOP) An initiative issued to

ensure that government departments and agencies are able to continue operation in case of natural, human-caused, or technological threats and national security emergencies.

Core Root of Trust Measurement (CRTM) The first trusted action executed at bootup. It measures the bootloader and sends the hash value to the TPM chip for storage in one of the platform configuration registers (PCR) before execution.

corporate owned, personally enabled (COPE) A policy by which employees are able to use corporate-owned devices for personal use.

corrective control A control that is reactive and provides measures to reduce harmful effects or restore the system being impacted.

counter mode A mode that essentially turns a block cipher into a stream cipher.

Counter Mode with Cipher Block Chaining Message Authentication Code Protocol (CCMP) A protocol based on the Advanced Encryption Standard (AES) encryption cipher.

cross-site request forgery (XSRF) A web attack that exploits existing site trust, such as unexpired banking session cookies, to perform actions on the trusting site using the already existing trusted account.

cross-site scripting (XSS) A web attack in which malicious executable code is placed on a website to allow the attacker to hijack a user session to conduct unauthorized access activities, expose confidential data, and log successful attacks back to the attacker.

cryptographic module Any combination of hardware, firmware, or software that implements cryptographic functions such as encryption, decryption, digital signatures, authentication techniques, and random number generation.

cryptography The process of protecting information by disguising (encrypting) it in a format that only authorized systems or individuals can read.

crypto-malware Malware that is specifically designed to find potentially valuable data on a system and encrypt it.

Cuckoo A malware analysis tool that provides results of what a file does when executed in an isolated environment.

curl A command-line tool that provides the ability to get and send data using URLs.

CVE/CVSS (Common Vulnerabilities and Exposure/Common Vulnerability Scoring System) A list of publicly known vulnerabilities that provides descriptions and references, along with severity ratings.

cyber kill chain A framework that is used to track the steps or phases that an attacker goes through as part of an intrusion.

D

dark web A part of the web that can't be accessed like regular websites but that requires the use of special software that provides secure communications.

data classification A system of organizing data into categories based upon the data sensitivity to help guide data protection measures.

data disposal The practice of disposing of equipment used by an organization.

Data Encryption Standard (DES) A block cipher that uses a 56-bit key and 8 bits of parity on each 64-bit chunk of data.

data execution prevention A security technology that can prevent security threats from executing code on a system.

data exfiltration The unauthorized transfer of data; also known as data theft.

data loss prevention (DLP) Security services that identify, monitor, and protect data during use, storage, or transfer between devices. DLP software relies on deep inspection of data and transactional details for unauthorized access operations.

decryption The process of turning ciphertext into plaintext.

defense-in-depth A term rooted in military strategy that requires a balanced emphasis on people, technology, and operations to maintain information assurance (IA).

demilitarized zone (DMZ) An area in a network that allows limited and controlled access from the public Internet. Also called a screened subnet.

denial of service (DoS) A type of attack that denies legitimate users access to a server or services by consuming sufficient system resources or network bandwidth to render a service unavailable.

detective control A control that warns that physical security measures are being violated.

deterrent control A control that is intended to discourage individuals from intentionally violating information security policies or procedures.

development and operations (DevOps) A term that originated from the recognition that organizational infrastructure should support development or the SDLC along with production capacity.

dictionary attack An attack in which software is used to compare hashed data, such as a password, to a word in a hashed dictionary. This is repeated until matches are found in the hashes. The goal is to match the password exactly to determine the original password that was used as the basis of the hash.

differential backup A backup that provides only the data that has changed since the last full backup. It is incomplete without the last full backup.

Diffie-Hellman (D-H) key exchange An early key exchange design in which two parties, without prior arrangement, can agree on a secret key that is known only to them.

Diffie-Hellman Ephemeral (DHE) An ephemeral version of D-H key exchange that uses a

different key for every conversation and supports perfect forward secrecy.

diffusion A method for mitigating the capability to identify patterns that might help break a cipher.

digital certificate An electronic document that includes the user's public key and the digital signature of the certificate authority (CA) that has authenticated the user. The digital certificate can also contain information about the user, the CA, and attributes that define what users are allowed to do with systems they access using the digital certificate.

Digital Signature Algorithm (DSA) A U.S. standard for the generation and verification of digital signatures to ensure authenticity.

disaster recovery plan (DRP) A plan that spells out actions to be taken in case a business is hit with a natural or human-caused disaster.

discretionary access control (DAC) An access control method in which access rights are configured at the discretion of accounts with authority over each resource, including the capability to extend administrative rights through the same mechanism.

distinguished encoding rules (DER) The binary form of a PEM certificate.

distributed denial of service (DDoS) An attack that originates from multiple systems simultaneously, causing even more extreme consumption of bandwidth and other resources than a DoS attack.

DLL injection A programming error that allows an attacker to run code within the context of another process, making it more difficult for an organization to trace the attack.

DNS poisoning An attack that involves redirecting legitimate traffic by changing the IP record for a specific domain.

dnsenum A tool that enumerates DNS by finding DNS servers and DNS records such as mail exchange servers, domain name servers, and the address records for a domain.

domain hijacking An attack that occurs when a domain is taken over without the original owner's knowledge or consent.

Domain Name System (DNS) A system that is responsible for translation of hierarchical human-readable named addresses into their numeric IP equivalents.

Domain Name System Security Extension (DNSSEC) A suite of specifications that provides protection against DNS attacks by authenticating DNS response data.

domain reputation Protection for registered domains that provides monitoring and threat intelligence.

dry-pipe fire suppression A sprinkler system with pressurized air in the pipes. If a fire starts, a slight delay occurs as the pipes fill with water. This system is used in areas where wet-pipe systems might freeze.

dumpster diving A technique used by an attacker that involves gathering useful information from discarded data.

DV certificate A certificate that is easily and quickly obtained that only verifies and includes the domain name.

E

EAP Flexible Authentication via Secure Tunneling (EAP-FAST) A proposed replacement to the Lightweight Extensible Authentication Protocol (LEAP) used for wireless authentication connections.

EAP Transport Layer Security (EAP-TLS) A protocol that uses certificate-based mutual authentication, negotiation of the encryption method, and encrypted key determination between the client and the authenticating server.

EAP Tunneled Transport Layer Security (EAP-TTLS) A protocol that is similar to PEAP but further extends TLS. With an established secure tunnel, the server authenticates the client using authentication attributes in the TLS wrapper.

edge computing Computing that happens near the edge of a network, close to where it's used or needed.

e-discovery The discovery process for electronically stored information.

eliciting information The use of varying techniques that can directly or indirectly lead to sensitive data loss or other compromise.

El Gamal An extension to the Diffie-Hellman design that is a complete public key encryption algorithm. It uses some of the key exchange elements from Diffie-Hellman and incorporates encryption on those keys.

elasticity The capability to expand and reduce cloud resources as needed.

electromagnetic interference (EMI) Electronic device interference that occurs when a device is in the vicinity of another device. EMI affects the performance of a device.

electromagnetic pulse (EMP) An electronic event that happens when a source emits a short-duration pulse of energy.

electronic codebook (ECB) A simple deterministic mode that divides a message into blocks and then encrypts each block on its own.

elliptic curve cryptography (ECC) A method in which elliptic curve equations are used to calculate encryption keys for use in general-purpose encryption.

Elliptic Curve Diffie-Hellman Ephemeral (ECDHE) A variant of the Diffie-Hellman key agreement protocol for ECC that uses an ephemeral mode of operation and supports perfect forward secrecy.

Encapsulating Security Payload (ESP) A method that provides confidentiality, data origin authentication, connectionless integrity, an antireplay service, and traffic flow confidentiality.

encryption The process of turning plaintext into ciphertext.

encryption algorithm A mathematical formula or method used to scramble information before it is transmitted over insecure media. Examples include RSA, DH, IDEA, Blowfish, MD5, and DSS/DSA.

end-of-life (EOL) Unsupported software that the vendor has retired.

ephemeral key A key that is used for only a single session.

escalation of privilege An exploitation technique that gives an attacker or tester access to a higher authorization and provides the capability to conduct more advanced commands and routines.

EV certificate A type of digital certificate that provides a high level of trust and security features proving the owner of the certificate.

evil twin A situation in which an unauthorized wireless access point has been set up to mount on-path attack.

exploitation framework A structure that helps in penetrating testing and risk assessments. Each exploitation framework contains a set of exploits for known vulnerabilities.

extranet A special internetwork architecture in which an organization's external partners and customers are granted access to some parts of its intranet and the services it provides in a secure, controlled manner.

F

federation A way to connect identity management systems by allowing identities to cross multiple jurisdictions.

file integrity checker A tool that computes a cryptographic hash such as SHA-1 or MD5 for all selected files. A database of the hashes is created, and the hashes are periodically recalculated and compared to the hashes in the database to check for modification.

File Transfer Protocol (FTP) A client/server data file transfer service for TCP networks that are capable of anonymous or authenticated access.

firewall A network system that monitors incoming and outgoing traffic and makes determinations to allow or deny the traffic based on policy.

framework A structure that generally includes more components than a guide and is used as a basis for implementing and managing security controls.

full backup A complete backup of all data. This is the most time- and resource-intensive form of backup, requiring the largest amount of data storage.

fuzzing An unknown environment for software testing in which semi-random data is injected into a program or protocol stack to detect bugs.

G

Galois/Counter Mode (GCM) A cryptographic block cipher mode of operation that provides for both integrity and confidentiality and that works in 128-bit blocks.

General Data Protection Regulation (GDPR) A regulation intended to strengthen data protection for all individuals within the European Union (EU).

geofencing The use of GPS coordinates or radio-frequency identification (RFID) to define a geographic perimeter.

GNU Privacy Guard (GPG) A tool that encrypts and decrypts email messages by using asymmetric encryption schemes such as RSA.

gray box (partially known environment) A testing method that combines white box and black box techniques. It can be thought of as being translucent as the tester has some understanding of or limited knowledge of the inner workings of the system being tested.

grep A command-line file manipulation command that searches files for patterns.

group policy A tool that eases administration in managing the environment of users in a Microsoft network. This can include installing software and updates or controlling what appears on the desktop. The group policy object (GPO) applies a group policy to users and computers.

guide Specific information about how standards should be implemented. A guide or guideline is generally not mandatory and provides recommendations or good practices.

H

hacktivist A threat actor who uses digital tools for malicious intent, based on political, social, or ideological reasoning.

hardware security module (HSM) A dedicated crypto-processor that is specifically designed for the protection of transactions, identities, and applications by securing cryptographic keys.

hash value The resultant output or data generated from an encryption hash when applied to a specific set of data. If it is computed and passed as part of an incoming message and then is recomputed upon message receipt, this value can be used to verify the received data when the two hash values match.

hash-based message authentication code (HMAC) A code that provides additional security to MAC by adding another integrity check to the data being transmitted.

hashing A methodology used to calculate a short, secret value from a data set of any size (usually for an entire message or for individual transmission units). This secret value is recalculated independently on the receiving end and is compared to the submitted value to verify the sender's identity.

head A command-line file manipulation command that displays the beginning of a text file or file fed to the command.

Health Insurance Portability and Accountability Act (HIPAA) U.S. legislation that includes data privacy and security provisions for protecting medical information.

heating, ventilation, air conditioning (HVAC) A form of environmental control that warms, cools, and transports air for the purpose of thermal and humidity regulation.

hoax A situation that seems like it could be legitimate but often results from people seeking to carry out various threats.

honeyfile A file used as bait intended to attract an attacker.

honeynet A network used as bait to attract an attacker.

honeypot A decoy system designed to attract hackers. A honeypot usually has all its logging and tracing enabled, and its security level is lowered on purpose. Such systems often include deliberate lures or bait, in the hopes of attracting would-be attackers who think they can obtain valuable items on these systems.

host-based IDS (HIDS) Systems that monitor communications on a host-by-host basis and try to filter malicious data. These types of IDSs are good at detecting unauthorized file modifications and user activity.

host-based IPS (HIPS) A software intrusion detection system capable of reacting to and preventing or terminating unauthorized access within a single host system.

hot site A physical site that is immediately available for continuing computer operations if an emergency arises. It typically has all the necessary hardware and software loaded and configured, and it is available continuously. Compare this with warm and cold sites.

HOTP (HMAC-based one-time password) An algorithm that relies on a shared secret and a moving factor or counter.

hping A packet assembler and analyzer that provides a number of security capabilities.

Hypertext Transfer Protocol (HTTP) A client/server protocol for network transfer of information between a web server and a client browser over the World Wide Web (WWW).

Hypertext Transfer Protocol over Secure Sockets Layer (HTTPS) A protocol used in a secured connection that encapsulates data transferred between the client and web server. It occurs on port 443.

hypervisor A virtualization platform that enables more than one operating system to run on a host computer at the same time. It controls how access to a computer's processors and memory is shared. A Type I native or bare-metal hypervisor is software that runs directly on a hardware platform. A Type II, or hosted, hypervisor is software that runs in an operating system environment.

I

identification A user or device presenting information such as a username, a process ID, a smart card, or another unique identifier, claiming an identity.

identity fraud The use of a person's personal information without

authorization to deceive or commit a crime.

IEEE 802.1X A standard designed to enhance the security of wireless networks.

impersonation A method by which someone assumes the character or appearance of someone else.

incremental backup A backup that includes only the data that has changed since the last incremental backup. It resets the archive bit.

indicator of compromise (IOC) Evidence that indicates a security breach or event has occurred.

industrial control system (ICS) A system that is considered to be critical to the infrastructure, such as manufacturing, a logistics and transportation network, energy and utilities, telecommunication services, agriculture, and food production networks.

influence campaign Coordinated actions that seek to affect the development, actions, and behavior of the targeted population.

Infrastructure as a Service (IaaS) A cloud computing model in which hardware, storage, and networking components are virtualized and provided by an outsourced service provider.

Infrastructure as Code (IaC) The incorporation of infrastructure configuration into application code. Also known as the programmable infrastructure.

initial exploitation An exploitation technique that commonly has only

regular user access, with no access to high-value areas.

initialization vector (IV) A fixed-size input of a random or pseudo-random value used with block cipher modes.

integer overflow A software programming error that can facilitate malicious code or a buffer overflow.

integrity measurement A method that uses attestation challenges from computed hashes of system or application information to obtain confidence in the trustworthiness and identity of a platform or software.

interconnection security agreement (ISA) An agreement between organizations that have connected or shared IT systems.

International Organization for Standardization (ISO) A body that provides best practice recommendations on information security management.

Internet Control Message Protocol (ICMP) A transport protocol in the TCP/IP suite that operates separately from TCP or UDP transfer. ICMP is intended for passing error messages and is used for services such as ping and traceroute.

Internet of Things (IoT) A network of connected devices that perform specific functions using embedded systems and sensors.

Internet Protocol Security (IPsec) A tool used for the encryption of TCP/IP traffic. IPsec provides security extensions to IPv4. It manages special relationships, called

security associations, between pairs of machines.

intranet A portion of the information technology infrastructure that belongs to and is controlled by an organization.

intrusion detection system (IDS) A sophisticated network protection system designed to detect attacks in progress but not to prevent potential attacks from occurring. Many IDSs actually can trace attacks back to an apparent source, and some can even automatically notify all hosts through which attack traffic passes that they are forwarding such traffic.

intrusive scan A vulnerability scan that tries to exploit a vulnerability.

ipconfig A tool that displays network settings such as IP address, subnet mask, and default gateway.

IP spoofing An attack that seeks to bypass IP address filters by setting up a connection from a client and sourcing the packets with an IP address that is allowed through the filter.

J

jailbreaking Removing the restriction to run only Apple-authorized apps on a device.

jamming attack An attack on a wireless network that is performed by setting up a nearby access point and using a dedicated wireless jamming device.

K

Kerberos A set of authentication services, including the authentication service (AS) exchange protocol, the ticket-granting service (TGS) exchange protocol, and the client/server (CS) exchange protocol.

key derivation function A function that derives a key, based on the password as the origin point.

key escrow A situation in which a CA or another entity maintains a copy of the private key associated with the public key signed by the CA.

key exchange A technique in which a pair of keys is generated and then exchanged between two systems (typically, a client and server) over a network connection to allow them to establish a secure connection.

key management The process of creating and managing cryptographic keys and digital certificates.

key stretching A technique that involves running a password through an algorithm to produce an enhanced key, usually of at least 128 bits.

keylogger A tool that monitors and sends keystrokes typed from an infected machine.

L

layered security The practice of implementing security at different levels or layers to form a complete

security strategy and provide better protection than by implementing an individual security defense.

LDAP injection A technique in which malicious input is applied to a directory server, which may result in unauthorized queries, granting of permissions, and even password changes.

least functionality The principle that, by default, systems provide a wide variety of functions and services, some of which are not necessary to support the essential operation of the organization.

least privilege An access control practice in which a logon is given only minimal access to resources required to perform its tasks.

Lightweight Directory Access Protocol (LDAP) A TCP/IP protocol that allows client systems to access directory services and related data. In most cases, LDAP is used as part of management or other applications or in browsers to access directory services information.

logger A command-line tool that is used to add logs to the local syslog file or a remote syslog server.

logic bomb A virus or Trojan horse designed to execute malicious actions when a certain event occurs or when a specified period of time goes by.

M

MAC spoofing An attack that involves spoofing the hard-coded

Media Access Control (MAC) address of a network card.

macro virus A virus inserted into a Microsoft Office document and emailed to unsuspecting users.

malware Malicious software used to cause damage or gain unauthorized access to systems.

mandatory access control (MAC) A centralized security method in which users are not allowed to change permissions on objects.

man-in-the-middle (on-path attack) An attack in which a hacker attempts to intercept data in a network stream and then insert his or her own data into the communication. The goal is to disrupt or take over communications.

mantrap (access control vestibule) A two-door configuration used in high-security facilities that allows only one person to pass at a time.

mean time between failures (MTBF) The point in time at which a device will still be operational, denoting the average time a device will function before failing.

mean time to failure (MTTF) The expected time to failure for a nonrepairable system.

mean time to recovery (MTTR) The average time that a device will take to recover from any failure.

memorandum of agreement (MOA) A document that outlines the terms and details of an agreement between parties, including each party's requirements and

responsibilities. Also known as an MOU.

memorandum of understanding (MOU) A binding, collaborative agreement entered into by two or more parties.

memory leak A programming error that reduces performance of a system and can cause an entire application or computer to become unresponsive. It has an impact on a system's availability.

message authentication code (MAC) A piece of information used to authenticate a message. It works like a hash to detect tampering.

message digest The output of an encryption hash that is applied to some fixed-size chunk of data. A message digest provides a profound integrity check because even a change to 1 bit in the target data changes the resulting digest value. This explains why digests are included so often in network transmissions.

Message Digest algorithm A hashing algorithm based on a message digest.

Microsoft CHAP (MSCHAP) An encrypted authentication mechanism that is similar to CHAP. It has two versions: MSCHAPv1 and MSCHAPv2.

mission-essential function An activity that needs to be immediately functional at an alternate site until normal operations can be restored.

MITRE ATT&CK A knowledge base and framework of different attack techniques to understand and defend against an attacker.

model verification A method used to automatically and thoroughly check whether a system model meets a given specification.

multifactor authentication A type of authentication that requires more than just a password for account access. Multifactor authentication involves two or more of the types of authentication (something you know, something you have, something you are, something you do, and somewhere you are), not simply multiple credentials or keys of the same type.

multipartite virus A virus that infects executable files and also attacks the master boot record of a system.

N

National Institute of Standards and Technology (NIST) An agency within the U.S. Department of Commerce that is responsible for developing measurement standards, including standards for cybersecurity best practices, monitoring, and validation.

near-field communication (NFC) A set of standards for contactless communication between devices.

netcat A network utility for gathering information from TCP and UDP network connections.

network-based IDS (NIDS) An IDS that monitors packet flow and tries to locate unauthorized packets that might have gotten through the firewall. A NIDS may be used to detect DoS attacks and unauthorized user access.

network-based IPS (NIPS)
A device or software program designed to sit inline with traffic flows and prevent attacks in real time.

Network Time Protocol (NTP)
A UDP protocol used for device clock synchronization that provides a standard time base over variable-latency networks. This is critical for time-synchronized encryption and access protocols such as Kerberos.

next-generation firewall   A firewall that goes beyond traditional port and IP address examination to include application and user awareness.

nmap   A network scanning tool used for locating network hosts, detecting operating systems, and identifying services.

nondisclosure agreement (NDA)   A legally binding document that organizations might require of their employees and other people who come into contact with confidential information.

nonresident virus   A type of virus that, when executed, looks for targets locally and even across the network.

normalization   The conversion of data to its anticipated, simplest known form.

nslookup   A command-line utility used for troubleshooting DNS.

NTLM (NT LAN Manager)   An older Microsoft authentication protocol that requires Active Directory and relies on Microsoft Windows user

credentials in the authentication process.

O

OAuth (Open Authorization)
A framework used for Internet token-based authorization that provides API authorization between applications.

obfuscation   The act of making something difficult to understand.

object identifier (OID)   A hierarchical globally unique identifier for an object.

OCSP stapling   A process that helps reduce the certificate validity request load by allowing a web server to "staple" a time-stamped OCSP response as part of the TLS handshake with the client.

offboarding   A process in which user identities that no longer require access to the environment are disabled or deactivated and then deleted from the environment, based on organizational policy.

onboarding   A process used to create an identity profile and the information required to describe the identity.

Online Certificate Status Protocol (OCSP)   An Internet protocol defined by the IETF that is used to validate digital certificates issued by a CA. OCSP was created as an alternative to certificate revocation lists (CRLs) and overcomes certain limitations of CRLs.

open source intelligence (OSINT) Information available for collection from publicly available information sources.

Open Vulnerability Assessment Language (OVAL) A community open standard for the transfer of information regarding security tools and services. It focuses on vulnerabilities, patch states, and configuration states.

Open Web Application Security Project (OWASP) A nonprofit organization that provides resources to improve the security of software.

OpenID Connect An identity layer based on OAuth 2.0 specifications used for consumer single sign-on.

order of restoration The order in which backup tapes are restored.

order of volatility In the evidence collection process, collection that occurs from the most volatile component to the least volatile.

OV certificate A type of certificate that provides stronger assurance than does a domain-validated certificate.

P

P12 An extension used for PFX-encoded certificates.

P7B A Base64-encoded certificate format used on Windows and Java Tomcat systems.

PAP (Password Authentication Protocol) A legacy plaintext authentication protocol for remote server access that does not support stronger authentication mechanisms.

pass the hash A type of replay attack in which the attacker provides the hashed password to an accepting authentication scheme.

passive reconnaissance Reconnaissance techniques that not require actively engaging with the targeted systems.

password attack An attack on a password using manual or automated techniques, such as dictionary, brute-force, spraying, and rainbow table attacks.

Password-Based Key Derivation Function 2 (PBKDF2) A key-stretching algorithm that applies a pseudo-random function to a password, combined with a salt of at least 64 bits, and then repeats the process at least 1,000 times.

password cracker A software utility that allows direct testing of user logon password strength by conducting brute-force password tests.

Payment Card Industry Data Security Standard (PCI DSS) A standard that governs the use and storage of credit card data.

perfect forward secrecy A mechanism to prevent the compromise of a private key used to create session keys from compromising past session keys.

persistence An exploitation technique that enables the tester to gain additional compromising information.

personal health information (PHI) Any medical data that can be used to identify an individual.

Personal Information Protection and Electronics Document Act (PIPEDA) A Canadian law governing the collection and use of personal information.

personally identifiable information (PII) Broadly, any data that can be used to identify an individual.

PFX A binary certificate format also known as PKCS#12.

pharming An attack that redirects victims to a bogus website.

phishing An attempt to acquire sensitive information by masquerading as a trustworthy entity via electronic communication, usually email.

physical control A control that forms the outer line of physical defense against direct access to data.

ping A network tool for testing the basic function of a network that is commonly used to test whether a remote host is alive or responding.

pinning A method that extends beyond normal certificate validation to help thwart on-path attacks.

plain old telephone service (POTS) The traditional audio circuit-switched telephone service, which predated modern broadband network connectivity using audio modem endpoint devices for remote data access. POTS is still used in many rural and underdeveloped areas that lack broadband infrastructure.

Platform as a Service (PaaS) The delivery of a computing platform, often an operating system with associated services, over the Internet without downloads or installation.

pointer dereference A programming error in which an application dereferences a pointer that it expects to be valid but that is really null, resulting in a system crash.

polymorphic virus A virus that can change form or signature each time it is executed, to avoid detection.

pop-up blocker A program used to block a common method of Internet advertising in which a window pops up in the middle of the screen, displaying a message, when you click a link or button on a website.

potentially unwanted program (PUP) Software that often is not wanted, although it may not be explicitly malicious.

PowerShell A command-line shell and scripting interface for Microsoft Windows environments.

Pretty Good Privacy (PGP) An encryption program that is an alternative to S/MIME.

preventive control A control that attempts to prevent unwanted events by inhibiting the free use of computing resources.

privacy enhanced mail (PEM) The most common format and extension for certificates.

privacy impact assessment (PIA) An assessment needed for any organization that collects, uses, stores, or processes personal information such as PII or PHI.

privacy threshold assessment An assessment used before a privacy impact assessment to determine whether a system contains personal information such as PII or PHI.

private key A key that is maintained on a host system or application.

privilege escalation A method of software exploitation that takes advantage of a program's flawed code. Usually, this crashes the system and leaves it in a state in which arbitrary code can be executed or an intruder can function as an administrator.

Protected EAP (PEAP) An encrypted form of the EAP authentication protocol, which couples EAP with transport encryption to protect credentials during transfer.

protocol analyzer A tool that troubleshoots network issues by gathering packet-level information across the network. It captures packets and decodes the information into readable data for analysis.

public key A key that is made available to whoever is going to encrypt the data sent to the holder of a private key.

Python A popular and widely used general-purpose programming language.

R

race condition A way in which a program executes sequences of code. It typically occurs when code sequences are competing for the same resource or interfering by acting at the same time.

RACE Integrity Primitives Evaluation Message Digest (RIPEMD) A group of hash functions developed within academia, based on the design of MD4.

radio-frequency identification (RFID) A wireless technology that was initially common to supply-chain and inventory tracking.

RAID (redundant array of inexpensive/independent disks) Multiple disks arranged as a large, high-performance logical disk to provide redundancy in case of disk failure.

rainbow table A table that consists of a large set of precomputed hash values for every possible combination of characters. May be used in brute-force cracking of passwords that have been hashed.

ransomware A form of malware that attempts to hold a person or company hostage, often for monetary gain.

Raspberry Pi A single-board computer with integrated peripherals that is commonly used for hobbies, projects, and prototypes.

real-time operating system (RTOS) A small operating system used in embedded systems and IoT applications that typically run in a SoC environment.

recovery point objective (RPO) The amount of time that can elapse during a disruption before the quantity of data lost during that period exceeds the business

continuity plan's maximum allowable threshold.

recovery site   The site an organization chooses for disaster recovery.

recovery time objective (RTO)   A measure of the time in which a service should be restored during disaster recovery operations.

redundancy   Replication of a component in identical copies to compensate for random hardware failures.

refactoring   A practice for software developers that involves identifying ways to make code more efficient through better design.

registration authority (RA)   A network authority that provides a CA with authentication of a client's certificate request and serves as an aggregator of information.

remote access Trojan (RAT)   A backdoor Trojan installed on a system that allows a remote attacker to take control of the targeted system.

Remote Authentication Dial-In User Service (RADIUS)   An Internet protocol used for remote-access services. It conveys user authentication and configuration data between a centralized authentication server and a remote-access server (RADIUS client) to permit the remote-access server to authenticate requests to use its network access ports.

remote wipe   A technique that involves deleting a handheld device's data remotely (for example, if the device is lost or stolen).

resident virus   A type of virus that resides in memory. By living in the memory of a system, the virus can be loaded each time the system starts or can infect other areas based on specific actions.

risk acceptance   The process of recognizing a risk, identifying it, and then accepting that it is sufficiently unlikely or of such limited impact that corrective controls are not warranted.

risk avoidance   A solution for eliminating a vulnerability that gives rise to a particular risk so that it is avoided altogether.

risk mitigation   The reduction in likelihood or impact of a risk's exposure.

risk register   A specialized software program, cloud service, or master document that provides a method to record information about identified risks.

risk transference   A strategy that involves moving risk to hosted providers who assume the responsibility for recovery and restoration or acquiring insurance to cover the costs of equipment theft or data exposure.

Rivest Cipher (RC)   One of the most commonly implemented ciphers for encryption security.

rogue access point   An unauthorized wireless access point.

role-based access control (RBAC)   A security method that combines MAC and DAC. RBAC uses profiles, which are defined for specific roles within a company, and then users are assigned to such roles. This facilitates administration

in a large group of users because when you modify a role and assign it new permissions, those settings are automatically conveyed to all users assigned to that role.

root of trust A sequence in which software images are authenticated by previously verified software before they are executed.

rooting A process that enables complete access to a mobile device. Root-level access allows a user to configure the device to run unauthorized apps and set different permissions by circumventing Android's security architecture.

rootkit A piece of software that can be installed and hidden on a computer, mainly for the purpose of compromising the system.

ROT13 A substitution cipher that rotates each letter by 13 places.

router A device that connects multiple network segments and routes packets between them. Routers split broadcast domains.

RSA algorithm An asymmetric cryptography algorithm that allows anyone to create products that incorporate different implementations of the algorithm, without being subject to license and patent enforcement.

rule-based access control An extension of access control that includes stateful testing to determine whether a particular request for resource access may be granted. When a rule-based method is in force, access to resources might be granted or restricted, based on conditional testing.

S

salt An additional input of random data to a function that hashes a password.

sandboxing A method that allows programs and processes to be run in an isolated environment, to limit access to files and the host system.

scalability The capability to handle the changing needs of a system, process, or application within the confines of the current resources.

scanless A port scanning utility that uses websites to do scanning and enables the user to remain anonymous.

script kiddie A threat actor who runs exploits developed by others but who can't write sophisticated code and might not even know how to program.

secure boot An action that permits a platform to record evidence that can be presented to a remote party in a platform attestation.

Secure Hash Algorithm (SHA) A hash algorithm pioneered by the National Security Agency and widely used in the U.S. government.

Secure Hypertext Transfer Protocol (S-HTTP) An alternative to HTTPS that was developed to support connectivity for banking

transactions and other secure web communications.

Secure/Multipurpose Internet Mail Extensions (S/MIME)   An Internet protocol specified in RFC 2633 and used to secure email communications through encryption and digital signatures for authentication. It generally works with PKI to validate digital signatures and related digital certificates.

Secure Shell (SSH)   A protocol designed to support secure remote login, along with secure access to other services across an insecure network. SSH includes a secure transport layer protocol that provides server authentication, confidentiality (encryption), and integrity (message digest functions), along with a user authentication protocol and a connection protocol that runs on top of the user authentication protocol.

Secure Sockets Layer (SSL)   An Internet protocol that uses connection-oriented, end-to-end encryption to ensure that client/server communications are confidential (encrypted) and meet integrity constraints (message digests). Because SSL is independent of the application layer, any application protocol can work with SSL transparently. SSL can also work with a secure transport layer protocol, which is why the term SSL/TLS appears frequently.

Security as a Service (SecaaS)   A subscription-based cloud services model that implements security in an organization.

Security Assertion Markup Language (SAML)   An Extensible Markup Language (XML) standard that allows a user to use single sign-on for affiliated but separate websites.

security baseline   A specific set of security-related modifications to patches and settings for systems and services that underpins the technical implementations of security. It is defined in an organization's security policy.

security information and event management (SIEM)   A set of tools that collects, correlates, and displays data feeds that support response activities.

security orchestration, automation, and response (SOAR)   A set of tools that aggregates intelligence from internal and external sources to provide fusion analysis and advanced security analytics and operations.

security through obscurity   Reliance on secrecy to provide security to an organization.

self-encrypting drive (SED)   A hard disk that continually performs full disk encryption.

sensor   A device (such as a network tap or a firewall log) that collects information about a network.

service-level agreement (SLA)   A contract between two companies or a company and an individual that specifies, by contract, a level of service to be provided. Supplying replacement equipment within 24 hours of loss is a simple

example of something an SLA might specify.

session hijacking An attack in which session cookies are stolen so the attacker can gain access to the site the user is currently connected to.

session key A randomly generated key that performs both encryption and decryption during the communication of a session between two parties.

Shibboleth A SAML-based, open source federated identity solution that provides single sign-on capabilities and federated services. It is popular in research and educational institutions.

shimming A sophisticated hack that requires the installation of a piece of code between two components that is capable of intercepting calls and redirecting them elsewhere.

shmishing An SMS phishing attack that uses text messaging as the attack vector.

Short Message Service (SMS) A text-based mobile communication system with a message size originally limited to 160 characters per message.

shoulder surfing Looking over someone's shoulder to obtain information.

sideloading A process in which a user goes around the approved vendor app marketplace and device settings to install unapproved apps.

signature-based monitoring A method of monitoring a network

that is based on finding a pattern or signature match.

Simple Network Management Protocol (SNMP) A UDP-based application layer Internet protocol used for network management. SNMP is specified in RFCs 2570 and 2574. In converting management information between management consoles (managers) and managed nodes (agents), SNMP implements configuration and event databases on managed nodes that can be configured to respond to interesting events by notifying network managers.

single loss expectancy (SLE) The expected cost per instance arising from the occurrence of a risk. The SLE is calculated as the product of the asset value and the risk's exposure factor (a percentage of loss if a risk occurs).

skimming An attack that involves copying data from a physical card by using a specialized terminal.

smart card A credit card–size device that contains an embedded chip that can store various types of data, such as a driver's license number, medical information, passwords and other authentication data, and bank account data.

sn1per An automated penetration testing scanner that enumerates and scans for vulnerabilities.

snapshot A picture that preserves the entire state and data of a virtual machine at the time it is taken.

social engineering The process of taking advantage of human behavior

to attack a network or gain access to resources that would otherwise be inaccessible. Social engineering emphasizes the well-known fact that poorly or improperly trained individuals can be persuaded, tricked, or coerced into giving up passwords, phone numbers, or other data that can lead to unauthorized system access, even when strong technical security measures can otherwise prevent such access.

Software as a Service (SaaS) A cloud computing model in which software applications are virtualized and provided by an outsourced service provider.

software-defined networking (SDN) A method by which organizations can manage network services through a decoupled underlying infrastructure that allows for quick adjustments based on changing business requirements.

software-defined visibility (SDV) Visualization combined with the capability to dynamically respond to events across software-defined networks.

software development life cycle (SDLC) A process that outlines the steps for developing software.

spam Unsolicited messages typically sent to a large number of recipients.

spam over Internet messaging (SPIM) A type of unsolicited messaging that is specifically sent over instant messaging platforms.

spear phishing A targeted version of phishing.

spyware Software that communicates information from a user's system to another party without notifying the user.

SSL stripping A technique that involves removing the encryption between a client and a website.

staging environment An SDLC environment that is primarily used to unit test deployment of code before it is put into production.

standard Specific mandatory controls based on policies.

standard operating procedure (SOP) A prescriptive procedure that provides step-by-step instructions to ensure a standardized and repeatable method for performing a task.

stealth virus A memory-resident virus that uses techniques to avoid detection, such as temporarily removing itself from an infected file or masking a file's size.

steganography A word of Greek origin meaning "hidden writing" that refers to hiding messages so that unintended recipients are not even aware that a message exists.

stream cipher A cipher in which plaintext bits are encrypted a single bit at a time and combined with a stream of pseudo-random characters.

Structured Threat Information (STIX) A standardized and structured language that represents threat information in a flexible, automatable, and easy-to-use manner.

supervisory control and data acquisition (SCADA) A subset of systems considered to be critical infrastructure systems.

supply-chain attack An attack that involves taking advantage of other vendors that an organization relies on.

symmetric key A single encryption key that is generated and used to encrypt data. This data is then passed across a network. After the data arrives at the recipient device, the same key used to encrypt the data is used to decrypt it. A secure method for sharing keys is required because the sender and the receiver both use the same key (which is also called a shared secret because the key should be unknown to third parties).

syslog A system logging protocol used to send logs or messaging events to a server.

system logging The process of collecting system data to be used for monitoring and auditing purposes.

system-on-a-chip (SoC) Integration between a microcontroller, an application, or a microprocessor and peripherals.

T

TACACS+ An authentication, access control, and accounting standard that relies on a central server to provide access over network resources, including services, file storage, and network routing hardware.

tactics, techniques, and procedures (TTP) Attack methods and activities associated with specific threat actors.

tail A command-line file manipulation command that is used to display the tail end of a text file or a file fed to the command.

tailgating Following closely behind someone who has authorized physical access in an environment.

tcpdump A command-line packet analysis tool that captures packets sent and received on an interface.

tcpreplay A command-line tool used for replaying network traffic from saved files such as tcpdump.

teaming Security team exercises conducted with teams with color names that represent different goals, such as attackers and defenders.

Temporal Key Integrity Protocol (TKIP) A protocol based on RC4 that is designed to overcome many of the limitations of WEP. It offers great improvements in message integrity and confidentiality.

tethering The sharing of a device's Internet connection with other devices through Wi-Fi, Bluetooth, or a USB cable.

theharverster A tool used to gather emails, domains, employee names, ports, and banners from varying sources.

threat actor An individual, a group, or an entity that contributes to an incident—or, more simply, a person or an entity that executes a given threat.

threat hunting A proactive approach to finding an attacker before alerts are triggered.

time of check/time of use (TOCTOU) A race condition that takes advantage of the time delay between checking and use.

TOTP (time-based one-time password) An algorithm that computes a one-time password from a shared secret key and the current time.

transitive trust Trust in which any domain that trusts Domain A also trusts all other domains that Domain A trusts.

Transport Layer Security (TLS) An end-to-end encryption protocol originally specified in ISO Standard 10736 that provides security services as part of the transport layer in a protocol stack.

Trojan horse A form of malware that appears to be useful software but has code hidden inside that attacks a system directly or allows the system to be infiltrated by the originator of the code when it is executed. A Trojan horse is software hidden inside other software. It is commonly used to infect systems with viruses, worms, or remote-control software.

Trusted Automated Exchange of Indicator Information (TAXII) A specification for machine-to-machine communication that allows organizations to share information with others, as desired.

Trusted Platform Module (TPM) A standard for secure crypto-processor chips that are used

to authenticate hardware devices such as PCs or laptops.

Twofish A block cipher that can encrypt using a chunk of data of any size. It is the successor to Blowfish.

typo squatting An attack that most commonly relies on typographic errors made by users on the Internet. Also known as URL hijacking.

U

Unified Extensible Firmware Interface (UEFI) An industry-wide standard managed by the Unified Extended Firmware Interface Forum that defines a standard interface between the OS, firmware, and external devices.

unmanned aerial vehicle (UAV) An aerial device or drone, which may be used for military, agriculture, cartography, and other purposes.

URL hijacking A simple method used frequently for benign purposes but that can be easily used for more malicious attacks that most commonly relies on typographic errors made by users on the Internet. Also known as typo squatting.

V

virtual desktop environment (VDE) An environment similar in form to server virtualization but with some differences, specifically in usage and performance demands.

virtual desktop infrastructure (VDI) The server-based virtualization technology that hosts and manages virtual desktops.

virtual local area network (VLAN) A software technology that facilitates the grouping of network nodes connected to one or more network switches into a single logical network. By permitting logical aggregation of devices into virtual network segments, VLANs offer simplified user management and network resource access controls for switched networks.

virtual private network (VPN) A popular technology that supports reasonably secure logical private network links across some insecure public network infrastructure, such as the Internet. VPNs are more secure than traditional remote access because they can be encrypted and because VPNs support tunneling (hiding numerous types of protocols and sessions within a single host-to-host connection).

virtualization technology A technology developed to allow a guest operating system to run along with a host operating system with one set of hardware.

virus A piece of malicious code that spreads to other computers by design, although some viruses also damage the systems on which they reside. Viruses can spread immediately upon being received or can implement other unwanted actions, or they can lie dormant until a trigger in their code causes them to become active. The hidden code a virus executes is called its payload.

vishing An attack in which the attacker uses fake caller ID to appear as a trusted organization and attempts to get the individual to enter account details by phone. Also known as voice phishing.

VM escape A situation in which a virtual machine breaks out of or escapes from isolation and has the capability to interact with the host operating system. VM escape doesn't affect bare-metal platforms.

VM sprawl A situation in which multiple underutilized virtualized servers take up more space and consume more resources than is justified by their workload.

voice over IP (VoIP) The delivery of voice communications over the Internet, which is subject to the same attacks as other Internet communication methods.

vulnerability scan A scanning method that identifies vulnerabilities, misconfigurations, and lack of security controls.

vulnerability scanner A software utility that scans a range of IP addresses, testing for the presence of known vulnerabilities in software configuration and accessible services.

W

warm site A backup site that has some of the equipment and infrastructure necessary for a business to begin operating at that location. Typically, companies or organizations bring their own computer

systems and hardware to a warm site, and the site usually already includes a ready-to-use networking infrastructure. It also might include reliable power, climate controls, lighting, and Internet access points. Compare with hot and cold sites.

Waterfall   A traditional SDLC model that starts with a defined set of requirements and a well-developed plan. Adjustments are confined to the current development stage.

watering hole attack   An attack in which the attacker focuses on a site frequently visited by the target. Similar to spear phishing but does not use email.

web application firewall   Software or a hardware appliance used to protect an organization's web server from attack.

wet-pipe fire suppression   A sprinkler system with pressurized water in the pipes. If a fire starts, the pipes release water immediately and offer the fastest and most effective means of water-based fire suppression.

whaling   The use of spear phishing tactics against high-profile targets such as executives within a company.

white box (known environment) A testing method in which the assessor has knowledge about the inner workings of the system or knowledge of the source code. Also called clear box or glass box testing.

whois   A free and publicly accessible directory from which domain names can be queried to discover contact and technical information about registered domain names.

Wi-Fi Alliance   A consortium of companies that has a major impact on wireless technologies. The organization contributes to the standards process and is responsible for certifying wireless devices.

Wi-Fi Protected Access (WPA) A wireless transport security service that uses TKIP 128-bit encryption in place of the weaker legacy WEP encryption standard.

Wi-Fi Protected Access Version 2 (WPA2)   WPA technology that replaced the original version. It improved the security of Wi-Fi connections by requiring the use of stronger wireless encryption than WPA required.

Wi-Fi Protected Setup (WPS) An extension of wireless standards that enables end users to easily establish secure wireless home networks. Originally known as Wi-Fi Simple Config.

Wired Equivalent Privacy (WEP)   A security protocol used in IEEE 802.11 wireless networking that was designed to provide security equivalent to that found in regular wired networks. It uses basic symmetric encryption to protect data sent over wireless connections so that sniffing of wireless transmissions does not produce readable data. Drive-by attackers cannot access a wireless LAN without additional effort and attacks. WEP is no longer considered secure.

Wireshark   A well-known packet analyzer that is similar to tcpdump.

worm A type of virus designed primarily to reproduce and replicate itself on as many computer systems as possible. A worm does not normally alter files; instead, it remains resident in a computer's memory. Worms typically rely on access to operating system capabilities that are invisible to users.

WPA-Enterprise Also known as WPA-802.1X mode, a form of WPA that requires security certificates and uses an authentication server from which the keys can be distributed.

WPA-Personal Also known as WPA-PSK (preshared key), a form of WPA that requires a password consisting of 8 to 63 characters; this same password must be used by all devices on the wireless network.

X–Z

X.509 A digital certificate that uniquely identifies a potential communications party or participant. An X.509 digital certificate includes a party's name and public key, and it can also include organizational affiliation, service or access restrictions, and other access- and security-related information.

XML injection An injection technique that is used to manipulate the logic of an application in order to perform unauthorized activity or gain unauthorized access by inserting undesirable Extensible Markup Language (XML) content into an XML message.

XOR A type of streaming operation commonly used with advanced cryptographic algorithms in which pseudo-random numbers are used in place of a string of ones.

zero-day An attack that exploits a vulnerability that is unknown to others—possibly even to the software developer.

Index

ICS, 228

MFD, 232

RTOS, 226–227

SCADA, 227–229

smart devices, IoT, 229–231

SoC, 226–227

special-purpose devices, 233

   aircraft, 235–236

   drones, 235–236

   implied trust, 236

   medical devices, 233–234

   resource constraints, 236

   UAV, 235–236

   vehicles, 234–235

surveillance systems, 233

EMM (Enterprise Mobility Management), 405

encryption

3DES, 289

applications, 173

blowfish, 288

cloud computing, 429

configuration management, 129–132

cryptography

   algorithms, 262

   asymmetric algorithms, 266–268

   blockchains, 275

   constraints, 276

   cryptocurrencies, bitcoin, 275

   data encryption process, 262

   digital signatures, 270–271

   ECC, 268

   FIPS 140-2, 273

   hashing, 271–272

   homomorphic encryption, 273–274

   IV, 262–263

   keys, 262–264

   nonces, 262–263

   nonrepudiation, 269, 270

   passwords, 262–263

   PFS, 268–269

   private key encryption, 267–268

   pseudo-random numbers, 262–263

   public key encryption, 266–268

   quantum cryptography, 268

   salting, 272

   session keys, 268–269

   steganography, 273–274

   symmetric algorithms, 264–266

   use cases, 274–275

   use of proven technologies, 272–273

data at rest, 129

data in motion, 129

data in processing, 129–130

data in transit, 129

data masking, 131

DES, 288–289

EFS, 322–323

embedded encryption, 404

enterprise-level encryption, 404

FDE, 322–323, 324, 403–404

homomorphic encryption, 273–274

IDEA, 288

keys, 286

mobile devices, 397

process, 262

redaction, 131

secure data destruction, 256

SED, 323

tokenization, 130–131

traffic management, 134–135

voice encryption, 404

VoIP, 404

endpoints

detection/response, cloud computing, 430

NAC, 366

protection. *See* host-based security

impact, 610–611

mission-essential functions, 607–608

MTBF, 609–610

MTTF, 609–610

MTTR, 609–610

qualitative risk management, 604

quantitative risk management, 604–605

risk acceptance, 600

risk analysis, 598

risk appetite, 599

risk assessments, 598, 602–604

risk avoidance, 599–600

risk awareness, 599

risk deterrence, 600

risk heat maps, 603–604

risk matrices, 603

risk mitigation, 600

risk response, 599–601

risk transference, 600

risks registers, 598–599

RPO, 608

RTO, 608

single points of failure, 607–608

SLE, 605

third-party risk management, 592–593

threat assessments, 601–602

secrets managers, cloud computing, 426

security information/event management, cloud computing, 430

threats, UTM, 357–358

mandatory vacations, 585

MANET (Mobile Ad hoc Networks), 410–411

man-in-the-browser (MITB) attacks, 59

man-in-the-middle (MITM) attacks, 31, 57, 58–59

manipulating drivers, 40–41

refactoring, 41

shimming, 41

Manning, Chelsea, 452

mantraps, internal security, 245

maps

risk heat maps, 603–604

threat maps, 83

masking data, 131

matrices, risk, 603

MCM (Mobile Content Management), 394–395

MDM (Mobile Device Management), 393–394

Measured Boot, 327

medical devices, embedded control systems, 233–234

Memdump command, 506

memory

application development, 179

leaks, 37

malware, 16

messaging, Internet, 7

metadata, 536

MFD (Multifunction Devices), 232

microservices, 148–149

Miller, Charlie, 235

MIME (Multipurpose Internet Mail Extensions), 287

mission-essential functions, 607–608

MITB attacks, 59

mitigating

incidents, 520

application control, 545–546

blacklists, 546

certificate revocation, 543

containment, 541–542

content filtering, 543

DLP, 543

firewalls, 544–545

REGISTER YOUR PRODUCT at PearsonITcertification.com/register
Access Additional Benefits and SAVE 35% on Your Next Purchase

- Download available product updates.
- Access bonus material when applicable.
- Receive exclusive offers on new editions and related products.
  (Just check the box to hear from us when setting up your account.)
- Get a coupon for 35% for your next purchase, valid for 30 days. Your code will be available in your PITC cart. (You will also find it in the Manage Codes section of your account page.)

Registration benefits vary by product. Benefits will be listed on your account page under Registered Products.

PearsonITcertification.com–Learning Solutions for Self-Paced Study, Enterprise, and the Classroom
Pearson is the official publisher of Cisco Press, IBM Press, VMware Press, Microsoft Press, and is a Platinum CompTIA Publishing Partner–CompTIA's highest partnership accreditation.
At **PearsonITcertification.com** you can

- Shop our books, eBooks, software, and video training.
- Take advantage of our special offers and promotions (pearsonitcertifcation.com/promotions).
- Sign up for special offers and content newsletters (pearsonitcertifcation.com/newsletters).
- Read free articles, exam profiles, and blogs by information technology experts.
- Access thousands of free chapters and video lessons.

Connect with PITC – Visit PearsonITcertifcation.com/community
Learn about PITC community events and programs.

PEARSON IT CERTIFICATION

Addison-Wesley · Cisco Press · IBM Press · Microsoft Press · Pearson IT Certification · Prentice Hall · Que · Sams · VMware Press

PEARSON

To receive your 10% off Exam Voucher, register your product at:

www.pearsonitcertification.com/register

and follow the instructions.